I0762219

MUSEUM BARBERINI

POTSDAM

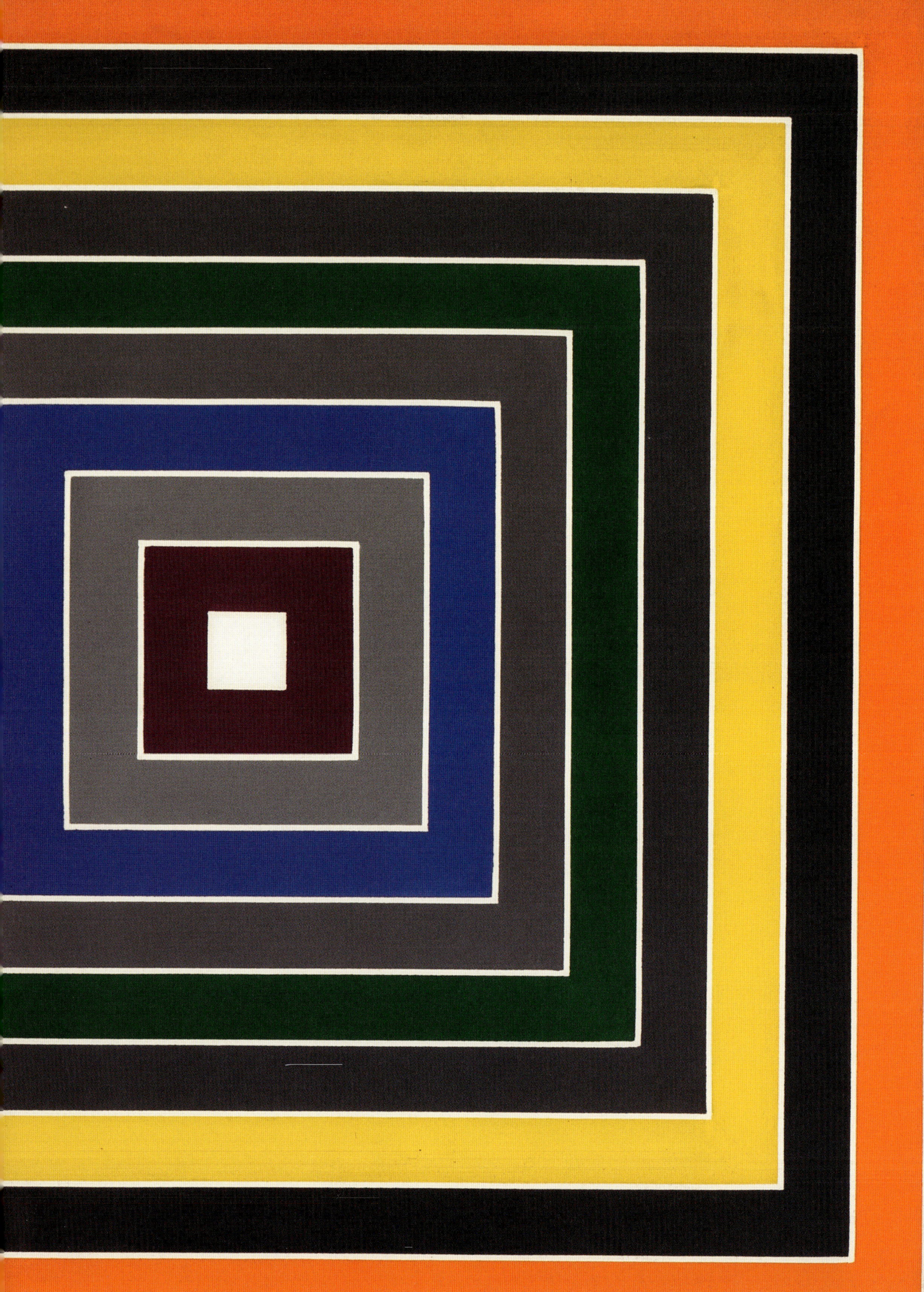

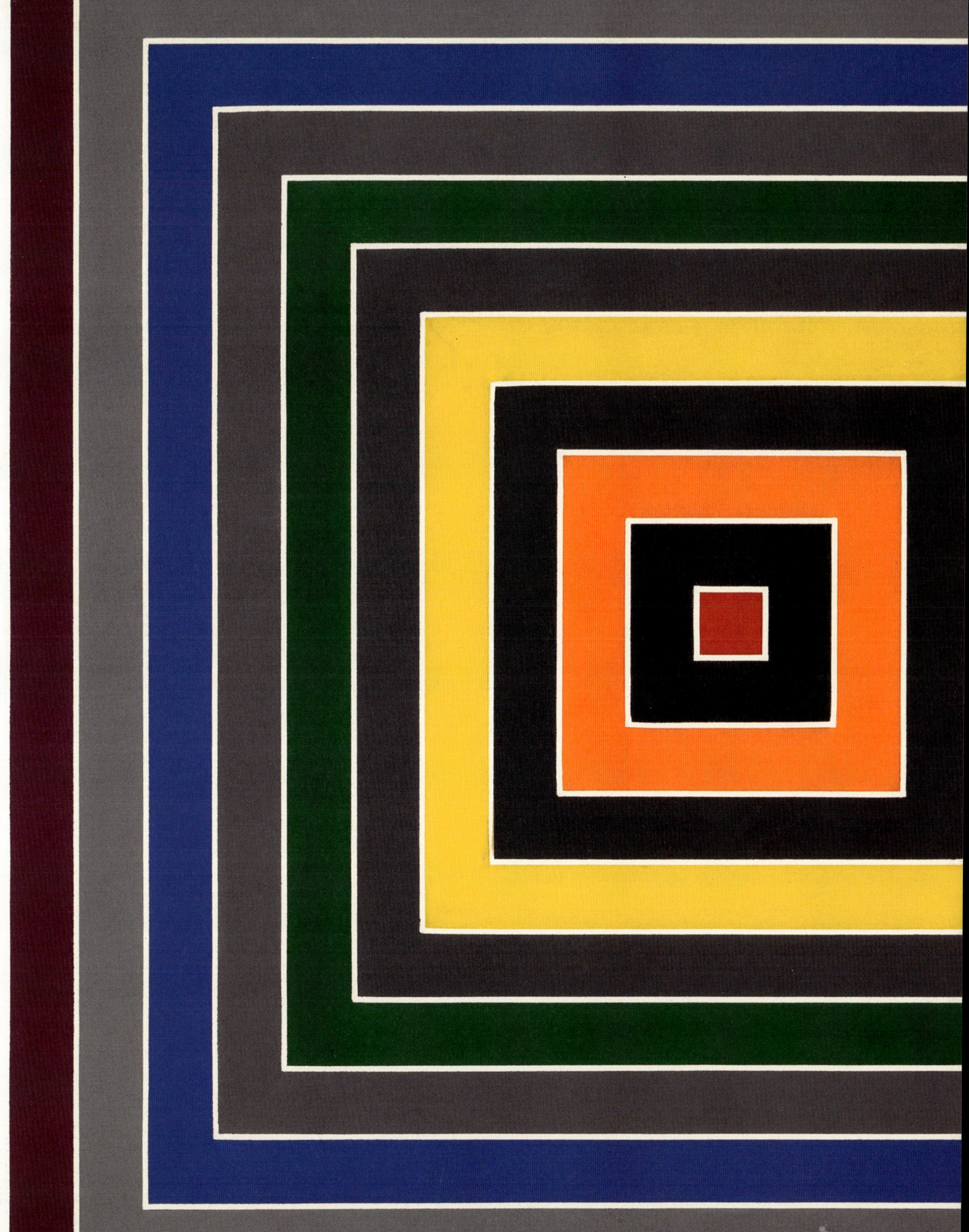

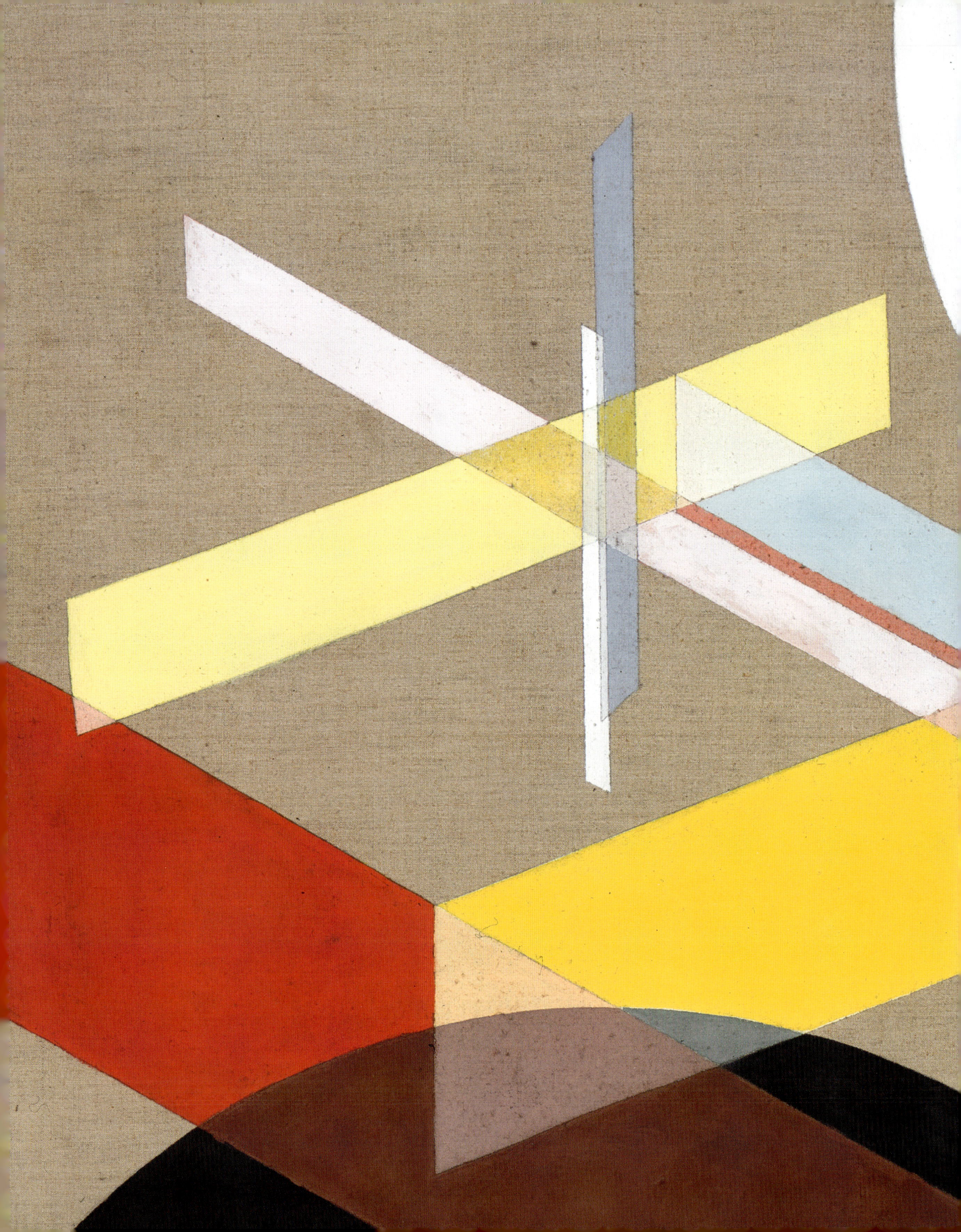

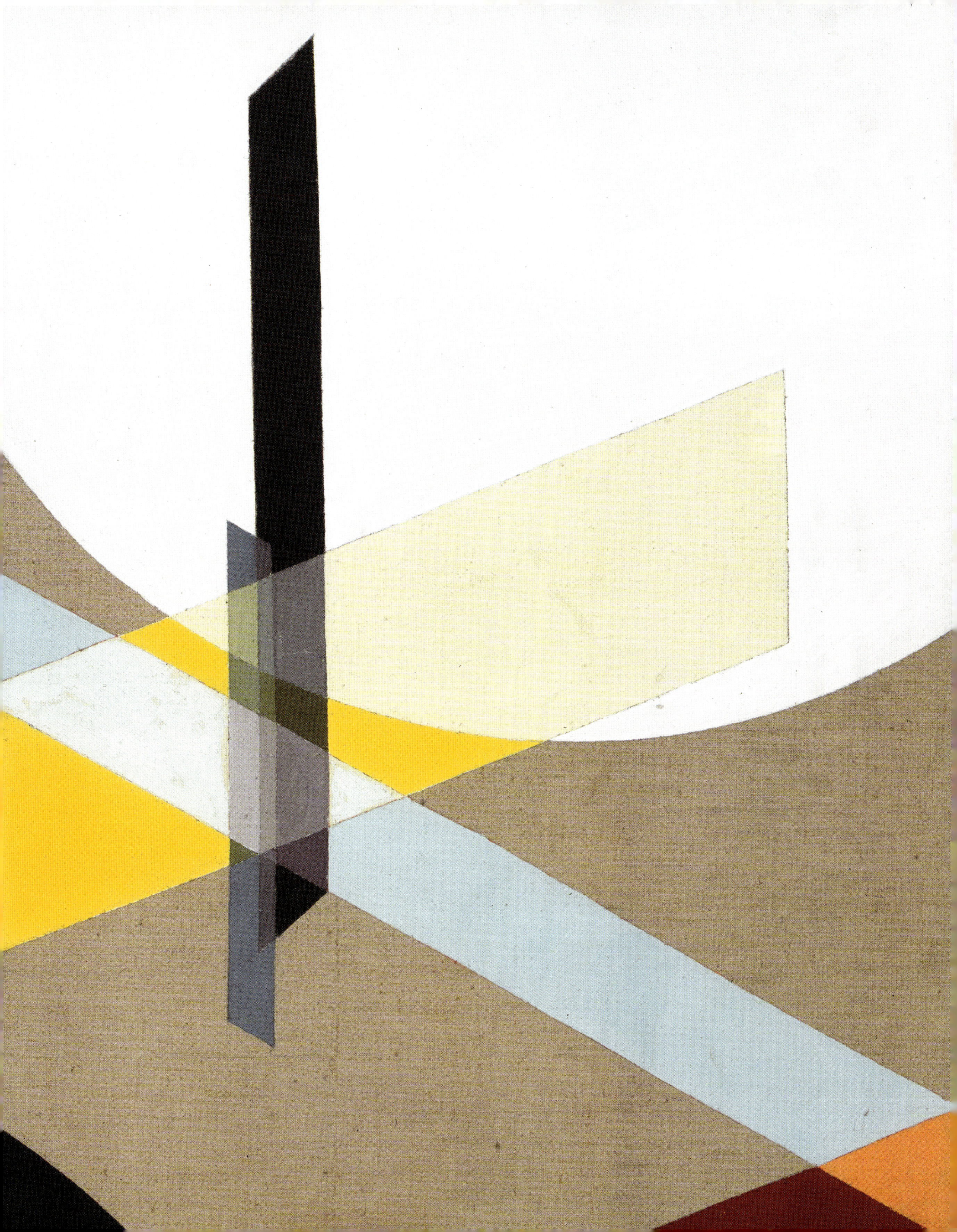

Kandinsky's Universe

Geometric Abstraction in the Twentieth Century

Exhibition and catalog:
Sterre Barentsen

Assistant curator:
Anna Heling

Edited by:
Ortrud Westheider
Michael Philipp
Nerina Santorius

With contributions by:
Sterre Barentsen
Max Boersma
John E. Bowlt
Altair Brandon-Salmon
Anna Heling
David Max Horowitz
Jeremy Lewison
Chen Min Loh
Céline Véronique Marten
Maria Mileeva
Nicoletta Misler

PRESTEL Munich · London · New York

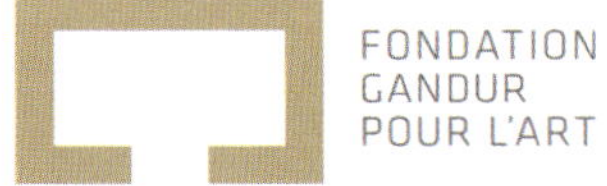

An exhibition of the Museum Barberini, Potsdam
With the generous support of the Fondation Gandur pour l'Art, Genève

Contents

Foreword

The history of geometric abstraction has generally been recounted as a series of episodes. Constructivism, the Bauhaus, De Stijl, Abstraction-Création, Hard Edge Painting, and Op Art have been interpreted as isolated movements, defined by national boundaries. The exhibition *Kandinsky's Universe: Geometric Abstraction in the Twentieth Century* sets a new course, tracing lines of connection in the history of geometric abstraction. Running through it like a common thread are the paintings of Wassily Kandinsky, which inspired multiple generations of artists worldwide. His doctrine of the "spiritual in art," formulated in 1911, continued to exert an influence even into the 1970s.

Until now, only a few exhibitions in the United States have focused on the connection between European and American geometric abstraction. *Kandinsky's Universe: Geometric Abstraction in the Twentieth Century* spans a wide arc: beginning with Constructivist works, the show explores artistic exchange in Eastern and Western Europe in the 1920s and 1930s, includes Great Britain for the first time, and traces the migration of ideas to the United States under the conditions of exile. It surveys a period of sixty years during which artists reduced painting to fundamental forms, sought to transcend pictorial boundaries by means of grids and color fields, and expanded their painterly possibilities and the imaginative space of their viewers again and again.

Kandinsky's Universe: Geometric Abstraction in the Twentieth Century illustrates the exchange of ideas and examines Kandinsky's seminal role. His painting *White Sound* from 1908 marks the beginning: painted in the style of the Blue Rider group, it shows how he already exploited the great promise of an isolated area of white in his Expressionist phase. As he wrote in *Concerning the Spiritual in Art,* "It is an absence that is not dead, but rather full of potential. White sounds like silence, a correlation that is easy to fathom. It is a nothingness characterized by youth or, more precisely, that void that comes before the beginning, before birth."[1]

To this day, geometric abstraction is sometimes accused of lacking content. Yet in the course of its history, it served as a vehicle for ideas ranging from the rise of the October Revolution in Russia, to Kandinsky's "great spiritual" as a level of cognition, to notions of collective authorship in the 1960s. Even in purity, even in negation, a statement is communicated. Repeatedly throughout the twentieth century, geometric abstraction offered a counterpoint to the Expressionist emphasis on the individual self: in 1915, the Constructivists bid farewell to the pathos of the Expressionists, while in the late 1950s Hard Edge Painting superseded Abstract Expressionism with its focus on subjective trauma. Even the juxtaposition of realism and abstraction was echoed in the counterplay of the Bauhaus versus New Objectivity or Pop Art versus Color Field Painting.

Artists of differing generations used the elemental formal vocabulary of geometric abstraction to allude to the discoveries of the natural sciences. For them, experimental and theoretical forays into the transcendental, into the tiniest particles and the furthest galaxies, legitimated their enthusiasm for nonobjective art: the first generation witnessed the discovery of the space-time continuum in Albert Einstein's theory of relativity, while Op Art artists lived through the moon landing of 1969, experiencing it on television. As Kandinsky wrote in 1914, "The crumbling of the atom was to my soul like the crumbling of the whole world. Suddenly the heaviest walls toppled."[2]

Geometric forms were reassuring; experiments on the canvas were a new kind of realism. Kandinsky's *Point and Line to Plane: Contribution to the Analysis of the Pictorial Elements,* published in 1926 in the Bauhausbücher series, continued to influence painters into the 1970s. Nowadays, the point, line, and plane are parameters for geometric modeling, better known as geodata. Although the technology behind it is highly abstract, it achieves the desired result. Kandinsky's universe gave rise to painting and sculpture that prefigured our present-day reality. The aim of these artists was not to do away with content, but to create paintings that offer new experiences of space and time, even to this day.

Daniel Zamani, curator at the Museum Barberini from 2018 to 2024, conceived the idea for this exhibition. In 2021 he had already devoted a show to the phenomenon of gestural abstraction with *The Shape of Freedom: International Abstraction after 1945,* presented at the Museum Barberini, the Albertina in Vienna, and Munchmuseet in Oslo. For *Kandinsky's Universe: Geometric Abstraction in the Twentieth Century,* he collaborated with Sterre Barentsen, who took over the project as curator. She organized the catalog and was able to secure loans from major German and international museums and private collections for the exhibition. Together we would like to thank the lenders for their trust.

The earnestness and vigor with which the development of geometric abstraction was accompanied by hundreds of authors in countless magazine and catalog articles is documented by the essays in this book. We would like to thank Sterre Barentsen, Max Boersma, John E. Bowlt, Altair Brandon-Salmon, David Max Horowitz, Jeremy Lewison, Maria Mileeva, and Nicoletta Misler for their contributions. The chronology, initiated by Sterre Barentsen and compiled together with Anna Heling, Chen Min Loh, and Céline Véronique Marten, juxtaposes the pioneering exhibitions with the most important scientific discoveries of their day. The universe of art thus takes its place in the Space Age: like the magazines, the exhibitions recorded in the chronology transcend generational and national boundaries and constitute first-rate and hitherto undervalued sources for the project of geometric abstraction.

We are grateful to the Hasso Plattner Foundation and to our museum founder for their support, which enables us to realize such ambitious projects. We hope that all of our visitors will enjoy immersing themselves in the spaces of abstraction. After all, it was a painting by Claude Monet—a *Grainstack,* as can be seen in the Hasso Plattner Collection—that prompted Kandinsky to create his first nonobjective image.

Ortrud Westheider
Director of the Museum Barberini
Potsdam

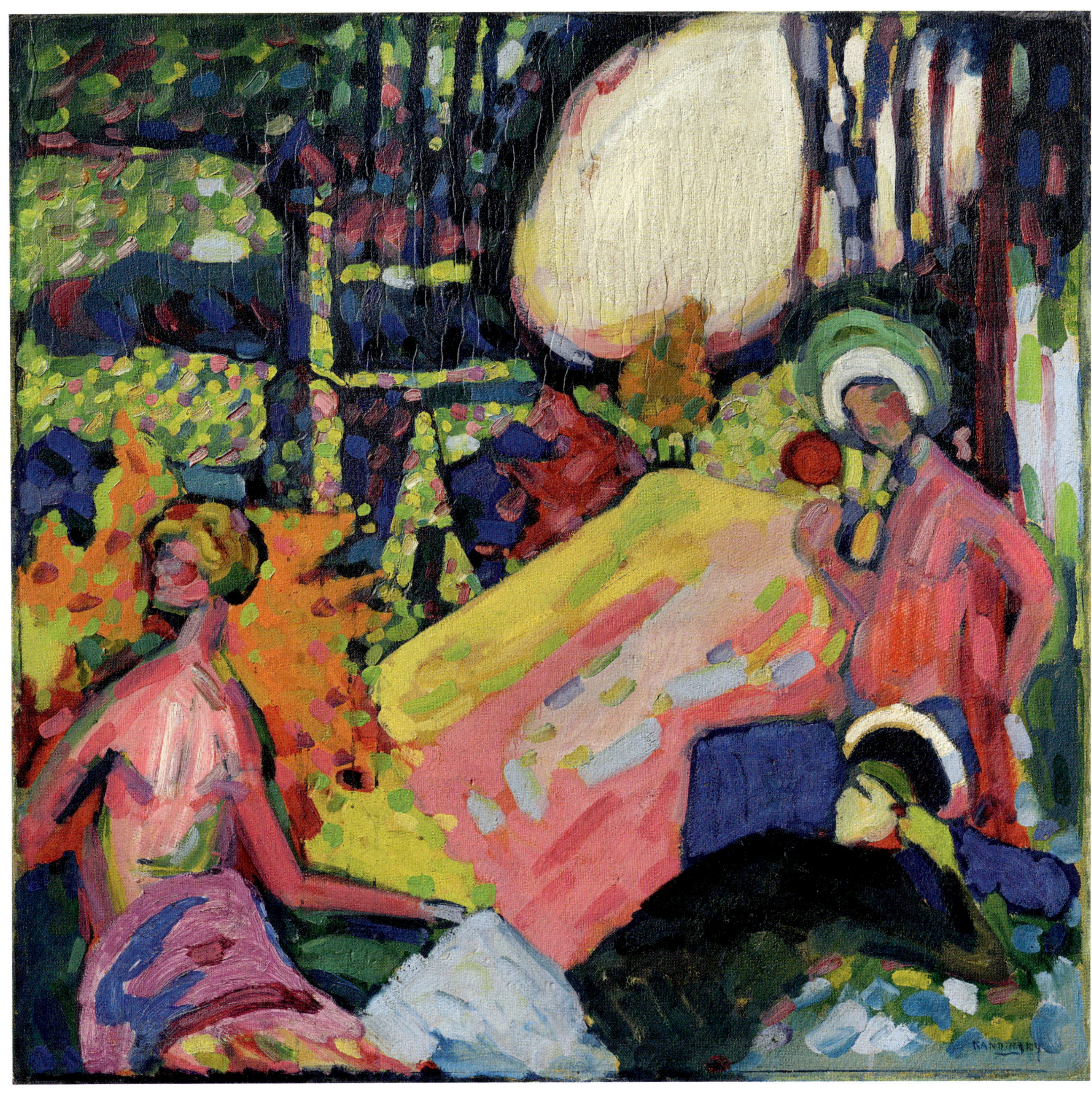

1 Wassily Kandinsky
White Sound, 1908
Private collection

Lenders

ASOM Collection
Galerie Berinson, Berlin
Staatliche Museen zu Berlin, Nationalgalerie, Marzona Collection
Staatliche Museen zu Berlin, Neue Nationalgalerie
Josef Albers Museum Quadrat Bottrop
Lehmbruck Museum, Duisburg
Kunstsammlung Nordrhein-Westfalen, Düsseldorf
Fondation Gandur pour l'Art, Genève
Kulturstiftung Sachsen-Anhalt, Kunstmuseum Moritzburg Halle (Saale)
Hamburger Kunsthalle
University of Hertfordshire Art Collection
Louisiana Museum of Modern Art, Humlebæk
Muzeum Sztuki, Łódź
Courtauld, London
Royal Academy of Arts, London
Solomon R. Guggenheim Museum, New York
Whitney Museum of American Art, New York
D. Wigmore Fine Art, Inc., New York
Sainsbury Centre, University of East Anglia, Norwich
Pier Arts Centre, Stromness, Orkney
Kröller-Müller Museum, Otterlo
Philadelphia Museum of Art
Fondation Beyeler, Riehen/Basel
Museum Boijmans Van Beuningen, Rotterdam
Fondation Marguerite et Aimé Maeght, Saint-Paul de Vence
Museum für Gegenwartskunst, Siegen
MOMus—Museum of Modern Art—Costakis Collection, Thessaloniki
Peggy Guggenheim Collection, Venice
ALBERTINA, Vienna—Private collection
National Gallery of Art, Washington
Haus Bill, Zumikon
Camille Graeser Stiftung, Zurich
Kunsthaus Zürich
Verena Loewensberg Stiftung, Zurich

Estate of Richard Anuszkiewicz
Collection of David and Kathryn Birnbaum
Estate of Carmen Herrera
Studio Paul Huxley
Richard Paul Lohse-Stiftung
Mercedes-Benz Art Collection
Nahmad Collection
Neil K. Rector & the Rector Artwork Trust
Estate of Julian Stanczak
Triton Collection Foundation
UK Government Art Collection

as well as numerous private collectors who wish to remain anonymous

Acknowledgments

We would like to thank the following for their support in making this exhibition possible:

Hendrik A. Berinson, Tobia Bezzola, Raphael Bouvier, Alla Chilova, Harry Cooper, Martha Craig, Veronica DaSilva, Bertrand Dumas, Lucy Economakis, Roger Emery, Megan Fontanella, Emily Ann Francisco, Sandra Gianfreda, Keith Gill, Taisse Grandi Venturi, Christine Hourde, Paul Huxley, Brigitte van Kann, Wan Hui Keoy, Tamar Kharatishvili, Ekaterina Klim, Ulf Küster, Olesia Lazarenko, Miriam Leimer, Emily Lenz, Jeremy Lewison, Egidio Marzona, Hugo Nathan, Julius Osman, Alivé Piliado, Alisa Podolyak, Neil K. Rector, Peter Sedgley, Xan Serafin, Simon Shaw, Jack Shear, Gražina Subelytė, Angela Thomas, Giulia Trabaldo Togna, Charlotte Webster, Emily Whittle, Deedee Wigmore, Calvin Winner, Allison Wucher,

and especially Daniel Zamani, who initiated the exhibition.

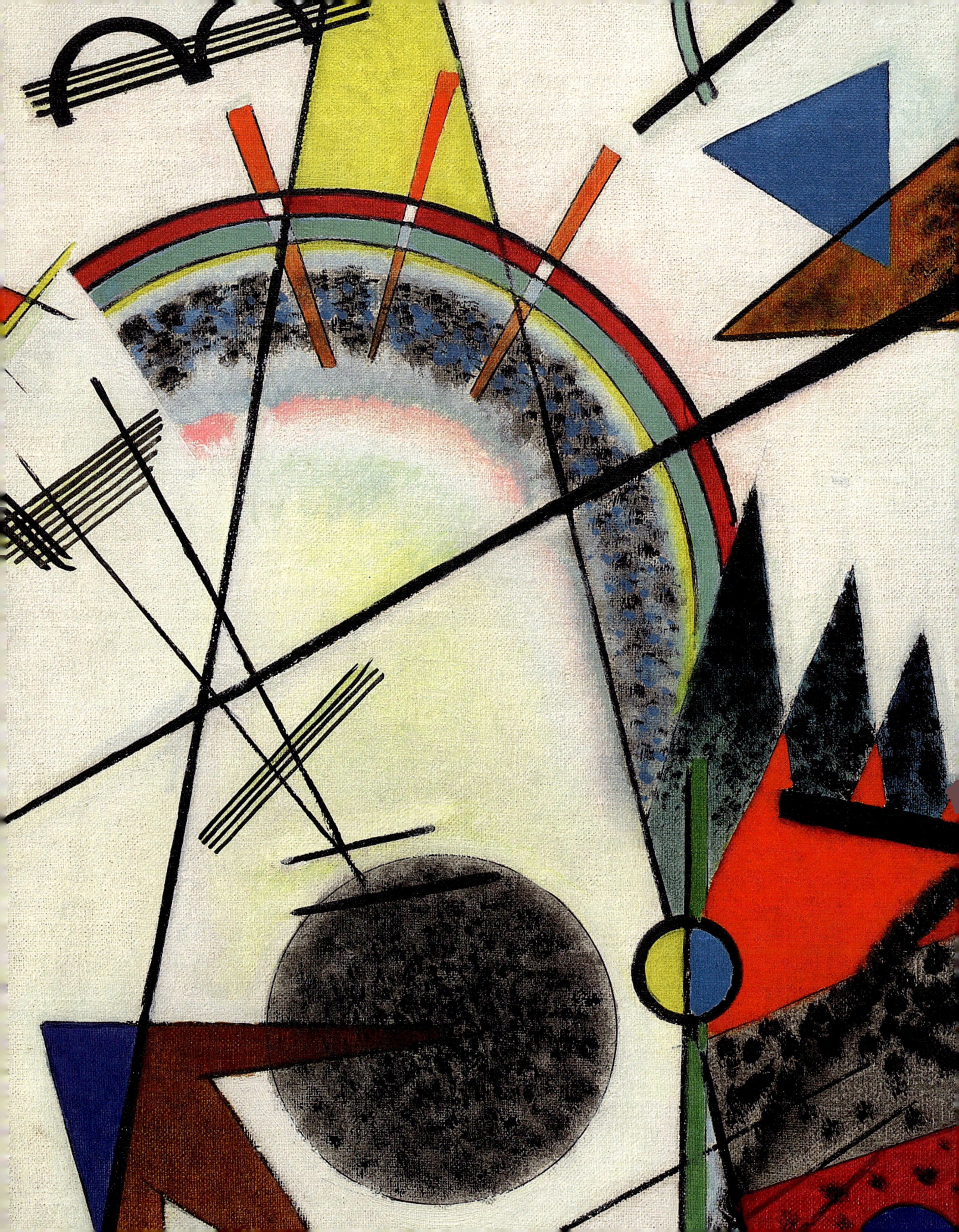

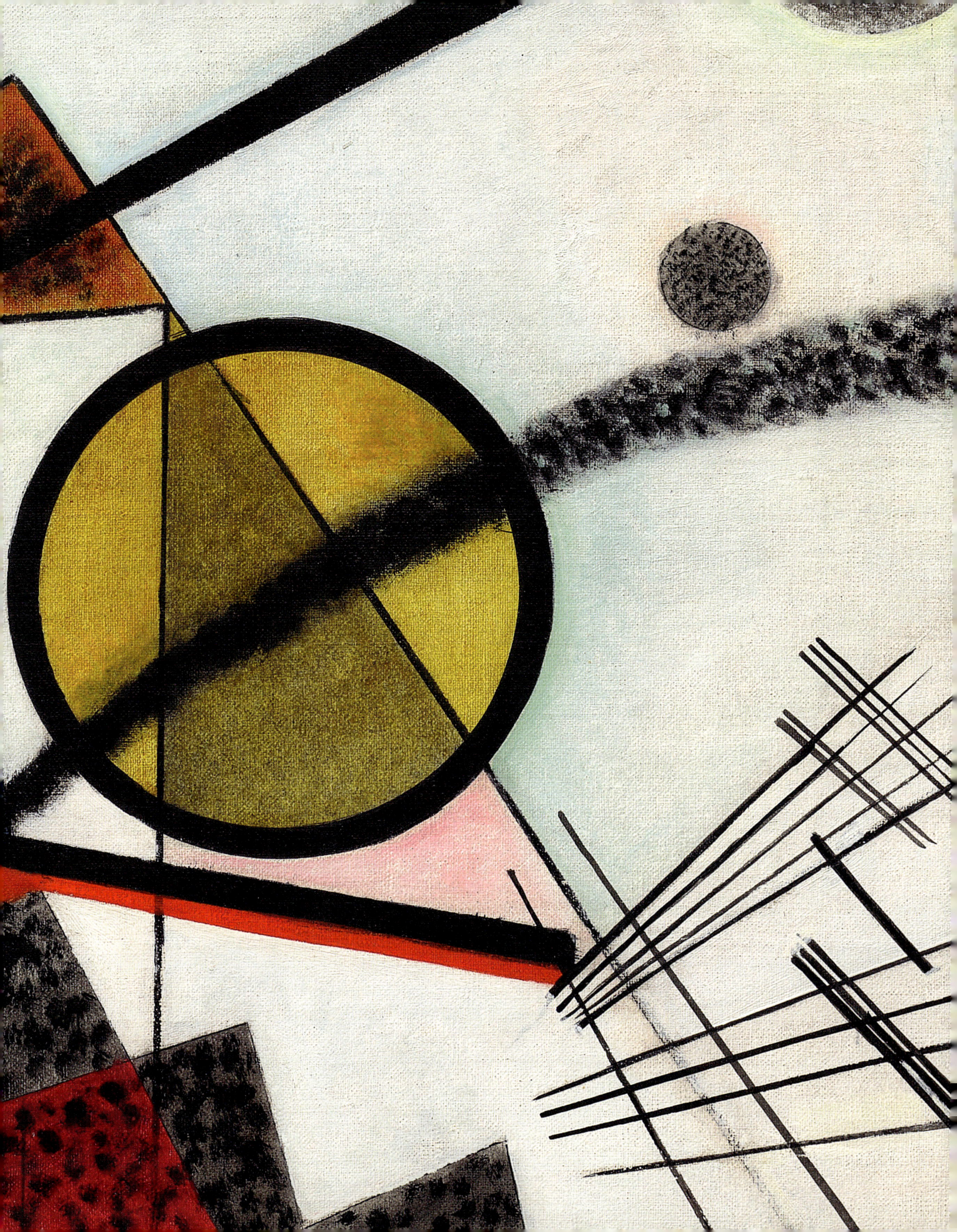

John E. Bowlt and Nicoletta Misler

Kandinsky's Synthesis

Bridging Art, Science, and Spirituality

A major paradigmatic shift in twentieth-century Western art was the departure from figurative representation in favor of abstraction, a shift often reduced to a precarious, almost neurotic, bipolarity: on one side, the strict geometrization of forms; on the other, the flowing abstraction of internal visions and extrasensory ideas. One of the leading protagonists of this tendency was Wassily Kandinsky, whose work highlights the synergies between art and science. Associated with diverse cultural and intellectual circles of Europe, Kandinsky had access to pioneering artistic and scientific experiments. His early treatise *Concerning the Spiritual in Art* already drew on neuroscience and spiritual concepts to suggest that geometric planes and colors possess universal, interrelated qualities. His engagement with scientific principles deepened in 1921 at the Russian Academy of Artistic Sciences in Moscow (RAKhN), where he collaborated with experts in fields such as psychology and crystallography, further probing the formal and psychological dimensions of art.

Kandinsky's paintings as well as his theoretical writings reveal that the abovementioned polarities—between geometric precision and lyrical abstraction, science and spirit, and the organic and inorganic—are far less rigid than assumed.[1]

THE SCIENCE OF ART

On December 29 and 31, 1911, Nikolai Kulbin, a painter, physician, and friend of Kandinsky, delivered *Concerning the Spiritual in Art* on Kandinsky's behalf. At the time, Kandinsky was living in Munich, where he had just published the German edition of his treatise.[2] The reading took place at the Second All-Russian Congress of Artists in St. Petersburg, a three-day gathering of painters, sculptors, art historians, and teachers that featured a wide variety of lectures and discussions. Kandinsky's contribution was among the most radical and provocative.

In the three-volume edition of the congress's transactions, a single full-page color illustration appeared (fig. 1): a triad of yellow triangle, blue circle, and red square. Kandinsky used this image to demonstrate the effects of different backgrounds on colors and to suggest that specific shapes and colors have intrinsic, universal relationships. This diagram serves as a

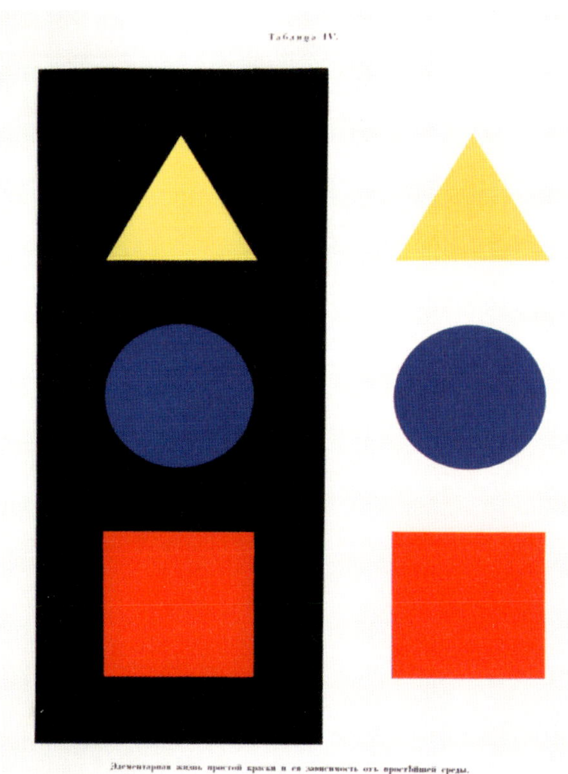

1
Wassily Kandinsky,
Elementary Life of the Primary Color and Its Dependence on the Simplest Locale,
in *Transactions of the All-Russian Congress of Artists,* St. Petersburg 1914, vol. 1, table 4

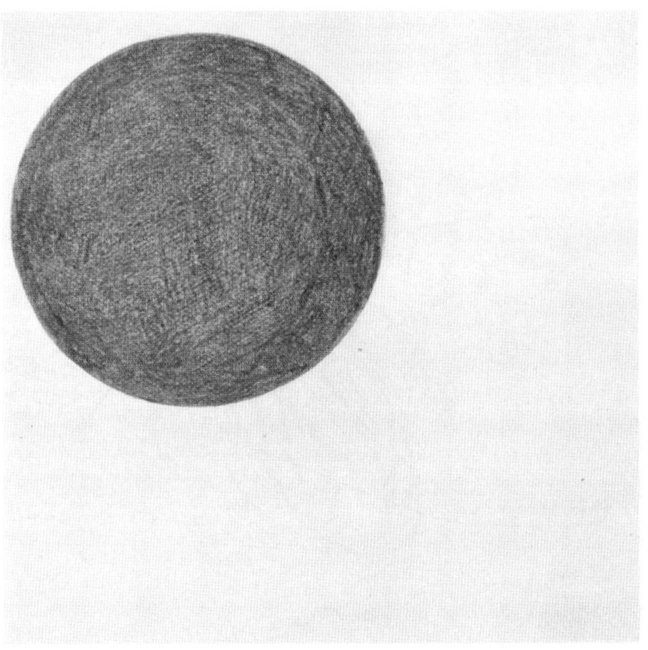

2
Kazimir Malevich,
The Basic Suprematist Element: The First Suprematist Form Created from the Square; 1913,
in Malevich, *Die gegenstandslose Welt* (The Nonobjective World), Bauhausbücher 11, Munich 1927, fig. 68

precursor to the stripped-down geometry that Kazimir Malevich developed in his Suprematist works, which he first exhibited in 1915 (→ p. 267).

Concerning the Spiritual in Art has been extensively discussed and annotated,[3] but it is especially relevant for understanding the geometric and formulaic elements of Kandinsky's creative output. All the versions of the treatise carry numerous illustrations of geometric figures. A central thesis of the paper is that a work of art can be at least partially "explained" by reason and deduction. Kandinsky theorizes that geometric forms—such as the triangle, square, and circle—have vibrational correspondences and, much like music notes, evoke certain emotions. For example, the triangle is sharp and active, symbolizing energy, movement, and change. Analyzing geometry can therefore help reveal the inner content of a composition. On this level, Kandinsky's arguments help us understand his own evolution from the free lyricism of the early period to the geometric compositions of the 1920s and 1930s.

Convinced that "every form has its content," Kandinsky was not alone in his pursuit of a geometric alphabet.[4] He shared his methodology with numerous artists, not least Malevich, who depicted squares, circles, triangles, and crosses to illustrate his theory of a Suprematist "alphabet" consisting of thirty-four black characters (fig. 2).[5] Considering this analogy, one might surmise that Kandinsky's *In the Black Square* from 1923 (cat. 21) was a comment on Malevich's *Black Square* of 1915 (fig. p. 72). For Kandinsky, there were ultimately two geometric orders: one mathematical and calculable, the other hermetic and approximate—a conflict of interests that accompanied and stimulated his artistic evolution.

The nervous tension and physical exertion Kandinsky seemed to experience as he painted his first abstract masterpieces—works not yet soberly geometric—are documented in a sequence of photographs of *Composition VII* taken by his partner at the time, artist Gabriele Münter. These images capture the spiritual labor—and pangs of creation—that Kandinsky endured between November 25 and 29, 1913 (fig. 3).[6] The final version of the large oil painting (fig. 4) was the culmination of at least twenty drawings and watercolors as well as six preliminary oil sketches. It was a long and elaborate process that, as Kandinsky affirmed, could be perceived as a metaphor for procreation: "A true work of art emerges 'from the artist.' Born of the artist, the artwork acquires an independent life, itself becoming a personality, an independent, thinking, breathing subject that also leads a material life."[7]

Kandinsky's *Concerning the Spiritual in Art* is concerned with the effort to reduce the intangible—inspiration, the soul, and harmony—into geometric forms and color vibrations, effectively the "materialization of spiritual values."[8] Kandinsky concluded that, for example, a "large, acute-angled triangle divided into unequal segments with the narrowest segment upwards—that is the spiritual life conceived as a precise scheme."[9] The triangle motif continued to haunt Kandinsky even during the Bauhaus years, as seen in paintings *Silent* (cat. 80) and *Above and Left* (cat. 78). His analysis of the basic elements of form (such as color, plane, volume, space, time, movement) coincided with a burgeoning "science of art."[10] Kandinsky was aware of the emerging discipline of *Kunstwissenschaft,* which was not only focused on historical or biographical analyses but also on the formal and psychological aspects of art. In the spring of 1920, as the founding director of the Institute of Artistic Culture (INKhUK), Kandinsky outlined its primary objective as the development of a science of art—an objective that he continued to pursue, even after he left the institute in January 1921, and helped shape when the Russian Academy of Artistic Sciences (RAKhN) was founded that same year.

NEUROSCIENCE, MEMORY, AND THEOSOPHICAL THOUGHT

Kandinsky's theory that geometric shapes and colors evoke specific emotional and spiritual responses seems to have been influenced by an unexpected source: the memory training experiments of neuroscientist Fedor Rybakov. Like Kandinsky, he explored psychological responses to color through instructive tables (figs. 5, 6). In his experiments, he studied how the selection and grouping of visual matches—recognizing patterns and connections between colors and shapes—could enhance memory retention. While Kandinsky referred to the "psychic effects of color," Rybakov spoke of their "higher psychic functions."[11]

Rybakov served as the head of the Department of Experimental Psychology and the Psychiatric Clinic at Moscow University, where Kandinsky also taught in 1919. A prominent psychiatrist and psychoanalyst, he specialized in environmental psychology, with a particular interest in the effects of mental "abnormality" on artistic and literary creativity, and vice versa.[12] Rybakov's Psychiatric Clinic, with its various laboratories, so-called cabinets, library, and photo-laboratory, may have inspired the departmental structure of RAKhN. Rybakov replicated this model on a smaller scale at the Moscow Psychoneurological Institute, which he cofounded and directed in 1920. Incidentally, in June of the following year, RAKhN occupied the institute building at 32 Prechistenka, where Kandinsky served as its vice president and chair of its Physico-Psychological Department.[13]

3
Gabriele Münter,
Four Documentary Photographs of the Creation of Kandinsky's "Composition VII," Munich, Ainmillerstrasse, 1913,
Gabriele Münter and Johannes Eichner Foundation, Munich

4
Wassily Kandinsky,
Composition VII, 1913,
Tretyakov Gallery, Moscow

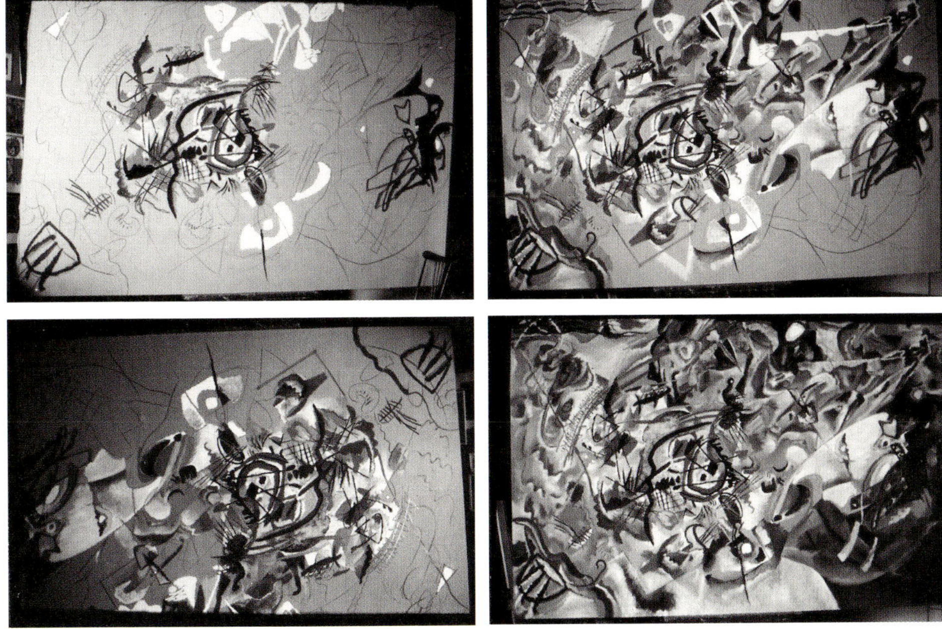

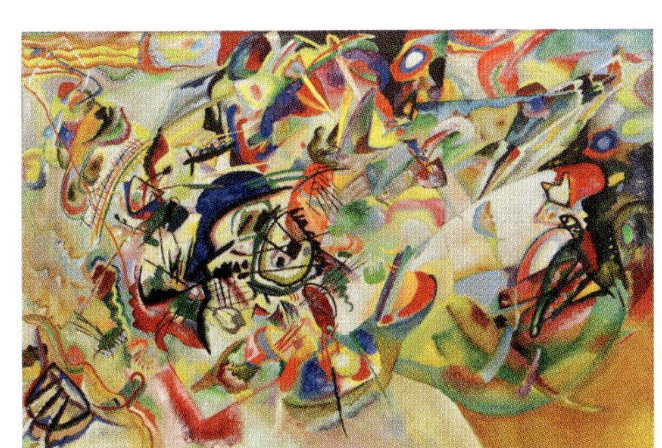

In developing his initial plan for the department, Kandinsky envisioned a program that had the aim of examining the visual arts from a synthetic perspective—incorporating aesthetic, formal, scientific, spiritual, and psychological viewpoints. By 1921–22, Kandinsky's department became the guiding force of RAKhN, addressing subjects such as Gestalt theory, hypnosis, dreams, psychoanalysis, physiology of perception and the unconscious, and their relation to the artistic process. Among these, the notion of "improvisation as the revelation of the unconscious" (a theme that particularly appealed to Kandinsky) received significant attention.[14] Kandinsky was intrigued by the intersection of psychological sciences and philosophical idealism. To advance this interest, during his brief tenure, he facilitated no fewer than nineteen lectures by leading psychologists, physicists, art historians, and philosophers—such as Ivan Ermakov, Semen Frank, Pavel Kapterev, Petr Lazarev, Aleksandr Samoilov, and Aleksei Sidorov—on the mechanics of perception.[15] They strove to demonstrate the influence of both "physiology" and "psyche" on the artistic process.

The prominent scientists who collaborated with Kandinsky in RAKhN's Physico-Psychological Department, especially the psychologists Georgy Chelpanov and Vladimir Ekzempliarsky, specialists in the art of mentally ill people, were undoubtedly familiar with Rybakov's research. It is reasonable to assume that Kandinsky and Rybakov, both mentors at Moscow University and advocates of the "physiological" and the "psychological," had been personally acquainted. Kandinsky also published his article "Whither the 'New' Art?" a year after Rybakov's 1910 essay, also on contemporary culture, with the very similar title "Whither are We Going?"[16] Kandinsky's colored chart for *Concerning the Spiritual in Art* shows a parallel to Rybakov's contemporaneous "Mnemonic for Geometric Figures and Colors" (fig. 6), while Rybakov's illustrations of "Fantasy" (fig. 7) could be elements from Kandinsky's *Improvisations,* foreshadowing Hermann Rorschach's projective inkblot method of psychological testing, developed a decade later.

However, Kandinsky's interest in the psychological and psychical matters, along with the very title of his primary work, *Concerning the Spiritual in Art,* points to another significant influence: Theosophy. This spiritual and philosophical movement sought to explore the hidden truths of existence, aligning closely with Kandinsky's artistic quest to transcend the materiality of his works. Although he was not a convinced Theosophist, Kandinsky was drawn by its claim to universality, syncretic nature, and core ideas of clairvoyance and consciousness hierarchy. He was familiar with Theosophical founder Helena Blavatsky—keeping her *Secret Doctrine* in

5
Fedor Rybakov,
"Attention with Choices,"
in Rybakov, *Atlas for Experimental Psychological Research on Personality,* Moscow 1910

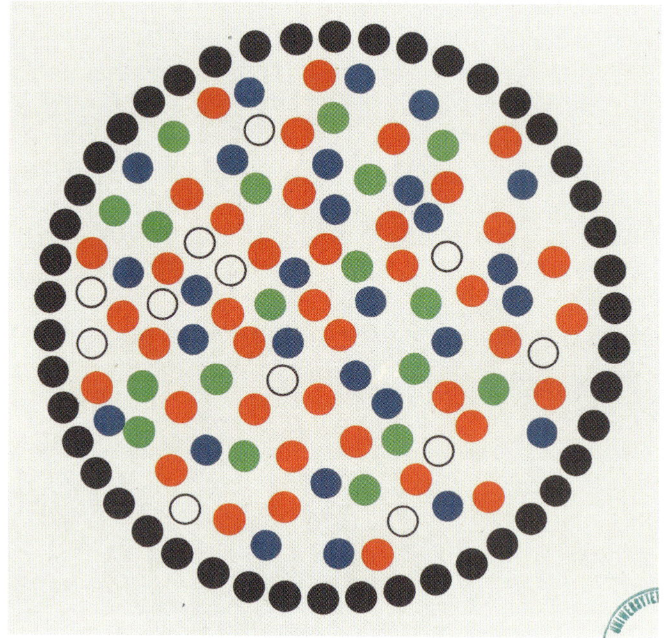

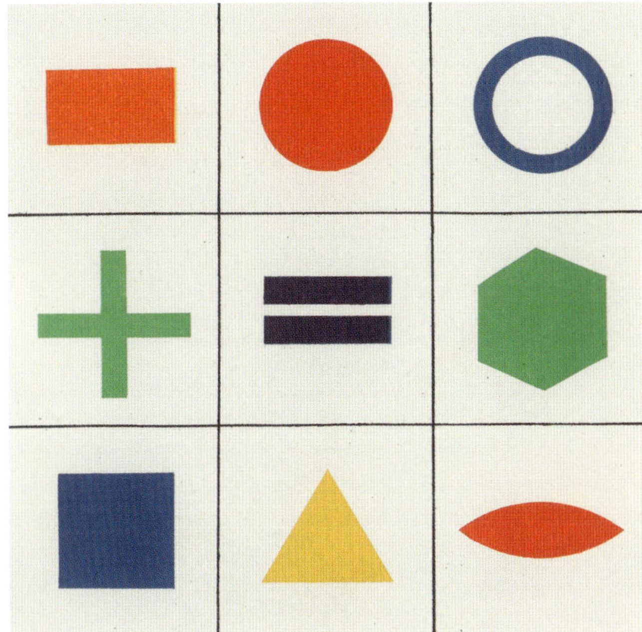

6
Fedor Rybakov,
"Mnemonic for Geometric Figures and Colors,"
in Rybakov, *Atlas for Experimental Psychological Research on Personality,* Moscow 1910

his Munich library—as well as Annie Besant and Charles Leadbeater's mystical *Thought-Forms,* published in 1905. The latter work, which proposed that emotions could project colored forms, resonated with Kandinsky's belief that the physical world was intertwined with unseen realms. As Besant and Leadbeater explained, the "physicist . . . finds himself bewildered by touches and gleams from another realm which interpenetrates his own, he finds himself compelled to speculate on invisible presences."[17]

Kandinsky's frequent use of words such as "spirit" and "soul" in his writings echoes Theosophical ideas.[18] There are also clear Theosophical analogies in his paintings, such as the bizarre floating form in *Woman in Moscow* of 1912 (fig. 8), which resembles the "thought-form" that Besant and Leadbeater attributed to the feeling of "vague pure affection" (fig. 9). According to them, this "cloud of pure affection . . . represents a very positive feeling. The person from whom it emanates is happy and in harmony with the world."[19] These loose Theosophical symbols reappear more geometrically in later works such as *Light in Heavy* (cat. 27) and *Arrow Toward the Circle* (cat. 38). Together, these influences suggest that Kandinsky's study of geometry was not only a visual exploration but also an intricate synthesis of scientific inquiry and metaphysical thought.

BRIDGING THE SENSES

Embedded within *Concerning the Spiritual in Art* is a reference to Aleksandra Vasilevna Zakharina-Unkovskaia, a Theosophist, violinist, and schoolteacher, who, as Kandinsky noted, carried out "successful experiments . . . with unmusical children—to encourage them to memorize a melody with the help of color or, at least, of colors."[20] Her ideas on synesthesia and the interrelationship between different sensory modalities—specifically between sound and color—resonated with Kandinsky's own theories. Kandinsky elaborated that "A. Zakharina-Unkovskaia has worked for many years on this project and has constructed a special, precise method of 'notating music from the colors of nature and of painting from the sounds of nature, to see sound in color terms and to hear colors in musical terms.'"[21]

A champion of Theosophy, Unkovskaia taught art and music as a single subject to children, believing that nature was the receptacle of synesthesia. To this end, she composed music to represent natural phenomena such as the shimmering surface of a lake, the stars shining, or clouds billowing, as in her score *Mysterious Painting.* She also designed charts to measure the ebb and flow of colors as music progressed, a kind of coordinational color organ,[22] and contributed a version of her treatise "Method of Color-Sound-Number" for the 1908 St. Petersburg exhibition *Art in the Life of the Child.*[23] Unkovskaia was excited by Kandinsky's theory and practice, referring to his prints as "pure music" and hoping to share her exercises in sound, color, and number with him.[24]

Unkovskaia lectured widely and in 1908 even visited author Lev Tolstoi to discuss her ideas, subsequently sending him an offprint of her "Method of Color-Sound-Number" from the journal *Vestnik teosofii* (Herald of Theosophy).[25] The following year she contributed to the fifth International Theosophical Congress in Budapest with an exposition of her "Method of Color-Sound-Number" and a concerto on her Guarneri violin.[26] According to various sources, Kandinsky attended the Budapest convention, where he would have made the acquaintance of Unkovskaia, listened to her lectures and violin recital,[27] and learned of her identification of colors, sounds, and numbers, according to which red is equal to *do* and one, orange to *re* and two, yellow to *mi* and three, and so on.[28]

Like Kandinsky, Unkovskaia believed in a second geometry that runs parallel to the visible, physical world: "Contemplation of geometric forms assists in the development of a serenity, while the reproduction of forms in nature and the expression of beautiful thoughts via versification in speech and song awakens a joyous feeling of beauty in the pupil."[29] Unkovskaia also spoke of the "inner content behind external forms,"[30] a concept reminding us of Kandinsky's frequent references to the "inner necessity" or "inner sound" within a work of art.

BLURRING BOUNDARIES

In this role at the Russian Academy of Artistic Sciences (RAKhN), Kandinsky grappled with the rigidness of traditional science, especially the division between organic and inorganic matter—a dichotomy mirroring the one between geometric and visionary abstractions. Kandinsky's oeuvre suggests that, for him, there was no opposition between these two forms of representation: one was spiritual, highly emotional, and transcendent, while the other was rational, materialistic, and immanent, yet they could be combined and transition into one another.

Even as Kandinsky left Moscow in December 1921 to join the Bauhaus, where he connected with more "rational" abstractionists such as Josef Albers (cats. 28–32), he never abandoned his inner vision. Biomorphic forms continued to dominate his ink drawings, watercolors, and oils, resembling small protoplasmic and organic beings. These forms share space with flying enigmatic "chessboards" and geometric shapes, as seen in his 1922 painting *White Cross* (cat. 3). The chessboard motifs in his Bauhaus works, however, were not without precedent. His 1920 painting *Composition No. 224 (On White 1)*, from his last years in Moscow, is characterized by energetic motion and free handling of geometric and curved shapes, where a checkered pattern decomposes as it stretches across the composition (fig. 10).

This synthesis of spiritual and geometric abstraction, where organic forms and structured patterns coexist, underscores Kandinsky's lifelong pursuit to blur the lines between the material

7
Fedor Rybakov,
"Fantasy," in Rybakov,
Atlas for Experimental Psychological Research on Personality,
Moscow 1910

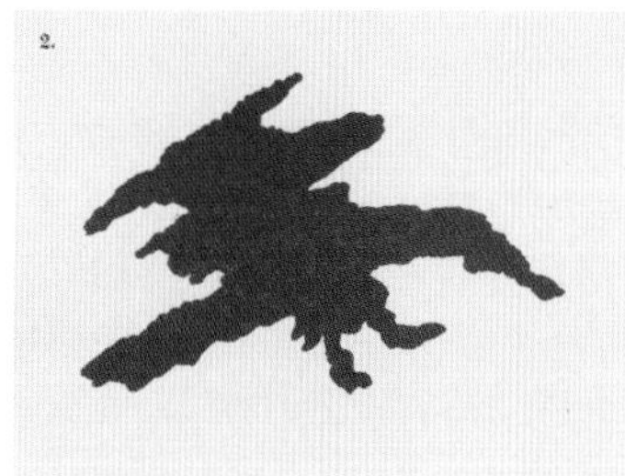

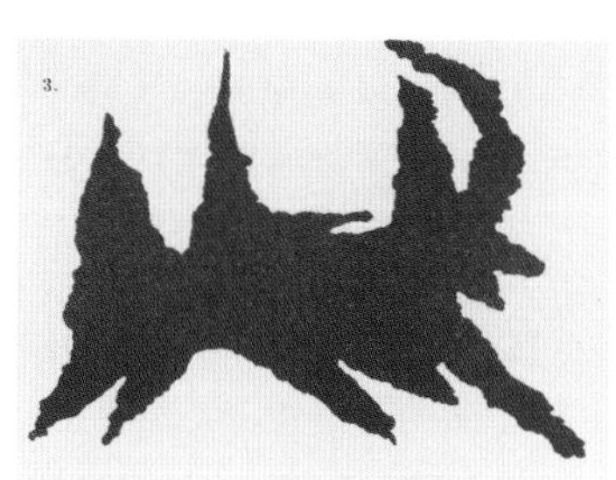

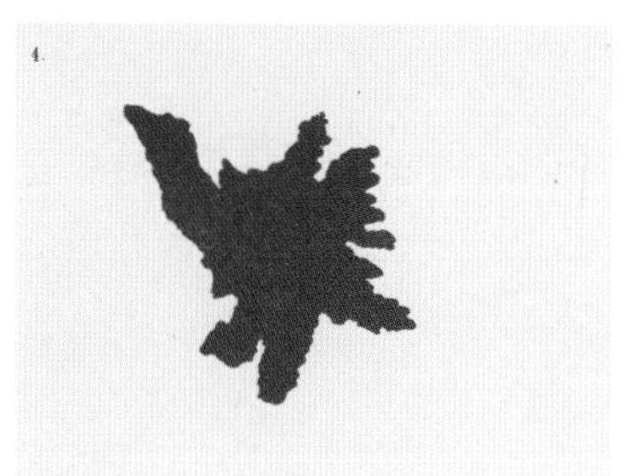

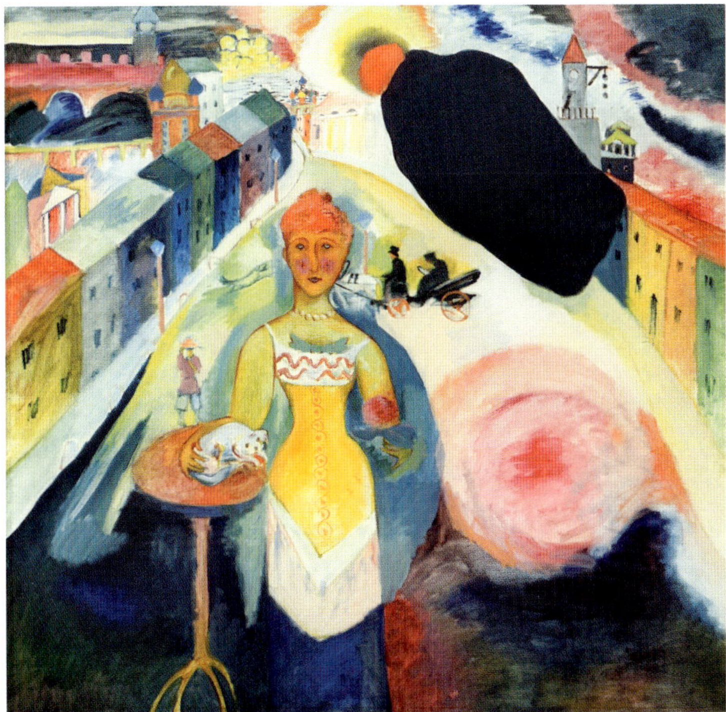

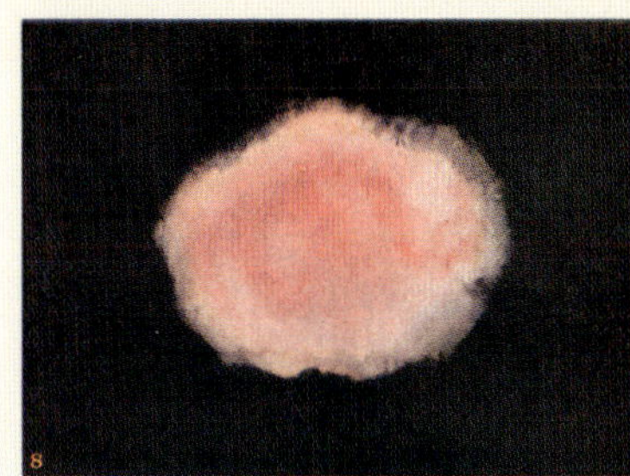

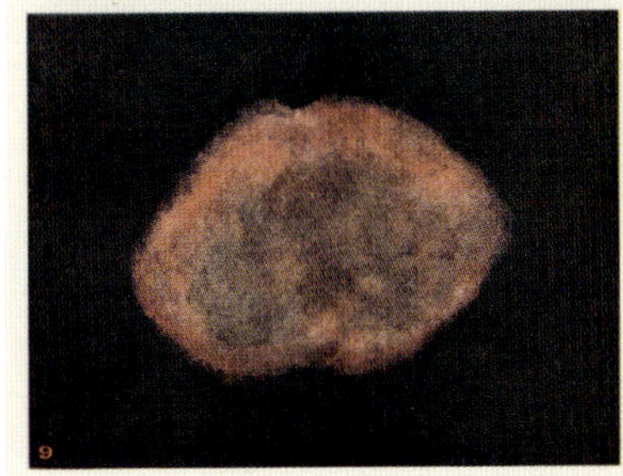

8
Wassily Kandinsky, *Woman in Moscow,* 1912, Städtische Galerie im Lenbachhaus, Munich

9
Annie Besant and Charles Webster Leadbeater, "Thought-Forms of Vague Pure Affection and Vague Selfish Affection," in Besant/Leadbeater, *Thought-Forms: A Record of Clairvoyant Investigation,* London 1905, figs. 8–9

and the mystical, the organic and inorganic—a pursuit that found a parallel in the lectures on crystal research at RAKhN.

CRYSTALLOGRAPHERS

In 1921 Kandinsky invited professional scientists to collaborate with him at RAKhN. In his paper "On a Method for Working with Synthetic Art," written in March 1921, he determined the types of scientists and artists who should be invited. Giving precedence to biologists, Kandinsky continued, "Specialists in mechanics should be added to mathematicians, while inviting crystallographers on the one hand, and engineers on the other, is of particular importance . . . crystallographers are concerned exclusively with the laws of nature which create phenomena very close to works of art."[31]

Kandinsky's belief that biological sciences could offer models for understanding human creativity, shares much in common with the ideas of Russian philosopher Semen Frank. His lecture "The Role of Art in the Positive Sciences," delivered at RAKhN on August 30, 1921, compared evolutionism with abstract art.[32] He suggested that, just as a biologist could conceptualize new beings within the evolutionary chain, an artist could envision new forms "at the frontier" of reality.[33] Frank concluded that contemporary art could reveal many unexplored aspects of reality, just as the pioneering work of mathematicians Bernhard Riemann and Nikolai Lobachevsky, which challenged the long-standing dominance of Euclidean geometry, opened up new ways of thinking about space.[34]

Among the scientists invited to be one of four members of the first working commission of Kandinsky's Physico-Psychological Department was physicist and crystallographer Nikolai Uspensky. His research focused on X-raying crystals, a topic he had begun researching in Munich in 1912, where Kandinsky may have already met him. Uspensky collaborated closely with physicist Georg Wulff, who was examining crystal structures at the Commercial Institute in Moscow. Building on their individual research they developed a research program focused on X-ray diffraction in crystals. As early as the spring of 1907, Wulff had presented a lecture series at the Polytechnic Museum in Moscow, offering a scientific analysis of symmetry in nature: covering examples from animal, vegetable, and mineral kingdoms. He discussed how symmetry governed the internal structure of both animate and inanimate matter. Later, Wulff studied the growth of crystals and traced an analogy between the various forms of growth in animals and plants, insisting in 1915 that the "ideas of a similarity between crystals and organisms are very attractive, because they instill hope that we might discover the secret bridge spanning the two fields of the inorganic and the organic worlds."[35] He expanded on this subject in his lecture "Rhythm in the Creations of Nature" at RAKhN on April 4, 1922.

The collaboration between scientists and artists at RAKhN was part of a broader twentieth-century enthusiasm for merging scientific inquiry with artistic creation. Russian avant-garde painter Pavel Filonov developed a unique theoretical and artistic approach known as Analytical Realism. This involved a deconstruction of form and structure, resulting in works that resemble complex crystalline compositions. Filonov regarded each of his works as a "formula of life," by which he meant that his paintings were not representations of the visible world, but a coded representation of the dynamics of life, growth, and transformation. The crystal, a model for inanimate matter, often served as a mental image or code. For example, in his *Formula of the Universe* from 1920–22 (fig. 14) he painted a transparent, rotating crystal beneath an arch at the center of the composition, a representation similar to the graphic illustrations of crystals (fig. 12) published in popular journals such as *Priroda* (Nature).

The scientific revolution at the threshold of the twentieth century included the advanced application of modern instruments such as the microscope, various electrical apparatuses, and X-rays. Avant-garde artists were fascinated by such inventions, inserting them into their artworks as seen in Marcel Duchamp's *Chocolate Grinder* (1913, Philadelphia Museum of Art) or Ivan Kliun's *Ozonator* (1914, Russian Museum, St. Petersburg). The artists, like their scientific colleagues, were aware of the epistemological implications of their own discoveries. They advanced a common philosophical query: wherein lies the boundary between the organic and the inorganic?

10
Wassily Kandinsky,
Composition No. 224
(On White I), 1920,
Russian Museum, St. Petersburg

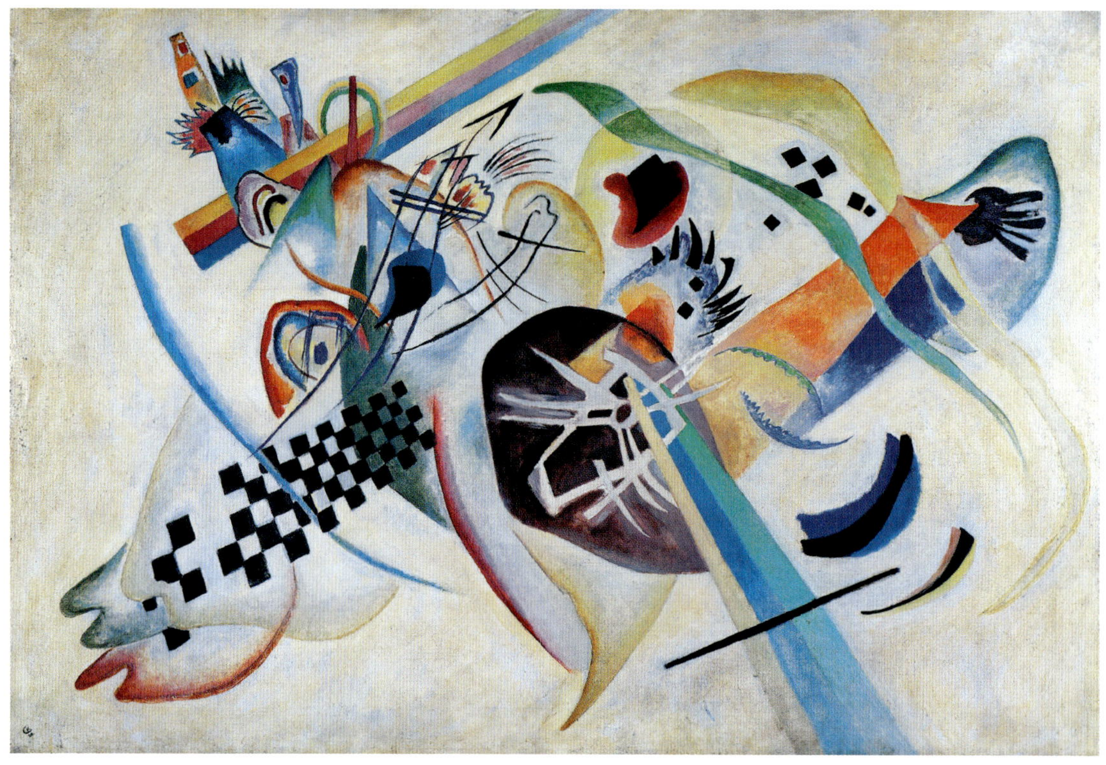

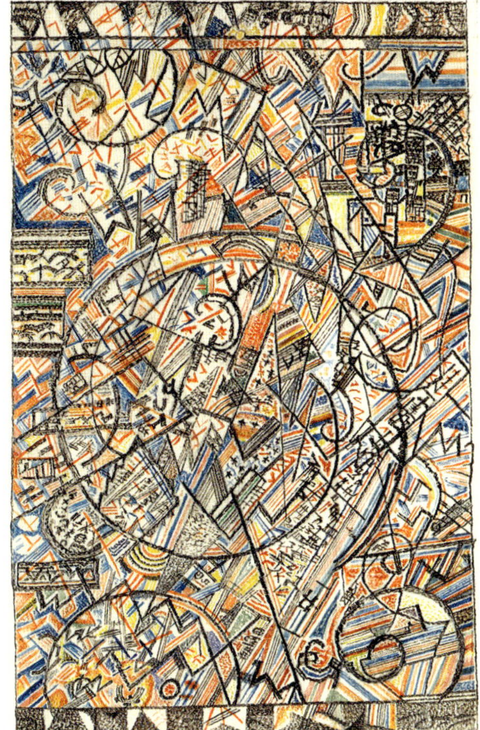

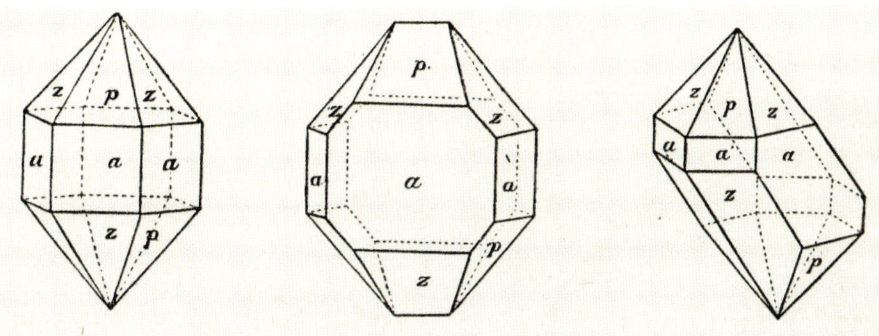

11
Pavel Filonov,
Formula of the Universe, 1920–22,
Russian Museum, St. Petersburg

12
Georg Wulff,
"Do Crystals and Plants Have Anything in Common?,"
in *Priroda* (January 1912), 45–46

THE CEREBRAL AND THE SENSUAL

Kandinsky never erred from his conviction that the cerebral must yield to the tactile, the calculated to the spontaneous and sensual. In one of his conclusive essays, "Line and Fish" from 1935, Kandinsky, perhaps meditating upon his long career, observed:

> *Approaching it in one way* I see no essential difference between a line one calls "abstract" and a fish. . . .
> This isolated line and the isolated fish alike are living beings with forces peculiar to them, though latent. . . .
> Because each being has an impressive "look" which manifests itself by its expression. . . .
> *But approaching it in another way* there is an essential difference between a line and a fish.
> And that is that the fish can swim, eat and be eaten. It has then capacities of which the line is deprived.
> These capacities of the fish are necessary extras for the fish itself and for the kitchen, but not for painting. . . .
> That is why I like the line better than the fish—at least, in my painting.[36]

Maria Mileeva

Circles of Exchange

Geometric Abstraction and the East-Central European Avant-Garde, 1920–1930

In January 1922 Ilya Ehrenburg imagined the evolution of geometric abstraction in the visual arts through the metaphor of circular development and transformation in his book *And Yet the World Turns,* which was published in Moscow and Berlin.[1] The original dust jacket featured a Cubist work by Fernand Léger (fig. 1). Léger's black-and-white composition of intersecting circles, lines, and patterns takes the form of a dynamic machinelike construction with subtle optical effects that suggest volume, rhythm, and movement. In his book, Ehrenburg defended Constructivism and discussed the "new architecture" of Vladimir Tatlin; the work of Léger, Jacques Lipchitz, El Lissitzky (cats. 13, 14, 18), Pablo Picasso, Aleksandr Rodchenko (cat. 6), and Theo van Doesburg (cat. 39); and a Charlie Chaplin film. Published amid an influx of art publications that sought to take stock of key developments in the visual arts across Europe, *And Yet the World Turns* is a largely forgotten treatise on contemporary avant-garde art.

As the title of Ehrenburg's book suggests, the period in the immediate aftermath of World War I was marked less by rupture in creative practices than by continuities that conjured a vision of circular and repetitive artistic interdependencies. Ehrenburg and many other artists and critics of the 1920s and 1930s were intent on determining the roots of geometric abstraction—both to lay their claim to it and show the significance of preceding "isms." One such example is the canonical diagram that art historian and curator Alfred H. Barr Jr. created for the cover of the catalog accompanying the exhibition *Cubism and Abstract Art* (fig. 2; → p. 272), held at the Museum of Modern Art in New York in 1936.[2] Barr's diagram is a one-directional and rigid conceptualization of the developments of modern art that led unequivocally with a forward thrust to "non-geometrical abstract art" and "geometrical abstract art" between 1890 and 1935. Both Ehrenburg and Barr represent a shared vision of progress and universality that was common among contemporary avant-garde groups and critics across America and Europe of the 1920s and 1930s. Nevertheless, Suprematism and Constructivism, which Barr's diagram dates to 1913 and 1914 in Moscow, took on a different meaning when the movements reached Berlin in the early 1920s.[3] It was the label of Constructivism that became an umbrella term for multiple international groups of artists that developed together and in parallel. While they had many shared concerns, there were key differences based on a set of social, cultural, and political conditions in the places where they emerged.

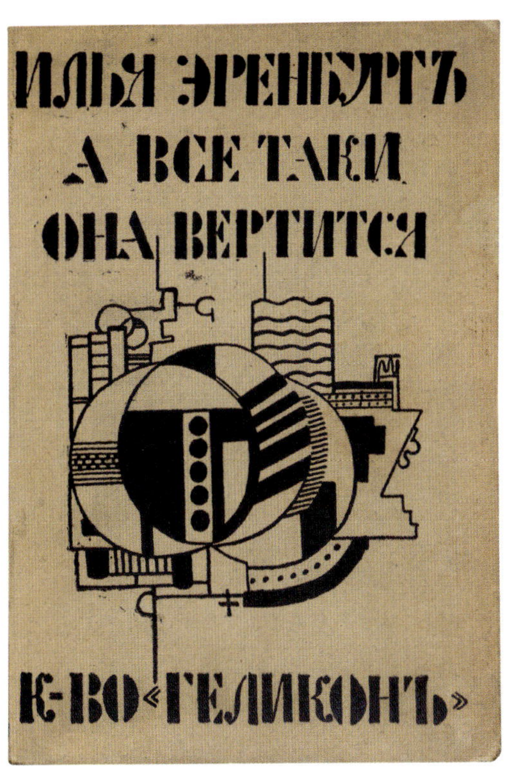

1
Fernand Léger,
illustration on the cover of
Ilya Ehrenburg, ed., *A vse-taki ona vertitsia* (And Yet the World Turns),
Moscow and Berlin 1922

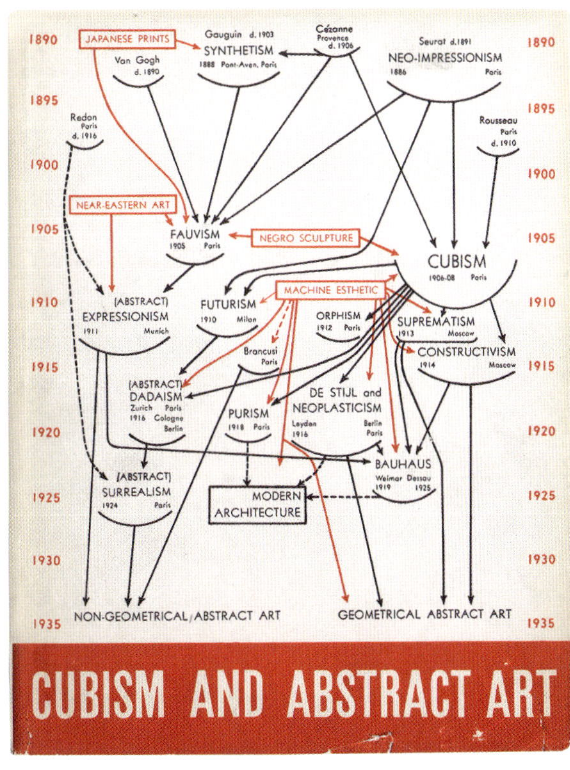

2
Alfred H. Barr Jr.,
cover of the exhibition catalog
Cubism and Abstract Art,
Museum of Modern Art,
New York 1936

CONSTRUCTING THE INTERNATIONAL

The end of World War I witnessed the collapse of the Romanov, Hohenzollern, Habsburg, and Ottoman Empires. As a result, emerging avant-garde groups migrated within a region of shifting national borders and sociopolitical conditions. This rich ethnic and cultural diversity of East-Central Europe is an important framework for studying the evolution of avant-garde groups and geometric abstraction.[4] The conditions of migration and pluralism can be described in the multiple contacts, statements, and publications organized around the Congress of International Progressive Artists in Düsseldorf in May 1922. Here, artists and avant-garde groups from France, Hungary, Italy, the Netherlands, Poland, and Soviet Russia took part in the first *International Exhibition.* The founding proclamation of the Union of Progressive International Artists in Düsseldorf stated, "Art needs the unification of those who create. Forgetting questions of nationality, without political bias or self-seeking intention, our slogan must now be: 'Artists of all nationalities unite.' Art must become international or it will perish."[5] The ability to move, participate in international events, fund and implement publishing projects, and transport artworks became an essential part of what it took to be a "progressive" and "international" artist in Europe during the early 1920s.

This essay will discuss artistic circulation in East-Central European art as a complex narrative, suggesting a range of hybridity, cross-border international activities, and local specificities that are often left out of homogenizing narratives of the self-professed universality of the avant-garde. Specifically, it will explore the development and migration of Constructivism between Berlin, Vienna, Vilnius, Warsaw, Łódź, and Kharkiv, cities that were undergoing rapid change with the emergence of new and reestablishment of old nation-states as a result of World War I and the crumbling of empires, giving the movement of geometric abstraction a sense of cultural and political hybridity.[6] Alongside the impact of Constructivism and Suprematism, artists across Europe were responding to movements such as Dada, Futurism, and De Stijl. This essay will consider these interrelated formations by examining a number of avant-garde publications that narrate the history of avant-garde movements by the artists themselves.[7] The style, language, and forms of geometric abstraction and its social applications were debated in books, anthologies, magazines, and exhibition catalogs that were produced in multiple locations and disseminated across Europe. Not only did these publications reproduce well-known artworks from across a broad geography; they also offered a blank canvas for innovative typographical experiments and theoretical pronouncements.

CHALLENGING NARRATIVES

In Ehrenburg's book *And Yet the World Turns,* the advances of the contemporary avant-garde were heralded by a reproduction of Aleksandr Rodchenko's *Project for a Kiosk* (fig. 3). While Rodchenko's sketch is a heavily simplified and abstracted representation of a human figure outside of a newsstand, the function of the building is clearly recognizable. The text included on the interlocking rectangular boards of the building reads "Down with Imp[erialism]" and "RSFR" (Russian Soviet Federative Socialist Republic), highlighting the propagandistic nature of the image. Rodchenko's geometric abstraction was radical in its promise to transform everyday life, which the Working Group of Constructivists in Moscow sought to enact.[8]

Not long after the publication of *And Yet the World Turns,* Ehrenburg and Lissitzky published the magazine *Veshch/Objet/Gegenstand* (Object), releasing two issues in Berlin in the spring of 1922 (fig. 4). This short-lived journal explored the evolution and exchange of artistic developments between Soviet Russia and Western Europe, with texts in German, French, and Russian. The main editorial statement of the first issue boldly proclaims "The Blockade of Russia Is Coming to an End," noting that "Art is today international, though retaining all its

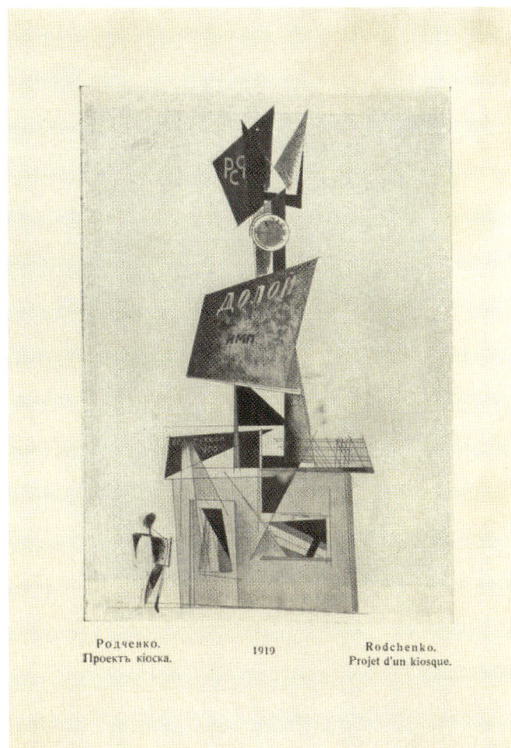

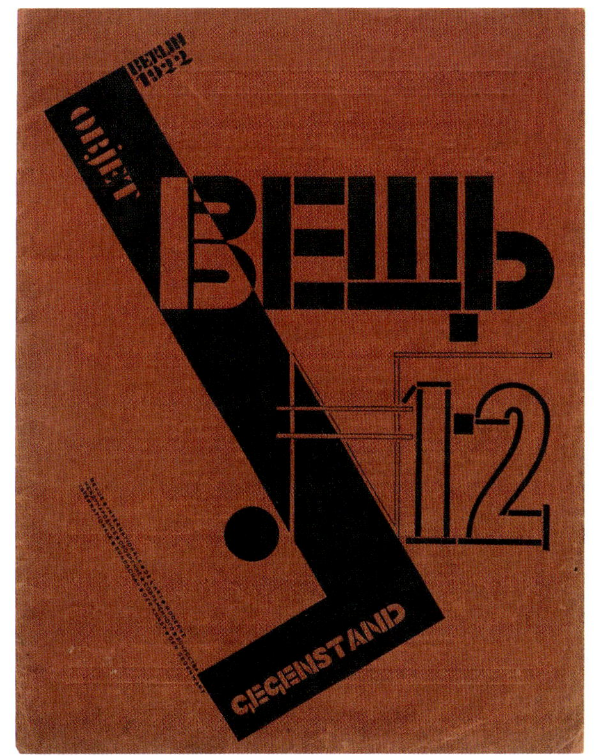

3
Aleksandr Rodchenko, *Project for a Kiosk*, 1919, reproduction in Ilya Ehrenburg, ed., *A vse-taki ona vertitsia* (And Yet the World Turns), Moscow and Berlin 1922

4
El Lissitzky and Ilya Ehrenburg, eds., cover of *Veshch/Objet/Gegenstand* (Object) 1–2 (March–April 1922)

local symptoms and particularities."[9] This announcement raises important questions about contact, transnational exchange, and cross-pollination of ideas between the multiple groups across Europe in the aftermath of World War I. Ehrenburg and Lissitzky prioritize "Russia" and present artistic narratives in geopolitical terms, demonstrating concerns with political and artistic hierarchies. Alfred H. Barr's diagram, on the other hand, presents a different view on artistic exchange—one that is supranational and unconstrained by the practicalities of national borders between Berlin, Cologne, Dessau, Leiden, Milan, Moscow, Munich, Paris, Weimar, and Zurich.

Ehrenburg and Lissitzky were referring to the diplomatic blockade of Imperial and Soviet Russia during the period of World War I, the October Revolution, the subsequent Civil War, and the two wars with Poland between 1919 and 1921. The publication of "The Blockade of Russia Is Coming to an End" resulted in a series of official state-sponsored events directed from Moscow, the most instrumental of which was the opening of the *First Russian Art Exhibition* on October 15, 1922, at Galerie van Diemen, Berlin (→ p. 268).[10] It was conceived as a commercial exhibition to raise funds for "the starving people of Russia."[11] Both *Veshch* and the exhibition signaled the emergence of Soviet cultural diplomacy, which became a well-oiled machine by the late 1920s and 1930s. After the signing of the Treaty of Rapallo in 1922, Germany became one of the first European powers to officially recognize and engage in diplomacy with the Bolshevik government. Although *Veshch* claimed it was "apart from all political parties," when read in the context of diplomatic relations, Ehrenburg and Lissitzky emerge primarily as shrewd propagandists, effectively speaking on behalf of the Moscow-based government.[12]

In his design of the cover for the *First Russian Art Exhibition* catalog, Lissitzky used striking typography to reconfigure the exhibition title as a radical image based on geometry, economy of form, order, and transparency (fig. 5). The more than seven hundred works by more than 167 artists that were featured in the exhibition went beyond the "Russian" scope promised by the title's ethnonational denominator.[13] Instead, it included work by artists from Armenia, Georgia, Latvia, Mongolia, Poland, and Ukraine. "Russia" clearly stood for the former Russian Empire. For example, prominent figures involved in the organization of the exhibition were Jewish artists from Ukraine: Soviet Commissar of Enlightenment Anatoly Lunacharsky was born in Poltava, and the exhibition's curators, David Shterenberg and Natan Altman, were born in Zhytomyr and Vinnytsia respectively. It has now been more than one hundred years since the *First Russian Art Exhibition,* and, since then, the focus has remained on the role, place, and significance of the "Russian avant-garde." This essay is aimed as an intervention in the histories of geometric abstraction in Europe that continue to prioritize the "Russian" contribution. The narrative of the *First Russian Art Exhibition* was an imperial construct, and its legacy continues to marginalize and erase "otherness."

The avant-garde in the late Russian Empire and early Soviet period was multinational and multiethnic, with artists and designers from countries such as Armenia, Georgia, Latvia, Lithuania, Poland, and Ukraine. The term *Russian avant-garde* came into its own in the 1960s.[14] Camilla Gray's book *The Great Experiment: Russian Art 1863–1922*, published in 1962, did much to endorse "Russian," while the coupling with "avant-garde" only began to be used as an all-inclusive umbrella in the 1970s and 1980s.[15] Western scholarship and museum exhibitions uncritically followed in the footsteps of "Russian" narratives, fueled by the growing art market for avant-garde art from the region since the 1990s.[16] During the 1920s East-Central European artists preferred designations of Futurist, Panfuturist, Suprematist, and Constructivist, as revealed in a recent scholarly effort to complicate these narratives.[17] To counter the hegemonic narratives that pivot geometric abstraction between Paris, Berlin, and Moscow, tethered between the binaries of Western and Russian art-historical discourses, art-historical studies that challenge the center-periphery paradigm continue to be instructive. An alternative approach that would narrate Eastern European art history as "horizontal, non-hierarchical and polycentric" was proposed by art historian Piotr Piotrowski.[18] An early key exponent of such a heterogeneous and non-hierarchical survey was the coauthored anthology by Lissitzky and Jean Arp ahead of the *International Exhibition of Modern Decorative and Industrial Arts* in Paris in 1925.[19] The cover of *Die Kunstismen/Les Ismes de l'art/The Isms of Art, 1914–1924* listed artistic tendencies that originated in different places, ranging from Futurism and Cubism to Constructivism and Suprematism, including lesser-known tendencies such as Merzism and Prounism between 1914 and 1924 (fig. 6).

5
El Lissitzky,
cover of the exhibition catalog
Erste Russische Kunstausstellung
(First Russian Art Exhibition),
Galerie van Diemen, Berlin 1922

6
El Lissitzky and Jean Arp, eds.,
Die Kunstismen/Les Ismes de l'art/
The Isms of Art, 1914–1924,
Erlenbach et al. 1925

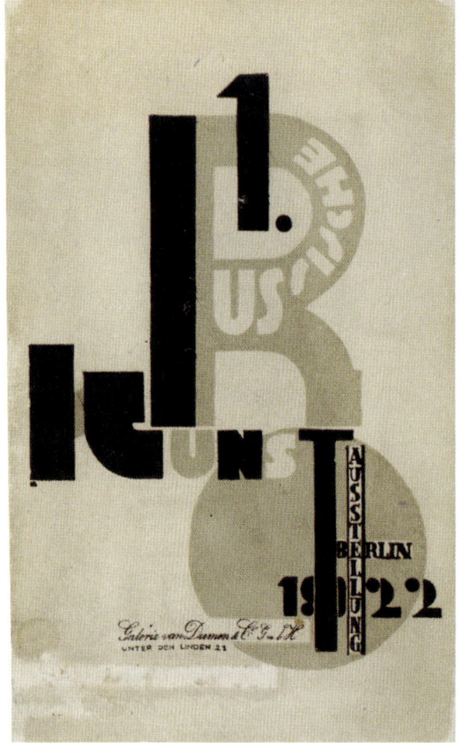

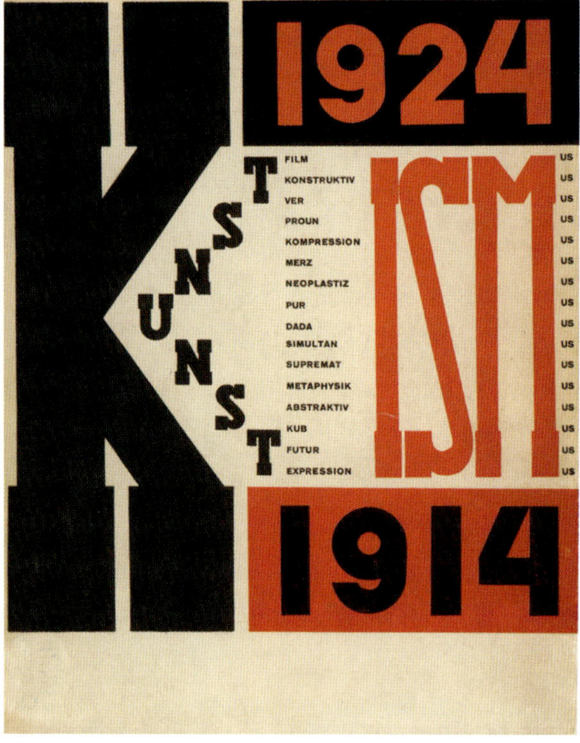

EXHIBITIONS AND THEIR CRITICS: HUNGARIANS IN VIENNA

The *First Russian Art Exhibition* opened in Berlin, which by 1922 had a population of émigrés from the former Russian Empire estimated to be over three hundred thousand.[20] The exhibition was widely reviewed in the press, and many figures of the international avant-garde traveled from across Europe to see it. Only three rooms were dedicated to bold nonobjective works of art that included Vladimir Tatlin's *Painterly Reliefs* and Aleksandr Rodchenko's *Hanging Constructions,* alongside Naum Gabo's *Constructions* (cat. 20) and Kazimir Malevich's Suprematist compositions (fig. p. 73). The remainder of the exhibition provided a survey of earlier and more traditional movements such as the Union of Artists, Mir Iskusstva, and Jack of Diamonds. The exhibition was intended as a propaganda stunt and has continued to shape the narrative of the development of twentieth-century art history and Russia's role in it for consumption abroad. In Lajos Kassák's review "The Russian Exhibit in Berlin," published in the Hungarian avant-garde magazine *Ma* (Today) that was issued in Vienna starting in 1920, the critic and artist declared that since World War I, "we have outgrown our love affair with Russian literature."[21] Kassák, who also served as the editor of the magazine, found fault with the state of literature after the Revolution and praised the new developments in visual arts. He had traveled to see the exhibition in person, describing Suprematism as "the first consciously new step" and movement in which "the Russian, the Asian power joins the European forces as a truly absolute value that is capable of multiplication. And characteristically its message is, instead of heaping on, a simplification, by getting rid of every externality deposited by civilization and aesthetics, to dig all the way back down to the essentials."[22] He continued to praise the language of basic geometric forms and the use of two basic colors—black and white—stating in reference to the Suprematists that "their debut was a revolutionary act."[23] At the same time, Kassák was scathing in his attack of Rodchenko's spatial constructions, which he called naive and insignificant. He argued that "in these days of locomotives doing 120 kilometers per hour, of giant cranes and vast bridges, these items seem to be superfluous games, impoverished both in intuition and in science."[24]

Kassák, like László Moholy-Nagy (cat. 19), moved to Vienna after the defeat of the short-lived Socialist Federative Republic of Councils in Hungary that lasted from March to August 1919. It was in Vienna that Kassák continued to publish *Ma* in exile starting in May 1920. He was committed to a strong internationalist position and addressed his readers both at home in Hungary and abroad by publishing a collective appeal "To the Artists of All Nations" to prioritize ethics and humanity over dictatorship of the proletariat.[25] In his rousing speech Kassák asserted, "We feel there is only one law, that of continual advance in the face of cosmic life; everything else is a cowardly avoidance of our true selves or a resigned waiting for death. . . . The revolution is our life, and our revolution is a most sacred credo of love."[26] In this call to arms, Kassák insisted on the unity of life and the revolution, but he was not speaking of a communist revolution, instead celebrating "the dictatorship of ideas."[27] Kassák developed his constructive idea in "Képarchitektúra" (Picture-Architecture), published in *Ma* in March 1922.[28] At the same time, Hungarian artists Sándor Ék, Jolán Szilágyi, Béla Uitz, and critic Alfréd Kemény experienced the artistic developments in Moscow firsthand when they attended the meeting of the Third International (Comintern) and visited the Higher Artistic and Technical Studios (VKhUTEMAS). Kemény called on Rodchenko and Gabo in their studios and took part in debates at the Institute of Artistic Culture (INKhUK), the birthplace of the Working Group of Constructivists. Even though *Ma* reproduced works by and writings about the Moscow Constructivists, they did not prioritize artistic developments in Soviet Russia. Instead, *Ma* was in favor of an inclusive, Pan-European movement.[29]

Taking on a challenge similar to Lissitzky, Ehrenburg, and Arp, Kassák published the anthology *Book of New Artists* together with Moholy-Nagy in Vienna in 1922 (fig. 7). The book explores the origin and evolution of contemporary art from Cubism, Futurism,

Neo-Primitivism, Dada, Constructivism, and cinema. With only a short introduction and more than one hundred high-quality illustrations of visual arts, architecture, music, and technology, it contains reproductions of works by many Constructivist artists across Europe, including Lissitzky and Malevich. Kassák juxtaposed works of art with feats of engineering and technology that celebrated industrialization and mechanization of the contemporary world. In the early 1920s, the anthology became the favored genre of avant-garde artists. The *Book of New Artists* was distinct in combining Dada and Constructivism in a single narrative, while also including Futurism, Expressionism, and Cubism—with Constructivism as the final "ism."

NEW PATHS: POLISH CONSTRUCTIVISM FROM VILNIUS AND WARSAW TO ŁÓDŹ

Polish Constructivism had its first exhibition not in Warsaw or Kraków but in Vilnius. *Wystawa Nowej Sztuki* (New Art Exhibition) opened at the Cine-Theatre Corso on May 20, 1923. Until Lithuanian independence was secured in 1922 through fierce fighting, Vilnius had remained a cosmopolitan regional center of the Russian Empire. Once the country became autonomous, Vilnius and a significant part of Lithuanian territory were partitioned to Poland. Vytautas Kairiūkštis (Witold Kajruksztis) and Władysław Strzemiński were instrumental in the organization of the *New Art Exhibition*.[30] The simple geometric composition of the exhibition catalog cover designed by Strzemiński reflected his first-hand knowledge of Malevich's Suprematism (fig. 8). Strzemiński studied at Moscow's First State Free Art Studios (Svomas), a precursor to VKhUTEMAS, during the time Malevich was on the faculty. Strzemiński arrived in Polish Vilnius in 1922 from Smolensk, having also studied in Vitebsk, where he was briefly a member of the Affirmers of New Art (UNOVIS), a short-lived but influential group headed by Malevich and Lissitzky. Upon his arrival to Poland, Strzemiński published "Notes on Russian Art" in Tadeusz Peiper's Paris-oriented magazine *Zwrotnica* (The Switch), in which he renounced Suprematism.[31]

The most recognized Polish journal to espouse and develop Constructivist ideas was the magazine *Blok,* which was started by a group of artists in Warsaw in 1924 and ran until 1926, publishing eleven issues (fig. 9). Key founders included Edmund Miller, Strzemiński, Mieczysław Szczuka, and Warsaw artists such as Teresa Żarnowerówna and Henryk Stażewski, who participated in the *New Art Exhibition* in Vilnius. Subtitled as *Revue d'art* and later *Revue internationale d'avant-garde, Blok* aspired to be internationally recognized. Its editorial offices were located in Warsaw, Kraków, Paris, Brussels, and Berlin.[32] The first issue of *Blok* from March 1924 advertised *The Block of the Cubists, Suprematists, and Constructivists,* an exhibition of the Vilnius group of artists at the Warsaw showroom of the Czech car manufacturer Laurin & Klement.[33] Alongside the abovementioned artists who participated in the Vilnius exhibition, the Laurin & Klement exhibition included Katarzyna Kobro (cat. 17), known for her abstract sculptures that explored spatial concepts. The editorial statement, in Polish and French, in the first issue of *Blok* promoted the collective and mechanized creative experience: "The demands of contemporary life place the principle of economy in the forefront. The principle of economy results in a great simplification of means—that is why the artist's handiwork is reduced to a minimum through mechanization."[34] In the joint issue 6–7 of that year, the editors included the fourteen-point manifesto "What Constructivism Is." Reiterating "the construction of a thing" and "a system of methodological collective work," the statement cites Van Doesburg, who argued for the importance of color, construction, and new architecture.[35] The editors explain that the term *construction* was borrowed from Ludwig Mies van der Rohe's article "Budowa" (Construction), which had been published in the first issue.[36] Reproductions of Merz assemblages by Kurt Schwitters and an essay on Dada, which Strzemiński and Szczuka commissioned from Schwitters, reaffirmed the role of Dadaism as an important movement that gave birth to Constructivism.[37]

To counter local criticism of imitation, Szczuka published "What We Are Doing," an editorial arguing that *Blok* "is not imitation, but an effort at paralleling the most recent art in France,

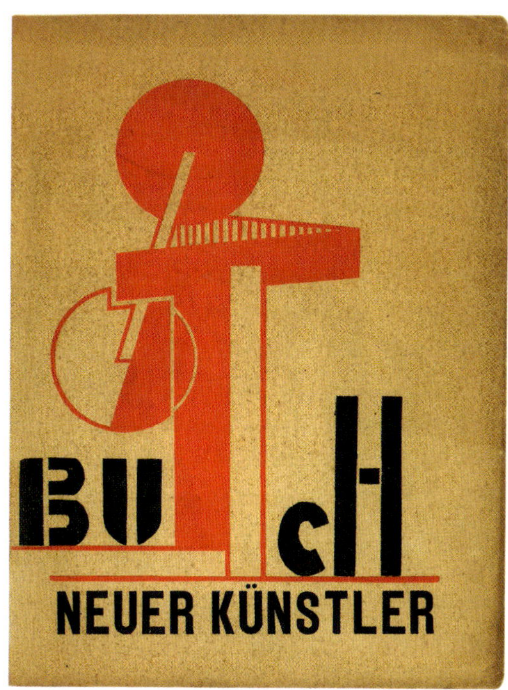

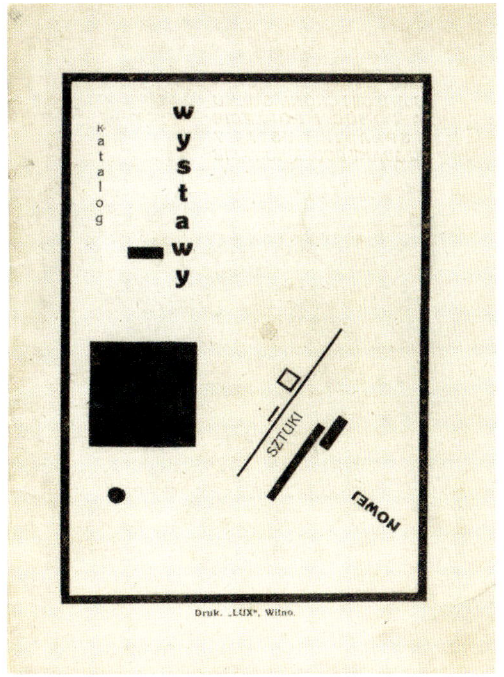

7
Lajos Kassák and
László Moholy-Nagy, eds.,
Buch neuer Künstler
(Book of New Artists),
Vienna 1922

8
Władysław Strzemiński,
cover of the exhibition catalog
Wystawa Nowej Sztuki
(New Art Exhibition),
ed. Vytautas Kairiūkštis,
Vilnius 1923

Germany, Russia, Holland, and Hungary, etc."[38] The focus was on mutual contacts and connections. When *Blok* was discontinued, it was followed by Praesens (1926–30), a project that combined design, new architecture, and social commitments. In 1928 the Praesens group published Strzemiński's treatise "Unism in Painting," which advocated his principles of organic unity in art.[39] In 1929 Blok and Praesens regrouped to form the a.r. group (Revolutionary Artists or Real Avant-Garde) in Łódź. With links to Paris, the a.r. group included artists, poets, and architects who shared the goal of synthesis. To this end, the a.r. group founded the International Collection of Modern Art at the Municipal Museum of History of Art in Łódź in 1931. The collection was assembled by Strzemiński, Kobro, and Stażewski, along with poets Julian Przyboś and Jan Brzękowski, from artist donations and was gifted to the museum in Łódź. Their ambition was to promote and popularize modern art in Poland through a museum of modern art; the a.r. library, a publishing arm that issued artists' writing; and a bulletin disseminating their activities with artistic communities at home and abroad. Stażewski and Brzękowski lived in Paris in the 1920s and were associated with the Cercle et Carré, Art Concret, and Abstraction-Création groups (→ p. 270). The Łódź collection aimed to illustrate the development of art from Cubism to abstraction through the work of Blok and Praesens artists, along with artwork from Abstraction-Création and Cercle et Carré, and by Max Ernst, Léger, and Picasso.[40] At the same time, Strzemiński was developing links with the artes group of artists (1929–35) in Lwów (now Lviv), aided by artist and art theorist Debora Vogel, who played a pivotal role in bridging new connections between Łódź and Lwów.[41]

CONSTRUCTIVE DYNAMISM: UKRAINIAN PANFUTURISM AND THE AVANT-GARDE PRESS

Another important context for the parallel and interrelated discourse of the avant-garde was in Kharkiv, Ukraine. As the Russian Empire collapsed, the Ukrainian National Republic declared its short-lived independence in January 1918. After the defeat of nationalist Ukrainian forces during the War of Independence (1917–21), the Bolsheviks established the Ukrainian Socialist Soviet Republic (UkSSR), with Kharkiv becoming its capital city until 1934. The new Soviet government initiated a policy of "Ukrainization" during the 1920s that promoted the development of national language and culture previously banned by Czarist Russia. Before this campaign was brutally suppressed under Stalin in the 1930s, Ukrainian culture experienced a growth experimentation and national awakening. During this period, many Ukrainian artists and intellectuals orientated themselves toward cultural developments in Western Europe, as well as advancing local knowledge and heritage.[42] This decision firmly asserted their inclusion in a "Pan-European intellectual community," a relationship that developed alongside the long-standing imperial relationship with Moscow and St. Petersburg/Petrograd/Leningrad in the East.[43]

One of the key representatives of avant-garde activities in Ukraine was Mykhailo Semenko, who was based in Kharkiv between 1926 and 1929.[44] Semenko supported the principles of Futurism and published a number of innovative literary-artistic projects, including *Mystetstvo* (Art) and *Semafor u maibutnie* (Semaphore into the Future). In his manifesto "What Panfuturism Wants," written in English, Semenko espoused a synthesis of Futurism, Cubism, Expressionism, and Dadaism.[45]

Nova heneratsiia (The New Generation, 1927–30) was the last avant-garde magazine to be published by Semenko before he was arrested and executed in 1937 under the Moscow-based Soviet government.[46] As a monthly dedicated to the "left formation of the arts," the magazine included contributions from key avant-garde artists and designers such as Vadym Meller (theater), Pavlo Kovzhun (book graphics), Anatol Petrytskyi (painting), Dan Sotnyk (photography), and Vasyl Yermylov (painting). *Nova heneratsiia* survived longer than the Moscow-based Constructivist magazines *LEF* (Left Front of the Arts) and *Novy LEF* (New Left), which was discontinued in 1928. Many *LEF* authors, including Kazymyr Malevych (Kazimir Malevich), who published twelve articles, continued to publish in *Nova heneratsiia*.[47] An important function of the journal was to publicize and review European artistic and literary developments with direct references from international journals. A key focus was forging links with the Bauhaus in Dessau, as well as making frequent references to international figures such as Marcel Breuer, Giorgio de Chirico, Paul Klee, Léger, László Moholy-Nagy, Enrico Prampolini, and Herwarth Walden.[48] Furthermore, *Nova heneratsiia* contained translations of key theoretical writings on architecture, film, typography, and art into Ukrainian by international avant-garde artists such as Leo Adler, Willi Baumeister, Erich Mendelsohn, and Jan Tschichold. Semenko's version of Futurism, or Panfuturism, which aspired to attain Pan-European recognition, was clearly expressed on the cover of the first issue of the magazine in 1927 with a reproduction of one of Oskar Schlemmer's designs for the *Triadic Ballet* from 1922–24 (fig. 10).

In 1930 two issues of the avant-garde almanac *Avanhard: Almanakh proletarskykh myttsiv Novoi heneratsii* (Avant-Garde: An Almanac of Proletarian Artists of the New Generation) showed a strong commitment to proletarian culture and a continued advocacy of the Panfuturist principles. This strong sentiment defined the local character of the Ukrainian almanac, which promoted an artistic system based on a commitment to the "destructive-constructive" method. The editorial of the avant-garde almanac argued, "The Panfuturist system combines the destructive processes in art, which is coming to an end, with the constructive process, which is beginning, considering these two processes as constituent parts of a single dialectical process leading to the development of the revolutionary formation of art."[49] Ukrainian avant-garde magazines and the almanac are important contributions to modernist histories of printed media that continue to be little noticed in research on avant-garde modernist journals and artist groups.

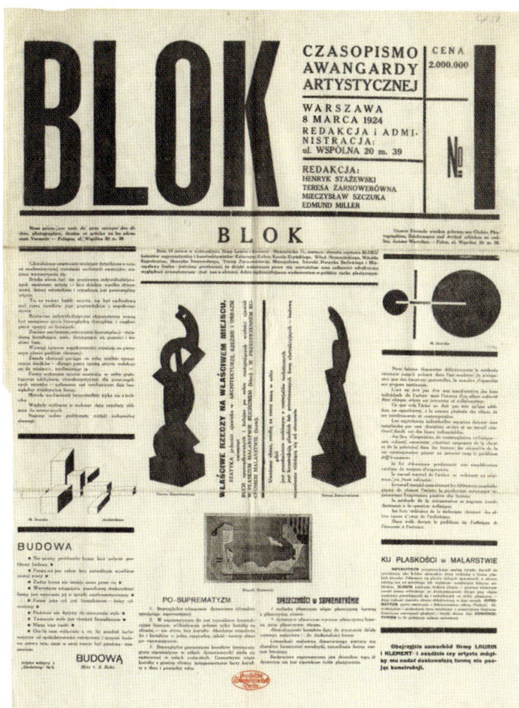
BLOK
CZASOPISMO AWANGARDY ARTYSTYCZNEJ
CENA 2.000.000
WARSZAWA 8 MARCA 1924
REDAKCJA i ADMINISTRACJA: ul. WSPÓLNA 20 m. 39
REDAKCJA: HENRYK STAŻEWSKI TERESA ŻARNOWERÓWNA MIECZYSŁAW SZCZUKA EDMUND MILLER
№ 1
BLOK
WŁAŚCIWE RZECZY NA WŁAŚCIWEM MIEJSCU.
BUDOWA
PO-SUPREMATYZM
KU PŁASKOŚCI w MALARSTWIE
BUDOWĄ

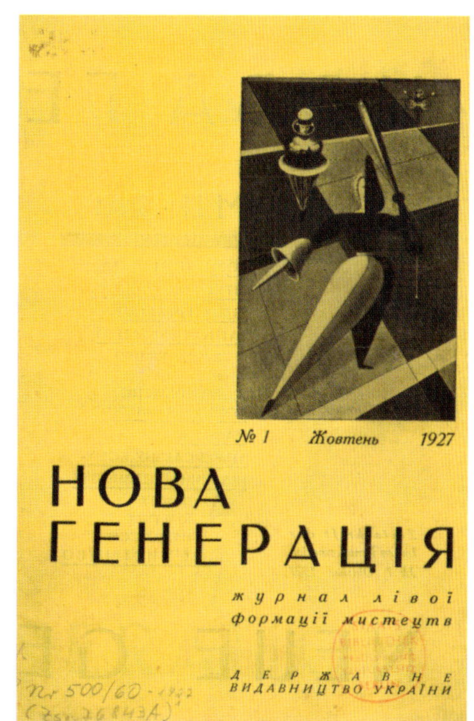
№ 1 Жовтень 1927
НОВА ГЕНЕРАЦІЯ
журнал лівої формації мистецтв
ДЕРЖАВНЕ ВИДАВНИЦТВО УКРАЇНИ

9
Henryk Stażewski, ed., cover of the first issue of *Blok* (Block), Warsaw 1924

10
Oskar Schlemmer, *Figurines in Space: Study for the Triadic Ballet,* ca. 1924, illustration on the cover of *Nova heneratsiia* (The New Generation) 1, ed. Mykhailo Semenko, Kharkiv 1927

CONCLUSION

East-Central European avant-garde artists, magazines, and groups present a complex web of international connections established during the short window of international mobility, professional opportunity, and revolutionary innovation during the 1920s and early 1930s. The 1920s witnessed the formation of multiple Constructivist groups whose theoretical ideas and visual forms circulated in print across newly formed national borders. The magazines discussed in this essay engaged in conversation, in which works of art were reproduced and international artists' texts appeared in translation. At the same time, the publications were shaped by the specific sociopolitical conditions of the cities in which they were produced and largely aimed at an urban and local readership. The exchange of ideas took both international and local paths. For many artists, this period of cultural exchange was followed by Stalinist and Nazi censorship and oppression. During and after World War II, many of the newly established connections were severed.

Sterre Barentsen

Rhythms of the City

The Influence of the Metropolis on Piet Mondrian's Geometric Abstraction

On a spring day between 1934 and 1938, while both artists were living in Paris, Piet Mondrian visited Wassily Kandinsky at his home in the Paris suburb of Neuilly-sur-Seine.[1] Nina Kandinsky recalled that on the day of his visit the chestnut trees outside were in full bloom, and her husband had set the table so that Mondrian could enjoy the view. As they sipped tea, Mondrian suddenly exclaimed, "Oh, how dreadful!" Puzzled, Kandinsky asked, "What is dreadful?" "Those trees," Mondrian replied. Kandinsky immediately offered to switch places, and Mondrian sat with his back to the window. Anecdotes of Mondrian's distaste for natural landscapes recur in various accounts—his biographer Michel Seuphor and artist Jean Arp described very similar encounters with the painter.[2]

The irony of Nina Kandinsky's account is that trees are a central motif in Mondrian's early work. In his Cubist paintings, he reduced their organic forms to a network of horizontal and vertical lines. This process of abstraction continued to evolve, gradually stripping away all traces of the natural world, until his art was reduced to black lines and planes of primary colors. Through this reduction—or rather, through this act of deconstruction—Mondrian sought to reveal a spiritual order. The more Mondrian distanced himself from nature, the more the geometric patterns and rhythms of the urban environment shaped his compositions.

Mondrian first articulated the connection between art and the metropolis in his seminal 1917–18 text "The New Plastic in Painting," published in the journal *De Stijl.* In this essay, he outlined the theoretical foundations of Neoplasticism for the first time:

> The truly modern artist sees the metropolis as abstract life given form: it is closer to him than nature, and it will more easily stir aesthetic emotion in him. For in the metropolis, nature is already tensed, ordered by the human spirit. The relationships and rhythm of plane and line in its architecture will move man more directly than the capriciousness of nature. In the metropolis, beauty is expressed more mathematically; it is here that the mathematical artistic temperament of the future will develop—here the New Style will emerge.[3]

This belief in the power of the city to inspire artistic innovation aligned with the ideals of the De Stijl group. The central debate within the group was whether the fine arts or the applied

1
Anonymous,
Garage du Départ, Rue du Départ, Paris, ca. 1913,
RKD—Netherlands Institute for Art History, The Hague

2
Piet Mondrian,
Paris Courtyard Façades, Rue du Départ, 1913–14,
private collection

3
Piet Mondrian,
Composition in Oval with Color Planes 2, 1914,
Kunstmuseum Den Haag, The Hague

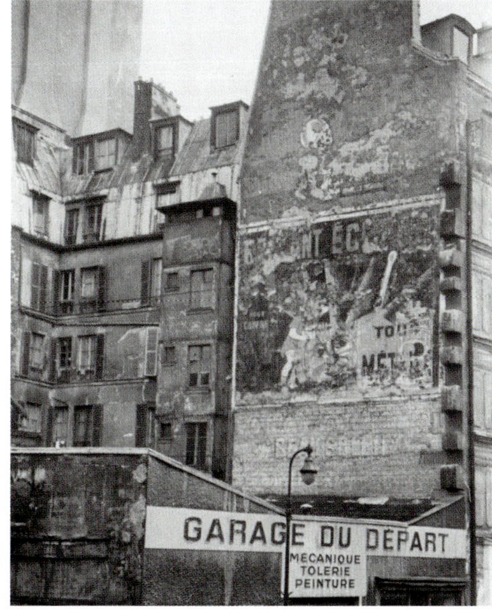

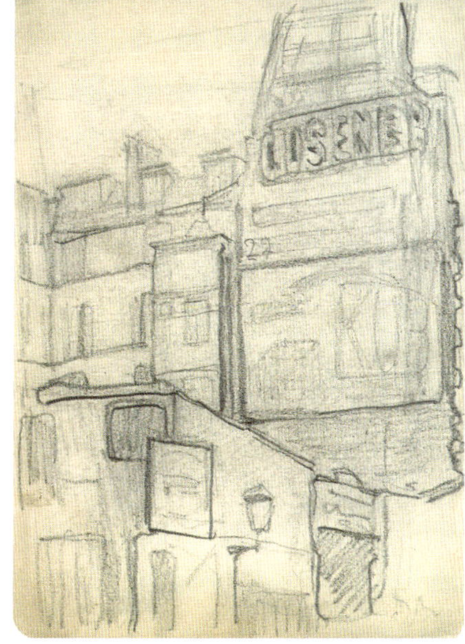

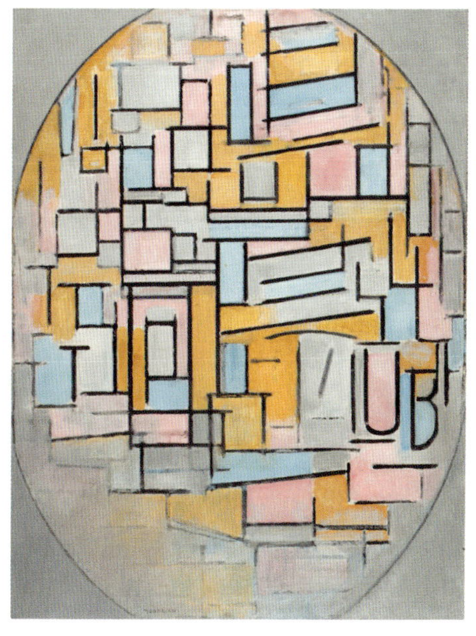

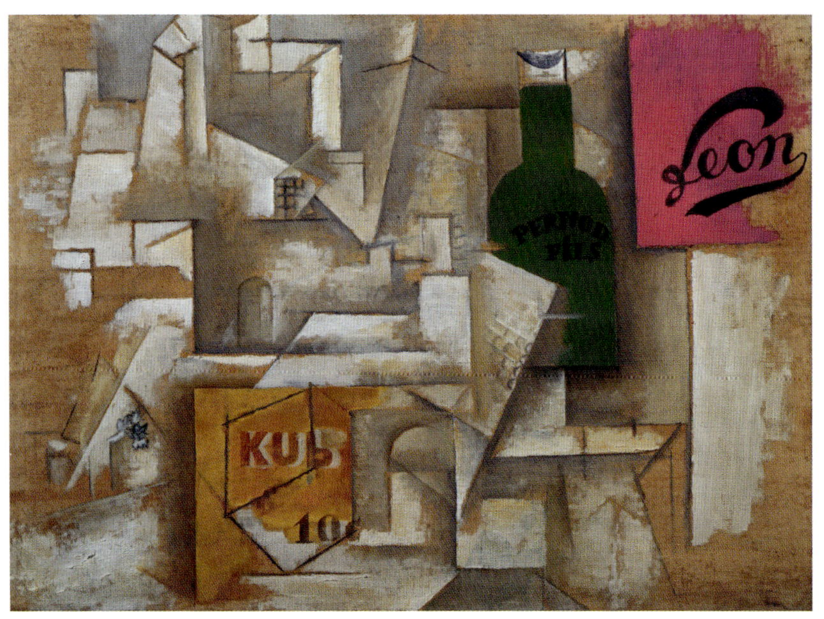

4
Pablo Picasso,
Landscape with Posters, 1912,
National Museum of Art,
Osaka

arts represented the highest expression of De Stijl's ideals. For Mondrian, the answer was clear: painting represented the purest expression of universal harmony, and he envisioned his works as models for the cities of the future. He wrote, "Our surroundings will fall short of abstract reality for a long time to come! But for that reason, Abstract-Real Painting is, for the time being, the saving substitute!"[4]

It was evident to Mondrian that his only option was to live in a metropolis. His initial move to Paris in 1912, at the age of forty, was driven by a growing desire to immerse himself in the world's most urban and cosmopolitan environment. His temporary return to the Netherlands two years later, however, was unplanned; the outbreak of World War I during a visit made it safer for him to remain in his neutral home country. In a letter to collector Salomon Slijper, he expressed his frustration with the situation, writing, "I think a metropolis is the only place where you can live. But 'Krieg ist Krieg' [war is war]."[5]

Mondrian's vision extended beyond depicting modern urban life; he also saw painting as a projection of what cities could become. His fascination with modernism and new developments motivated him to relocate to Paris from 1912 to 1914 and again from 1919 onward. Even when he was forced into exile, moving to London in 1938 and then to New York in 1940, he continued his study of the metropolis.

PAINTING IN PLANES

As Mondrian's sketchbooks show, he focused his attention on the city during his first stay in Paris from 1912 to 1914. Near his studio in Montparnasse, on the corner of Boulevard Edgar Quinet and Rue du Départ, stood a cluster of half-demolished buildings. A large advertisement was painted on one of the exposed walls (fig. 1). With loose pencil lines, Mondrian outlined the details of windows, doors, and façades, and sketched out larger planes, such as billboards and jutting projections (fig. 2). In addition, he faintly penciled in the letters *KUB,* a reference to a popular brand of broth. Since industrialization, the spread of advertising reflected societal changes toward mass consumption in the city.

Mondrian's sketch served as the basis for his painting *Composition in Oval with Color Planes 2* (fig. 3), in which the KUB advertisement becomes more prominent. The letters are embedded in a grid of overlapping rectangles, squares, and lines that guide the viewer's eye across the canvas. Only the curves of the letters *U* and *B* break up the maze of straight lines and catch the viewer's attention. The inclusion of the KUB billboard may also be a nod to Pablo

Picasso's 1912 work *Landscape with Posters* (fig. 4), which shows colorful advertising posters, including one for KUB broth, that stand out against fragmented architectural shapes in muted browns and beiges. Unlike Picasso's usual focus in his Cubist still lifes on objects for private consumption—items that might be found on his café table—his *Landscape with Posters* highlights the prominence of urban advertising.[6] The advertising boards, consisting of layers of torn and pasted images, mirrored the assemblage techniques pioneered by the Cubists. The unexpected and random juxtapositions that emerged when different posters were hung side by side throughout the city contributed to a shift in the aesthetic sensibilities of the early twentieth century.[7]

In contrast to the slow pace of changes related to urban planning, the billboards and posters of Paris were in constant flux; their cycles of emergence, decay, damage, defacement, and replacement reflected the fast pace of the modern city (fig. 5). Captivated by this dynamic environment, Mondrian felt that "electric signs, posters, technical constructions of all kinds, compensate for the dearth of new architecture."[8]

By the 1910s large billboards began to cut through the urban architecture in Paris (fig. 6), making a strong impression on Mondrian. In his essay "The New Plastic Expression in Painting" of 1926, Mondrian wrote that despite Paris's historical buildings and traditions, the city's intense and accelerated life had a tendency toward abstraction.[9] The metropolis inspired him to capture its rhythm, sounds, and impressions in a painting style suited for modern life. Significantly, Mondrian argued that the aesthetics of the urban landscape increasingly resembled the language of abstraction, especially observing that "the enormous planes of the buildings, often colored by advertising, encouraged painting in planes."[10]

Mondrian's remark about billboards motivating him to "paint in planes" connects him to other pioneers of geometric abstraction, particularly Kazimir Malevich (cat. 4), who was also influenced by urban architecture (fig. 8). Malevich drew inspiration from aerial photographs (fig. 7; → S. 267), which revealed an unexpected geometry, transforming familiar urban forms into abstract, two-dimensional elements.[11] This aerial perspective defamiliarized the city and allowed it to be seen as a geometric whole. Similarly, the flat, often garish billboards added new aspects to the architecture of the city, causing visual interruptions. Their two-dimensional surfaces, suspended in the three-dimensional reality of urban space, seemed to suggest an alternate reality.

EMBRACING MODERNITY

Mondrian was likely inspired to look more closely at the billboards in Paris by the lecture *Contemporary Achievements in Painting,* held by artist Fernand Léger at the Académie Vassilieff in 1914. Given Mondrian's admiration for Léger's Cubist paintings and the lecture's proximity—just five hundred meters from his studio—it is likely that he was in the audience or read it in the journal *Les Soirées de Paris,* where it was published in June 1914.[12]

In his lecture, Léger argued that contemporary painting should reflect the technological and cultural advancements of the time, using billboards as a prime example of a modern visual expression. He likened the contrasts in his artwork to the abrupt presence of billboards in the cityscape, which he described as "brutally cutting across a landscape."[13] At the time Léger was working on his *Contrast of Forms* series (fig. 9), which is characterized by rhythmically patterned surfaces composed of cylindrical and cubic units. As the title suggests, the series explores several contrasts: the interplay of curves and straight lines, the juxtaposition of three-dimensional shapes against planes, and the dynamic use of primary colors—red, blue, and yellow. These "pictorial contrasts" mirror the tensions of the modern environment.[14] Léger's focus on these fundamental elements resonated with Mondrian, who acknowledged Léger as "perhaps the closest forerunner of the New Plastic," or Neoplasticism, a style that sought to establish a new visual language through pared-down abstract forms and rhythmic compositions.[15]

Léger bemoaned the bourgeois critique that large billboards disrupted Paris's traditional aesthetic, instead seeing the sharp contrasts between forms and colors as capturing the dynamism of modern life. Léger explained, "This yellow or red poster, shouting in a timid landscape, is the best of possible reasons for the new painting; it topples the whole sentimental literary concept and announces the advent of plastic contrast."[16]

For De Stijl artists such as Theo van Doesburg, Vilmos Huszár, and Bart van der Leck, advertising became a medium through which modern art could interact directly with the public.[17] They were commissioned to design billboards and advertisements, allowing them to change the cityscape in a relatively rapid manner. Huszár, who designed a billboard for Miss Blanche Virginia Cigarettes, even argued that "the highest that can be attained in art" should be exhibited "right on the street, right in front of the great public, most of whom have never visited an art collector or museum . . . . Whoever believes in 'art for the people' has no better means of achieving his goal than advertising art."[18]

AN INCREDIBLE MACHINE

The Paris Mondrian returned to in 1919 was a changed city. The war economy had attracted numerous workers, including many from the French colonies, to the factories in the suburbs. The population boom expanded the city into its surroundings. Jazz cafés, many of which were opened by African American soldiers, had sprung up in Montmartre; in these establishments, Mondrian would dance the Foxtrot, the Shimmy, and the One Step. The city exhibited the complexities of a globalized mass society, characterized by dislocation and cultural intermingling. Mondrian found himself in a Paris that was larger, more diverse, and culturally vibrant.

The first two texts written by Mondrian after his arrival reflected the essence of this transformation. In the spring of 1920, while observing the bustling Boulevard des Capucines, Van Doesburg encouraged Mondrian to describe the "incredible machine" of sounds and movements.[19] In the first of these literary works, "Les Grands Boulevards," he attempted to encapsulate the city's pulse through a vivid collage of auditory and visual impressions. Employing a literary style that mirrors Cubist fragmentation and incorporates elements of Futurist and Dadaist poetry, the text begins with the sounds "Ru-h ru-h-h-h-h-h-h. Poeoeoe. Tik-tik-tik-tik."[20] Mondrian conveys the rhythm of the modern metropolis, shifting between

5
Anonymous,
33, Rue de Viarmes, Paris, 1907,
Musée Carnavalet, Paris

6
Albert Harlingue,
Bébé Cadum Posters, Paris, ca. 1925

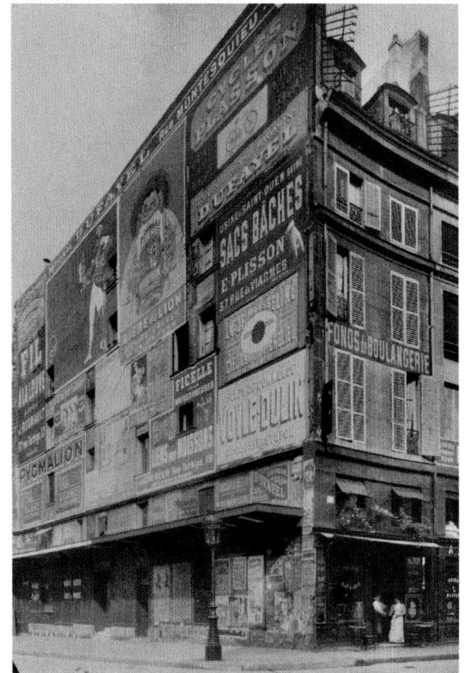

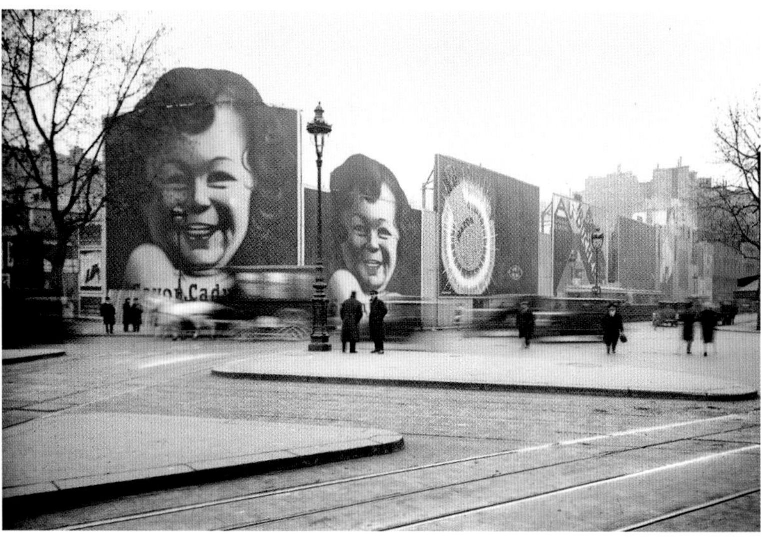

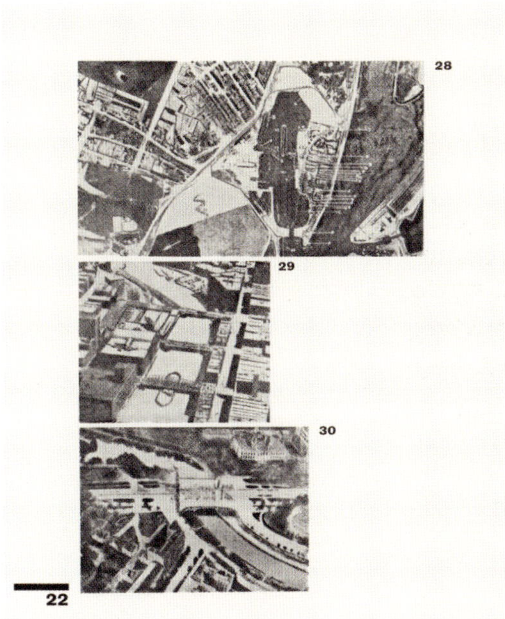

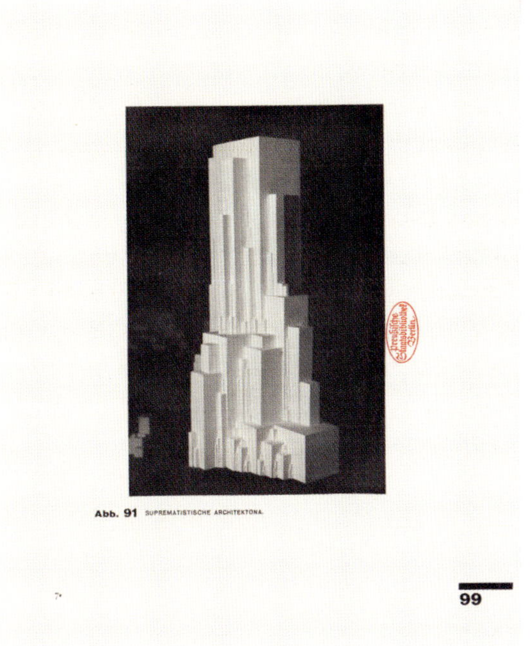

7
Kazimir Malevich,
The Inspiring Environment ("Reality") of the Suprematist,
in Malevich, *Die gegenstandslose Welt* (The Nonobjective World),
Bauhausbücher 11,
Munich 1927, 22

8
Kazimir Malevich,
Suprematist Architectons, 1927,
in Malevich, *Die gegenstandslose Welt* (The Nonobjective World),
Bauhausbücher 11,
Munich 1927, 99

observations of urban life and philosophical musings on the limits of truth and the relativity of time and space. He explores the essence of Paris, noting how everything contributes to a universal rhythm, blending individuals and the city into one.

For Mondrian, the metropolis, like art, could pervade the fabric of society. In 1920 he wrote a second text, which remained unpublished during his lifetime.[21] It describes a bustling scene at a restaurant, frequented by workers, intellectuals, and families, in which Mondrian picked up on the phrases around him: "'Du pain, s'il vous plait.' 'Merci, madame.'" And as he looked at the writing on the window—"TNAR-UATS-ER, gigantic letters on the three glass panels above the white. The words tell their meaning on the outside: RESTAURANT"—he fell into ontological musings on the unity between internal and external identities.[22]

How should these texts be interpreted? Is there a relationship between them and the irregular grid compositions Mondrian created around the same time? Mondrian scholars have often framed his paintings as abstracted from reality. Any traces of the real in his work are said to appear only through the "referential banality" of painting titles that refer to specific locations or through the "treacherous banality" of interpretations of the grid as a map.[23] However, recent studies have opened up new perspectives. They challenge the portrayal of Mondrian as a reclusive and ascetic artist, and instead present a socially engaged painter who was immersed in the cultural currents of his time.[24] A prolific writer, Mondrian reveals a deep connection to his surroundings in his writings, as he expressed in 1926: "It would be a great mistake to think of Neo-Plastic work as totally abstracted from life. Precisely through its relationships and pure plastic means, it can express life more intensely."[25]

URBAN ALGORITHMS

The first painting Mondrian worked on after his arrival in Paris in 1919 marks a significant departure from his earlier oeuvre. In *No. VI / Composition No. II* (fig. 10) the planes are larger than in the compositions he had developed on in the Netherlands, and the grid is irregular. Mondrian continued to work on the painting for several years, lightening the yellow panels and separating each plane with thin, wavering black lines.[26] This meticulous approach reflects Mondrian's idea of "equivalence," with no single element dominating the composition. The background was eliminated, along with any hierarchical structure. Planes and lines dissolve into the overall

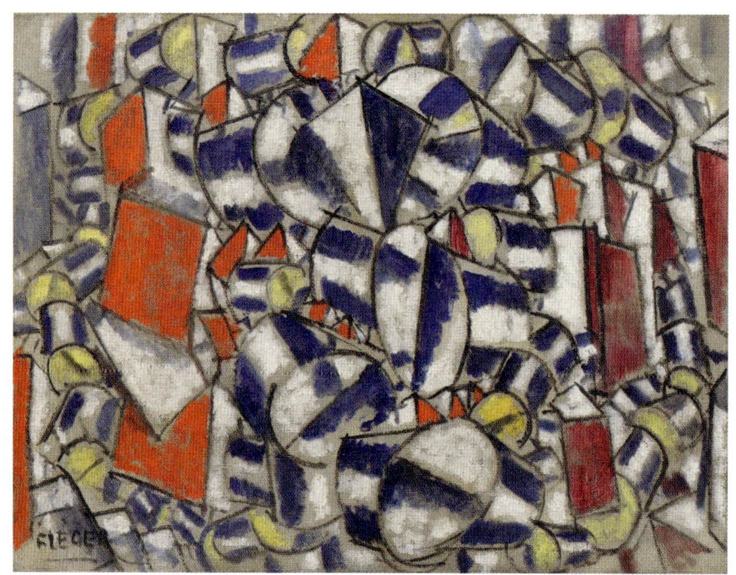

9
Fernand Léger,
Contrast of Forms, 1913,
Solomon R. Guggenheim Museum,
New York

composition, leaving behind only proportions and relationships. This invention of Neoplasticism—a system of irregular planes, primary colors, and lines—was something that Mondrian would continue to refine in Paris, London, and New York.

Prior to World War I, Mondrian had been influenced by the Cubism of Picasso, Braque, and Léger. Now he found that most Parisian artists were still working in the same prewar Cubism. In 1919 Léger painted *The City* (fig. 11), which captured rhythms of modern life, much like Mondrian's own literary texts of the same period: "Les Grands Boulevards" and "Palm Sunday." An ode to Paris, the Léger painting features overlapping elements—streets, chimneys, industrial structures, and billboard letters—that merge with cylindrical forms, geometric shapes, and vibrant colors.[27] The energetic composition conveys the chaos of urban life while adhering to the Cubist tradition of fragmenting recognizable elements. Léger's depiction of real objects made Mondrian increasingly frustrated, feeling that the Parisian art scene was primarily concerned with appeasing a commercial market. Musing on this disillusionment, he concluded, "In the face of all that, I remain a loner."[28]

Mondrian shared a similar dissatisfaction with his own texts "Les Grands Boulevards" and "Palm Sunday." In 1932 he reflected on this period in a letter to Lodewijk van Deyssel, admitting, "Since [1920] I have done nothing further in writing than to clarify my conception of art and life. I found that in literature I could not go beyond a deepened Futurism—thus still descriptive. I see no possibility of 'pure plastic' in literary art."[29] Turning away from literature, Mondrian sought new ways to express his vision through painting. Mondrian's decision to make his grids irregular—a departure from his last Dutch works, in which checkerboard grids maintained uniform proportions—was not one he made easily and one discussed at length with Van Doesburg.[30] It could be seen as a response to the metropolis itself, a place filled with constant opposing relationships—between people of different classes, genders, races, occupations, and ages, as well as between old buildings and garishly vibrant advertising billboards.

A photograph taken from Mondrian's studio window by artist László Moholy-Nagy (fig. 12; see also cat. 19), either in the summer of 1927 or 1930, reveals the city's energy permeating his workspace. Moholy-Nagy framed the composition so that the windowpane and balcony in the foreground create a grid of black lines that overlays the image. Behind it, the pulsating city unfolds with planes formed by rooftops and an advertisement for shoes, reading "CHAUSSURES." A locomotive passes by, emitting steam so intensely that its whistle seems almost audible. Considering the difference between a city and a village in 1927, Mondrian observed, "The noise of vehicles, etc., contains opposing relationships, whereas church bells have only the rhythm of repetition. Unconsciously the new culture is being built here."[31]

NEW DIMENSIONS

In "Les Grands Boulevards" and "Palm Sunday," Mondrian explored the challenge of capturing a city in constant flux—a place where today's boulevard is never quite the same as tomorrow's, and where the view shifts based on one's perspective, whether from the vantage point of a café, an airplane, or a car: "Toot, toot. The automobile too can provide the opportunity for everything (inside). On the outside, it is part of the whole on the boulevard."[32] His preoccupation with the ever-changing appearance of the metropolis touches on a core issue that had motivated the Cubists: how to represent three-dimensional objects on a flat canvas. While the Cubists fragmented their subjects and juxtaposed them against broken planes, Mondrian sought something beyond mere depiction. He aimed to express the essence of the boulevard in its entirety—including the transformation of its smells, tastes, sights, temperature over time and space.

More broadly, Mondrian's concerns with capturing the essence of space, time, and movement relate to the theories of multiple dimensions popular in European artistic circles at the time. Theo van Doesburg, for example, viewed the fourth dimension as integral to the evolution of abstract art, exploring it in his 1919 painting *Composition in Gray (Rag-time)* (cat. 39). When Kazimir Malevich launched Suprematism in 1915, he explicitly linked it with the concept of the fourth dimension in the titles he gave to some of his paintings.

The book *Tertium Organum* by Russian philosopher and mystic P. D. Ouspensky was particularly influential in artistic circles. In it, the author uses the metaphor of flight to explain how consciousness might expand beyond the limitations of the three-dimensional world.[33] Just as a person in a balloon perceives a vast landscape from above—seeing connections and relationships invisible on the ground—so too could human consciousness rise above ordinary perceptions to access planes in higher dimensions. For Ouspensky, this represented transcending the boundaries of time and space, enabling the mind to perceive the world in its full, multidimensional complexity.

In the context of painting, this idea resonated with abstract artists such as Kandinsky and Malevich, who were seeking to represent more than just the surface of objects. By painting abstract planes, they sought to represent not only three-dimensional space but also the flow of time, movement, and unseen connections—allowing them glimpses of realms beyond ordinary dimensions.

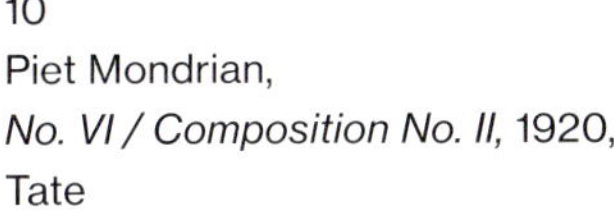

10
Piet Mondrian,
No. VI / Composition No. II, 1920,
Tate

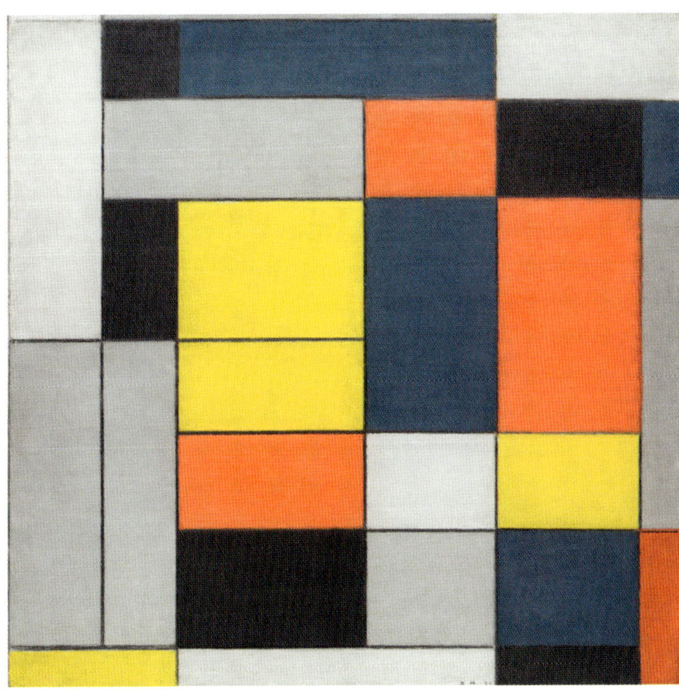

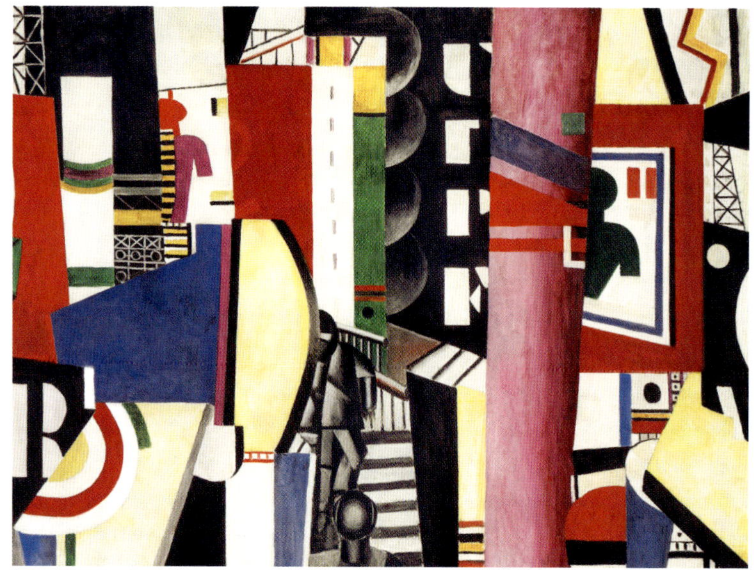

11
Fernand Léger,
The City, 1919,
Philadelphia Museum of Art

As Mondrian's texts reveal, the artist was grappling with these ideas. During this period, Mondrian spent significant time with Van Doesburg, who was temporarily living in Paris. While Mondrian ultimately dismissed Van Doesburg's enthusiasm for the fourth dimension as "loose talk,"[34] the concept of immeasurable space continued to play a role for him, symbolizing a universal balance—a spiritual or cosmic order that transcended the material world.[35]

SILENCED BEATS

There was one place in the city that Mondrian saw as a microcosm of an emerging urban culture: dance bars. In his essay "Jazz and Neoplasticism" of 1927, Mondrian views jazz as a symbol of this new culture.[36] He focuses particularly on bars, where rhythm transcends form and traditional constraints are diminished.

There were a number of jazz bars in Montmartre that had been opened by African American soldiers after World War I. While opportunities for black artists were limited in the United States—particularly under Jim Crow laws dictating that they could only perform at segregated venues—French society in the interwar period was fascinated by African American music, particularly jazz, which was seen as modern and exotic.

"In the bar we find the childlike experience that eludes the people of modern society with their grim seriousness," Mondrian writes. "No link with the old remains, for in the bar only the Charleston is seen and heard. The structure, the lighting, the advertisements—even in their disequilibrium serve to complete the jazz rhythm. All ugliness is transcended by jazz and by light."[37] In bars, social divisions and old values are irrelevant, and rhythm pervades every aspect of life. Mondrian's preoccupation with rhythm is paralleled in his paintings, around 1932 he began accentuating the canvas with double lines to create a stronger sense of rhythm in his compositions (fig. p. 127; see also cat. 42).

This emerging culture was soon disrupted by the rise of Nazism. "Progress has made the Metropolis. Evil has chased man out of some of them," Mondrian wrote in his notes in New York in 1941.[38] He may have been reflecting on his own journey. In 1938 he left Paris—a city where he had lived for over twenty years—and moved to London, where fellow artists sought refuge from the increasingly unstable political climate, as the looming threat of World War II grew. African American jazz performers who had stayed in Paris were singled out for arrest and internment after the German troops marched into Paris on June 14, 1940.[39] Nearly four million people in the Paris region fled their homes in June 1940. On their way south, they encountered evacuees from northern and eastern France, as well as from Belgium, the Netherlands, and

Luxembourg, all fleeing the advancing German soldiers. When the German troops arrived in Paris, they found a nearly deserted city, with only one-fifth of the population remaining.[40]

When Paris fell, Mondrian wrote from London-Hampstead to Barbara Hepworth (cats. 58, 79), who had left London for Cornwall, "It is impossible to do creative work now."[41] A few months later, on September 7, 1940, Germany sent over three hundred bombers and six hundred fighter planes to attack London.[42] On the third night of the assaults, a bomb exploded near Mondrian's house, smashing the windows.[43] Amid the fires that had broken out due to the air raids, the artist managed to take a train to Liverpool, where he had arranged to board the Cunard Line's RMS *Samaria* at the docks. The dance bars that once symbolized a new cultural harmony fell silent, and European art metropolises became places of exodus.

TRANSATLANTIC RHYTHMS

During his first summer in New York, in 1941, Mondrian spent a lot of time alone. He became enamored with the city's vibrant energy and geometric harmony. Charmion von Wiegand, a journalist, artist, and close friend to Mondrian in New York, describes how:

> He never tired of the visual delights of New York City. Everywhere he went he saw parallels with his ideas and work. In some cases these were the result of his anonymous influence. The geometric patterns of modern linoleum, the black and white tiles of Riker's lunch counters, the carefully proportioned shapes of windows, the spare verticals of skyscrapers—were these not related to the De Stijl compositions of the First World War?[44]

For his first ever solo exhibition at Valentine Gallery in January 1942, Mondrian meticulously reworked the paintings he had brought with him into exile, which later became known as the "transatlantic paintings." They were meant to have a rhythmic quality that Mondrian referred

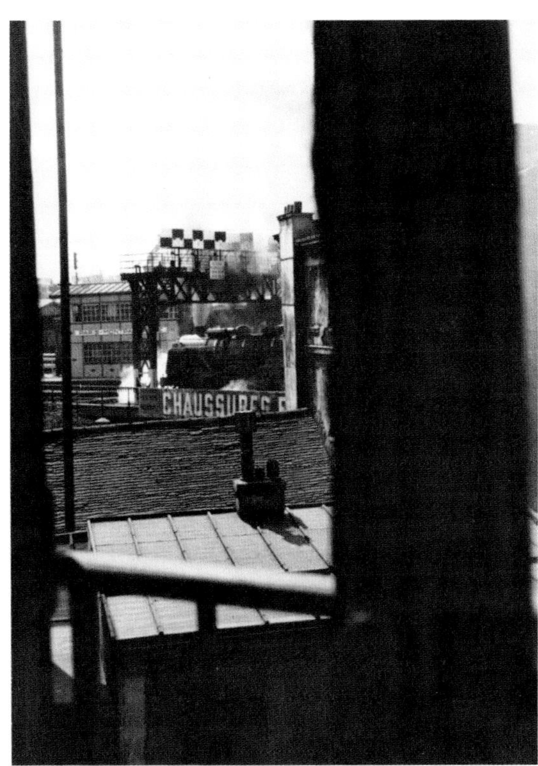

12
László Moholy-Nagy, *Montparnasse from Mondrian's Studio,* 1927 or 1930, Kunstmuseum Den Haag, The Hague

to as "Boogie Woogie."[45] For his second New York exhibition in March 1943, he reworked and renamed several more paintings, including *Place de la Concorde* (fig. 13) and *Trafalgar Square* (fig. 14), originally completed in Paris and London, respectively. The works show the characteristic white planes, a grid of vertical and horizontal black lines, and the three primary colors. However, Mondrian added colored blocks that appear to hover independently in their assigned spaces, and act as focal points in the otherwise rigid structure. The repetition of these blocks generates a rhythm or beat throughout the grid.

The works are signed with "PM" and two completion dates, in the case of Trafalgar Square "39" and "43." The two dates mark them as works created by an immigrant in both the old and the new world.[46] Mondrian exhibited the paintings with *Broadway Boogie Woogie* (fig. 15), which he had started and completed in New York. The three paintings are named after busy squares and streets in the heart of cities, where metropolitan life is most concentrated, emphasizing the deep connection to the cities that influenced his artistic evolution—particularly significant given that Mondrian had not titled his paintings with references to places or objects since 1913. Wiegand interprets the works as celebrations of urban transformation:

> These works celebrate the city of man—the city as symbol of transformation—just as the medieval age celebrated the city of God. Mondrian's late work is a paean of praise to the great cities of the twentieth century. For him they were the place of action where the struggle for a better world must take place. In his last years he forswore his abstract titles for concrete names: Trafalgar Square, Place de la Concorde, Broadway Boogie-Woogie. Three cities shaped him, and he in turn shaped them into a plastic image—a concrete image of how they could be made whole, and how man could find himself through them.[47]

13
Piet Mondrian,
Place de la Concorde, 1938/1943
Dallas Museum of Art

14
Piet Mondrian,
Trafalgar Square, 1939/1943
Museum of Modern Art, New York

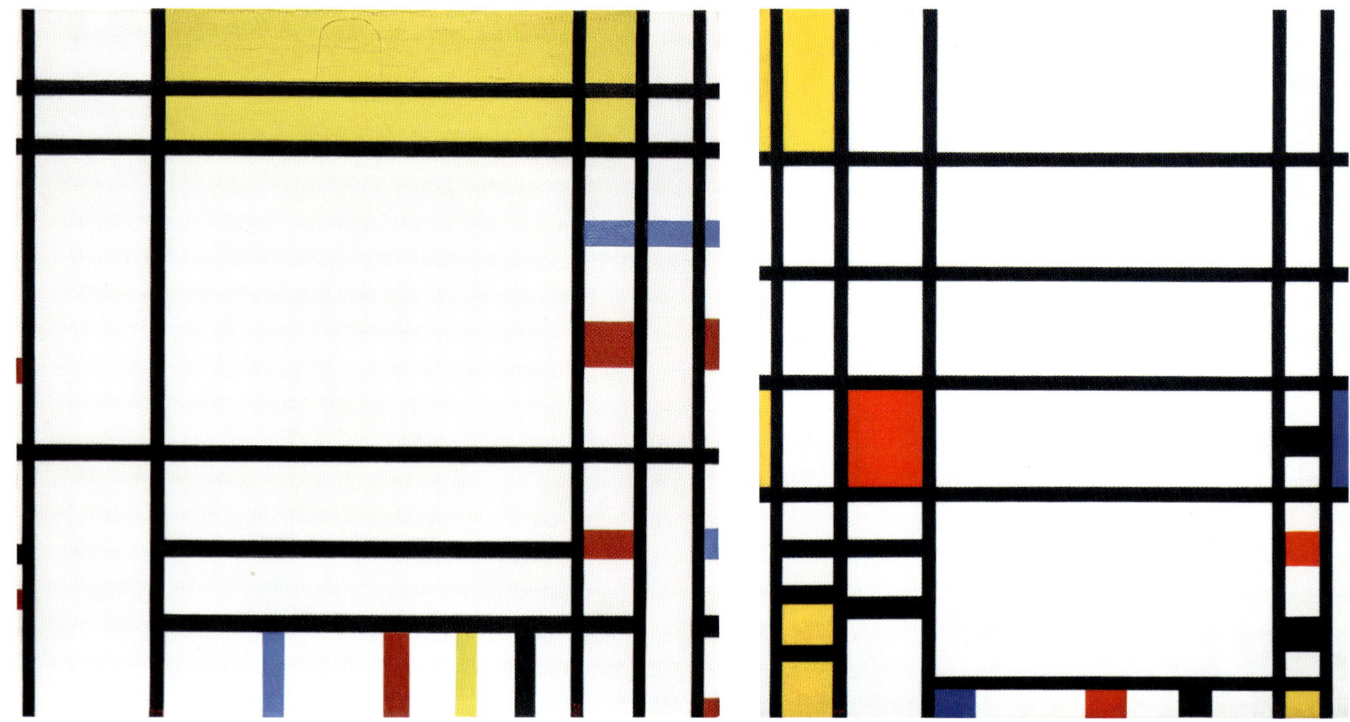

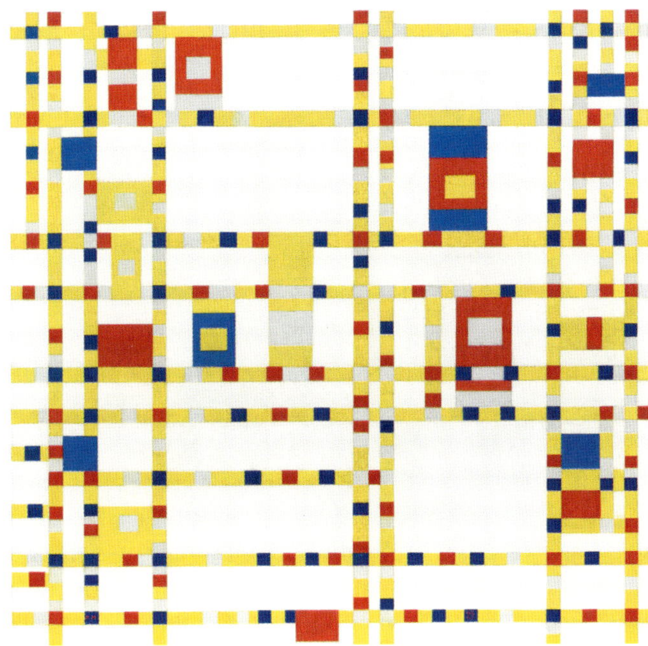

15
Piet Mondrian,
Broadway Boogie Woogie, 1942–43,
Museum of Modern Art,
New York

Rather than being merely artistic responses to New York's urban landscape, Mondrian's late works can be viewed as integrating cultural, political, and musical elements, mirroring Mondrian's engagement with African American culture and the broader sociopolitical context in the US.[48] Mondrian's artistic evolution cannot be understood without recognizing the influence of the metropolis. The dynamic, structured, and ever-changing environment of the city played a crucial role in shaping his artistic vision. Mondrian's experiences in Paris, London, and New York brought him into direct contact with the rhythms, contrasts, and complexities of urban life, which resonated with his pursuit of equilibrium and a new artistic reality.

The metropolis, for Mondrian, was not merely a backdrop but a symbol of modernity that encapsulated the spirit of the age. His works, particularly the "transatlantic paintings," reflect a celebration of the city's potential to inspire a new cultural and artistic paradigm. Through his exploration of the geometric forms and rhythmic patterns found in urban spaces, Mondrian envisioned the city as a force that could transcend the limitations of traditional art and represent the possibilities of a future where art and life are intertwined. Mondrian saw in the metropolis a model for the future—a space where human creativity and rhythms of modern life converge to create a new, universal aesthetic.

Jeremy Lewison

An Art Without Content? Hard Edge Painting, 1958–1968

In memory of David Anfam (1955-2024)

At the cessation of hostilities in 1945, Europe was exhausted. The vibrant prewar centers of art—Paris, Berlin, and London—had lost their allure. Many artists had emigrated to the United States; others had left the metropolitan environs for rural retreats, and some had perished either in the conflict or in the concentration camps. Few of them had remained in occupied Paris or bomb-ravaged Berlin or London.

In Britain, the energy of the prewar modern movement influenced by Paris-based artists—notably Piet Mondrian (cats. 40, 41) and Jean Hélion (cats. 50, 51)—had dissipated. Ben Nicholson (cats. 59–62) had returned to painting landscapes and still lifes, partly for commercial reasons but also in response to his and Barbara Hepworth's wartime relocation from the city to Cornwall. Hepworth (cats. 58, 79) also retreated from purist, internationalist, geometric abstraction to combine its legacy with a response to the ancient Cornish stones, sea, and landscape around Carbis Bay, where she and Nicholson lived. In England, a landscape-derived abstraction came to the fore in the 1950s in the work of Terry Frost (cat. 77), Patrick Heron, and Peter Lanyon, all based in or near St. Ives.

It was not until 1956, with the arrival of the *Modern Art in the United States* exhibition at the Tate Gallery, that British artists were fully exposed to American Abstract Expressionism. The impact of this show and the subsequent exhibitions *The New American Painting* and *Jackson Pollock* at the end of the decade diverted the attention of the middle and younger generations of artists toward New York from Paris.[1] The center of power had moved. The marked influence of Cubism and De Stijl on the middle-generation artists, who had spent time in postwar Paris, was replaced by that of Abstract Expressionism. Art school students were energized by the scale and immediacy of this painting.

However, the impact of Abstract Expressionism was so pervasive that by the late 1950s it had become somewhat academic. This was also the case in New York, where even an early advocate such as critic Clement Greenberg abandoned his promotion of this existentialist, emotional approach to painting for what became known as Post-Painterly Abstraction, particularly the work of Morris Louis and Kenneth Noland (cat. 83). Under Greenberg's influence, formalist writing replaced existentialist criticism; Harold Rosenberg, the originator of the widely

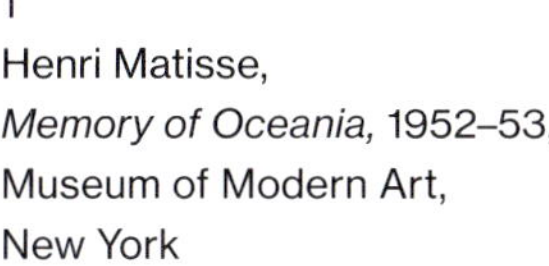

1
Henri Matisse,
Memory of Oceania, 1952–53,
Museum of Modern Art,
New York

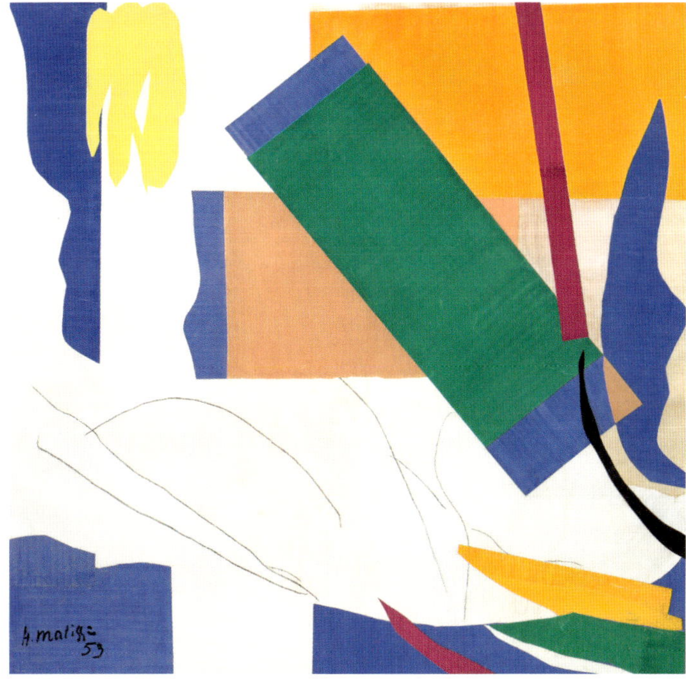

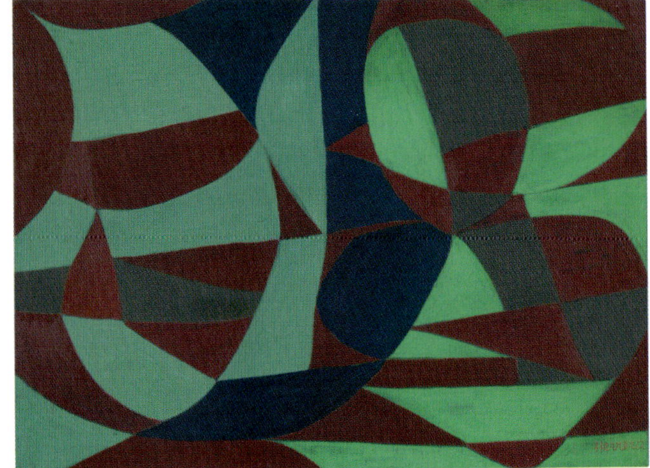

used term *action painting,* was drowned out by Greenberg, his existentialist approach becoming seemingly irrelevant to the new art.

As painter and writer Walter Darby Bannard, a disciple of Greenberg, wrote from the vantage point of 1966, "Abstract Expressionism was repudiated point by point: painting within drawing replaced drawing with paint; overt regularity replaced apparent randomness; symmetry replaced asymmetric balancing; flat, depersonalized brushing or open, stained color replaced the smudge, smear and spatter .... The entire visible esthetic of Abstract Expressionism was brutally revised. These were the 'hardedge' [*sic*] artists; many of them are the Op, Minimal and Color artists of today."[2]

The discussion that follows focuses on the social, political, and cultural context in which Hard Edge Painting emerged and suggests a way of understanding its apparent refusal of meaning from the vantage point of the present.

2
Carmen Herrera,
Blanco y Verde, 1959,
Estate of Carmen Herrera,
Whitney Museum of American Art,
New York

3
Carmen Herrera,
Green Garden, 1950,
Estate of Carmen Herrera,
Tate

A NEW CLASSICISM?

The term *Hard Edge* was first aired in Jules Langsner's introduction to the catalog of the exhibition *Four Abstract Classicists* that opened at the San Francisco Museum of Art in 1959 before touring to the Los Angeles County Museum of Art. The following year, it traveled to the Institute of Contemporary Arts in London (ICA) and Queen's University in Belfast with a revised title, *Four Abstract Classicists: West Coast Hard-Edge,* with the first part of the title offset in a considerably smaller typeface on the front cover of the catalog. The exhibition comprised the work of Karl Benjamin, Lorser Feitelson, Frederick Hammersley, and John McLaughlin. In 1961 Lawrence Alloway, a regular contributor to magazines who had recently completed his tenure as assistant director of the ICA, objected to the association of this art with classicism, noting that "an art that rests so squarely on the intensity and motility of color is not usefully described as 'classical.'"[3] In his introduction, however, Langsner suggested that the four artists themselves had adopted this description. Langsner regarded Hard Edge Painting as classical by reference to Abstract Expressionism: "The classicist seeks ordered relationships of a kind seldom found in the helter-skelter of raw existence.... To achieve impeccable order the classical artist consciously edits ideas rising to the surface from the unconscious. A classical work is deliberated rather than produced spontaneously," and refrains from external reference. "Abstract Classicist painting is hard-edged painting. Forms are finite, flat, rimmed by a hard, clean edge. These forms are not intended to evoke in the spectator any recollections of specific shapes he may have encountered in some other connection.

They are autonomous shapes, sufficient unto themselves as shapes." Langsner noted they have uniform, flat colors, and that color and shape were indistinguishable and mutually dependent.[4]

Notwithstanding the rather specious view that Abstract Expressionist paintings were neither edited nor deliberated, his definition could apply equally to the work of Mondrian as that of McLaughlin, whereas Alloway felt that the "aims and effects" of these more recent abstract painters "are quite different." Earlier geometric artists used shapes as "symbols of a comprehensive order." The Hard Edge painters had no "intention of using geometry as the basis of rules for art. . . . Early abstract theory, on the contrary, abounds in nostalgia for absolutes."[5] Implied in Langsner's discussion, according to Alloway, is that classicism was historically hard and precise where Romanticism was "fuzzy and personally autographic." Alloway pointed to the work of French Neoclassical painter Jean-Auguste-Dominique Ingres as confounding that theory.[6] He felt that Hard Edge painters were not concerned with order and stability but rather with the decisive importance of the edge in upsetting the figure-ground relationship and in transforming a painting into an object. Like Langsner, he presents Hard Edge Painting as the depiction of autonomous shapes with no external referents, but for Alloway, optical drama, including illusionism, was a key element.

There was no group or alliance of Hard Edge artists and, indeed, there is little agreement as to which painters may be described as such. Gene Davis (cat. 86), Feitelson, McLaughlin, Jack Youngerman, and British painter Robyn Denny may have been regularly regarded as Hard Edge painters, while the paintings of Al Held (cat. 89), Ellsworth Kelly (cat. 88), Kenneth Noland, and Frank Stella (cats. 81, 84, 85) appeared to contain shapes with hard edges, yet seemed to have concerns of a different nature. Similarly, the early works of Paul Huxley (cat. 87) might be considered Hard Edge but for their biomorphic overtones and abstracted references to things observed. The 1960s was a period in which both figurative artists, such as those associated with Pop Art, and abstract painters rejected the brushstroke's expressiveness, favoring smooth and impersonal fields of color.

THE SOURCES OF HARD EDGE

It is often suggested that Hard Edge Painting was developed in response to Abstract Expressionism, but this was not always the case. Many artists were responding to prewar modernism in Europe. Ellsworth Kelly, for example, who was working in Paris in the late 1940s and early 1950s, was unaware of Jackson Pollock, Mark Rothko, and Clyfford Still. Instead, he looked to the art of Jean Arp and Sophie Taeuber-Arp (cat. 56), with whose work he became acquainted in 1950 after meeting Arp through an introduction by critic Michel Seuphor. Arp's use of chance

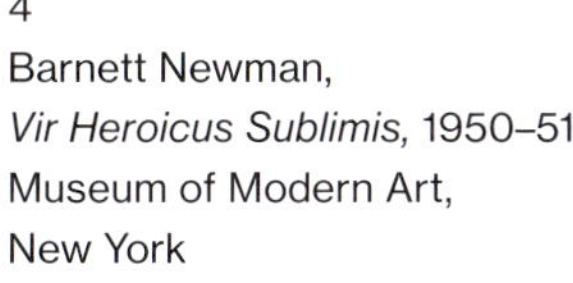

4
Barnett Newman,
Vir Heroicus Sublimis, 1950–51,
Museum of Modern Art,
New York

and collage attracted him and helped him create early examples of Hard Edge Painting. Like Kelly, John McLaughlin arrived at his signature motifs during the early 1950s, before Abstract Expressionism was widely known, and came to it through his interest in Kazimir Malevich (cat. 4) and Piet Mondrian. He would compose his paintings by placing colored strips of paper on the canvas and, when satisfied with the composition, would make notes of their placement and draw them in on the canvas before painting, making changes to the colors as desired. His process was intuitive, not logical.[7] Al Held, who painted in a manner related to Abstract Expressionism and Tachisme in his Paris years, came to Hard Edge Painting not simply through his exposure to the geometric paintings of Auguste Herbin (cat. 49) but through the cutouts of Henri Matisse, shown in a 1961 exhibition at the Museum of Modern Art in New York. Indeed, collage was an important catalyst for creating Hard Edge paintings. Held, Kelly, McLaughlin, and Youngerman, for example, all understood the potential of color and shapes to create space while simultaneously lying absolutely flat—an observation they made of Matisse's cutouts (fig. 1).

Immediately after the war, Paris had been a magnet for young artists, particularly Americans, who were able to stay there thanks to the financial support of the US government under the terms of the GI Bill. Paris became a center for geometric abstraction as well as Tachisme. Geometric abstraction was promoted by Galerie Denise René, but it rarely showed American artists. Foreign artists coming to Paris tended to exhibit at the annual Salon des Réalités Nouvelles, which was a multinational exhibition foregrounding experimental art, particularly of the nonobjective variety. It was there that Cuban artist Carmen Herrera, who arrived in Paris from New York in 1948, acquired knowledge of the history of abstraction and its contemporary developments. Herrera increasingly simplified her work as she eliminated inessential forms and, like Kelly and Youngerman, employed an impersonal facture, but in her Paris years her painting remained rooted in geometric abstraction. Later, after returning to New York, her works became somewhat larger, although never as large as those of her American counterparts, and she found it hard to attract galleries to mount exhibitions. The optical ambiguity and pared-down nature of her paintings as evidenced in *Blanco y Verde* (fig. 2) and *Diptych (Green & Black)* (cat. 91) show a marked development from such early geometric works as *Green Garden* (fig. 3), but her work always retained a memory of her geometric abstract beginnings.

5
Ad Reinhardt,
Abstract Painting, 1961,
Städel Museum, Frankfurt am Main;
on permanent loan from
the Adolf Luther Foundation

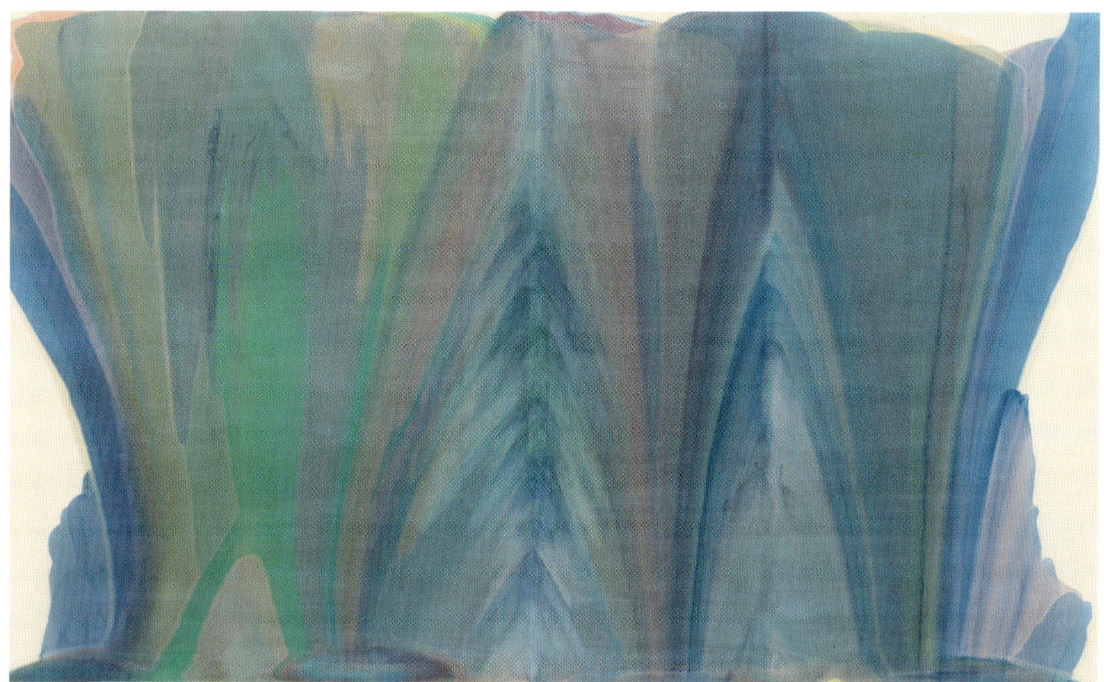

6
Morris Louis,
Tet, 1958,
Whitney Museum of American Art,
New York

In London, a number of artists rejected gesture and fast painting, having seen the works of Barnett Newman in *The New American Painting,* and responded by making works that were environmental in scale and eliminated evidence of brushstrokes. These were shown in exhibitions such as *Place* at the ICA in September 1959 and *Situation: An Exhibition of British Abstract Painting* at the Royal Society of British Artists (RBA Galleries) the following year. Scale, impersonal facture, clear definition, an interchangeability or an ambiguity of figure and ground, and the elimination of autographic marks and gestures, along with the self, were key elements of these paintings. For New York artists, Newman's (fig. 4) exhibition at French & Company in New York in 1959 was equally important in exemplifying the expansive, impassive field of color.

ART IS ART

The roots of Hard Edge were quite varied. Although Barnett Newman's work played a key role, notwithstanding its symbolic content, Ad Reinhardt, not represented in *Modern Art in the United States* and *The New American Painting,* had been theorizing and championing for many years an abstract art that eliminated content, whether authorial, associational, or representational. Looking back in 1965, American critic Barbara Rose, then married to Frank Stella, was uncertain how much Reinhardt's writings "helped to change the climate," but she observed that his "dicta, arcane as they may have sounded when first handed down from the scriptorium, have become canonical for the young artists."[8] Against the idea of interpreting paintings, Reinhardt (fig. 5) was in favor of subjectless paintings that were impersonal, boring—"I finally made a program out of boredom" he claimed retrospectively[9]—and nonreferential. In his celebrated "25 Lines of Words on Art: Statement," published in *It Is* in the spring of 1958, Reinhardt declaimed:

> Art is art. Everything else is everything else.

And four paragraphs further on:

> Painting "about which no questions can be asked."
> Painting as "not as a likeness of anything on earth."

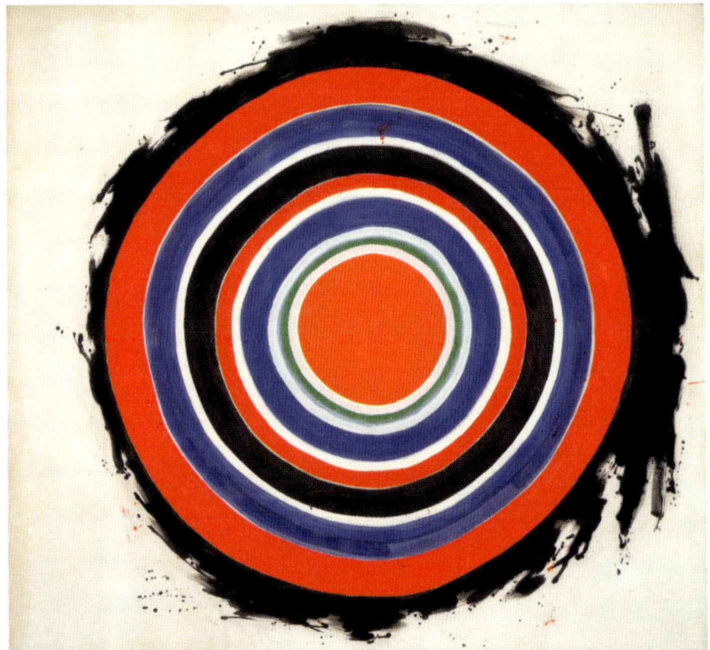

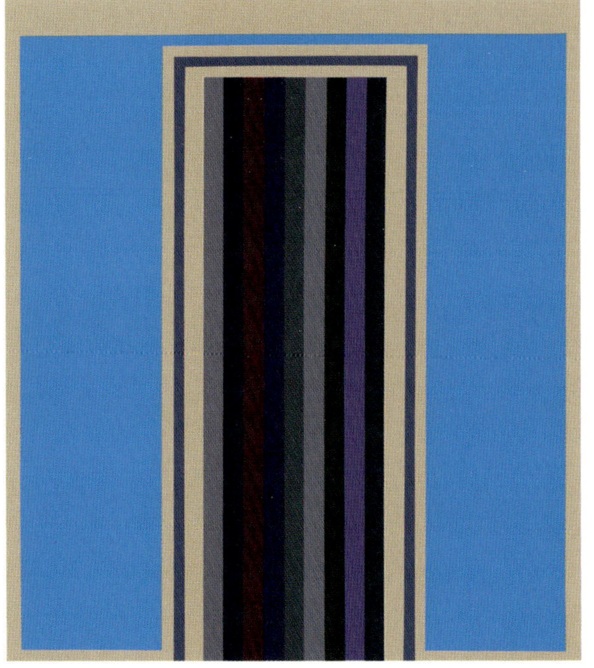

7
Kenneth Noland,
Beginning, 1958,
Hirshhorn Museum and Sculpture Garden, Smithsonian Institution, Washington, DC

8
Robyn Denny,
Ted Bentley, 1961,
New Art Centre, Salisbury

Reinhardt proposed painting as “central, frontal, regular, repetitive” that consisted of “outlines, monotones, blankness, quiescence, premeditation.” It was to be “extremely impersonal,” which he regarded as “the truly personal.”[10] Painting was simply paint on canvas. It was not to be mimetic or representational; it would not express any psychological state.

There are echoes of Reinhardt’s writing in the theories of Clement Greenberg, whose criticism changed direction in the late 1950s. He shifted from acknowledging the relationship between the works of Jackson Pollock and Willem de Kooning to world events, to emphasizing modernism as a progression toward the autonomy of painting, where good painting—and Greenberg placed great emphasis on his ability to judge the good from the bad—was defined by “literalness.” By this he meant that a painting should do what only painting could do, determined by its fundamental characteristics of paint on a flat surface. Greenberg saw the course of modernism, from Édouard Manet onward, in terms of continuous reduction from illusionism to flatness, from representation to art placing stress on color as hue, from narrative painting to one purged of all literary matter. His exemplars from around the late 1950s were Morris Louis (fig. 6) and Kenneth Noland, whom he described as painters of Post-Painterly Abstraction—where “painterly” meant Abstract Expressionist. Michael Fried, a follower of Greenberg, concurred that the history of painting from Manet onward was characterized by “the withdrawal of painting from the task of representing reality . . . in favor of an increasing preoccupation with problems intrinsic to painting itself.”[11] Painting, according to Fried, was self-critical, that is, each development sprang out of a critique of what immediately preceded it; painting was a means of solving the problems of painting rather than commenting on the world.

As early as 1939, Greenberg put forward a view that from medieval times onward the painter’s principal concern was formal: “As long as there was general agreement as to what were the worthiest subjects for art, the artist was relieved of the necessity to be original and inventive in his ‘matter’ and could devote all his energy to formal problems. For him, the medium became privately, professionally, the content of his art, even as his medium is today, the public content of the abstract painter’s art.”[12] Of course, he ignored the possible pious intentions of the artist, his (because principally in those days it was male artists) interest in the gospel stories or stories of ancient myth as providing lessons in morality, and he also ignored the possibility, indeed the likelihood, that form and meaning were inextricably linked.

Nor did he take into consideration the imaginative effort required to conceive scenes for which there was no documentary evidence. In 1959 Greenberg reached a position where he felt that abstract art's lack of referentiality came as "a relief" because it "does not have to mean, or be useful for, anything other than itself." Abstract art, he claimed, should be capable of being "taken in in a glance"; it should be "static," and "its unity should be immediately evident."[13]

Although Louis and Noland had been inspired by the stained paintings of Helen Frankenthaler and Pollock's black pourings on unprimed canvas, they created works that apparently made no reference to external objects and could be seen immediately as a whole in a single glance. Unlike Jasper Johns's series of target paintings that he began in 1955, Noland's 1959 works featured abstract concentric circles, centrally placed on the canvas without the symbolic associations of a target. Louis's poured paintings were concerned with color and hue, and he instrumentalized the framing edge. Both artists made flatness—a property unique to painting—a key characteristic by allowing the paint to be absorbed into the warp and weft of the canvas.

Noland saw Pollock's all-over painting as a dead end and stated that "the only thing to do would be to focus from the center out."[14] The emphasis on the boundaries of the canvas would soon lead to paintings being regarded as objects. In some of the early circles such as *Beginning* (fig. 7), Noland clearly embraced the legacy of Abstract Expressionism in the use of splatters and ragged brush marks. Later paintings in the series and in series that followed—chevrons, diamonds, and parallel lines—were more controlled and precise. The surfaces became increasingly depersonalized, although his choice of colors was always intuitive.

Noland had learned the value of juxtaposing colors from Josef Albers (cats. 28–32), but he worked on a much grander scale than the latter. He used color in a way that could create space like, for example, Hans Hofmann, who referred to the "push and pull" of color in his essay "Search for the Real" of 1948 and frequently in his teaching. Like the Abstract Expressionists, Noland's large-scale paintings encouraged an embodied experience because the juxtaposition of colors would cause them to pulse. The scale of the work was set at the limit of human reach. Noland underwent years of Reichian therapy, and it is possible, as Mollie Berger writes, that his concentric circles "emit energy akin to a beat or a pulse, as the circles expand and radiate across the space of the canvas. Its beating pulse, when perceived by the viewer, visualizes the Reichian goal of attending to one's own pulsing center in order to connect with the flow of life in the world beyond."[15] Berger's approach posits the view that the meaning of Noland's work extends beyond the merely formal, *contra* Greenberg and Fried. Wilhelm Reich's theories and Reichian therapy, in general, were widely known in New York in this period and were considered helpful in the recovery from the trauma of World War II.

The approach of critics to Noland's paintings was purely formal. Michael Fried and Kenworth Moffett emphasized the placement of Noland's designs within the canvas, their relationship to the framing edge, the corners, or the center. Fried admired the way in which Noland anchored the composition to the top corners in a work such as *Half-Time* (cat. 83), allowing him to "prize the chevron away from the bottom edge." This would also allow him to "dispense with lateral symmetry in other paintings since the image would always be anchored by the corners and they would no longer have to be perpendicular."[16] Thus, there followed a series of paintings in which the apex of the chevron was offset from the center. Fried and Moffett extolled the flatness of the works and their opticality, the disembodied nature of color that resulted from the staining process using liquid, acrylic paint. Although his colors seem bounded by hard edges, the fact that they are stained softens the geometry. There is always a slight fuzziness to Noland's colors that precludes them from being true, Hard Edge paintings.

THE DEATH OF THE AUTHOR

The apparent impersonality of these works was common to the production of a number of painters. Frank Stella determined the width of stripes in his paintings by the width of the stretcher bars or the width of the house painter's brushes he employed. Symmetry was an important characteristic of his painting in this phase; "Ken Noland has put things in the center and I'll use a symmetrical pattern, but we use symmetry in a different way [to European geometric painters]. It's nonrelational. In the newer American painting we strive to get the thing in the middle, and symmetrical, but just to get a kind of force, just to get the thing on the canvas. The balance factor isn't important. We are not trying to jockey everything around," Stella explained to Bruce Glaser in the mid-1960s.[17] Noland and Stella were not balancing elements in a composition, unlike European painters of geometric abstraction such as Mondrian.

Stella worked in modular formats and in series to eliminate the need to make decisions. From his point of view, once the painting was conceived, it could be executed by anyone following his rules (although it never was). The paint surface itself was to be "pedestrian," and the paint applied with simplicity, in contrast to Abstract Expressionist tendencies toward drama.[18] In *Slieve More* (cat. 81), for example, the composition reflects the framing edge, the shape of the canvas. The painting became an object, anti-illusionistic, representing nothing but itself. Stella felt that the role of the artist was to make nothing but "a thing . . . All I want anyone to get out of my painting, and all I ever get out of them, is the fact that you can see the whole idea without any confusion. . . . What you see is what you see," he stated echoing, probably unknowingly, a statement by Lawrence Alloway.[19]

In response to such painting—or perhaps to the zeitgeist—art criticism moved from interpretation to description, from describing the subjective experience of the work to revealing the visual language. The author's voice was no more a part of criticism than it was of paint-

9
Frank Stella,
Die Fahne hoch!, 1959,
Whitney Museum of American Art,
New York

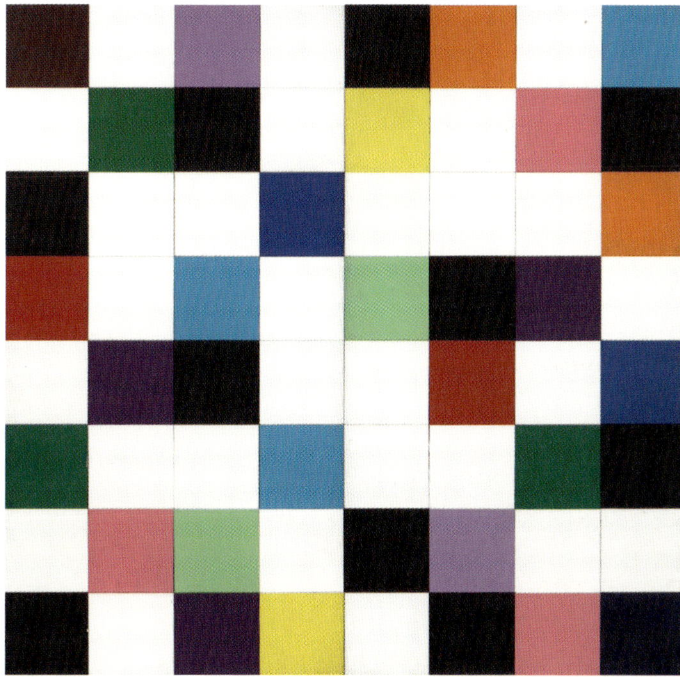

10
Ellsworth Kelly,
Colors for a Large Wall, 1951,
Museum of Modern Art,
New York

ing. According to the prevailing orthodoxy, grammar and syntax became more important to painting than meaning.

Some musicians and writers took a similar approach. Composer John Cage advocated the removal of the composer from the composition of music. Sounds would be determined by operations of chance, for example, in Cage's case by the *I Ching* (Book of Changes). In an article about contemporary developments in music, Leonard B. Meyer described how contemporary music had moved away from linearity—where patterns could be apprehended and outcomes anticipated—to a form that does not direct the listener to points of culmination and arouses no expectations. It simply is. He saw parallels between music and the visual arts in works where artists avoid symmetry,[20] perspective, and the presence of recognizable objects or patterns that may structure visual experience. Similarly, in literature, Meyer pointed to the progressive weakening of the importance of plot, character, and conventions of grammar. [21] The following year, Susan Sontag wrote a powerful refutation of interpretation, stating that interpretation "makes art manageable, conformable. . . . The flight from interpretation seems particularly a feature of modern painting. Abstract painting is the attempt to have, in the ordinary sense, no content; since there is no content there is no interpretation." If content is eliminated, she believed, the viewer would be able to see the object for what it is. The painting would be more "real." "The function of criticism should be to show *how it is what it is,* even *that it is what it is,* rather than to show *what it means.*"[22] In 1967 Roland Barthes would write about the death of the author, the elimination of the importance of biography and intentionality in the discussion of literary works. French novelist Alain Robbe-Grillet was already well known from the mid-1950s onward for novels with no plot, no narrative, and no authorial commentary that concentrated on the description of things. He was frequently invoked by artists and critics alike, regardless of whether they had read his books or were familiar with his literary theories.[23]

The pursuit of the impersonal was ultimately futile, for however much a smooth finish or lack of brushwork or semiautomated execution was intended to remove the personality of the artist from the artwork, the work of all these artists still retained a personal, identifiable look. A painting by Frank Stella is unmistakably by him; an Ellsworth Kelly painting has a signature look; a painting by Ad Reinhardt has an unmistakable appearance. Alloway had already pleaded this case in 1960 when he wrote, "The personal is not expunged by using a neat technique;

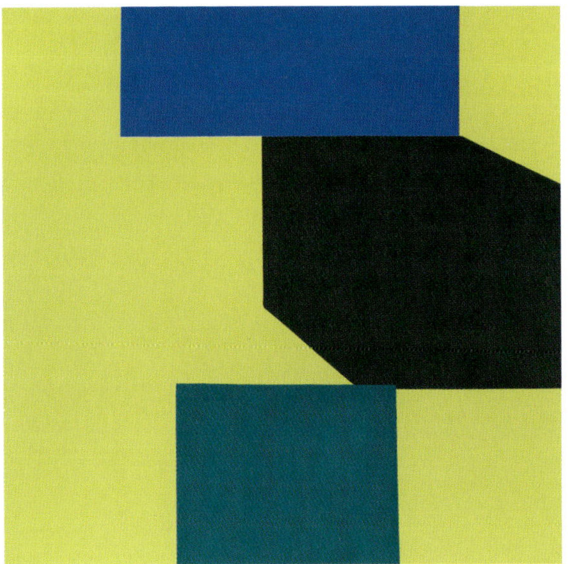

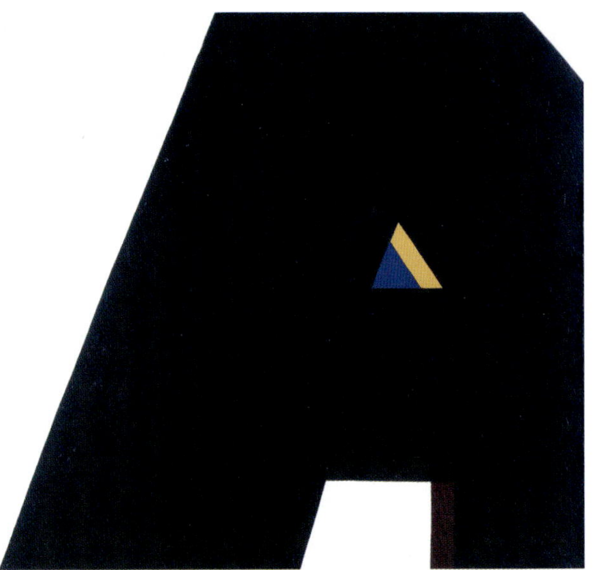

anonymity is not a consequence of highly finishing a painting. The artist's conceptual order is just as personal as autographic traits."[24] But Hard Edge paintings were broadly nonreferential, with some exceptions. For example, Kelly's work was often based on photographs he took, shadows he observed, or architectural details. Robyn Denny's paintings (fig. 8) were inspired by science fiction and circuitry that carried data streams in cyberspace.[25]

There were critics at the time who refuted the view that paintings by Noland, for example, were purely formal and optical. British critic Norbert Lynton, writing about Noland's 1963 exhibition that opened in the new Kasmin Gallery in London, bucked the formalist trend when he wrote that Noland's paintings were expressive of "sun and heat, God and infinity, water, well, depth and womb, danger and target, wheel and fire. Of course, their optical punch is enormous, and they mutate richly in the mind's eye, but their deeper appeal lies in their ethereal insubstantiality."[26] There was no getting away from meaning. How should Stella's titles *Arbeit Macht Frei* or *Die Fahne hoch!* (fig. 9) be regarded? Can their associations with Nazi ideology really be overlooked as early commentators tended to do?[27] The series of black paintings to which these two works belong are endowed with titles that, as Robert Rosenblum has pointed out, "allude to a wide spectrum of human sorrows, from New York tenements (*Arundel Castle*) and a Chicago cemetery (*Getty Tomb*) to a London insane asylum (*Bethlehem's Hospital*) and the Nazi concentration camps at Auschwitz (*Arbeit Macht Frei*)."[28] Far from being limited to what you see, the titles ensure such paintings resonate beyond the facts of their appearance. Even Morris Louis's late paintings are now seen by some writers as relating to post-Holocaust recovery.[29]

The idea that artists disengaged from meaning is less than certain. Moreover, once out of the artist's hands, a painting can be interpreted in whatever way the viewer wants. There is no denying intentionality, even if the intention was to deny an intentional reading. Those whose works were not limited to purely formal aspects may have been influenced by the weight of Clement Greenberg and his allies, leading them to keep silent.

11
Paul Huxley,
Untitled No. 89, 1967,
Studio Paul Huxley

12
Al Held,
The Big A, 1962,
Staatliche Museen zu Berlin,
Nationalgalerie

THE NEW COOL-ART

By the mid-1950s the trauma of World War II had become internalized, and the younger artists turned away from the excess of emotional outpouring they perceived in Abstract Expressionism for something more measured. The imagery had become clichéd or exhausted, and there was a need to invent a new language. As novelist James Baldwin put it in a question-and-answer session following a talk he gave on October 22, 1960, in San Francisco, "The world in which we live has to be named all over again."[30]

The Hard Edge look of painting emerged as an expression of the new spirit. Brian O'Doherty wrote in 1964 in an article in the *New York Times* that the anonymity of the facture, the machine-like appearance, and the lack of spontaneity in the new painting mark "the arrival of a new generation, a cool, hip generation that has gone beyond *angst* to indifference," an indifference in response to nuclear threats and "the atrocities of the social machine grinding down individuality and feeling." The new generation was apparently neutral, politically uncommitted, and suppressed emotion in the making of machinelike objects.[31] For O'Doherty, this was an expression of nihilism, whereas for Irving Sandler it represented a "new cool-art."[32] Yet, it might also be possible to say that the new generation was responding to its social environment of mass production, the buzz of consumer society with its refrigerators, televisions, washing machines, vacuum cleaners, Cadillacs, and the optimism of postwar reconstruction. In postwar industrial society, the handmade seemed rather quaint. As early as 1957, art historian Meyer Schapiro judged that Abstract Expressionist paintings were "the last hand-made, personal objects within our culture."[33]

The bright colors available in acrylic paint were used by Pop and abstract artists alike and were found in the new plastic furniture and clothes. These were paintings for a reconstructed world that had a strong relationship to architecture and the built environment. Ellsworth Kelly (fig. 10), for example, wanted to establish "a closer contact between the artist and the wall,"[34] not by creating easel paintings to be hung on the walls of the bourgeoisie but by creating objects of color. He even integrated the wall into some of his compositions. Like many artists at this time, Kelly was interested in the figure-field relationship, at times negating it, at other times exploring ambiguity. While flatness was important, illusion and negating illusion could be equally salient. Paul Huxley (fig. 11; cat. 87) had made similar moves toward playfulness in 1967 in a series of paintings that contrasted flatness and the illusion of volume, while always asserting the two-dimensionality of the canvas. Op Art explored the confounding of the eye further; the edge of each color was crucial.

Lawrence Alloway had remarked upon the importance of the edge in his introduction to *6 American Abstract Artists* in 1961. In discussing the works of Ellsworth Kelly, Alexander Liberman (cat. 92), Agnes Martin (cat. 99), Ad Reinhardt, Leon Smith, and Sidney Wolfson, he contended that the surfaces of their work were "immaculate, but by no means static; and the edges of their forms are hard and clear enough to permit alternative positive and negative readings. Doubt about which of the two adjacent areas is dominant is typical of these painters, most of whom have abolished the traditional primacy of figure-field relationships."[35] The trajectory was toward eliminating the figure-ground relationship, and Michael Fried commended Kelly's exhibition at Betty Parsons Gallery in 1964 for achieving this. He noted that Kelly had eliminated the suggestion of biomorphic forms of previous works and had also dispensed with "the ambiguities between figure and ground, and the image and framing edge." In the new work, Fried detected a greater emphasis on "the unitary impact" the paintings make upon the viewer echoing Clement Greenberg's requirement that a painting should be capable of being taken in in a glance.

Painting had come a long way from prewar geometric art. Alloway had defined the distinction between Hard Edge and geometric art in an article in *Architectural Design* in 1960. In geometric art, the picture became a "games board" on which "form has been treated as discrete entities, a procedure which led to the definition of the picture plane as a sort of tray which carried small objects," whereas

> forms are few in hard-edge and the surface immaculate. . . . Immaculate surface is essential because all the painted areas must be equal. Both sides of the edge are on the same plane. There is no illusion of overlapping or figure-field relationships. The whole picture becomes the unit; forms extend the length of the painting, or are restricted to two or three tones. The result of this spareness is that the spatial effect of figures on a field is avoided. The sharp boundaries of a hard-edge painting do not break the plane. There is no illusion of volumes behind the paint and no implication of atmosphere before it. What you see is precisely what there is. Yet what you see is usually optically ambiguous. Positive and negative interact as shapes in hard-edge, united in a single plane. The inseparable relationship of forms in a kind of absolute neighbourliness is the result of the tonal and planar economy of these painters.[36]

13
Al Held,
The Dowager Empress, 1965,
Whitney Museum of American Art,
New York
(Cat. 89)

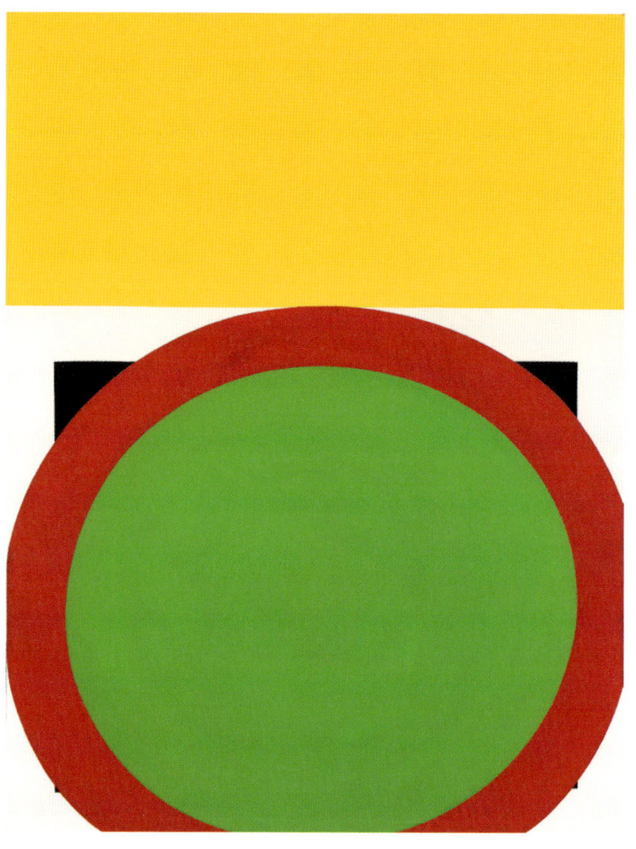

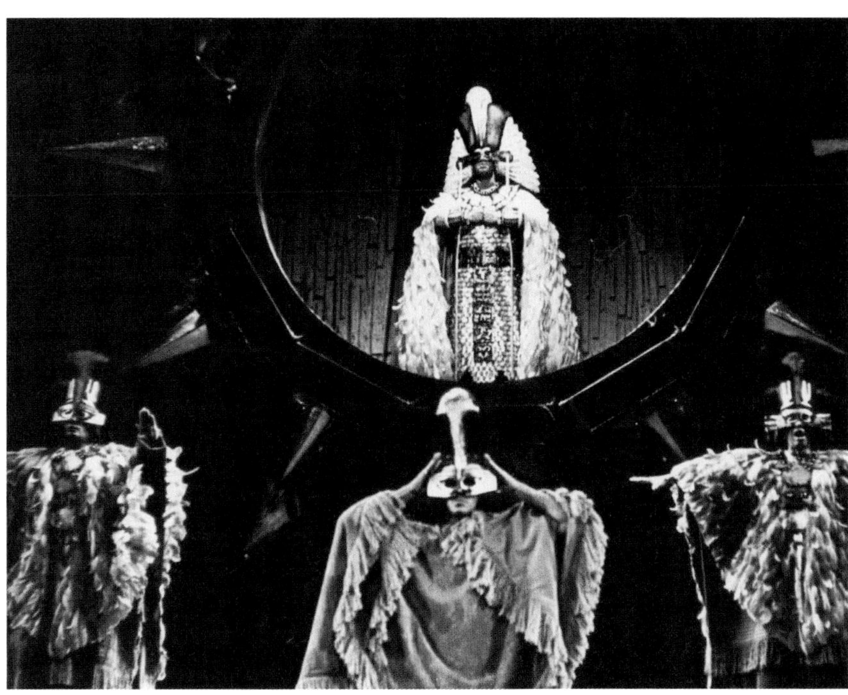

14
Scene from the Broadway production of Peter Shaffer's play *The Royal Hunt of the Sun,* 1965

Alloway's description of the attachment of color areas to the plane undermined by optical ambiguity is perfectly encapsulated in Al Held's *The Dowager Empress* (fig. 13), which celebrates flatness while at the same time suggesting layers of color. The painting juxtaposes complementary colors (red and green) that constantly flip backward and forward. The scale of the work makes for an overwhelming retinal and bodily experience, one that absorbs and repels. The tension between two and three dimensions in his work had been a key characteristic of the paintings depicting typographic forms of 1964–65, in which he broke away from the Greenbergian dogma of flatness. In paintings such as *The Big A* (fig. 12), Held took Hard Edge to a new position of referentiality, which could be cryptic but bold. There was something cartoonish and dramatic about them and earlier works such as *Y and I* (1961, private collection), although Matisse's cutouts were their obvious inspiration. The tension between flatness and depth and the corporeal response created by the juxtaposition of colors was a key element of these works that ran counter to the total flatness required by Greenberg or the purely optical experience favored by Fried.

What Held created was a theatrical space. In *The Big A,* the viewer is tempted to think that a space will open up between the two upstanding black elements of the A, but the white areas to the left and beneath, which are in the same plane, close this down. The only space is in front of the painting—between the viewer and the object. Similarly, in *The Dowager Empress* the triangles of black that seemingly emerge from behind the red circle, top and bottom, implying a hidden square—echoes of Malevich here—tempt the viewer to think there is depth to the painting, but they remain in the same plane as all the other colors. With nowhere to go, the viewer's gaze is returned by the object before him. For a spectator coming across the scene of the painting being viewed by another visitor, Held creates a space in front of the painting that is occupied and articulated by the first viewer. The space in which this viewer stands is what theater director Peter Brook was to call "the empty space." "I can take any empty space and call it a bare stage," he wrote in 1968. "A man walks across this empty space whilst someone else is watching him, and this is all that is needed for an act of theatre to be engaged."[37] Held's paintings are theatrical; the paintings act like backdrops. The title references a highly influential figure in Chinese and Russian imperial societies, the widow of the deceased emperor. Yet, with its simple geometric forms *The Dowager Empress* resembles Mesoamerican art, and there are also echoes of Michael Annals's set design for Peter Shaffer's *The Royal*

Hunt of the Sun (fig. 14), which played in New York from October 1965. Motion is implied by the cutting off of the bottom of the red circle, as though it were descending like the sun.

Alloway was to evolve his position and later did not deny the link between Hard Edge Painting and earlier geometric art, as his introduction to the catalog of *Systemic Painting,* his 1966 exhibition at the Guggenheim Museum in New York, makes clear. But Hard Edge Painting, he observed, did not come with the baggage of absolutism or the appeal to the ideal suggested in the work of artists such as Malevich or Mondrian. Meaning, he contended, came not from reference to "absent events or values" but from the presence of the work. "This does not mean we are faced with the art of nothingness or boredom as has been said with boring frequency. On the contrary, it suggests that the experience of meaning has to be sought in other ways."[38] If it was through the presence of the work, the key question was present to whom? For presence requires human interaction and thus a flow between perceiving body and object.

Alloway, who moved to New York in 1961 to become a curator at the Guggenheim Museum, had lined himself up against Greenberg, Fried, and their coterie. He did not accept that painting was merely a formal exercise and an experiment in opticality, but the Greenbergian dogma held sway, at least in the US. In Europe, there were other perspectives. Hard Edge Painting was noticeably absent from *Painting and Sculpture of a Decade, 54–64,* a panoramic exhibition at the Tate Gallery in 1964, which suggests either its force was spent or the curators of the exhibition, Lawrence Gowing and Alan Bowness, were too committed to painterly painting. Ellsworth Kelly, Kenneth Noland, and Ad Reinhardt were included, but none of the mainstream Hard Edge painters. Hard Edge, like Abstract Expressionism, became academic and began to be critiqued by the succeeding generation of minimalist artists who returned to painterly means—Brice Marden, Robert Ryman, and others—and some of whom invested their works with muted but legible emotion that Hard Edge painting shunned. Frank Stella himself abandoned the rigors of his early approach to create flamboyant works that might be called baroque. In the end, Hard Edge painting, which was suited to formalist analysis, was too limited in its outlook. Just as formalism eclipsed existentialism, it was eventually overturned by a return to an interest in the social, psychological, metaphysical, and existential context of art.

AN ART OF RELEVANCE

The climate in America had changed. The new generation was not scarred by World War II but traumatized by the Vietnam War, a series of political assassinations, and a rampant capitalist, consumerist society. The rise of feminism and the civil rights movement and the growing tendency to politicize art, particularly Conceptual art, meant that Hard Edge abstraction began to be seen as a decorative irrelevance, precisely because it had erroneously been seen through a formalist prism. Ellsworth Kelly recalled at the end of his life, "I know once during the Vietnam War I did a series of very colorful paintings in New York, and what people said was, 'This is too cheerful. Who wants to see these happy colors right now with these awful headlines in the papers, and all the boys and women there in the war.' So I said, 'I'm a little ashamed that I'm so cheerful,' and the next set of paintings was all gray. And then I didn't sell any of them."[39] There could be no better testimony to the growing perception of the apparent irrelevance of this work.

In retrospect, this seems like a misunderstanding. A painting by Kelly has relevance to the built environment; it makes you not only see color but feel it. There is a phenomenological aspect to the work. In one of his last interviews, Kelly remarked,

> I don't like decoration—it's like bad painting. Because, to me, a painting really has to really mean something. To me, I mean. It's hard to say what it means except what you feel and what you can do with it by looking and investigating. I think Diane Arbus said, "If you investigate enough, everything becomes abstract," and I like that, so I use it. Everything has to relate to the architecture, like that door back there that's open—it's a tall rectangle of dark next to white. I always felt there's too much in some of the pictures. I mean, I like Kandinsky very much and Léger, who both work in colors, but Kandinsky can have a lot of little things. But I've always wanted my works to have their own large space, and to be able to relate to that shadowed door and to everything else in the room.[40]

Similarly, Al Held's move into more spatially complex paintings was equally meaningful to him. They reflect a changed perspective: "I began to see the world as increasingly complex, contradictory, and paradoxical. This provoked my formal move away from flatness to spatial illusionism, simply to get more information into the paintings."[41] If Hard Edge went out of fashion, it was not for lack of meaning, but perhaps lack of relevance to the moment in the eyes of the beholder. For the artists, it continued to have meaning in relation to the world.

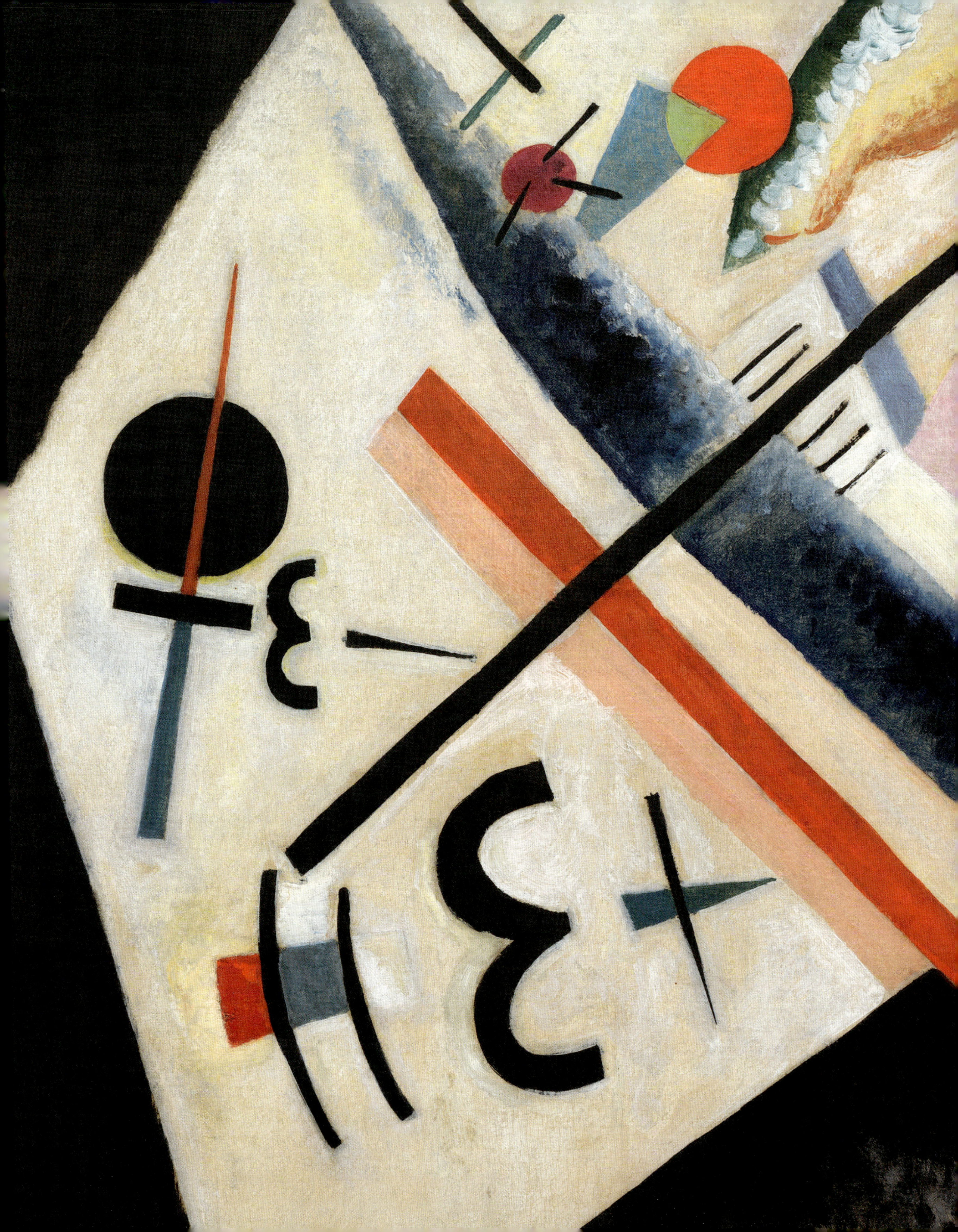

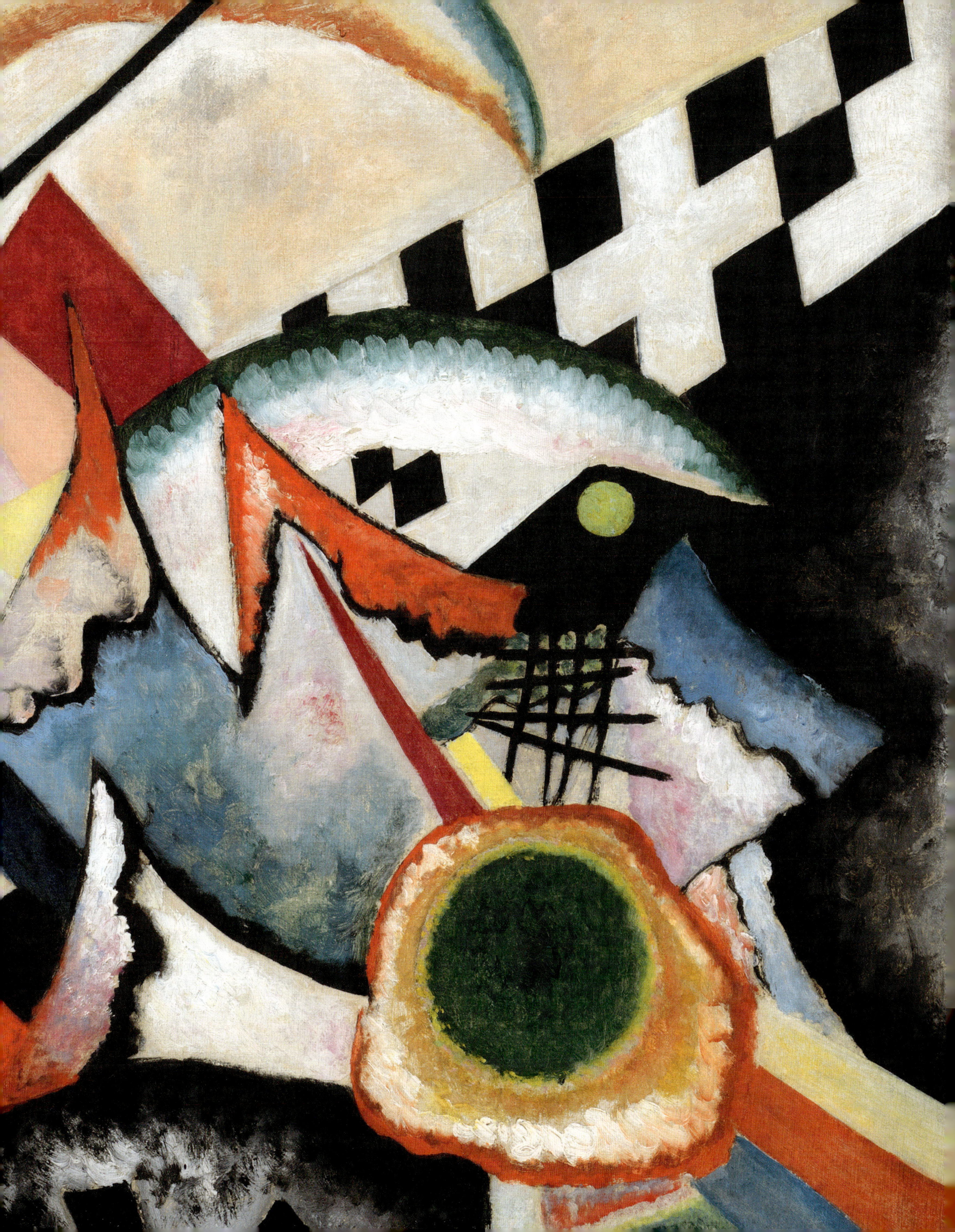

Max Boersma

Spirit and Technology

Geometry in Abstract Art

Wassily Kandinsky played a key role in the development of the artistic avant-garde at the beginning of the twentieth century. He developed a style of Expressionism characterized by bold colors and simplified forms. In his theoretical work *Concerning the Spiritual in Art,* formulated in 1911, he explored geometric shapes as central means of expression.

In 1914, after the outbreak of World War I, Kandinsky returned from Munich to Moscow, where early Constructivist artworks were already emerging. Their abstract visual language employed lines and geometric planes. The Constructivist movement envisioned a future in which art and technology as well as spirit and intellect were united. Geometric abstraction became an expression of a utopian vision of progress.

In 1917 most artists in Russia dedicated their work to the service of the revolution, but Kandinsky's insistence on the spiritual made him an outsider. In 1922 he returned to Germany.

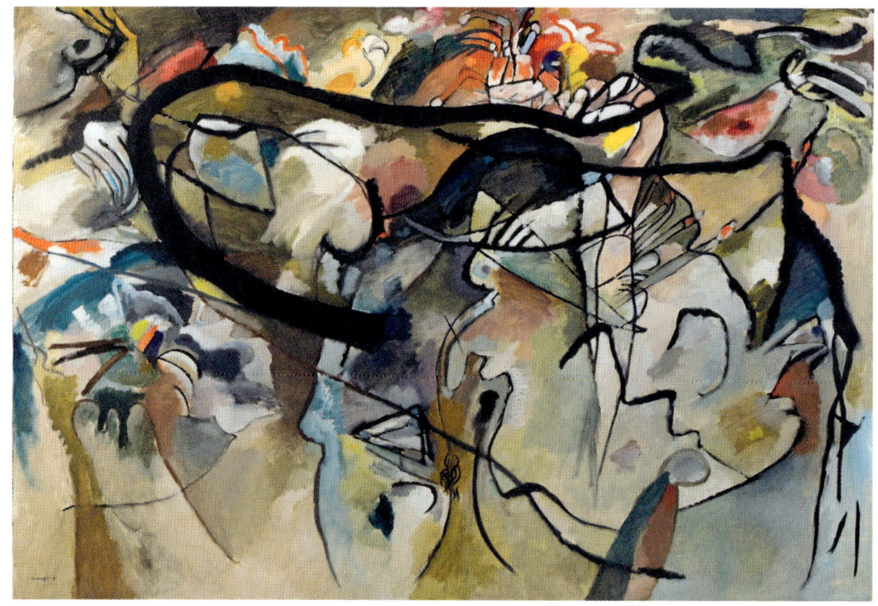

1
Wassily Kandinsky, *Composition V*, 1911, private collection

What is the meaning of a line? A dot? A square? A triangle? In the period of the October Revolution and its immediate aftermath, painters associated with Suprematism and Constructivism had very different—and often fiercely opposed—answers to these seemingly simple questions. Such issues even became matters of intensive, state-funded research and debate within the early Soviet Union. Painter Wassily Kandinsky, born in Moscow and raised in Odesa, initially developed his abstract art in Munich, where he founded the Blue Rider artist association in 1911. His return to Russia with the outbreak of World War I placed him in the center of these heated artistic discussions. In fact, geometric abstraction flourished in Russia not directly thanks to Kandinsky, but more often as an explicit reaction against his work. Eventually, these clashes compelled the artist not only to return to Germany, but also rethink his own painterly approach.

In December 1911 Kandinsky stimulated the widespread emergence of European abstract art with his first public display of nonrepresentational paintings. Included in this inaugural exhibition was the painter's 1911 *Composition V* (fig. 1), boldly demonstrating this new conception of painting and immediately setting off a chain reaction among painters across Europe and the United States. At nearly two by three meters in size, Kandinsky's immense canvas leaves behind any fixed relationship to the natural world. Instead, line and color churn and pulsate—at times gathering in dense clusters of activity, at others spreading and unfurling across the surface. "Every work of art," Kandinsky wrote, "comes into being in the same way as the cosmos—by means of catastrophes, which ultimately create out of the cacophony of the various instruments that symphony we call the music of the spheres."[1] Playing out this tentative drama of creation and negation, *Composition V* was a breakthrough work, a widely received pronouncement that modernist painting was abandoning referential form.

But this radically new paradigm of painterly production immediately presented a problem. What determined whether a particular work was successful—in other words, a "symphony," rather than a "cacophony"? In his influential treatise *Concerning the Spiritual in Art,* published in December 1911 in tandem with his exhibition, Kandinsky introduced his central principle of "inner necessity" to address precisely this concern. With this notion, the artist described how the composition of a painting was guided by a profound emotional response, dictating its forms and colors. Elsewhere, he went as far as to suggest the work itself already existed prior to its material production. "The birth of a work of art is of cosmic character. The originator of the work is thus the spirit," he explained. "Thus, the work exists in *abstracto* prior to that embodiment which makes it accessible to the human senses."[2]

In his writings, Kandinsky often mentioned geometric figures such as triangles, squares, and circles, but the shapes in his paintings were sinuous, unbounded, and fluid. As late as 1919, having resettled in Moscow, Kandinsky explicitly argued that lines and forms must resist fixity and instrumental determination. Accordingly, he rejected the use of drafting tools such as rulers and compasses. His canvases sought to materialize a liberated expressivity, lending maximum freedom to the hand and brush.

Rather than Kandinsky, it was Kazimir Malevich (cat. 4) who initiated the movement of geometric nonobjective painting in Russia. Born in Kyiv to Polish parents, Malevich developed an aesthetic doctrine and movement known as Suprematism. Conceived as a form of "painterly realism," his approach paradoxically gave the medium new life by reducing it to its brute materiality, exemplified by his *Black Square* from 1915 (fig. 3). Art historian T. J. Clark observes that Malevich's works sought the coexistence of the four seemingly incompatible pictorial qualities: "flatness, hardness, separateness, and weightlessness."[3] At the same time, works such as his *Suprematist Composition: Airplane Flying* (fig. 4) subtly court associations with celestial space and new technology, including the vertiginous perspectives of aerial photographs and aircraft in flight. Reflecting space-travel fantasies of his time, Malevich referred to such paintings as "aerial Suprematism," although he later deemed them too illusionistic.[4] Above all, Suprematism committed itself to the destruction of all academic and representational convention in painting, giving total autonomy to color and form; in tandem with this, Malevich's treatment of geometry was deliberately intuitive, distinguishing between an ideal mathematical figure and its painterly materialization.

Initially a disciple of Malevich, El Lissitzky formulated his own agenda for nonobjective painting starting in 1919. Known by the acronym *Proun,* short for "Proekt utverzhdeniya novogo" (Project for the Affirmation of the New), it combined the vacated ground and simple geometric idiom of Suprematism with a generally more constrained palette and varied technical means. The competing volumes and overlapping surfaces of his sparse *Proun 30* (cat. 13) reveal Lissitzky's complex method of spatial construction. Neither remaining flat nor offering a consistent perspectival system, each element of the work possesses its own distinct spatial logic, clashing with those of the others. Prevented from studying fine art in Imperial Russia due to exclusionary quotas on Jewish applicants, Lissitzky instead trained in architectural engineering, first in Germany and later in Russia. With this proficiency in technical drawing, he conceived of his *Prouns* as a generative

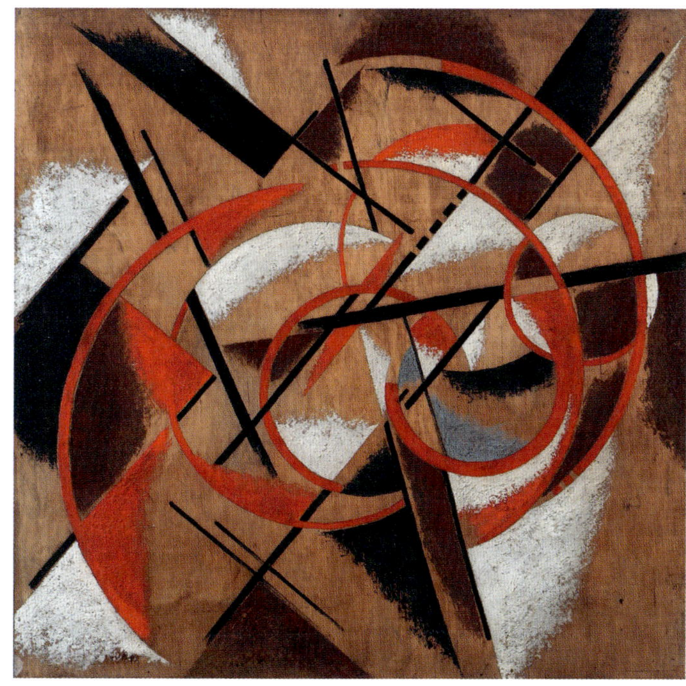

2
Liubov Popova,
Spatial Force Construction, 1920–21
MOMus—Museum of Modern Art—Costakis Collection, Thessaloniki
(Cat. 5)

intersection of painting and architecture—a way to reimagine the built environment. Moving back to Germany in late 1922, Lissitzky was an important bridge between artistic ideas in Russia and Western Europe, helping to stimulate a broader shift toward geometric form across Europe.

An embrace of the "technical" was one of the defining characteristics of the Constructivists. In 1921 this influential group of artists and theorists formed under the auspices of Moscow's Institute of Artistic Culture (or INKhUK), where Kandinsky served as a founding director. Seeking a new role for the artist within socialism, many figures associated with Constructivism transformed their practices from an initial embrace of nonobjective painting into new relationships with photography, graphic design, textiles, and other forms of industrial production. Painted before the group's official formation, Aleksandr Rodchenko's rigorously geometric *Linearism* (cat. 6) came out of a systematic scrutiny of the individual elements of painting—in this case, the functions of line. In contrast to Kandinsky's concept of artistic creation arising from "inner necessity," Rodchenko probed the medium's various formal and technical necessities, aided by geometric instruments in direct defiance of Kandinsky's prohibitions. "I really need to apply myself to the ruler, claim it as my own," Rodchenko once jotted in a notebook.[5] The work demonstrates Rodchenko's adherence to a depersonalized, antisubjective approach to painting, testing new tools, techniques, and materials as if working in a laboratory. Conceived less as a harmonious, stand-alone picture and more as just one experiment in an ongoing scientific process of research, Rodchenko's work studied line as a foundational element in painting, design, and construction in general, investigating its capacities to structure and divide, join and section, animate and fix.

While sharing an interest in the diagrammatic, Liubov Popova's *Spatial Force Construction* (fig. 2) has a material presence that overwhelms the restrained and strictly linear language of technical drawing. Popova formulated that "construction in painting = the sum of the energy of its parts," aptly describing how her work derives its total potency from the brash interplay of straight and curved lines, highly textured passages of contrasting red, black, gray, white, and brown, and large areas of bare wooden support.[6] Like Rodchenko, Popova saw in the rigorous scrutiny of painting's elements a means of repositioning the artist as a technical expert.

Around the time of her *Spatial Force Construction,* Popova was among a group at INKhUK—which also included Rodchenko—that passionately debated the difference between

3
Kazimir Malevich,
Black Square, 1915,
Tretyakov Gallery,
Moscow

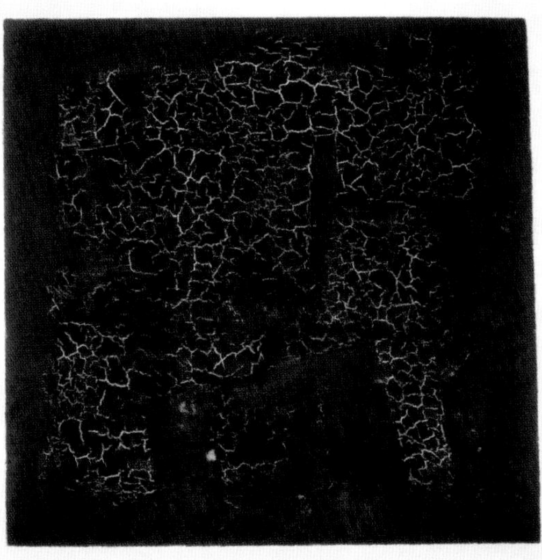

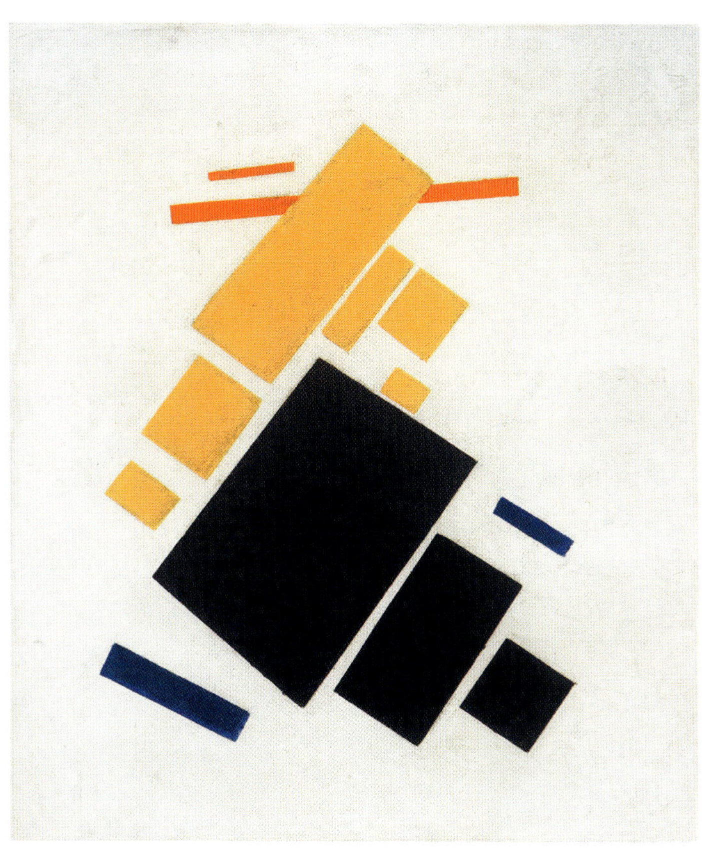

4
Kazimir Malevich,
Suprematist Composition: Airplane Flying, 1915 (dated 1914 on reverse), Museum of Modern Art, New York

notions of "composition" and "construction." As art historian Maria Gough has examined, the participants saw this distinction as urgently necessary to give their production a more rational and objective foundation and overcome the distinctly subjective principles of Kandinsky.[7] The debate would prove inconclusive, and instead, its virulent critique of painting ultimately led to the formation of the Constructivist group, which would call for the abandonment of the medium in favor of other forms of production. While initially resistant to their program, Popova joined their collective declaration in November 1921, and thus *Spatial Force Construction* features among the last of her painted works. Subsequently, her focus turned to the design of strikingly geometric textile patterns, pivoting from the unique art object to collaboration with industry.

In part due to the vocal resistance of the Constructivists, Kandinsky left Moscow and returned to Germany in December 1921. Shortly after his arrival, he was offered a teaching position at the Bauhaus in Weimar, a major turning point in his career. Created in 1923, his painting *In the Black Square* (cat. 21) clearly reacts and responds to the developments of the previous decade. Its numerous straight lines, circles, and semicircles were executed with tools once anathema to the artist, and the black enclosure, white ground, and title itself are obvious references—if not provocations—to Malevich. In his new institutional home, Kandinsky did not abandon his earlier expressive and spiritual commitments, but he did demonstrate their capacity to absorb other influences and adapt to differing contexts. Framed as a continuation of *Concerning the Spiritual in Art,* the artist's book *Point and Line to Plane: Contribution to the Analysis of the Pictorial Elements* of 1926 encapsulated the theoretical and pedagogical basis of this new period, serving as a foundational text in the development of geometric abstraction.

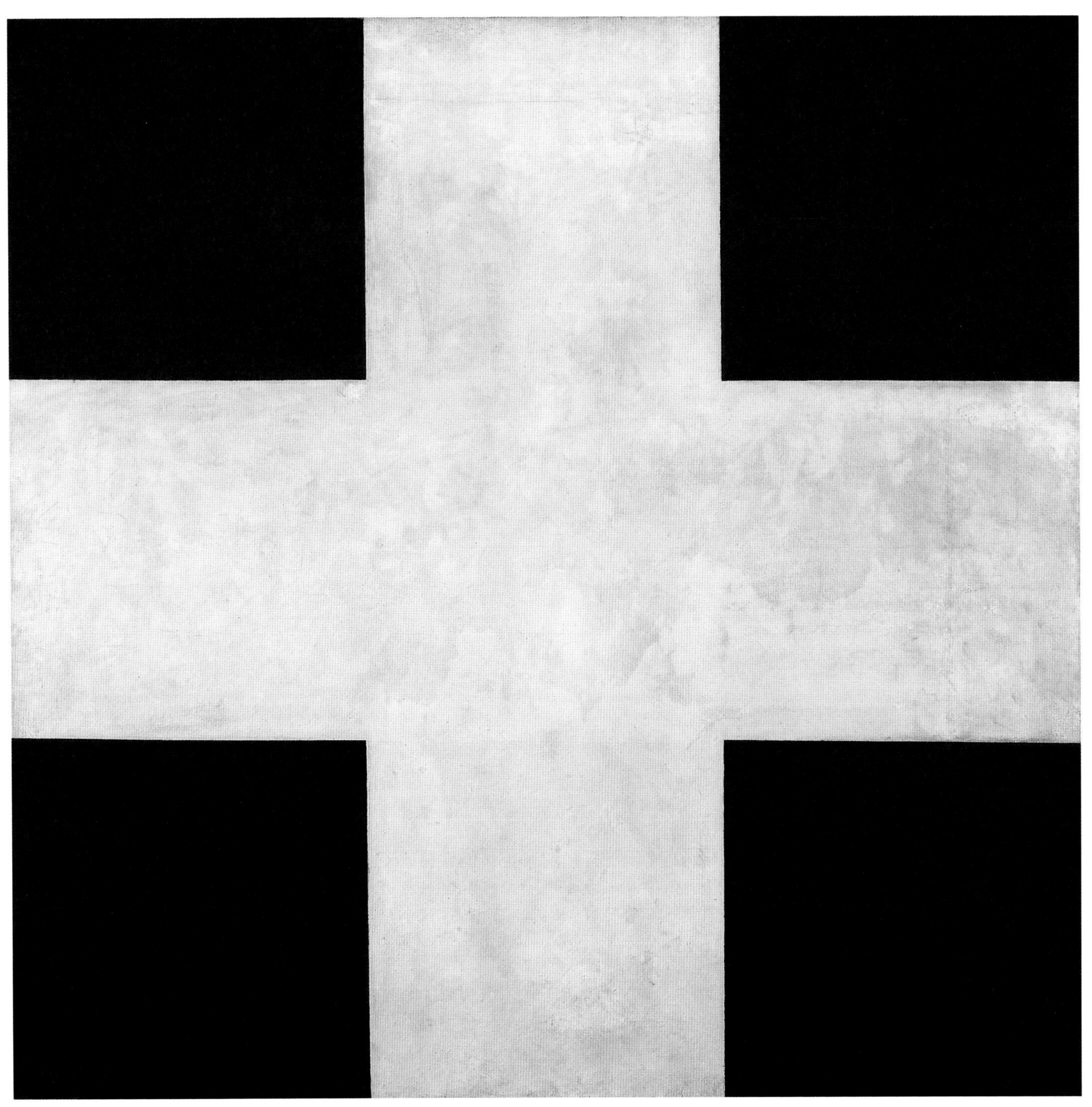

2 Ilya Chashnik
Suprematist Cross, 1923
MOMus—Museum of Modern Art—Costakis Collection, Thessaloniki

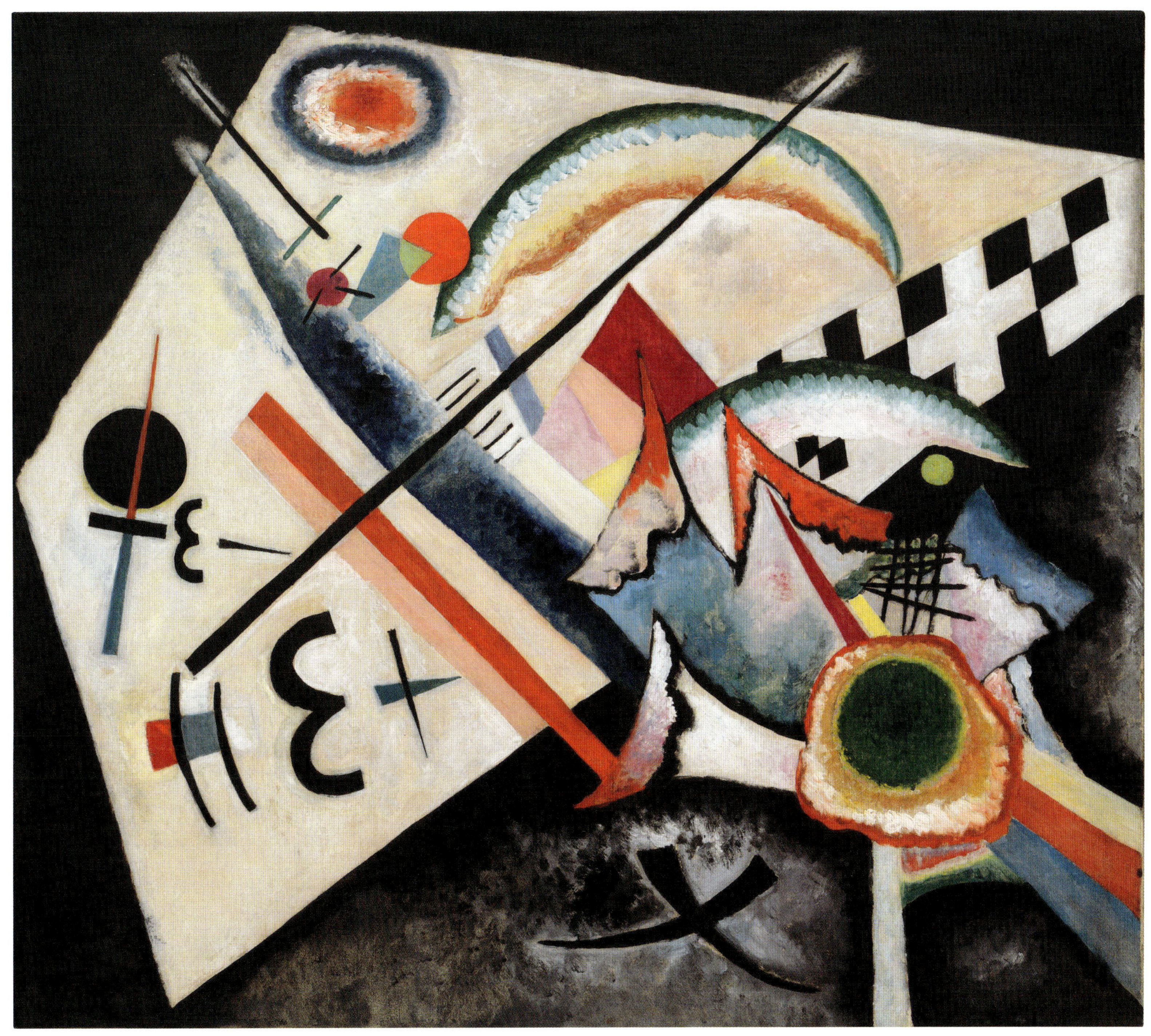

3 Wassily Kandinsky
White Cross, 1922
Peggy Guggenheim Collection, Venice

4 Kazimir Malevich
Architectons and Figurines, late 1920s
ALBERTINA, Vienna—Private collection

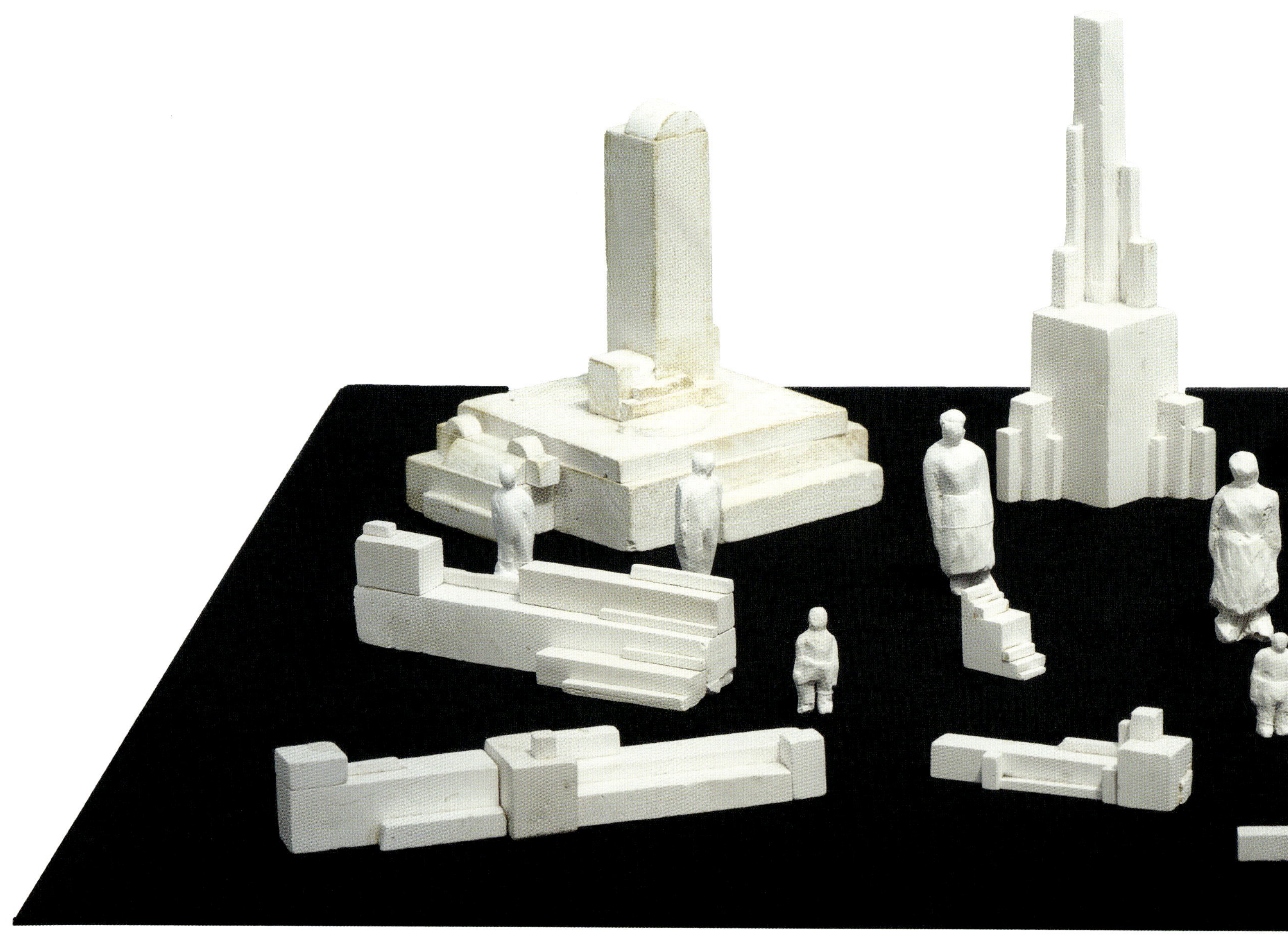

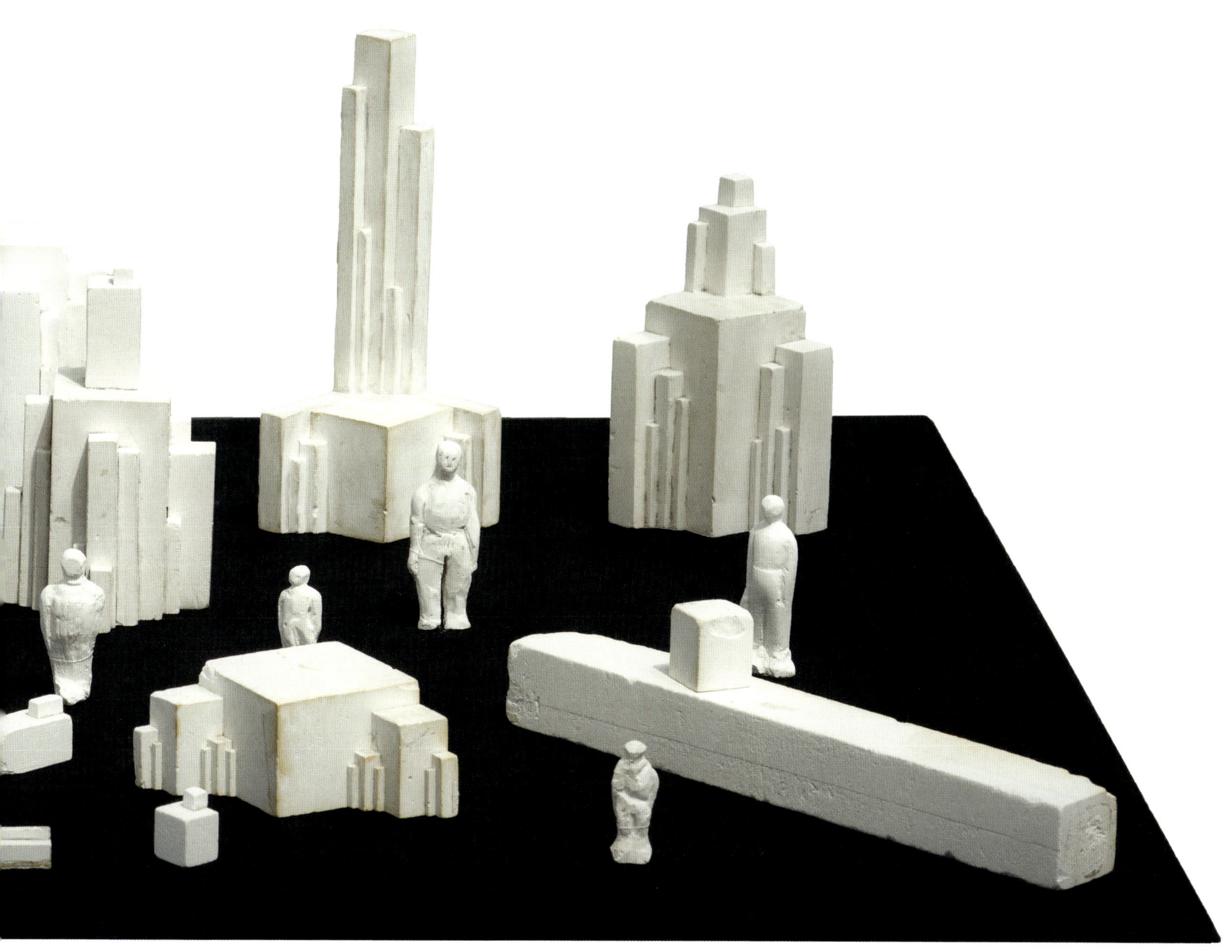

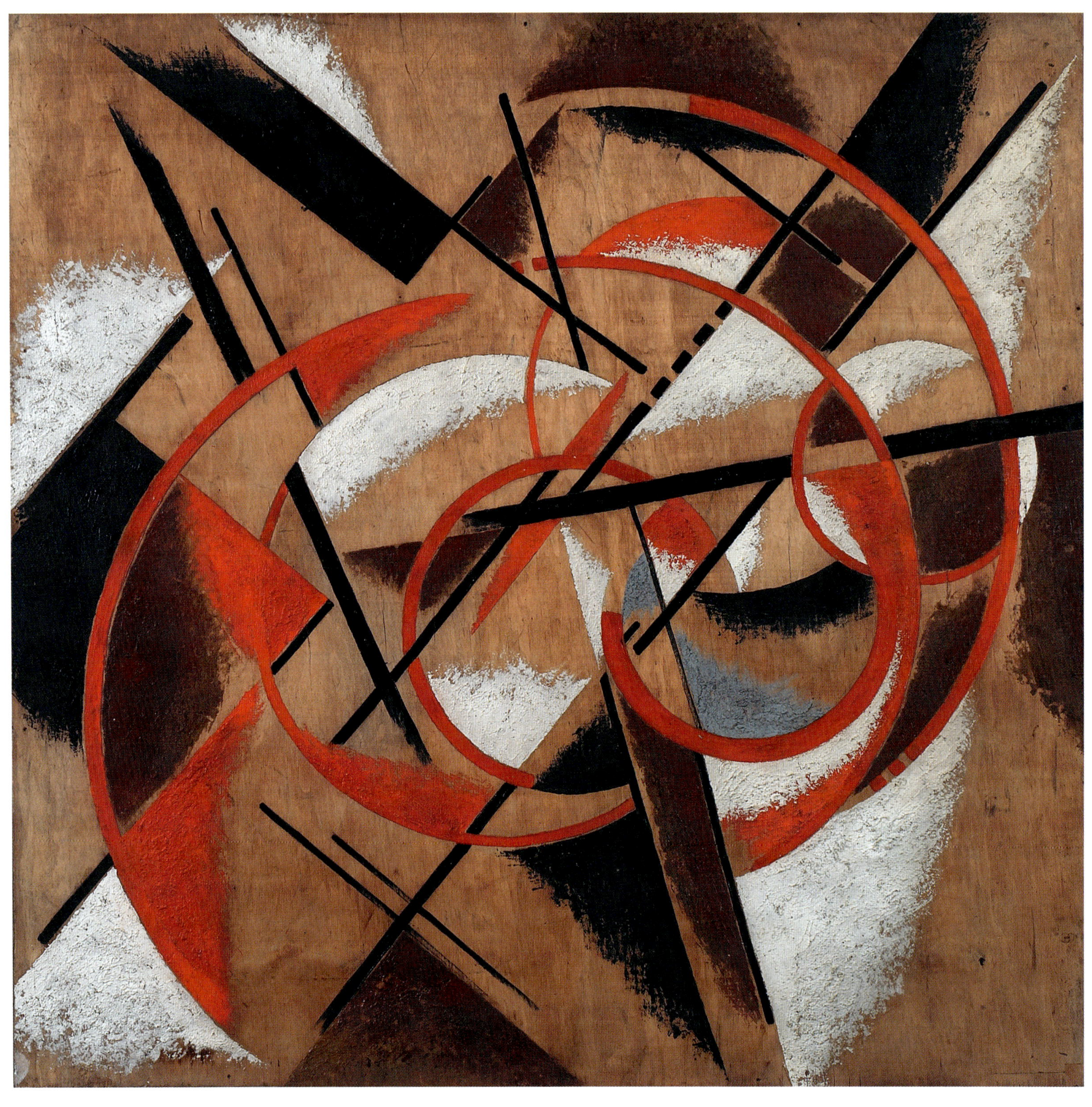

5 Liubov Popova
Spatial Force Construction, 1920–21
MOMus—Museum of Modern Art—Costakis Collection, Thessaloniki

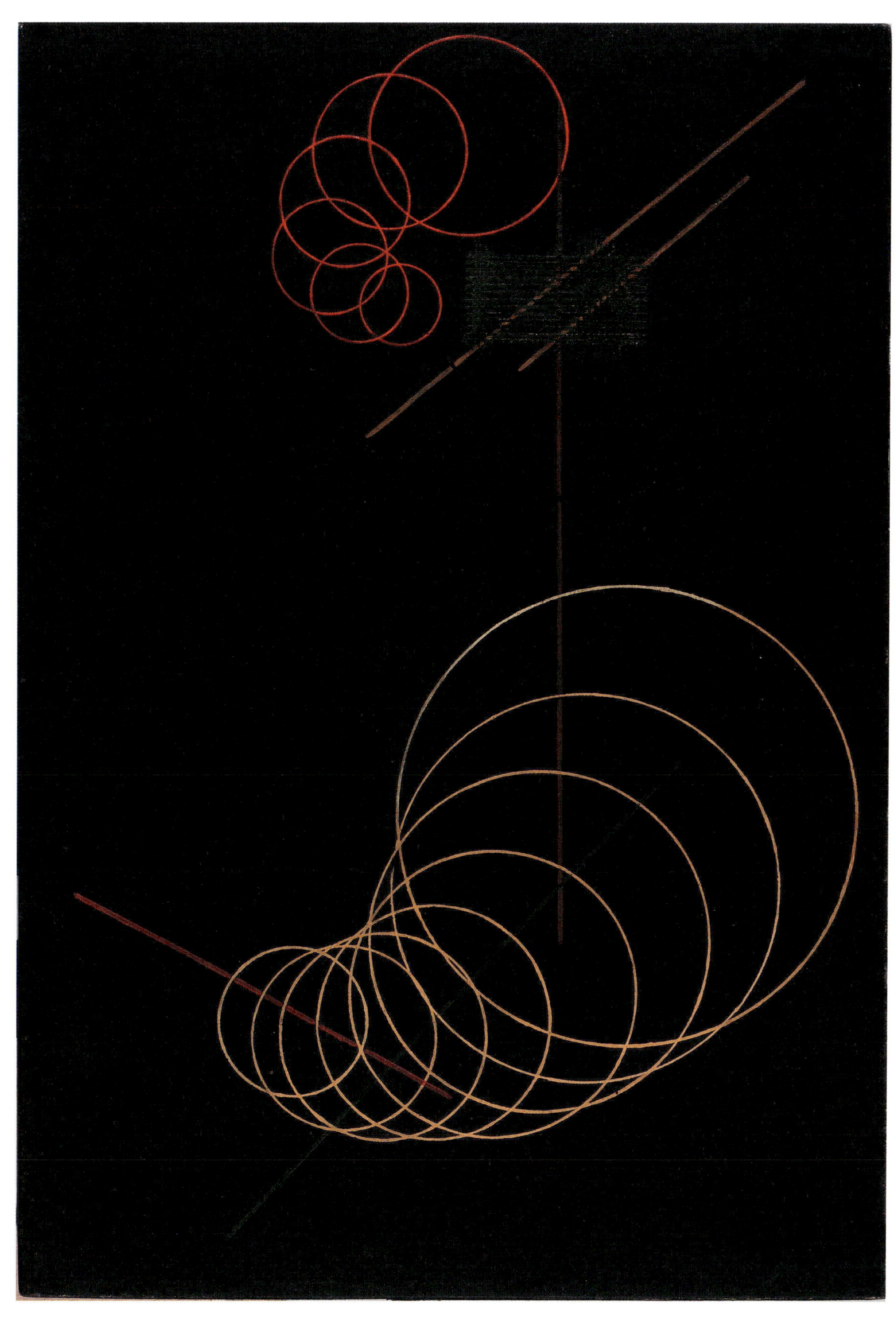

6 Aleksandr Rodchenko
Linearism, 1920
MOMus—Museum of Modern Art—Costakis Collection, Thessaloniki

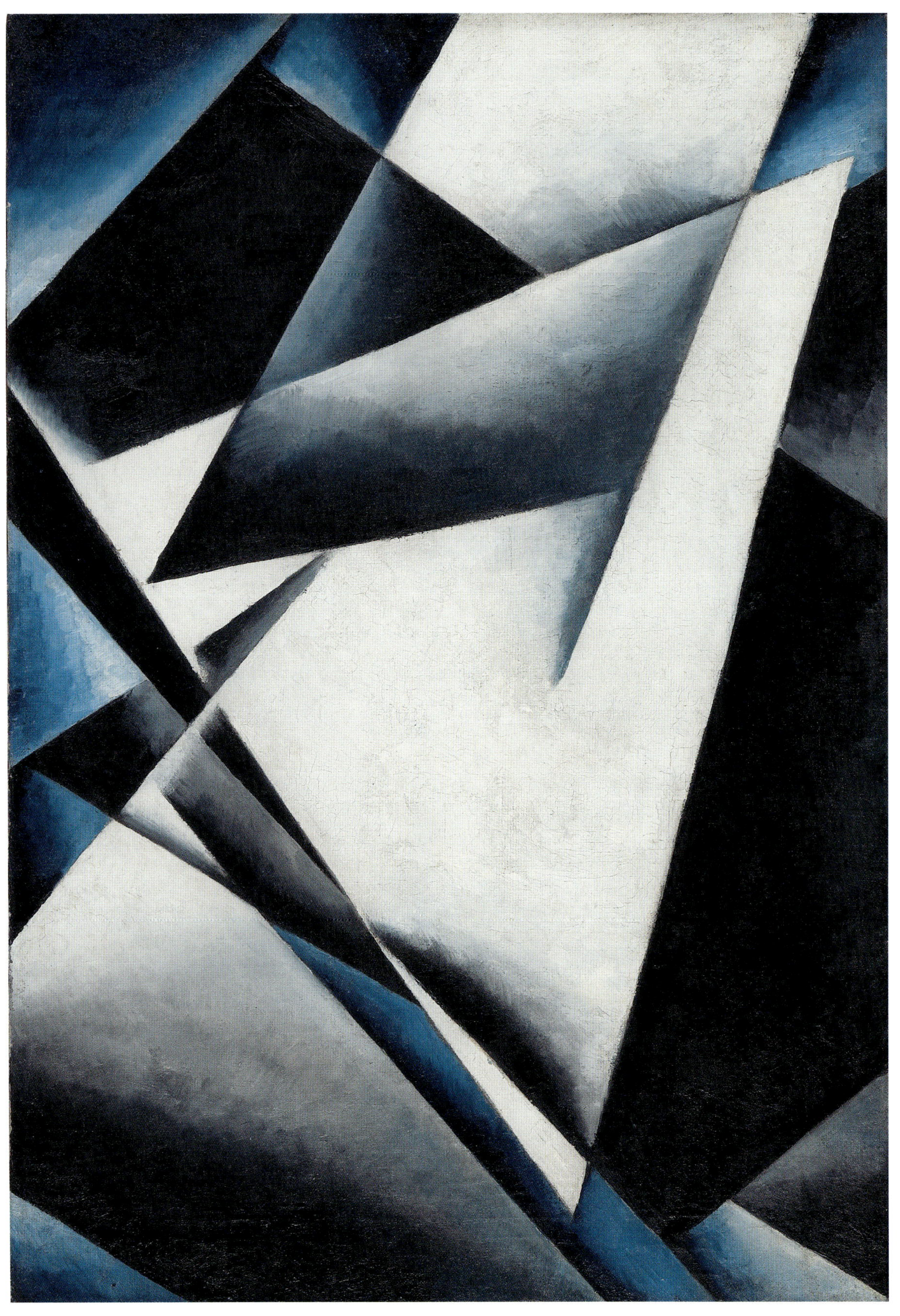

7 Liubov Popova
Painterly Architectonics, 1918–19
MOMus—Museum of Modern Art—Costakis Collection, Thessaloniki

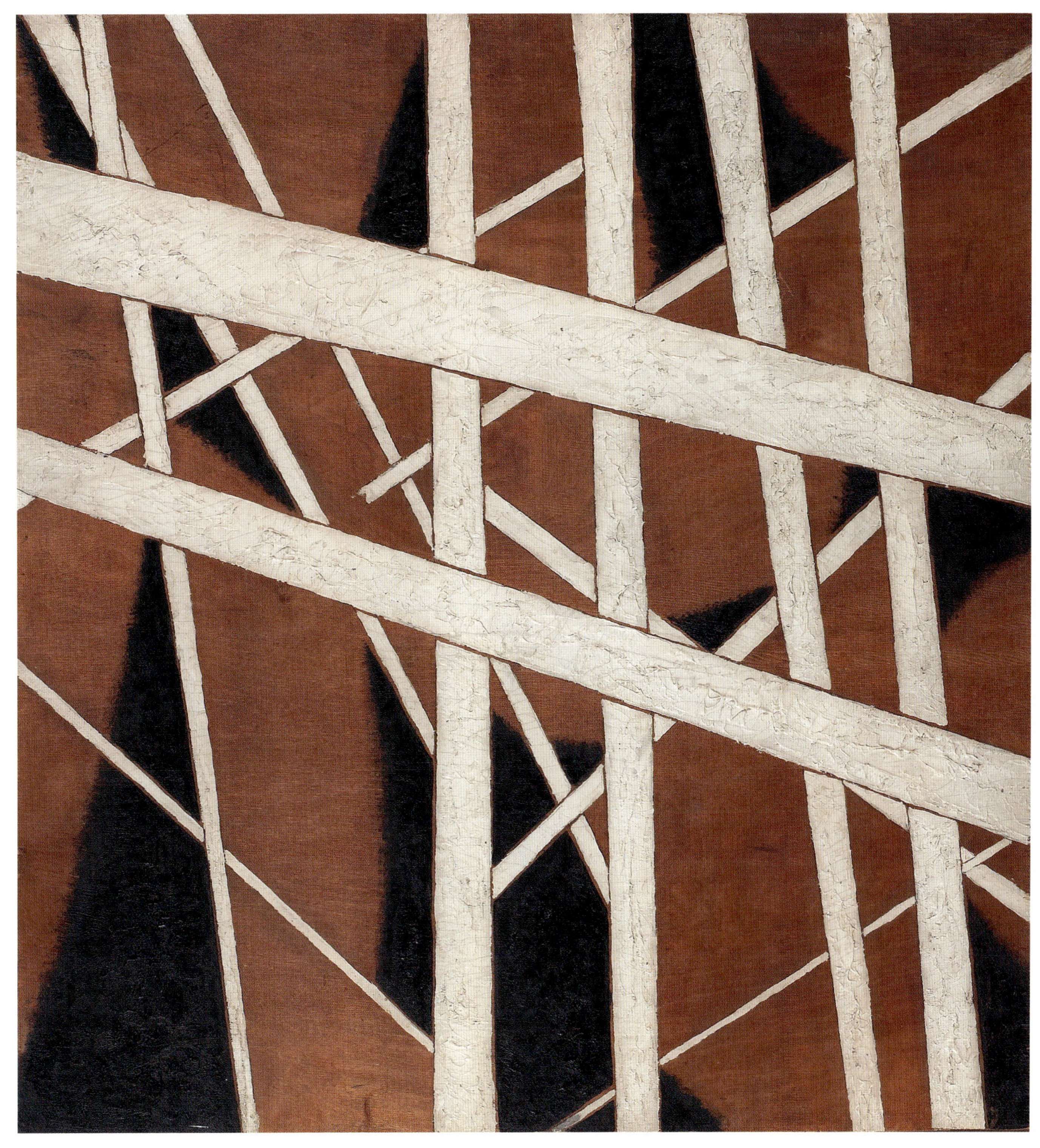

8 Liubov Popova
Spatial Force Construction, 1921
MOMus—Museum of Modern Art—Costakis Collection, Thessaloniki

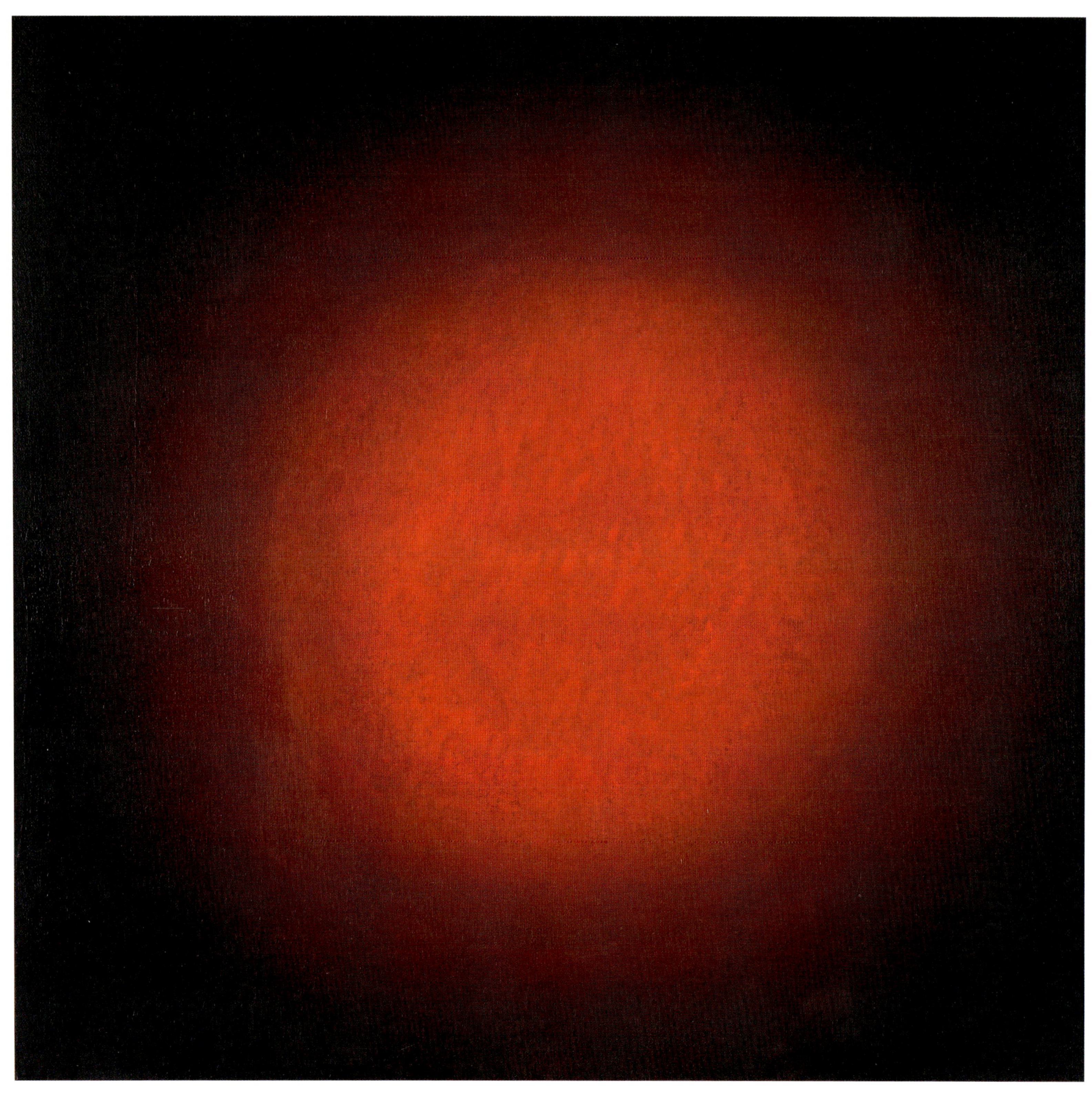

9 Ivan Kliun
Red Light: Spherical Composition, 1923
MOMus—Museum of Modern Art—Costakis Collection, Thessaloniki

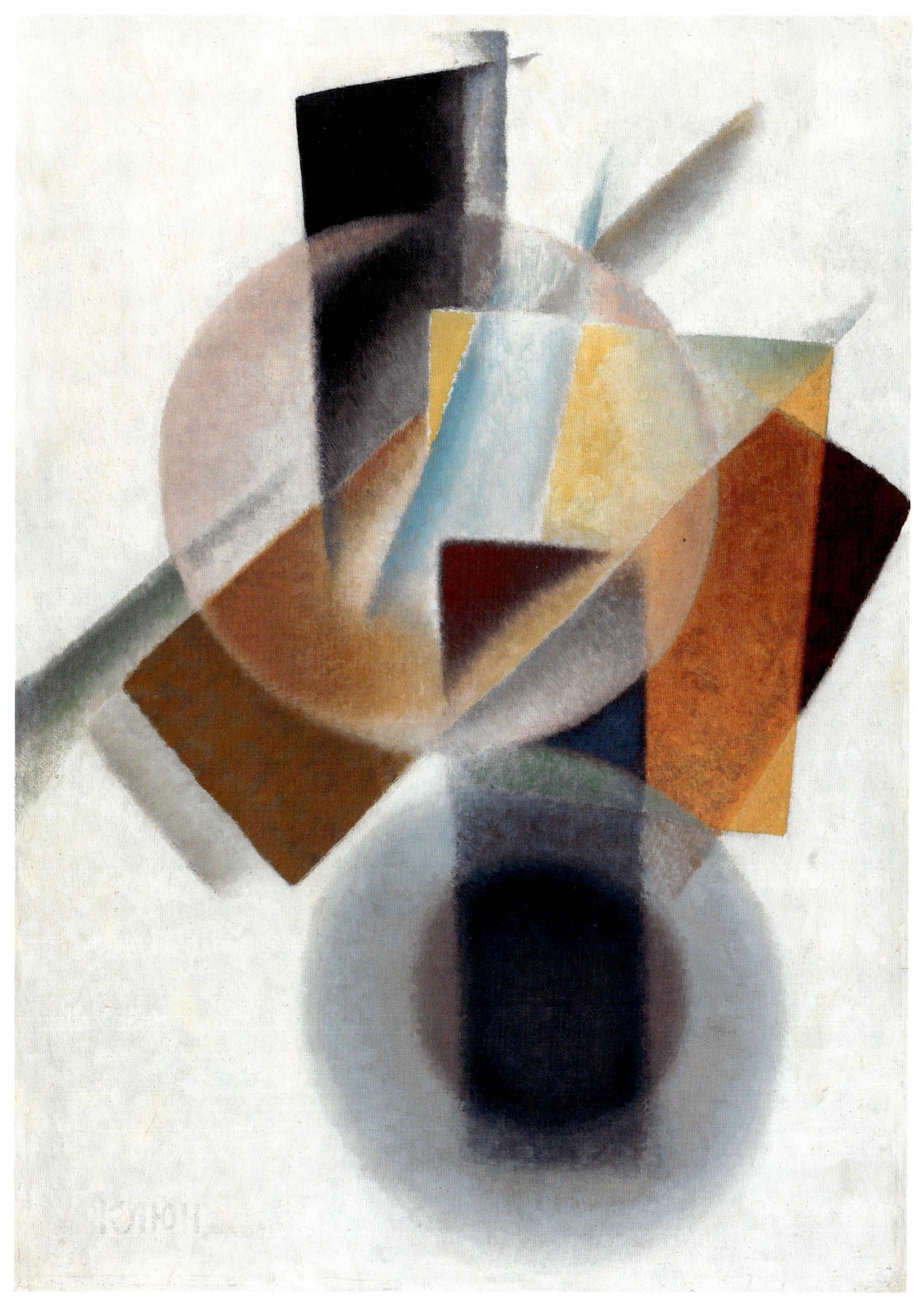

10 Ivan Kliun
Non-Objective Spherical Composition, 1920–25
MOMus—Museum of Modern Art—Costakis Collection, Thessaloniki

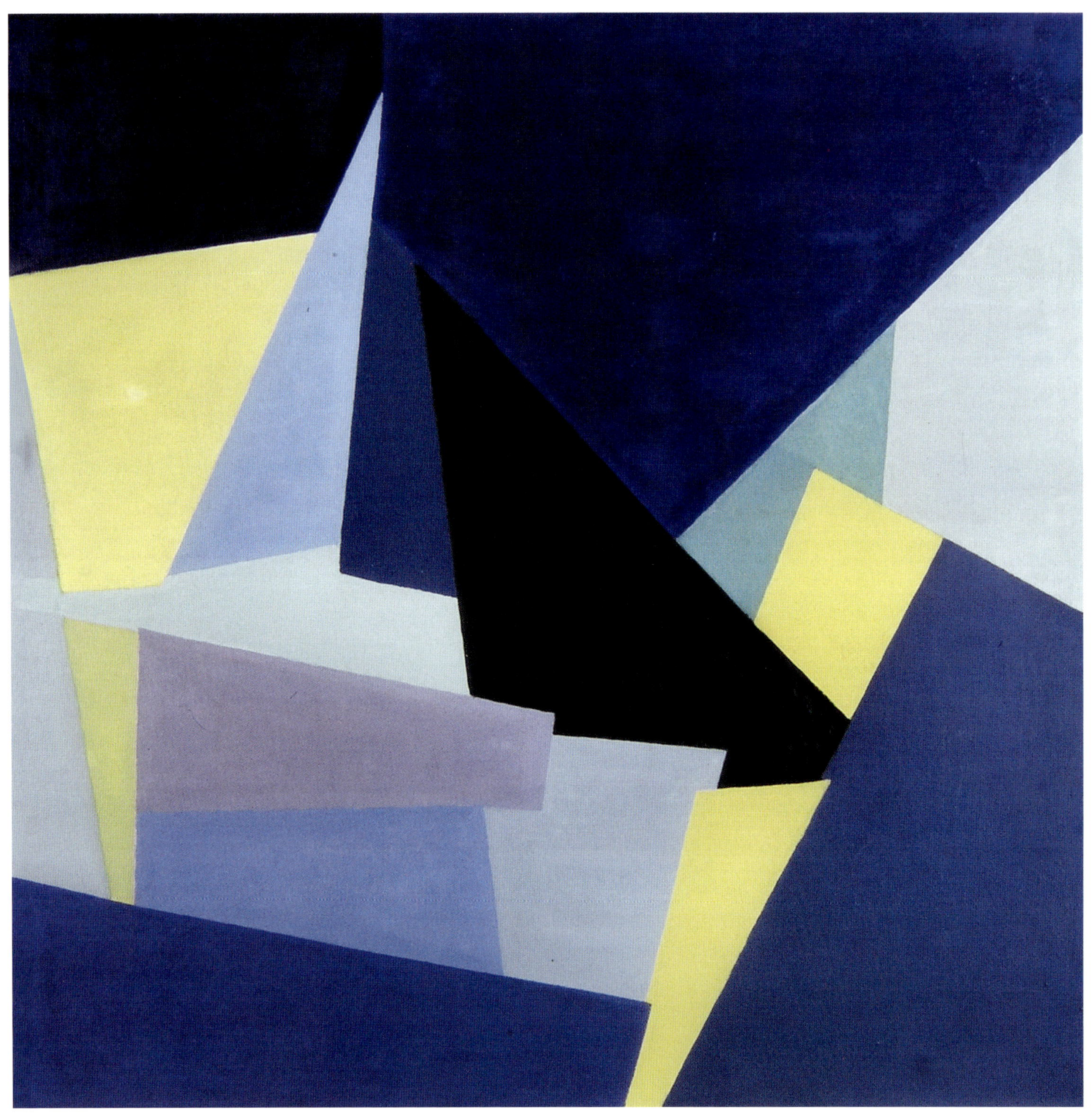

11 Boris Ender
Abstract Composition, 1919–20
MOMus—Museum of Modern Art—Costakis Collection, Thessaloniki

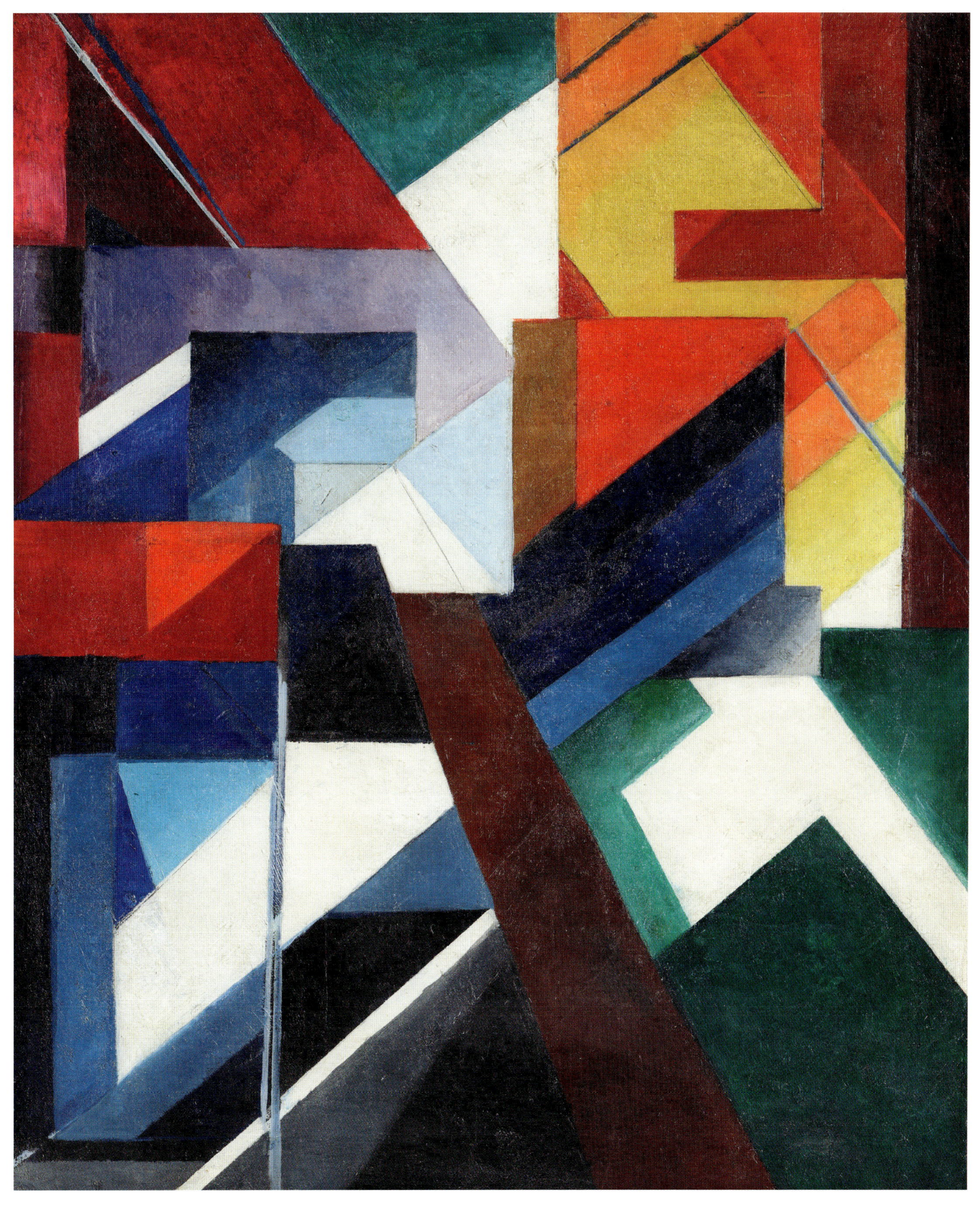

12 Aleksandra Ekster
Construction of Colors, 1921
ALBERTINA, Vienna—Private collection

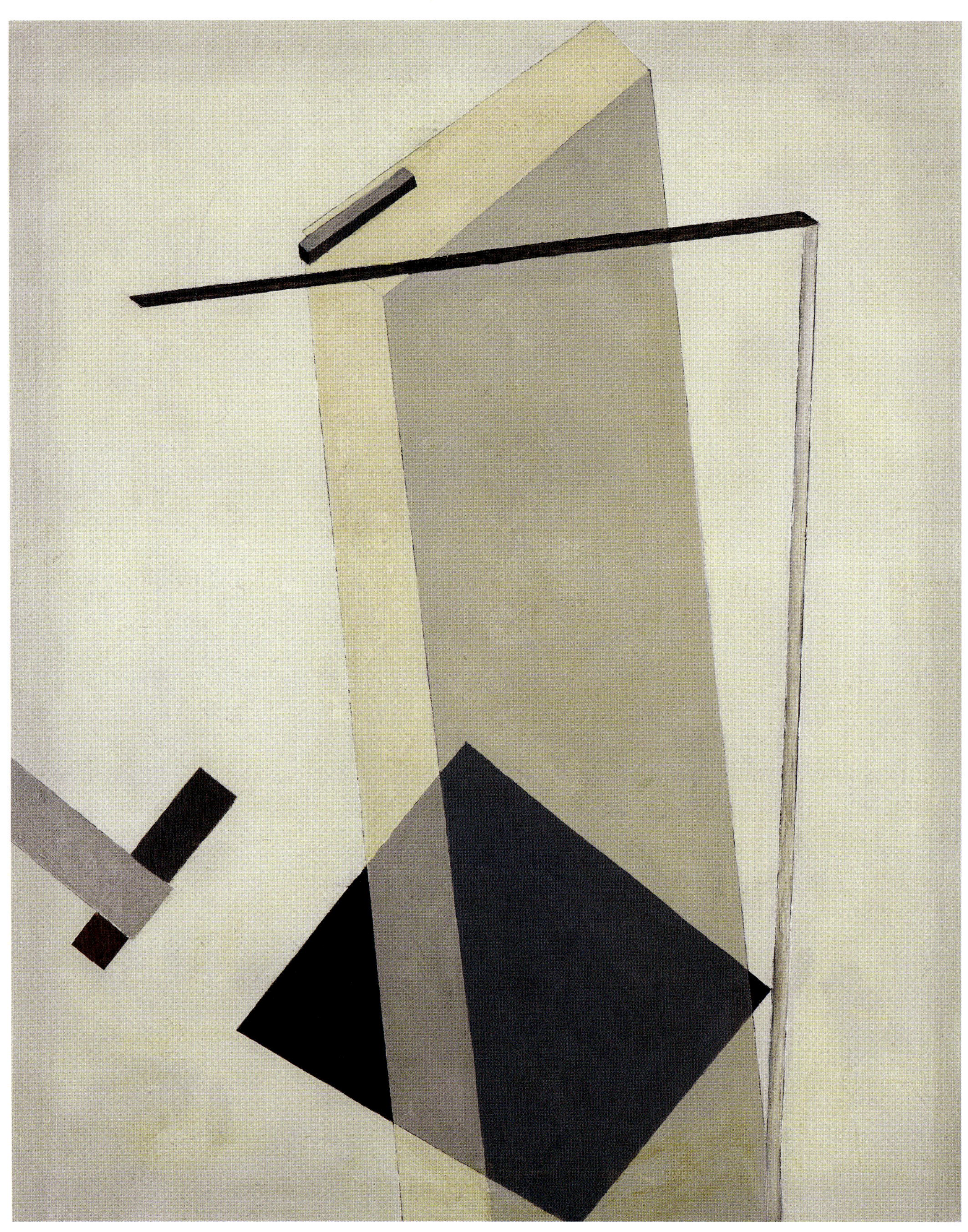

13 El Lissitzky
Proun 30, 1919–20
Kulturstiftung Sachsen-Anhalt,
Kunstmuseum Moritzburg Halle (Saale)

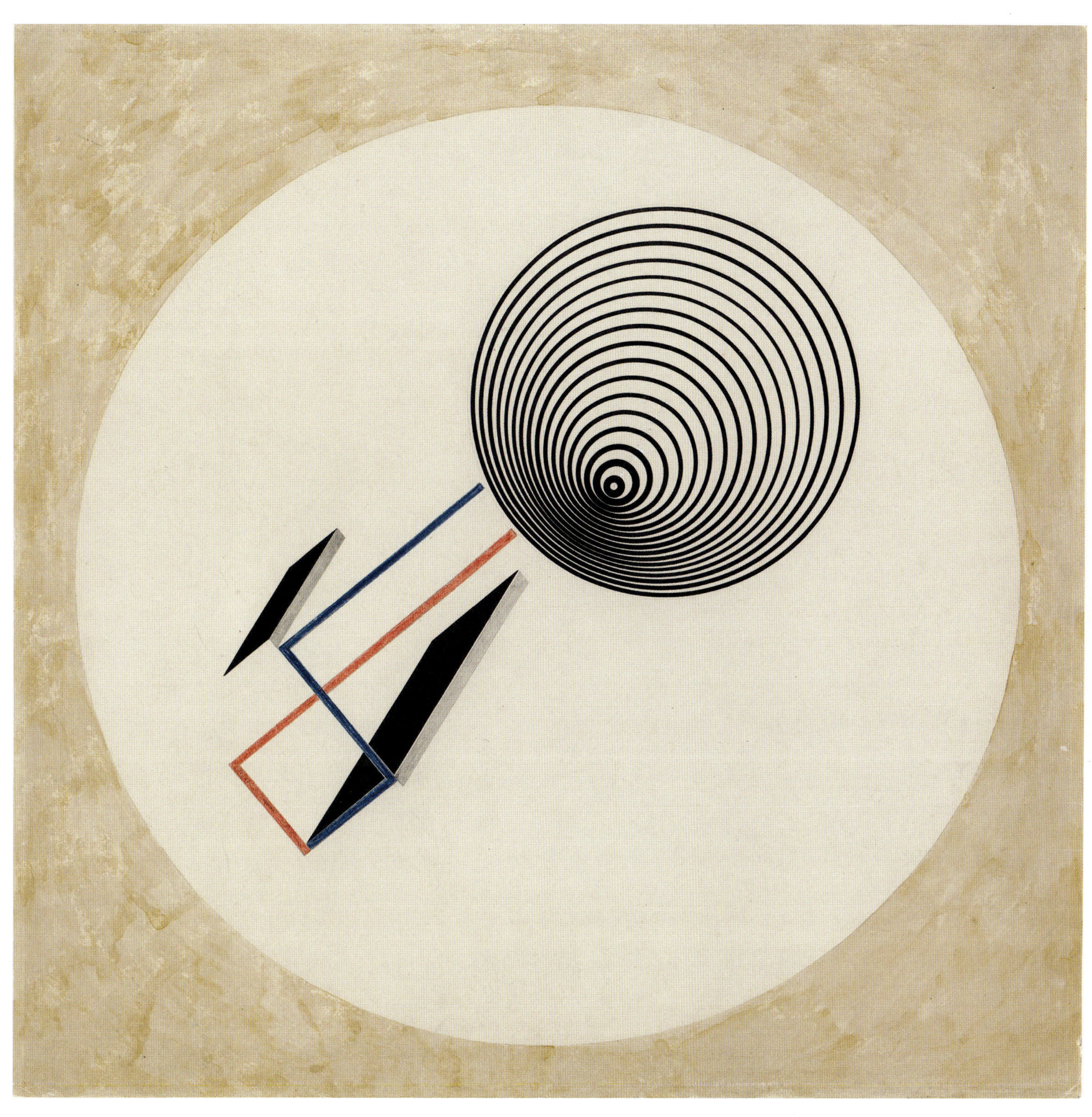

14 El Lissitzky
Proun 93 (Conic), ca. 1923
Kulturstiftung Sachsen-Anhalt,
Kunstmuseum Moritzburg Halle (Saale)

15 Antoine Pevsner
Construction in the Third and Fourth Dimension, 1961
Lehmbruck Museum, Duisburg

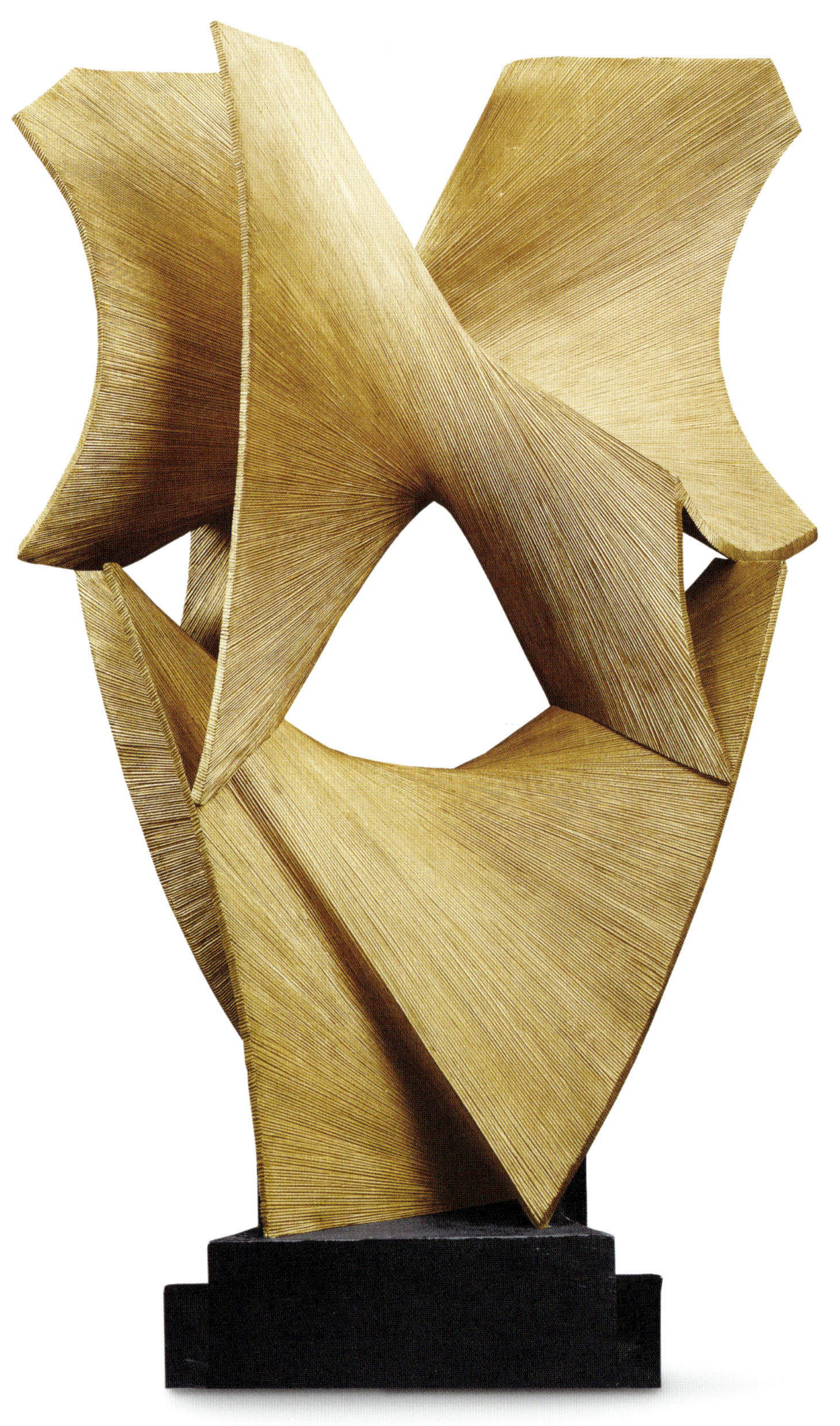

16 Antoine Pevsner
Column of Peace, 1954
Kröller-Müller Museum, Otterlo

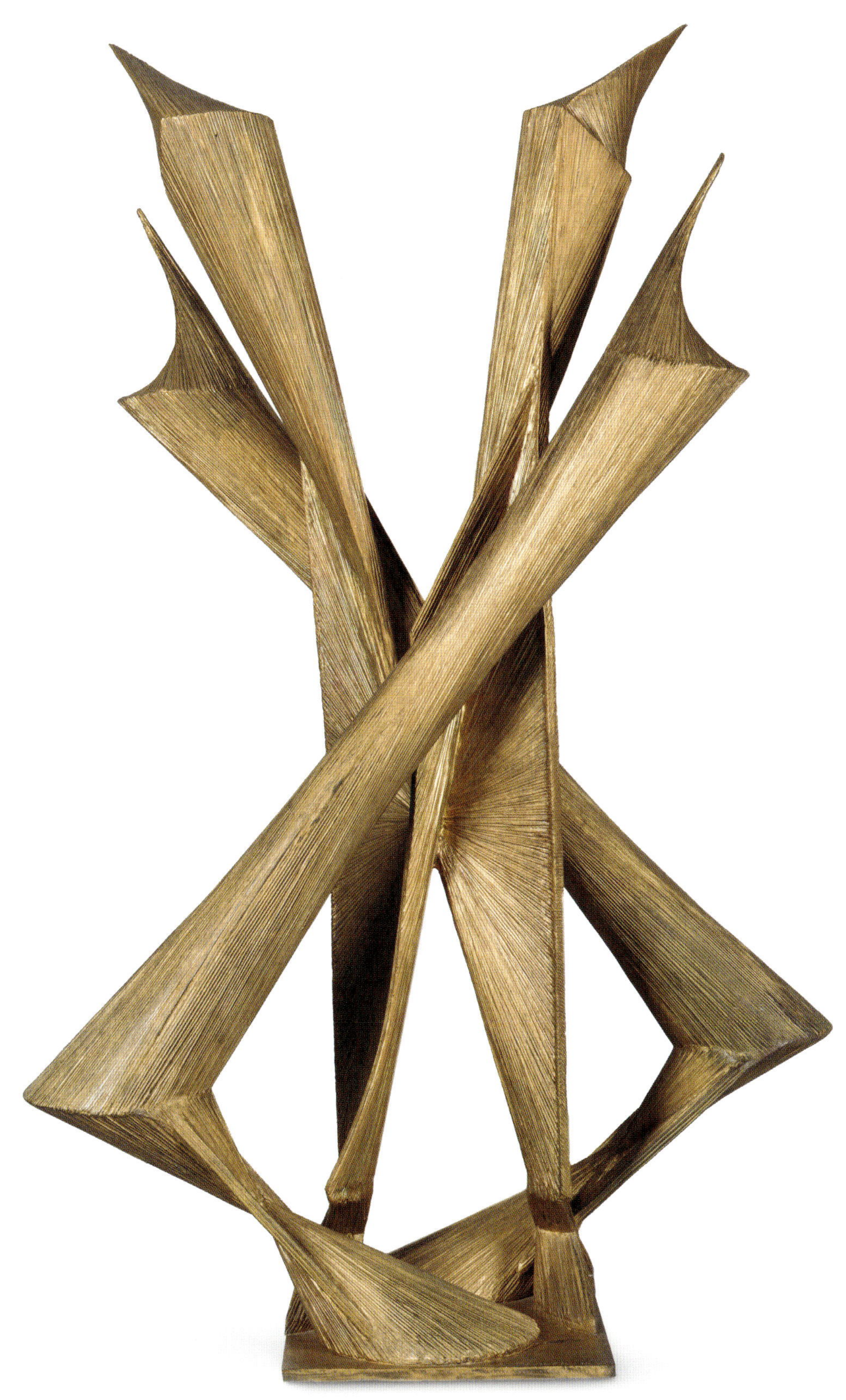

17 Katarzyna Kobro
Spatial Composition (6), 1931
Muzeum Sztuki, Łódź

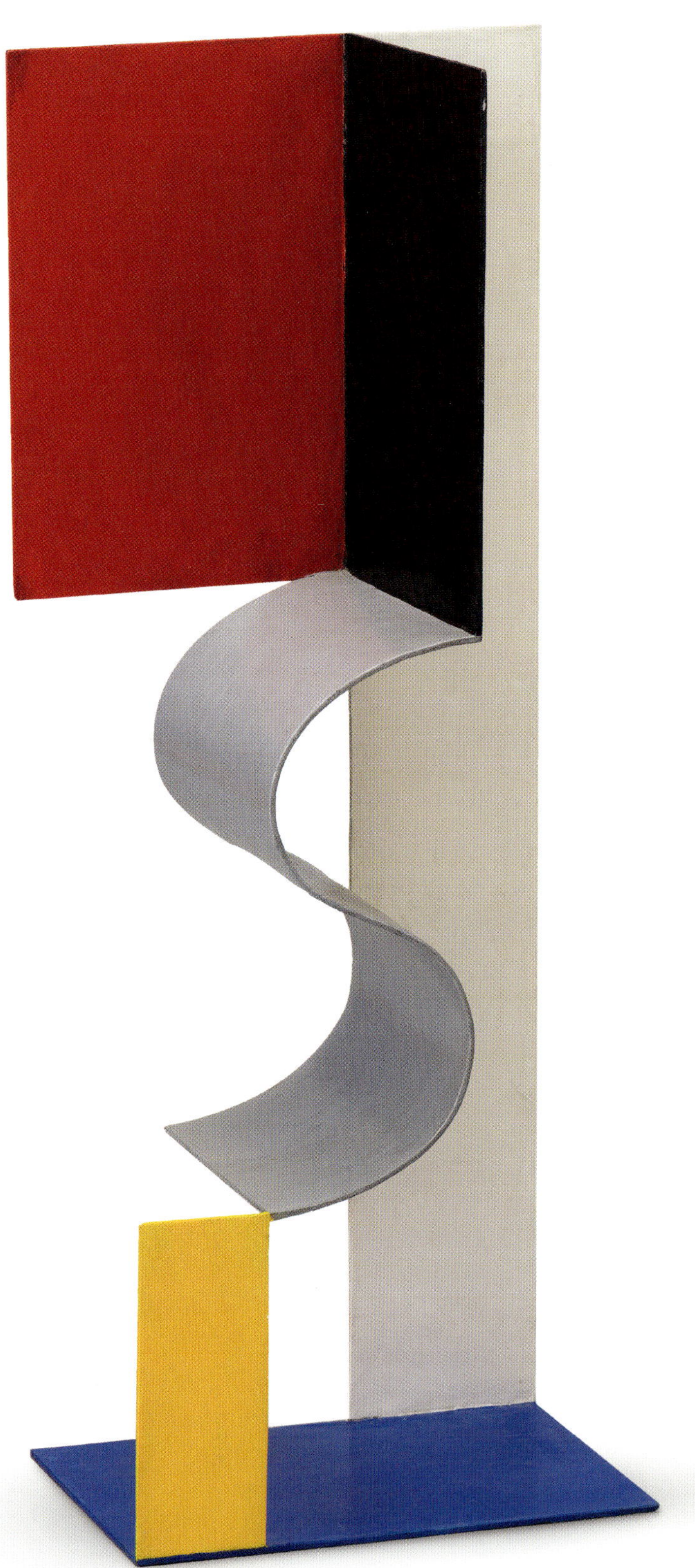

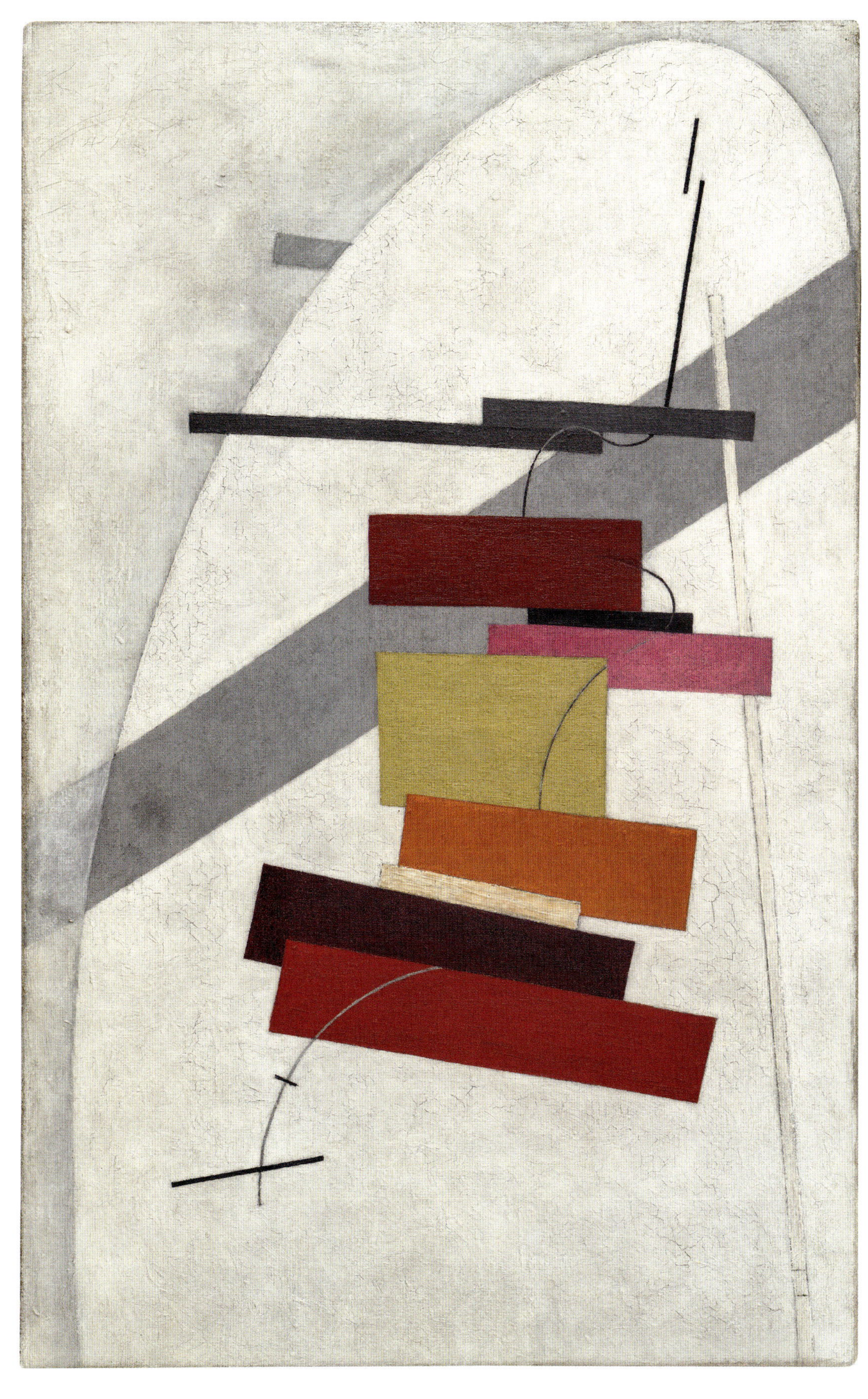

18 El Lissitzky
Untitled, 1919–20
Peggy Guggenheim Collection, Venice

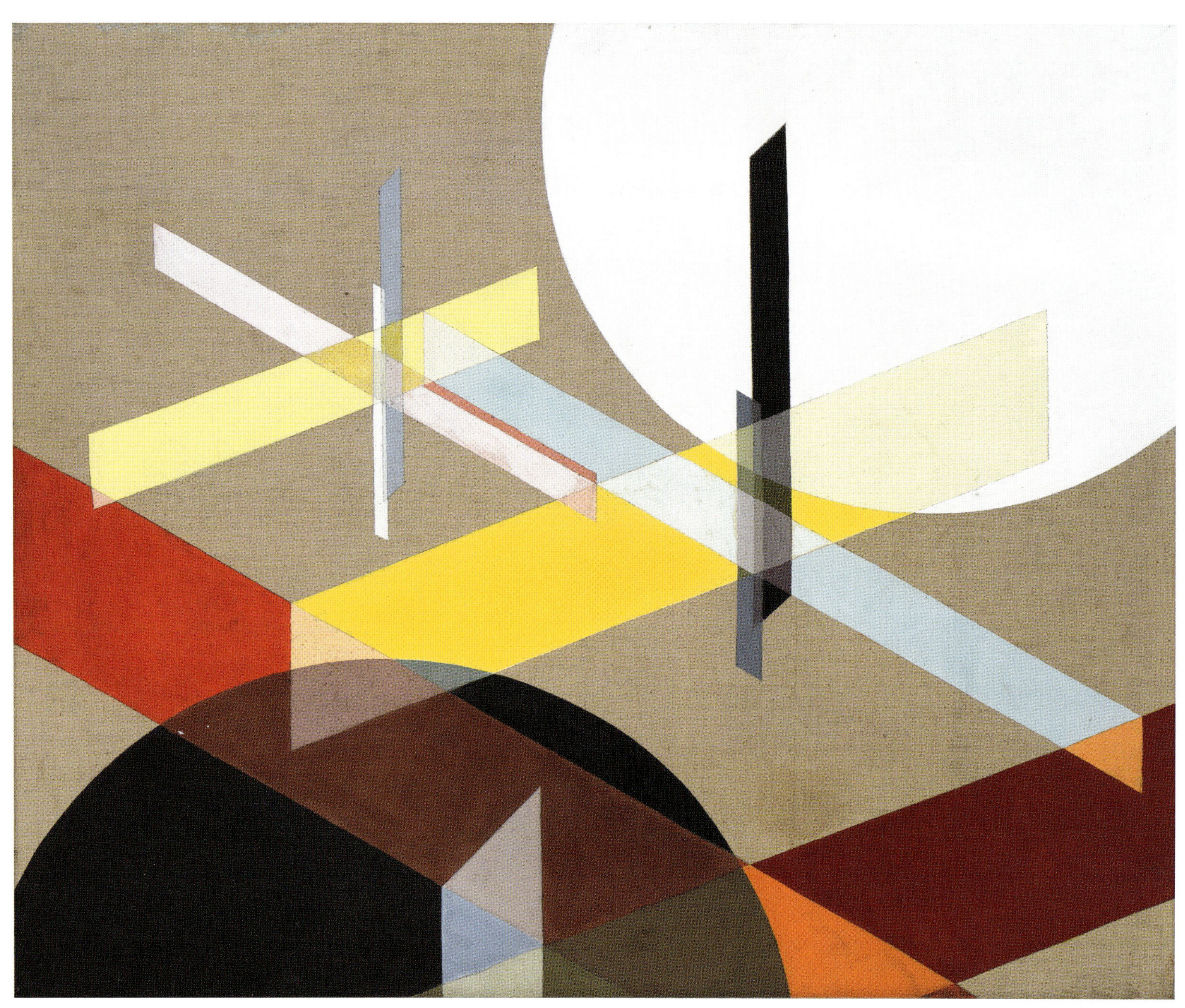

19 László Moholy-Nagy
Composition Z VIII, 1924
Staatliche Museen zu Berlin, Neue Nationalgalerie

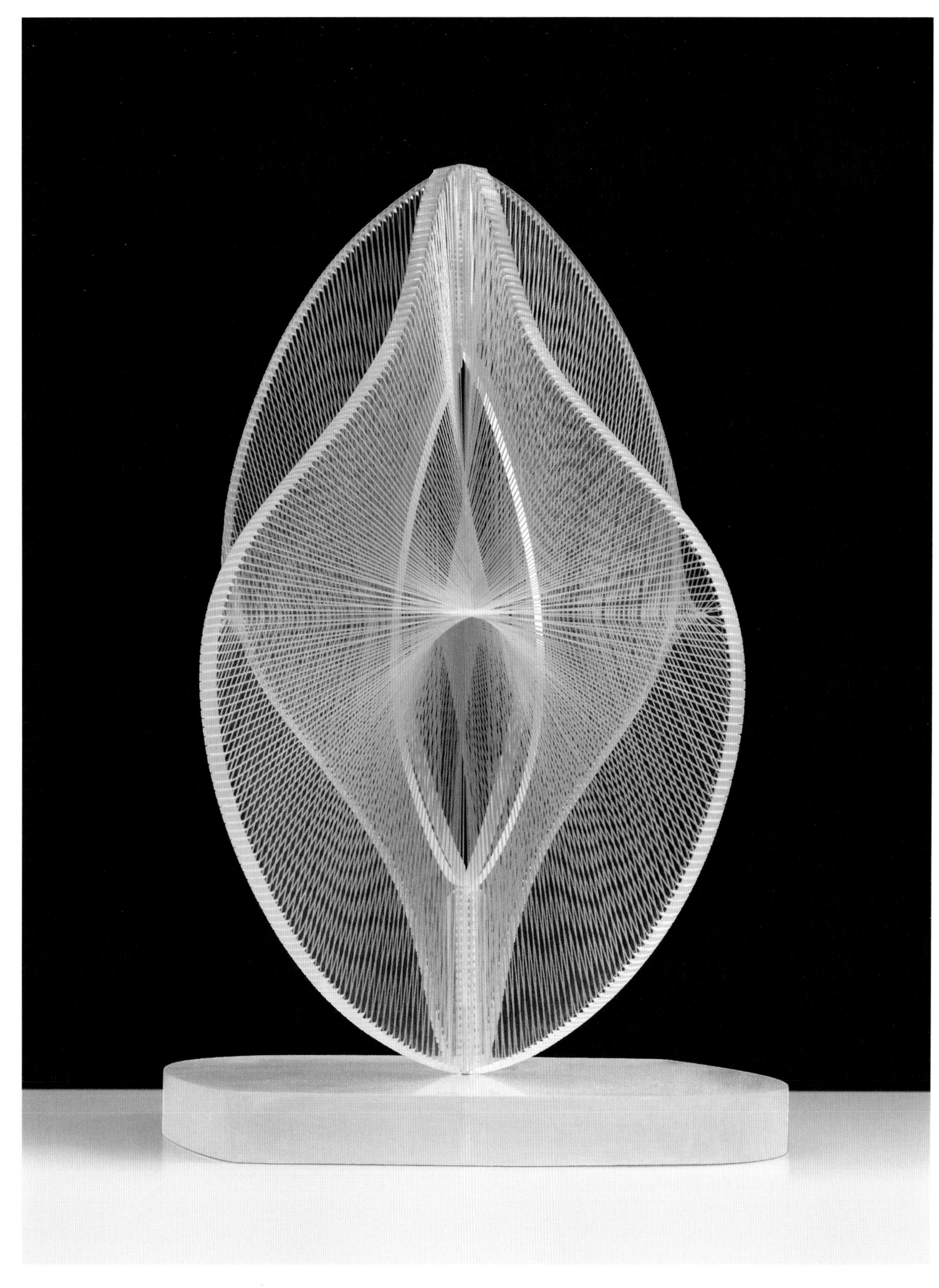

20 Naum Gabo
Linear Construction in Space no. 2, 1969
Triton Collection Foundation

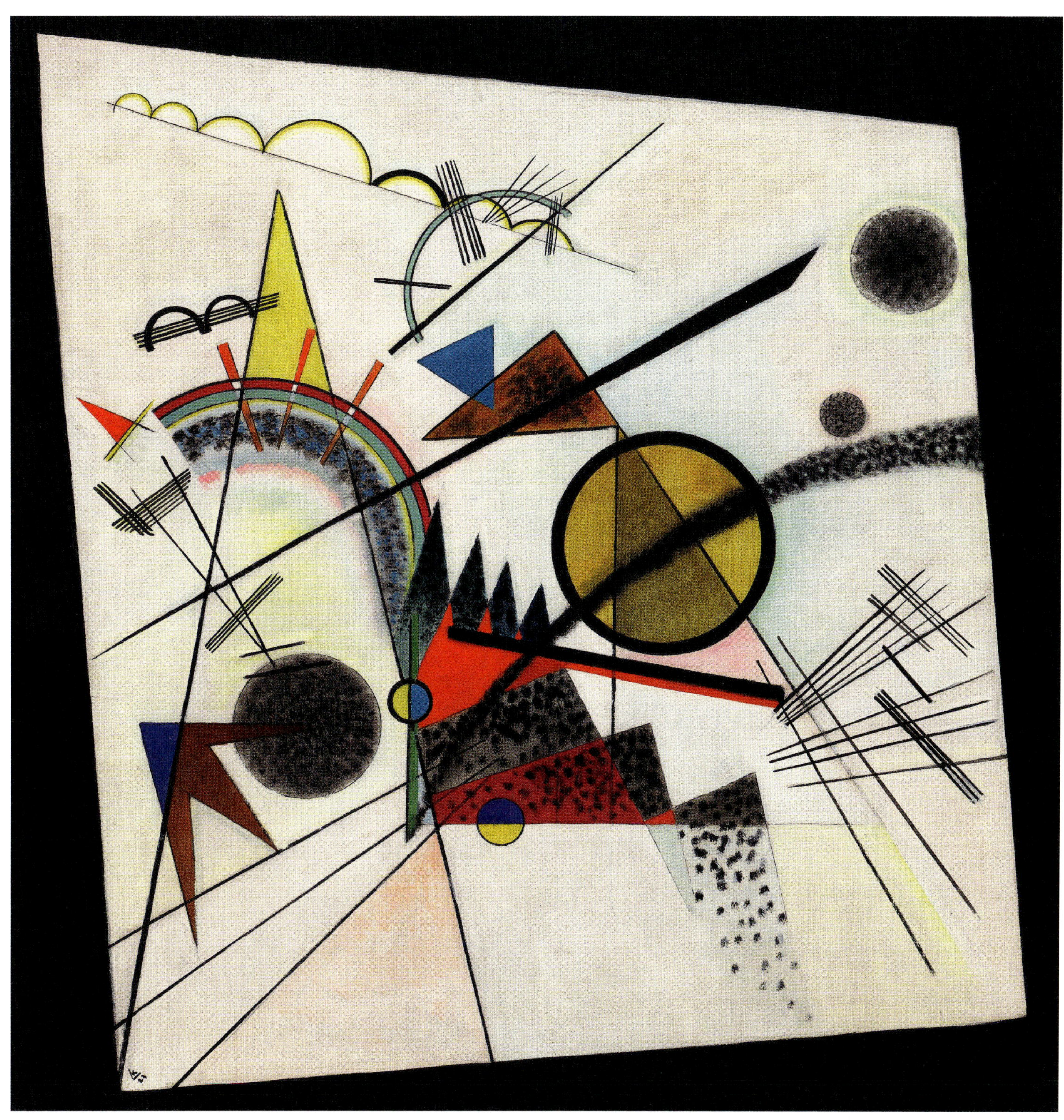

21 Wassily Kandinsky
In the Black Square, 1923
Solomon R. Guggenheim Museum, New York

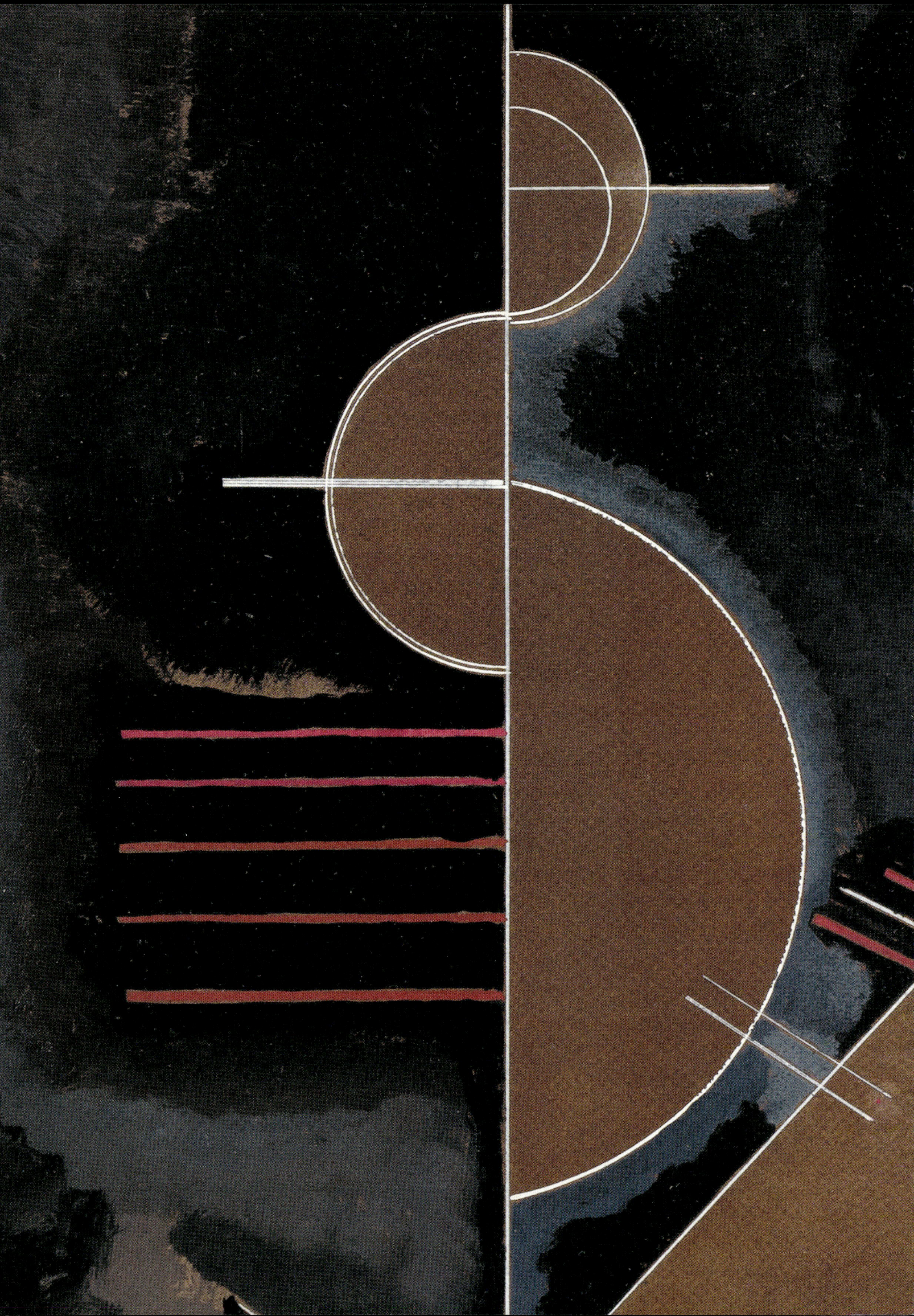

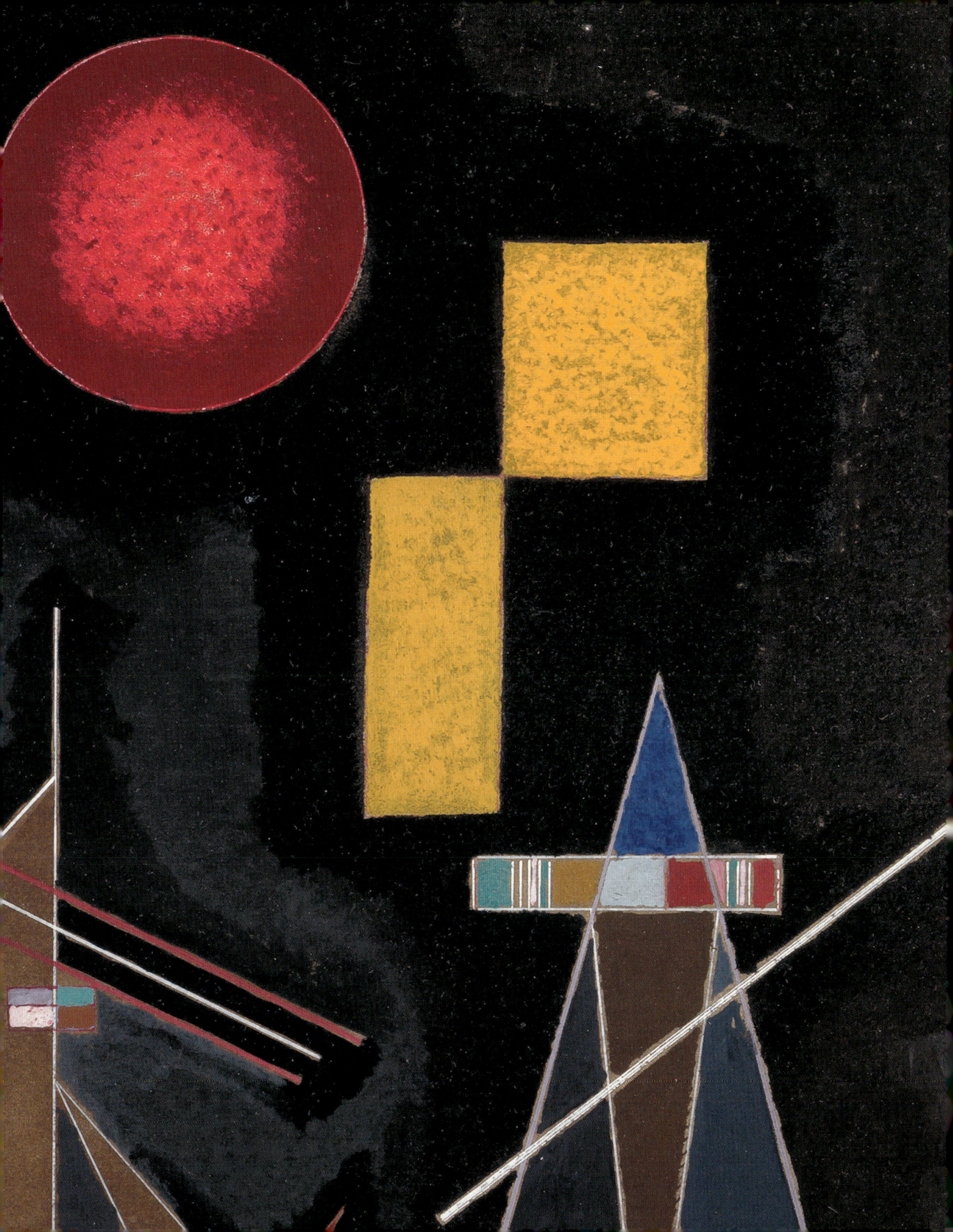

Max Boersma

Universal Language of Abstraction

Bauhaus and Concrete Artists

At the Bauhaus, founded in Weimar in 1919, Wassily Kandinsky saw an opportunity to further develop and convey his theories within a circle of other avant-garde artists. He began to align his paintings with a geometric visual language. In his book *Point and Line to Plane* of 1926, he explored what he considered to be the fundamental building blocks of art and their emotional impact.

The focus on color and form shaped the teaching of Kandinsky and other instructors at the Bauhaus such as Josef Albers, László Moholy-Nagy, and Johannes Itten. They laid the foundation for the development of Concrete Art during World War II. Former Bauhaus student Max Bill preferred the term *concrete* to *abstract* for describing art made without reference to nature. Concrete Art was characterized by bold colors in structured patterns, often drawing on math and science for inspiration.

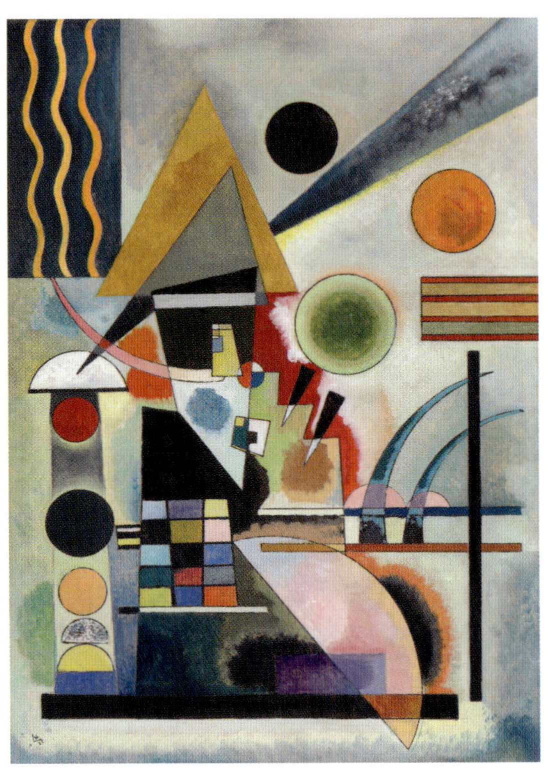

1
Wassily Kandinsky,
Swinging, 1925,
Tate

Abstract painting held a contradictory status at the Bauhaus. Opened in 1919, the legendary school employed several leading modernist painters as faculty, yet for many years, "free painting" had no official place in its curriculum. Instead, the Bauhaus committed itself to merging art with craft and training a new generation of industry-minded designers. After Kandinsky returned to Germany from Russia at the end of 1921, he accepted an offer from founding director Walter Gropius to teach at the recently formed institution. The Bauhaus would remain the painter's home for more than a decade, as he followed its relocations from Weimar to Dessau and finally to Berlin. Teaching was a core part of Kandinsky's artistic career, and his activities at the school had a substantial impact on later developments in abstraction. Prominent among these shifts was the reformulation of abstract painting into *Concrete Art,* a term championed by one of Kandinsky's most notable students and one that the Bauhaus master himself later endorsed.

During his Bauhaus period, Kandinsky completed his second major theoretical publication: *Point and Line to Plane,* which was issued in 1926 as the ninth volume in the iconic Bauhausbücher series. *Point and Line to Plane: Contribution to the Analysis of the Pictorial Elements,* is a systematic analysis of the elements of art, presenting three chapters that move sequentially from examinations of "point" and "line" to the "basic plane." Building on his earlier writings, Kandinsky framed his project as a quasi-scientific pursuit, yet one grounded in highly subjective, at times synesthetic principles that he saw as a critique of the excessively materialist and positivist culture of European modernity. The publication was a first step toward what he imagined as an "elementary dictionary," one that "in its further development, will lead to a 'grammar' and, finally, to a theory of composition . . . applicable to 'Art' as a whole."[1] Despite holding that the experiences of pictorial art could not be captured in written forms, Kandinsky analogized his effort to a "living dictionary" in its dual capacity for stability and change, akin to how words perpetually emerge, fade into disuse, and migrate across foreign languages.

While not intended to explain or decode its author's work, *Point and Line to Plane* offers some clear parallels to Kandinsky's paintings. For instance, the dominant yellow triangle in *Swinging* (fig. 1) is no doubt consistent with the artist's claim that certain colors are predisposed by their inherent "sound" to take on particular shapes: yellow correlates to the acute angle and triangle, red to the right angle and square, and blue to the obtuse angle and circle.[2] The vertical wavelike lines at the top left and the pair of ascending blue curves at the center right, too, closely analogous to figures that appear as illustrations in the artist's book, signal the combinatory logic of his painting practice at this moment. Kandinsky's publication also sheds light on the overall feeling sought by some paintings. The title and corresponding arrows of *Above and Left* (cat. 78) certainly connect to how the artist understood each direction to bear a distinct affect and poetic connotation. Within a particular composition, movement up and to the left were both linked with liberatory sensations of looseness and lightness as well as passages into the distance, while downward and rightward trajectories implied, respectively, the earth and home. Kandinsky viewed such associations as broadly fixed, and while recognizing them as culturally coded, he imagined international art institutions might bring divergent aesthetic systems into a future universal "harmony."

Other Bauhaus masters demonstrated little interest in the expressive and spiritual foundations of Kandinsky's thinking. Hungarian painter, photographer, and designer László Moholy-Nagy (cat. 19) represented a markedly different position, actively courting relationships between nonobjective painting, technology, and new media. The formal precision and reduced color palette of his 1927 painting *A19* (fig. 2) reflects this depersonalized and mechanized ethos, one indebted to the broad international impact of Constructivism. Moholy-Nagy's two contributions to the Bauhausbücher series—*Painting, Photography, Film* (1925) and *From Material to Architecture* (1929)—attest to the artist's wide-ranging, cross-media interests, celebrated for their future-facing arguments as well as their progressive typographic design (also by Moholy-Nagy). More broadly, the book series disseminated not only the writing and work of prominent Bauhaus faculty such as Walter Gropius, Paul Klee, and Oskar Schlemmer, but also enabled the school to ally itself with other major artists, including Piet Mondrian (cats. 40, 41), Theo van Doesburg (cat. 39), and Kazimir Malevich (cat. 4). However, after the Bauhaus was forced to relocate first to Dessau and then to Berlin due to political repression, the school was permanently closed in 1933 following the Nazis' rise to power. Its closure signaled the end of the artistic experimentation and international collaboration that had characterized the interwar period in Germany.

One significant legacy of Kandinsky—as well as the Bauhaus more generally—can be traced via the career of a prominent student: Swiss designer, artist, and architect Max Bill (cat. 33). Attending the school between 1927 and 1928, Bill participated in the "free painting" classes held by Kandinsky and Klee, and looking back on these years, he described the Russian painter as one of his most crucial teachers. Both Kandinsky and Bill moved during the 1930s to Paris, where they remained in regular contact and were active in the Abstraction-Création

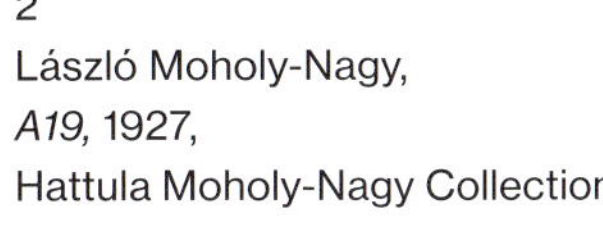

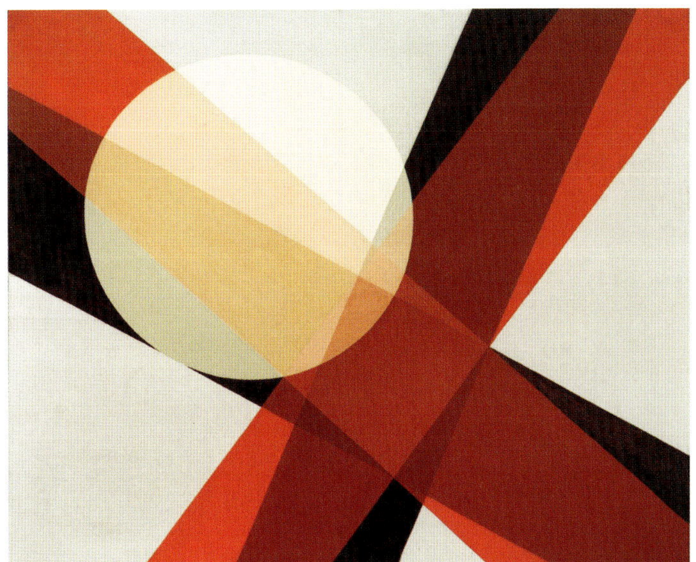

2
László Moholy-Nagy,
A19, 1927,
Hattula Moholy-Nagy Collection

circle (→ p. 270). In the postwar years, Bill became closely associated with the rise of Swiss modernism across art and design. In 1953 he acted as the founding director of the Hochschule für Gestaltung Ulm, a design school conceived as a direct successor to the Bauhaus.

Starting in the 1930s, Bill adopted and expanded the concept of Concrete Art, borrowing the term from Van Doesburg. Framed against the notion of "abstraction" as the formal reduction and simplification of forms from nature, "concrete" art utilized only the means and principles of art itself—such as form and color—without any external reference, literary association, or spiritual meaning. In this period, Bill developed an increasingly mathematical conception of artistic production, demonstrated in works like *fifteen variations on one theme* (fig. 3). Within this series of sixteen lithographic prints, the first sheet establishes the "theme:" a centrally positioned equilateral triangle opens on one side to become a square, which then becomes a pentagon, and so forth, until arriving at a final octagon. The subsequent fifteen "variations" reimagine this geometric sequence through a range of alternative graphic devices. Promoting his notion of Concrete Art, Bill regularly included Kandinsky in his exhibitions and writings, arguing for the continuity of their projects. In fact, the elder painter himself embraced the term *concrete* in the late 1930s, likewise preferring it to *abstract* for characterizing his work during his Paris years (cats. 55, 57).

Through a series of exhibitions (→ p. 274) across the following decade, a group of artists emerged known as the Zurich Concretists, which included Bill alongside Camille Graeser (cat. 35), Verena Loewensberg (cat. 34), and Richard Paul Lohse (cats. 36, 37) as its primary proponents. These four core artists maintained a shared commitment to nonrepresentational, geometric modes of production, although each had distinct motivations and methods. For example, Lohse—who started his career in graphic design—devised a standardized, serialized, and anonymized approach to painting around 1942–43, which he considered as directly aligned with his left politics and support for the antifascist resistance. His canvas *Thirty Vertical Systematic Color Series in a Yellow Rhombic Form* (fig. 4) consists of a strict system of gradated colors, with each of its thirty stripes spanning the full chromatic spectrum while starting from a different hue. As frequently encountered within his oeuvre, the work's dual dating to both 1943 and 1970 indicates the moment of the painting's initial concept or plan, as well as its material execution more than twenty-five years later. Inspired by twelve-tone music and group theory in mathematics, Lohse endeavored to render the logic of his practice fully consistent and transparent. His serial method allocated equal space to each color and ensured no color repeats in the

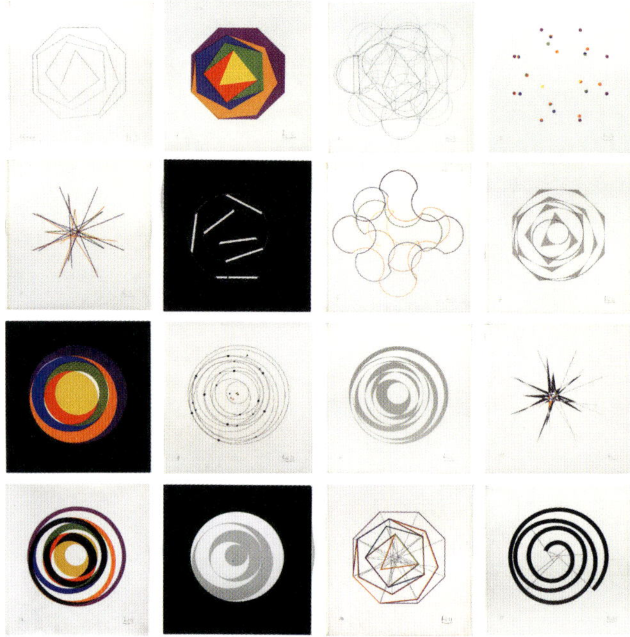

3
Max Bill,
fifteen variations on one theme,
1935–38,
Mercedes-Benz Art Collection

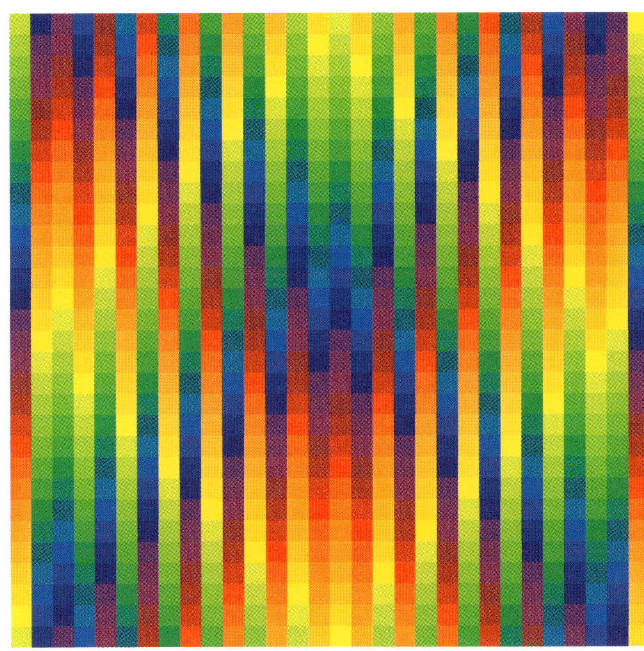

4
Richard Paul Lohse,
Thirty Vertical Systematic Color Series in a Yellow Rhombic Form, 1943/1970,
Richard Paul Lohse-Stiftung
(Cat. 36)

same column or row. Through this process, Lohse sought to model notions of social equality and materialize a "radical democratic principle," in his words, extending the egalitarian efforts of Constructivism and De Stijl.[3]

By contrast, Verena Loewensberg committed her practice neither to the mathematics of Bill nor the utopian values of Lohse. Turning to painting from a background in textiles and dance, she seemingly worked by means of a balance of predetermination and discovery, rather than on the basis of a fixed theory or formal operation. "In some instances, I'll have an idea for the picture in my mind's eye," Loewensberg once explained, ". . . in others, a picture might emerge from a mental process that is beset with all manner of detours."[4] In her work *Untitled* (cat. 34) from 1965, a pale lavender square is set as a diamond in the center of the canvas, anchoring four irregular quadrilaterals and a surrounding pattern of triangles paired by color. With its repeating yet intuitive geometries and unexpected combination of primary, secondary, and pastel hues, Loewensberg's painting makes light of the occasionally doctrinaire ideals and high seriousness of her male counterparts. Even while participating in virtually every significant exhibition for the emergence and elaboration of Concrete Art in Switzerland, she nonetheless charted a more individual and improvisatory path.

As the only Bauhaus student among the Zurich group, Bill was no doubt the most adamant about connecting the project of Concrete Art back to Kandinsky. Following the Russian painter's death in 1944 and the end of World War II, he worked actively to preserve his former teacher's reputation and memory. Bill published a retrospective article on Kandinsky in 1946 (referring to his teacher's work as "pure, concrete painting") as well as a monograph on his career in 1951.[5] Most significantly, Bill designed and helped edit republications of Kandinsky's landmark books and essays across the 1950s, including both *Concerning the Spiritual in Art* and *Point and Line to Plane,* which ran in numerous editions. Appropriately, in his introduction to the latter publication, Bill framed Kandinsky in terms clearly designed to establish the lineage of Concrete Art, arguing that the work of the Bauhaus master represented the true "beginning of a new, autonomous structuring and ordering of artistic means."[6]

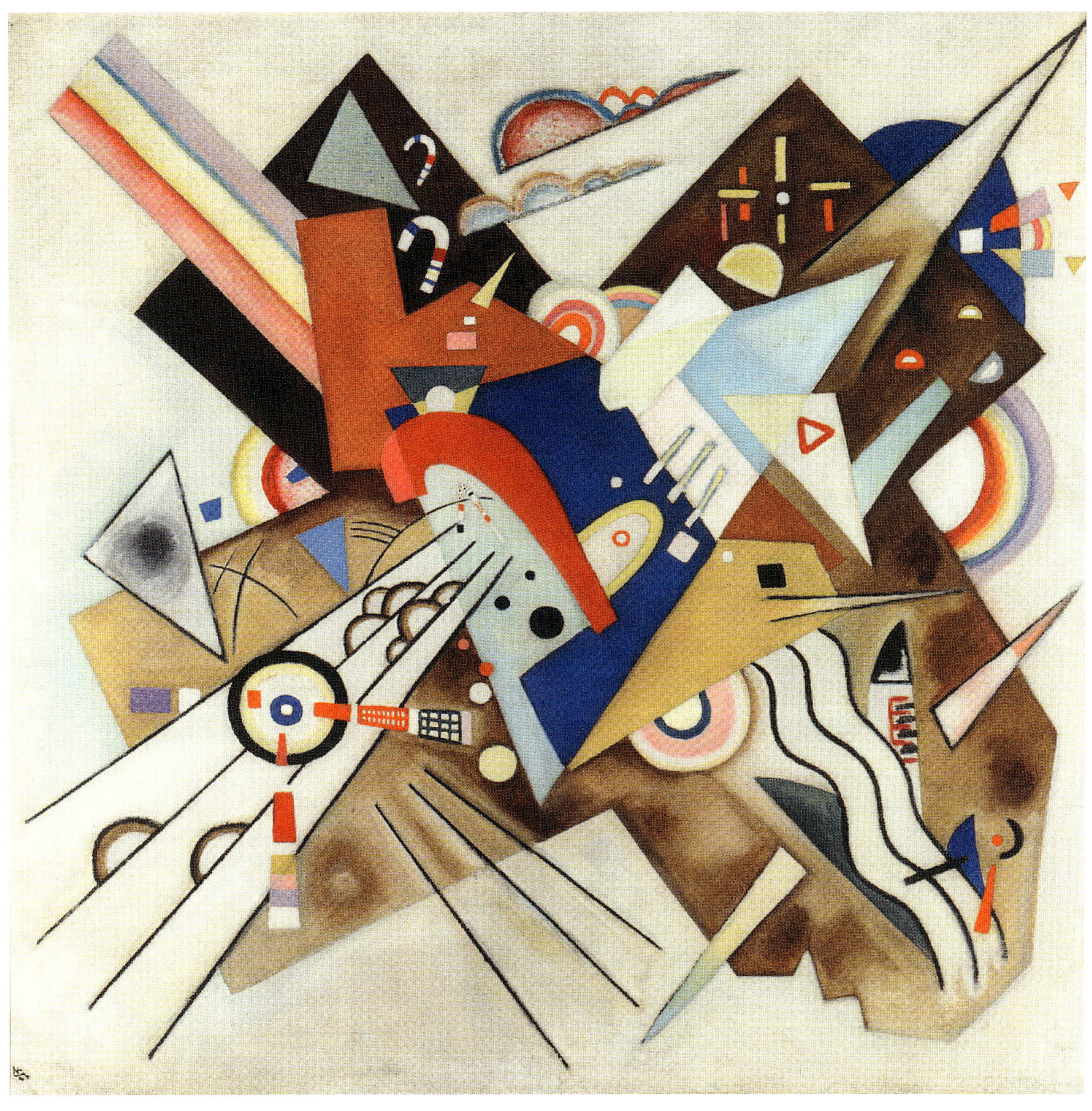

22 Wassily Kandinsky
Emphasized Corners, 1923
Nahmad Collection

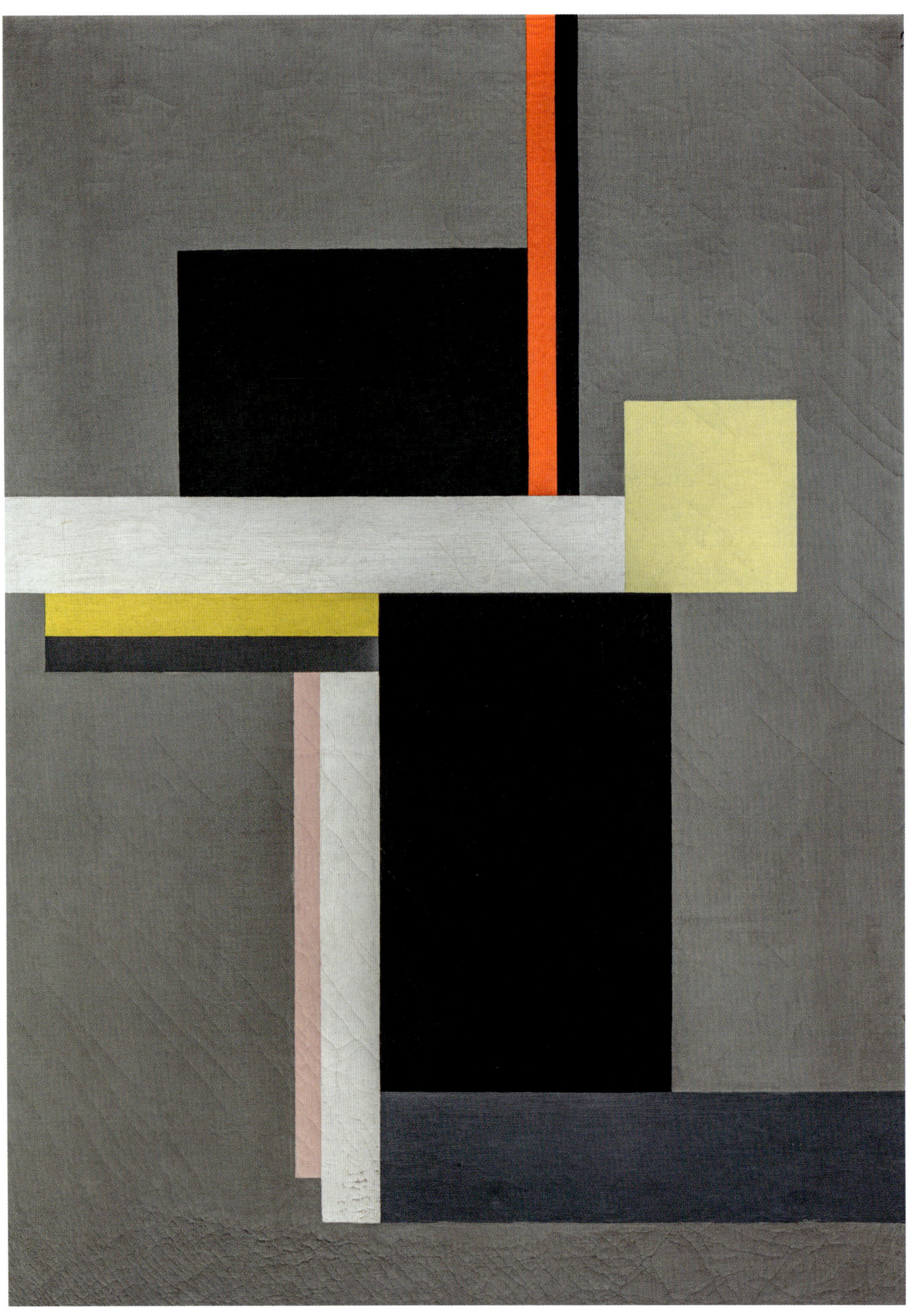

23 Walter Dexel
Composition 1924 VI, 1924
Galerie Berinson, Berlin

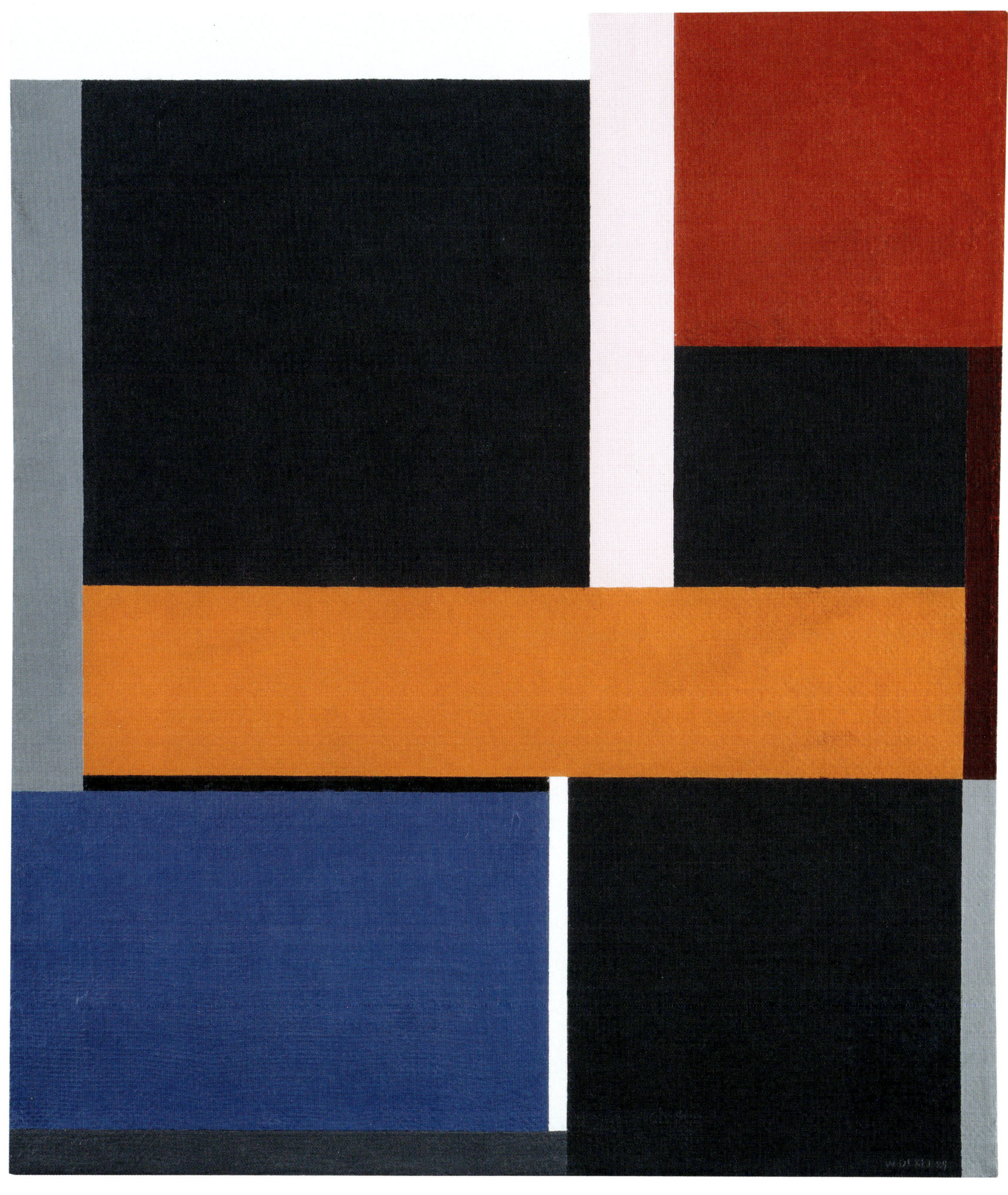

24 Walter Dexel
Composition 1924 II, 1924
Hamburger Kunsthalle

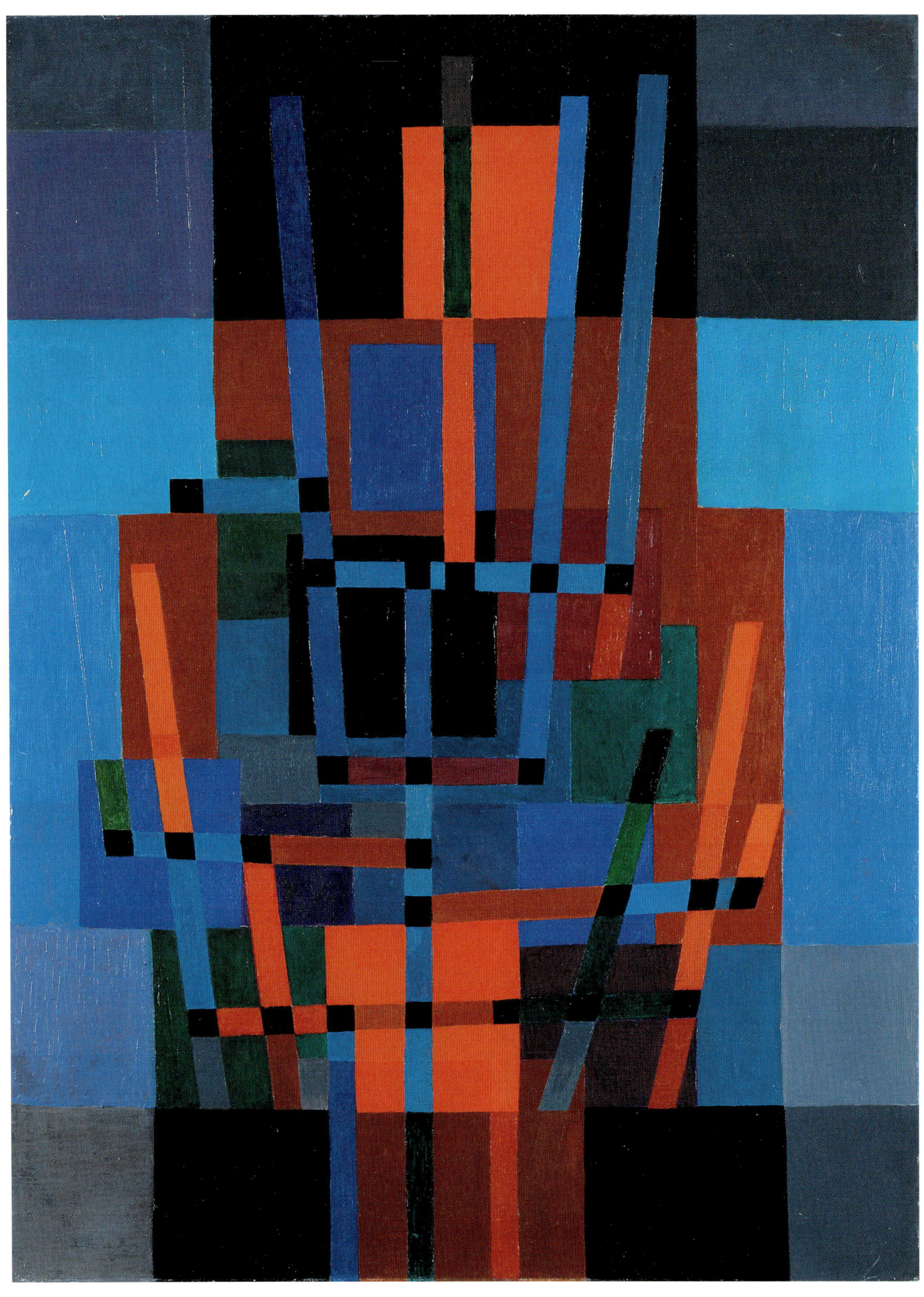

25 Johannes Itten
Sticks and Planes, 1955
Mercedes-Benz Art Collection

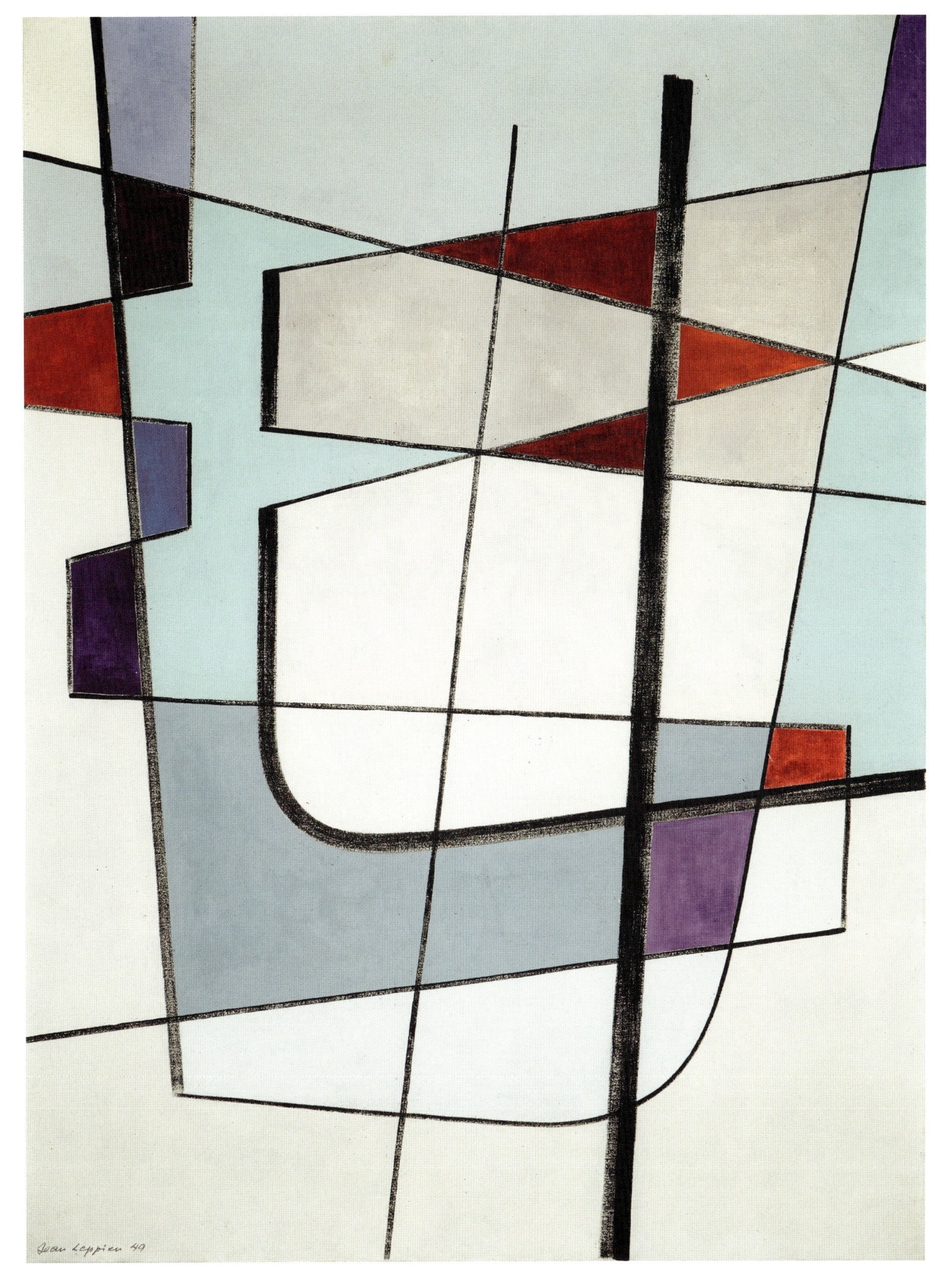

26 Jean Leppien
LXVIII, 1949
Fondation Gandur pour l'Art, Genève

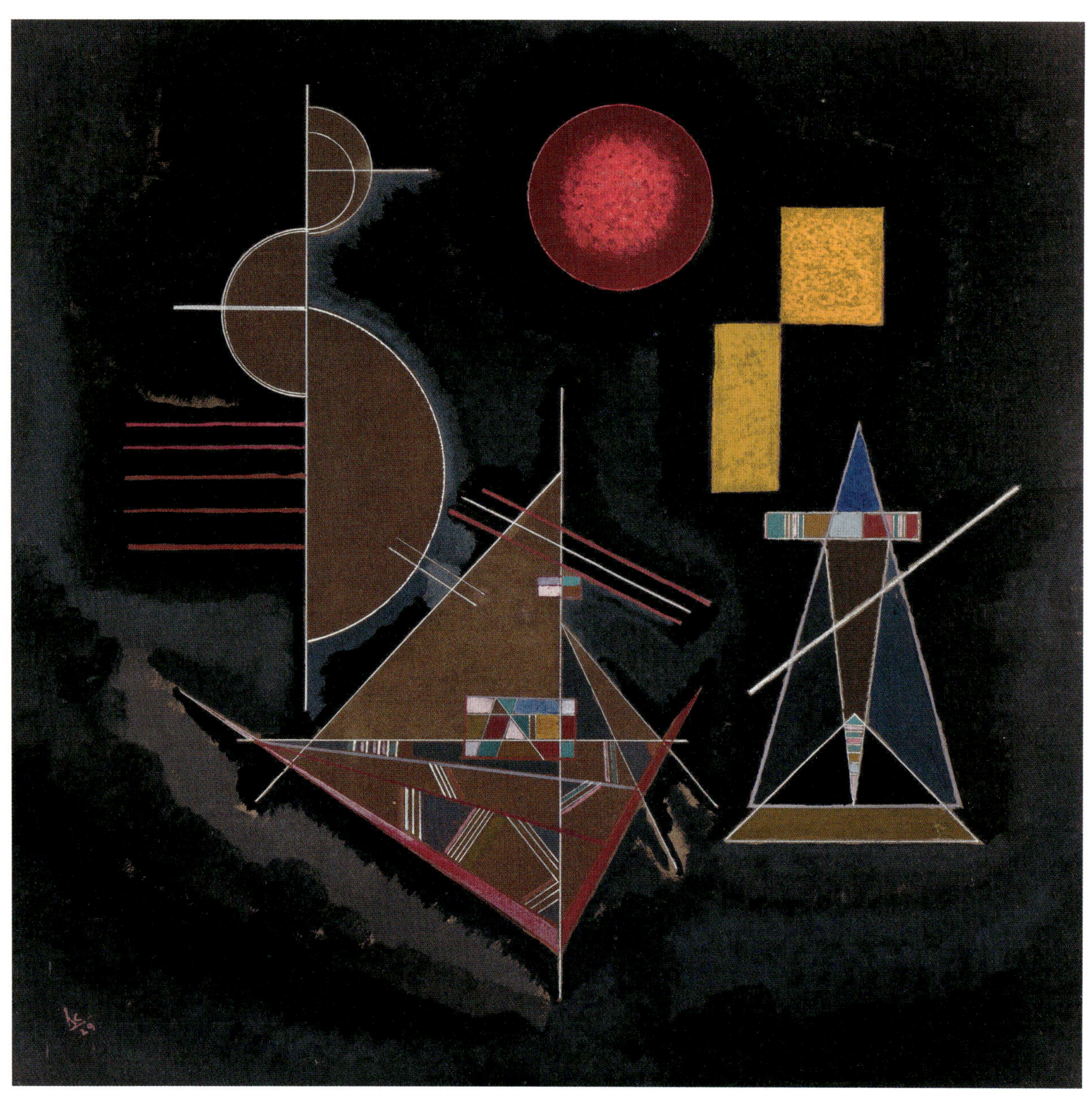

27 Wassily Kandinsky
Light in Heavy, 1929
Collection Museum Boijmans Van Beuningen, Rotterdam

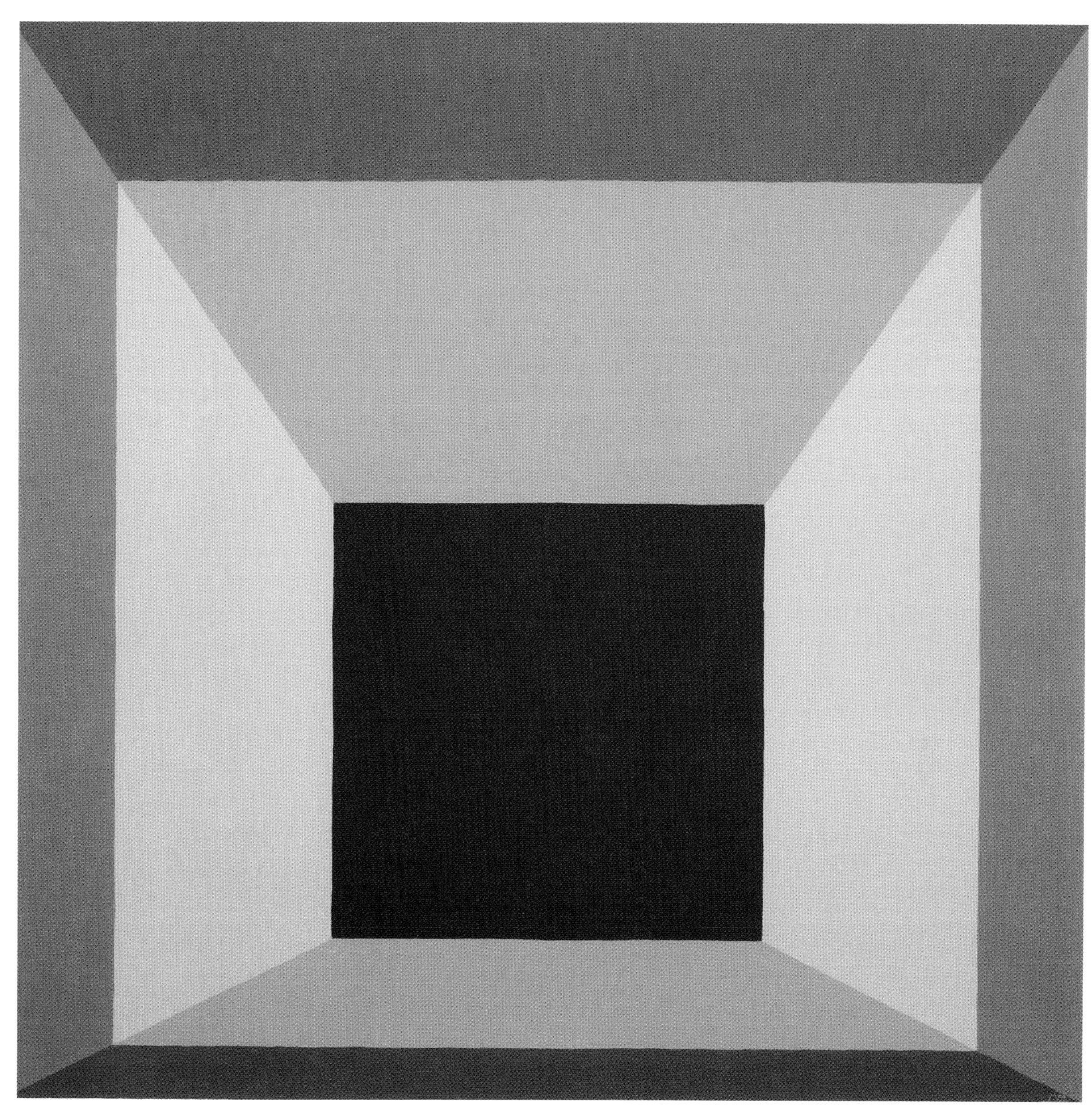

28 Josef Albers
Homage to the Square: Mitered Square, 1967
Josef Albers Museum Quadrat Bottrop

29 Josef Albers
Homage to the Square, 1967
Josef Albers Museum Quadrat Bottrop

30 Josef Albers
Study for Homage to the Square: Reticence, 1965
Josef Albers Museum Quadrat Bottrop

31 Josef Albers
Study for Homage to the Square: Corona, 1968
Josef Albers Museum Quadrat Bottrop

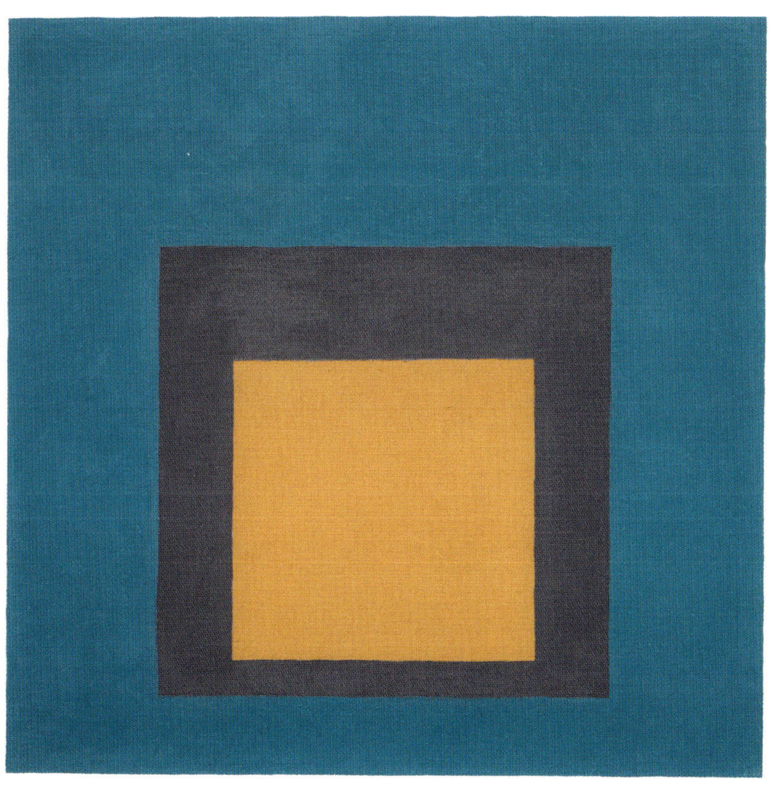

32 Josef Albers
Study for Homage to the Square, 1965
Josef Albers Museum Quadrat Bottrop

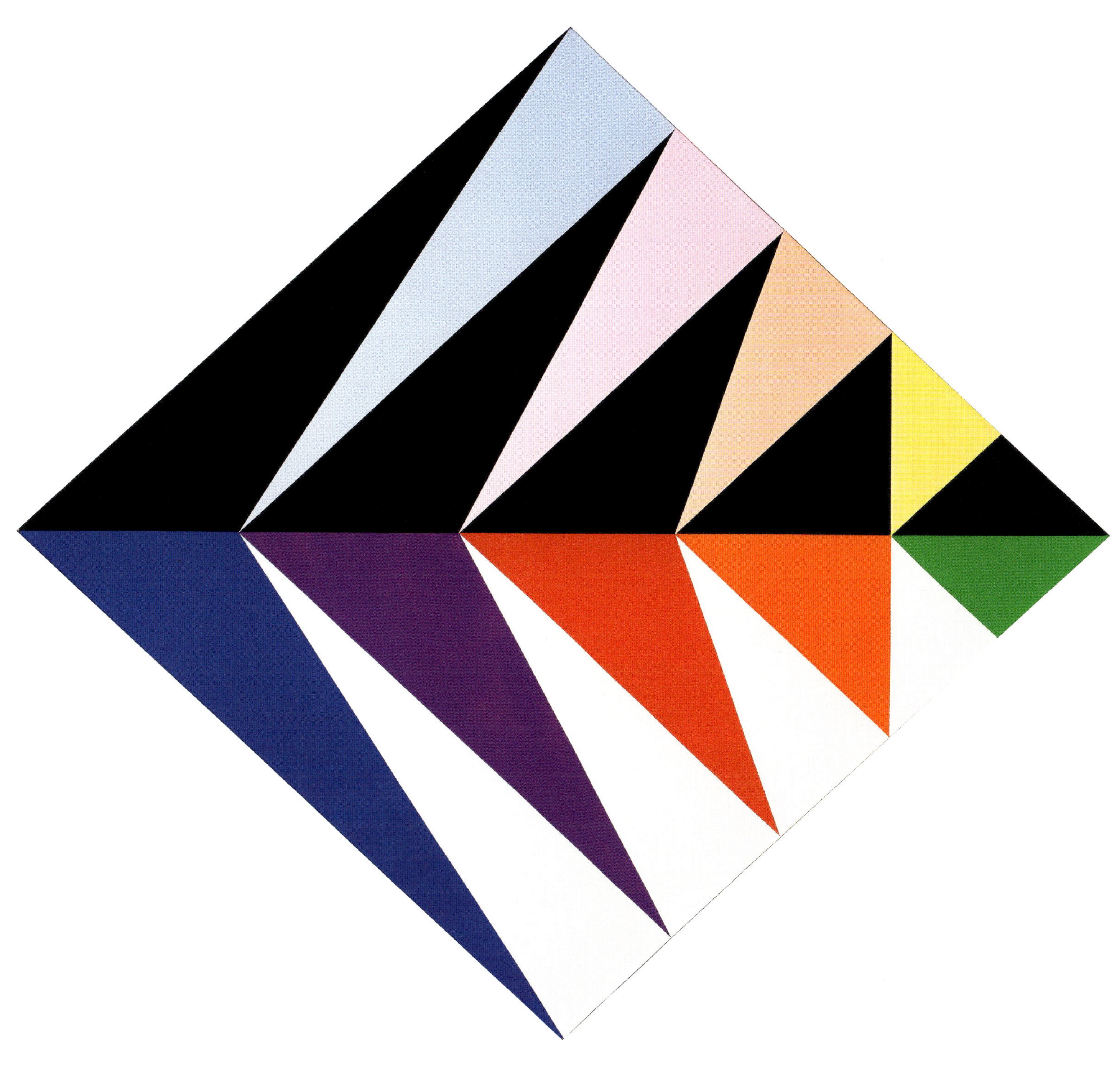

33 Max Bill
reflections from dark and light, 1975
Haus Bill, Zumikon

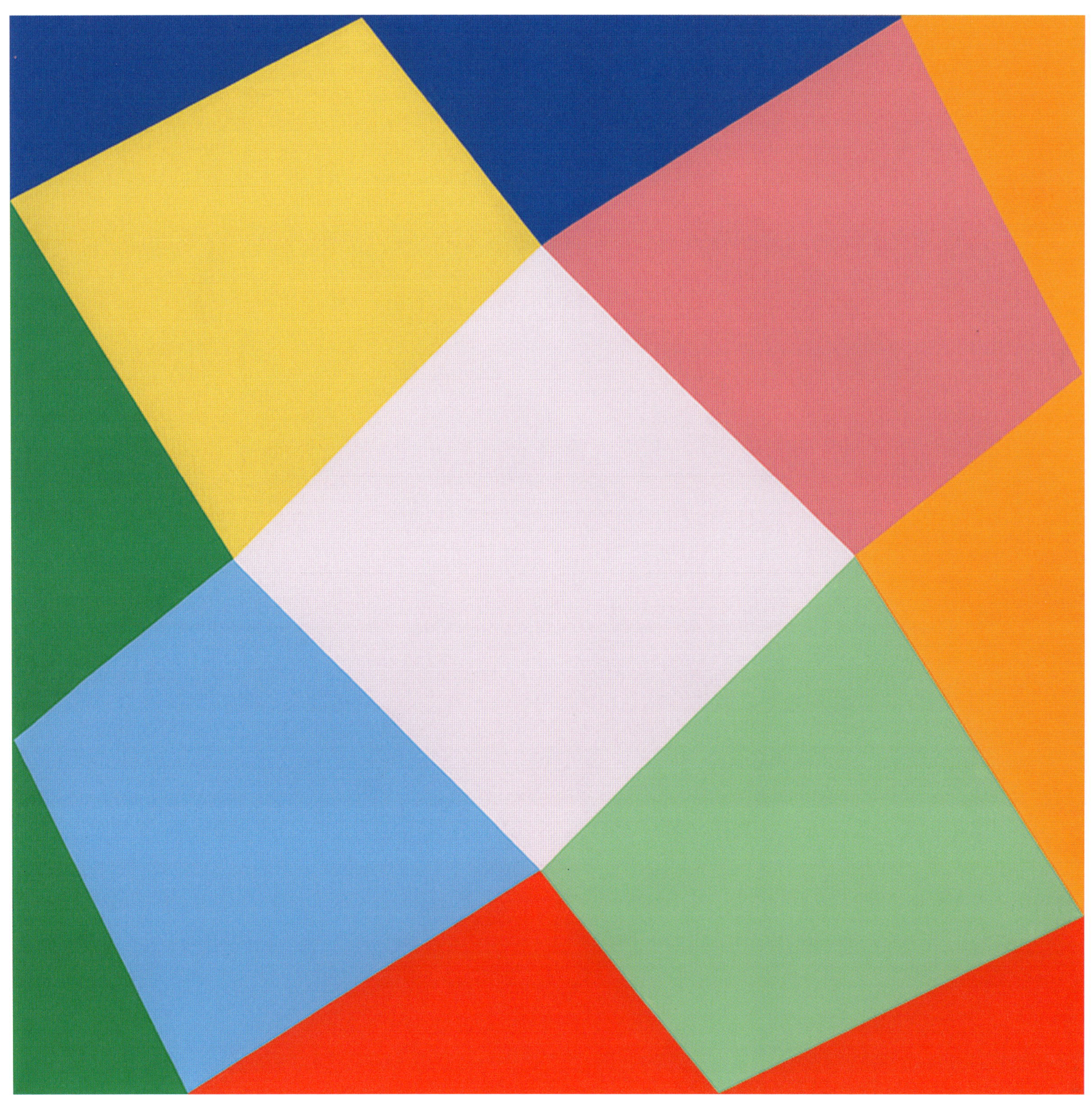

34 Verena Loewensberg
Untitled, 1965
Verena Loewensberg Stiftung, Zurich

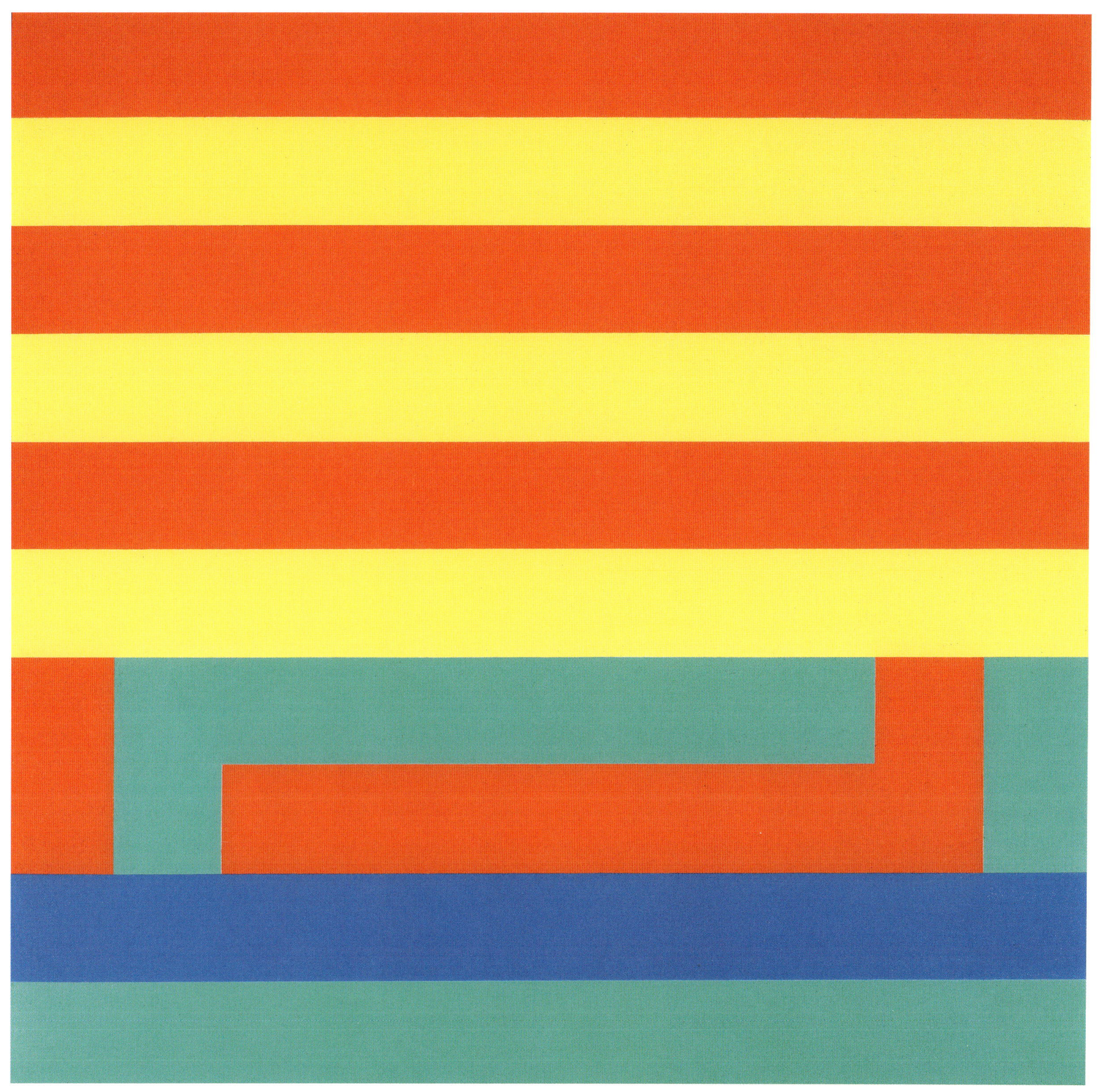

35 Camille Graeser
1 : 2 : 3 : 4, 1969
Courtesy Camille Graeser Stiftung, Zurich

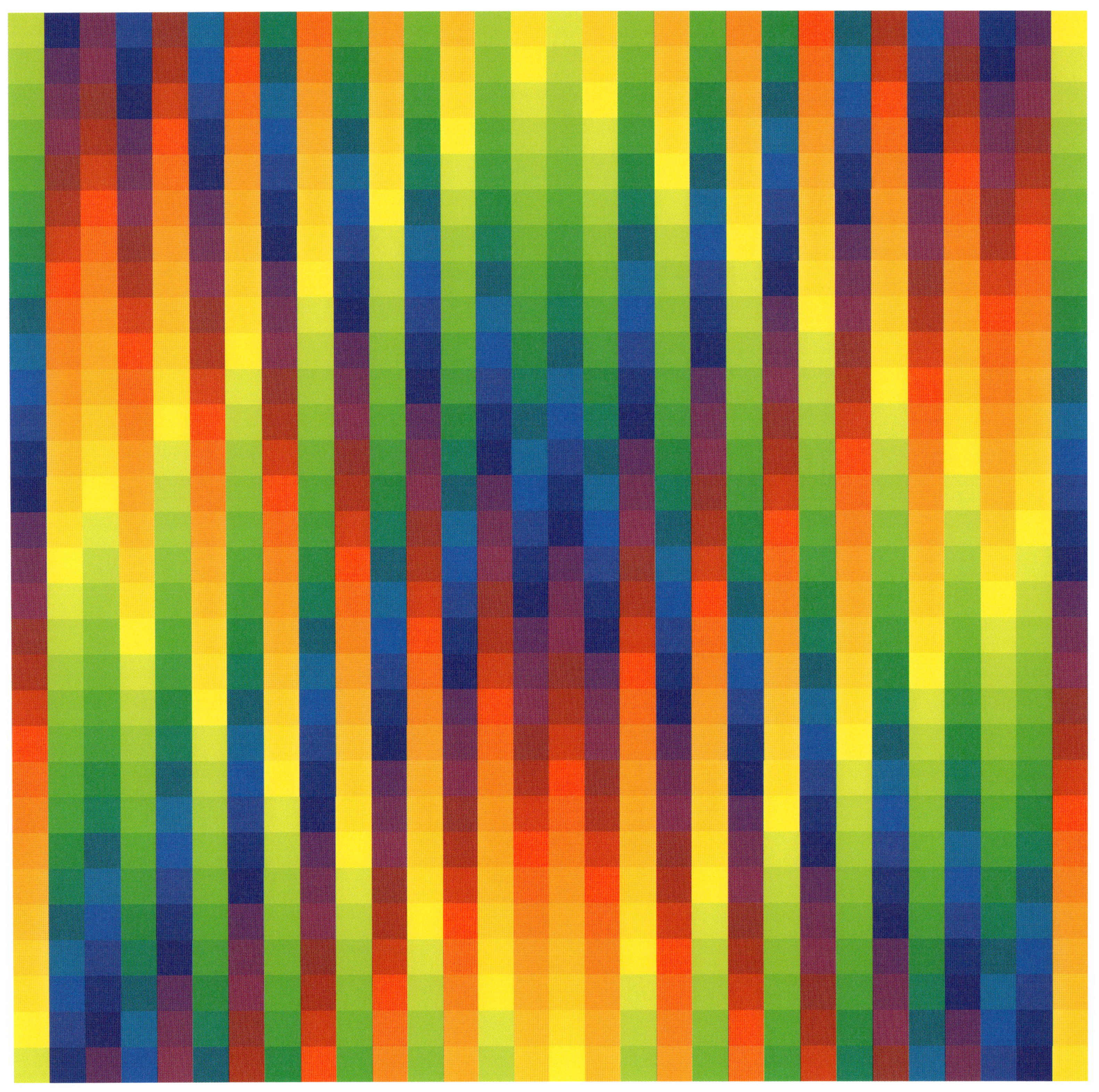

36 Richard Paul Lohse
Thirty Vertical Systematic Color Series in a Yellow Rhombic Form, 1943/1970
Richard Paul Lohse-Stiftung

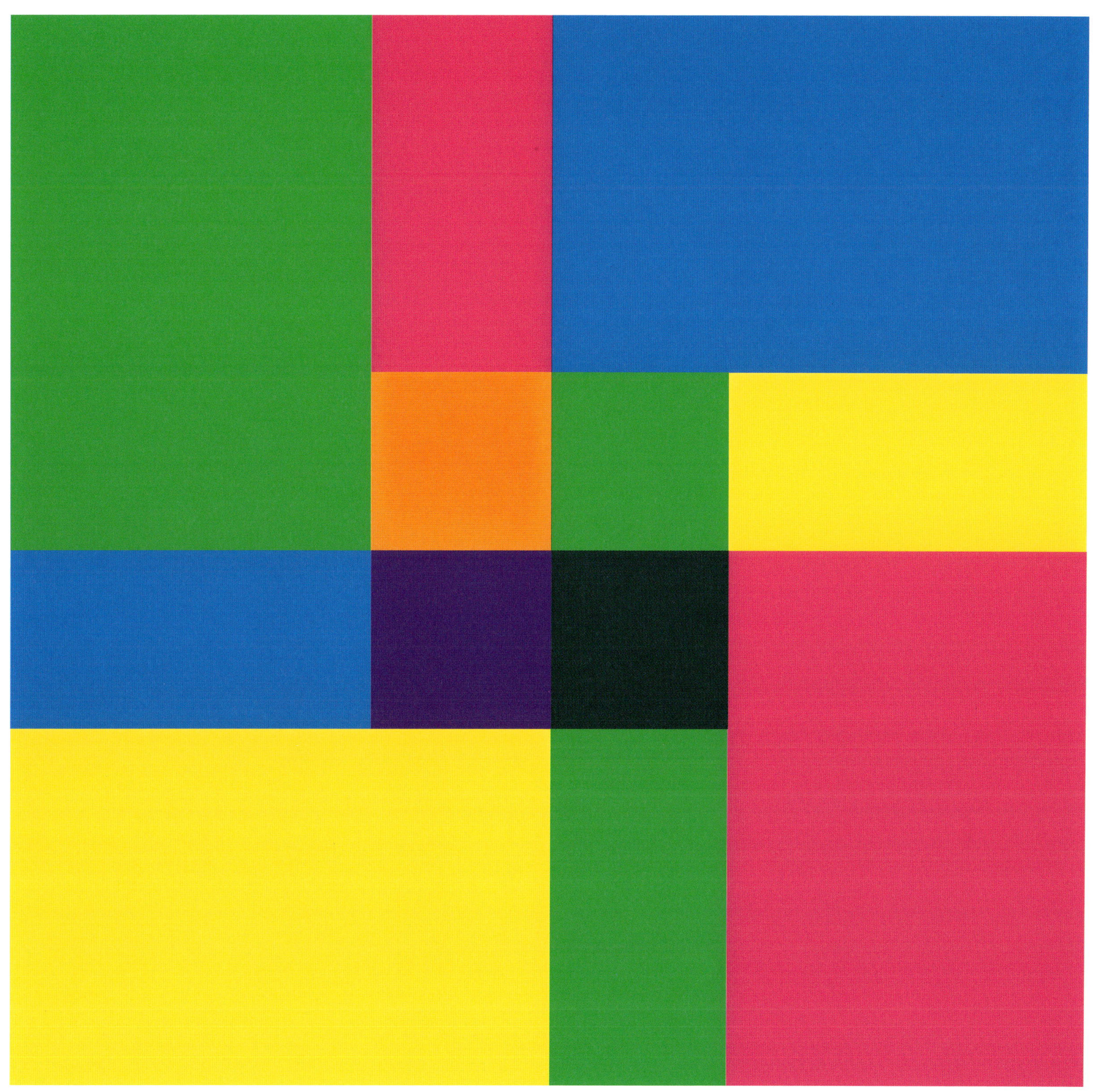

37 Richard Paul Lohse
Center of Four Squares as a Result of the Four Cross Surfaces, 1952/1971
Richard Paul Lohse-Stiftung

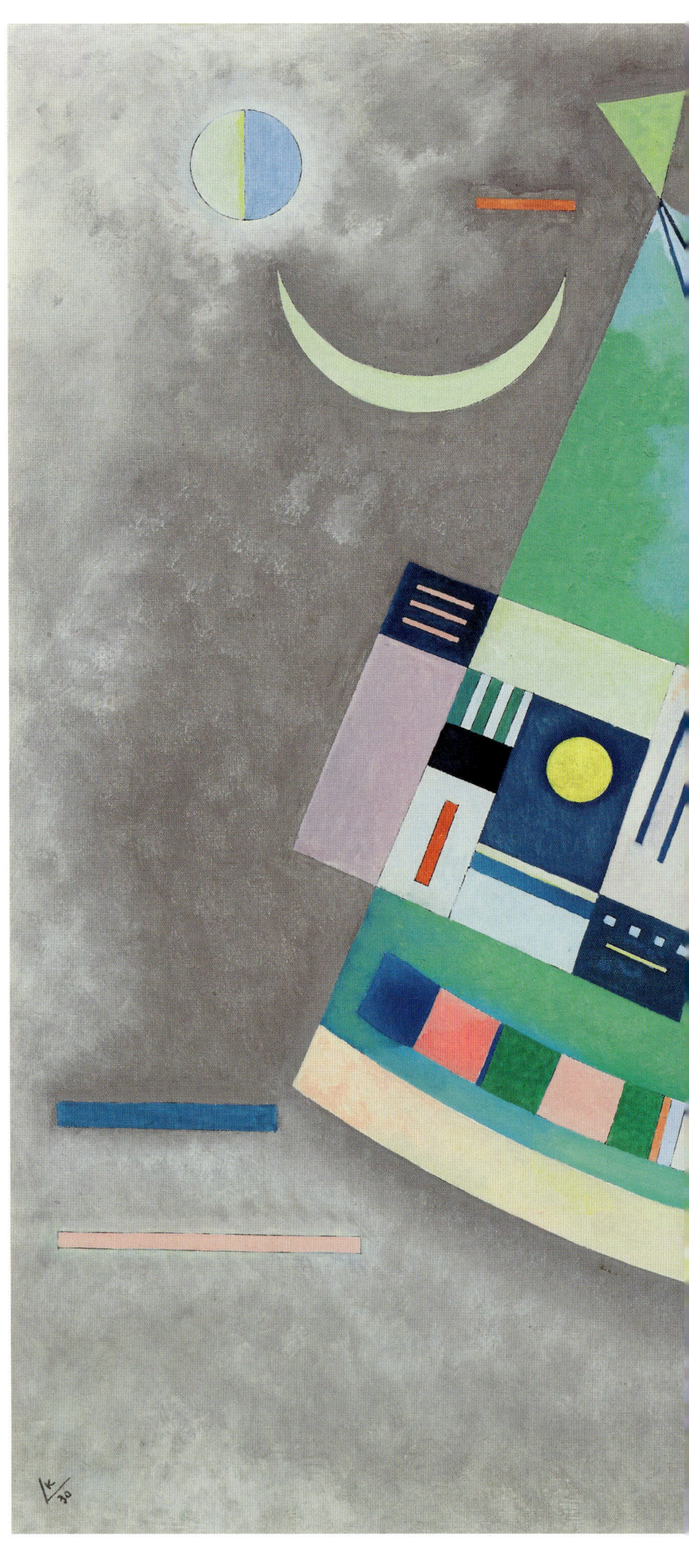

38 Wassily Kandinsky
Arrow Toward the Circle, 1930
Nahmad Collection

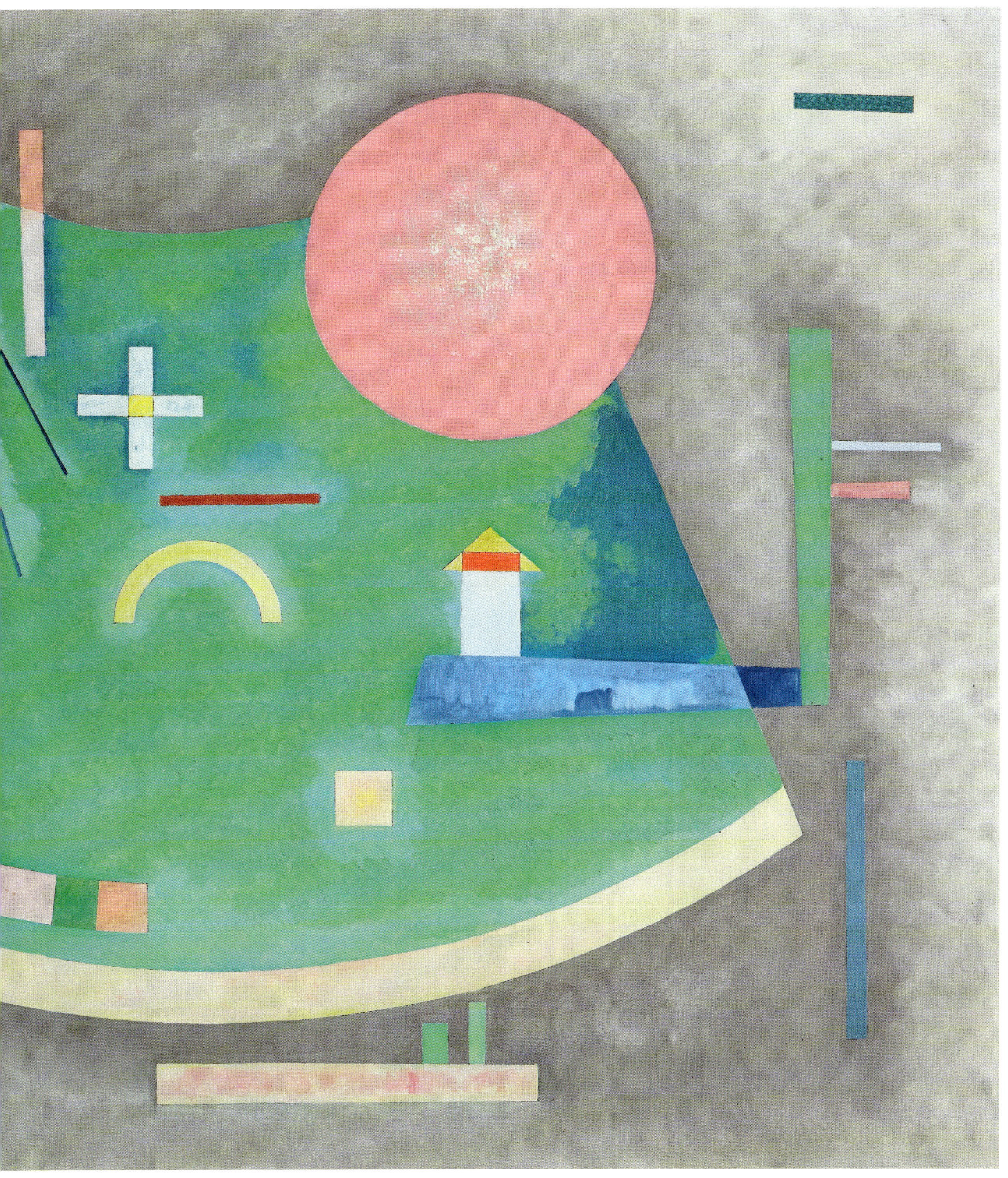

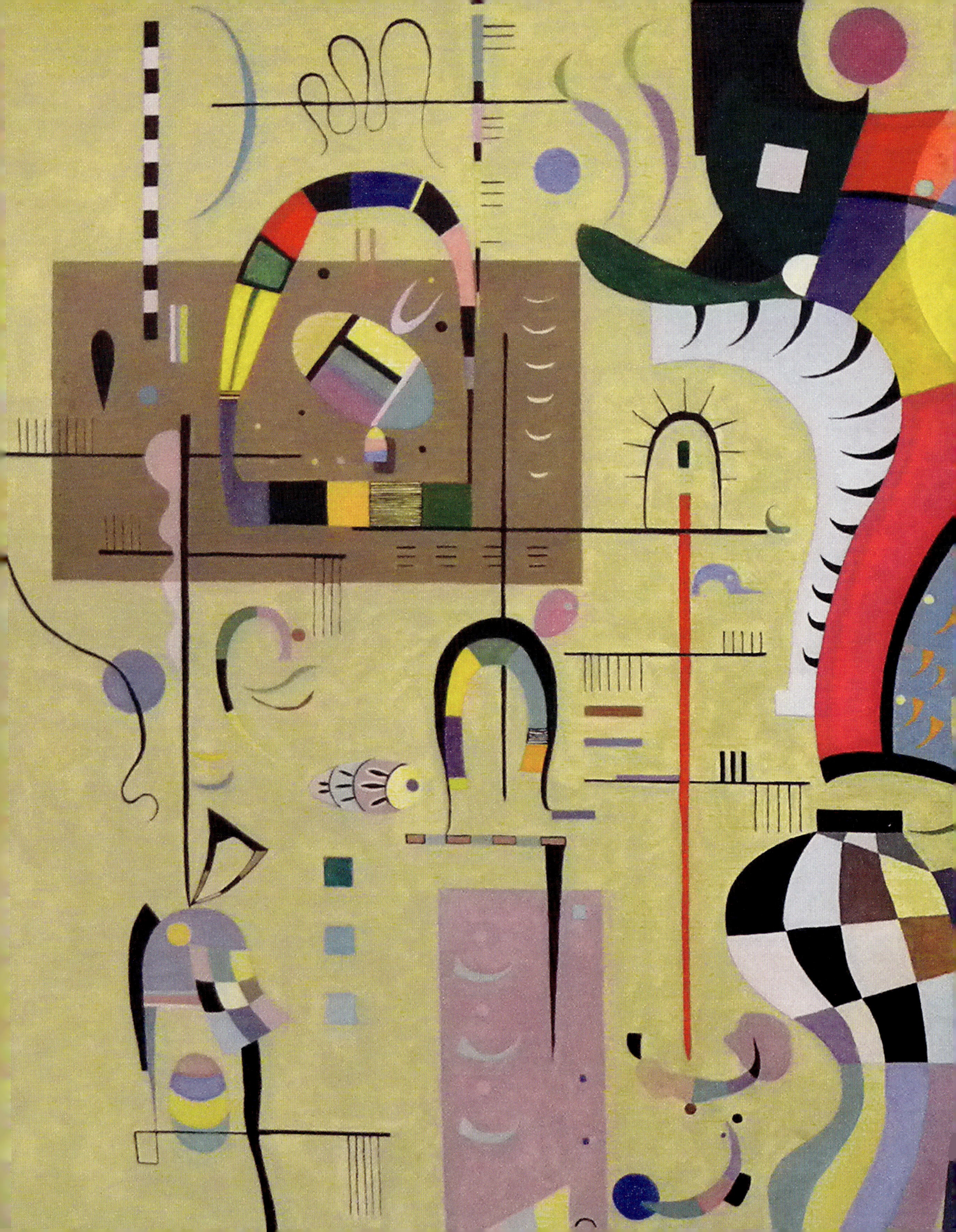

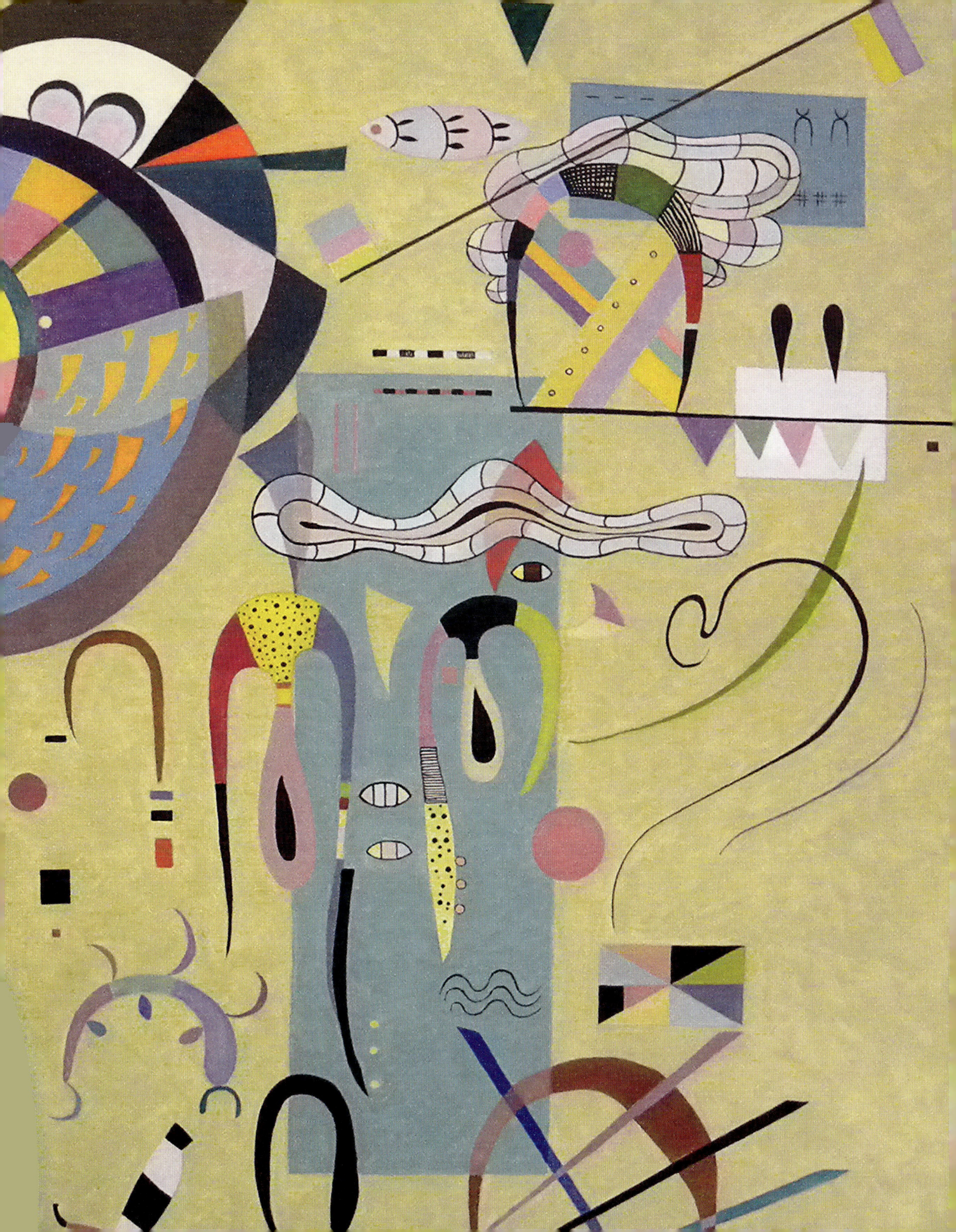

Sterre Barentsen

Straight Lines, Flowing Forms

International Abstraction in Paris

After the Nazis forced the Bauhaus to close in 1933, Wassily Kandinsky emigrated to Neuilly-sur-Seine, near Paris, where he encountered abstract artists from an international avant-garde that included Piet Mondrian, Marlow Moss, and César Domela. These artists had developed a strict compositional formula using grid structures. In contrast, Alexander Calder, Sophie Taeuber-Arp, and Jean Hélion incorporated playful shapes into their work. Kandinsky engaged with these artists, part of the Abstraction-Création group, but also exchanged ideas with their counterparts, the Surrealists, who focused on the unconscious mind. Despite this, Kandinsky saw himself as a lone figure.

His Parisian works feature organic forms that appear fantastical yet were often inspired by scientific literature. Regardless of the disillusionment with progress brought by the rise of totalitarian regimes, Kandinsky continued to see art as a realm for exploring spirituality.

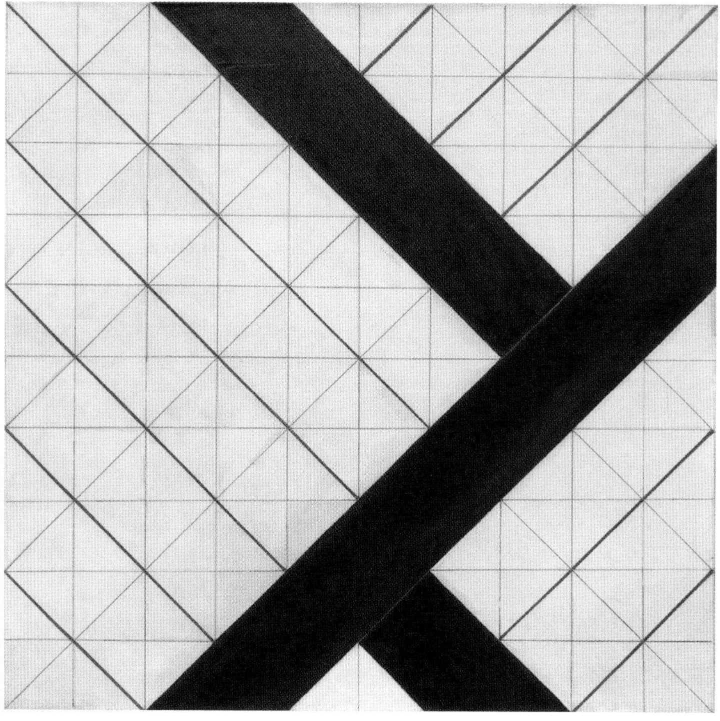

1
Theo van Doesburg,
Counter-Composition VI, 1925,
Tate

The utopian ideals that once defined geometric abstraction came under pressure in the 1930s. The forced closure of the Bauhaus by the Nazi regime in 1933 and the *Entartete Kunst* (Degenerate Art) propaganda exhibition of 1937 (→ p. 273) marked a sharp rejection of modernist art, which was viewed as a threat to Nazi ideology and ultimately forced many artists into exile. In the Soviet Union, Constructivism was similarly stifled by Stalinist policies, which favored Socialist Realism for propagating communist ideology. During this period, Paris emerged as a refuge for many artists who were fleeing totalitarian regimes, among them Wassily Kandinsky. In the French capital, international expressions merged with local variations of geometric abstraction, such as late Cubism and the grid compositions developed by Piet Mondrian after his arrival in Paris in 1919 (cats. 40, 41).

The De Stijl movement, founded in the Netherlands by artists such as Mondrian and Theo van Doesburg (cat. 39) during World War I, had a significant impact on the Parisian art scene. Their approach focused on stripping art down to its most essential forms, using primary colors and reducing compositions to vertical and horizontal lines. This purity of form was believed to reveal a deeper, underlying reality, aligning with the artists' interest in theosophy and idealistic philosophies. In this, they saw the potential for a universal language that transcended cultural and individual limitations. By the mid-1920s, however, the relationship between Mondrian and Van Doesburg began to fray. Mondrian returned to Paris after World War I, while Van Doesburg spread the ideas they had developed together throughout Europe and introduced them to the Bauhaus. The tension came to a head when Van Doesburg introduced diagonal lines into his work, breaking from De Stijl's rigid adherence to vertical and horizontal elements. His *Counter-Composition VI* (fig. 1) shows a grid of diagonal, vertical, and horizontal lines, creating the impression that a layer had been removed, revealing an underlying structure. On the basis of his series of *Counter-Compositions,* Van Doesburg founded a new movement, Elementarism, which sealed the final break. Mondrian left the De Stijl movement in 1925, marking the end of their revolutionary collaboration. Their personal and ideological differences had dissolved their shared vision for a universal art form.

Shortly after distancing himself from De Stijl, Mondrian attracted attention through his participation in the Paris exhibition *L'Art d'aujourd'hui: Exposition internationale* in 1925 (→ p. 269). This shift in Mondrian's career coincided with his embrace of new artistic dialogues. Since

1927 British artist Marlow Moss had been part of the international art circle in Paris. Alongside artists such as César Domela (cat. 43) and Jean Gorin (cat. 45), Moss was part of a second generation of abstract geometric artists who gathered around Mondrian. Born Marjorie Jewel Moss, she adopted the name Marlow and wore masculine-presenting clothes. By 1930 she was painting Neoplastic images. Moss adopted a distinctive approach that included painting two lines close to each other (cat. 42), which she developed by experimenting with the golden ratio. Initially skeptical of Moss's mathematical technique, Mondrian ultimately incorporated the "double line" into his own work by 1931 (fig. 2), recognizing it as a means to add dynamism and rhythm to his compositions. This evolution in Mondrian's style was reflective of his broader desire to capture the rhythm of modern music and city life. Mondrian explored this theme in his writings, including in the essay "Jazz and Neo-Plastic" from 1927, in which he discussed rhythm's ability to fracture and liberate.[1] Like the metropolis, jazz was a celebration of modern life and a motor to bring dynamic vitality into his compositions. Jazz was the future. In the 1920s, Paris was teeming with dance venues and jazz bars, many of which were operated by African American soldiers. The modern atmosphere and influx of new ideas invigorated Mondrian's work, illustrating the profound impact of cross-generational and international influences.

By the late 1920s, Surrealism had emerged as a dominant force in Paris, its realist dreamlike depictions setting it at odds with the principles of abstraction. In response to Surrealism's ascendancy, proponents of abstract art formed the group Abstraction-Création in 1931 in Paris. It aimed to champion and promote nonrepresentational art through exhibitions (→ p. 270) and publications. Yet the influence of Surrealism began subtly permeating the works of several abstract artists. Notably, French artist Jean Hélion, who initially adhered to Mondrian's principles of Neoplasticism, gradually introduced elements that broke from the rigid structures (cat. 50). By 1935 his style had evolved significantly; in his work *Untitled* (cat. 51), the traditional grid was replaced with overlapping rounded shapes that suggested a Surrealist influence with their shaded, organic forms. This marked a definitive move away from the rigid abstract-mathematical principles

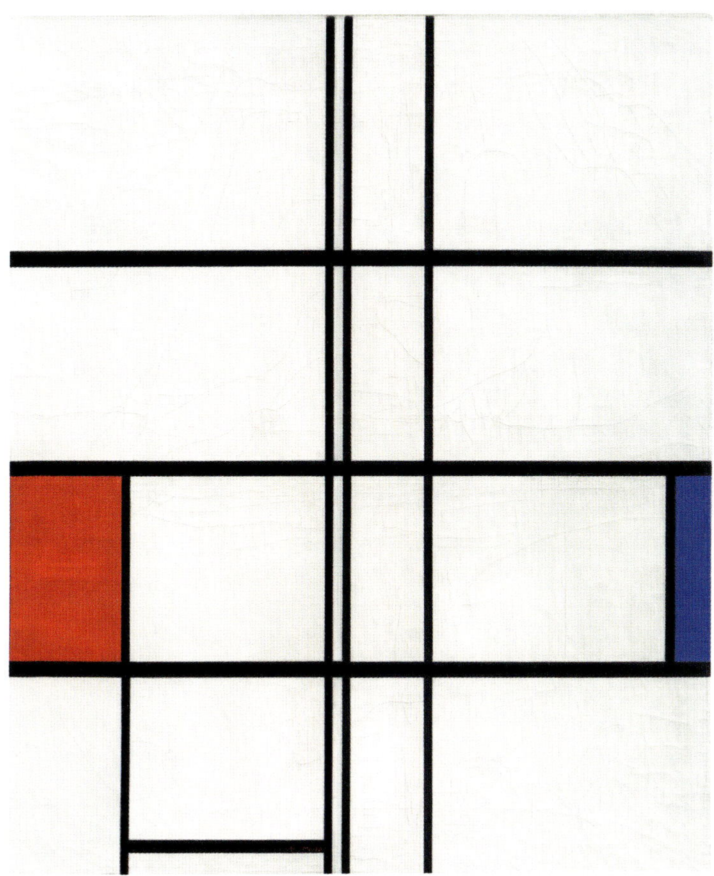

2
Piet Mondrian,
Composition in White, Red and Blue, 1936,
Staatsgalerie Stuttgart

he had once championed. Hélion's growing sympathy for Surrealist motifs became unmistakable in 1934, when he severed his ties with the group Abstraction-Création.

Kandinsky also began to adopt Surrealist elements in his work. He had moved to Paris in 1933 at the age of sixty-six, after the closure of the Bauhaus. Kandinsky was actively involved in the local art scene until the German occupation of Paris began in 1940. He became a member of Abstraction-Création, participated in exhibitions, and spent much time painting and writing. During this period, Kandinsky's style evolved significantly. One of Kandinsky's notable works from his time in Paris, *Accompanied Center* (fig. 3), bursts with vibrant and colorful geometric shapes—arcs, circles, and squares—and small creatures and individual eyes that float in the yellow space. Despite Kandinsky's denials of Surrealist influences, the similarities between his work and that of Joan Miró are striking. Kandinsky met Miró soon after his arrival in Paris, and the influence is apparent in Kandinsky's use of whimsical elements similar to those in Miró's *The Harlequin's Carnival* (fig. 4), which showcases a joyous array of playful creatures.[2]

When discussing Kandinsky's style during his Paris years, the focus is often on his developments rather than on the elements the painter consistently adhered to. Unlike the Surrealists, Kandinsky's works did not concern themselves with dreams and the unconscious. Thin, hairlike lines and geometric shapes in pure colors continue to adorn *Accompanied Center*. In the lower-right corner, three lines projecting outward intersect with a fourth, forming a lattice structure similar to the composition in his Bauhaus painting *Above and Left* (cat. 78). At the center of the painting, a large abstract form, nearly resembling a tropical bird with its opulent colors and taillike shapes, is anchored in a geometric vocabulary. The planes and checkerboard patterns of earlier works now fluidly curve around it.

Kandinsky's work often sought to evoke the spiritual through cosmic imagery, pointing to unseen realities beyond our sight. His later works reveal his interest in scientific disciplines such as embryology, botany, and zoology, which focus on organic life. In her analysis of *Accompanied Center,* art historian Vivian Endicott Barnett highlights a specific element: a horizontal, wavy, segmented shape in the upper-right corner, which she describes as a "clearly biological reference."[3] The form is reminiscent of the anatomical cross sections of a freshwater polyp found in the encyclopedia *Die Kultur der Gegenwart* (The Culture of the Present), which Kandinsky also referred to in his treatise *Point and Line to Plane.*[4] Kandinsky's fascination with scientific discoveries persisted. He shifted his focus from the telescope to the microscope

3
Wassily Kandinsky,
Accompanied Center, 1937,
Nahmad Collection
(Cat. 57)

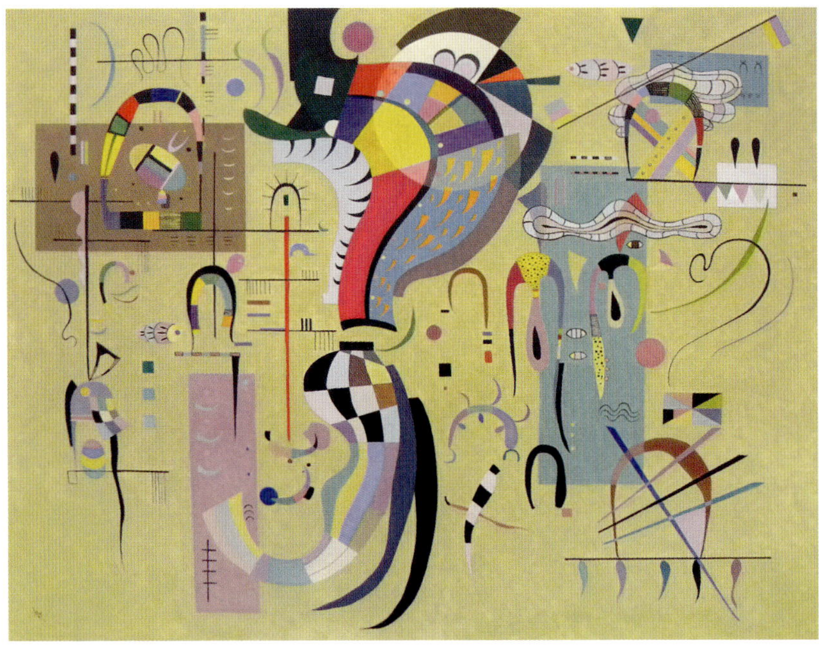

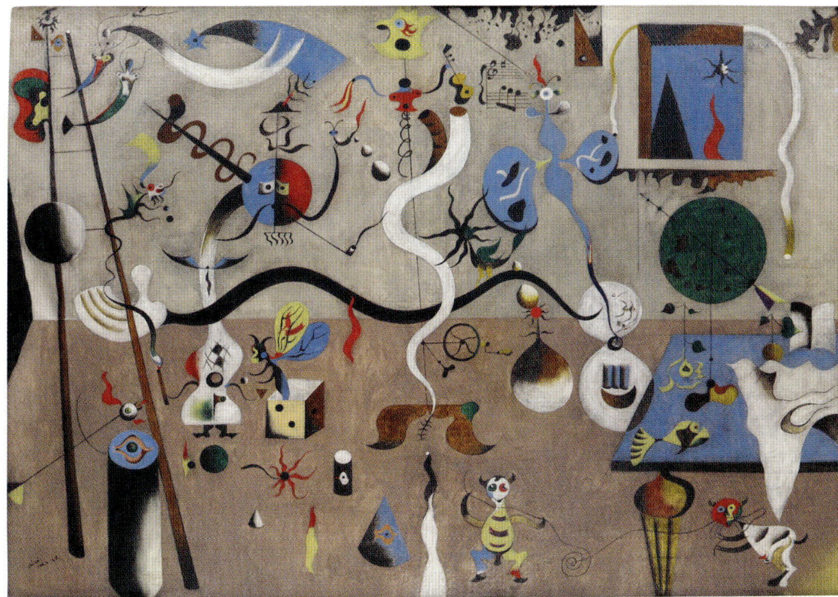

4
Joan Miró,
The Harlequin's Carnival, 1924–25,
Buffalo AKG Art Museum

(→ p. 271), exploring organic forms that conveyed a spiritual narrative of beginnings and regeneration. This shift from macro- to microcosm underscores an evolution in his work, while maintaining his profound interest in the hidden dimensions of reality.

The first decades of the twentieth century were marked by radical experimentation and a profound sense of idealism as artists sought to redefine the boundaries of art. By the 1930s, however, the utopian spirit of the previous decades began to wane, overshadowed by political, social, and economic crises. After the outbreak of World War II and the German occupation of Paris, numerous artists, gallery owners, and critics emigrated to the United States. Despite the exodus, the Parisian artistic community sought to recover after the war with the founding of the Salon des Réalités Nouvelles in 1946, attracting both established and emerging artists. The Salon became a leading center for geometric abstraction. American artists, often funded by the governmental reintegration assistance for US soldiers, the GI Bill, continued to flock to Paris.[5] Artists Carmen Herrera (cat. 91) and Ellsworth Kelly (cat. 88), who later found success in the New York art scene of the 1960s, began their careers in 1950s Paris. The decades-long exchange between artists of different generations and nationalities in Paris fostered ongoing dialogues and occasional conflicts, but also encouraged artists to adopt elements from different styles. Their interactions—marked by collaboration, divergence, and personal development—transformed artistic expression, furthering artistic individuality.

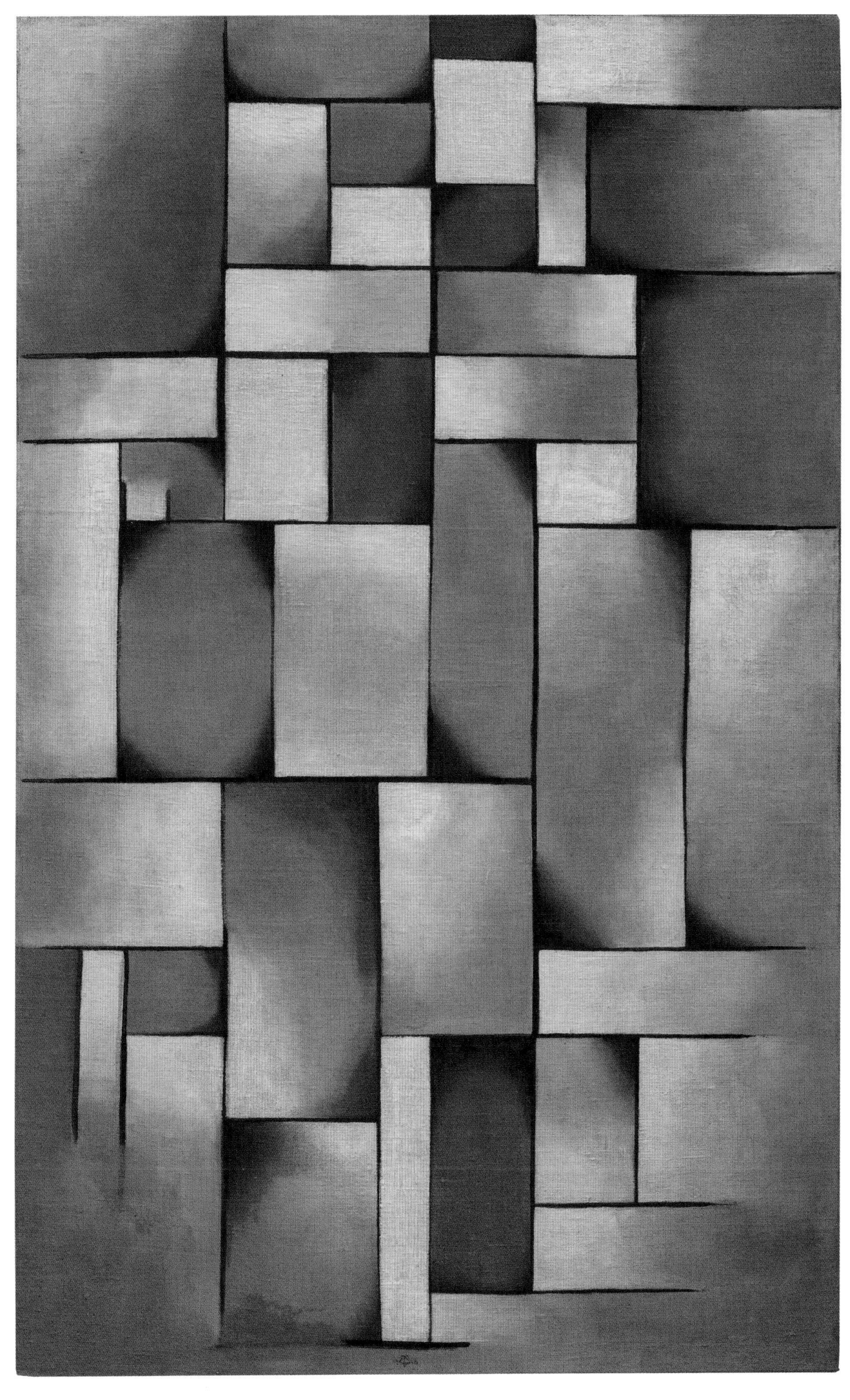

39 Theo van Doesburg
Composition in Gray (Rag-time), 1919
Peggy Guggenheim Collection, Venice

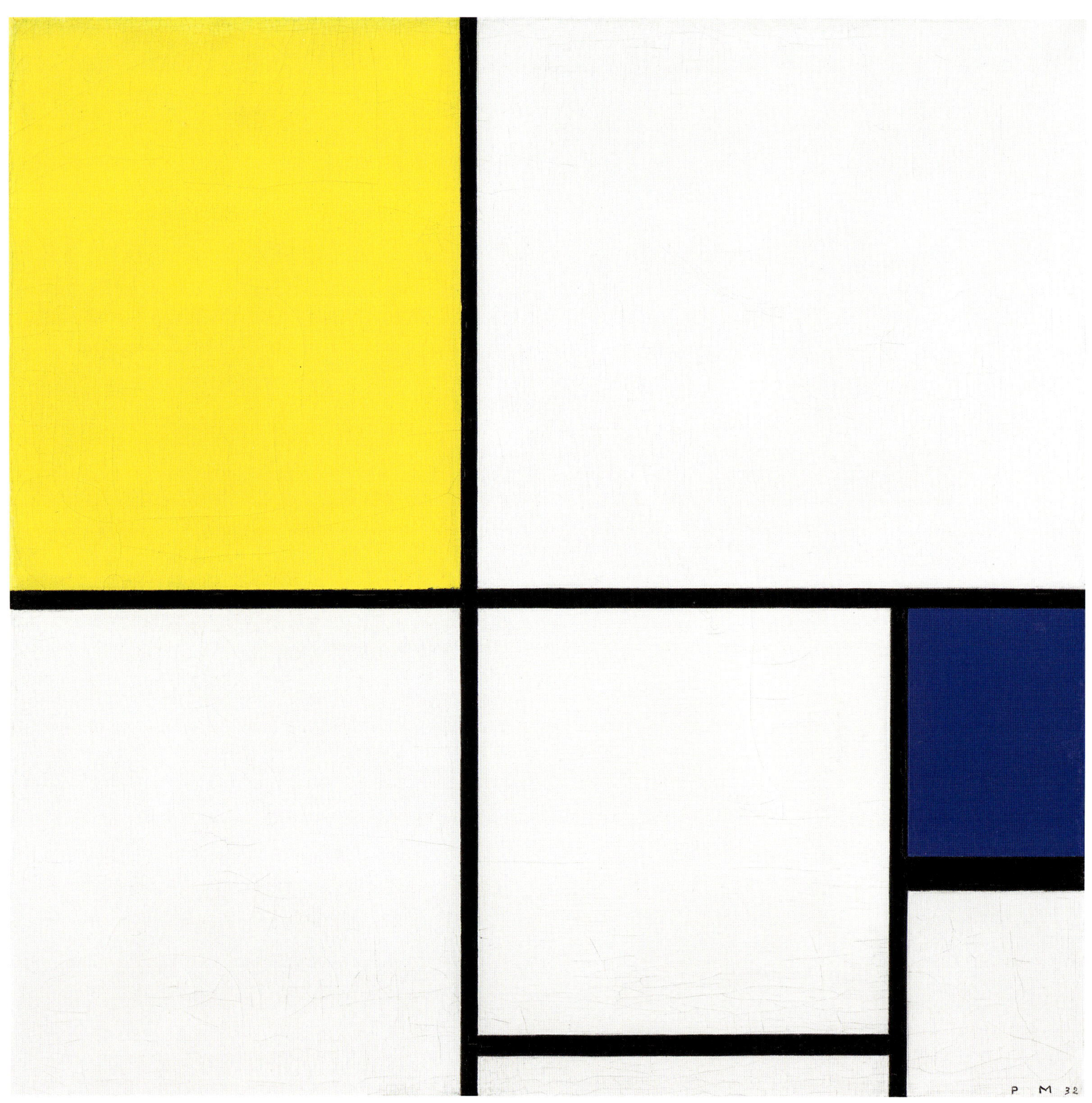

40 Piet Mondrian
Composition with Yellow and Blue, 1932
Fondation Beyeler, Riehen/Basel

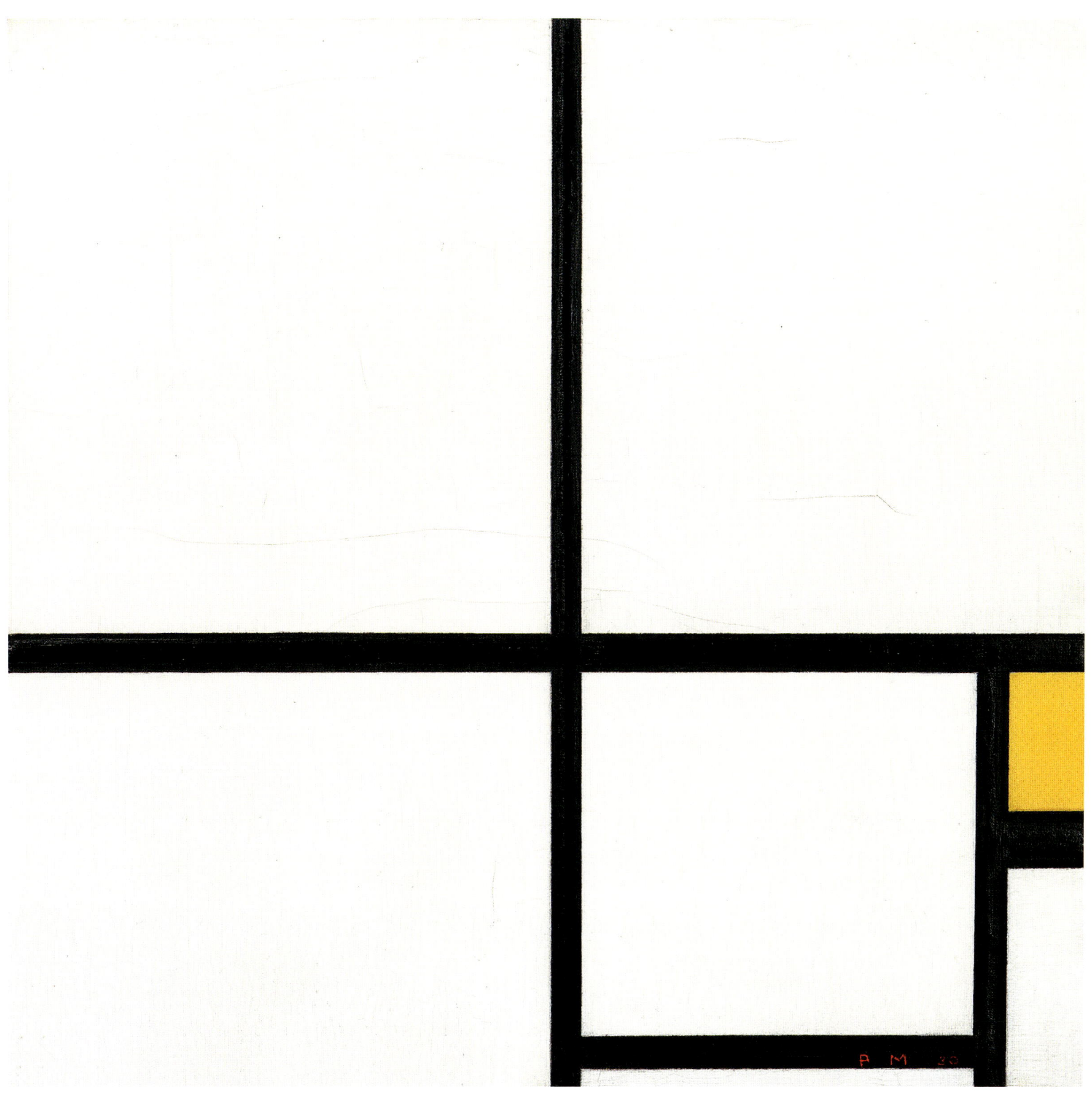

41 Piet Mondrian
Composition with Yellow, 1930
Kunstsammlung Nordrhein-Westfalen, Düsseldorf

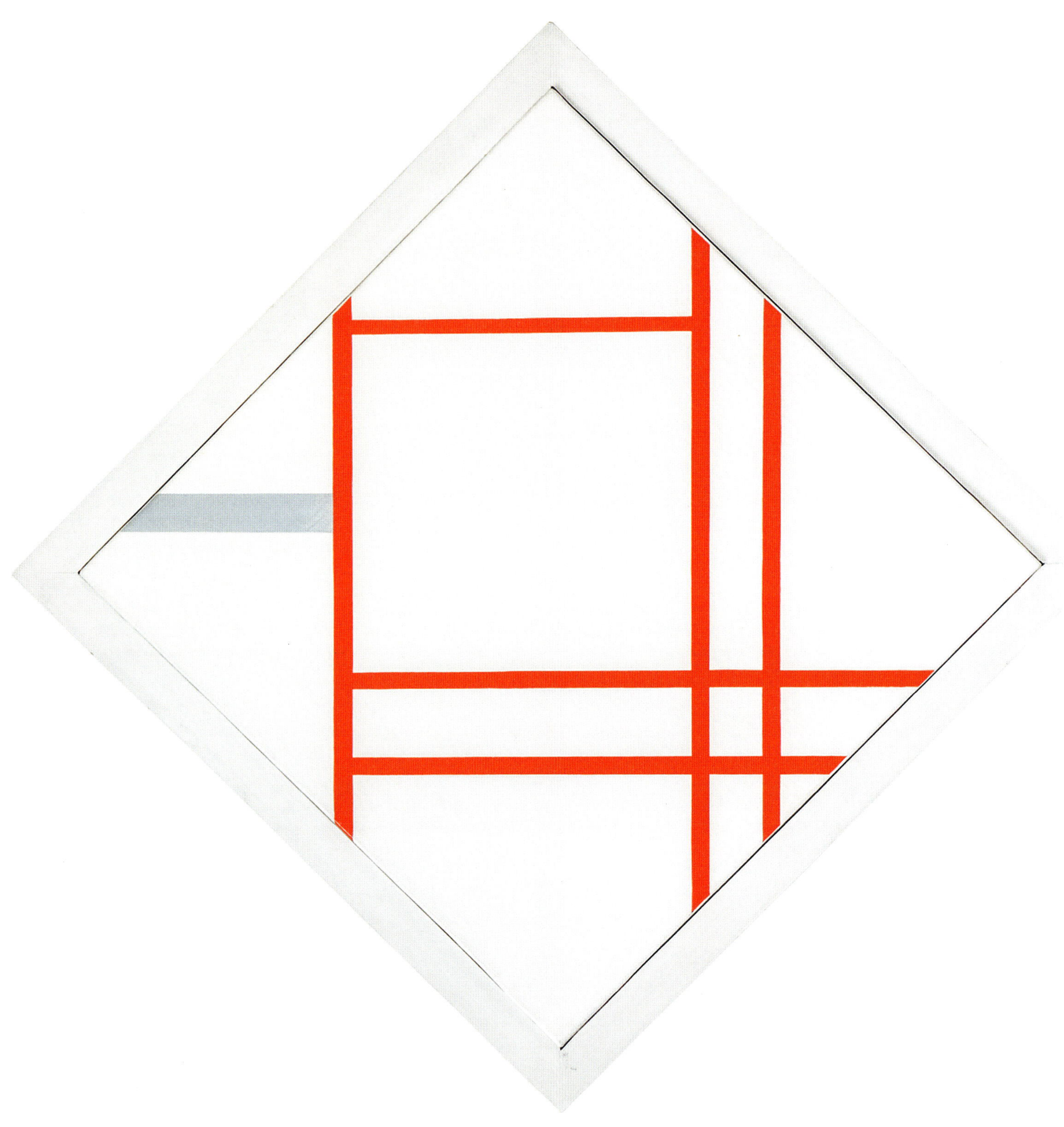

42 Marlow Moss
Composition in White, Red and Gray, 1935
Private collection, The Netherlands

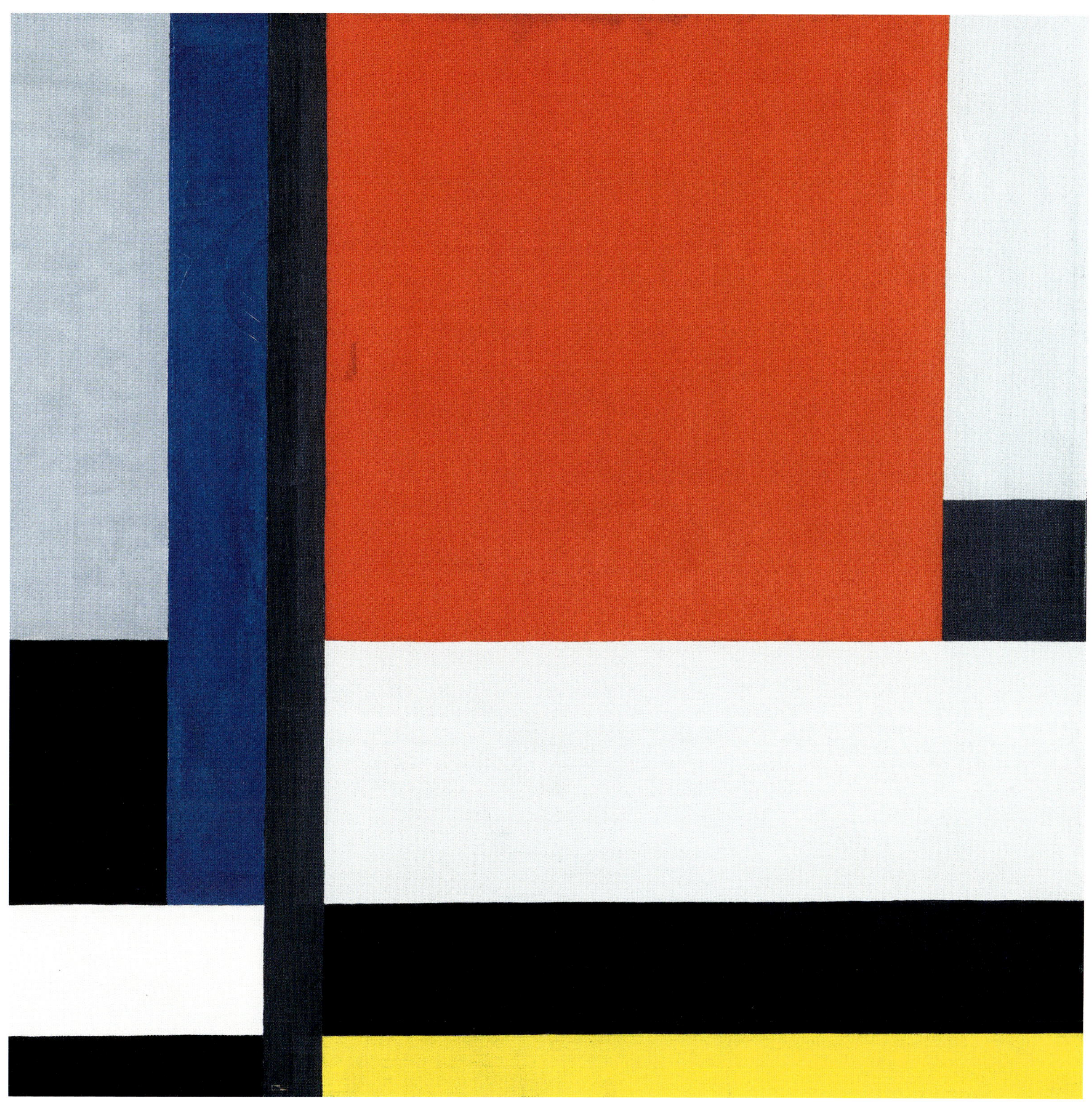

43 César Domela
Neoplastic Composition 5a, 1924
Triton Collection Foundation

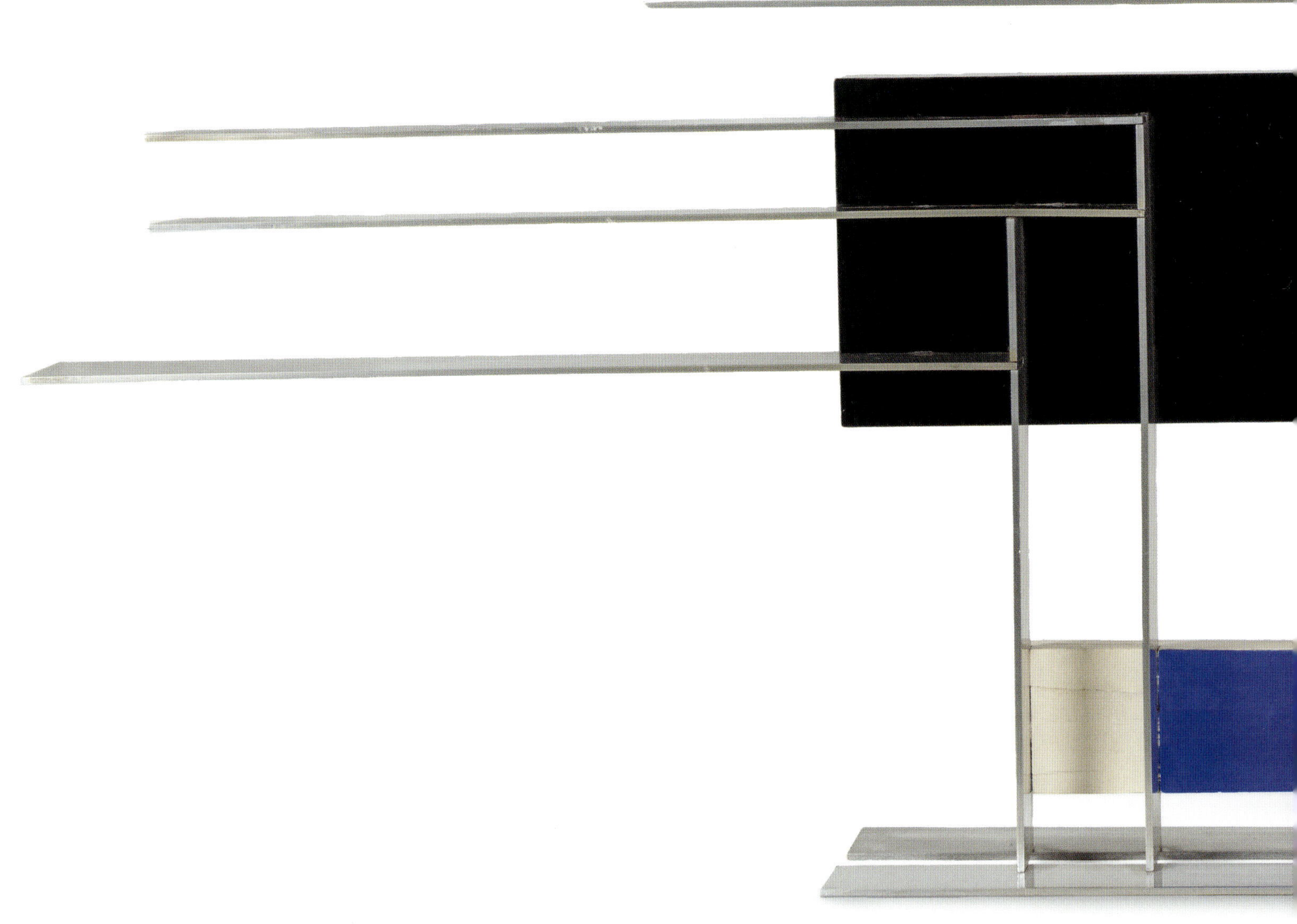

44 Marlow Moss
Relief, 1957
Kröller-Müller Museum, Otterlo

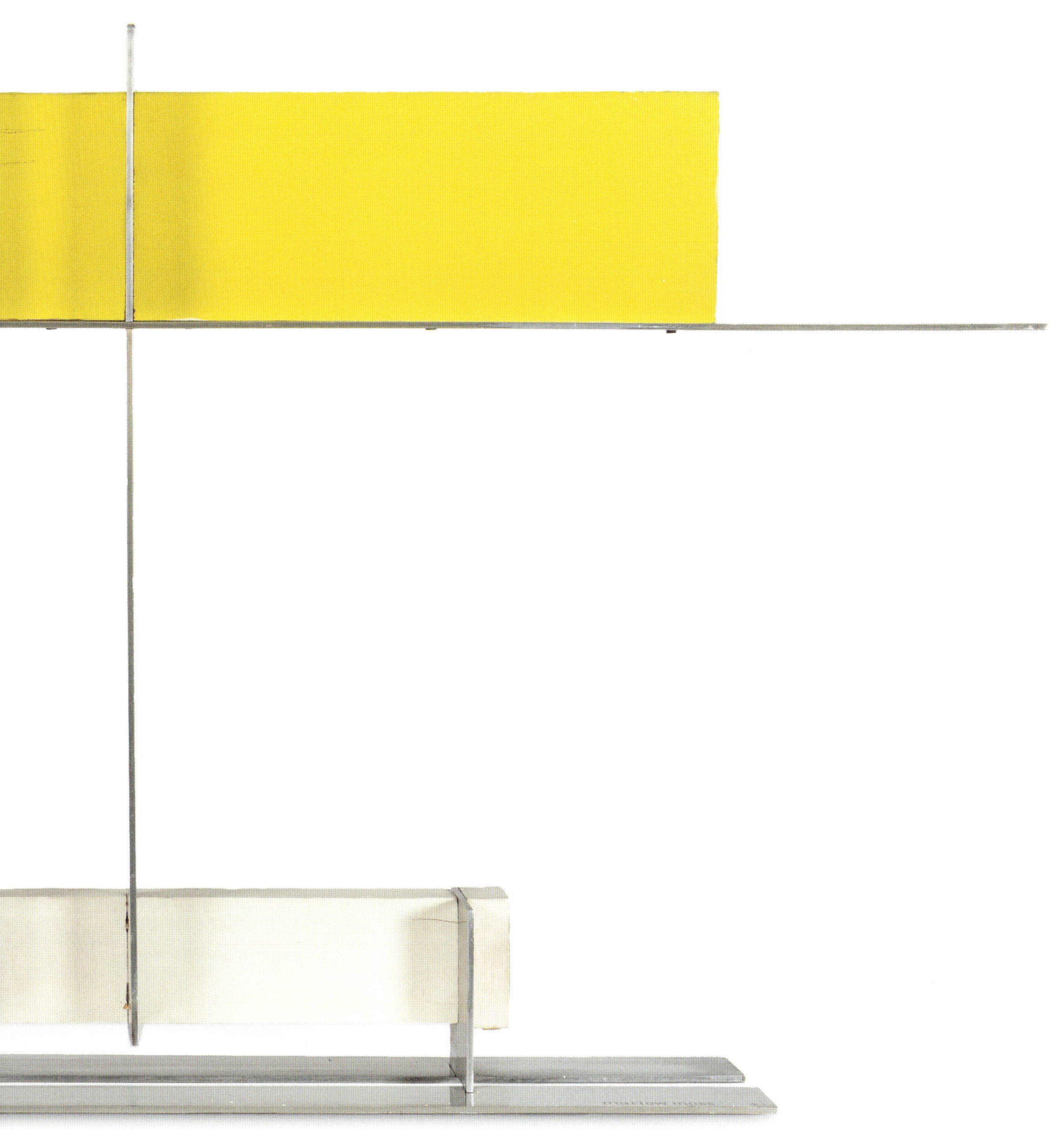

45 Jean Gorin
Spatio-Temporal Plastic Composition, 1962
Kröller-Müller Museum, Otterlo

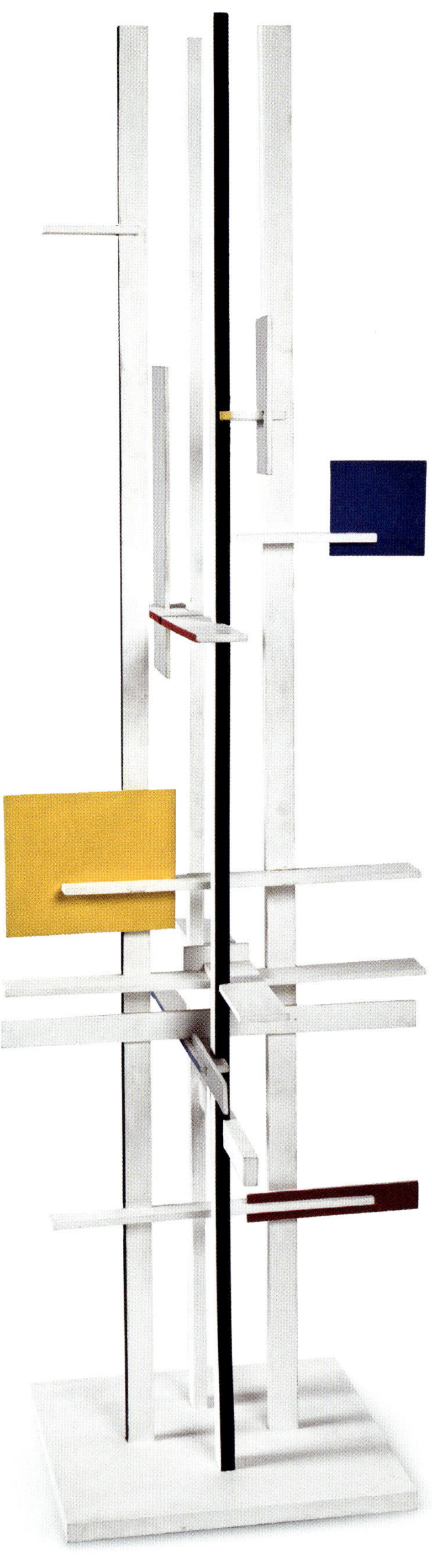

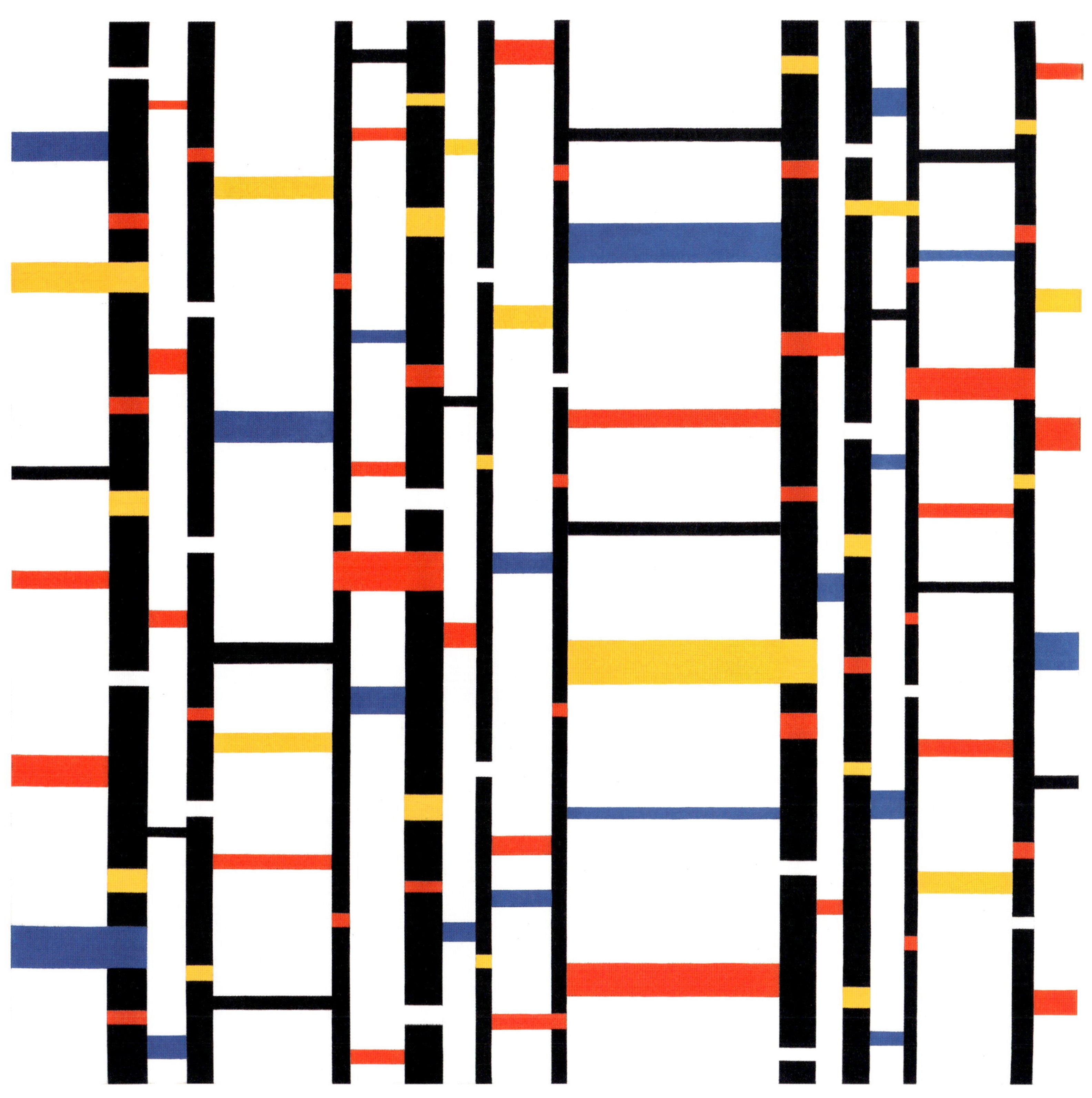

46 Burgoyne Diller
Third Theme, 1946–48
Whitney Museum of American Art, New York

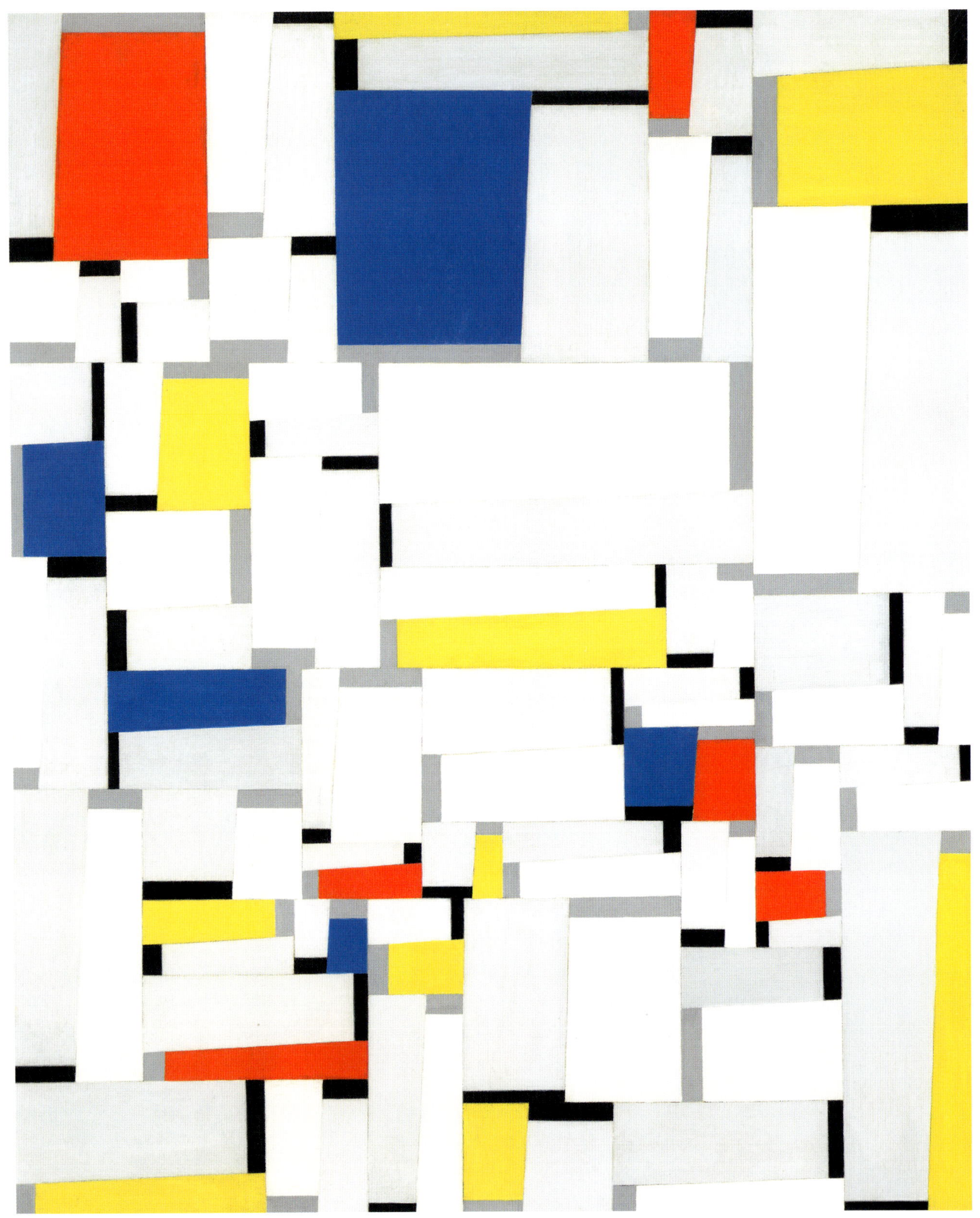

47 Fritz Glarner
Relational Painting, 1949–51
Whitney Museum of American Art, New York

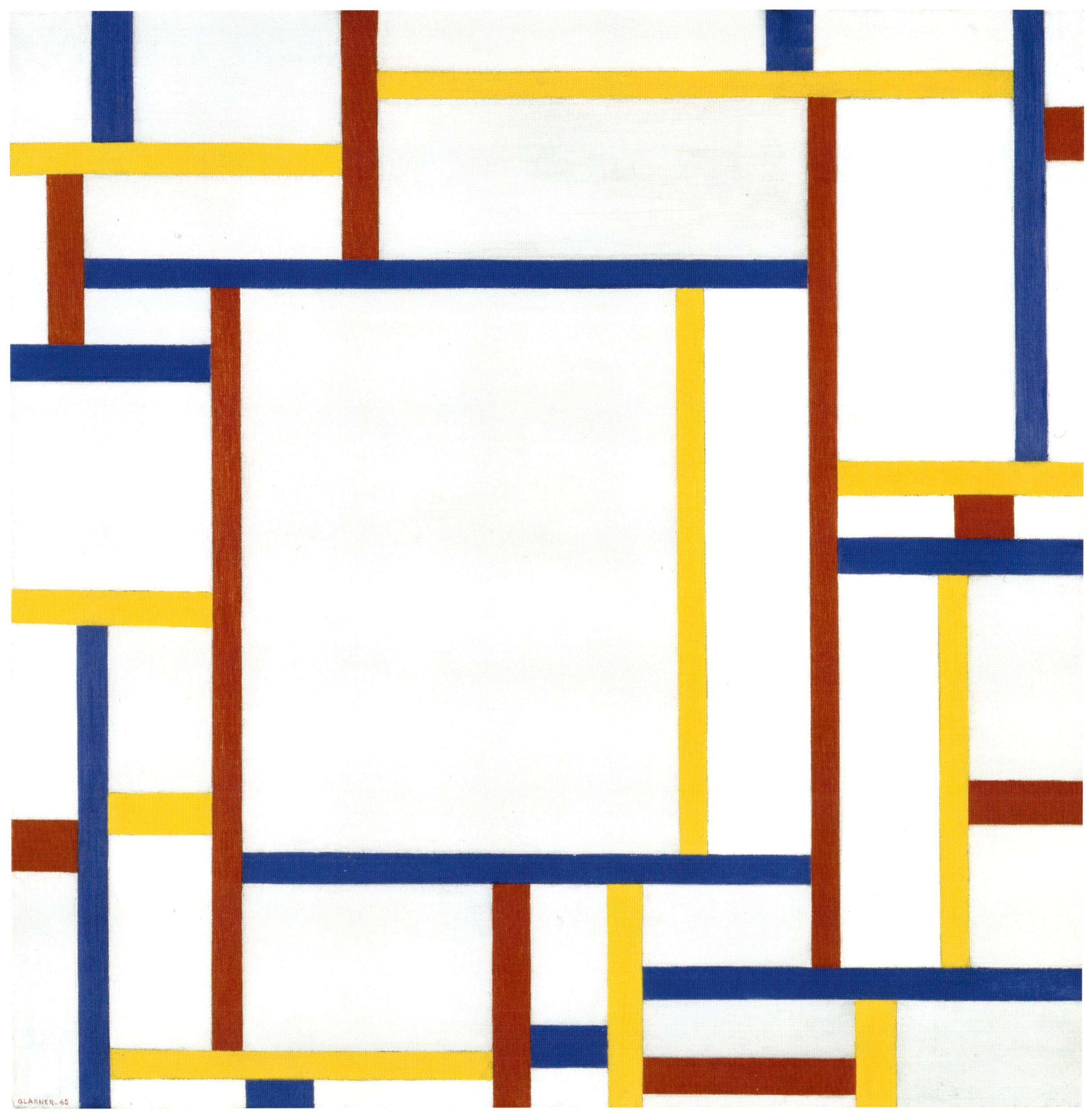

48 Fritz Glarner
Painting (white), 1945
Kunsthaus Zürich

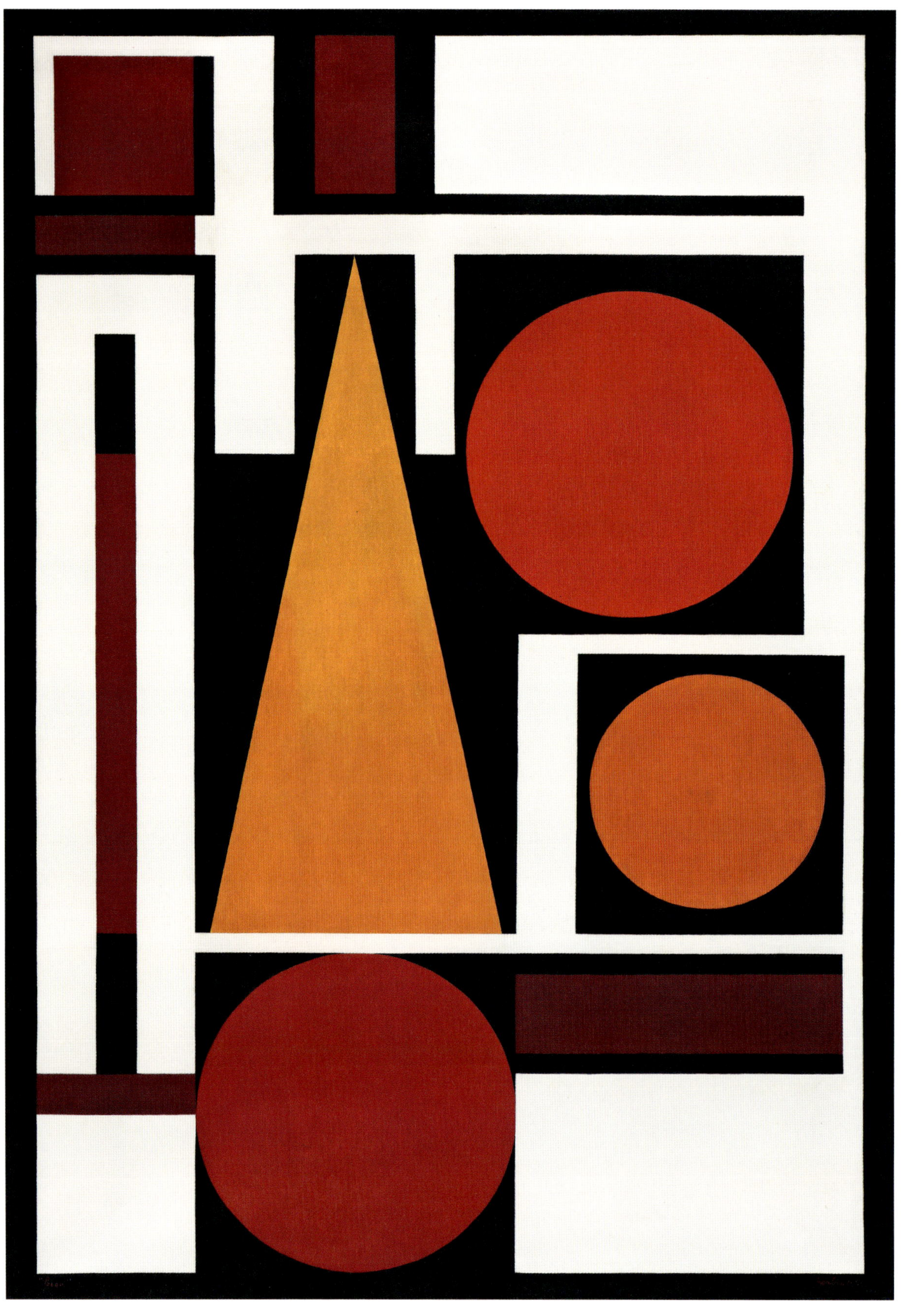

49 Auguste Herbin
Good, 1952
Fondation Gandur pour l'Art, Genève

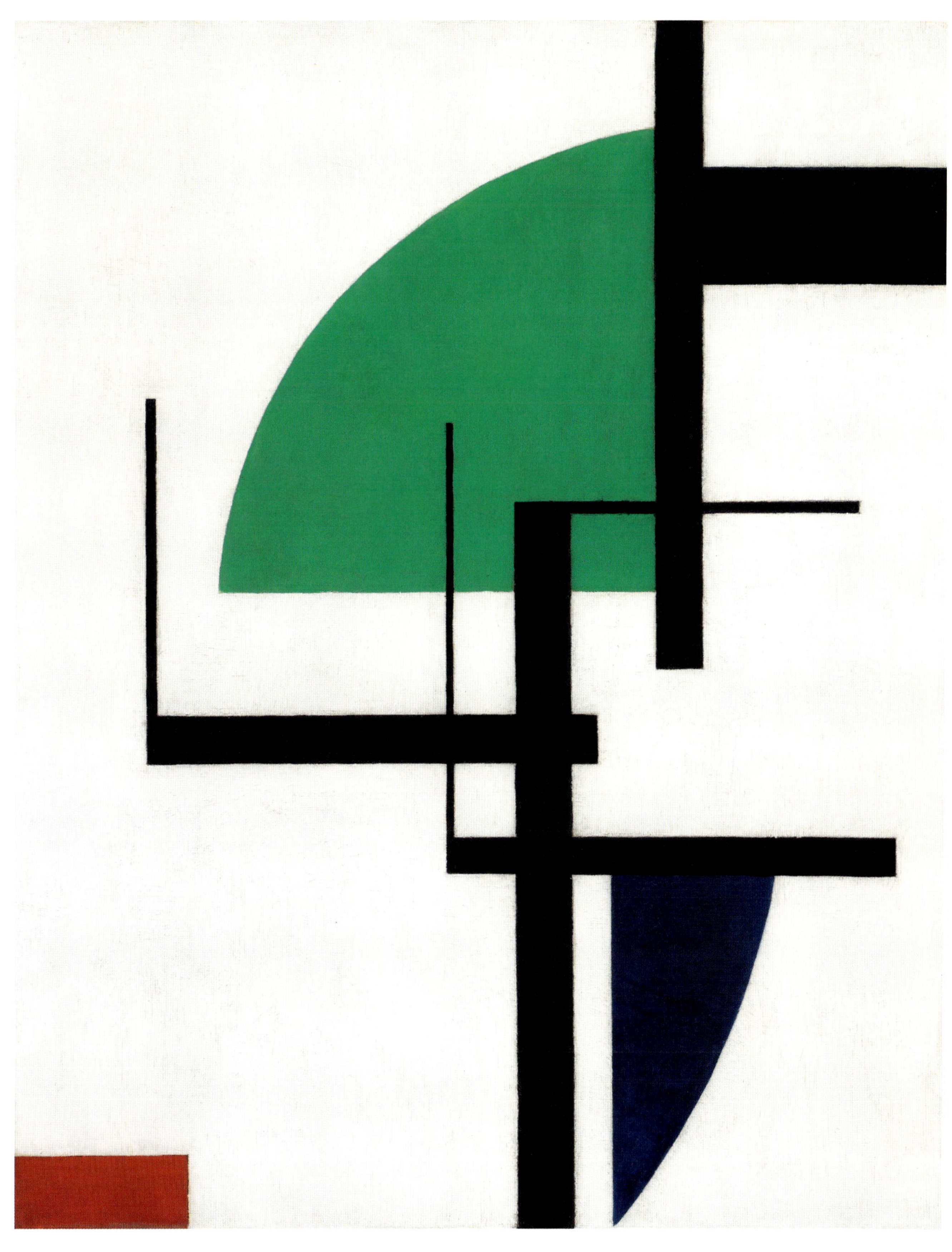

50 Jean Hélion
Abstract Composition, 1932
Fondation Gandur pour l'Art, Genève

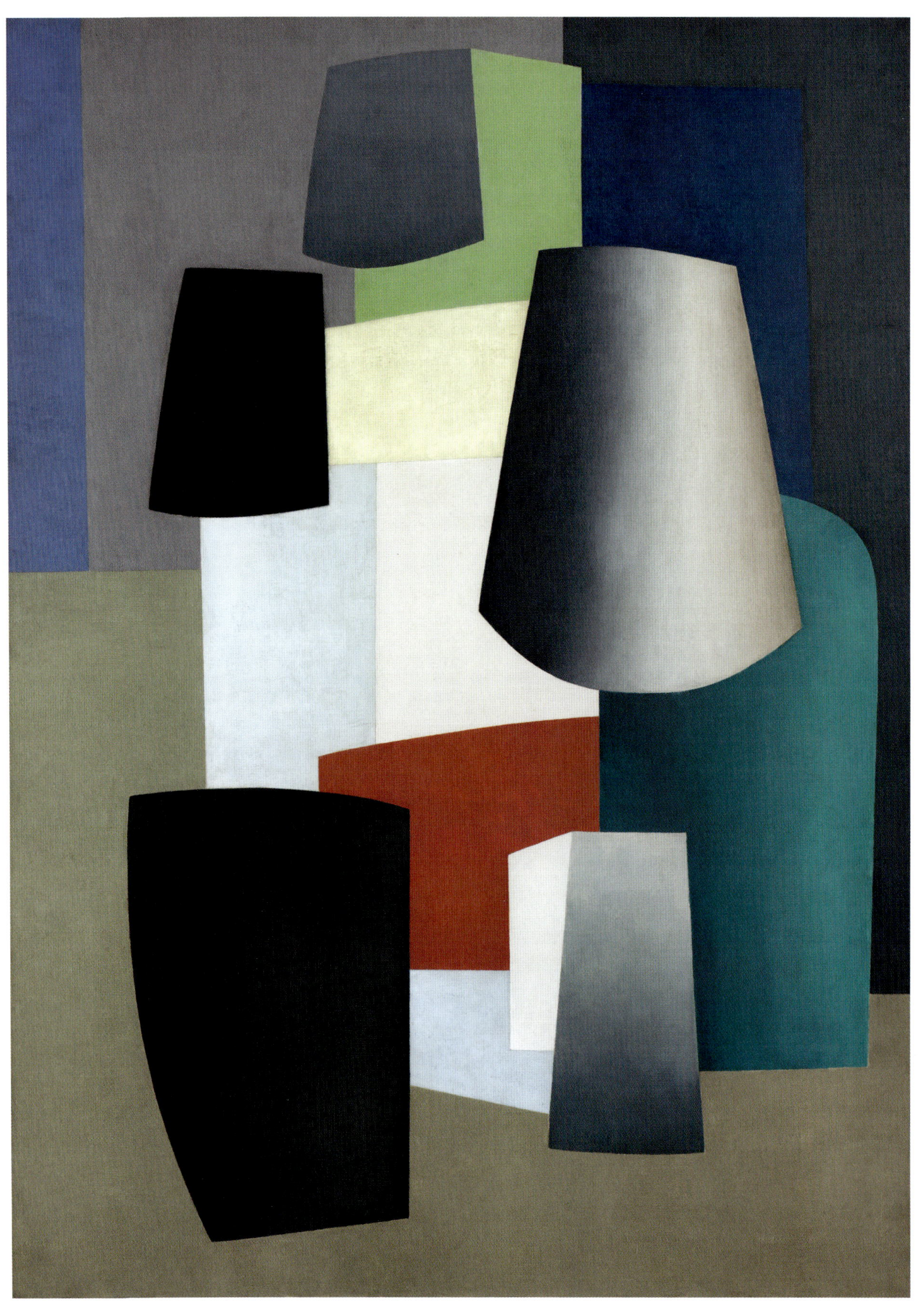

51 Jean Hélion
Untitled, 1935
Fondation Gandur pour l'Art, Genève

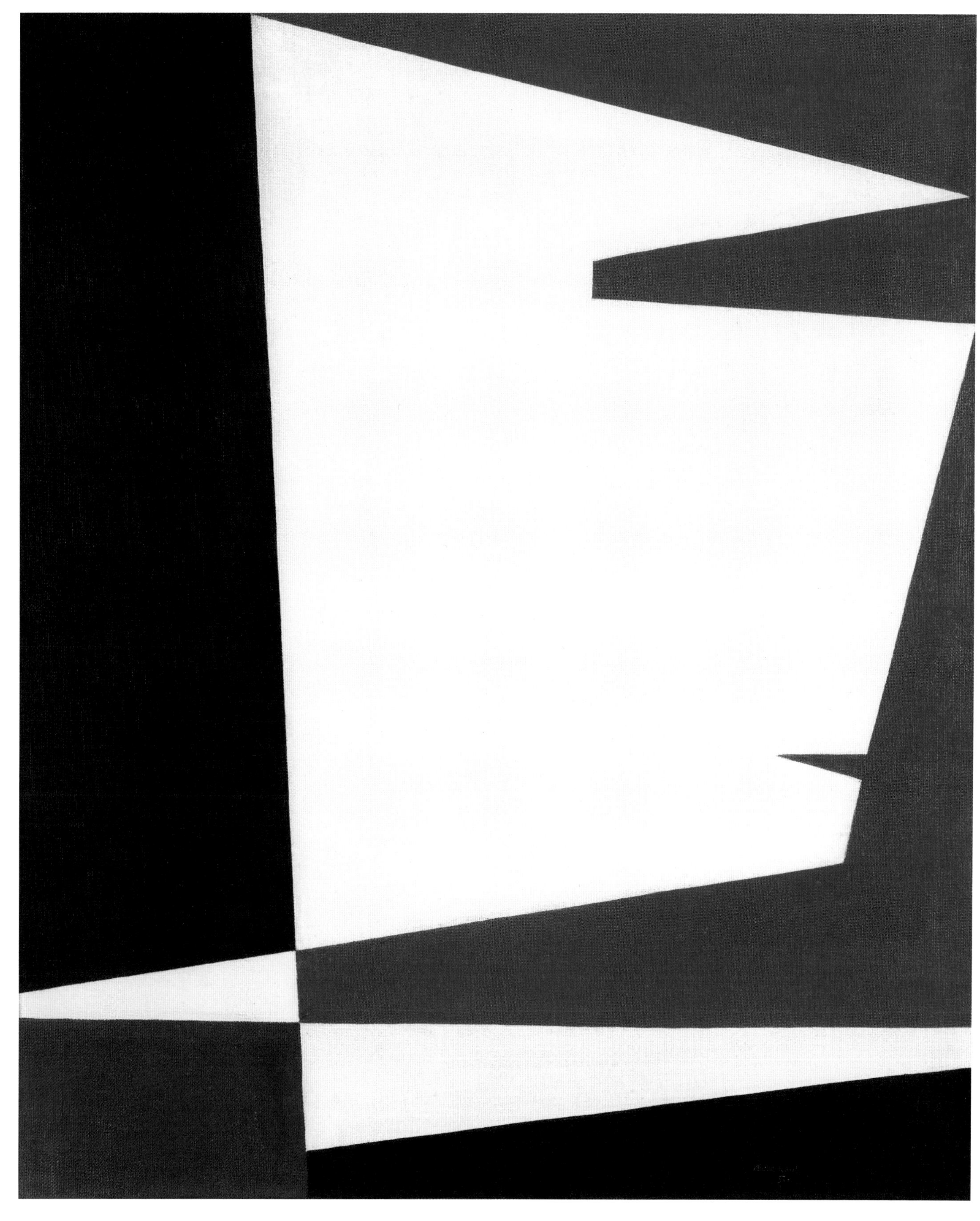

52 Jo Delahaut
Clostra, 1950
Fondation Gandur pour l'Art, Genève

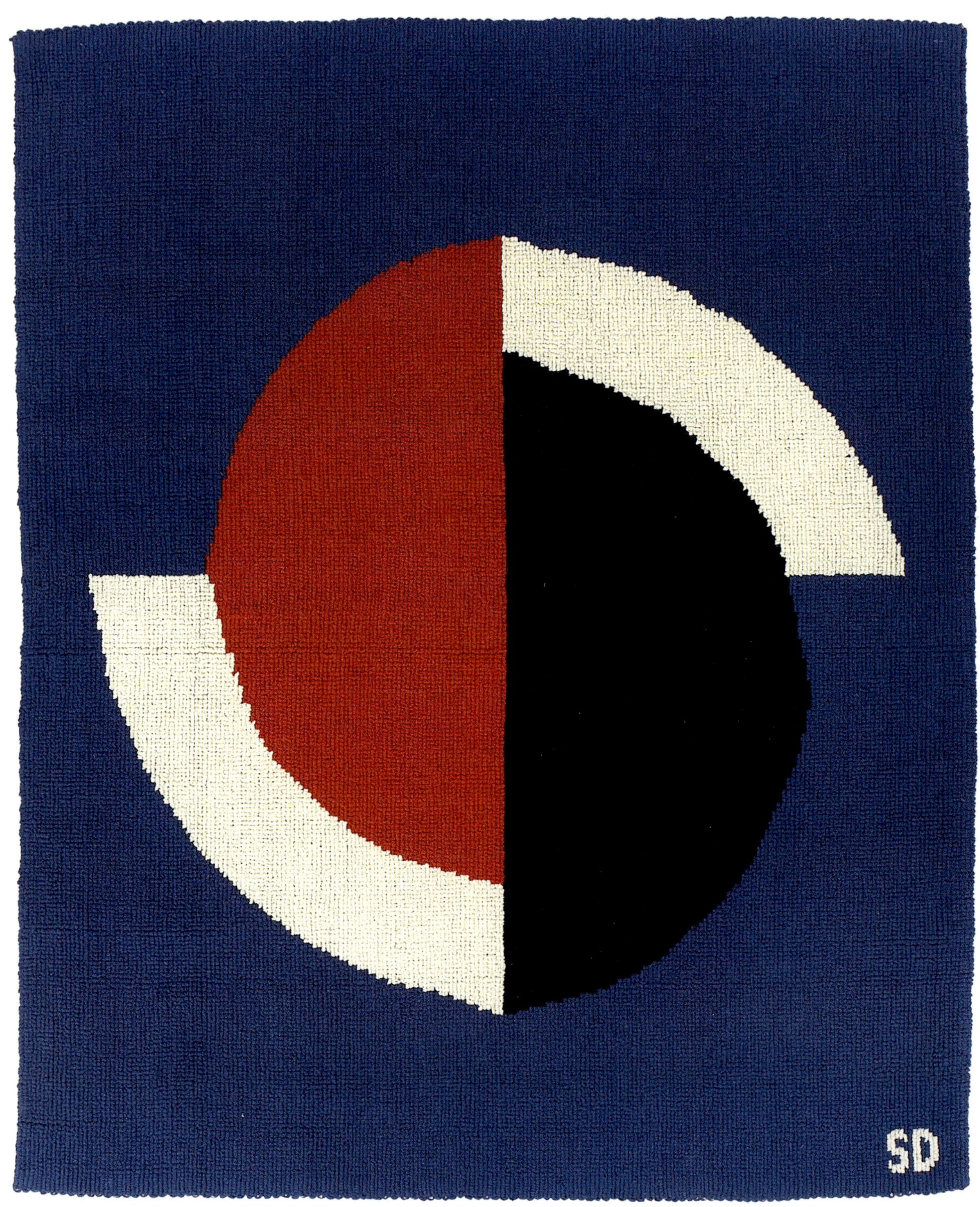

53 Sonia Delaunay
Bing, 1967
Sainsbury Centre, University of East Anglia

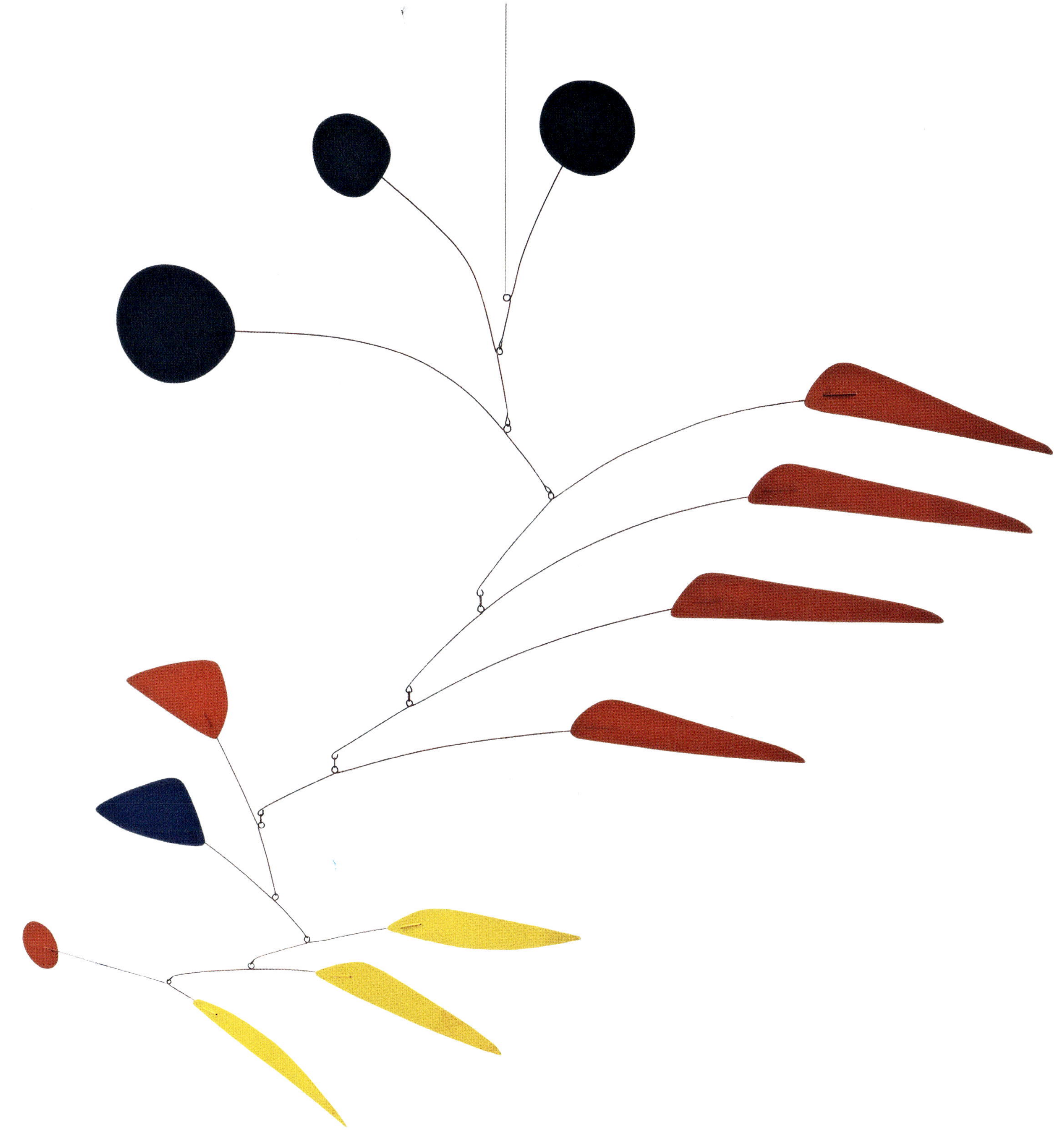

54 Alexander Calder
Untitled, 1963
Fondation Gandur pour l'Art, Genève

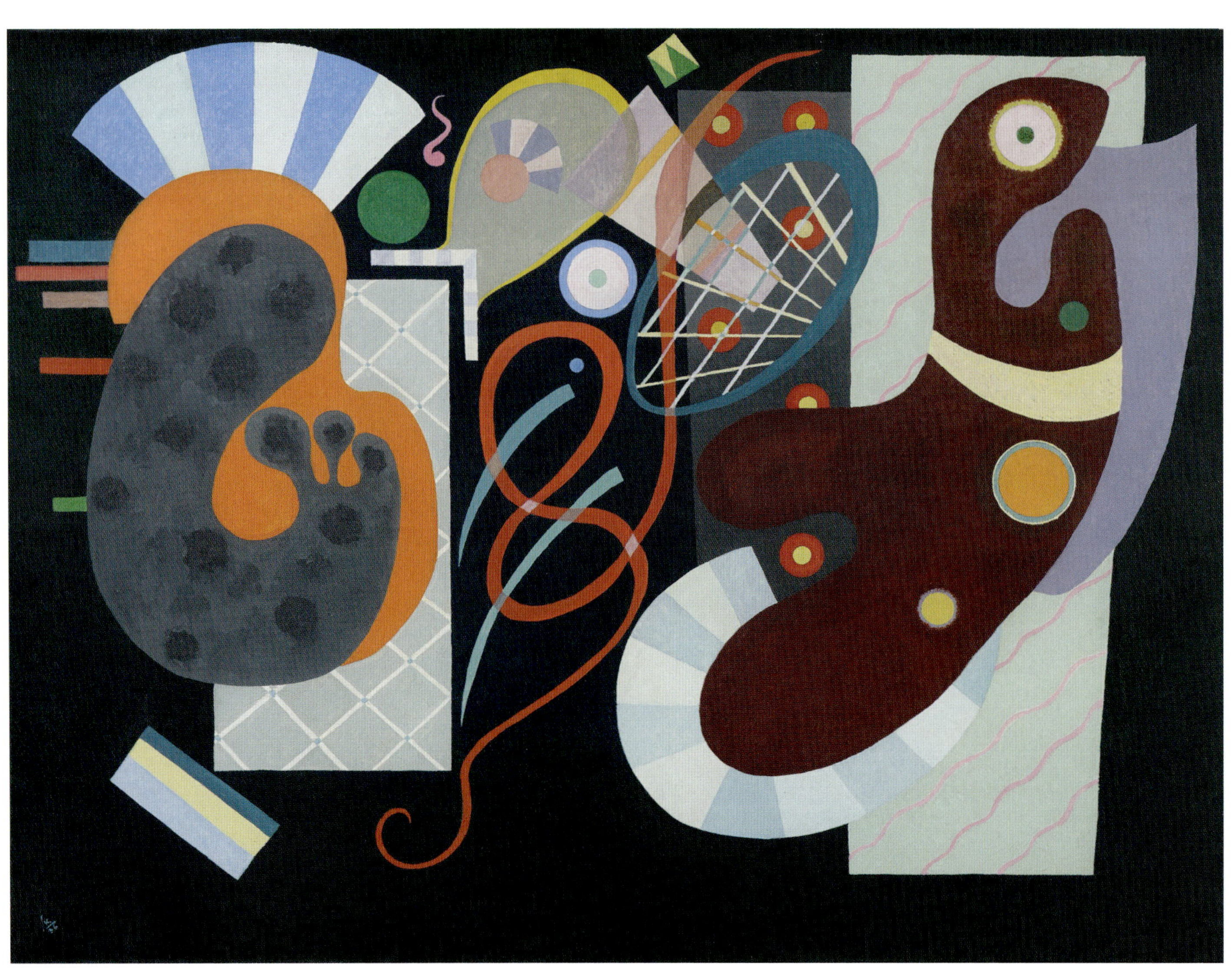

55 Wassily Kandinsky
Red Knot, 1936
Collection Fondation Marguerite et Aimé Maeght, Saint-Paul de Vence

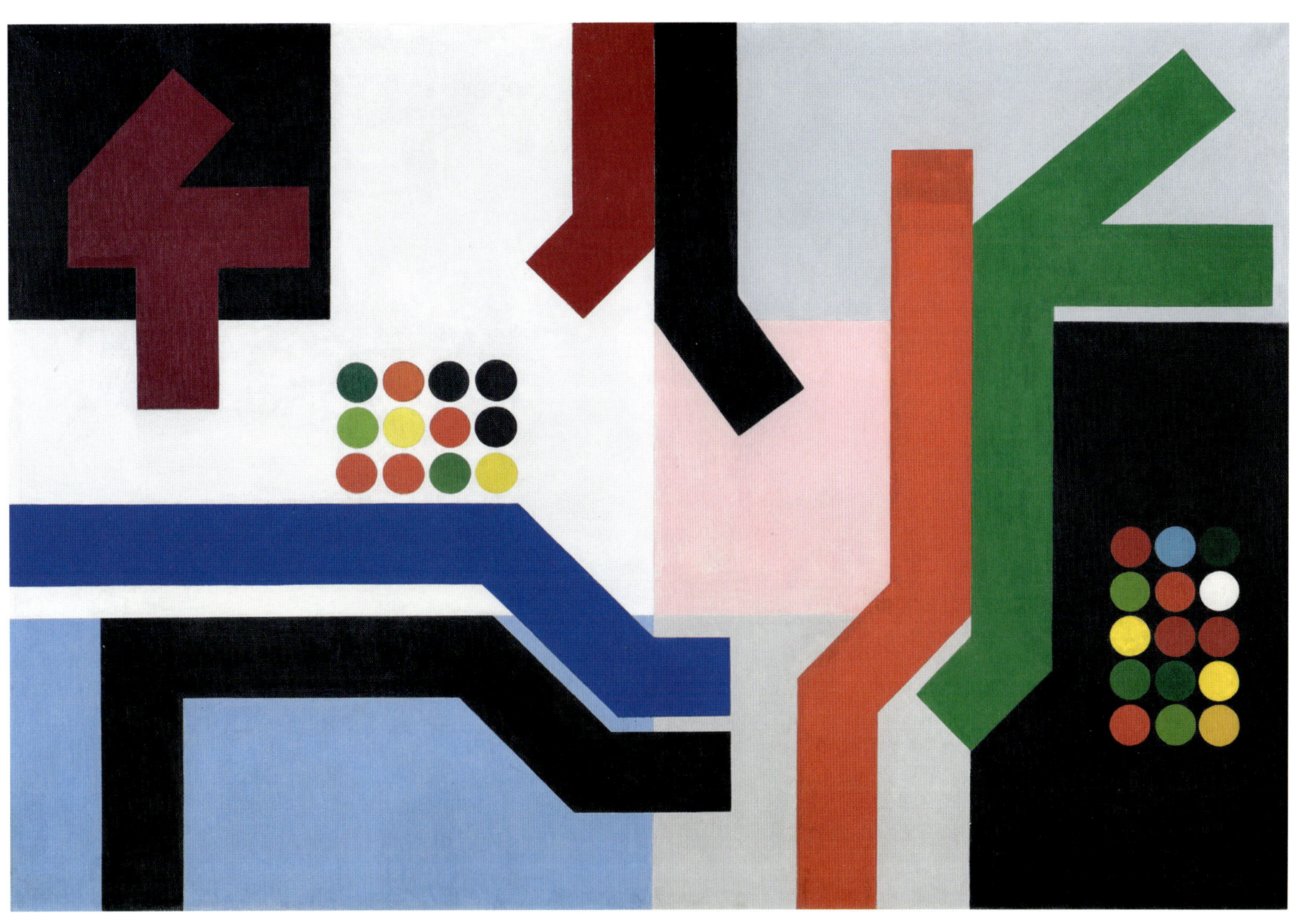

56 Sophie Taeuber-Arp
Twelve Spaces with Planes, Angular Bands, and Laid with Circles, 1939
Kunsthaus Zürich

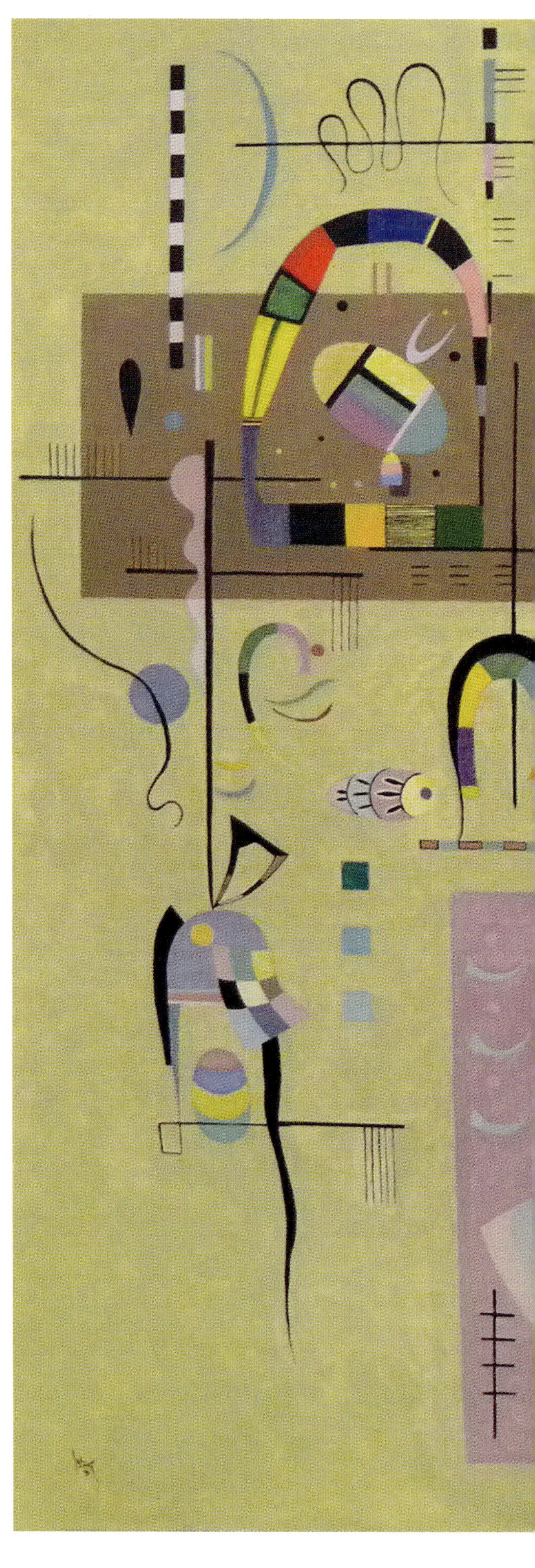

57 Wassily Kandinsky
Accompanied Center, 1937
Nahmad Collection

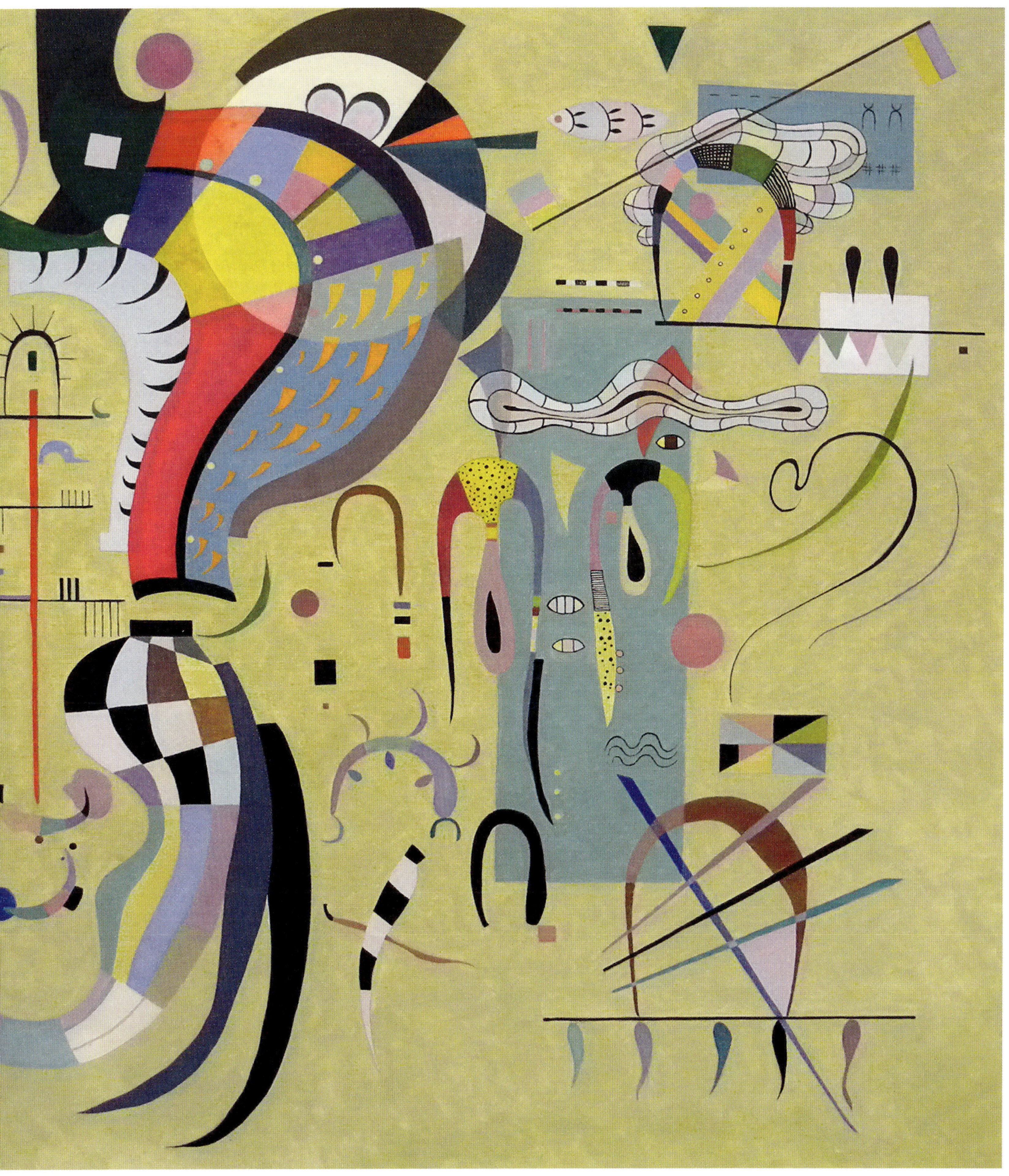

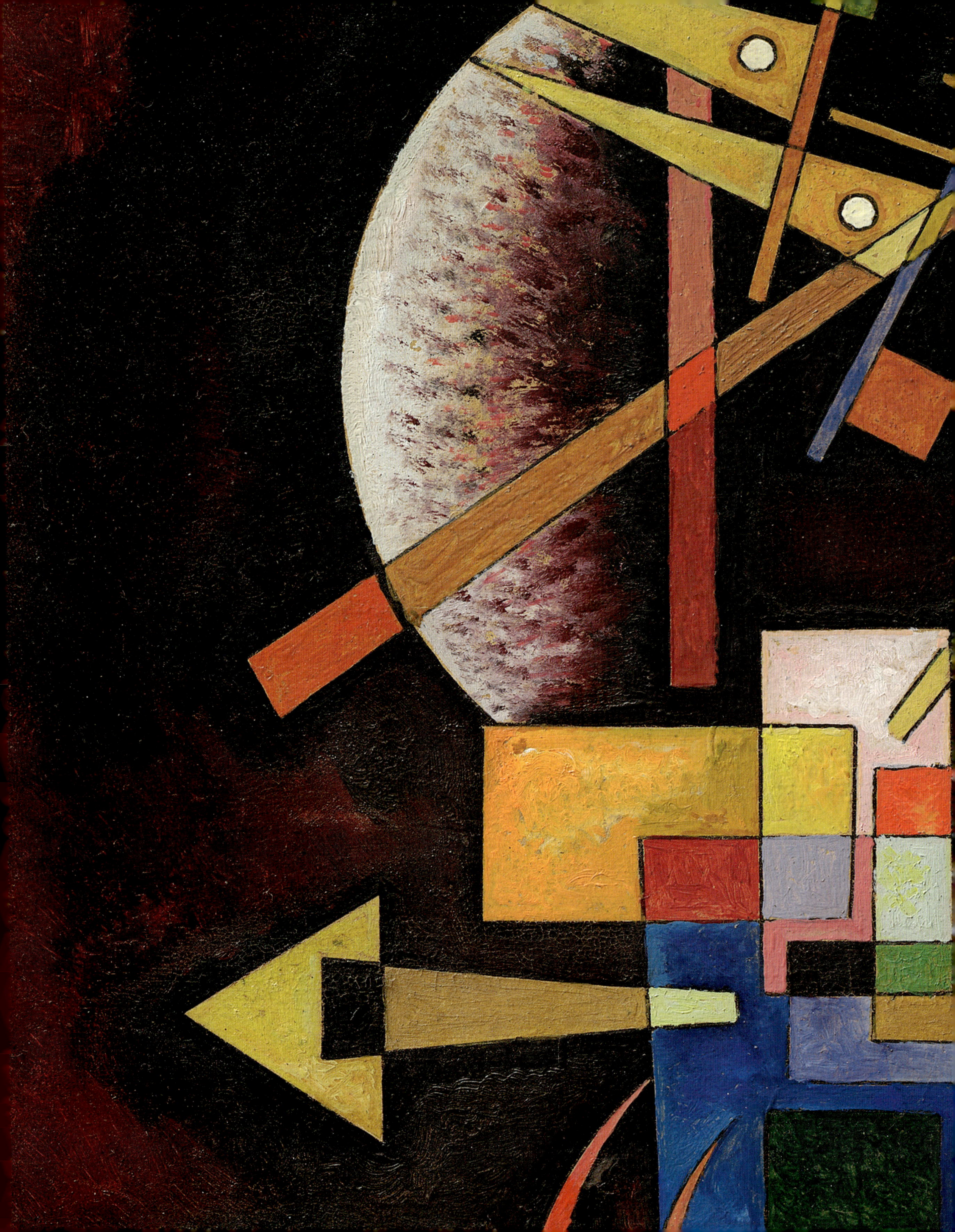

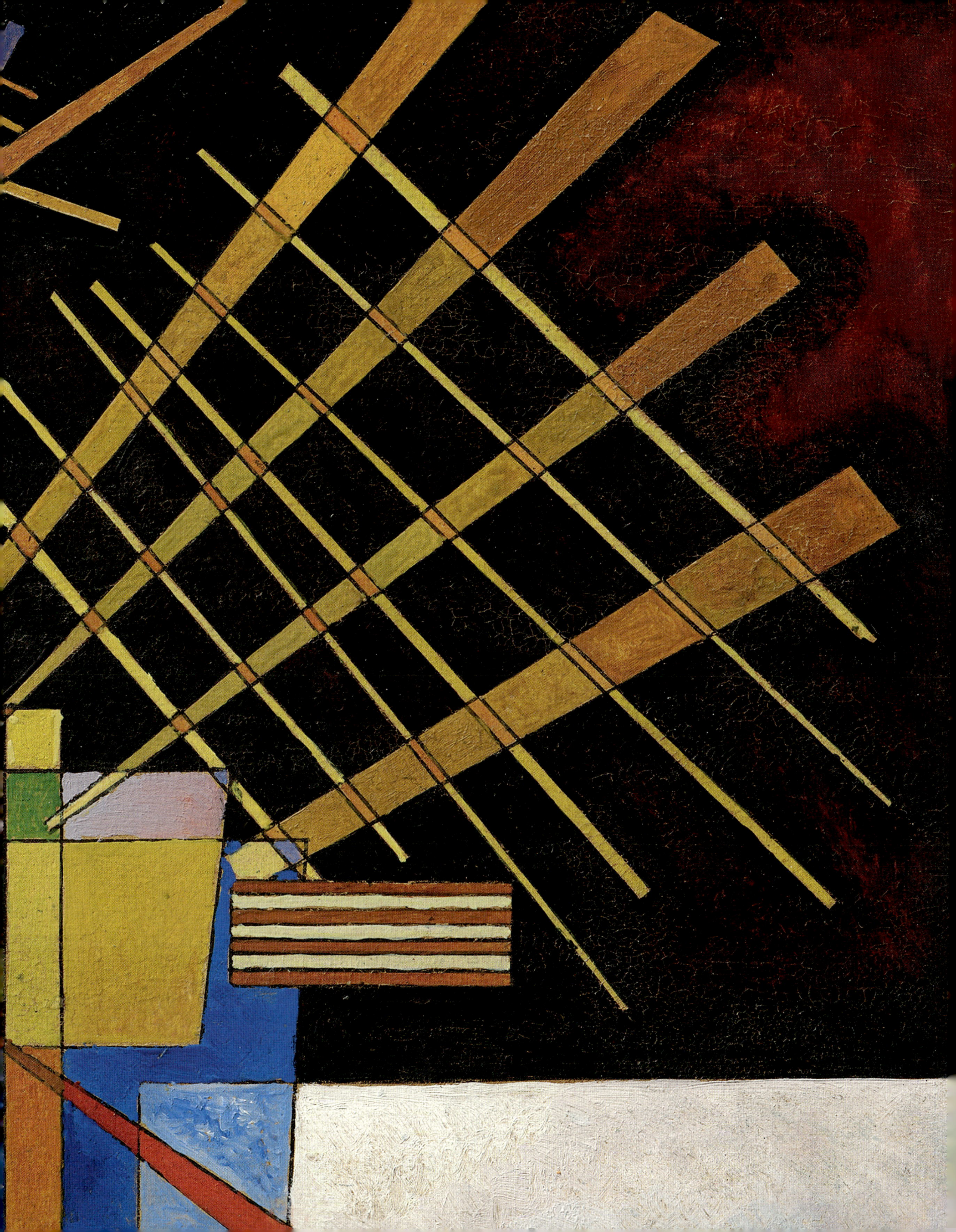

Altair Brandon-Salmon

Balanced Forces

Constructivist Utopias in British Art

In the face of impending war, many artists fled to Great Britain during the 1930s. London became a new center for geometric abstraction, providing refuge for artists such as Piet Mondrian, László Moholy-Nagy, and Naum Gabo before they moved to the United States. Barbara Hepworth and Ben Nicholson had already brought geometric abstraction into three dimensions through reliefs and sculptures.

After World War II, the Constructionist group was founded in London, drawing inspiration from the prewar Constructivists. These artists used newly developed synthetic materials such as plastic, acrylic, and fiberglass, combined with wood and aluminum. Their reliefs resemble industrial products from the 1950s, reflecting the optimistic drive for modernization that shaped postwar reconstruction.

A series of interlocking, off-white planes is balanced by two circles, one large, the other small. Ben Nicholson's *1934 (painted relief)* (fig. 1) is one of his first all-white reliefs. After visiting Piet Mondrian (cats. 40, 41) in his studio in Paris in April 1934, he embarked on a series of constructions, composed of different levels of board painted white in such a meticulous manner that the final object seems to have hardly been touched by human hands. With the elemental nature of the form and the purity of the color, they aspire to a universal image. Their design aims to transcend cultural specificities. Both sculpture and painting at once, this unity reflects the ambition of British abstract artists to create works that transcend distinctions between form and subject. As sculptor Barbara Hepworth (cats. 58, 79) declared in 1934, "The present moment is the only real time."[1] By casting off convention and any commitment to representation, a revolution in art was felt to be possible. The time was now.

British abstract artists, despite their differences, were anchored by a conviction that art should function as an autonomous object in space, resulting in work that was, to quote postwar critic Lawrence Alloway, "complete in itself."[2] This desire for unity in the artwork arose at a moment of political change in Britain. Between the 1930s and the 1960s, the country faced the Great Depression, World War II, the end of the British Empire, and a political turn toward social democracy. During these convulsions, abstract art promised to be a progressive force that could transform society. The postwar generation of Constructionists, such as Anthony Hill (cats. 65, 73), Kenneth Martin (cats. 67, 68), and Mary Martin (cats. 63, 64, 70–72, 74), experimented with industrial materials, while lionizing the Constructivists and De Stijl from the prewar avant-garde.

Abstract art was at the center of the avant-garde in London during the 1930s. Hepworth and Nicholson (cats. 59–62) were at work in Hampstead, where they were joined by Mondrian. They had visited Pablo Picasso in Paris in April 1933, while the *Abstract and Concrete* exhibition (→ p. 271), which toured Oxford, Liverpool, London, and Cambridge in 1936, featured the pair of them alongside Alexander Calder (cat. 54), Wassily Kandinsky, and László Moholy-Nagy (cat. 19).[3] Mondrian's late painting *Trafalgar Square* from 1939/1943 (fig. p. 48), painted in London and significantly reworked in New York, hints at the cosmopolitan networks running through Britain in the 1930s, which shaped a particularly geometric approach to abstraction. Like many European artists such as Marcel Breuer, Naum Gabo (cat. 20), and Walter Gropius, Mondrian fled from Nazi threat, arriving in London in 1938. The air raids on London in 1940 dispersed many of the émigrés to the United States, while Nicholson, Hepworth, and Gabo retreated to Cornwall in the far southwest of England and established an artist colony at St. Ives.

1
Ben Nicholson,
1934 (painted relief), 1934,
University of Hertfordshire
Art Collection
(Cat. 60)

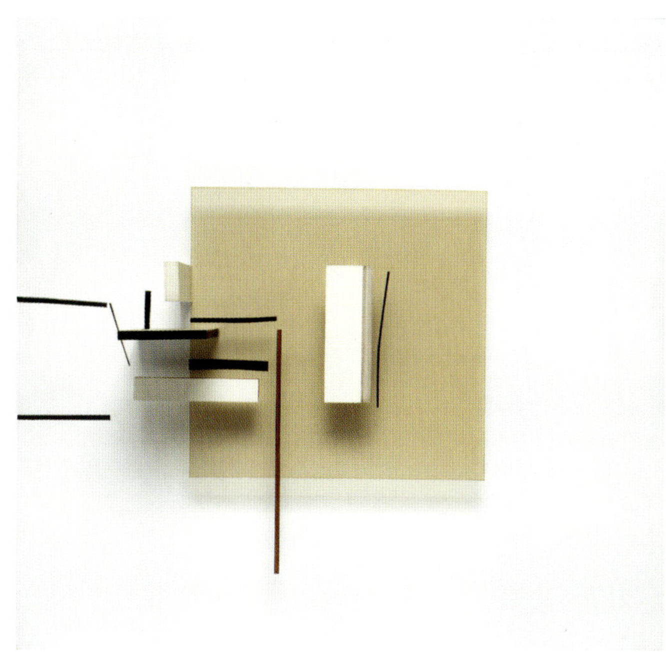

2
Victor Pasmore,
Synthetic Construction (White and Black), 1965–66,
Tate

London in the 1950s, after war and austerity, had been cut off from the main strands of abstract art in Europe and America during the preceding decade. Few abstract works were on show, and reproductions were confined to black-and-white illustrations in modernist books from the 1930s. A Mondrian from 1927 that was shown at the Royal Academy in 1951 created an enormous excitement among younger artists. A new generation of artists briefly coalesced around a series of exhibitions, beginning with *Nine Abstract Artists: Their Work and Theory* at the Redfern Gallery in 1955. Its catalog, authored by Alloway, was the first major postwar publication on abstract art. The artists called themselves the Constructionists, a term coined by influential American artist and theorist Charles Biederman, in reference to prewar Constructivism and an attempt to reawaken Britain's connection to the modern movement.[4] Their work was harder-edged and more industrial than Cornish abstraction, which was given to biomorphic forms and references to the landscape.

At *Nine Abstract Artists,* Kenneth Martin showed *Mobile Reflector* from 1953 (cat. 67), made of aluminum painted red, yellow, and white. Martin had built his first mobile in 1951, under the influence of the older artist Victor Pasmore (cat. 66), who had transitioned from representational painting to abstract art in the late 1940s. Martin's mobiles were not Surrealist jeux d'esprit in the style of Alexander Calder, but an interplay of binary qualities: "Heavy and light, solid and plane," as Alloway noted.[5] The white arrows appear as vectors of motion, the assemblage moving on several axes simultaneously, while the heart-shaped red and yellow flats of metal act as signals of emotion. This is a "hot" sculpture, not cold, a machine operating according to airflows and physics, the movement of the audience registering in how it twists and turns. It seems appropriate that mobiles were sites of experimentation in the early 1950s, as the jet age dawned, and human flight was seen simultaneously as a harbinger of technological progress and of terrifying destruction. Martin's mobiles were meant to activate space—to make the audience conscious of it—and to fulfill Hepworth's dictum for art to continually exist in the present.

The defiantly open constructions of Pasmore (fig. 2), usually in metal, wood, and plastic, were intended to create a new relationship between viewer and object. Roger Hilton, one of the Constructionists, said that "ideally [art] should be a kind of anonymous presence" when confronting the viewer.[6] This was no mere formalist ambition. The Constructionists, self-consciously emulating the Russian and Eastern European avant-garde of the 1910s and 1920s, sought to create a modern world in which painting, sculpture, and architecture would be unified

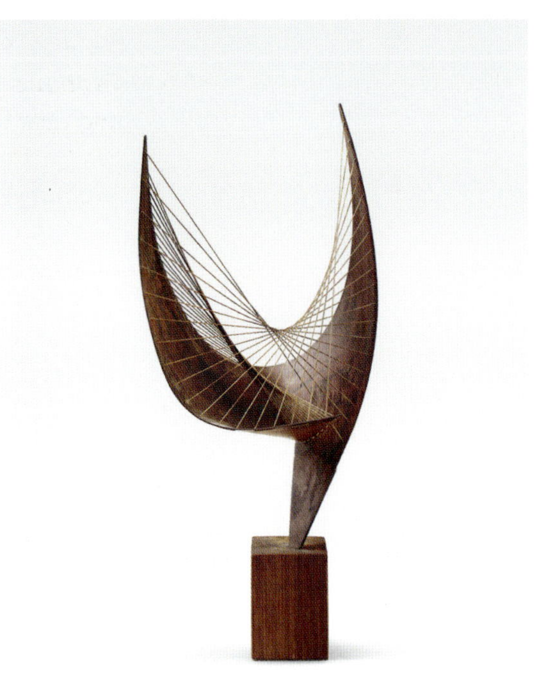

3
Barbara Hepworth,
Orpheus (Maquette I), 1956,
Pier Arts Centre, Stromness, Orkney
(Cat. 79)

and in so doing, produce a radical new politics. This bore fruit in the public art Pasmore created for the Festival of Britain in 1951 and his later architectural designs for Peterlee New Town (1955–77) in County Durham.[7] It has been argued that culturally and politically, the 1950s in Britain was felt to be a "clear field," where revolutionary change was possible after the election of a Labour government in 1945 brought sweeping nationalization of industries—politically committed art, for the Constructionists, meant art that moved away from the Neoromanticism that celebrated British culture, and toward the universal language of abstraction.[8] Science fiction and revolutionary politics seemed to go hand in hand. No wonder John Ernest and Anthony Hill worked on the landmark exhibition *This Is Tomorrow* (→ p. 275) at the Whitechapel Art Gallery in 1956; Robby the Robot from the sci-fi movie *Forbidden Planet* made an appearance at the opening, and Pop artist Richard Hamilton showcased a monumental painting of the iconic robot at the exhibition. If the Constructionists' dreams of transforming art did not survive contact with the cultural convulsions of the 1960s, when "pop" (in art, music, and film) became the chief agent of change, the work they created still embodies a hope for a new kind of society.

This desire for the universal, expressed in a world that was divided into West and East, capitalist and communist, comes full circle with Barbara Hepworth's *Orpheus (Maquette I)* from 1956 (fig. 3). Hepworth, formed in the febrile atmosphere of the 1930s, is the intergenerational link with the Constructionists of the 1950s. Instead of working in marble or wood, she used bronze, cold rolled, to create an open form, its wings bound by strings in a complex geometric pattern. It shows Hepworth experimenting with new processes, using flat sheets of metal to shape and enfold space. This approach marked a departure from traditional carving methods, aligning her work with Naum Gabo's *Linear Constructions in Space* (fig. 4), a series he developed in the early 1940s, while he, Hepworth, and Nicholson were in Cornwall.

Orpheus (Maquette I) is one of a series of related works generated in response to a commission from Mullard Ltd, a manufacturer of electronic components, for their head office at Torrington Place in Bloomsbury, London. That led to *Theme on Electronics (Orpheus)* from 1956 (private collection), which was made of brass and had a rotating, motorized base. Hepworth's tactics are reminiscent of the Futurists and Kenneth Martin's interest in mobiles, but unlike the Constructionists, Hepworth liked to balance between abstraction and something more suggestive. In classical Greek mythology, Orpheus could charm all living creatures with his lyre. A parallel can be drawn between the sculpture's bands of strings and the lyre. Yet Orpheus also descended into the underworld to rescue his wife, Eurydice: this story of death and rebirth perhaps resonated with Hepworth. She went on a cruise of Greek islands in August 1954 after the death of her son, Paul, in 1953, and began naming her sculptures after ancient Greek characters and sites.

As an ode to electronics, the sculpture seems to vibrate with life. Indeed, the curving ellipses are powerfully suggestive of movement, soaring from the wooden base. Hepworth could have been thinking of the possibility of conquering space (a term that by 1956 was redolent of outer space; → p. 276) through electronics, with near-instantaneous communication and ever-faster mobility. Hepworth was funneling the forces of the present into *Orpheus,* so that the final form—elegant, effervescent, flowing—addresses the hopes and visions of her time. The Constructionists longed to shake off the weight of the past, so that something new and universal could be created for all people. It was the hope of a decade when political and technological utopia was felt to be just around the corner. A hope that inevitably would be disappointed, except in the art it produced. Hepworth's *Orpheus* still yearns for freedom.

4
Naum Gabo,
Linear Construction in Space No. 4,
1958–59, Kunsthalle Mannheim

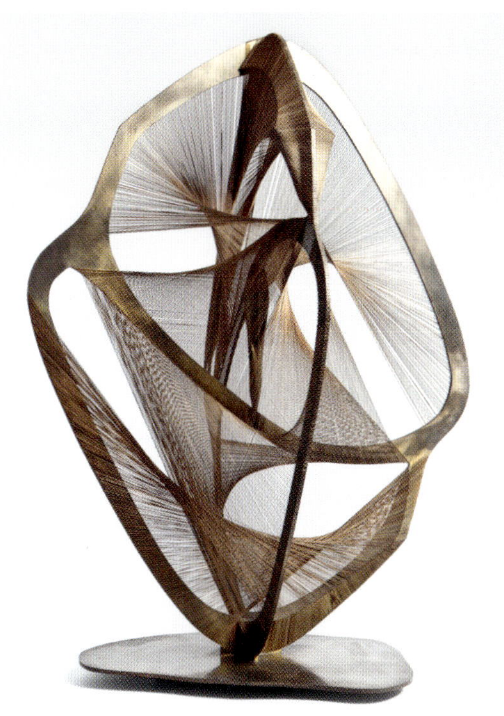

58 Barbara Hepworth
Conoid, Sphere and Hollow III, 1937
UK Government Art Collection

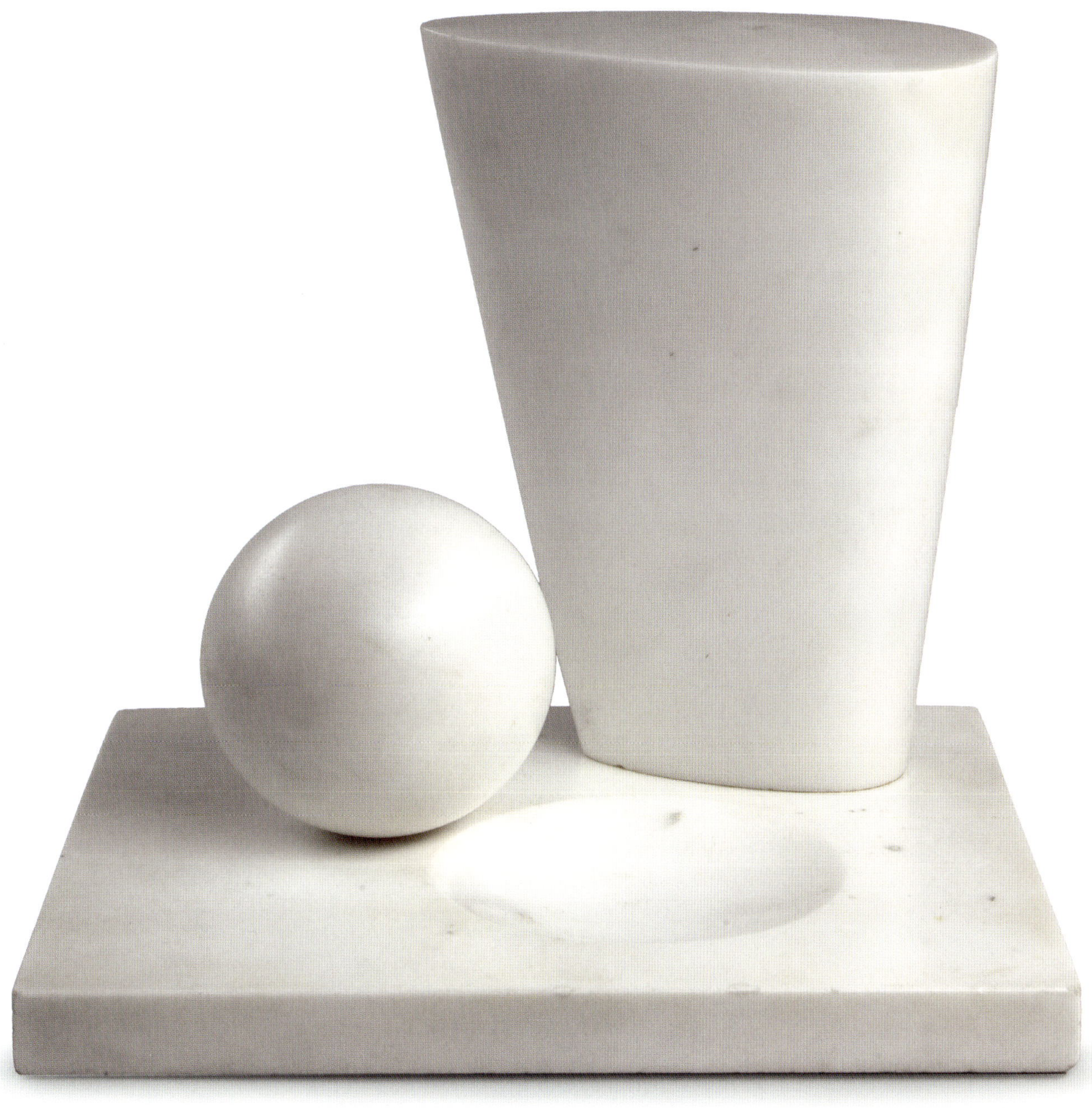

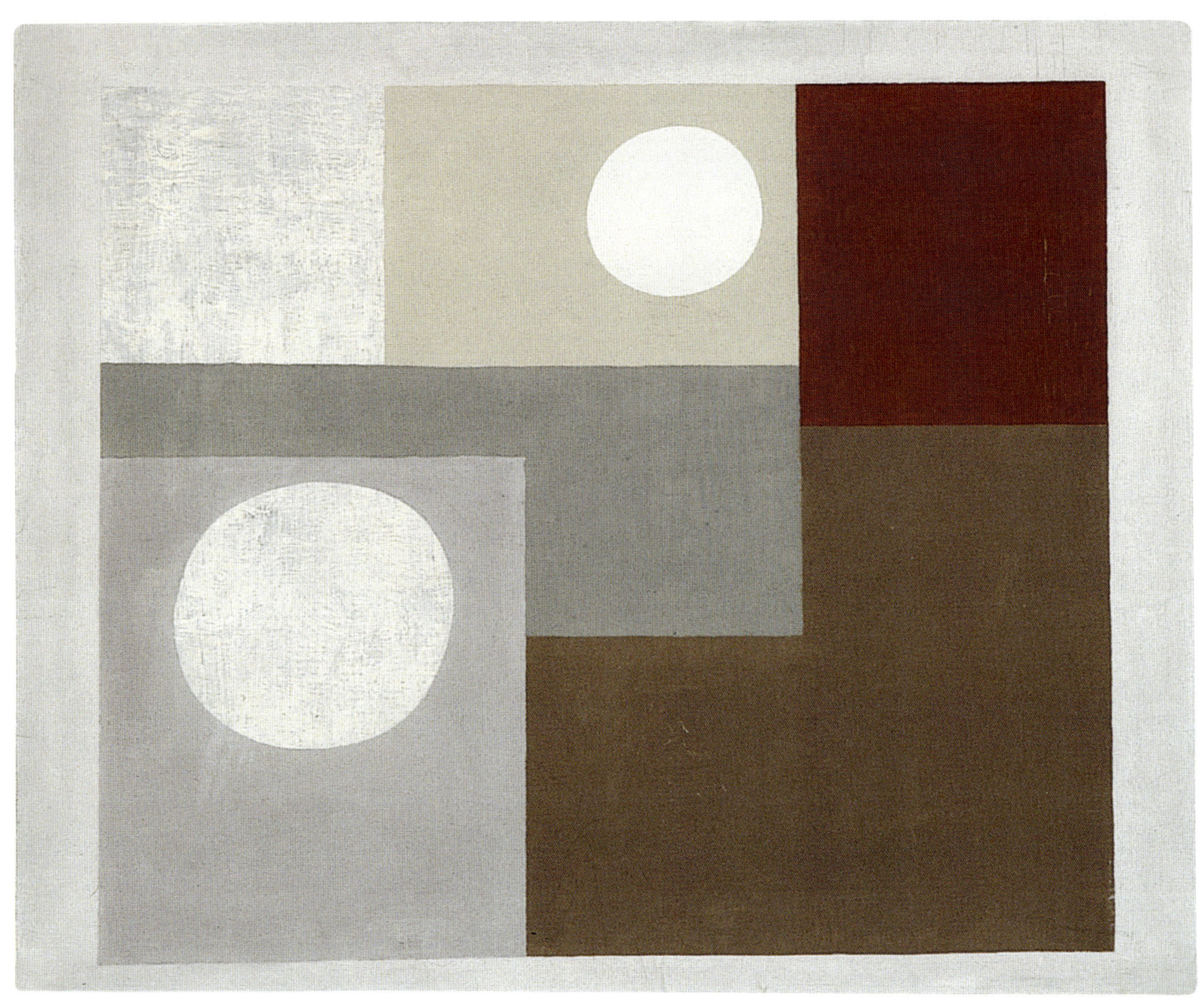

59 Ben Nicholson
1934 (painting), 1934
Pier Arts Centre, Stromness, Orkney

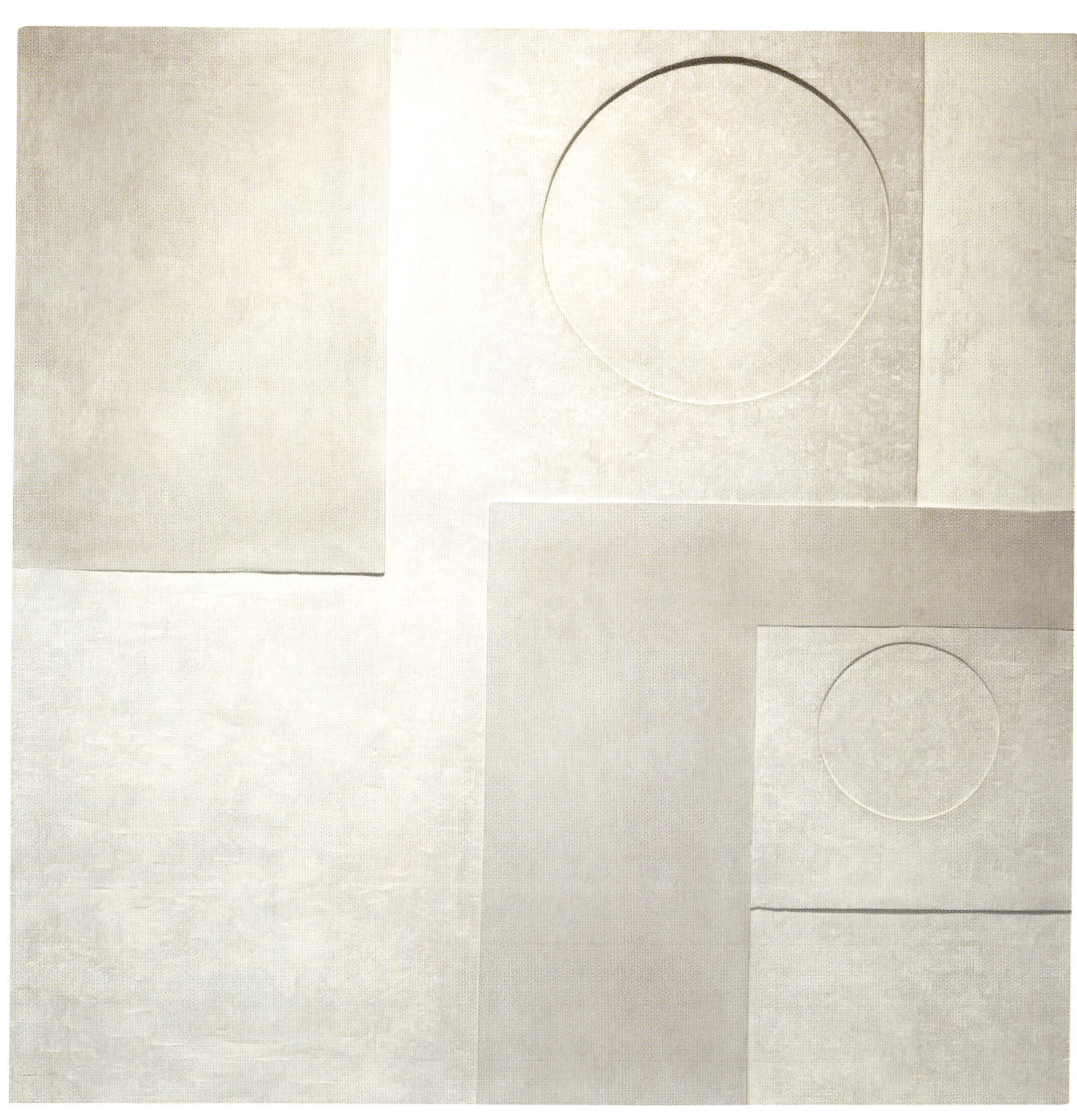

60 Ben Nicholson
1934 (painted relief), 1934
University of Hertfordshire Art Collection

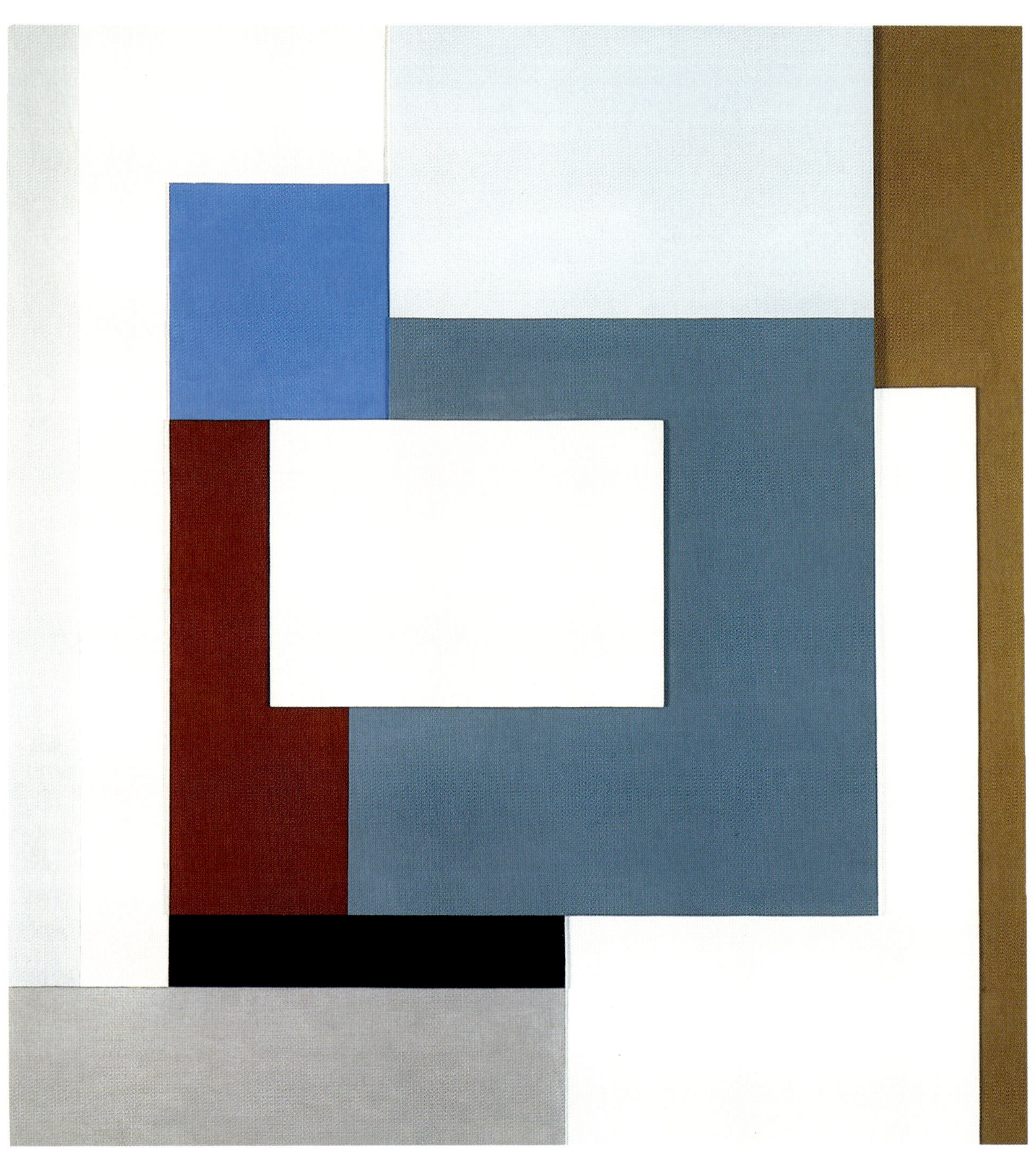

61 Ben Nicholson
1939 (painted relief), 1939
Pier Arts Centre, Stromness, Orkney

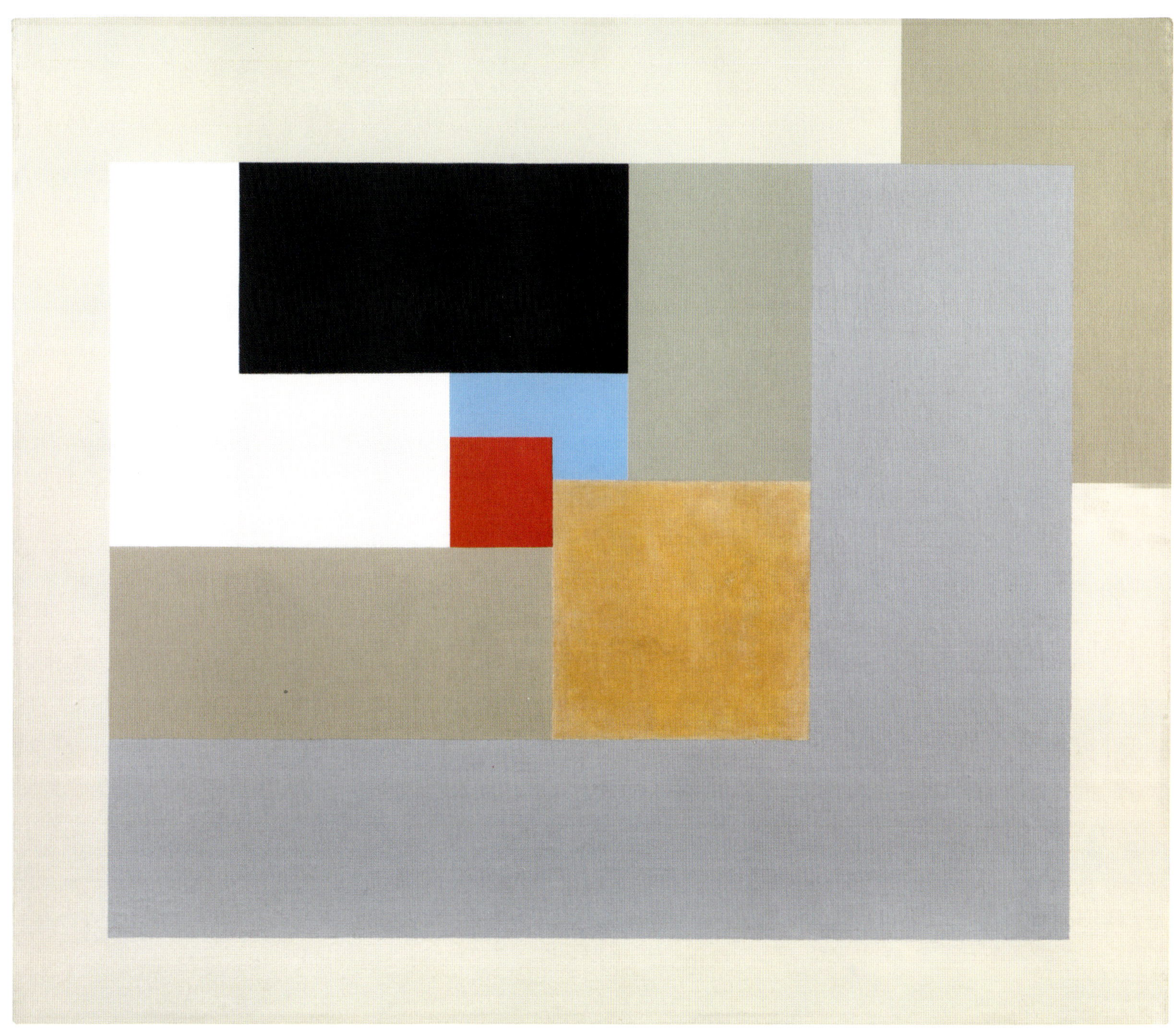

62 Ben Nicholson
Painting 1937, 1937
Courtauld, London
(Samuel Courtauld Trust)

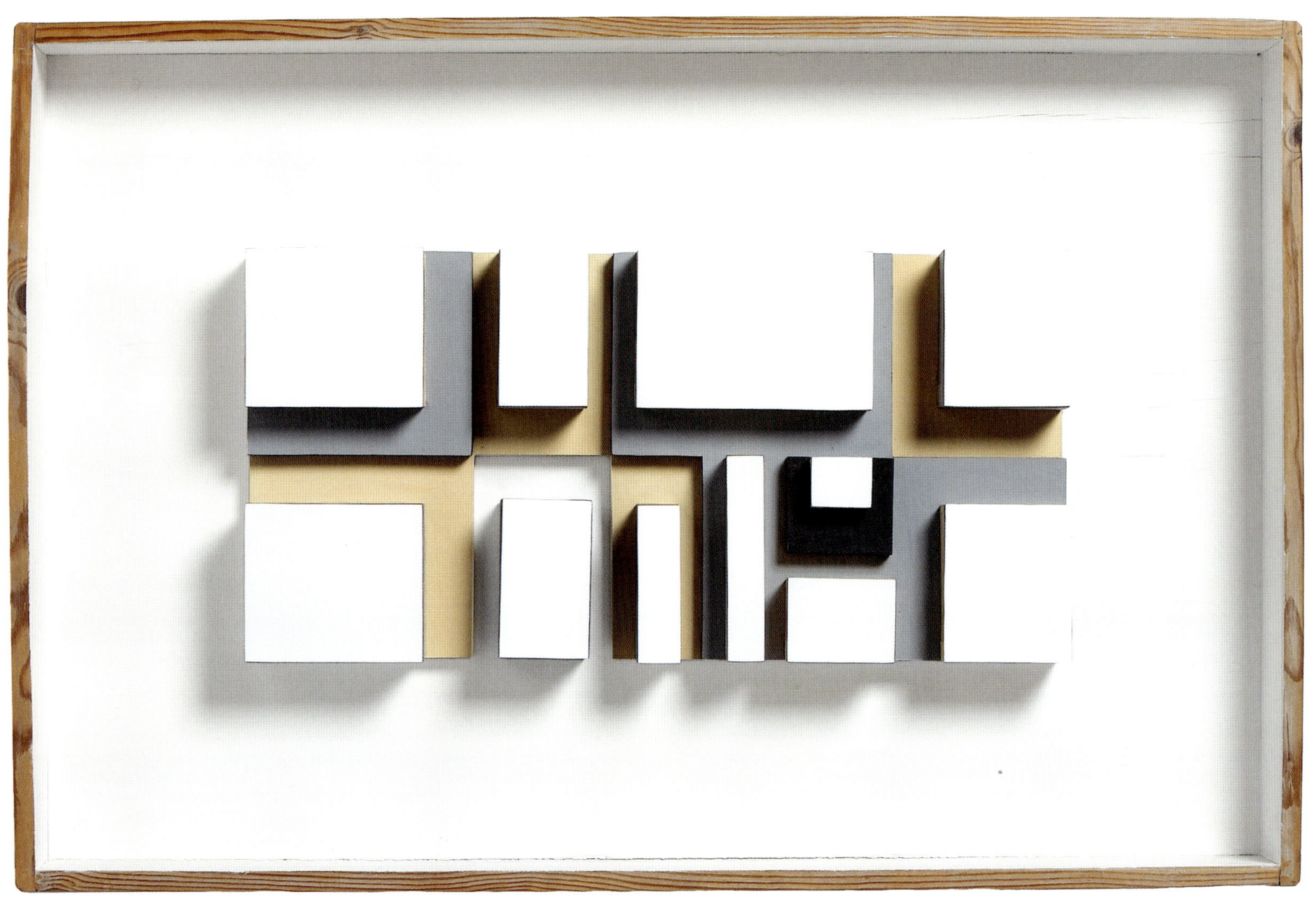

63 Mary Martin
White-Faced Relief, 1959
Sainsbury Centre, University of East Anglia

64 Mary Martin
Climbing Form, 1957
Sainsbury Centre, University of East Anglia

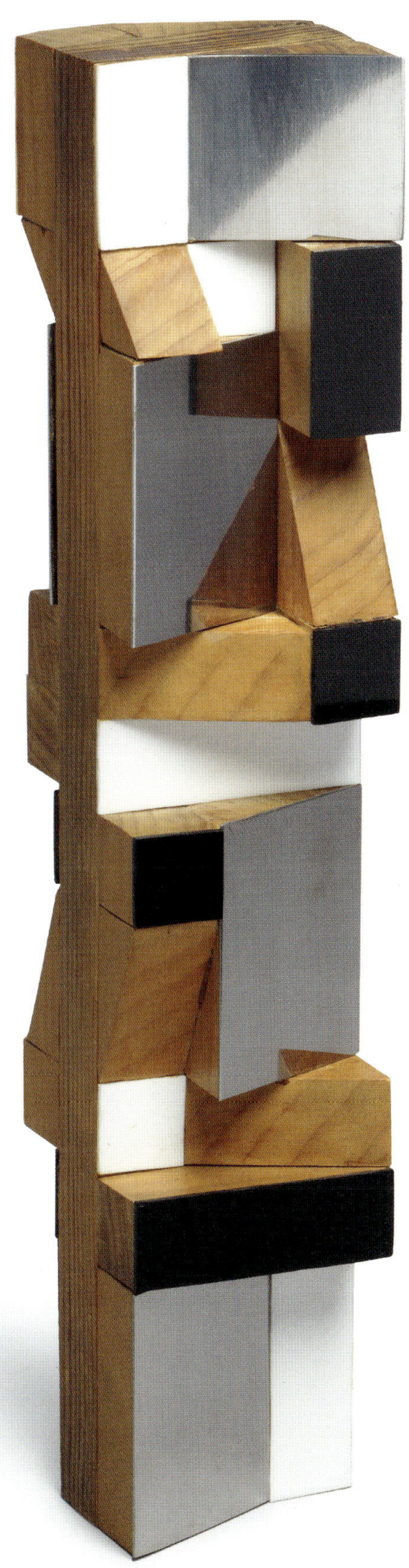

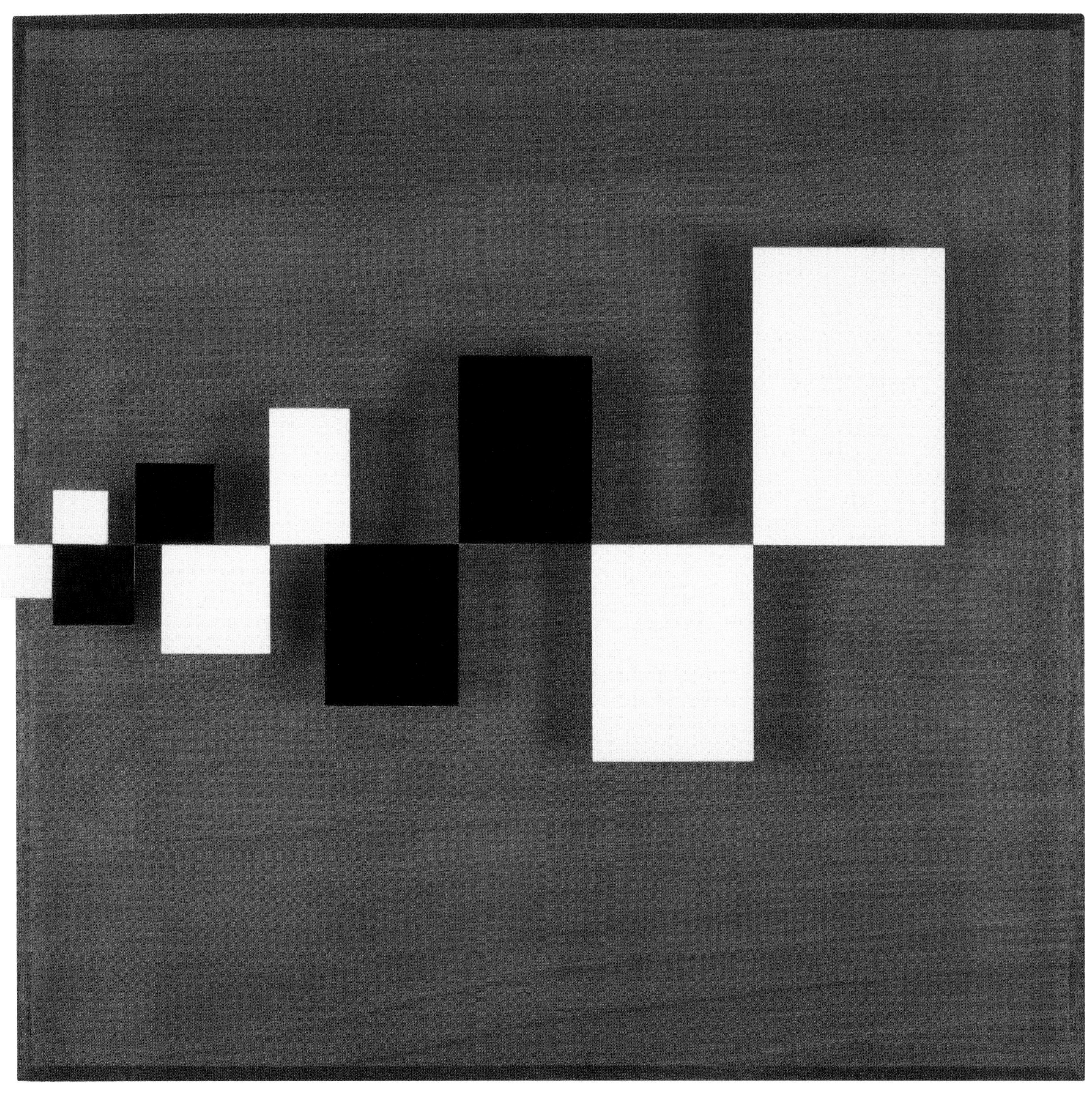

65 Anthony Hill
Progression of Rectangles, Version II, 1954–59
Sainsbury Centre, University of East Anglia

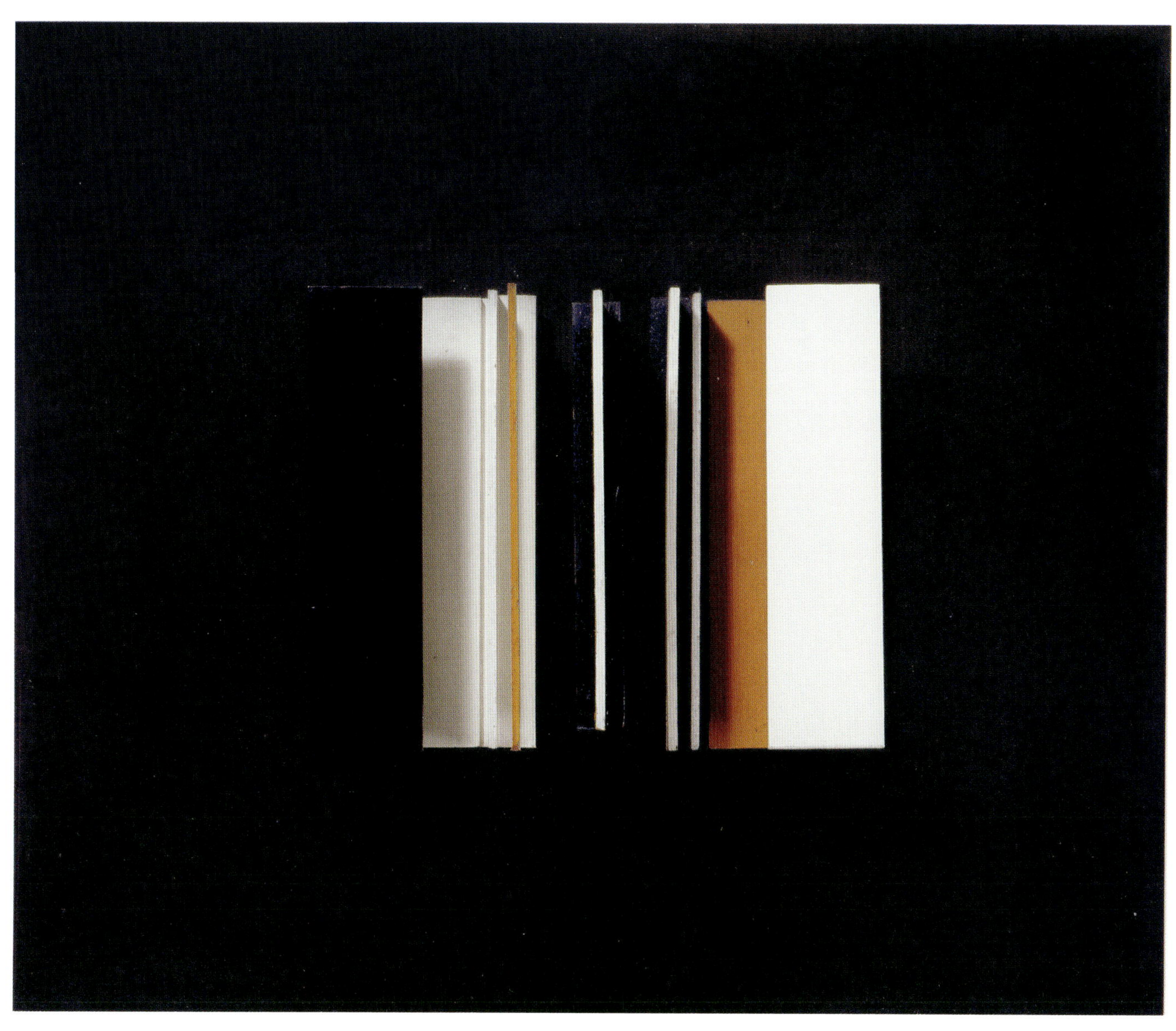

66 Victor Pasmore
Transparent Relief Construction in Black, White & Ochre, 1956–57
Sainsbury Centre, University of East Anglia

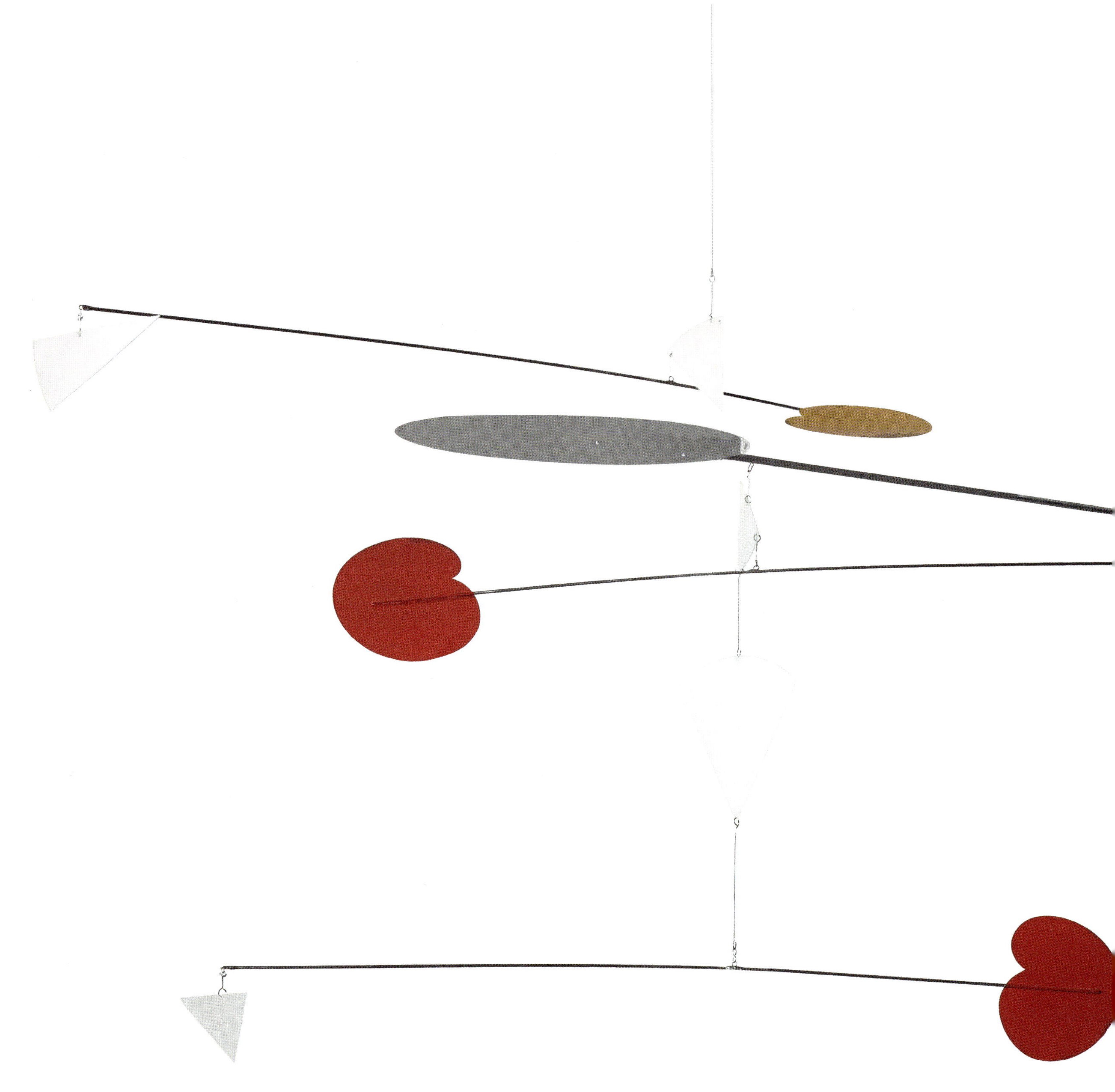

67 Kenneth Martin
Mobile Reflector, 1953
UK Government Art Collection

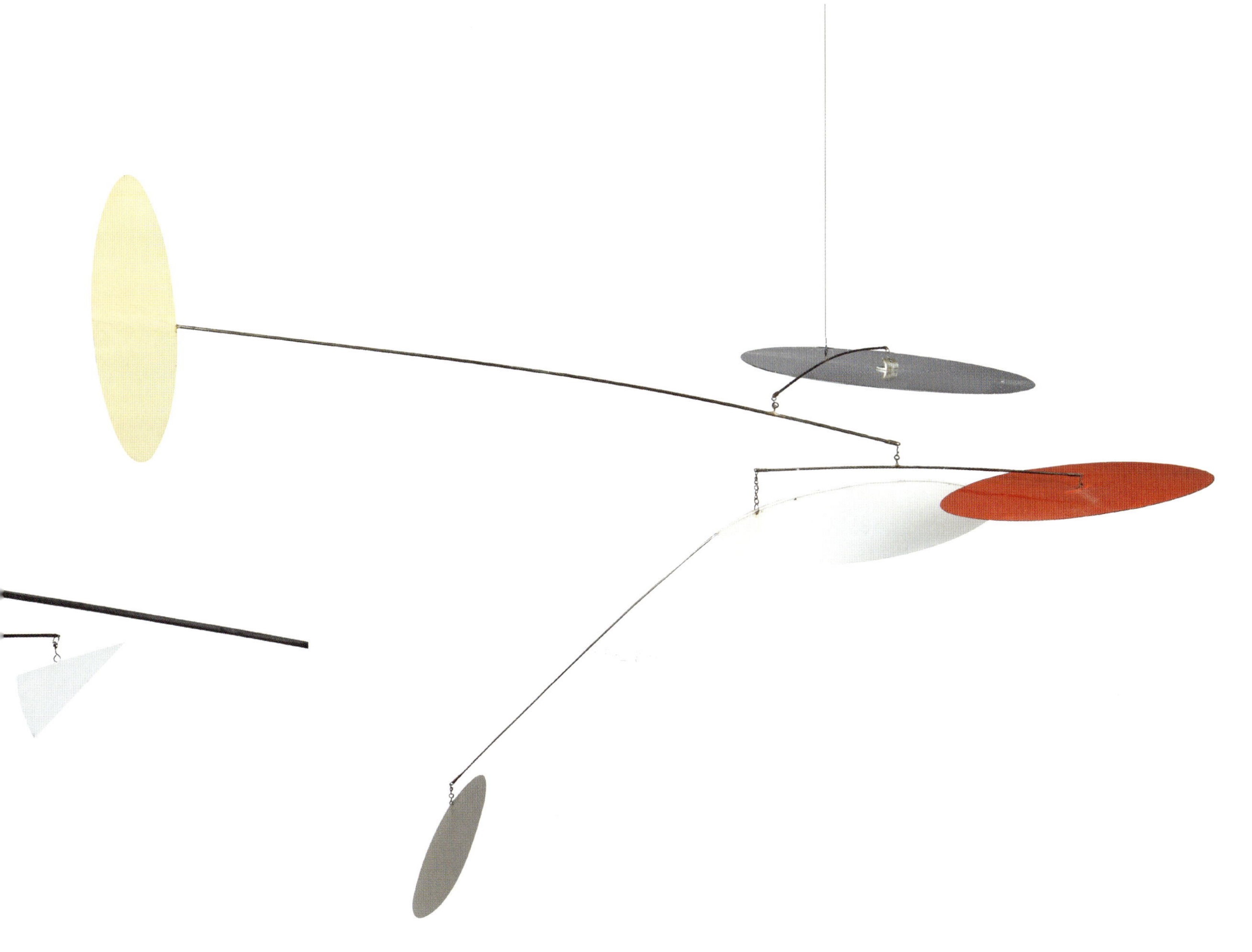

68 Kenneth Martin
Mobile Reflector: Elliptic Motif, 1955
Sainsbury Centre, University of East Anglia

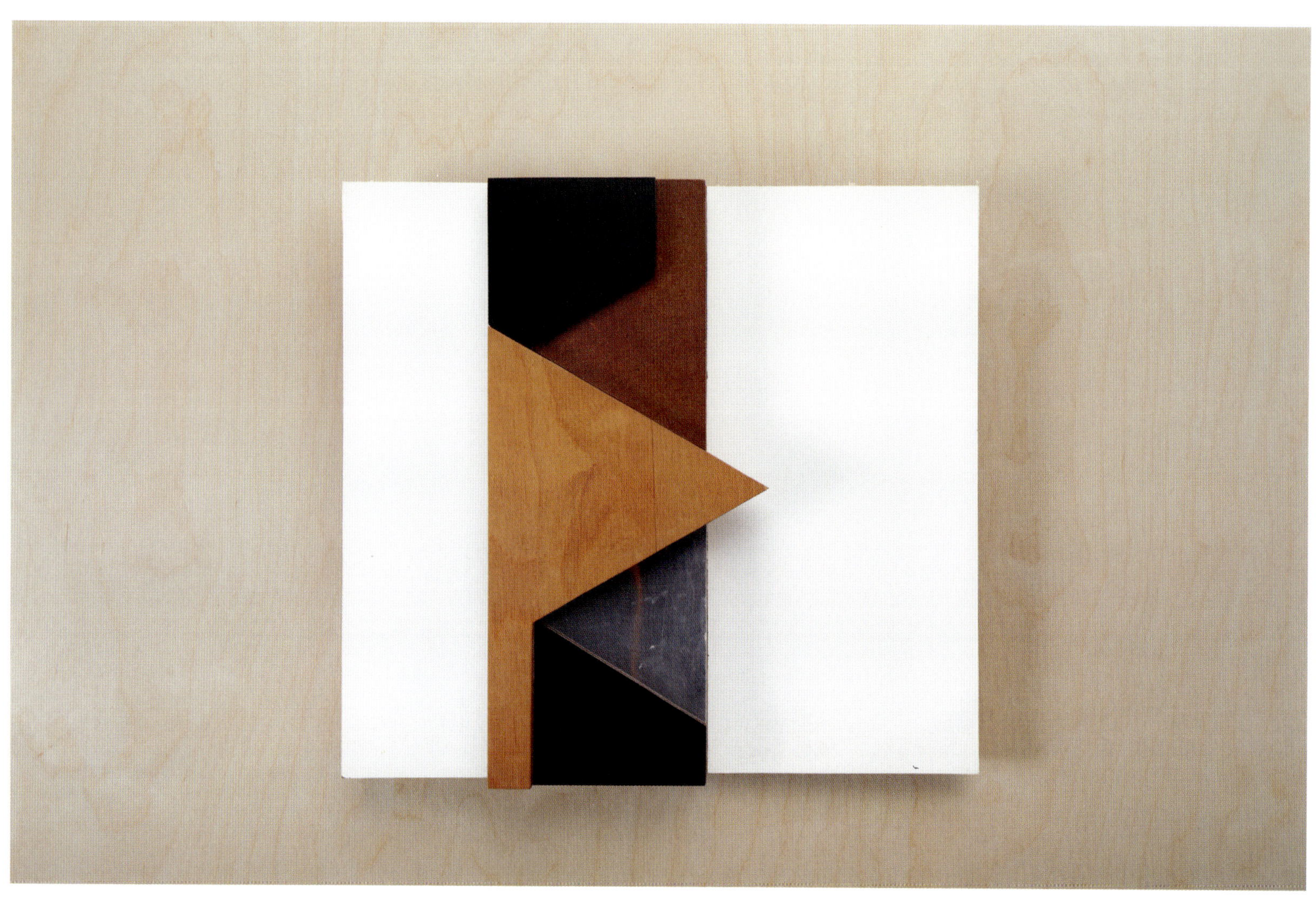

69 John Ernest
Relief: Triangular Motif II, 1959
Sainsbury Centre, University of East Anglia

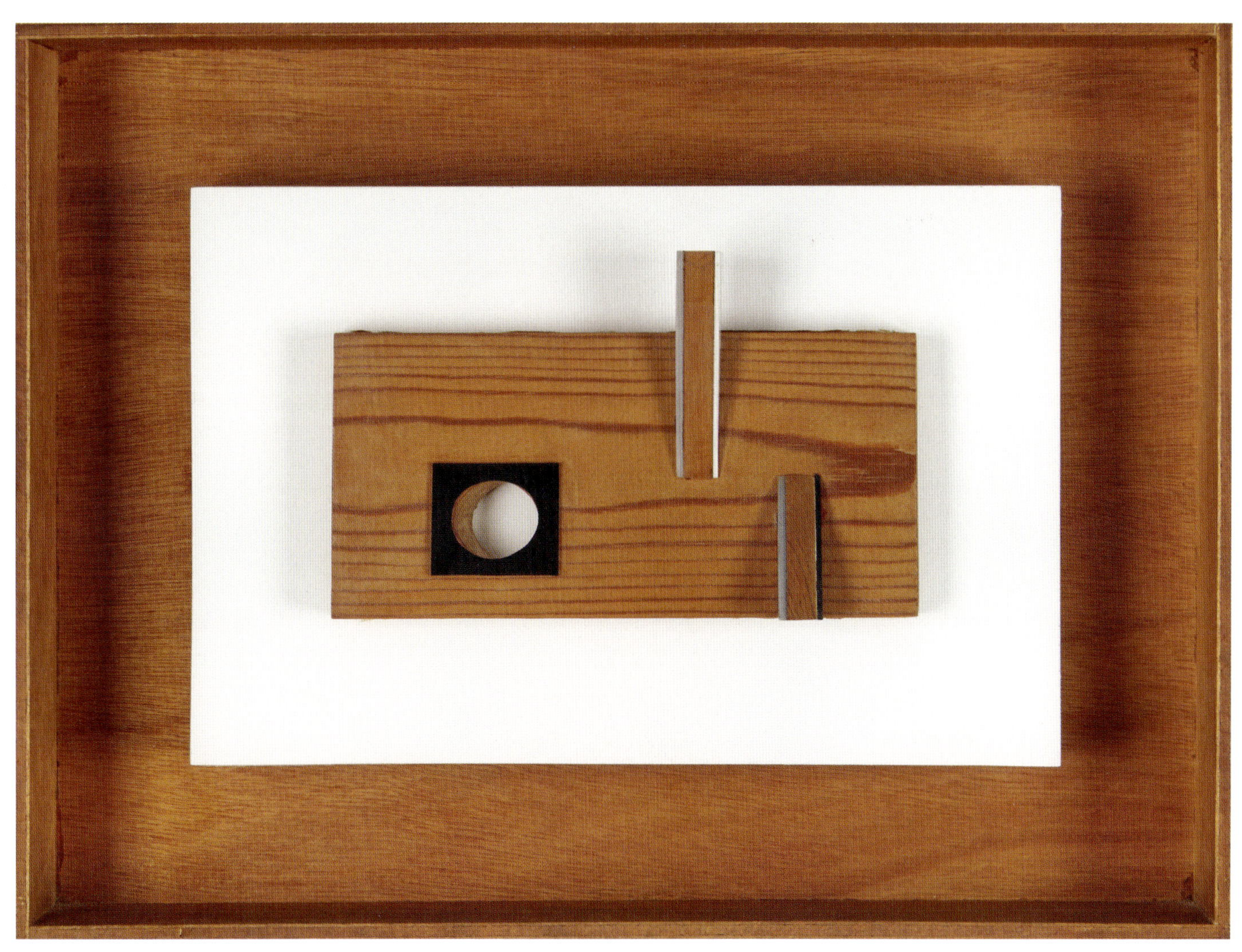

70 Mary Martin
Pierced Relief, 1959
Sainsbury Centre, University of East Anglia

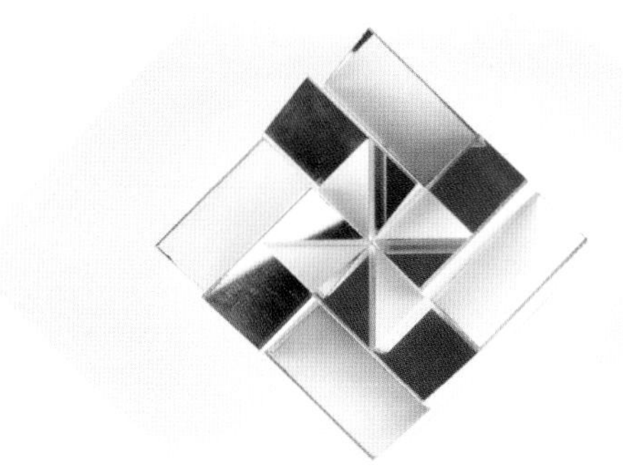

71 Mary Martin
Rotation, 1968
Sainsbury Centre,
University of East Anglia

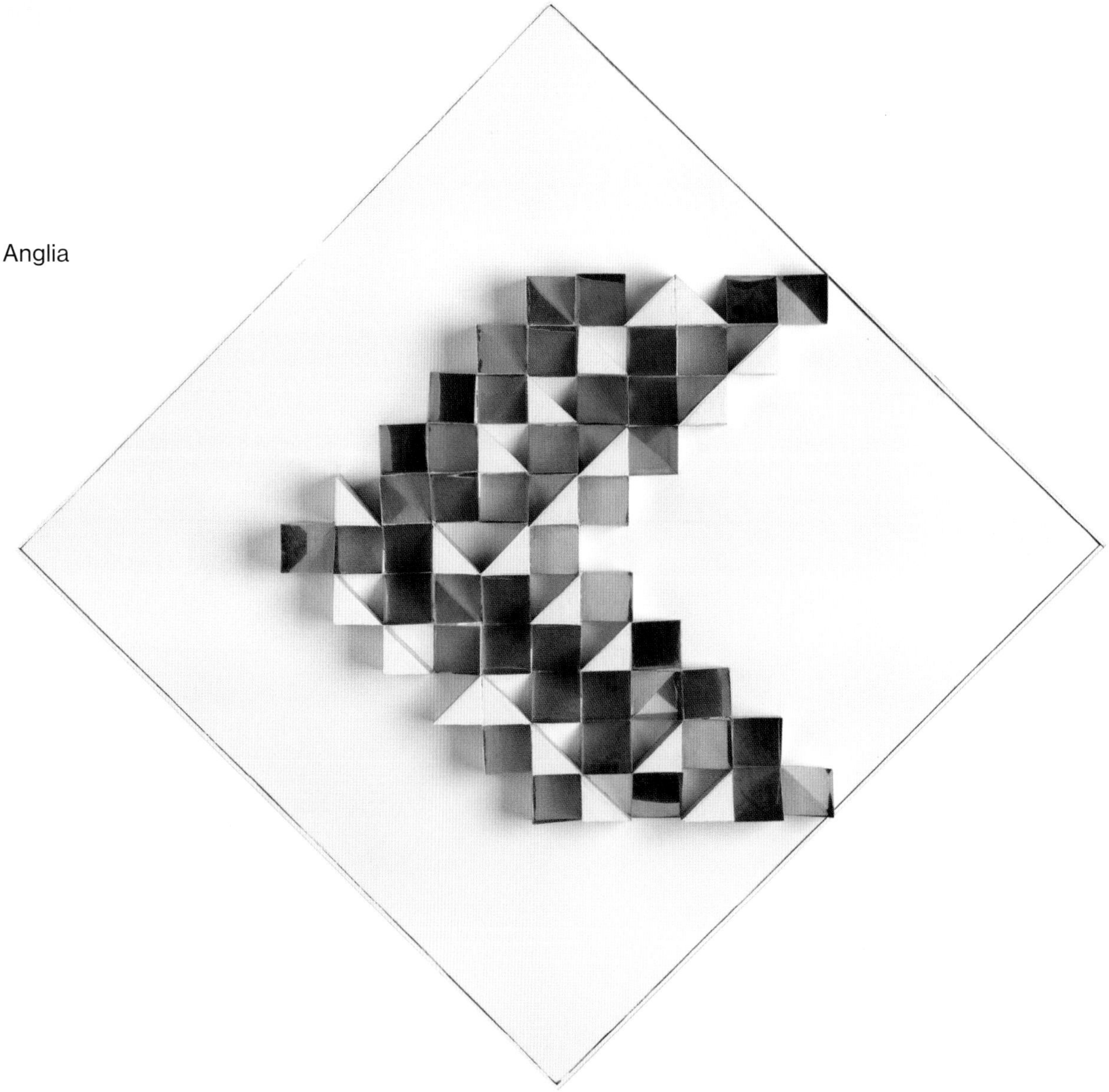

72 Mary Martin
White Diagonal, 1963
UK Government Art Collection

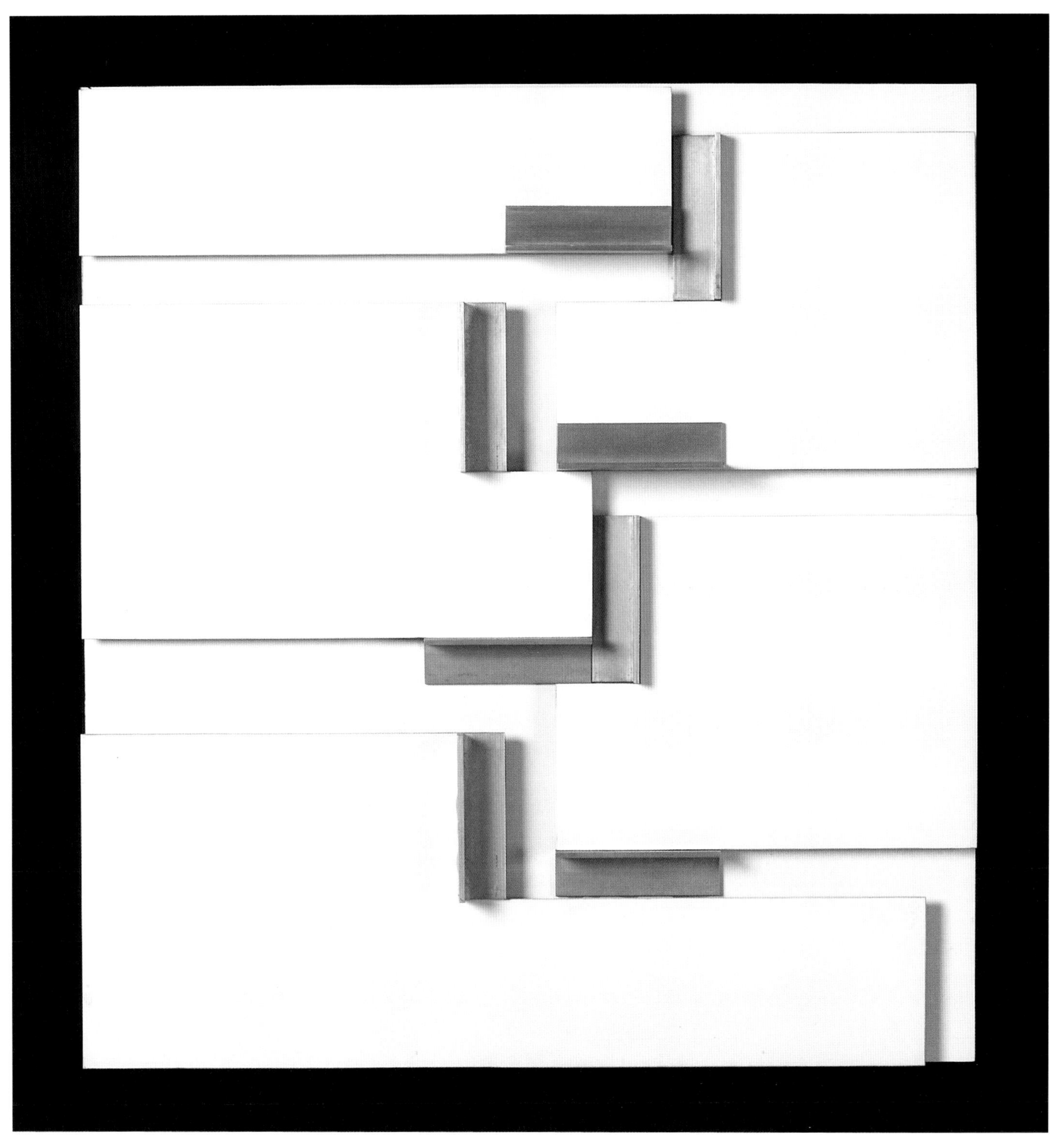

73 Anthony Hill
Five Regions Relief, 1960–62
Sainsbury Centre, University of East Anglia

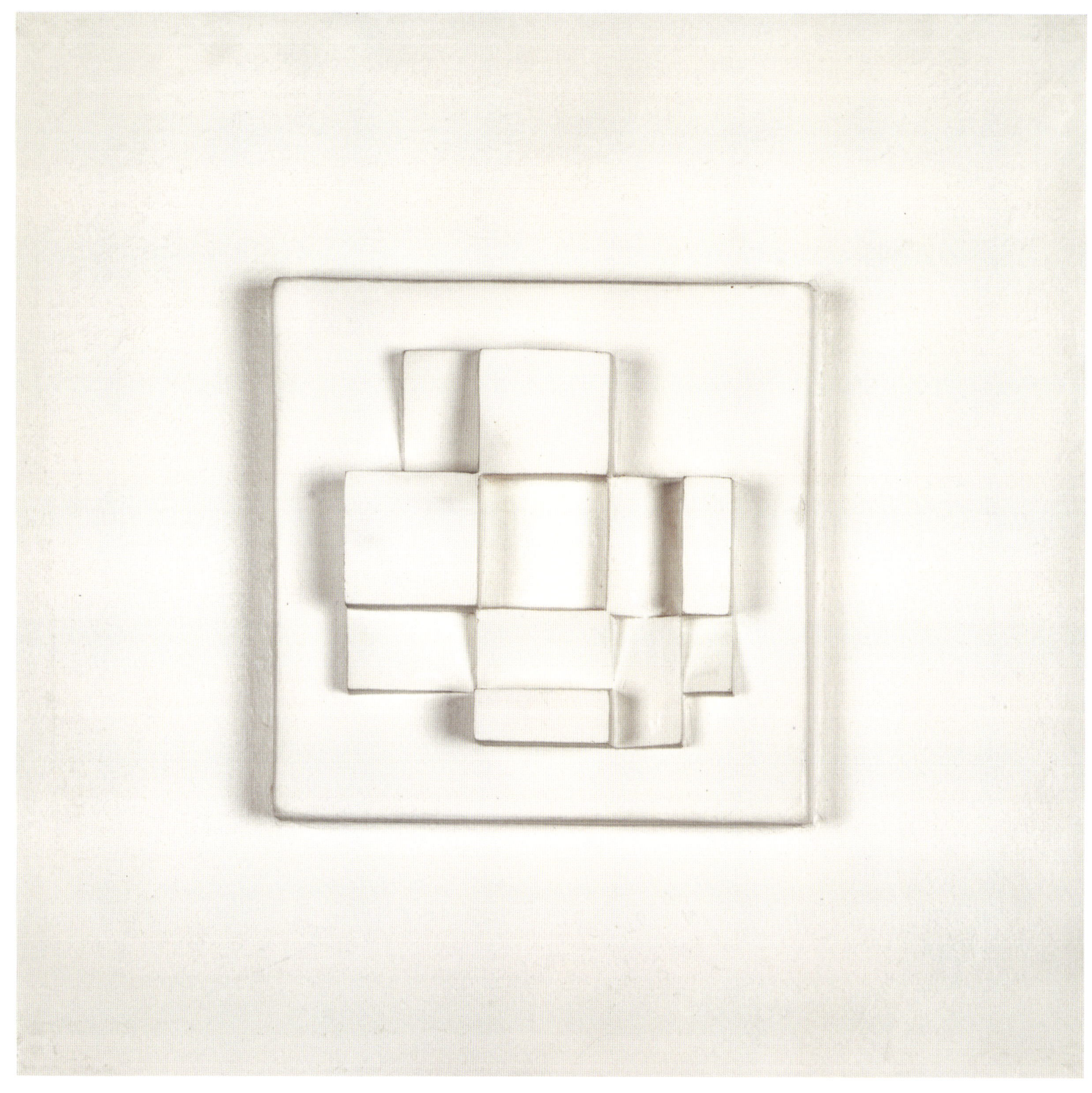

74 Mary Martin
Spiral Movement, ca. 1971
Sainsbury Centre, University of East Anglia

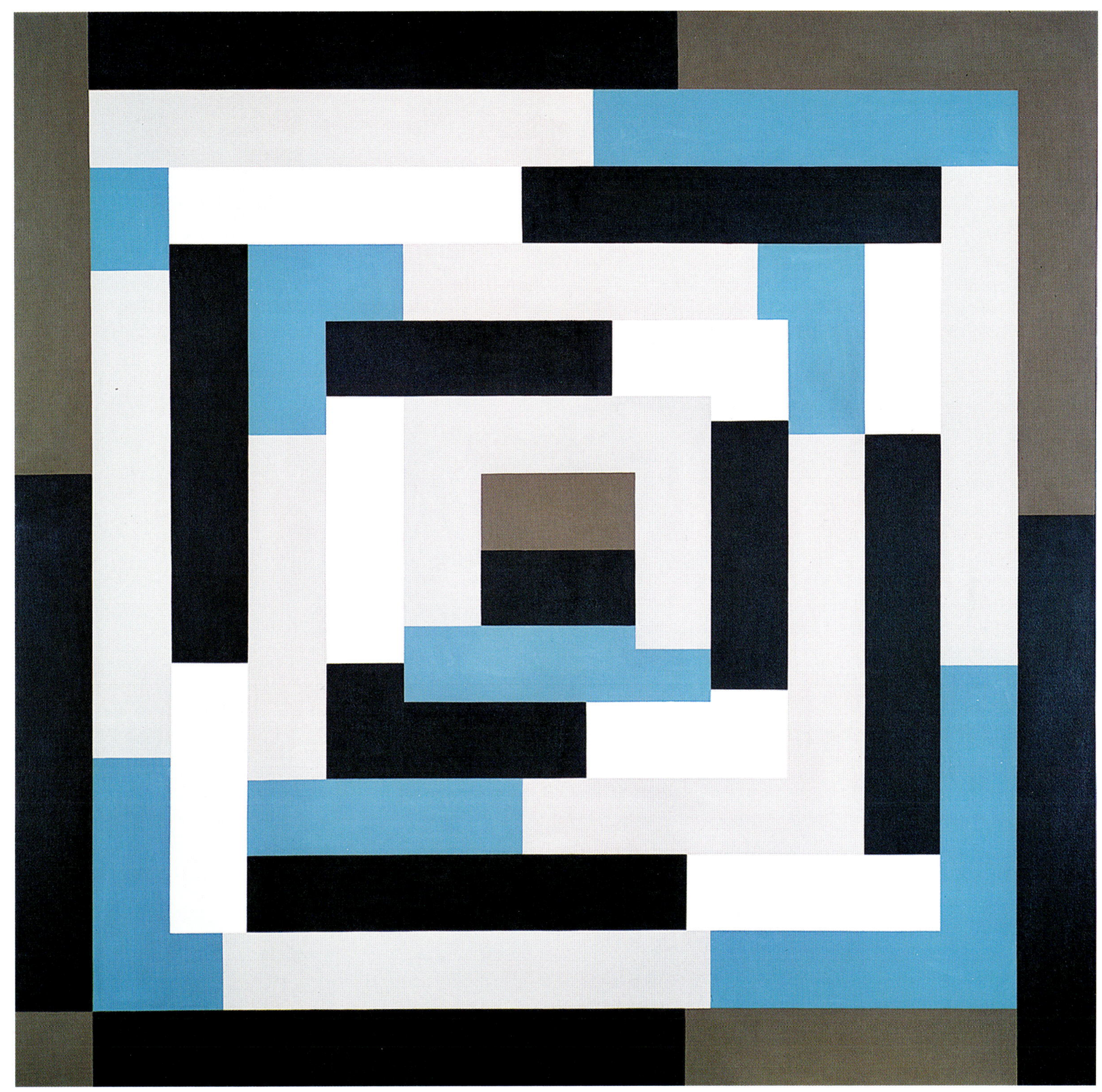

75 Mary Webb
Fritton, 1971
Sainsbury Centre, University of East Anglia

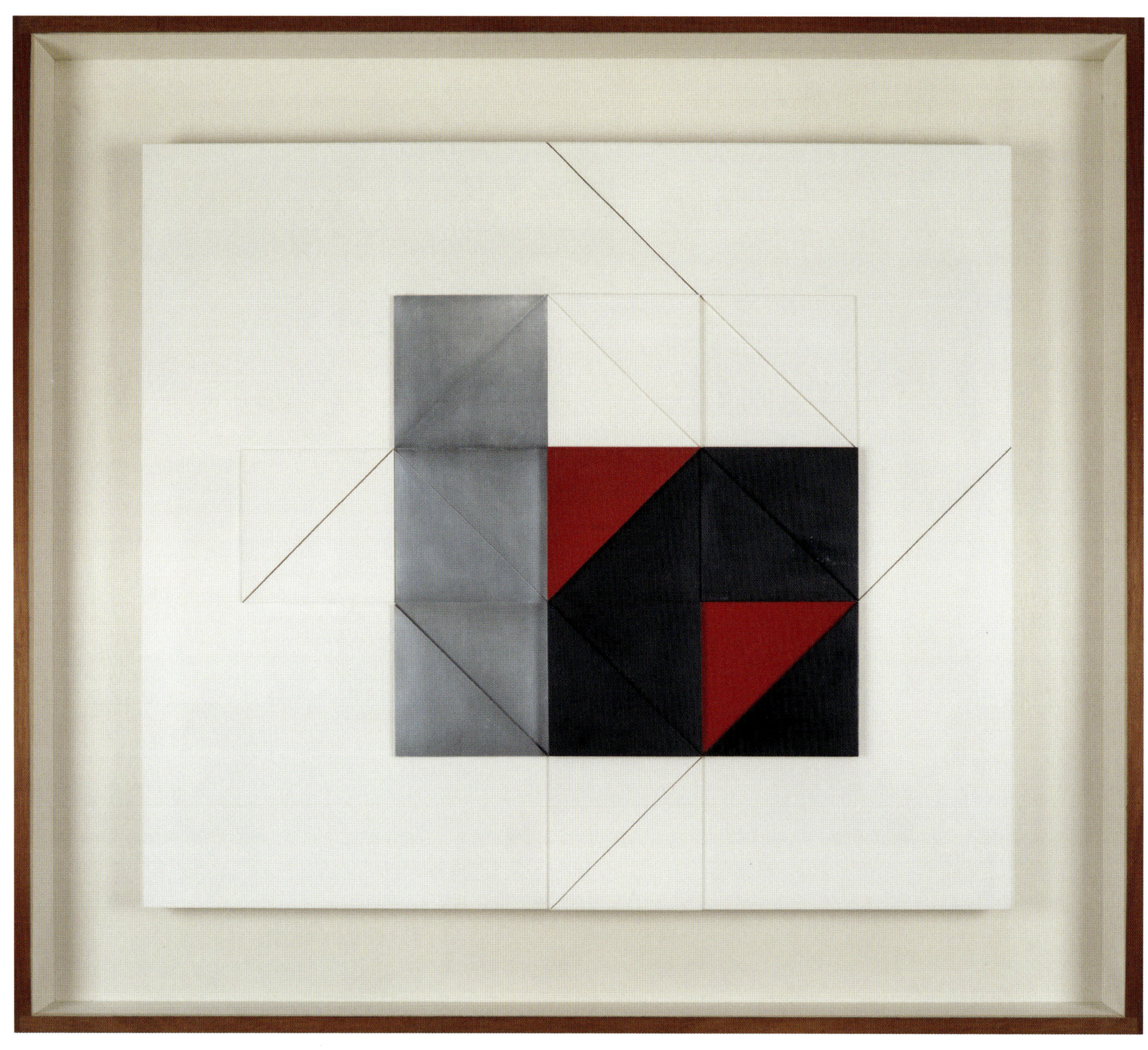

76 John Ernest
Mosaic Relief III, 1964
Sainsbury Centre, University of East Anglia

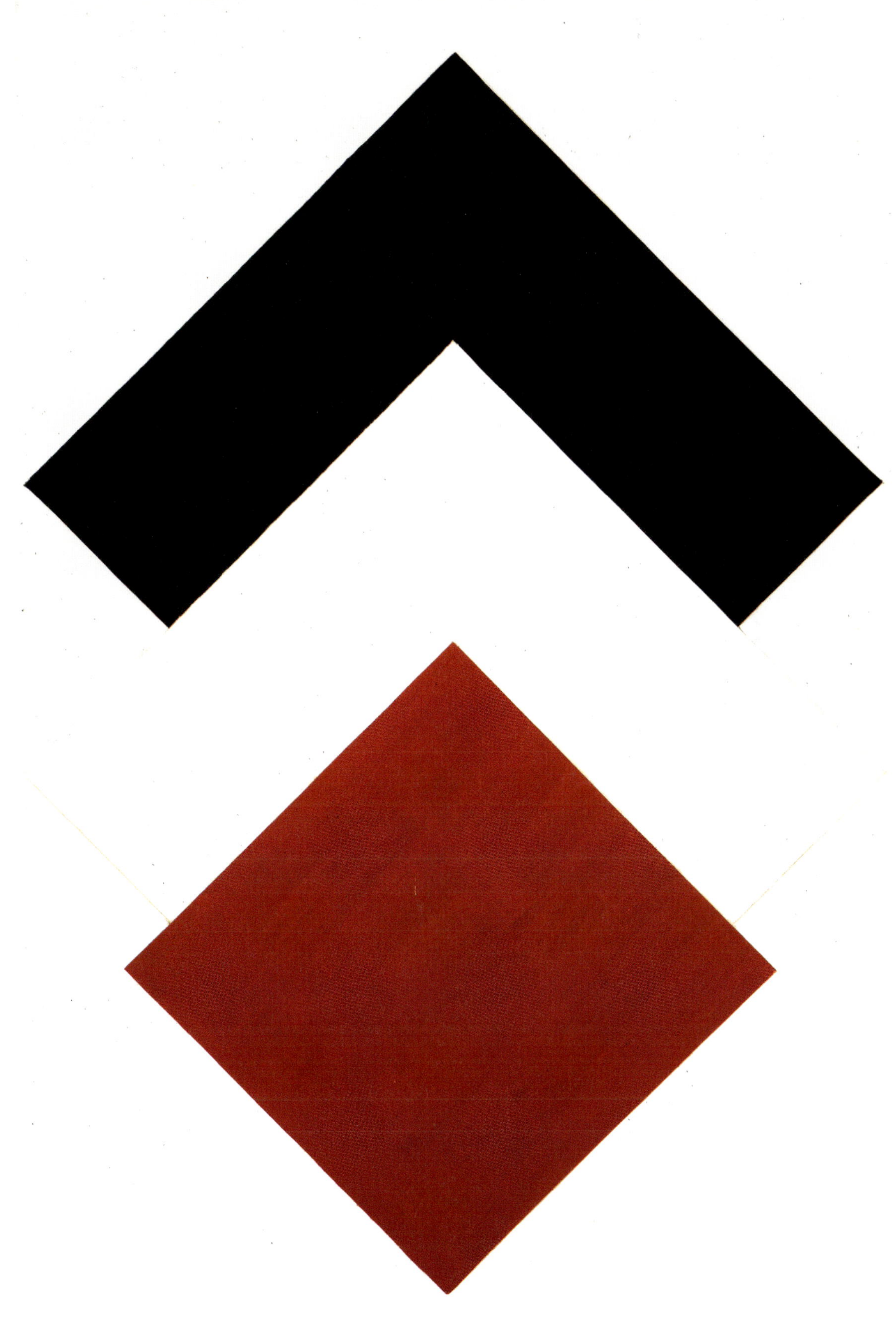

77 Terry Frost
Red, Black and White, 1977
Royal Academy of Arts, London

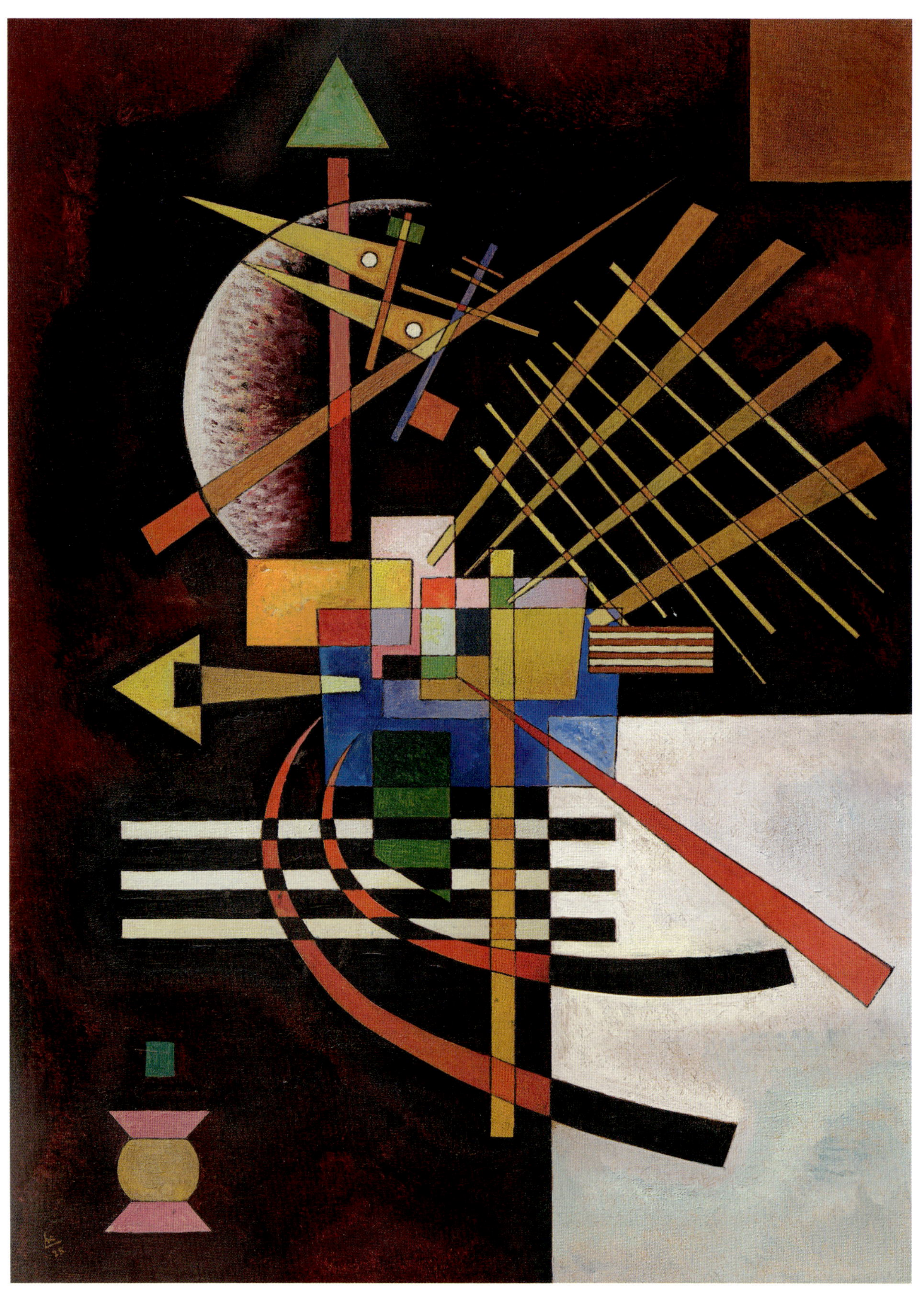

78 Wassily Kandinsky
Above and Left, 1925
Private collection

79 Barbara Hepworth
Orpheus (Maquette I), 1956
Pier Arts Centre, Stromness, Orkney

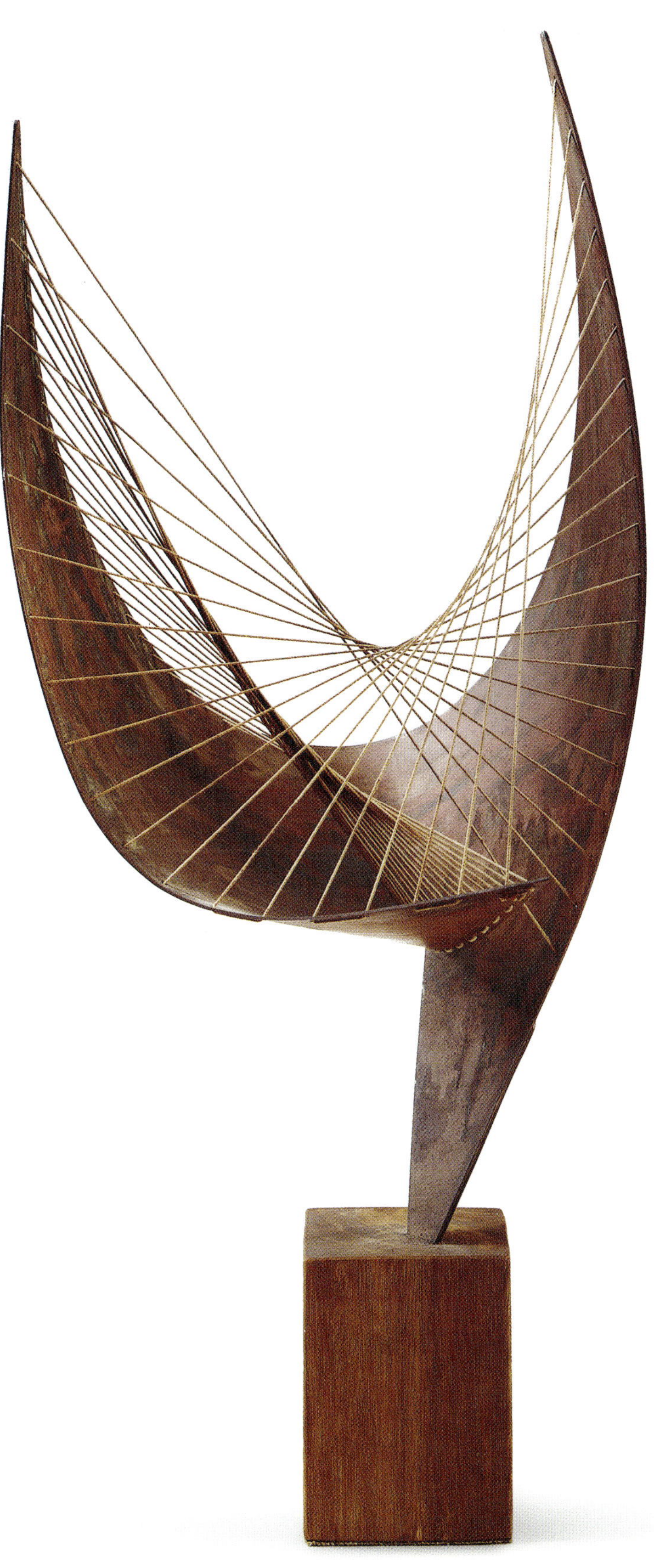

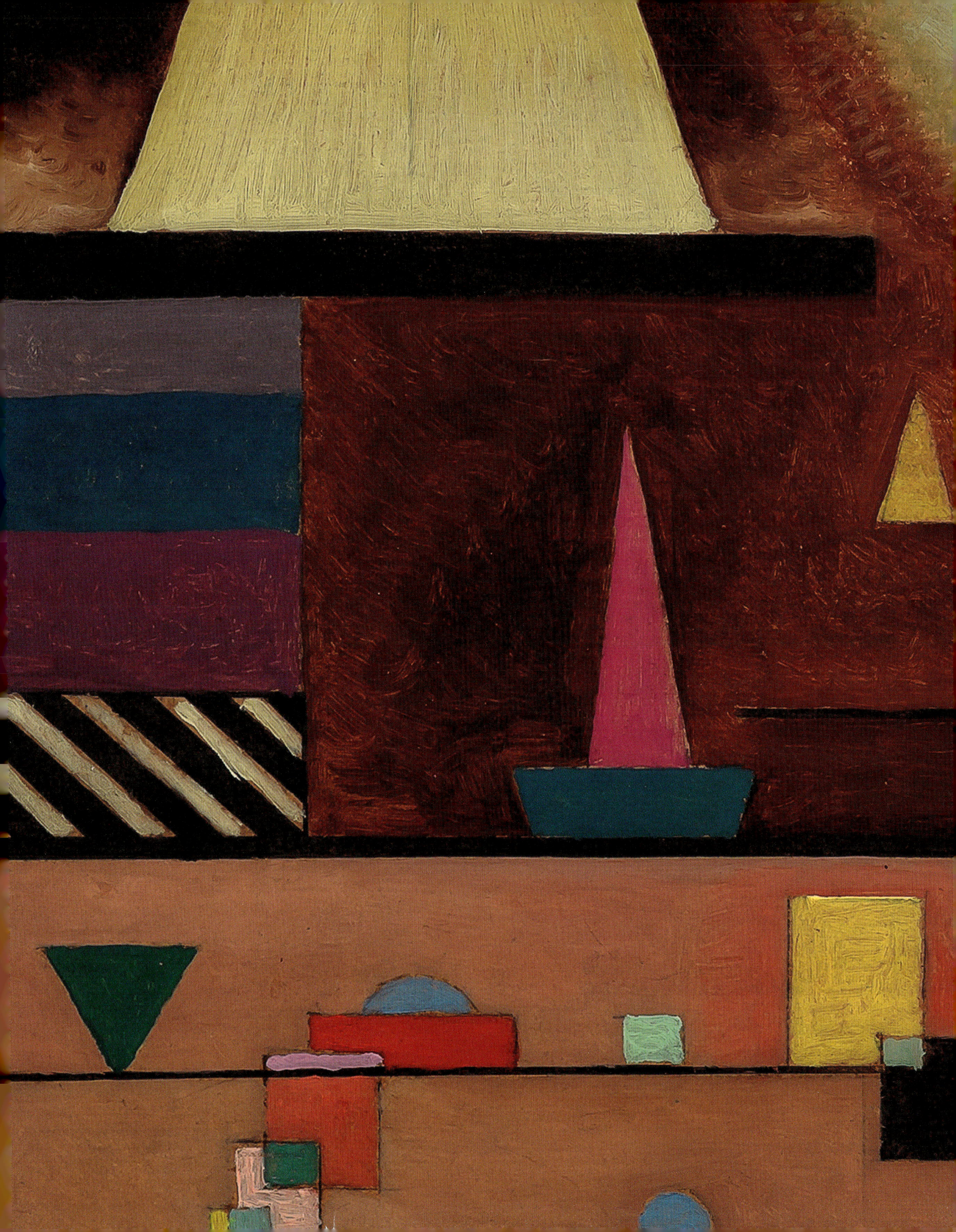

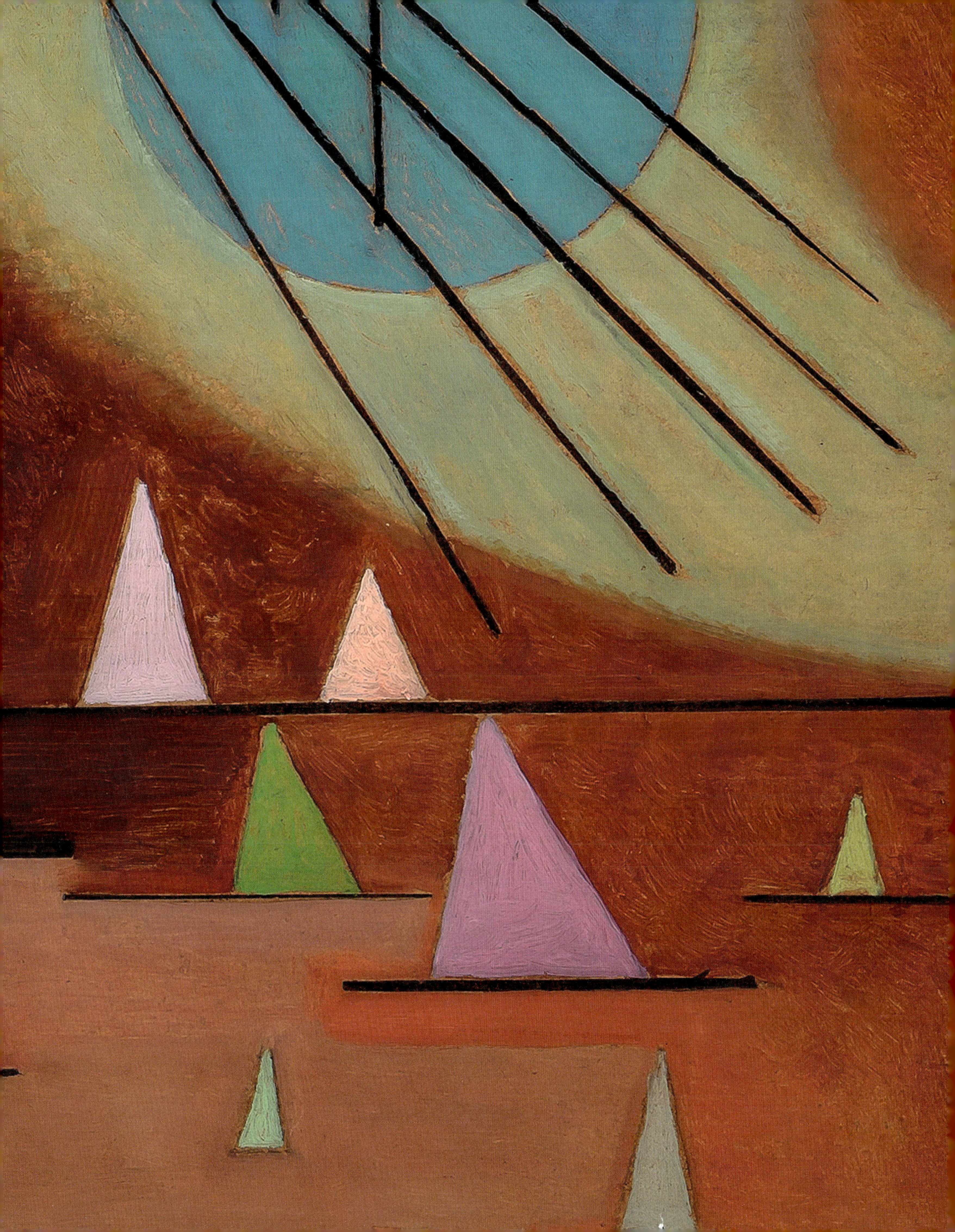

David Max Horowitz

The Essence of Form

Hard Edge Painting and Minimalism

In the 1960s, geometric abstraction in the United States embraced a trend toward monumental formats. Artists such as Frank Stella, Ellsworth Kelly, and Carmen Herrera focused on clear geometric shapes, sharp outlines, and vibrant colors. This style, known as Hard Edge, was characterized by a cool, matter-of-fact approach that contrasted with the expressive painting dominating the New York art scene in the 1950s.

Another trend of the time took a Minimalist approach, distinguishing itself from vibrant Hard Edge paintings by creating objects that combined elements of sculpture and painting. Prioritizing simplicity, order, and repetition, the works resemble serially produced objects rather than individually crafted pieces. Despite the seemingly detached style, references to jazz rhythms can still be found in the works of Gene Davis, and Buddhist spirituality in those of Agnes Martin.

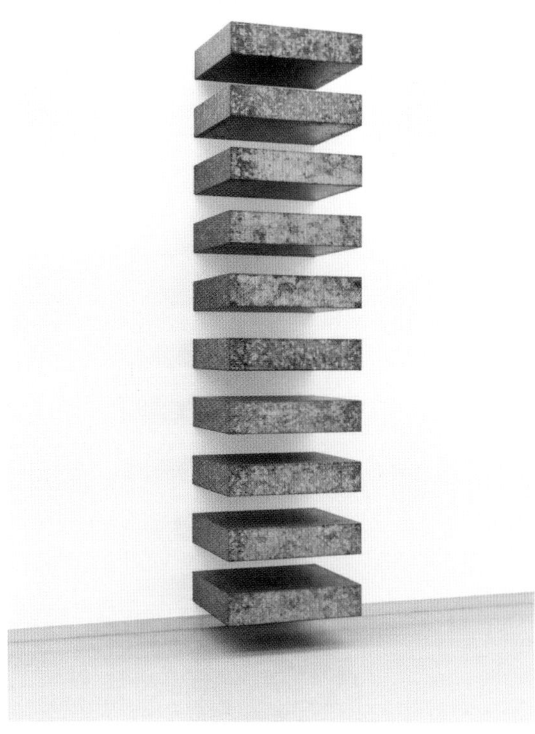

1
Donald Judd,
Untitled, 1968–69,
Kröller-Müller Museum,
Otterlo

By the mid-1960s, discussions of contemporary abstraction in the United States revolved around two movements: Color Field Painting and Minimalism. Frequently, they were placed in vociferous opposition to one another. Within the context of that clash, Color Field's apologists claimed Minimalist artworks, regularly drained of hue, radically simplified, and with little in the way of internal incident, had strayed too far from the essential elements that made art worthwhile. Those on the side of Minimalism, for their part, felt Color Field painters were clinging to regressive attitudes about individual creativity and composition, and that their use of color, shape, and part-to-part relationships was arbitrary and obsolete.

From today's perspective this discordance might seem unexpected, especially if one focuses on one of the major Color Field styles, Hard Edge. Both Hard Edge and Minimalism emphasize bold forms, eschewing tonal variations to create a strong correspondence between color and shape. Both are characterized by meticulous surfaces that show few traces of artistic process or humanizing imperfections. Both eliminate overt expression, external reference, and illusionism, and emphasize the physical realities of the materials.

Despite their aesthetic and theoretical similarities, proponents of Hard Edge Painting and Minimalism found themselves in disagreement. One of the primary champions of Hard Edge Painting was critic Clement Greenberg—though he preferred the term *post-painterly abstraction* (→ p. 276). In his era-defining essay "Modernist Painting" of 1960, Greenberg declared, "The essence of Modernism lies, as I see it, in the use of characteristic methods of a discipline to criticize the discipline itself, not in order to subvert it but in order to entrench it more firmly in its area of competence."[2] In his telling, this self-critical approach had, over the preceding century, led painters to stress the medium's defining feature: the flatness of the support. Accordingly, illusionistic depth was progressively eliminated. In illustrating this argument, he drew together a context for Hard Edge Painting, given its resolutely abstract, frontal compositions.

The writings of artist Donald Judd (cat. 102) helped set the terms for Minimalism—though he himself never embraced the label. In his essay "Specific Objects" of 1964, he identified a new tendency, which he claimed was neither painting nor sculpture, but something in between.

The power of these works arose from their unified, insistent physicality, their presence in real space, and their break with conventional artistic categories. This characterization strongly suits his own works, such as his "stacks" series (fig. 1). Though he does not cite Greenberg and is at odds with him on many fronts, Judd employs a similar logic. He describes the visual arts as undergoing a self-critical process focused solely on materiality, and he retains, and even strengthens, Greenberg's rejection of illusion and his implicit dismissal of communicative content.

These resemblances are revealing, but they do not negate the deep divergences. Judd advocated a rupture from European Modernism, while Greenberg advanced a vision of continuity. The artist rejected the critic's emphasis on medium-specificity and instead challenged traditional artistic categories. Along the way, he dismissed the prospects of painting as such—the mode of artmaking most prized by Greenberg.

The kinds of frictions represented by these two foundational texts were enough to create a structural schism in how these two movements have generally been understood. As is regularly the case when histories are constructed, much that did not fit neatly into these dominant frameworks was omitted or distorted. Artists were swept under headings with which they did not identify. Ellsworth Kelly (cat. 88) chafed at the Hard Edge label. Agnes Martin (cat. 99), whose work was often shown with Minimalists in the 1960s, insisted she was an Abstract Expressionist. Jo Baer (cat. 100), who was also categorized as a Minimalist, went on to write a broadside against the movement in 1967, propelled especially by its denigration of painting.

Some artists were even claimed by both sides, no one more so than Stella. Michael Fried, who was openly hostile to Minimalism, championed the painter as an exemplar of late modernism. When Stella had his first retrospective at the Museum of Modern Art in New York in 1970, curator William Rubin positioned the artist's work as staunchly opposed to Minimalist sensibilities. Yet Stella was widely seen as helping establish that very tendency with his early paintings. Their concentric, regularly spaced, monochromatic bands suggested a systemic logic that served as an antidote to the individualistic choices necessitated by composition. His use of shaped canvases (cat. 81), along with their deep stretchers, made

2
Agnes Martin,
The Tree, 1964,
Museum of Modern Art,
New York

the paintings appear object-like, rather than portals into an optical space. As such, Judd singled out Stella's work as generative in "Specific Objects"; Greenberg went on to dismiss it for the same reasons.

The inability to establish clean margins between Hard Edge Painting and Minimalism was not the only shortcoming in how these two tendencies were theorized. Though there were good reasons they took root, these approaches often missed the motivations of individual artists, many of whom were concerned with emotion, expression, and societal issues. This was even recognized, if left relatively unaddressed, by both Greenberg and Judd. In a 1963 text on Kenneth Noland (cat. 83) and two other painters, Greenberg declared, "And yet the color, the verticality, the concentricity, and the interlocking are not there for their own sakes. They are there, first and foremost, for the sake of feeling . . . . And if these paintings fail as vehicles and expressions of feeling, they fail entirely."[3] For his part, Judd was asked in a 1964 interview, "Are you suggesting an art without feeling?" He replied, "No, you're reading me wrong."[4]

There is an oft-cited anecdote about Kelly's work that the artist found instructive. A child looking at his *Painting for a White Wall* (fig. 3)—a work consisting of five abutted monochrome panels—pointed to each section, naming the color aloud. This story has been seen as an indication of the linguistic implications and literalism of Kelly's art, driving toward more theoretical questions. However, that interpretation is not inevitable or necessarily total. When children are first able to indulge in this kind of recognition and expression, the experience is accompanied by apparent pride and delight. Those affective charges can be felt to resonate with Kelly's art. His bold colors and forms often have a bounce of jubilation about them.

Occasionally the abstract forms the artists used are suggestive of external interests. Noland's pared-down geometries have been revealed to stem from his experience in Reichian therapy, with its focus on the physical manifestation of psychic events. This grounding draws out the soothing and salutary effects of the consistent balance and clarity of his compositions. In a very different vein, Miriam Schapiro (cat. 90) used vulval forms—most famously in *Big Ox* from 1967 (fig. 4)—a strategy she employed to bring an explicitly feminist charge to a male-dominated style.

Other artists were driven by more spiritually inflected aspirations. Alexander Liberman (cat. 92) regularly utilized circles in his work. In his thinking, they were not just a geometric form but a sign of a higher, transcendent unity. Agnes Martin, meanwhile, evoked Zen Buddhism along with the beauty of nature—the latter suggested in titles such as *Summer Sky II* (cat. 99) and *The Tree* (fig. 2)—when discussing her delicate, stripped-down, monochromatic grids. These points of view evoke the spiritual utopianism more commonly expected of early-twentieth-century abstract artists, perhaps none more so than Wassily Kandinsky.

3
Ellsworth Kelly,
Painting for a White Wall, 1952,
Glenstone Museum, Potomac

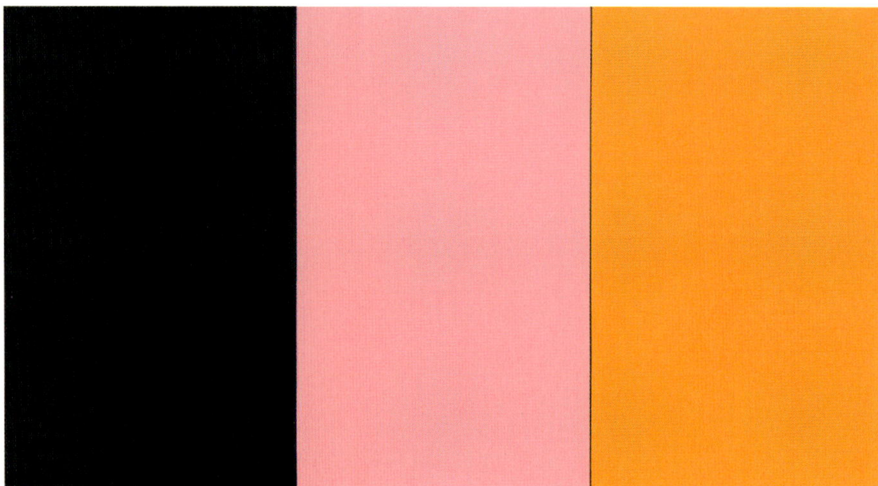

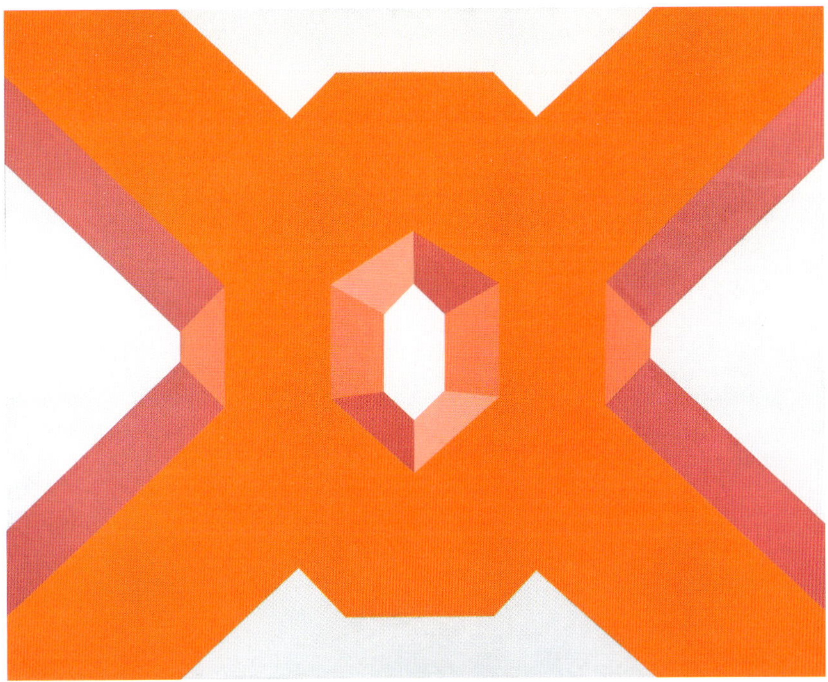

4
Miriam Schapiro,
Big Ox, 1967,
private collection

The grid, as seen in the work of Martin and François Morellet (cats. 93–97), was endemic to Minimalism. To many, it seemed like the height of a detached, logical approach, freed from the burdens of expression or the expectations of composition. However, critic and curator Lucy Lippard identified its power to contain multitudes, writing, "The grid is music paper for color, idea, state of mind. It is a standard measure. It repeats the traditional shape of the canvas itself. It implies, illogically, logic and harmony and unity, and is therefore all the more interesting to alter or destroy, no matter how slightly." The truth of this description had been demonstrated decades earlier by Wassily Kandinsky. Within his omnivorous style, the grid had been deployed to all of these ends, many of them demonstrated with particular clarity in his painting *Grid and Other Shapes* (private collection, 1937).

Compared to Greenberg's and Judd's more rigid and polemical takes, Lippard's insights may be less useful when it comes to neat categorization and summation. However, in identifying a supposedly simple, mute form as an adaptable scaffolding for diverse content, she offers another way to think about the period. Her broader view can encompass the wide range of motivations that these artists brought to their work, as they pushed abstraction in new directions—far beyond its surface.

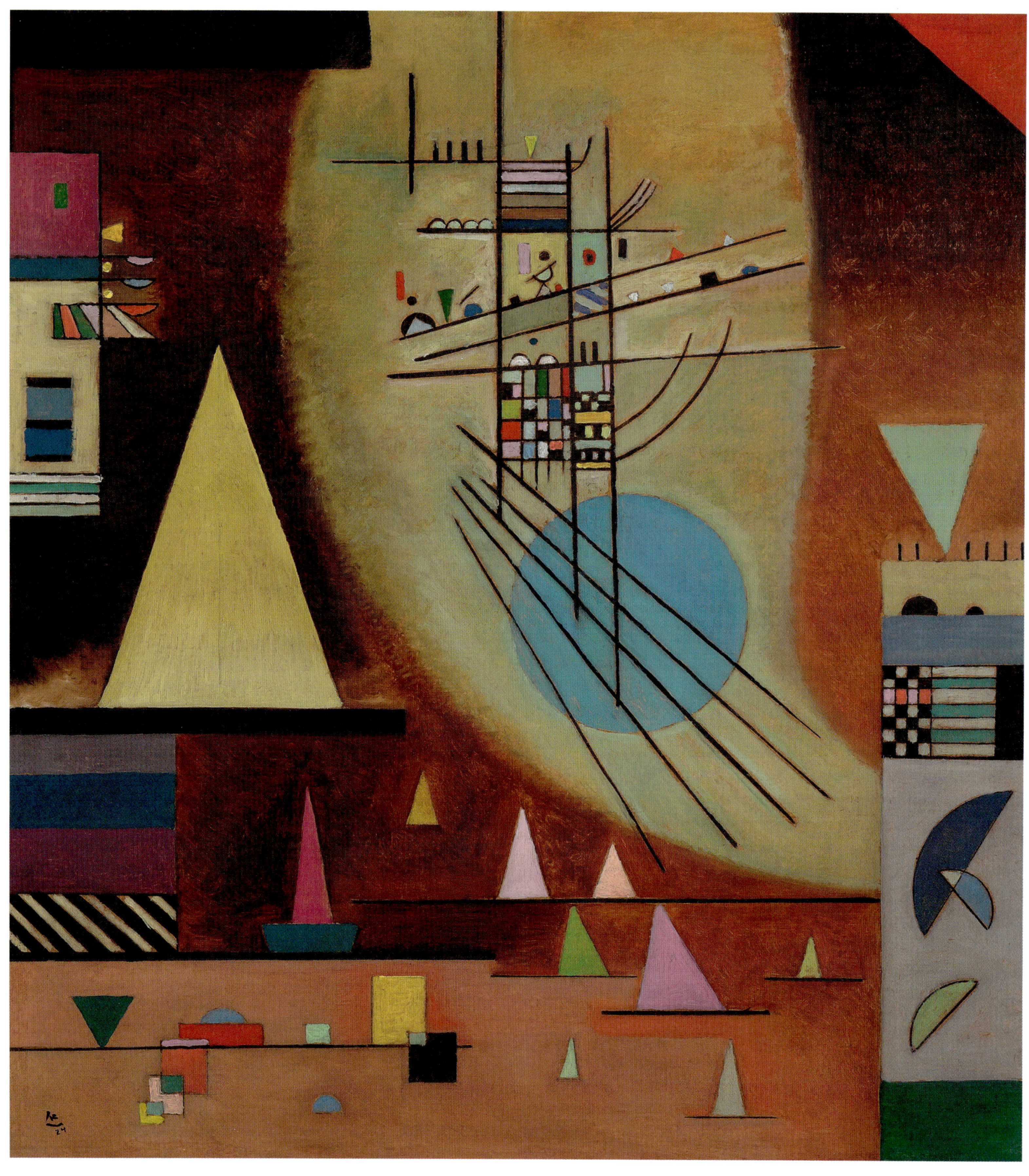

80 Wassily Kandinsky
Silent, 1924
Collection Museum Boijmans Van Beuningen, Rotterdam

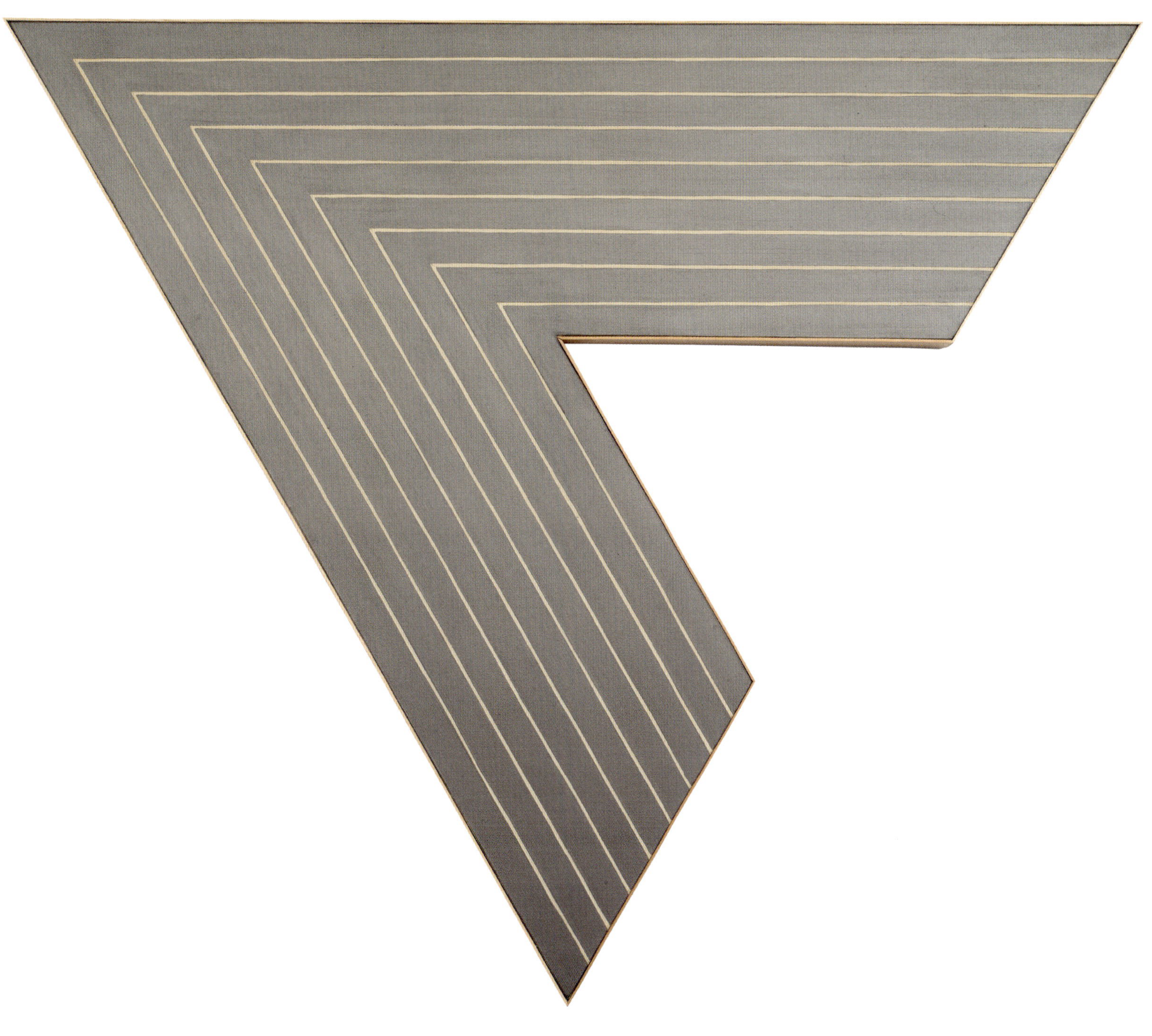

81 Frank Stella
Slieve More, 1964
Private collection, Switzerland

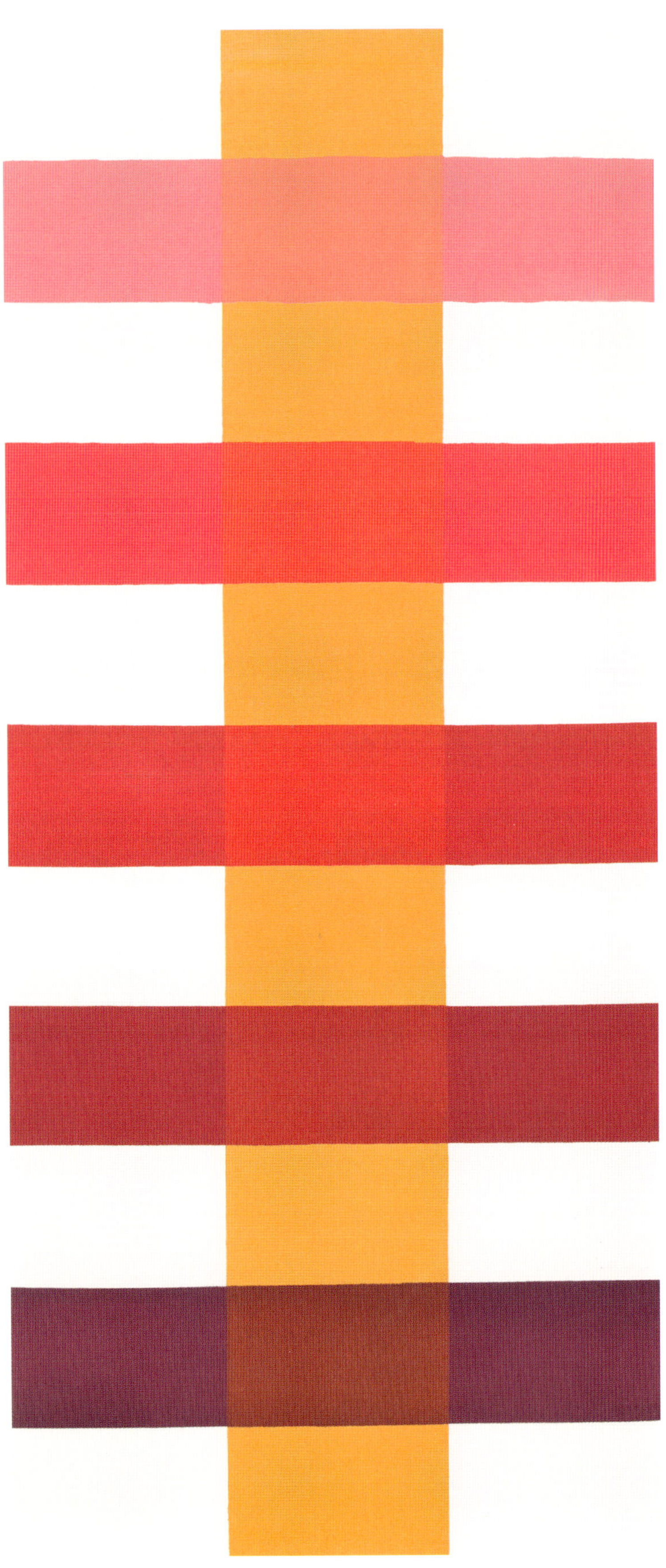

82 Paul Reed
Coherence, 1966
National Gallery of Art, Washington

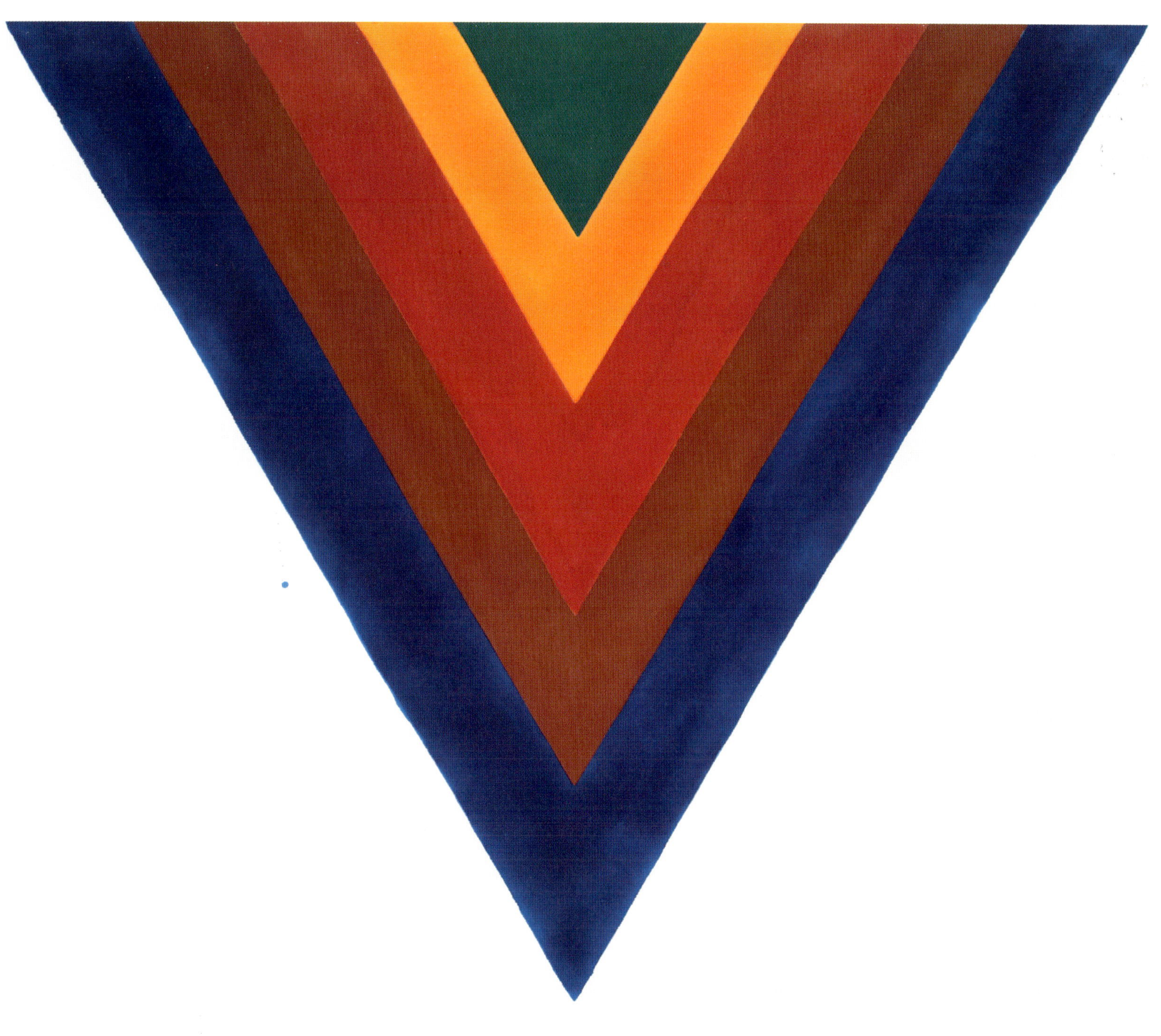

83 Kenneth Noland
Half-Time, 1964
ASOM Collection

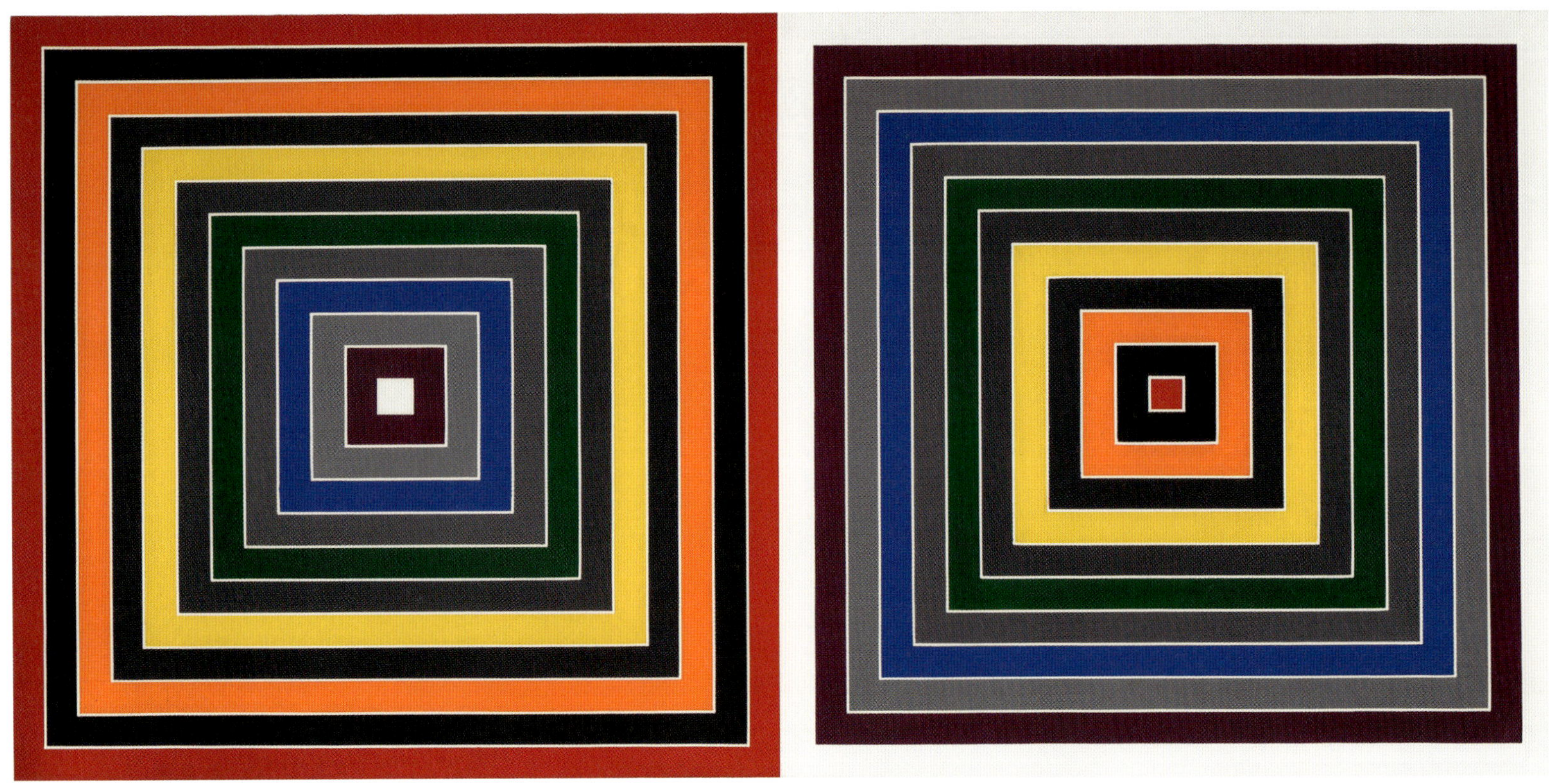

84 Frank Stella
Double Scramble, 1978
Private collection

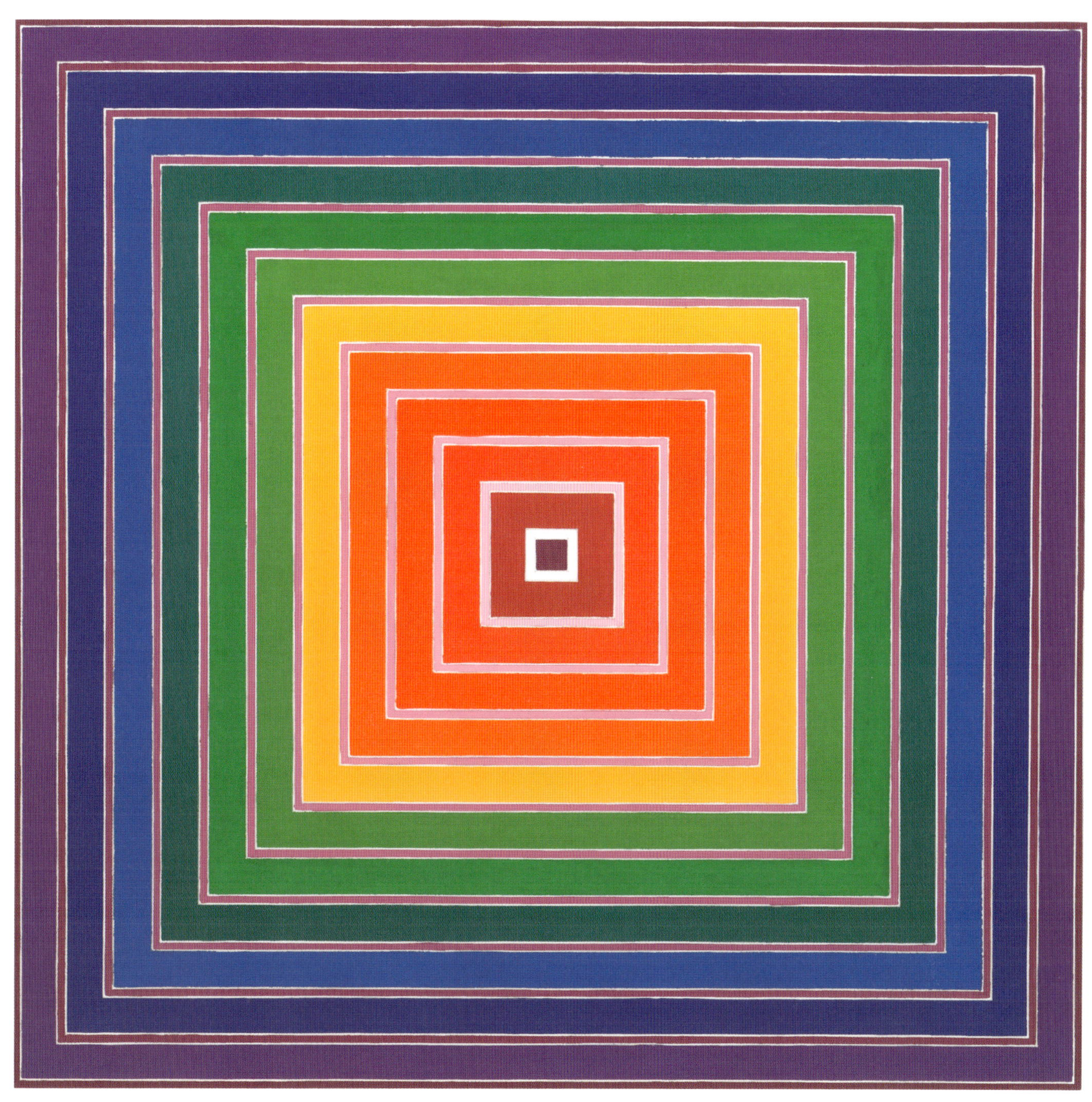

85 Frank Stella
Sacramento Mall Proposal #4, 1978
National Gallery of Art, Washington

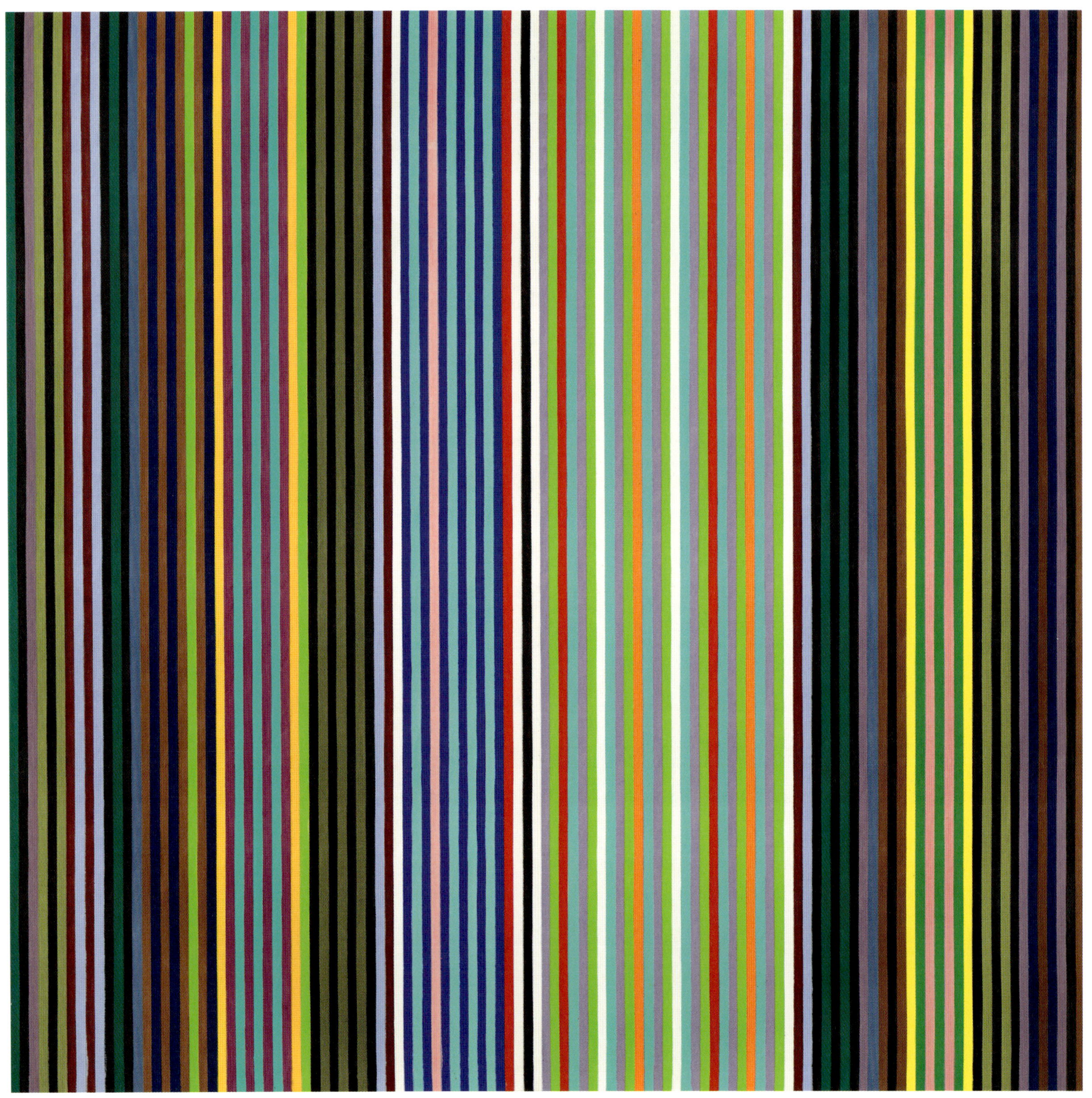

86 Gene Davis
Black Popcorn, 1965
National Gallery of Art, Washington

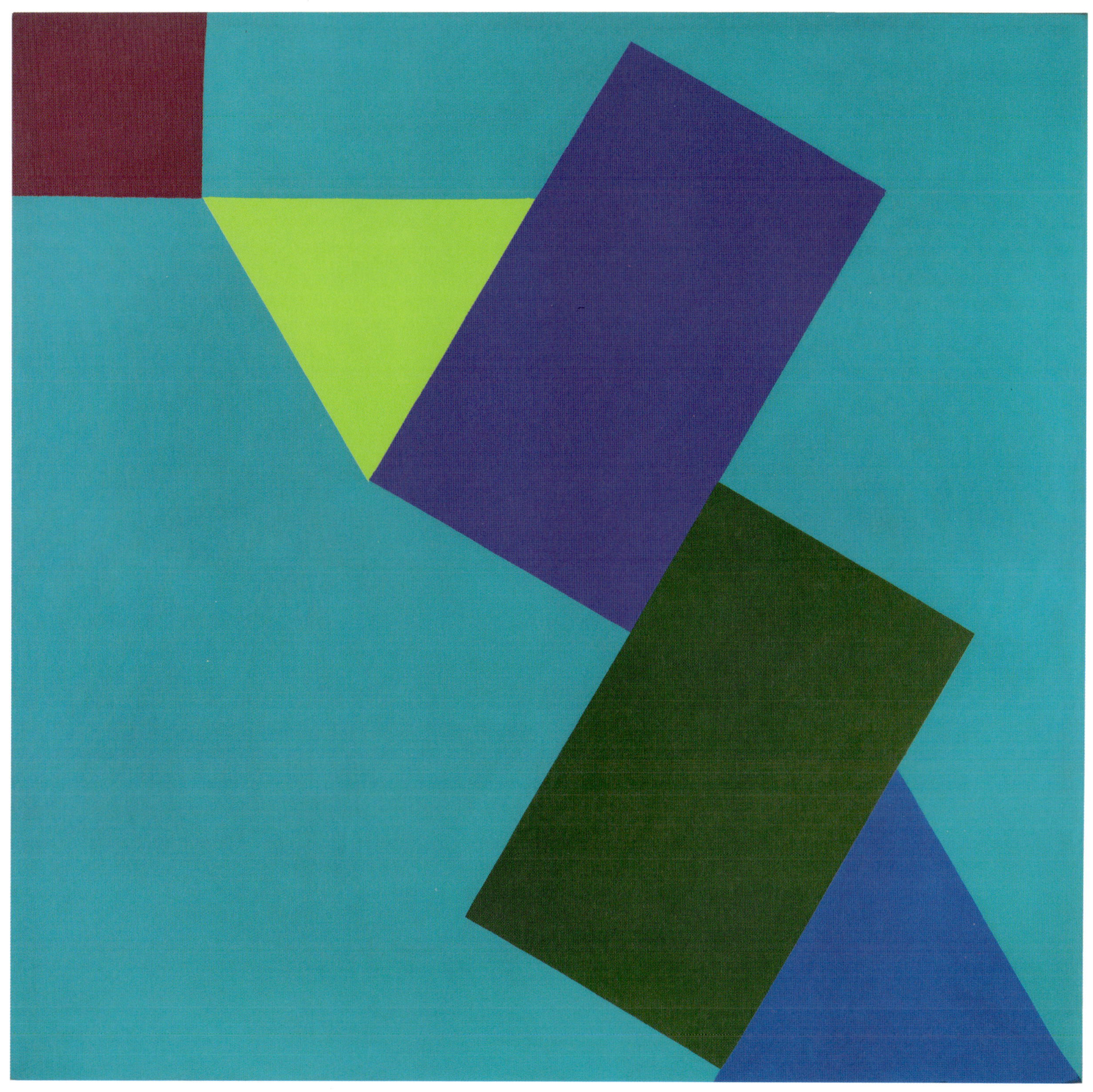

87 Paul Huxley
Untitled no. 51, 1966
Studio Paul Huxley

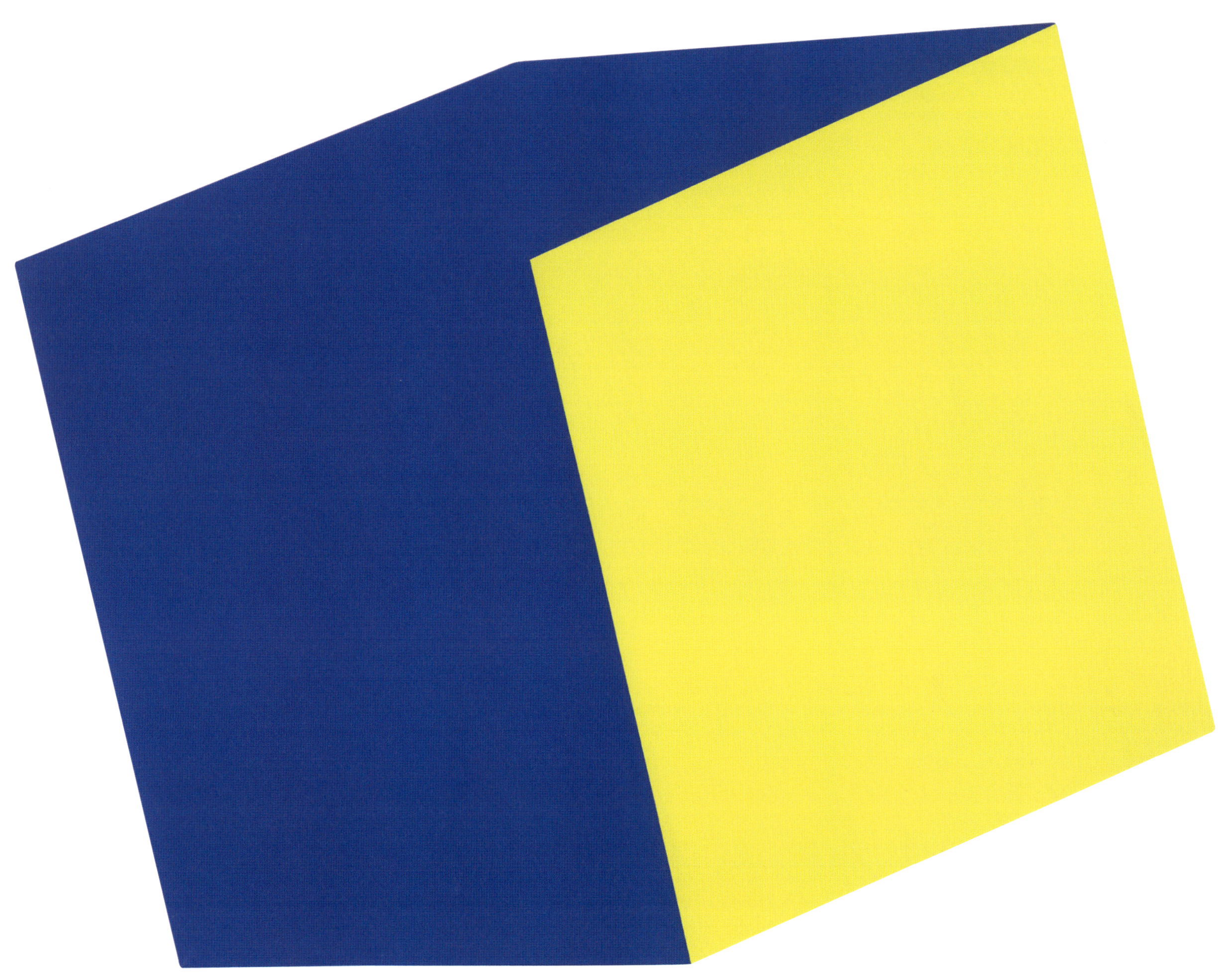

88 Ellsworth Kelly
Blue Yellow, 1968
Private collection

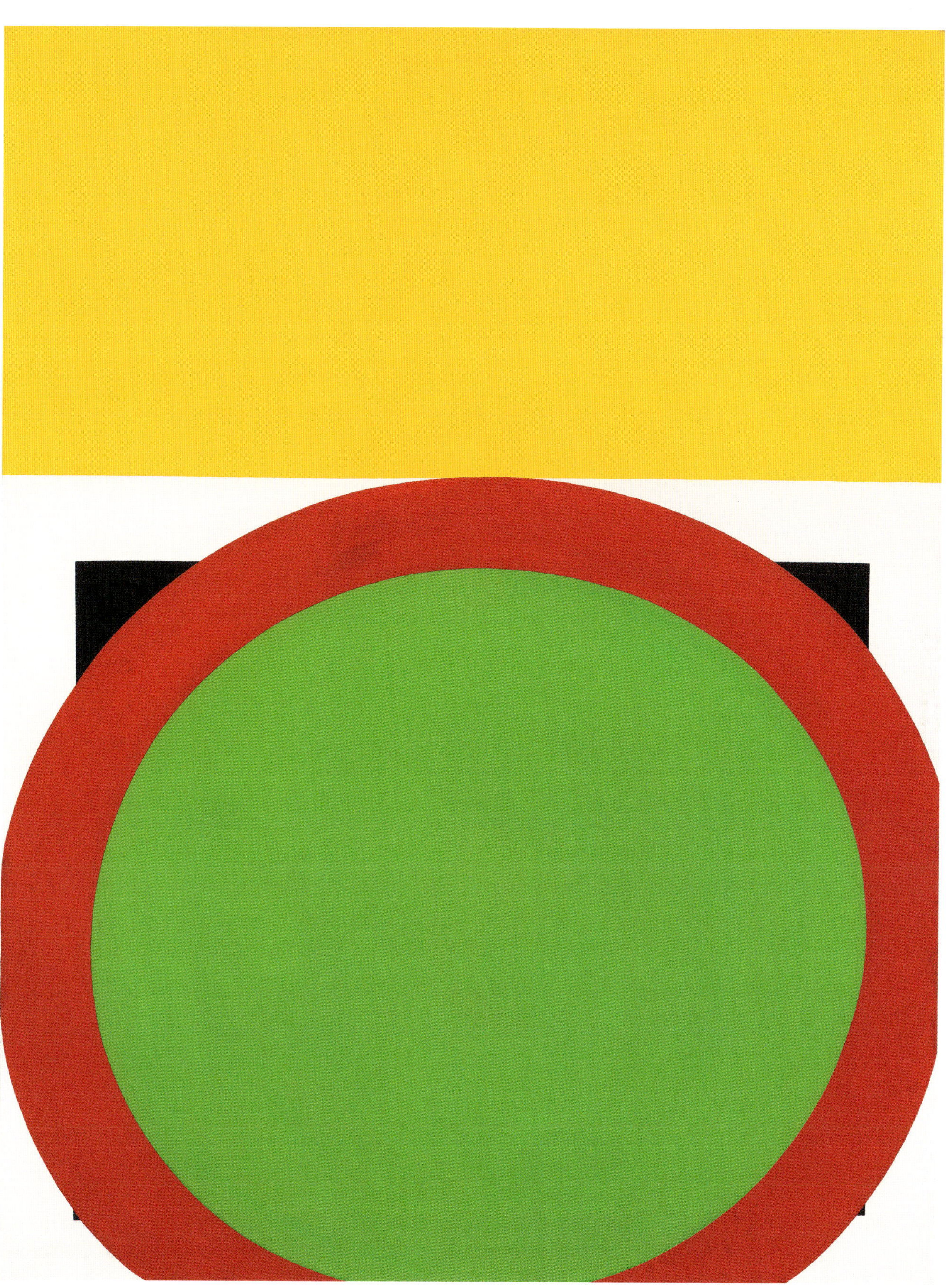

89 Al Held
The Dowager Empress, 1965
Whitney Museum of American Art, New York

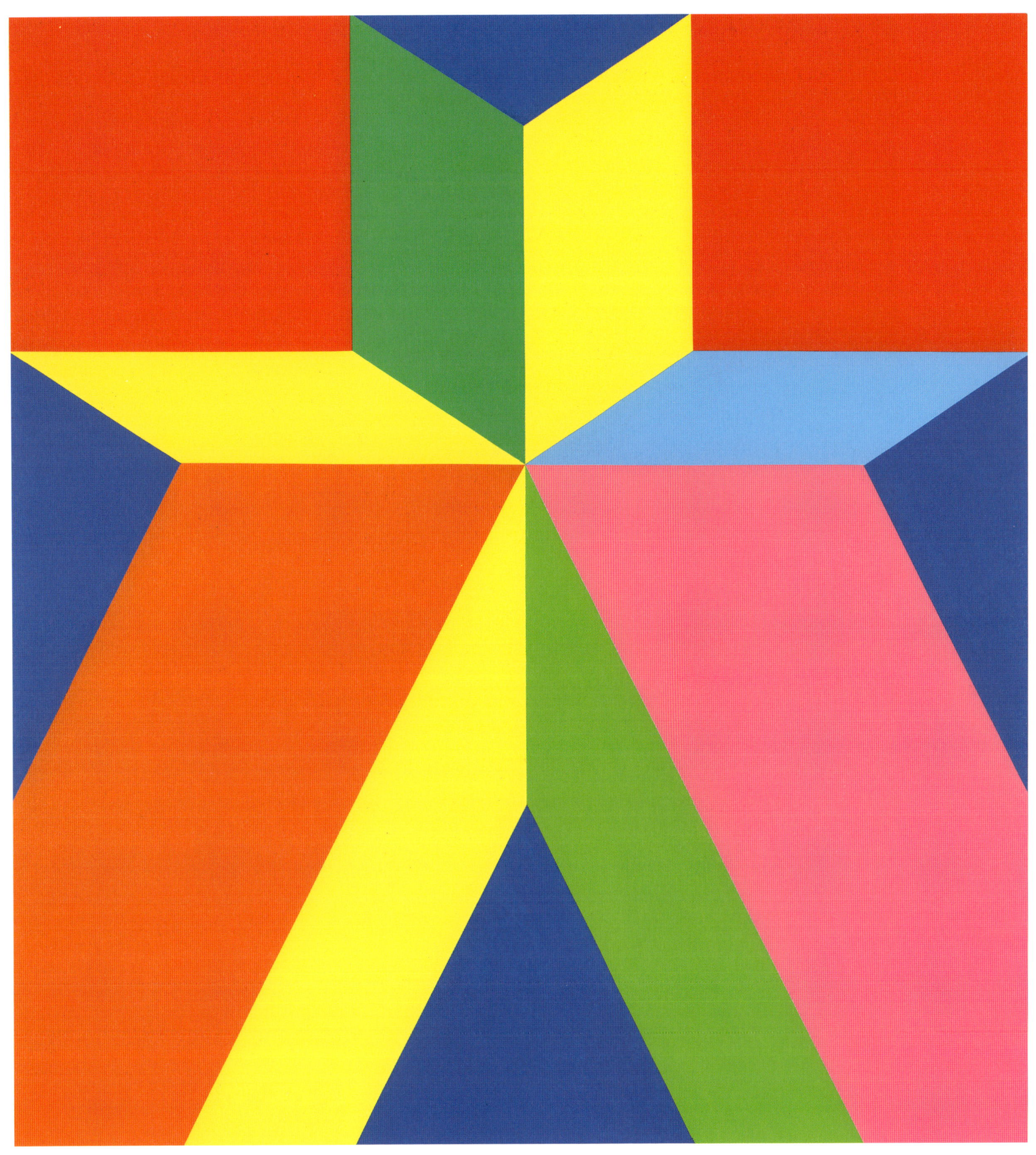

90 Miriam Schapiro
Jigsaw, 1969
Whitney Museum of American Art, New York

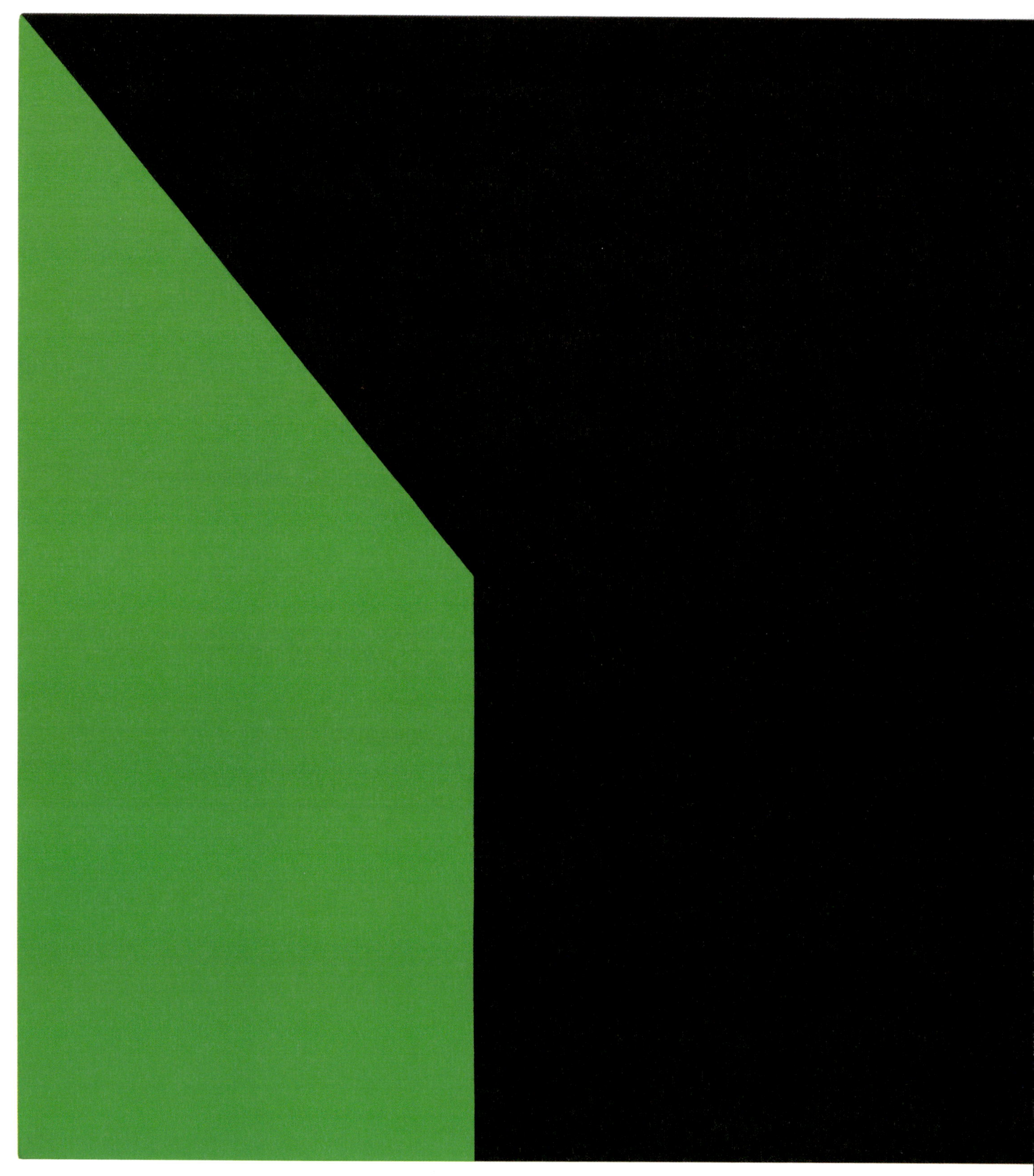

91 Carmen Herrera
Diptych (Green & Black), 1976
Estate of Carmen Herrera;
Courtesy private collection and Lisson Gallery

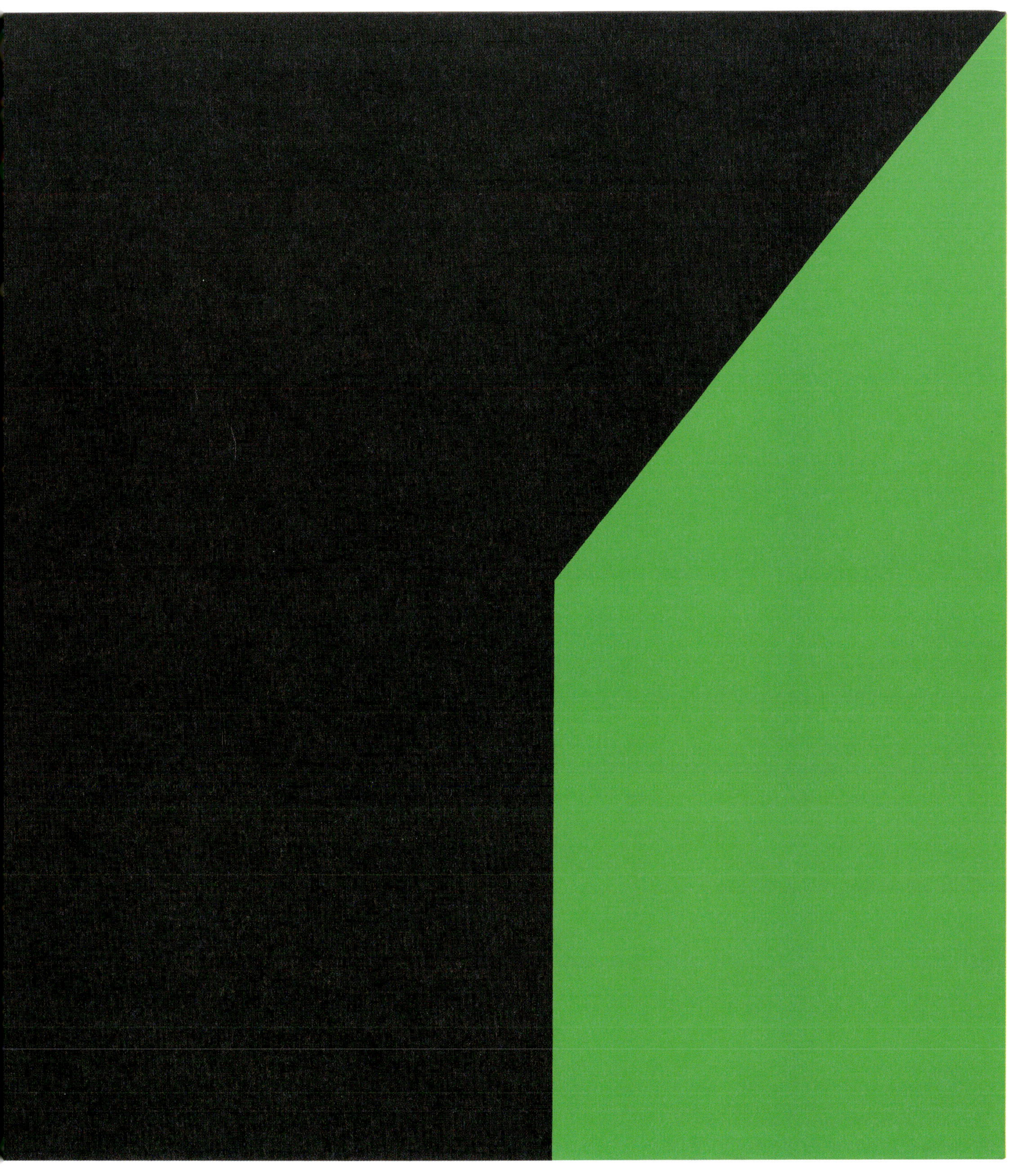

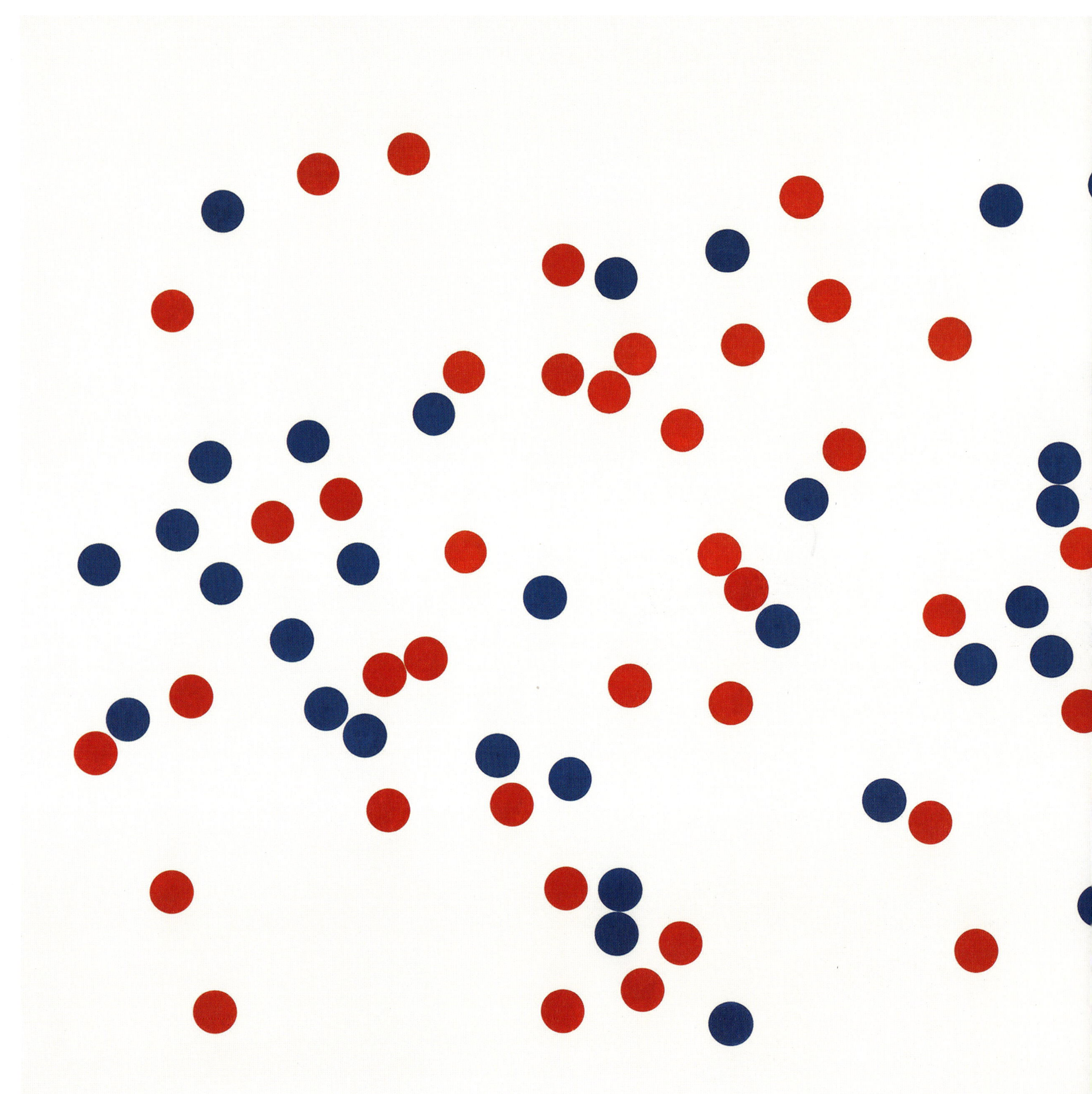

92 Alexander Liberman
Blue Opposite Red, 1959
Whitney Museum of American Art, New York

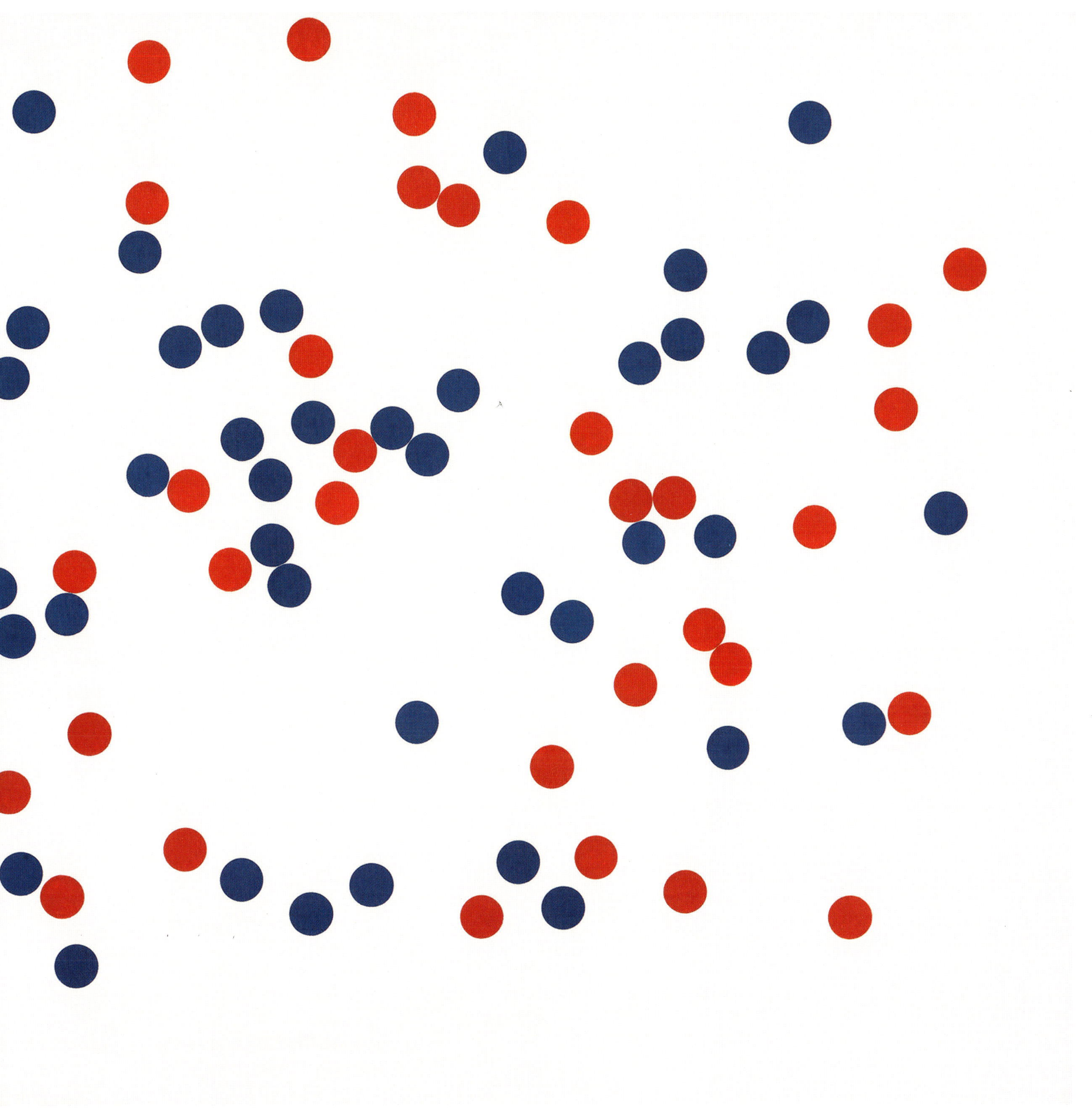

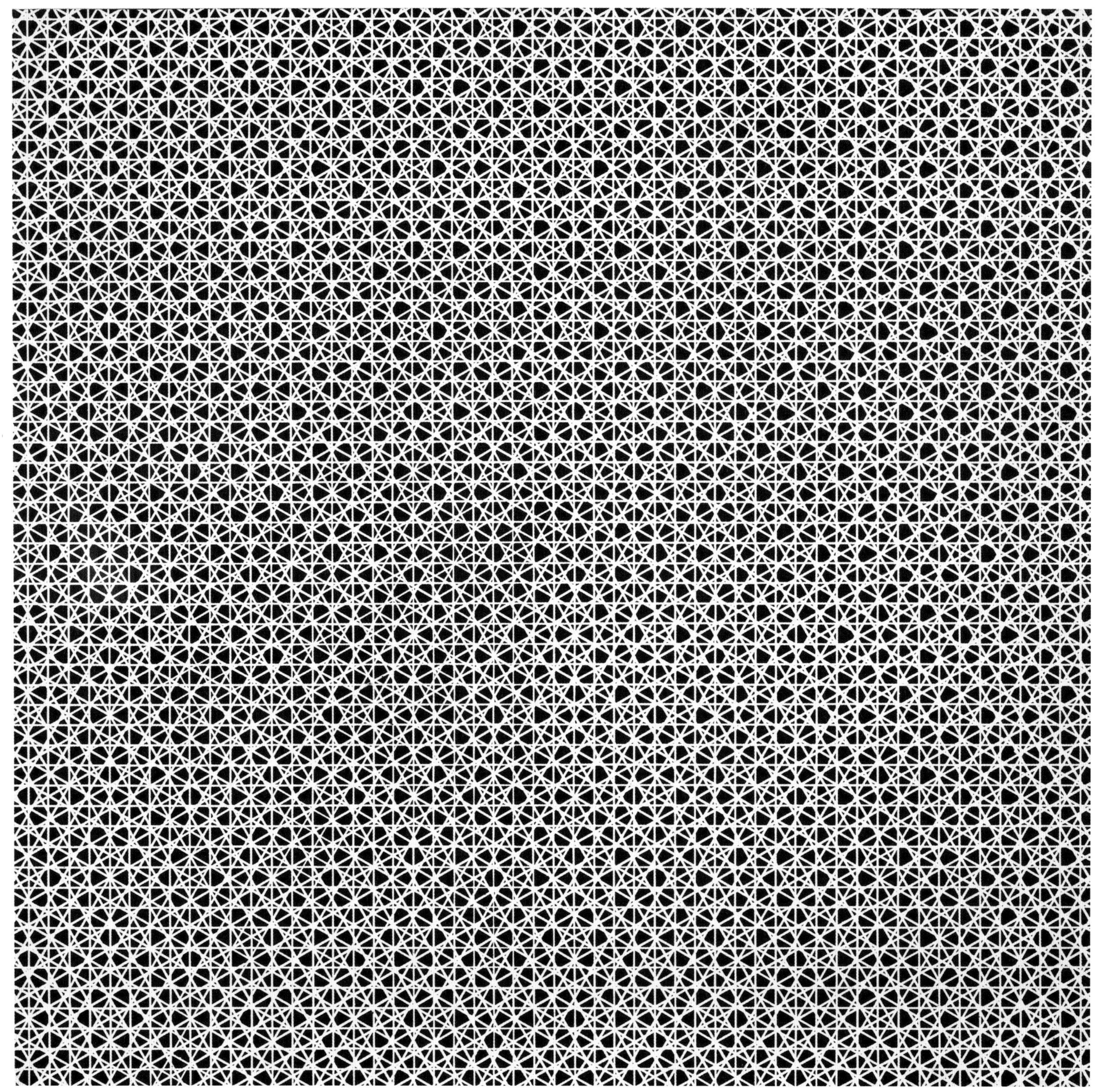

93 François Morellet
3 Double Grids 0° 30° 60°, 1971
Fondation Gandur pour l'Art, Genève

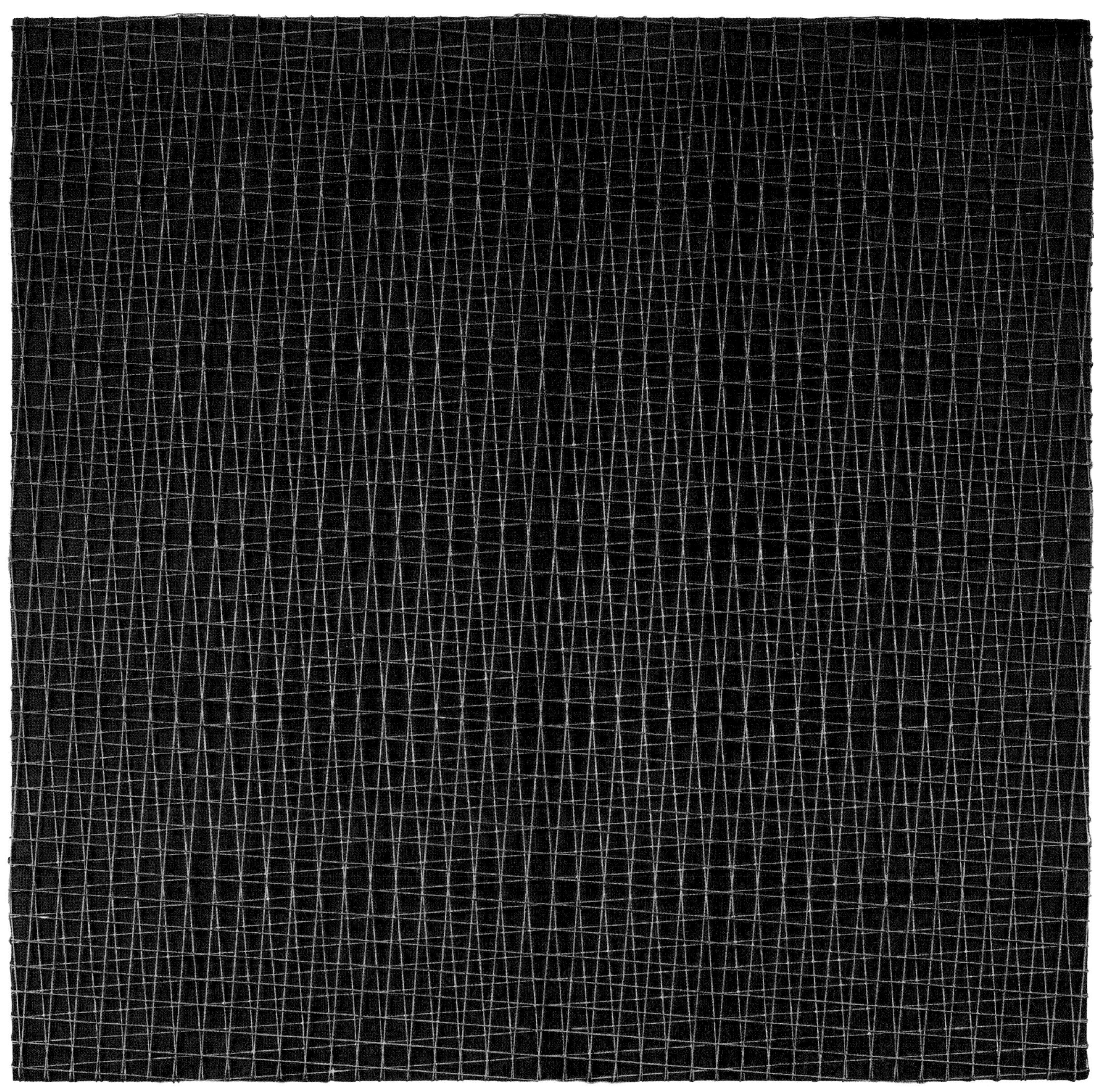

94 François Morellet
2 Wire Grids −4° +4° (# 19 mm), 1972
Fondation Gandur pour l’Art, Genève

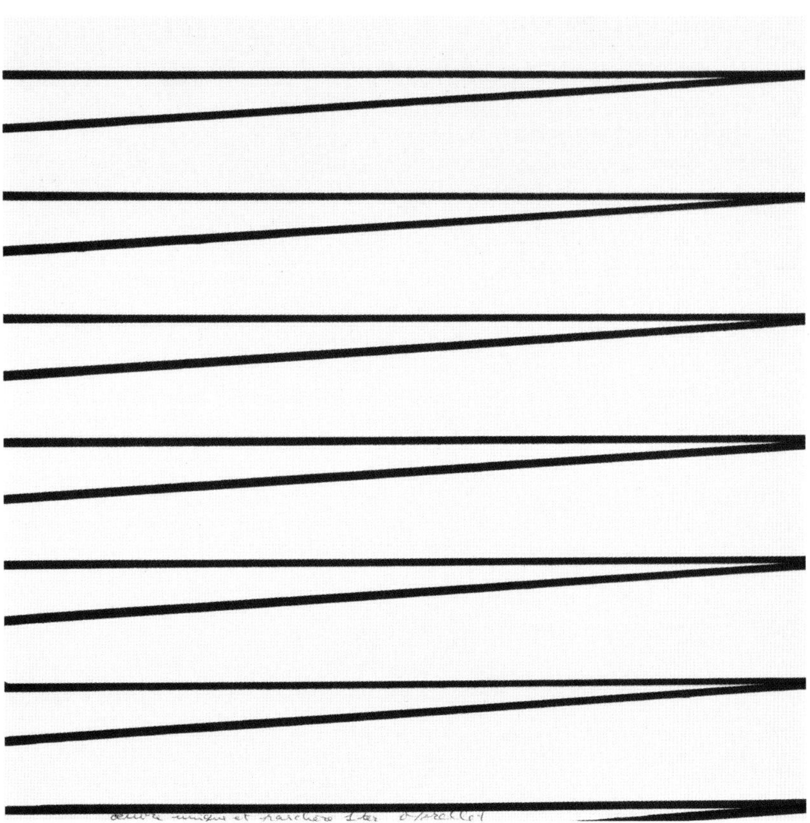

95 François Morellet
The 1st Unique and Inexpensive Work, 1970
Fondation Gandur pour l'Art, Genève

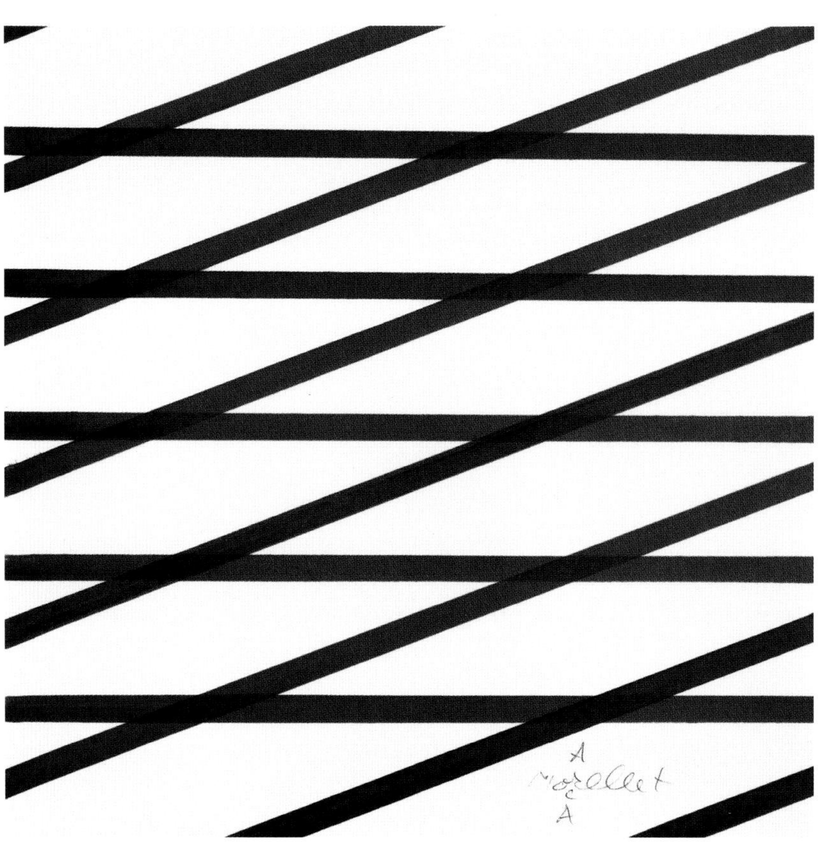

96 François Morellet
Untitled, 1970
Fondation Gandur pour l'Art, Genève

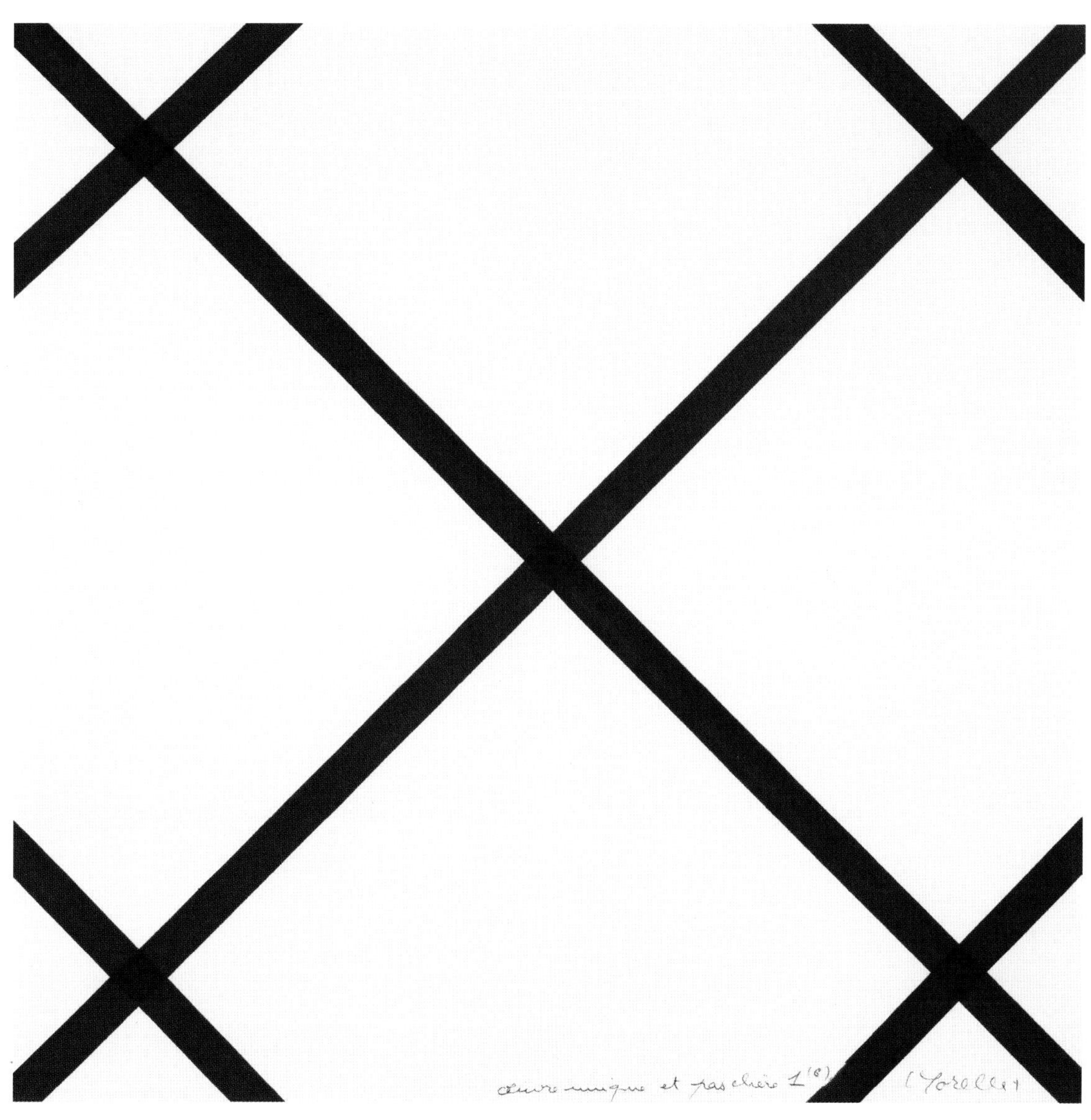

97 François Morellet
Unique and Inexpensive Work 1 (6), 1970
Fondation Gandur pour l'Art, Genève

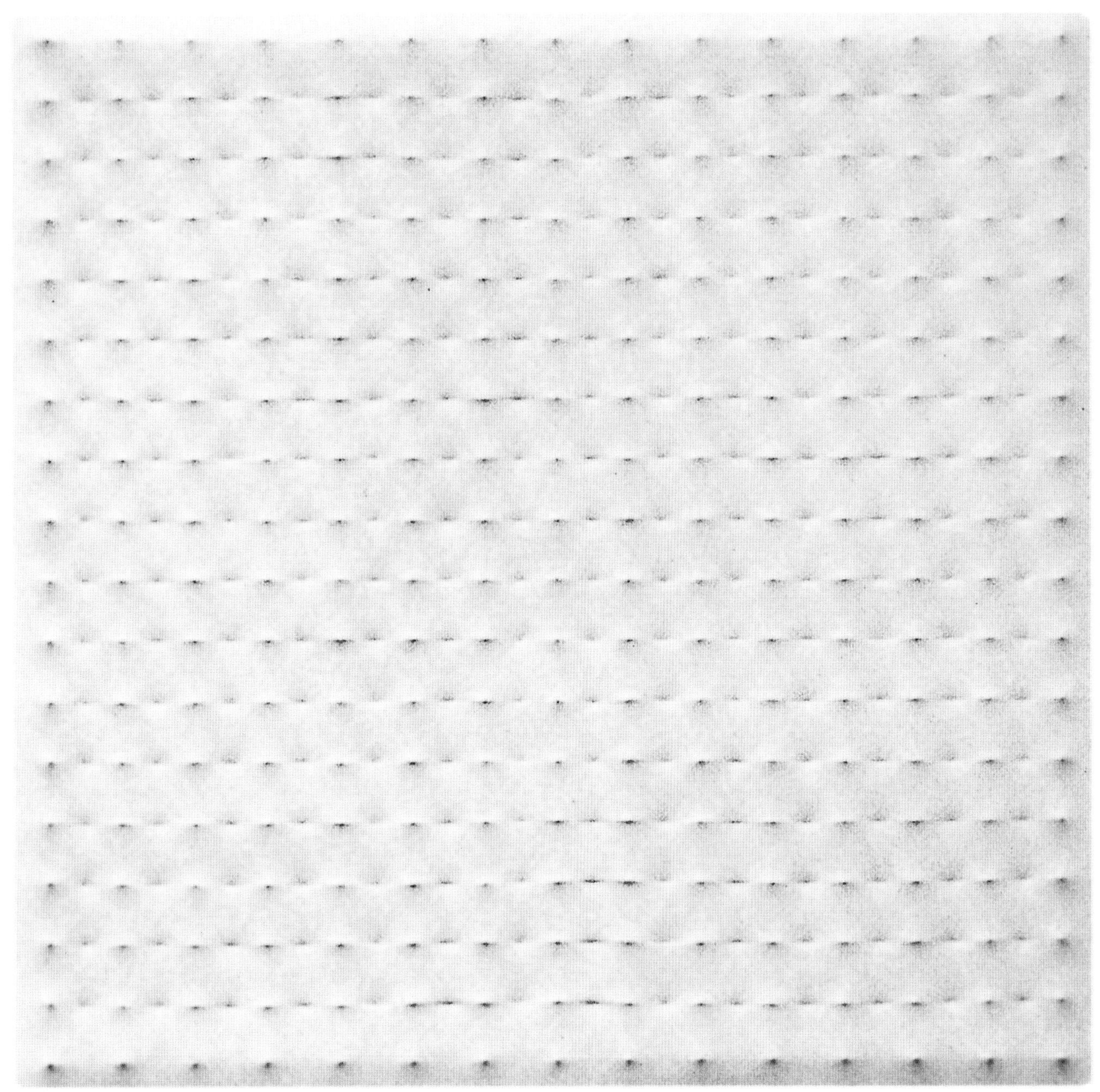

98 Enrico Castellani
White Surface No. 18, 1964
Mercedes-Benz Art Collection

99 Agnes Martin
Summer Sky II, 1967
Private collection

100 Jo Baer
White Side Bar (blue line), 1972–75
Louisiana Museum of Modern Art, Humlebæk

101 Aurélie Nemours
Composition (Divide), 1961
Fondation Gandur pour l'Art, Genève

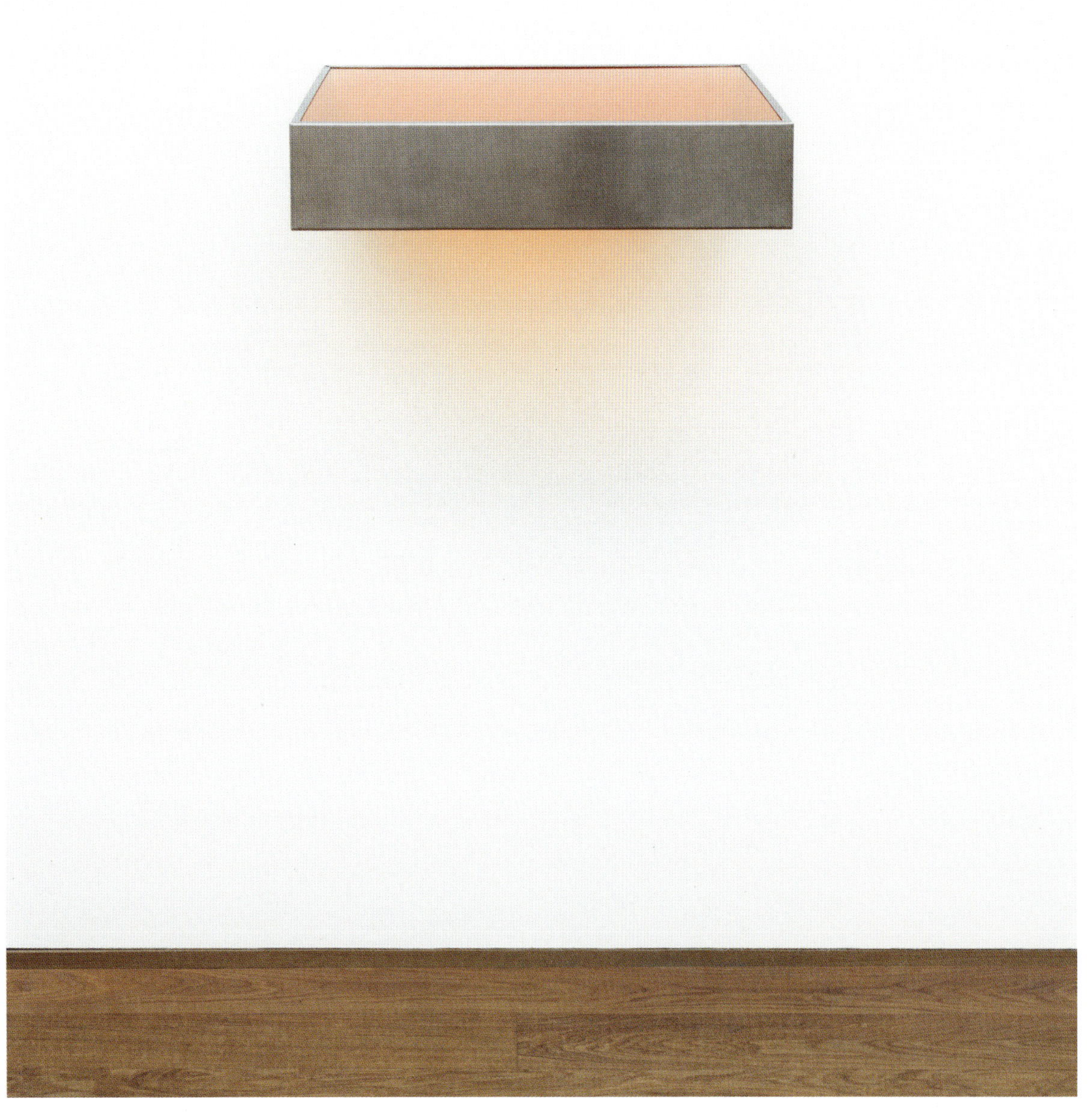

102 Donald Judd
Untitled, 1969
Staatliche Museen zu Berlin, Nationalgalerie, Marzona Collection

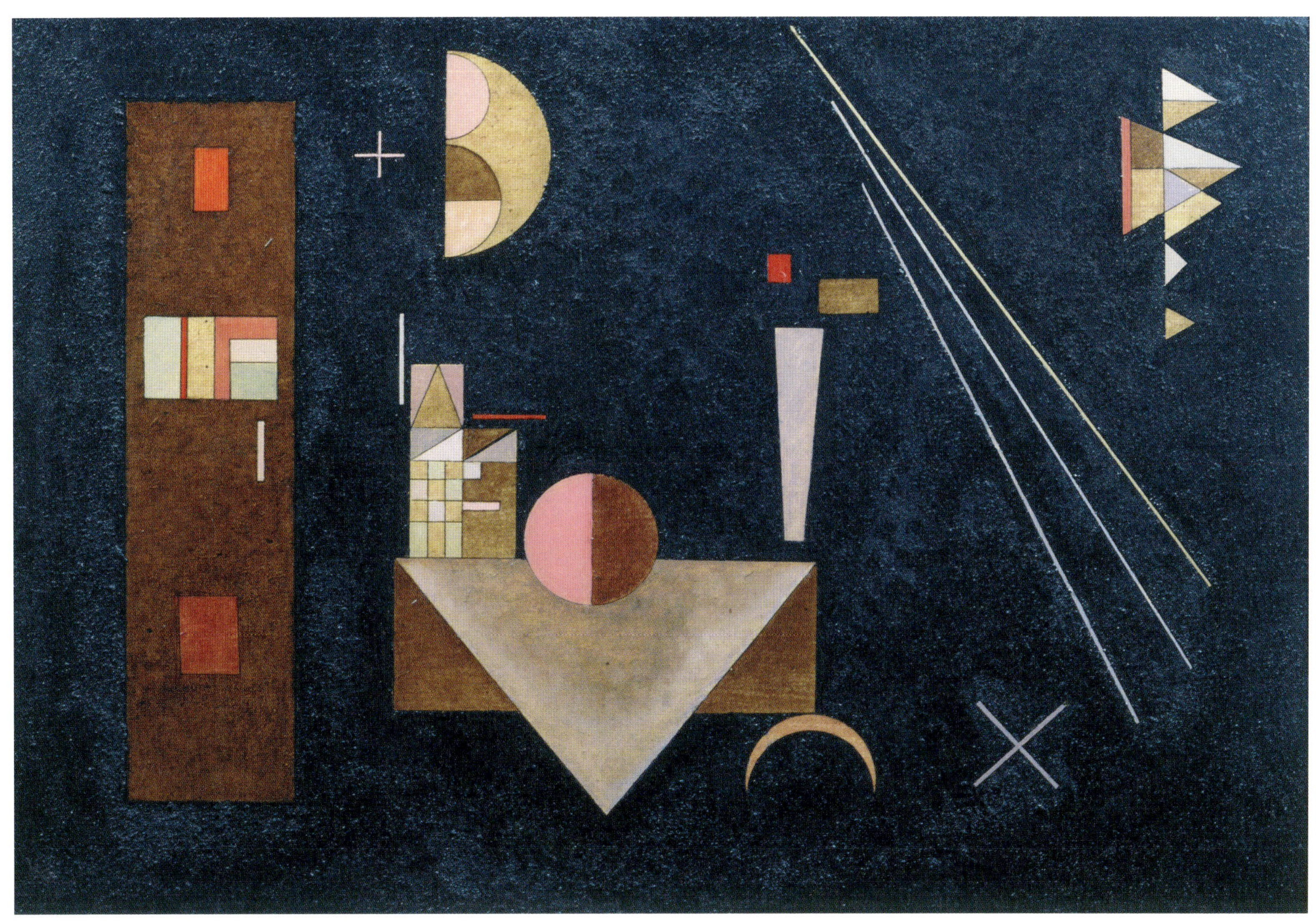

103 Wassily Kandinsky
Two Crosses, 1929
Private collection

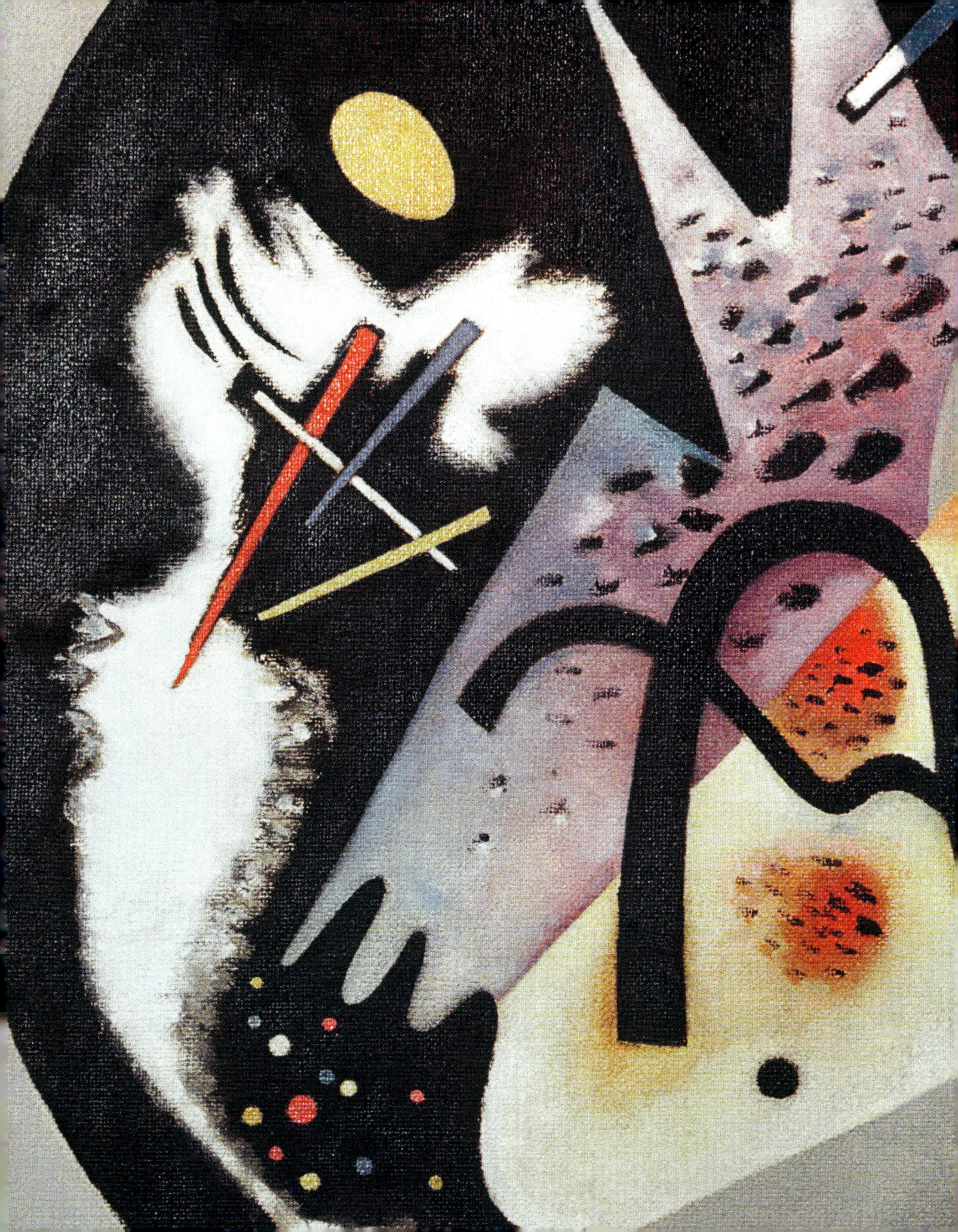

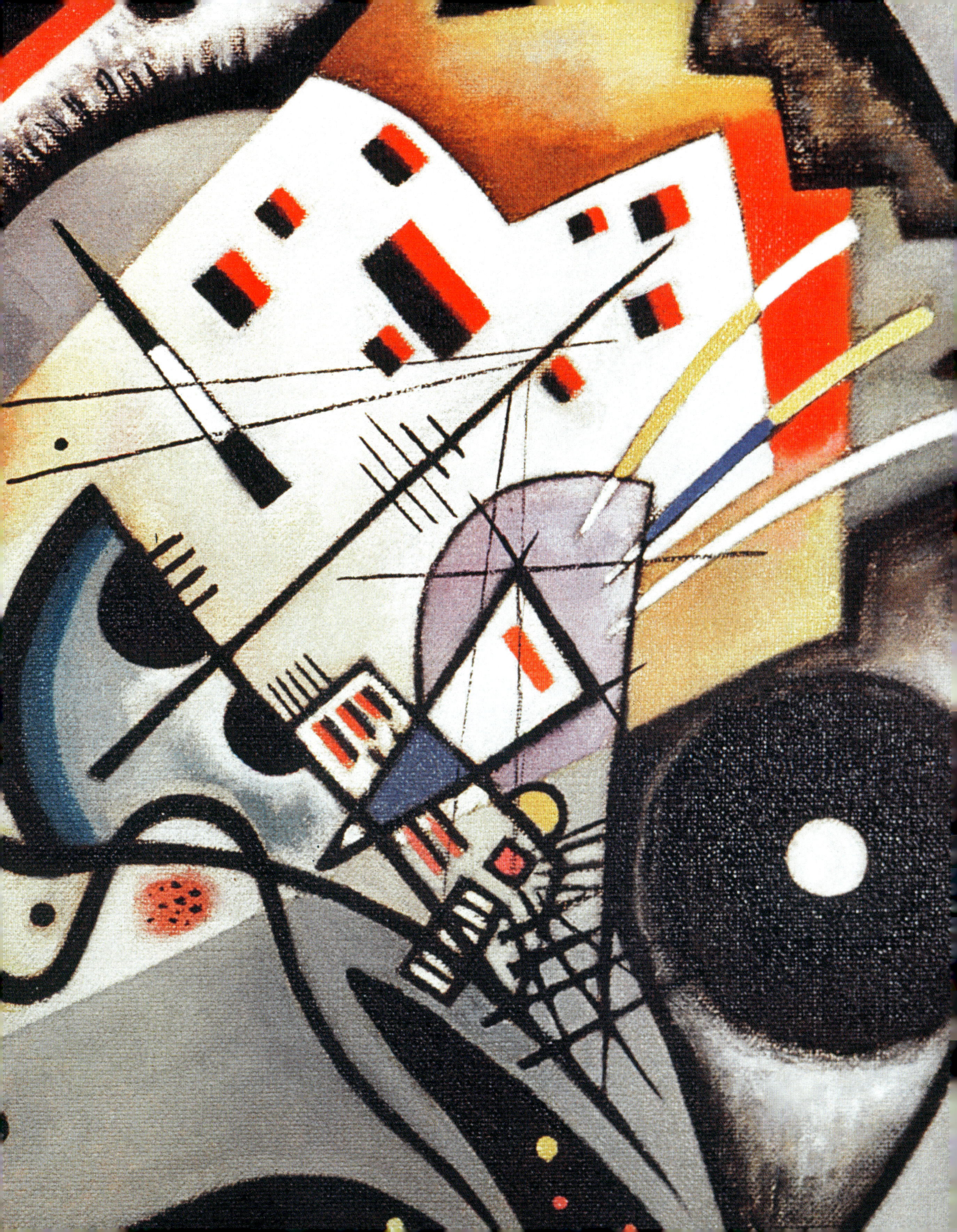

Sterre Barentsen

Space Age Op Art in the Sixties

Op Art pushed the boundaries of visual perception, making two-dimensional images appear spatial, and static paintings seem to move. The act of seeing becomes an active experience.

As early as the 1910s, Wassily Kandinsky and Kazimir Malevich experimented with visual elements that appear to float or convey a sense of movement. Op Art later built upon these ideas, combining insights from the Bauhaus on the effects of colors and shapes with the 1960s fascination for technology, space exploration, and television imagery.

Bridget Riley and Victor Vasarely created geometric patterns with stark black-and-white contrasts. Meanwhile in America, students of former Bauhaus master Josef Albers continued his distinctive work with squares in vivid colors.

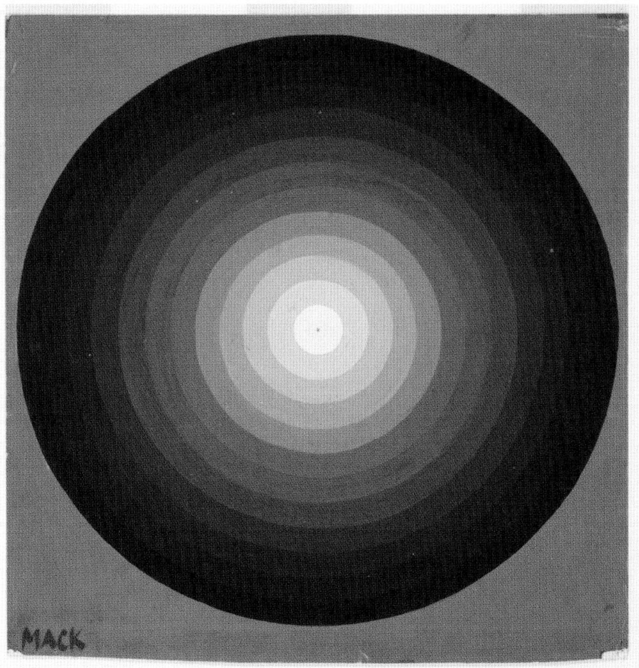

1
Ludwig Hirschfeld-Mack, *Exercise in Advancing and Receding Values,* 1922–23, Harvard Art Museums/ Busch-Reisinger Museum

Optical Art, or Op Art for short, took the art scene by storm as the latest trend after the exhibition *The Responsive Eye* (→ p. 277) at the Museum of Modern Art in New York achieved groundbreaking success in 1965. It was the best attended in MoMA's history up to that point. The exhibition brought together works by artists from fifteen countries under the banner of "perceptual abstraction." Their compositions were unharmonious and charged with tension, seemingly unstable, with forms that appeared to collapse inward and swell outward, flickering and twitching. It defined a movement that united art with technology and the science of optics.[1]

While viewers came in droves to see paintings that seemed to move and flicker, the critical responses to the exhibition were scathing. Lucy Lippard called it "an art of little substance with less to it than meets the eye"; Barbara Rose scoffed that Op Art "goes Pop art one better by being considerably more mindless," while Rosalind Krauss described it as "perpetual gimmickry."[2] Yet no other art movement so incisively captured the zeitgeist of the 1960s. Leaning into the futuristic and psychedelic aesthetic of the decade, it explored the astral realms of space, the "glitches" of television screens, and the pseudotechnological language of science fiction. In so doing, it continued the experiments of Constructivism and the Bauhaus, which had demonstrated that the play of geometric forms and colors alone was enough to bring canvases to life.

Checkerboard patterns had already aroused considerable interest at the Bauhaus, where students experimented with black-and-white design elements and created compositions that seemed to advance or recede in space (fig. 1). Wassily Kandinsky incorporated these patterns into paintings such as *White Cross* (cat. 3), *Silent* (cat. 80), and *Composition No. 224 (On White I)* (fig. p. 26), with artificial black-and-white grids that resemble planes from another dimension. The checkerboard pattern formed the basis of many Op Art experiments, since its contrasts gave rise to pulsating effects that maximized pictorial tension. In paintings such as *Vegaviv II* (cat. 108), artist Victor Vasarely—who in the late 1920s had trained at the private art school Műhely in Budapest, known as the "Hungarian Bauhaus"—used the pattern to produce swelling, spherical effects. The distribution of various geometric forms keeps the viewer's eye in motion and prevents it from focusing on any single location.

Vasarely continued to develop his geometric patterns in the series *Planetary Folklore,* which is based on the combination of two geometric forms. The primary shape is a square, which serves as a background and contains within it another shape—such as a smaller square, or perhaps a circle, rhombus, rectangle, diamond, or triangle. Each shape is filled with a uniform color, making it possible to create infinite variations. These pairs of shapes and colors form a kind of alphabet—or algorithm. One example is the work *Boglar I* (cat. 109), which consists of green and blue circles arranged in squares, with a lighter, bilious green center. Vasarely found a new use for the modern grid by integrating the technological and cultural influences of his time. With their sharp edges and artificial colors, the modular compositions of *Planetary Folklore* anticipate the aesthetic of computer games.

The launch of Sputnik 1 by the Soviet Union in 1957 marked the beginning of the Space Race (→ p. 276), a period of intense competition between the United States and the Soviet Union. This event not only ignited political rivalry, but also prompted intense interest in outer space in contemporary popular culture and propaganda. Polish artist Wojciech Fangor had spent the 1950s creating paintings in the style of Socialist Realism, which had been declared the official artistic movement in Poland in 1949. Toward the end of the decade, he began designing round, abstract forms that resembled blurred, hazy planets. The works are reminiscent of the astral images of Wassily Kandinsky and the foggy spheres on black backgrounds created by Ivan Kliun (cat. 9). While early modern artists had used cosmic references to evoke spirituality and allude to the existence of unseen realities beyond the visible world, Fangor, enthralled by space, adopted the pictorial language of the Sputnik era. Works such as *B13* (cat. 112) and *B15* (cat. 113) show rings of opaque color within soft-edged spheres, with bright white centers glowing like the afterimage of a dying star. The captivating effect of this cosmic pictorial language in the 1960s probably contributed to Fangor's international success: he was given a solo exhibition at the Solomon R. Guggenheim Museum in New York in 1970, a rare honor for an Eastern European artist during the Cold War. British artist Peter Sedgley created a similar series of concentric circles (fig. 2), with colors that seem to change as they are illuminated with preprogrammed sequences of light. Sedgley's integration of light and color lends a kinetic quality to these otherwise static works and reflects the artist's interest in the relationship between visual perception and technology.

While the art of Fangor, Sedgley, and Vasarely is associated with images from the world of cybernetics or astronomy, the smooth, anonymous surfaces of paintings by British artist Bridget Riley find their pendant in the television screen (→ p. 272). In *Tremor* (cat. 104), Riley covers the entire canvas with a pattern of triangles. Their curving sides are convex or concave,

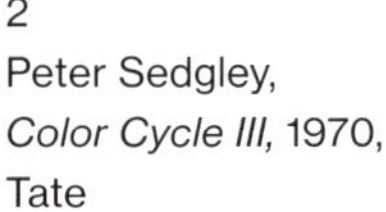

2
Peter Sedgley,
Color Cycle III, 1970,
Tate

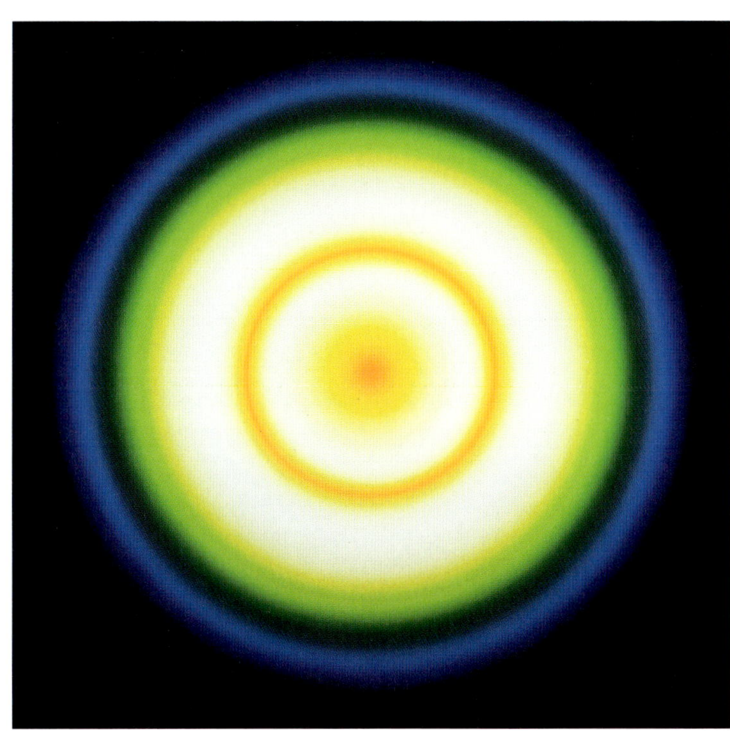

causing them to pulsate and shimmer. This intricate repeating pattern is associated with the pixelation of a television monitor, so that the painting seems to flicker like a screen. In later works such as the paintings *Clepsydra 1* (cat. 123) and *Shih-Li* (cat. 124), Riley introduces color: here, pastel lines in a repeating, wave-shaped pattern evoke a dizzying sensation of movement. Such paintings allude to the visual language of electronic glitches.

Op Art, which emerged at the same time as Happenings, offered an immersive experience—one that at times blurred the boundary between immersion and overwhelm. The sight of such works could elicit feelings of physical revulsion, nausea, or pounding headaches in their viewers. While the other major art trend of the same years, Pop Art, embraced elements of advertising, posters, and commercial packaging, Op Art adopted the visual language of television. In the 1960s, television became the dominant medium of popular culture, and its powers of fascination gave rise to the fears reflected in the negative critical response to the exhibition *The Responsive Eye* at MoMA.[3] In the magazine *ARTnews,* critic Thomas B. Hess reported that audiences "'bob and wave' in front of the exhibits, shake their heads back and forth, make little jumps, like penguins at a mating dance, to get the biggest retinal kicks." Hess was so contemptuous of the exhibition-goers that he called them "peripatetic zombies."[4]

The expression "Pop goes Op" was widespread in the press. Op Art was viewed as a short-lived fad in a rapidly accelerating cycle of fashionable currents. However, this neglects its connections to prewar modernism. Bridget Riley referred to *The Thinking Eye,* by Paul Klee, as "one of my Bibles in the 1960s," and used this compilation of Klee's pedagogical notes and lectures to create for herself a self-imposed Bauhaus curriculum.[5] In it, Klee gave a lesson on how movement can be suggested with a grid, using his painting *Town Castle Kr.* (fig. 3) as an example: by pulling on the corners and changing the sizes in a grid of squares, waves of motion can be produced across the canvas, causing some sections to seem to project outward or collapse inward. The instructions in the margin next to the image read: "Try to achieve the greatest possible movement with the least possible means."[6] It is easy to imagine Riley accepting this challenge when she created her first work of Op Art, *Movement in Squares* (fig. 4).

The influence of the Bauhaus on Op Art is most obviously manifested in the series of paintings *Homage to the Square* (cats. 28–32) by Bauhaus master Josef Albers. In the exhibition *The Responsive Eye,* these works received their own, chapel-like space. When the Bauhaus

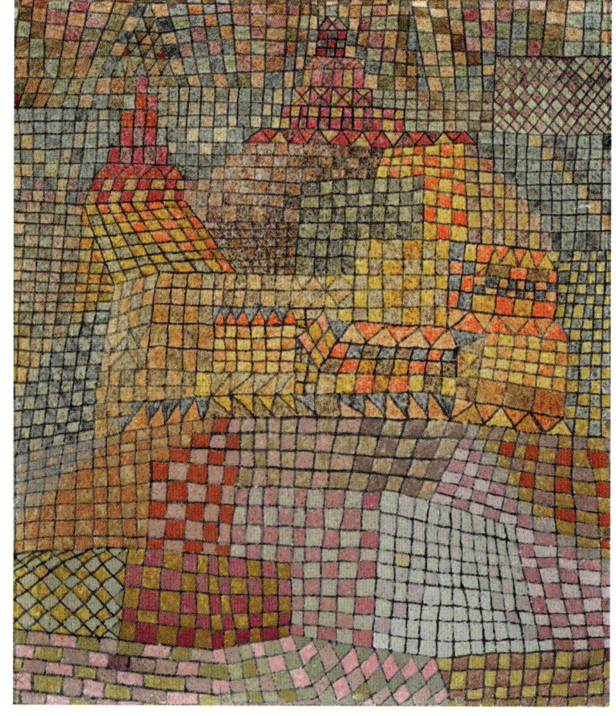

3
Paul Klee,
Town Castle Kr., 1932,
private collection

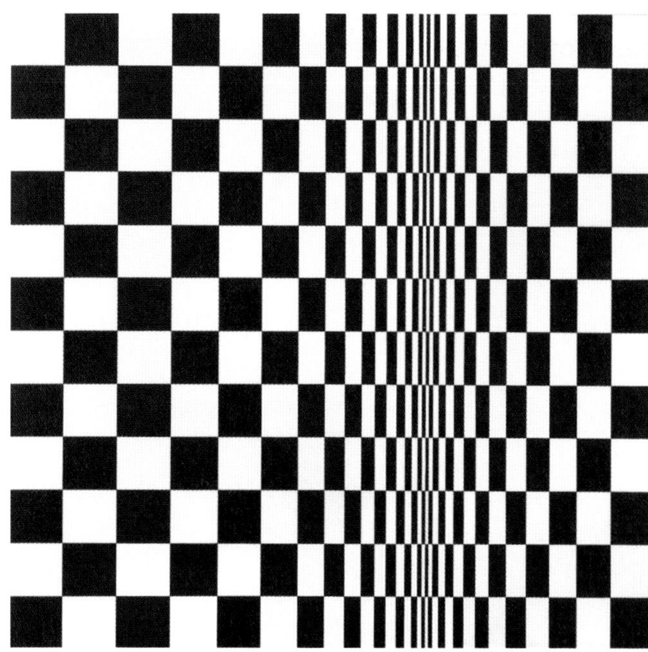

4
Bridget Riley,
Movement in Squares, 1961,
Arts Council Collection,
Southbank Centre, London

was forced to close in 1933, its masters and students scattered throughout the world. Josef Albers became an influential art educator in the United States: after his time at Black Mountain College in North Carolina, he was appointed director of the School of Art at Yale University in 1950. It was during this period that he began creating his first studies for *Homage to the Square,* a series that features three or four nested squares in various colors. In these works, the layers of opaque color at times seem transparent, at times superimposed. Albers created over a thousand of these works, which exerted a strong influence on a younger generation of American artists. In 1963 his color theory text *Interaction of Color* was published, accompanied by 150 silkscreens of *Homage to the Square.*

Inspired by Albers's teaching, his students Richard Anuszkiewicz and Julian Stanczak also adopted the square as a geometric framework for their paintings. In works such as *Monument Valley* (cat. 119), Anuszkiewicz used razor-sharp lines to create a pattern of concentric squares. A warm color palette of red, orange, and yellow is arranged in a gradient toward the center, contrasting with thin lines in cool tones of purple, green, and blue. Through the use of the newly developed acrylic paints, Anuszkiewicz maximized contrasts between complementary colors. Stanczak, his roommate at Yale University, likewise explored the tension between warm and cool colors in paintings such as *Green Light* (cat. 114) and *Firefly* (cat. 115). Using a grid pattern across the entire canvas, he created the illusion of multiple transparent layers overlapping at various angles. While Albers's works remained subtle and, with their relatively static compositions, concentrated on the interaction of color and form, the younger generation embraced his formal teachings on color theory, but pushed the contrasts to an extreme.

Op Art of the 1960s reflected the aesthetic and cultural currents of its time. This new art movement expressed a fascination with technology and scientific experimentation, capturing the spirit of a new visual culture shaped by television and digital aesthetics. Its appeal lay in making the act of seeing an active experience. This intense visual experience mirrored both the optimism and the anxieties provoked by technological innovations.

Translated from German by Melissa M. Thorson

104 Bridget Riley
Tremor, 1962
Lambrecht-Schadeberg Collection,
Museum für Gegenwartskunst Siegen

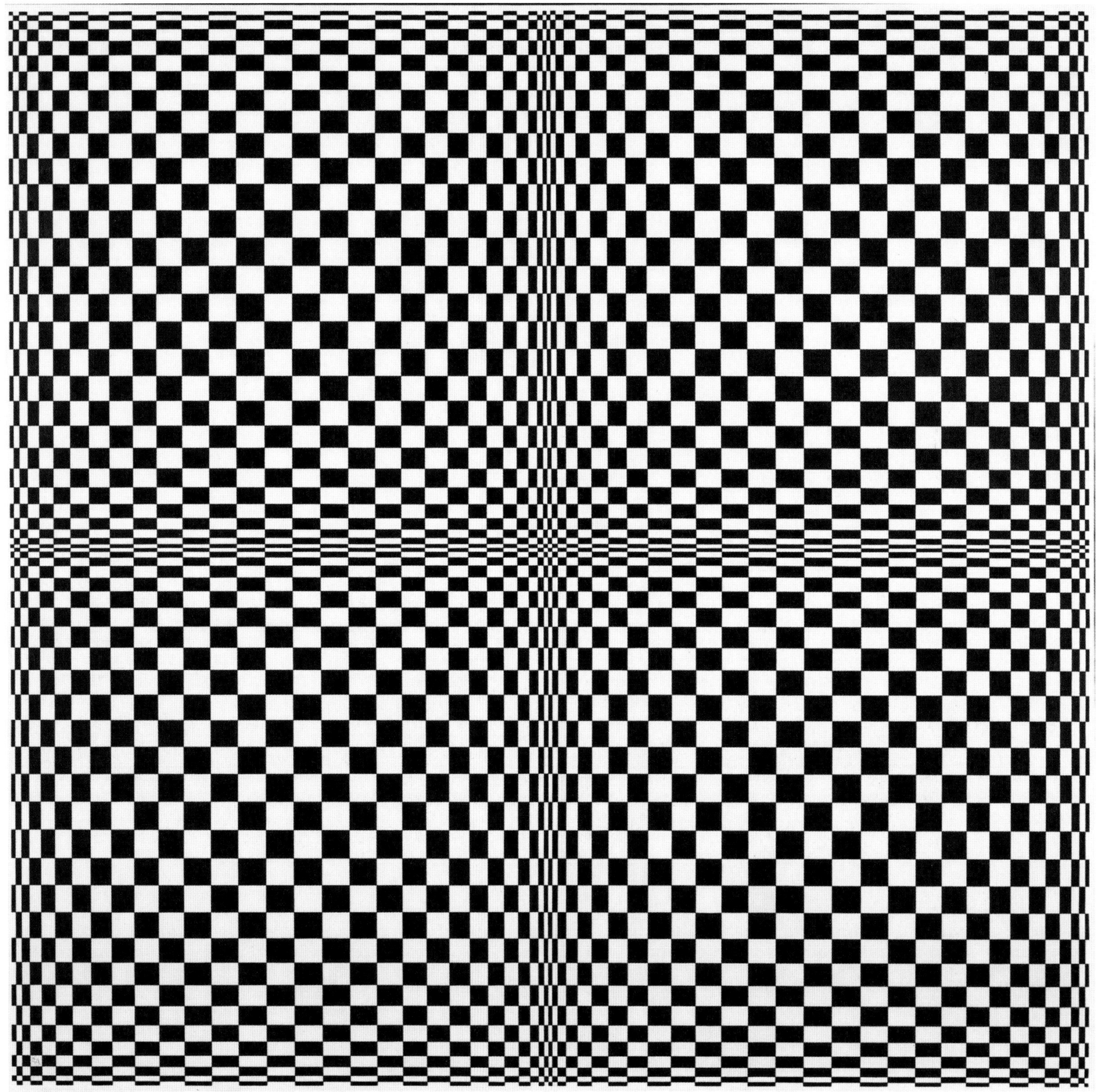

105 Edna Andrade
Color Motion 4-64, 1964
Philadelphia Museum of Art

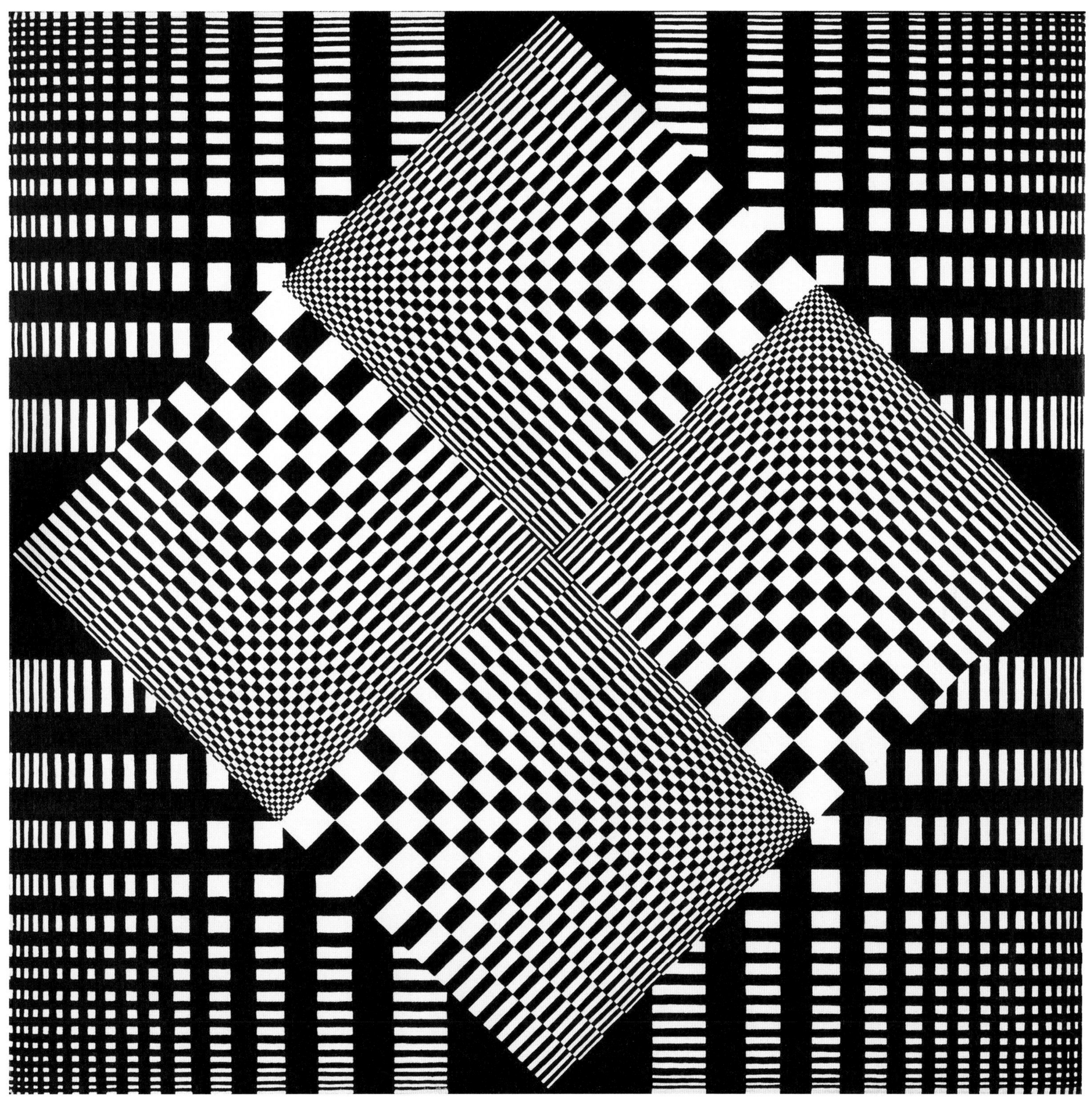

106 Margaret Wenstrup
Whirligig, 1964
D. Wigmore Fine Art, Inc., New York

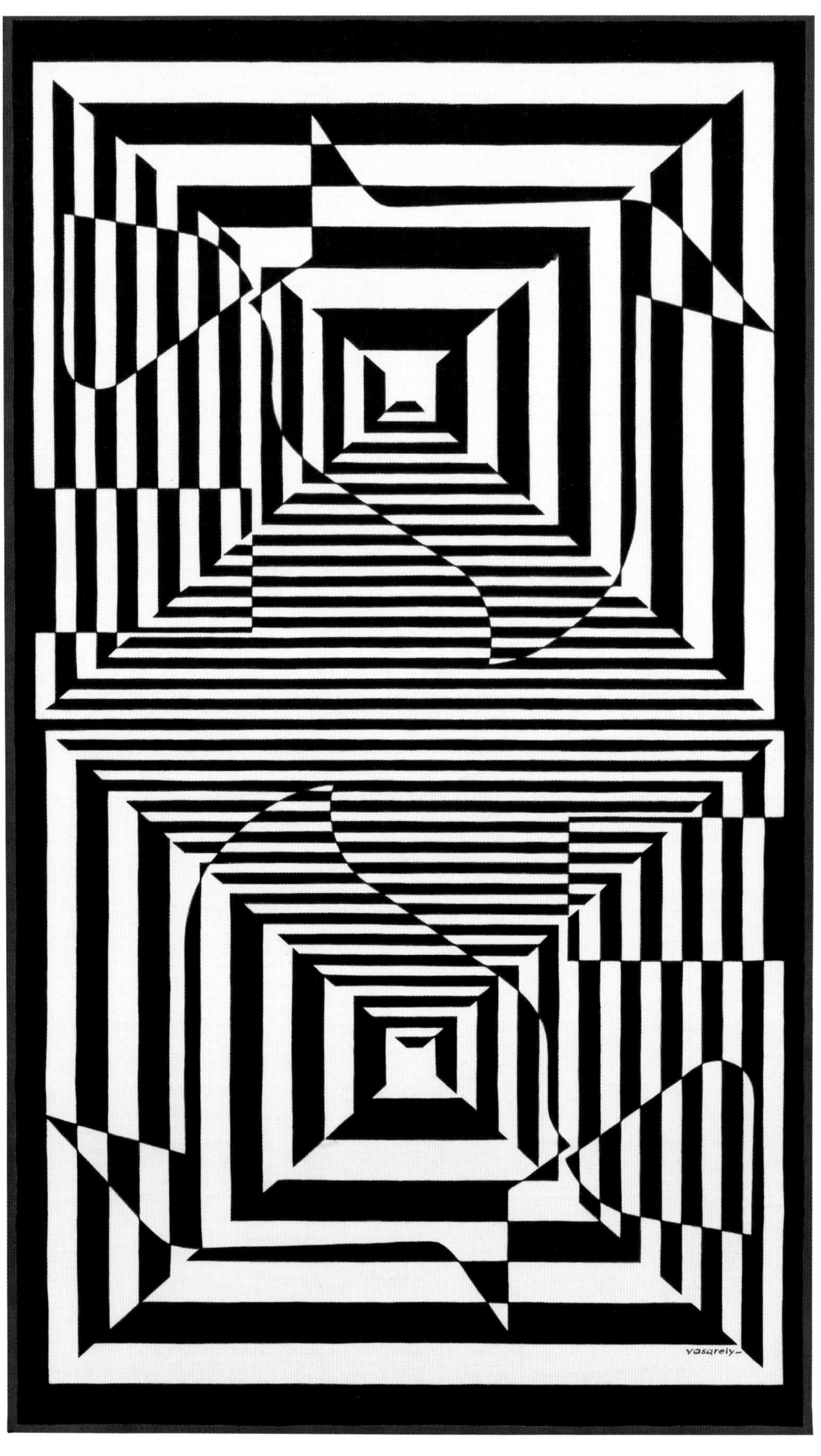

107 Victor Vasarely
Yabla, 1961
ASOM Collection

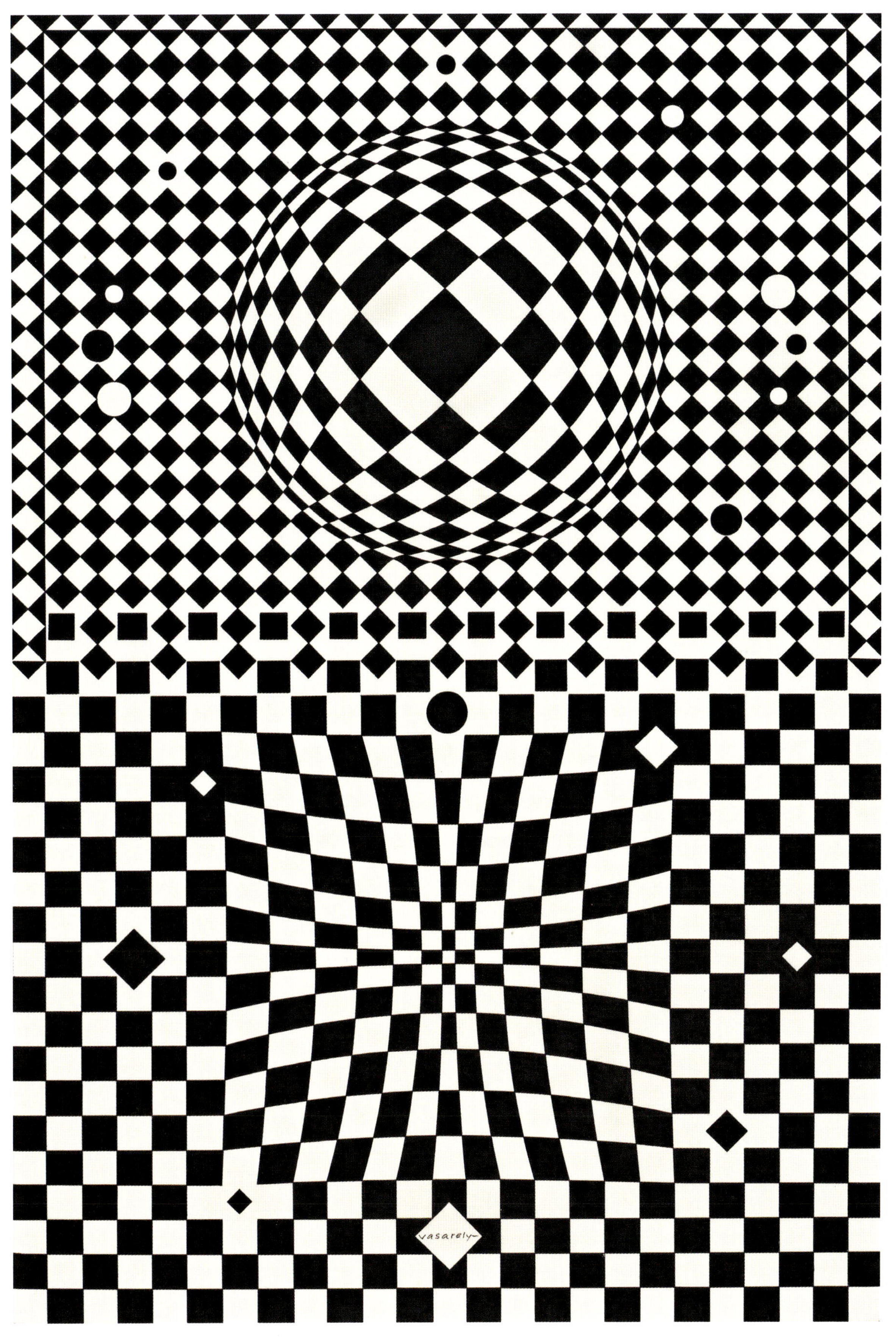

108 Victor Vasarely
Vegaviv II, 1955
Fondation Gandur pour l'Art, Genève

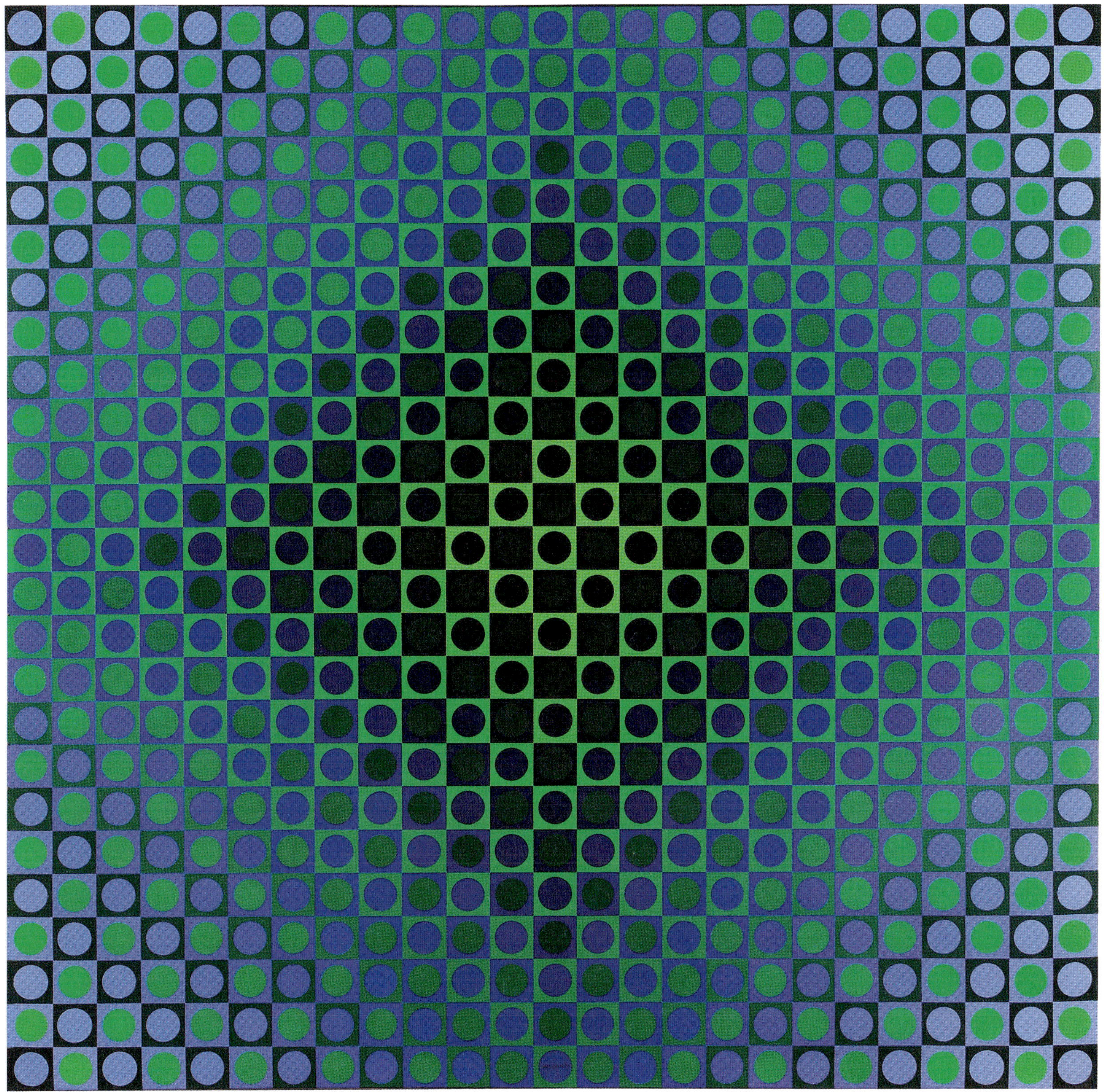

109 Victor Vasarely
Boglar I, 1966
ASOM Collection

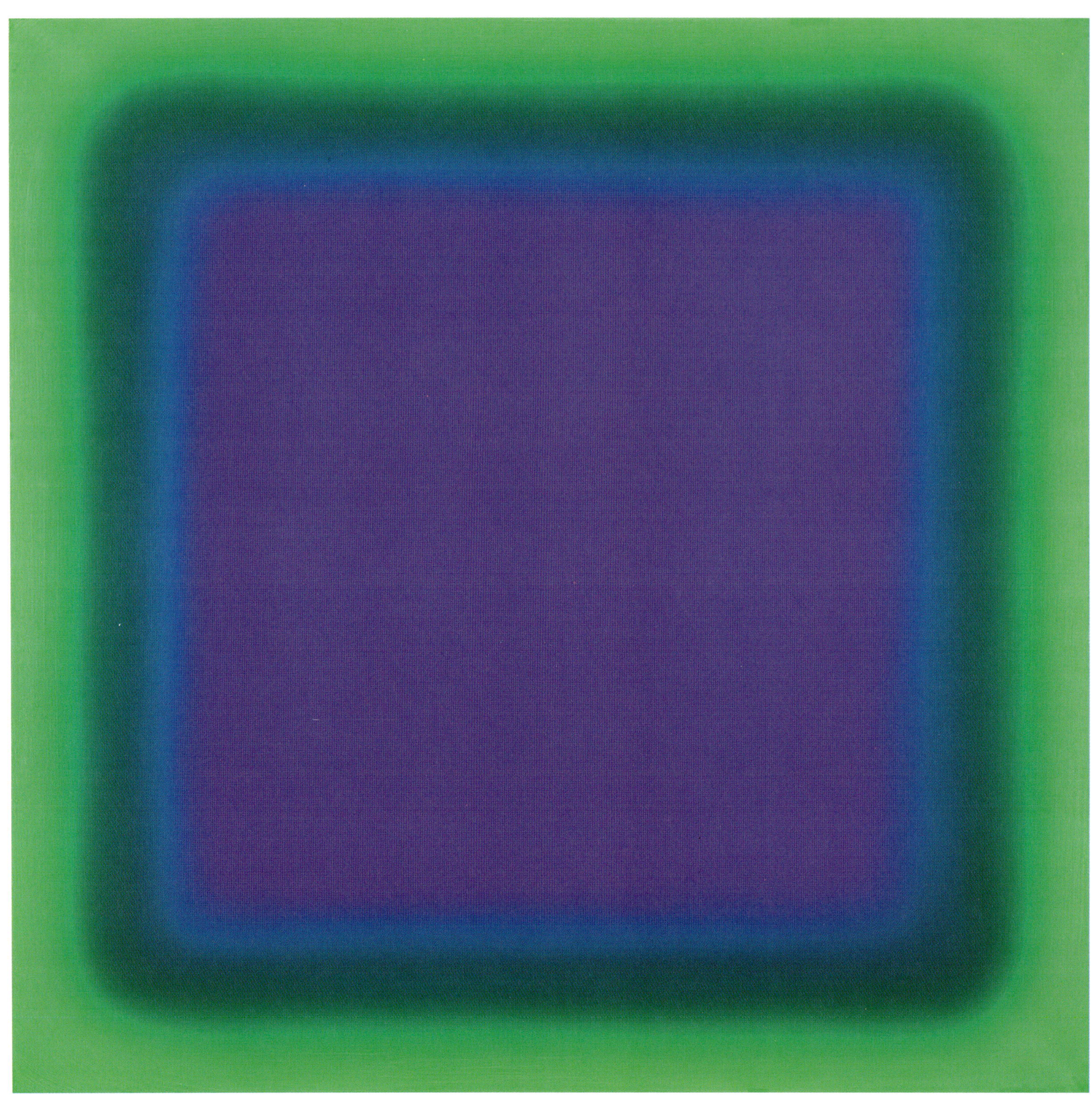

110 Wojciech Fangor
M37, 1967
ASOM Collection

111 Wojciech Fangor
M70, 1966
ASOM Collection

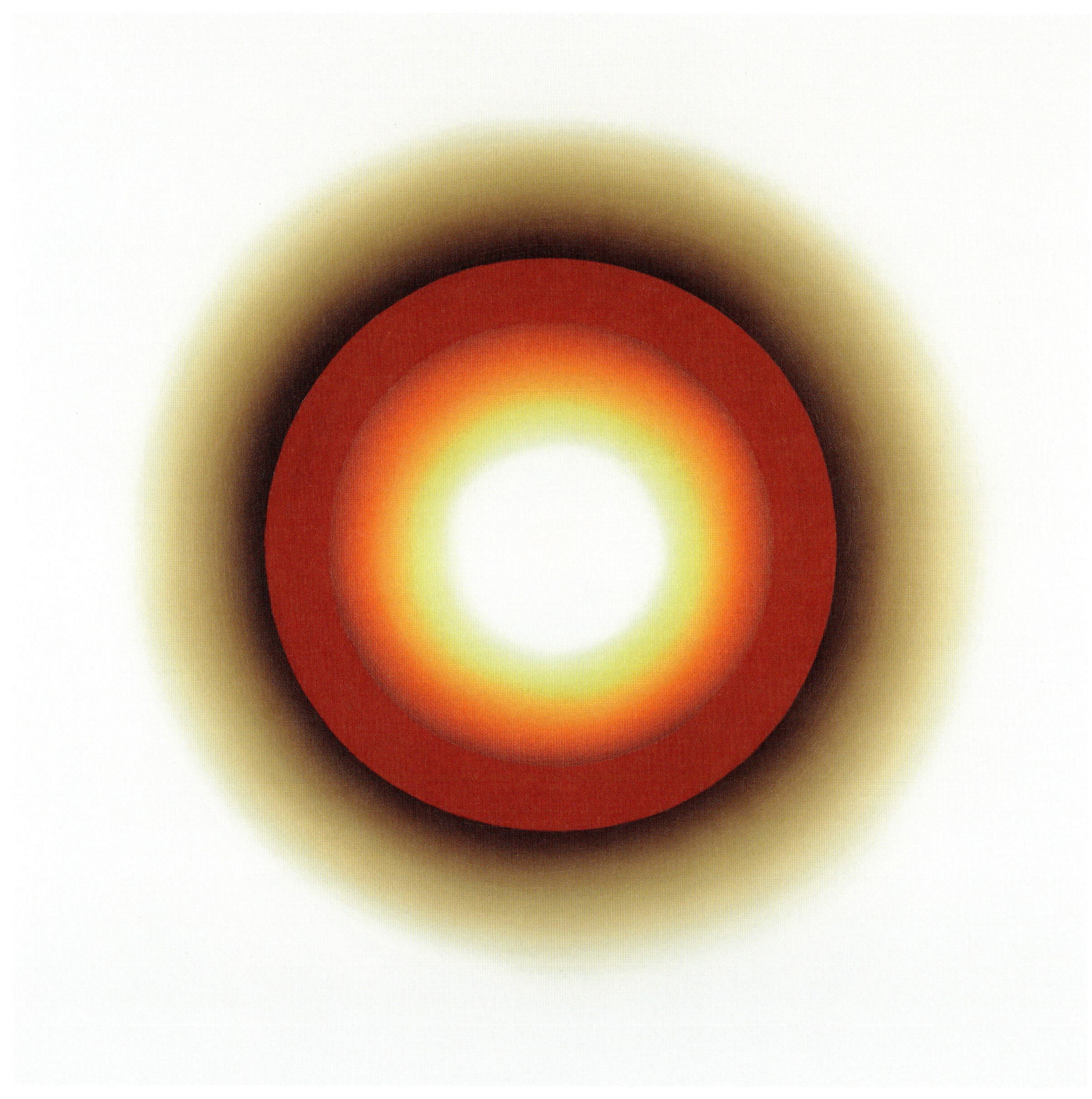

112 Wojciech Fangor
B13, 1964
ASOM Collection

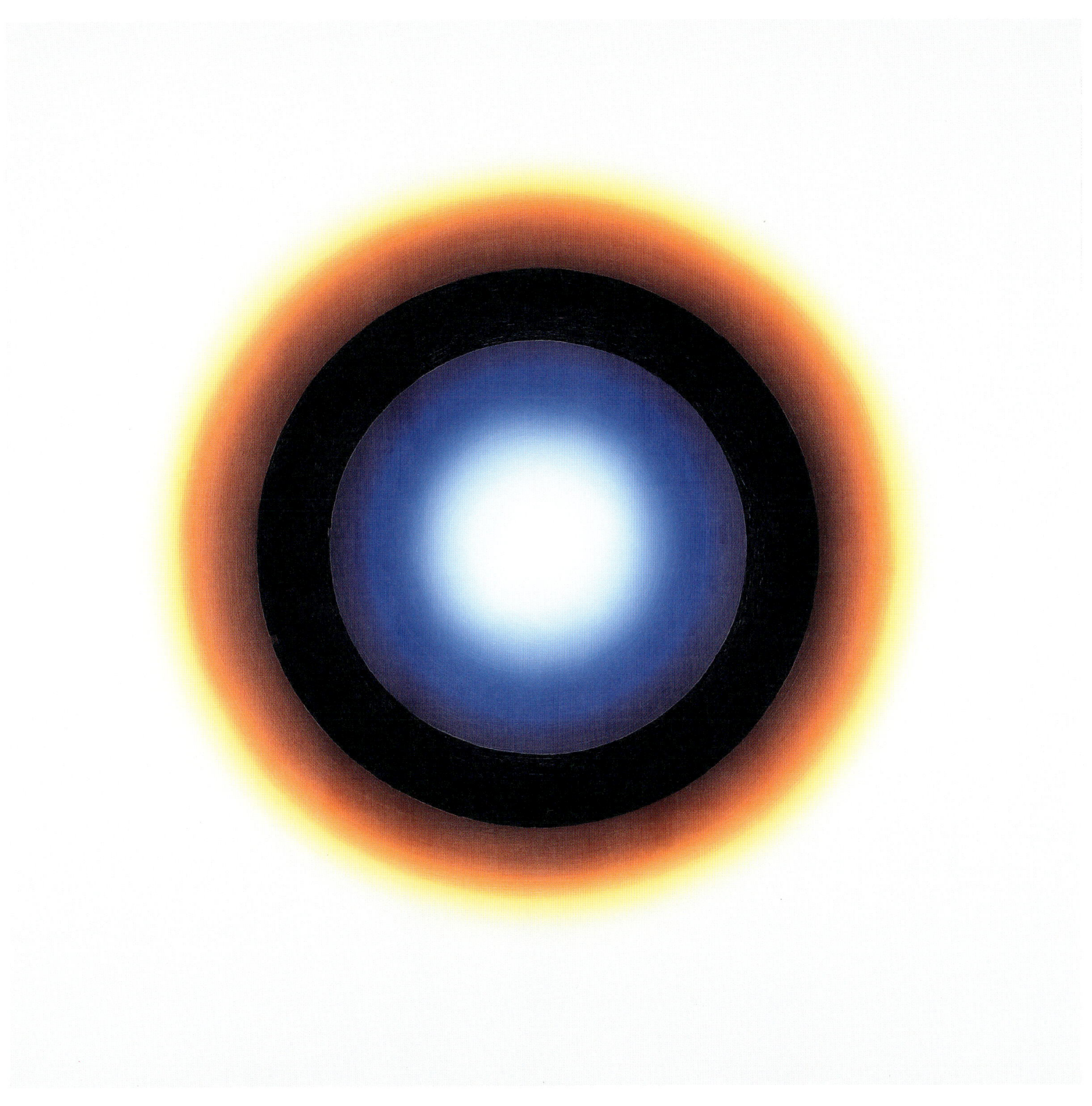

113 Wojciech Fangor
B15, 1964
ASOM Collection

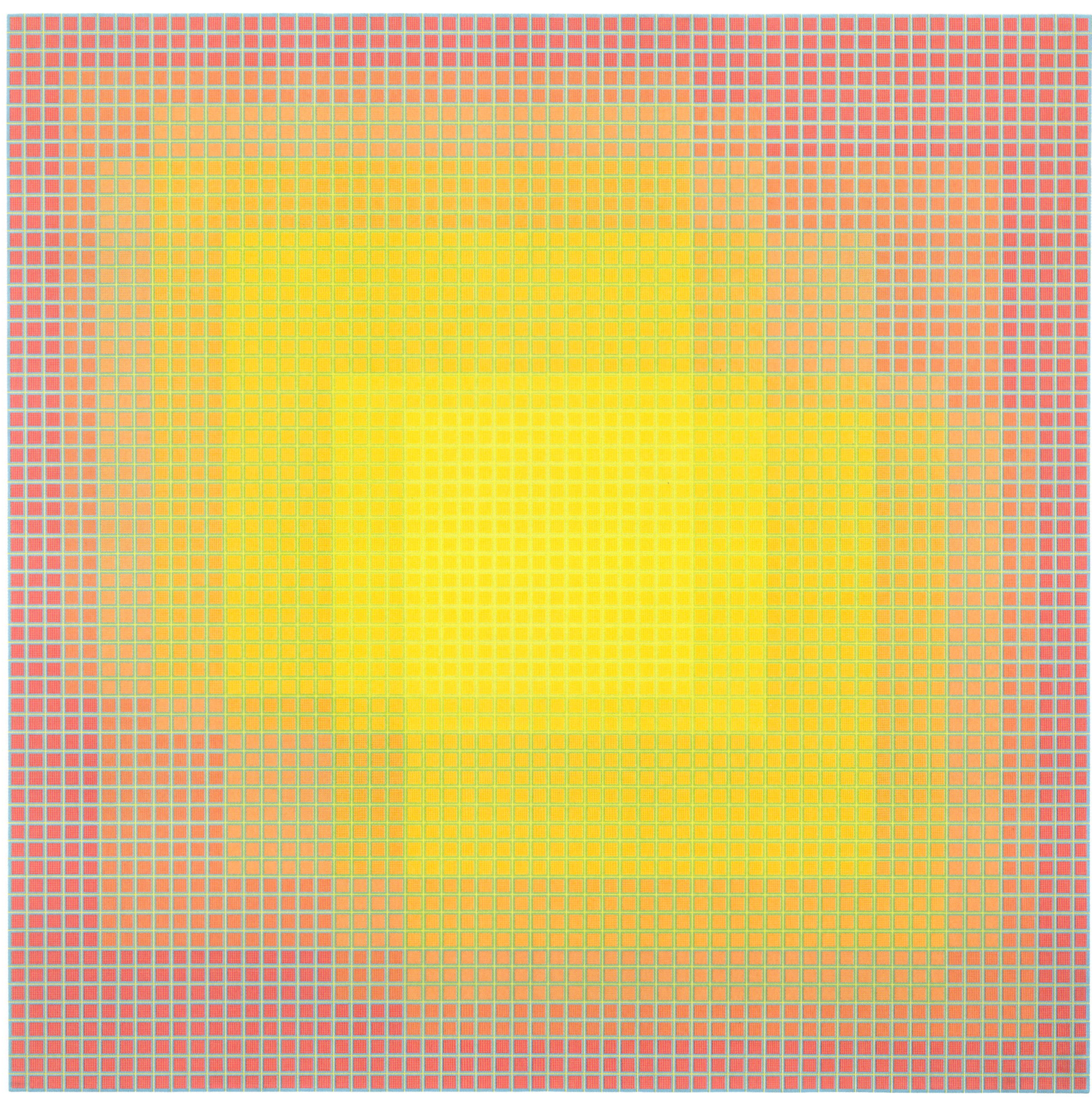

114 Julian Stanczak
Green Light, 1973
Collection of the Estate of Julian Stanczak,
courtesy of The Mayor Gallery, London

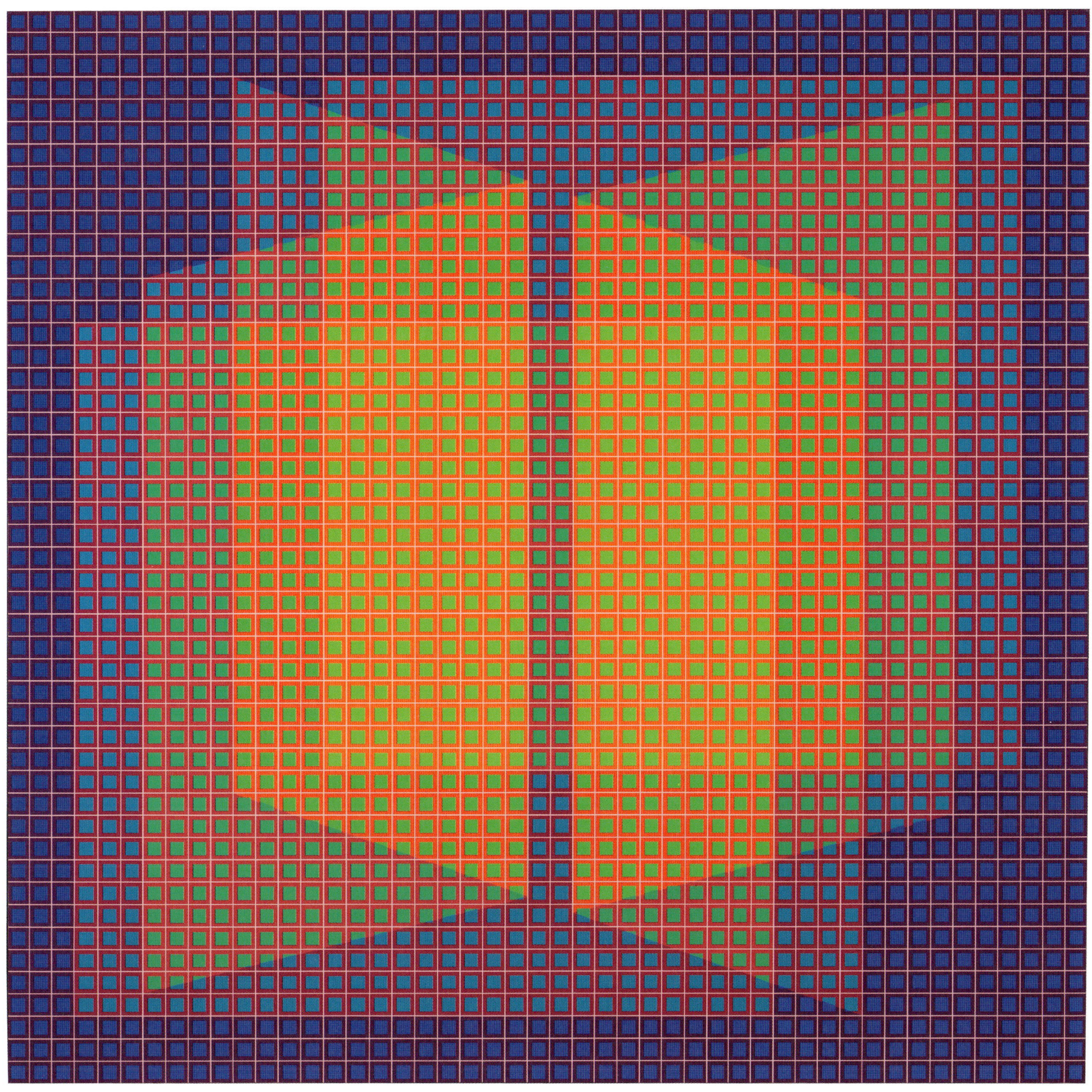

115 Julian Stanczak
Firefly, 1973
Collection of David and Kathryn Birnbaum

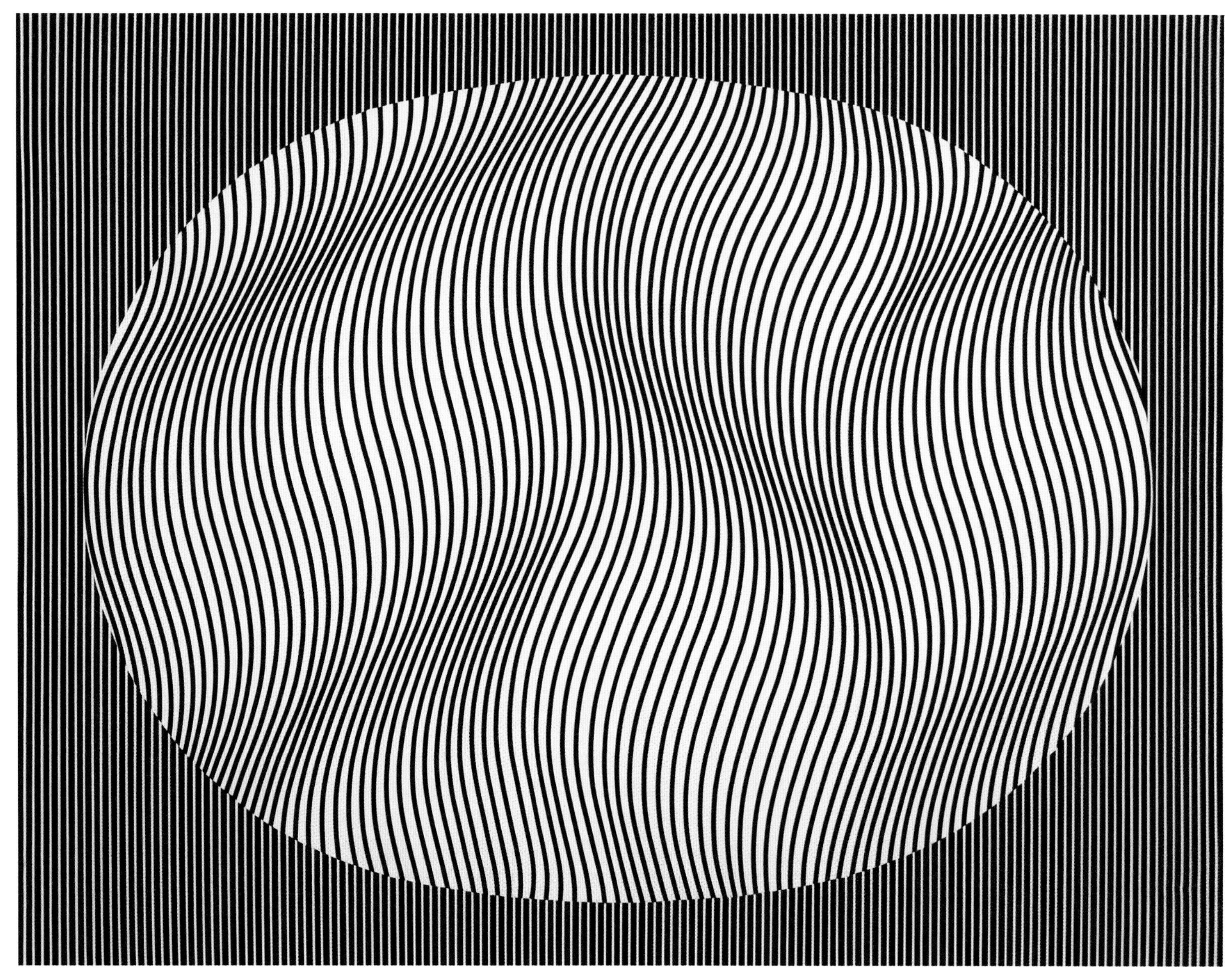

116 Julian Stanczak
Repulsive Attraction, 1965–66
Courtesy of Neil K. Rector & the Rector Artwork Trust

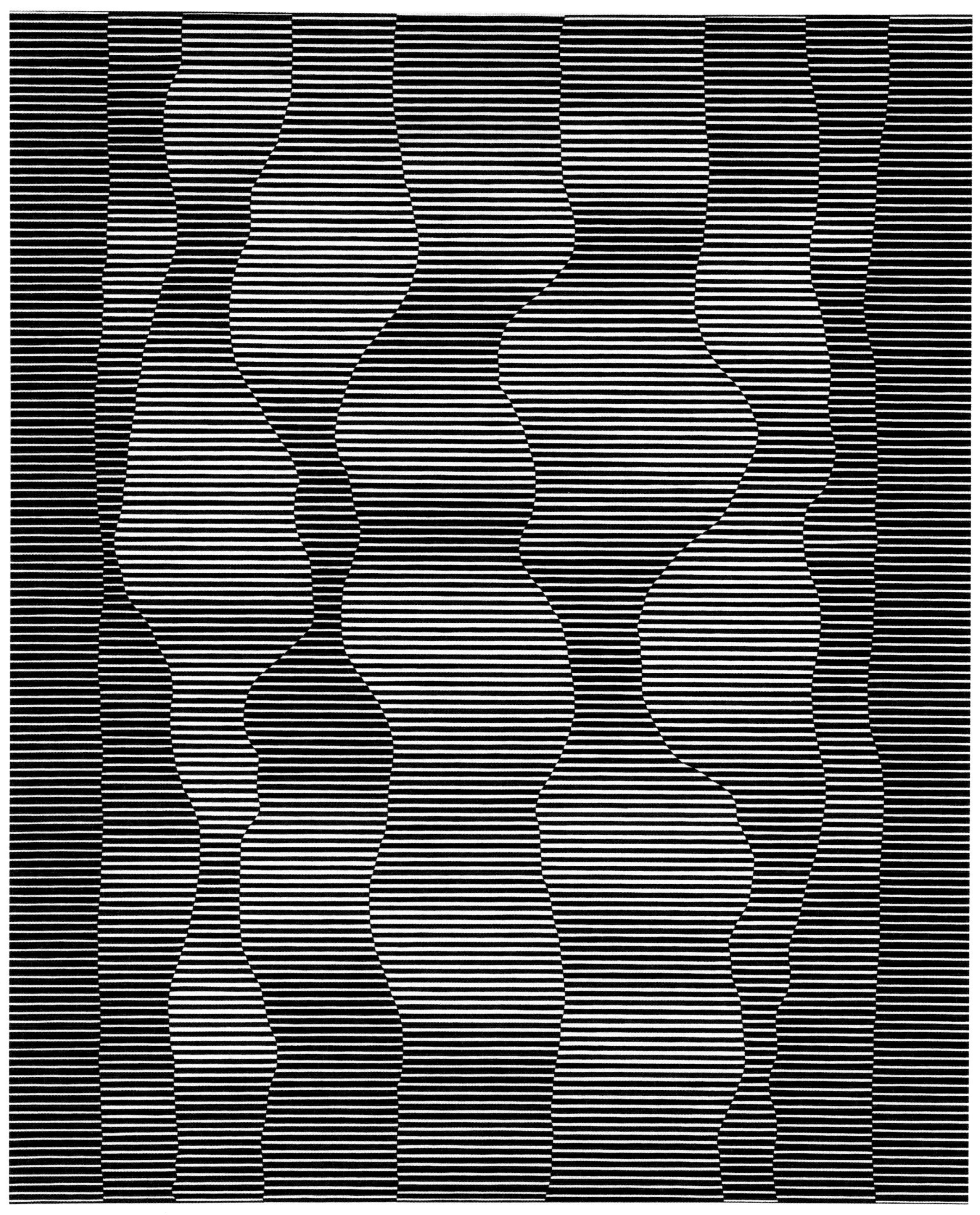

117 Julian Stanczak
Ephemeral Movement, 1965
Collection of the Estate of Julian Stanczak

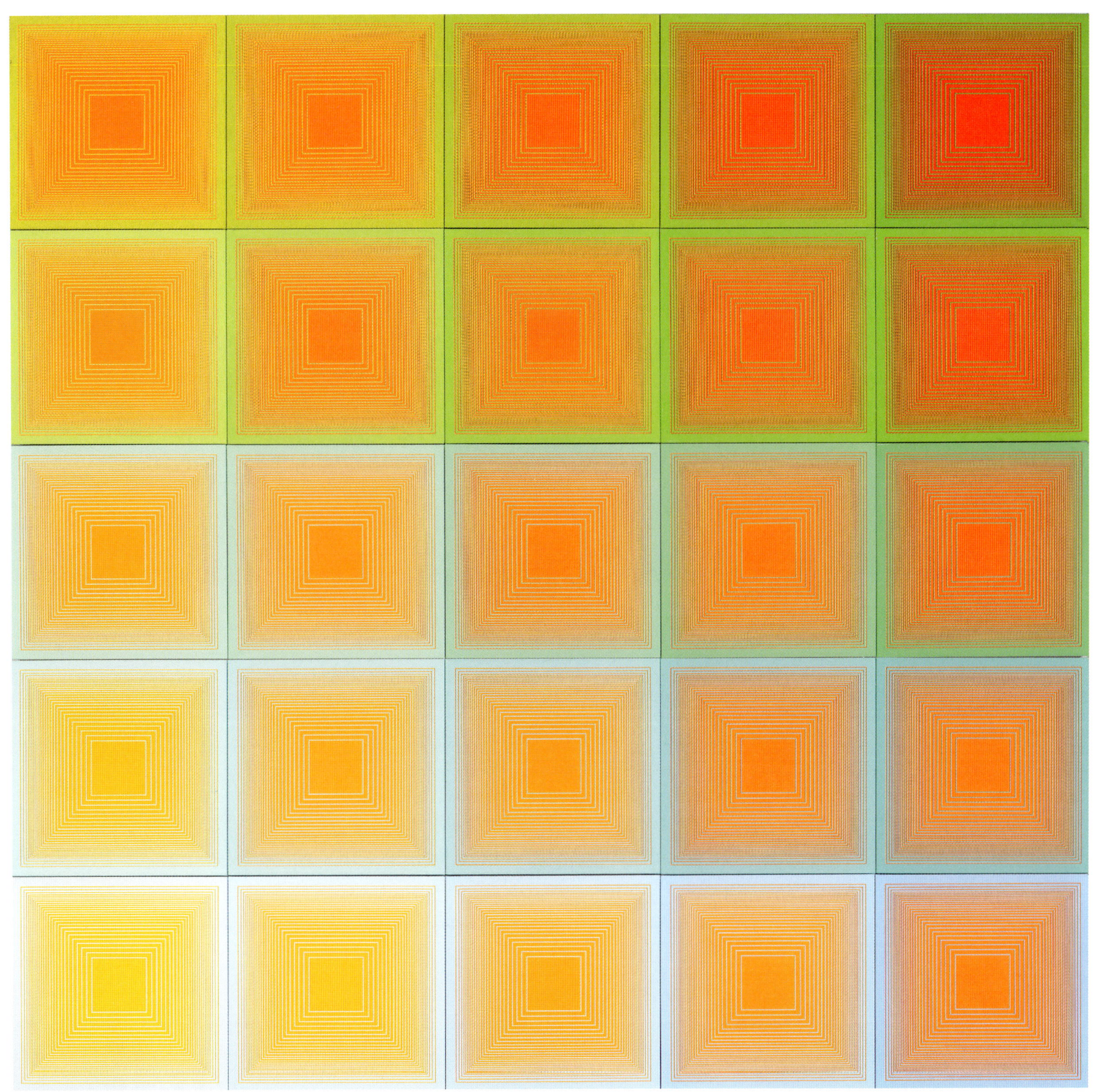

118 Richard Anuszkiewicz
Orange Delight, 1969
Whitney Museum of American Art, New York

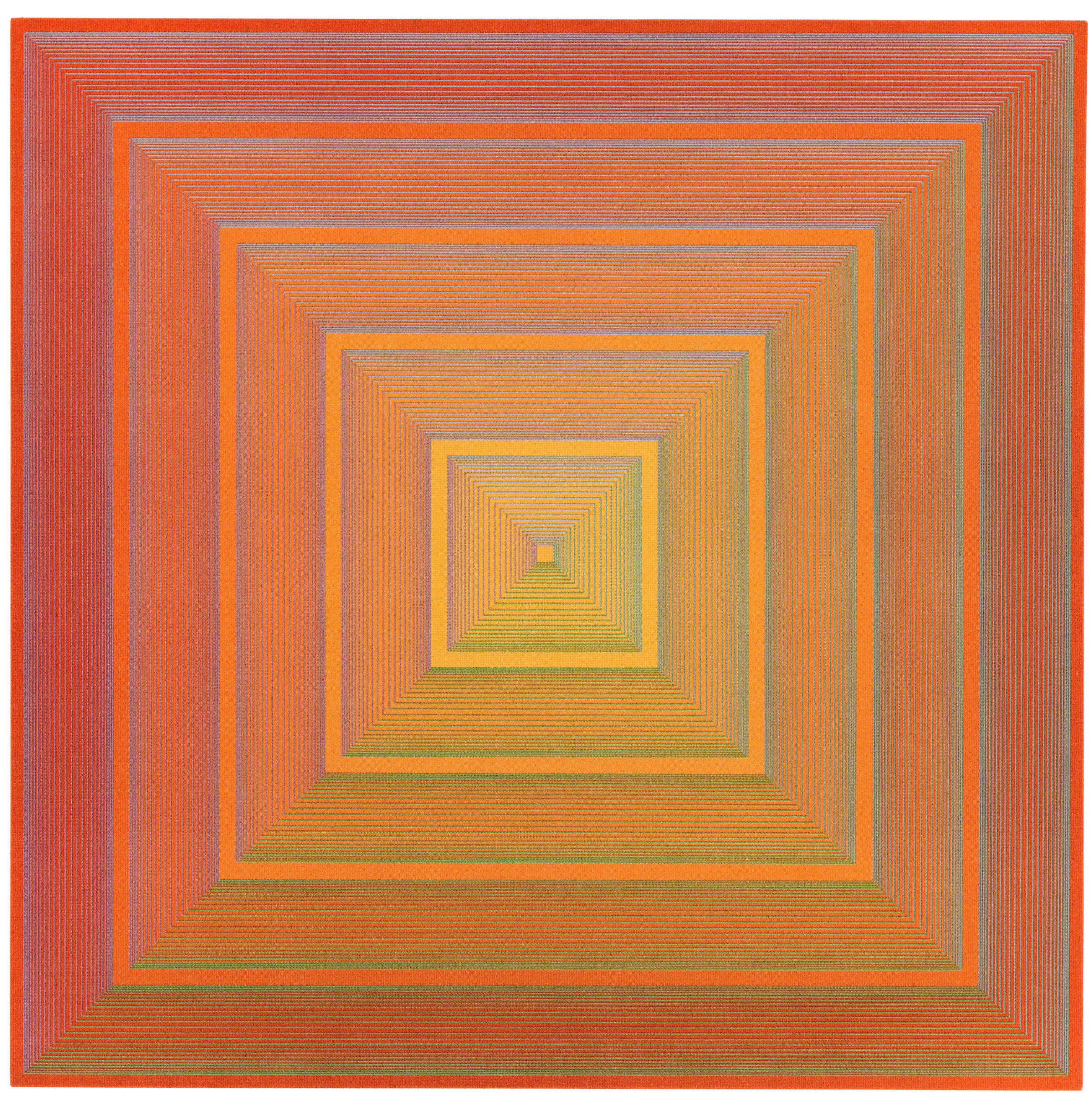

119 Richard Anuszkiewicz
Monument Valley, 1970
Estate of Richard Anuszkiewicz

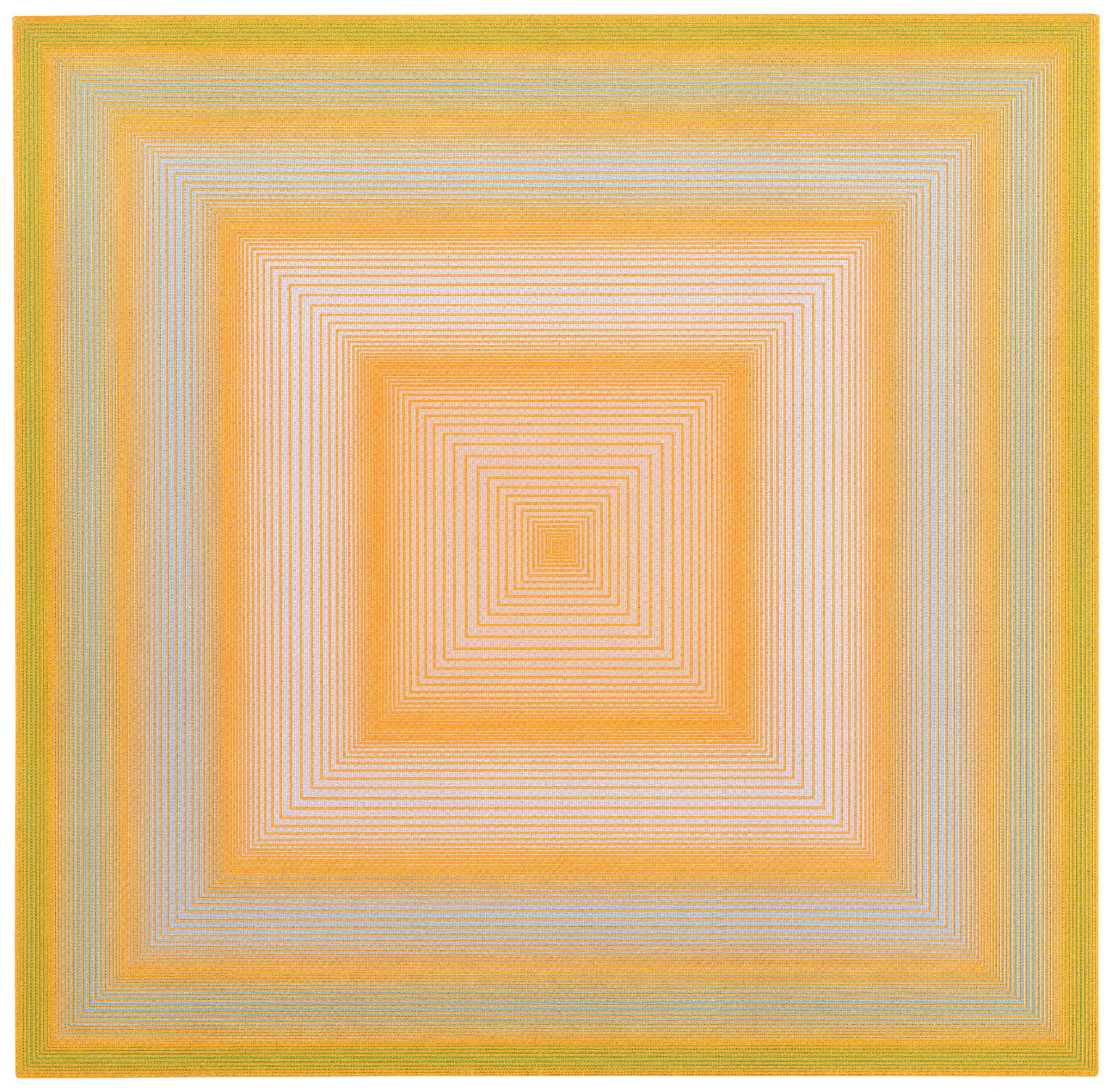

120 Richard Anuszkiewicz
Untitled, 1972
ASOM Collection

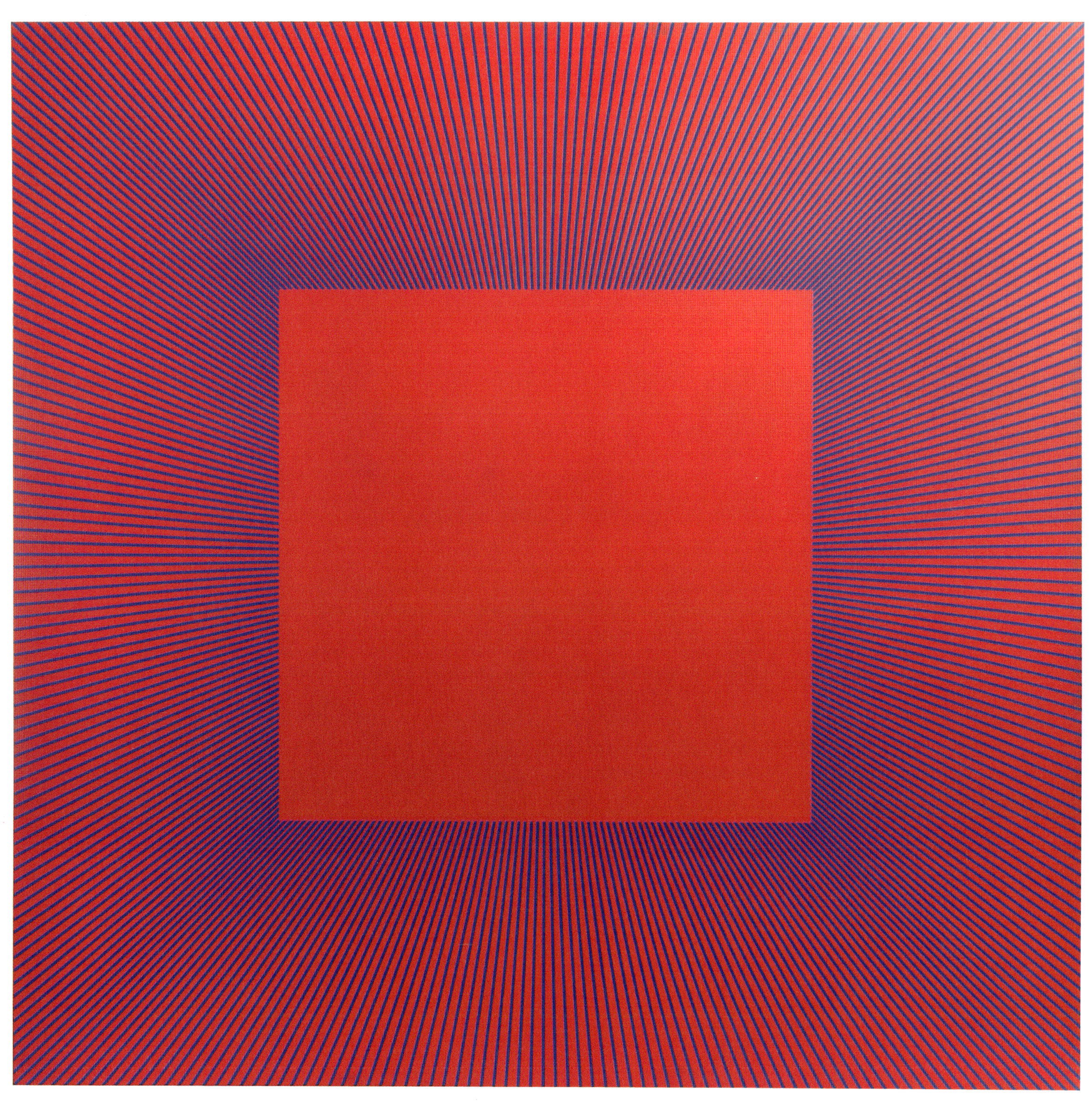

121 Richard Anuszkiewicz
Metamorphosis of Cadmium Red—Blue Line, 1979
Estate of Richard Anuszkiewicz

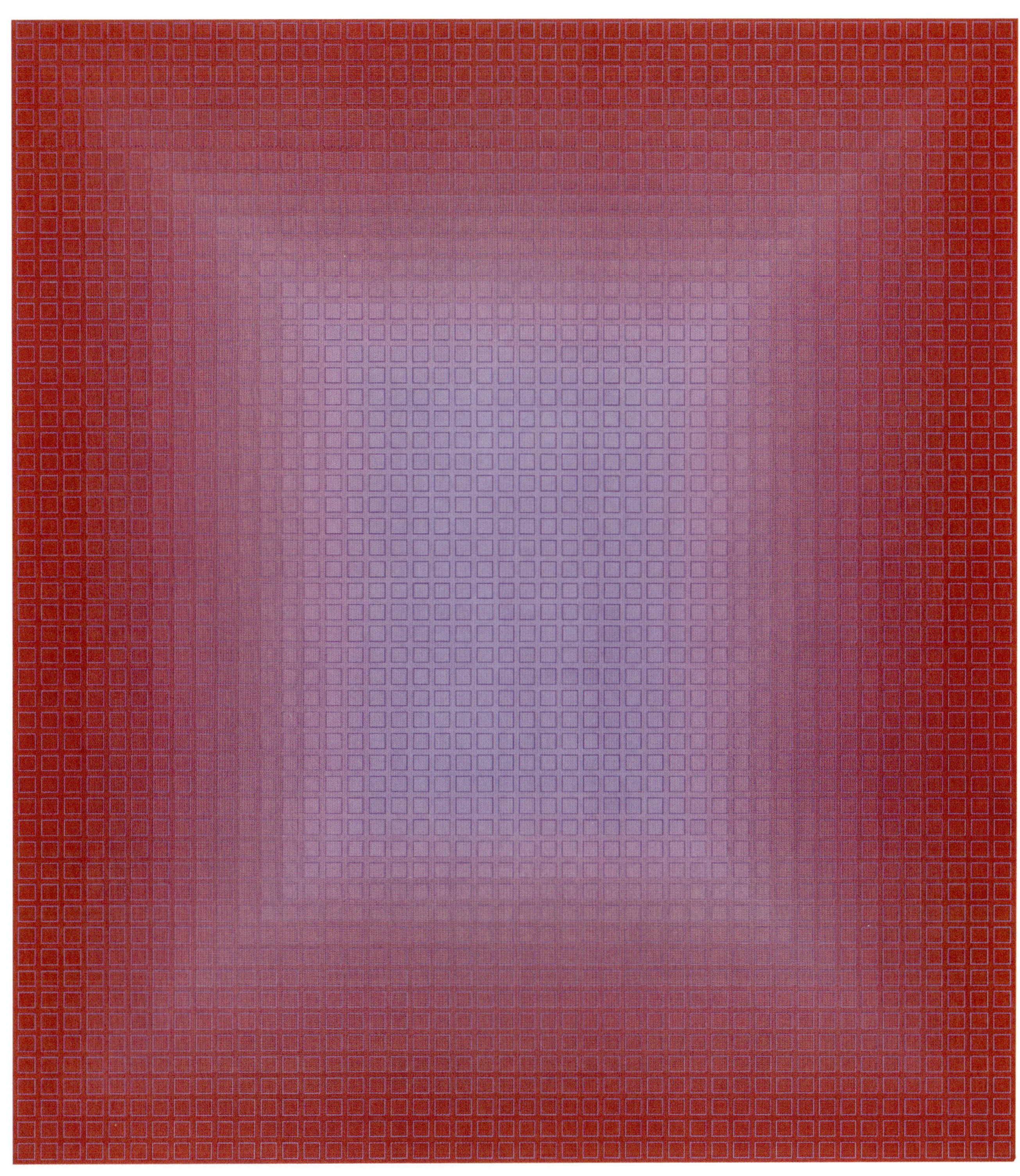

122 Julian Stanczak
Late Glow, 1977
Collection of the Estate of Julian Stanczak

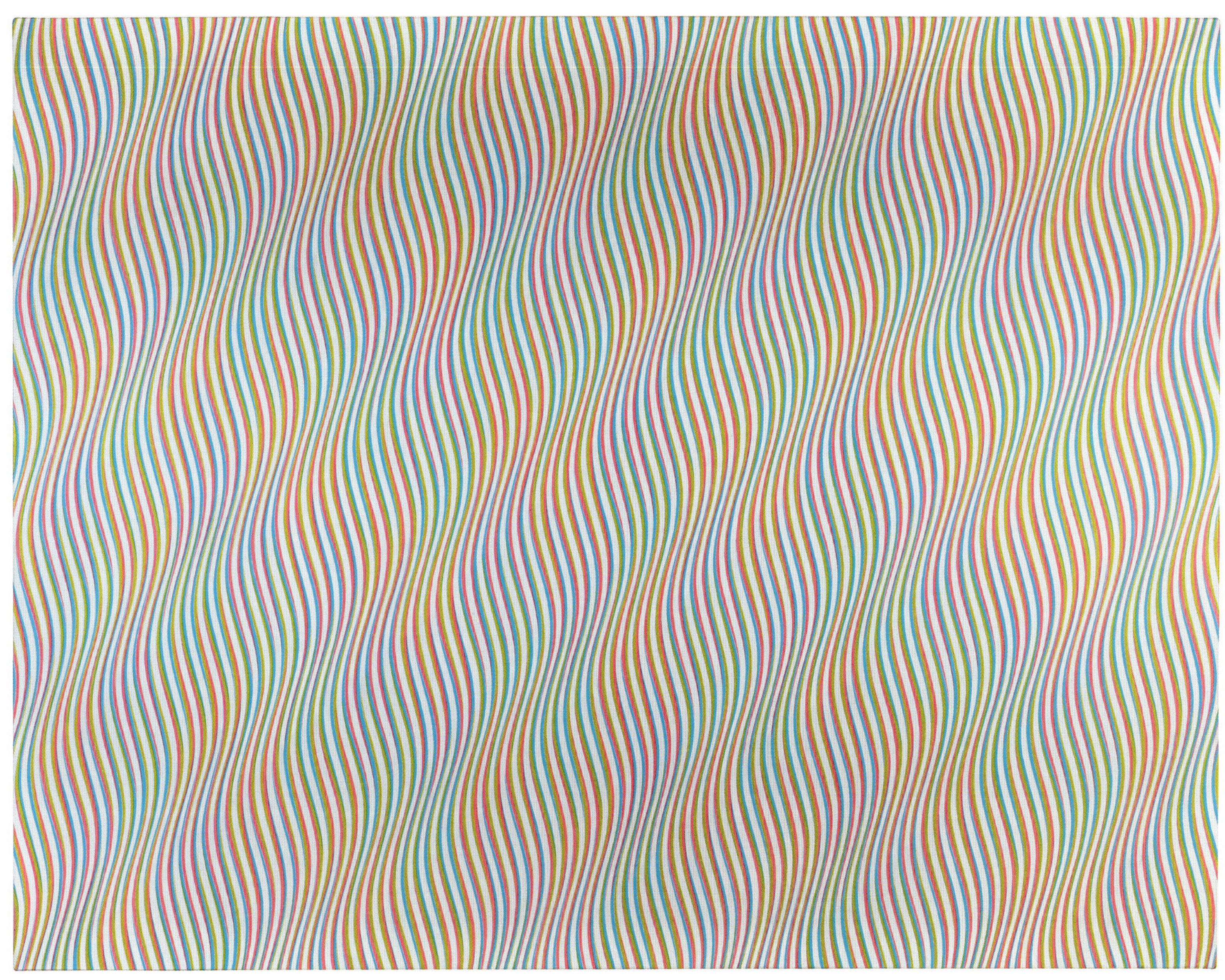

123 Bridget Riley
Clepsydra 1, 1976
Lambrecht-Schadeberg Collection,
Museum für Gegenwartskunst Siegen

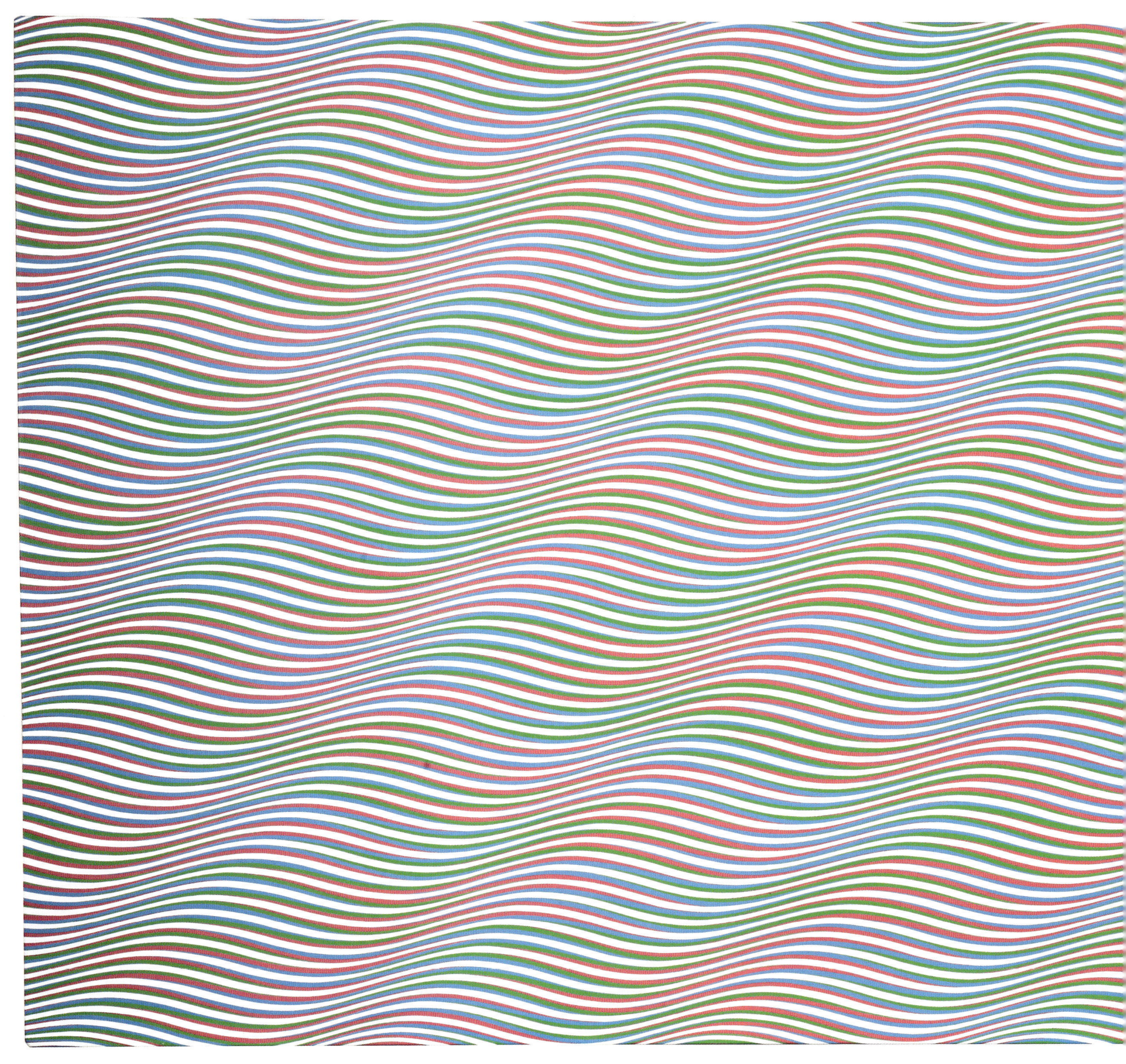

124 Bridget Riley
Shih-Li, 1975
ASOM Collection

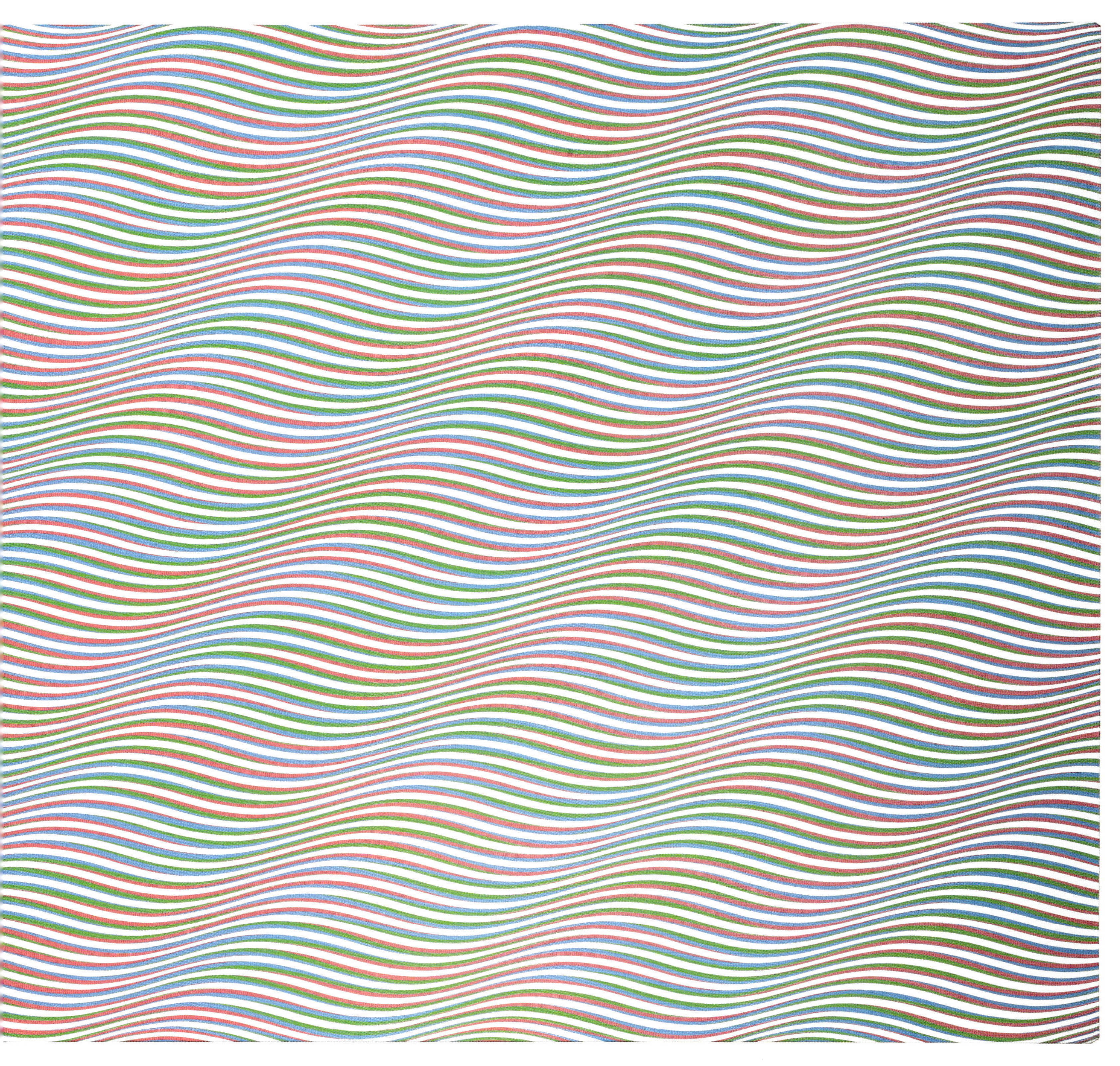

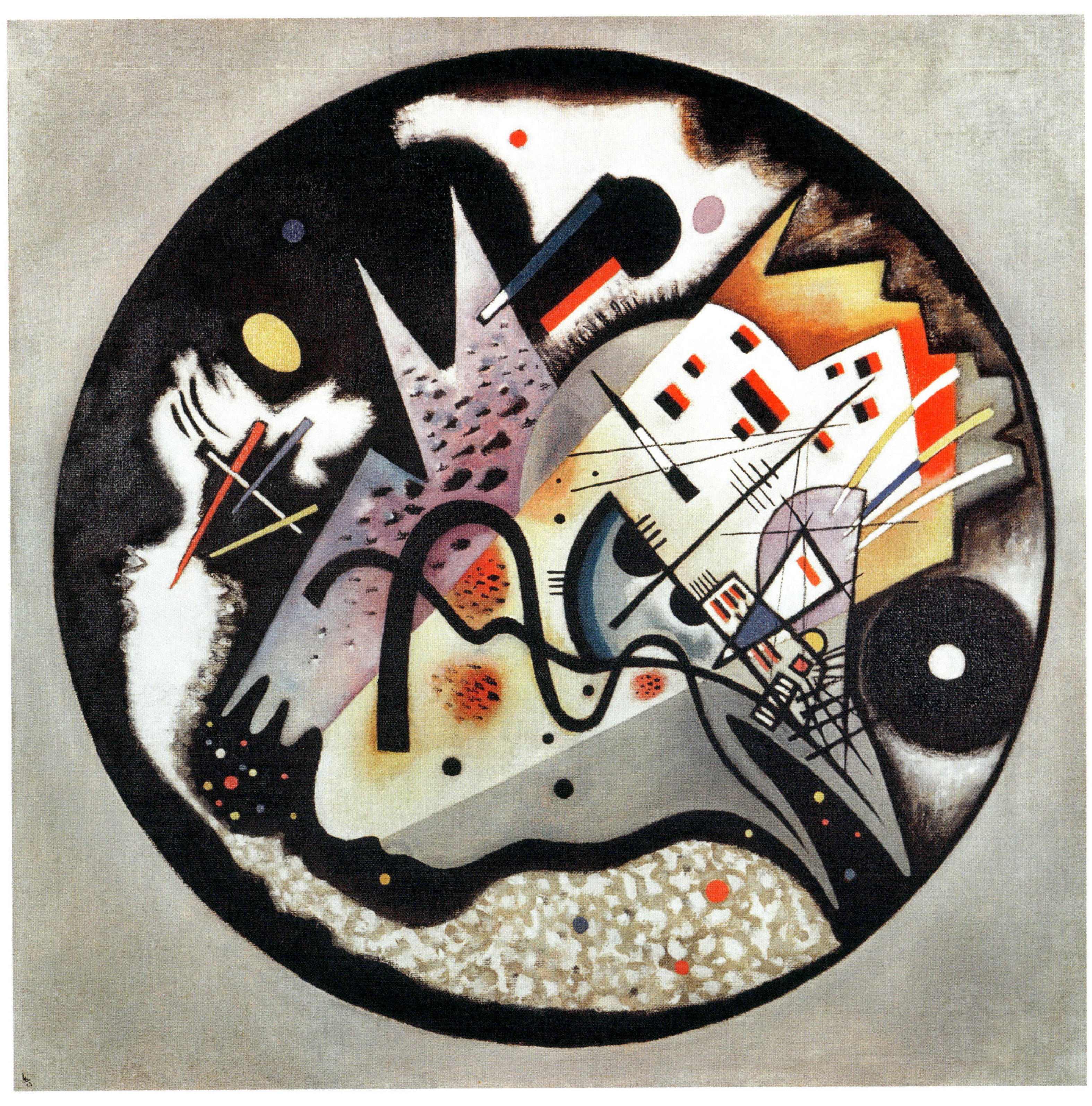

125 Wassily Kandinsky
In the Black Circle, 1923
Private collection

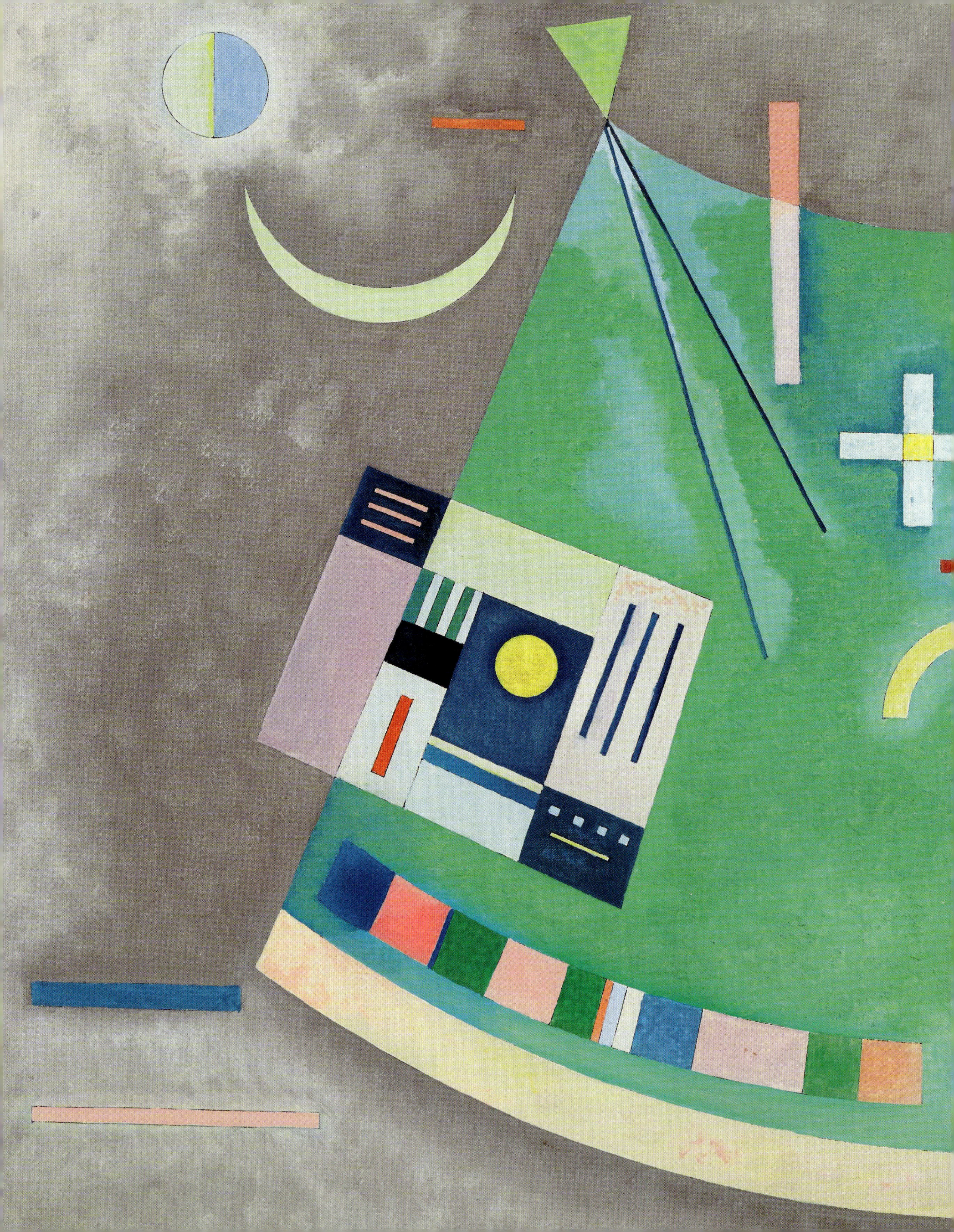

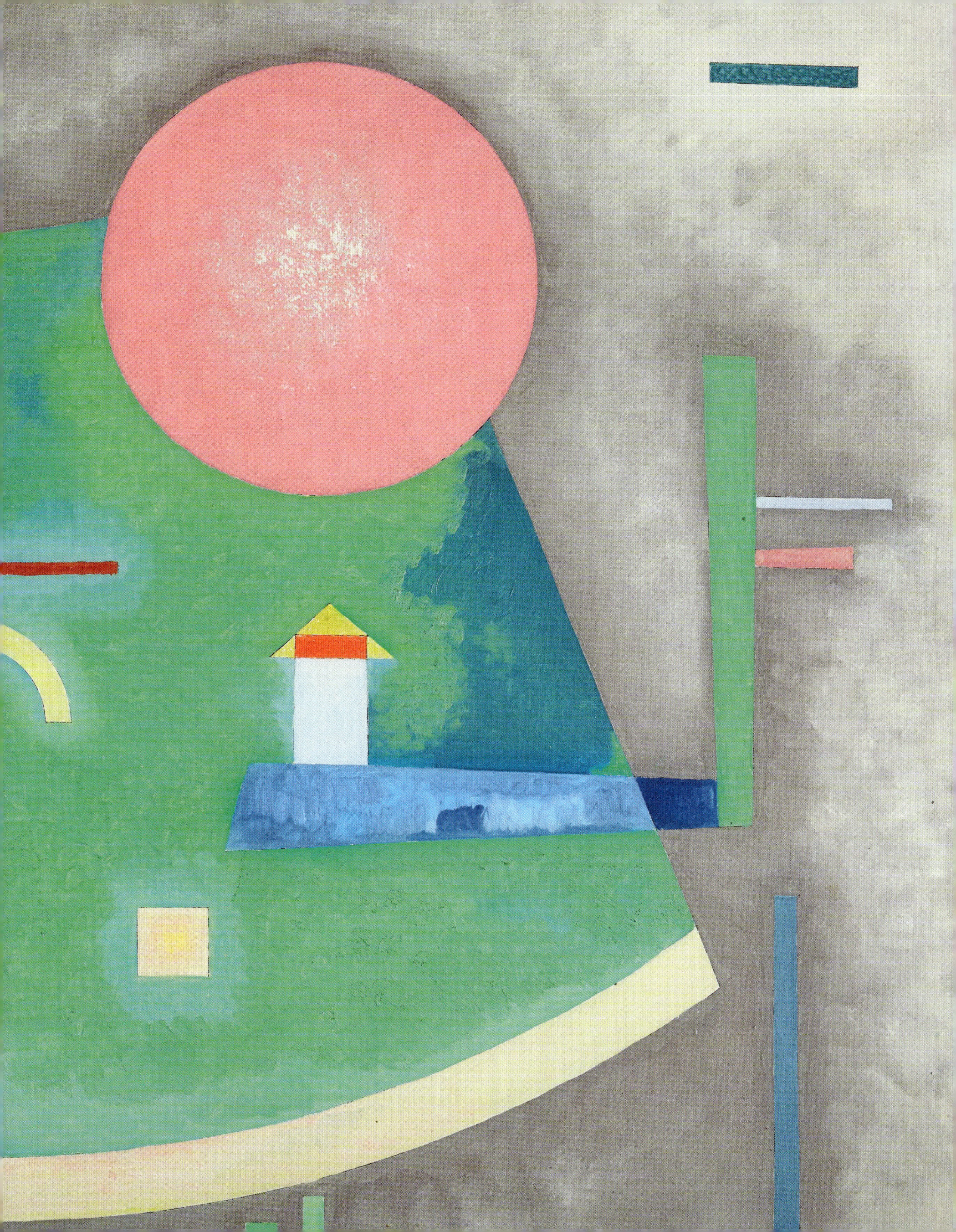

Notes

FOREWORD

Ortrud Westheider
pages 10–13

1 Kandinsky 2024, 72–74.
2 Wassily Kandinsky, *Reminiscences* (1913), in Kandinsky 1994, 357–82, here 364.

ESSAYS

Kandinsky's Synthesis: Bridging Art, Science, and Spirituality
John E. Bowlt and Nicoletta Misler
pages 18–27

1 The spiritual, the occult, and the "Other" in modern Western art has been the subject of numerous publications, although particular mention should be made of the following two sources: Los Angeles 1986 and Frankfurt am Main 1995.
2 Kandinsky 1977.
3 For a detailed textological discussion of the several versions of "Concerning the Spiritual in Art," see Nadezhda Podzemskaia, *V. Kandinskii o dukhovnom v iskusstve: Pol'noe kriticheskoe izdanie* [W. Kandinsky on the Spiritual in Art: Complete Critical Edition], Moscow 2020, 2 vols.
4 Quoted in the Russian text of Wassily Kandinsky's lecture, "O dukhovnom v iskusstve (Zhivopis')" [On the Spiritual in Art (Painting)], in *Trudy Vserossiiskogo s'ezda khudozhnikov* [Proceedings of the All-Russian Congress of Artists], ed. Il'ia Repin et al., Petrograd 1914, 3 vols., here 1, 47–76. The lecture is republished in Natal'ia Avtonomova et al., eds., *V. V. Kandinskii: Izbrannye Trudy* [Selected Works], Moscow 2001, 2 vols., here vol. 1, 96–156. Further translations here are from this reprint, including this quotation on 115.
5 Kazimir Malevich, *Suprematizm: 34 risunka* [Suprematism: 34 Drawings] (1919), Vitebsk 1920.
6 Magdalena Moeller, "Kandinsky a Monaco: Avvio all'astrazione," in Rome 2000, 25–26.
7 Kandinsky 2024, 104.
8 Vasilii Kandinskii, "K voprosu o forme" [On the Problem of Form] (1913), in Avtonomova 2001 (see note 4), vol. 1, 210–34, here 210.
9 Kandinskii 2001 (see note 4), 100.
10 Vasilii Kandinskii, "Tochka i liniia na ploskosti: K analizu zhivopisnykh elementov" [Point and Line to Plane: Toward an Analysis of the Painterly Elements], in Avtonomova 2001 (see note 4), vol. 2, 96–156, here 99.
11 Kandinskii 2001 (see note 4), 110; Fedor Rybakov, "Predislovie" [Preface], in *Atlas dlia eksperimental'no-psikhologicheskogo issledovaniia lichnosti* [Atlas for Experimental Psychological Research on Personality], Moscow 1910, unpaginated.
12 See Fedor Rybakov, *Sovremennye pisateli i bol'nye nervy: Psikhiatricheskii etiud* [Modern Writers and Sick Nerves: A Psychiatric Study], Moscow 1908; Petr Gannushkin, *Vliianie kul'tury i tsivilizatsii na dushevnye zabolevaniia* [The Influence of Culture and Civilization on Psychic Illnesses], Moscow 1914.
13 See Misler 2002, 173–85.
14 Sergei Kotliarevskii, "Improvizatsiia kak raskrytie bessoznatel'nogo: Znachenie bessoznatel'nogo v sovremennoi nauke i filosofii s gipnozom i snovideniem [Improvisation as Disclosure of the Subconscious: The Meaning of the Subconscious in Modern Scholarship and Philosophy with Hypnosis and Dreams]: Tezis [Thesis]," typescript, RGALI (Russian State Archive of Literature and Art, Moscow), call no. f. 941, op. 1, ed. khr. 3, l. 23.
15 For information on the role of Sidorov and his colleagues at RAKhN, especially in the fields of psychology and dance, see Irina Sirotkina, "Nauka o tantse: Khoreologiia Alekseia Sidorova" [The Science of Dance: The Choreology of Aleksei Sidorov], in *Mezhdunarodnyi zhurnal issledovanii kul'tury* [International Journal of Cultural Research], 4 (2022), unpaginated.
16 See Fedor Rybakov, "Sovremennaia intelligentsia i 'ozverenie' nravov" [Modern Intelligentsia and the Bestiality of Morals], in Rybakov et al., *Kuda my idem? Nastoiashchee i budushchee russkoi intellgentsii, literatury, teatra i iskusstv: Sbornik statei i otvetov* [Whither Are We Going? The Present and Future of Russian Intelligentsia, Literature, Theater, and the Arts: A Collection of Articles and Answers], Moscow 1910; and Vasilii Kandinskii, "Kuda idet 'novoe' iskusstvo?" [Whither the "New" Art?], in *Odesskie novosti* [Odesa News] (February 9, 1911), 2.

[17] Besant/Leadbeater 1905, 12.

[18] See, for example, the contributions from Ivan Aksenov and Aleksandra Unkovskaia to the rubric entitled "Otdel dukhovnykh iskanii" [Division of Spiritual Quests], in *Vestnik teosofii* 1 (1909), 91–95 and 2 (1909), 98–101; also see Aleksandra Unkovskaia, "i v dushe svoei razlivaetsia bol" [pain spilled into his soul], in Unkovskaia, "Son starogo skripacha" [Dream of an Old Violinist], in *Vestnik teosofii* 12 (1908), 41–45, here 42; or "samoe nachalo zhizni dushi … eto osnovnaia nota [kotoraia] nemedlenno sozdaet otzvuki" [the beginning of the soul is like the keynote which creates an infinite number of resonances], in Unkovskaia, "Metoda tsveto-zvuko-chisel" [Method of Color-Sound-Number], in *Vestnik teosofii* 1 (1909), 77–82, here 79.

[19] Besant/Leadbeater 1905, 40.

[20] Although recognized as an accomplished violinist and important Theosophist in her day, Unkovskaia—and her connection with Kandinsky—have not been the subject of extensive critical investigation. For some commentary on her "color-sound-number" theory and the manifest relevance to Kandinsky see, for example, Nadezhda Kargapolova, "Muzyka i rannie sinteticheskie zamysly V. Kandinskogo" [Music and Early Synthetic Concepts by W. Kandinsky], in *Izvestiia Ural'skogo gosudarstvennogo universiteta* [Bulletin of the State Ural University] 35, 2005, 114–19; and Irina Vanechkina and Bulat Galeev, "Kandinskii i Skriabin" [Kandinsky and Scriabin], in *Mnogogrannyi mir Kandinskogo* [The Multifarious World of Kandinsky], ed. Natal'ia Avtonomova et al., Moscow 1998; also see Lindsey Macchiarella, "Skryabin's Prefatory Action and Mysterium: Libretto, Sketches, and Divine Unity," PhD diss., Florida State University, Tallahassee 2016.

[21] Kandinskii 2001 (see note 4), 151.

[22] Nadezhda Kargapolova, *Muzykal'nye idei v teoreticheskom i khudozhestvennom nasledii Kandinskogo* [Musical Ideas in Kandinsky's Theorical and Artistic Legacy], dissertation, Altai State University, Barnaul 2003.

[23] *Iskusstvo v zhizni rebenka* [Art in the Life of the Child], exh. cat., St. Petersburg 1908, 23. Other contributors included toymaker Nikolai Bartram and sculptor and Theosophist Vasilii Vatagin; see the exhibition reviews in *Knizhnyi vestnik* [Book Herald] 18–19 (1908), 136; and Aleksandr Benua (Benois), "Vystavka 'Iskusstvo v zhizni rebenka'" ["Art in the Life of the Child" Exhibition], in *Rech'* [Speech] 289 (November 28, 1909).

[24] Kargapolova 2003 (see note 22).

[25] The copy containing Unkovskaia's dedication to "Dear Lev Nikolaevich Tolstoi" is in the Library of the "Iasnaia Poliana" Lev Tolstoi Museum and Estate, inventory no. KP (GIK): MZYaP KP-1807/429. Unkovskaia first published her essay "Metoda tsveto-zvuko-chisel" [Method of Color-Sound-Number] in 1909 (see note 18). The essay was published as a booklet in Petrograd in 1916 and was also widely circulated as a separate offprint, sometimes with a slightly different title such as "Metoda tsveto-zvuko-chislo."

[26] See the report in *Kaluzhskii kur'er* [Kaluga Courier] 59 (June 2, 1909), 2–3.

[27] See, for example, Maria Carlson, *No Religion Higher Than Truth: A History of the Theosophical Movement in Russia, 1875–1922,* Princeton 1993, 187.

[28] Unkovskaia 1909 (see note 18), 80.

[29] Unkovskaia 1916 (see note 25), 7.

[30] Unkovskaia 1909 (see note 18), 78.

[31] Vasilii Kandinsky, "On a Method for Working with Synthetic Art" (1921), in *Experiment* 8,1 (January 2002), 187–92.

[32] Semen Frank, "Rol' iskusstva v pozitivnykh naukakh," lecture delivered at the presidium of the Scientific-Artistic Commission at RAKhN on August 30, 1921. Typescript in the collection of the Wassily Kandinsky Papers 1911–1940 at the Getty Research Center, Los Angeles, call no. 86/A32850/910/OCLC/805/ Record No. 009775, 6.

[33] Ibid.

[34] Ibid.

[35] Georgii Vul'f, "Kak rastut kristally" [How Crystals Grow], in *Priroda* [Nature] (September 1915), 1107–08. See also Georgii Vul'f, "Est' li chto-libo obshchee u kristallov i rastenii?" [Do Crystals and Plants Have Anything in Common?], in *Priroda* (January 1912), 45–46.

[36] Wassily Kandinsky, "Line and Fish," in *Axis* 2 (1935), 6 (italics in the original).

Circles of Exchange: Geometric Abstraction and the East-Central European Avant-Garde, 1920–1930
Maria Mileeva
pages 28–37

[1] Il'ia Ehrenburg, *A vse-taki ona vertitsia* [And Yet the World Turns], Moscow and Berlin 1922. Russian-Jewish writer and critic Ehrenburg spent extensive periods of time before World War I in France to escape political persecution in Imperial Russia.

[2] See New York 1936.

[3] Forgács 2022.

[4] As art historian Timothy O. Benson argued, "From the perspective of its participants the avant-garde was becoming pluralistic, not centered in one place but constantly shifting in among various sites of exchange, where multiple views and approaches were debated and absorbed." Benson claimed that during the 1920s "the avant-garde was itself becoming migratory, as artists' mobility increased." Timothy O. Benson, "Introduction," in Los Angeles 2002, 12–21, here 16. For the latest approaches to the migration and dislocation of modernism, see Schuldenfrei 2024.

[5] "Gründungsaufruf der Union internationaler fortschrittlicher Künstler," in *De Stijl* 4,4 (May 1922), 199–202, here 199; English translation in "Founding Proclamation of the Union of Progressive International Artists," trans. Nicholas Bullock, in Benson/Forgács 2002, 388–402, here 389–90.

[6] The essay does not touch on avant-garde groups and activities in Romania, the former Czechoslovakia, the Kingdom of Serbs, Croats, and Slovenes (later Yugoslavia), and other East-Central European nation-states, where forms of geometric abstraction were developing during the period of the 1920s and 1930s.

[7] See Brooker et al. 2013. See also *Graphic Modernism: From the Baltic to the Balkans, 1910–1935,* exh. cat., New York Public Library, 2007; and London 2008.

[8] Kiaer 2008.

[9] [El Lissitzky und Ilja Ehrenburg], "Blokada Rossii Konchaetsa" [The Blockade of Russia Is Coming to an End], in *Veshch'/Gegenstand/Objet* 1–2 (March–April 1922), 1–4, here 1; English translation in Bann 1974, 53–57, here 55.

[10] See Berlin 1922. The exhibition traveled to the Stedelijk Museum Amsterdam in the spring of 1923.

[11] Berlin 1922, 2.

[12] Lissitzky/Ehrenburg 1922 (see note 9), 3; English translation in Bann 1974, 56.

[13] Ulrich Schmid, "What Did 'Russian' Mean in the Early Twentieth Century," in Leimer/Wünsche 2022, 21–24.

[14] Éva Forgács, "How the New Left Invented East-European Art," in *Centropa* 3,2 (May 2003), 93–104, here 102–03; and Konstantin Akinsha, "Naming the Russian Avant-Garde," in Cologne 2020, 16–31.

[15] Gray 1963.

[16] For recent examples, see New York 2002a and Paris 2018.

[17] Mansbach 1999; Los Angeles 2002; Howard 2006; Hock et al. 2019; Levinger 2022; and Oliver A. I. Botar et al., eds., *Cannibalizing the Canon: Dada Techniques in East-Central Europe,* Leiden and Boston 2024.

[18] Piotr Piotrowski, "How to Write a History of Central-East European Art?," in *Third Text* 3,1 (January 2009), 5–14, here 8–9; Agata Jakubowska and Magdalena Radomska, eds., *Horizontal Art History and Beyond: Revising Peripheral Critical Practices,* New York and London 2024.

[19] El Lissitzky and Hans Arp, eds., *Die Kunstismen/Les Ismes de l'art/The Isms of Art, 1914-1924,* Erlenbach et al. 1925.

[20] Steven A. Mansbach, "Władysław Strzemiński's Textual Radicalism," in *Władysław Strzemiński: Readability of Images,* ed. Paweł Polit and Jarosław Suchan, Łódź 2015, 35–50, here 38–39.

[21] Lajos Kassák, A berlini orosz kiállitáshoz [On the Russian Exhibit in Berlin], in *Ma* 8,2–3 (December 1922), unpaginated; English translation in Benson/Forgács 2002, trans. John Bátki, 409–10, here 409.

[22] Ibid.

[23] Ibid.

[24] Ibid., 410.

[25] Lajos Kassák, "An die Künstler aller Länder!" [To the Artists of All Nations!], in *Ma* 5,1–2 (May 1920), 2–4, here 2; English translation in Benson/Forgács 2002, trans. John Bátki, 418–20, here 418–19.

[26] Ibid.

[27] Ibid.

[28] Lajos Kassák, Képarchitektúra [Picture-Architecture], in *Ma* 7,4 (March 1922), 52–54; English translation in Benson/Forgács 2002, trans. George Cushing, 427–31.

[29] N. [Nikolai Nikolaevich] Punin, "Tatlin üvegtornya" [Tatlin's Glass Tower], in *Ma* 7,5–6 (May 1922), 31; English translation in Christina Lodder, "Art into Life: International Constructivism in Central and Eastern Europe," in Los Angeles 2002, 172–98, here 197n34.

[30] For a full list of the participants in the exhibition, see *Constructivism in Poland,* 1923–1936: Blok, Praesens, a.r., exh. cat., Museum Folkwang, Essen 1973; and *The 70th Anniversary of the New Art Exhibition, Vilnius,* 1923, exh. cat., Muzeum Sztuki, Łódź 1993.

[31] Władysław Strzemiński, "O sztuce rosyjskiej-notatki" [Notes on Russian Art], in *Zwrotnica* [The Switch] 3 (1922), 79–82, and 4 (1923), 110–14; English translation in Benson/Forgács 2002, trans. Wanda Kemp-Welch, 272–80.

[32] News of *Blok* appeared in *De Stijl* 8 (1924), 411.

[33] Krisztina Passuth, "The Exhibition as a Work of Art. Avant-Garde Exhibitions in East Central Europe," in: Los Angeles 2002, 226–246, here 234.

[34] Editorial statement, in *Blok* 1 (March 1924), unpaginated; English translation in Benson/Forgács 2002, trans. Wanda Kemp-Welch, 491.

[35] "Co to jest konstruktywizm" [What Constructivism Is], in *Blok* 6–7 (September 1924), unpaginated; English translation in Benson/Forgács 2002, trans. John E. Bowlt, 496.

[36] Ludwig Mies van der Rohe, "Budowa" [Construction], in *Blok* 1 (March 1924), unpaginated.

[37] Kurt Schwitters, "Dadaizm," in *Blok* 6–7 (September 1924), unpaginated; English translation in Przemysław Strożek, "Polish Responses to Dadaism: The Voices on Dada, Contacts and Interpretations," in Botar et al. 2024 (see note 17), 55–76, here 67.

[38] Mieczysław Szczuka, "To co my robimy . . ." [What We Are Doing . . .], in *Blok* 2 (April 1924), 8; English translation in Przemysław Strożek, "Cracow and Warsaw: Becoming the Avant-Garde," in Brooker et al. 2013, 1184–1207, here 1203.

[39] Władysław Strzemiński, *Unizm w malarstwie* [Unism in Painting], Warsaw 1928; English translation in Benson/ Forgács 2002, trans. Wanda Kemp-Welch, 649–57.

[40] The room became known as the Neoplastic Room at the Muzeum Sztuki in Łódź after World War II. It remained closed between 1950 and 1960, as a result of the repressive measures that followed the introduction of Soviet Socialist Realism as the official method in Poland in 1949. See Paulina Kurc-Maj and Anna Saciuk-Gąsowska, eds., *The International Collection of Modern Art of the "a.r." group,* Łódź 2019.

[41] See Montages: *Debora Vogel and the New Legend of the City,* exh. cat., Muzeum Sztuki, Łódź 2017; and Piotr Łukaszewicz and Andrij Bojarow, *Artes: nowocześni plastycy lwowscy* [Art: Modern Łwów Artists], Wrocław 2023.

[42] Tetiana Zhmurko, "The Tragic Sensuality of the Kharkiv Avant-Garde," in Madrid 2022, 56–60.

[43] Myroslav Shkandrij, *Modernists, Marxists and the Nation: The Ukrainian Literary Discussion of the 1920s,* Edmonton 1992. On Pan-European community and networks, see Forgács 2003 (see note 14); Klara Kemp-Welch, *Networking the Bloc: Experimental Art in Eastern Europe 1965-1981,* Cambridge, MA, and London 2018; Jérôme Bazin et al., eds., *Art beyond Borders: Artistic Exchange in Communist Europe (1945-1989),* Budapest 2016.

[44] Another important figure in the creation of artist almanacs in Kharkiv was Valer'ian Polishchuk, the initiator of the movement known as Avanhard (Avant-Garde) that promoted "Constructive Dynamism" (Spiralism). He published a number of journals, including *Biuleten' Avanhardu* (Bulletin of the Avant-Garde, 1928), *Mystets'ki materialy avanhardu* (Artistic Materials of the Avant-Garde, 1929), and *Avanhard* (Avant-Garde, 1929), which featured Constructivist designs by Vasyl' Iermylov. *Avanhard* had a strong internationalist outlook and included contributions in Yiddish, German, and Esperanto. See Oleh S. Ilnytzkyj, "From Under Imperial Eyes in Kyiv and Kharkiv Magazines," in Brooker et al. 2013, 1341–62, here 1351.

[45] Mykhailo Semenko, "What Panfuturism Wants," in *Semafor u maibutnie: Aparat panfuturystiv* [Semaphore into the Future: The Apparatus of Panfuturists] 1 (May 1922), 12.

[46] Thirty-six issues were published between 1927 and 1930. See Myroslava M. Mudrak, "Nova heneratsiia (1927–1930)," in Madrid 2022, 78–84.

[47] Kazimir Malevich was born in Kyiv to Polish parents and worked most of his life in Imperial and Soviet Russia. He is a representative of a hybrid, multinational identity common among the international avant-garde of the period in question.

[48] For a recent exhibition that considers the links of Enrico Prampolini with the Polish avant-garde, see *Enrico Prampolini: Futurism, Stage Design and the Polish Avant-Garde Theatre,* exh. cat., Muzeum Sztuki, Łódź 2017.

[49] "Vid redaktsii" [Editorial], in *Avanhard: Al'manakh proletars'kykh myttsiv Novoi heneratsii* [Avant-Garde: An Almanac of Proletarian Artists of the New Generation], no. "a" (January 1930), 2; English translation in Ilnytzkyj 2013 (see note 44), 1360.

Rhythms of the City: The Influence of the Metropolis on Piet Mondrian's Geometric Abstraction
Sterre Barentsen
pages 38–49

1 Nina Kandinsky, *Kandinsky und ich: Mein Leben mit einem großen Künstler,* Munich 1999, 178.
2 See Harry Holtzman, "Piet Mondrian: The Man and His Work," in Mondrian 1986, 1–10, here 7; and Geoffrey T. Hellman, "Lines and Rectangles," The Talk of the Town, in *New Yorker* (March 1, 1941), 9.
3 Piet Mondrian, "De Nieuwe Beelding in de Schilderkunst: Van het natuurlijke tot het abstracte, d.i. van het onbepaalde tot het bepaalde" [The New Plastic in Painting: From the Natural to the Abstract: From the Indeterminate to the Determinate], in *De Stijl* 1,11 (September 1918), 187–96, here 188n8; English translation in Mondrian 1986, 47–64, here 59, note t.
4 Piet Mondrian, "Natuurlijke en abstracte realiteit: Trialoog (gedurende een wandeling van buiten naar de stad): 6e Tooneel" [Natural Reality and Abstract Reality: A Trialogue (While Strolling from the Country to the City): Scene 6], in *De Stijl* 3,2 (December 1919), 485–87, here 486. Unless otherwise indicated, all translations are by Sterre Barentsen.
5 Letter from Piet Mondrian to Salomon Slijper (Laren, April 2, 1916), in *The Mondriaan Papers,* https://edition.mondrianpapers.org/record/1385?q=wereldstad (accessed on September 27, 2024).
6 Kirk Varnedoe and Adam Gopnik, "Advertising," in *High & Low: Modern Art and Popular Culture,* exh. cat., Museum of Modern Art, New York 1990, 231–368, here 251.
7 Stuart Wrede, "The Modern Poster," in *The Modern Poster,* exh. cat., Museum of Modern Art, New York 1988, 11–38, here 12.
8 Piet Mondrian, "Liberation from Oppression in Art and Life (1939–1940)," in Mondrian, *Plastic Art and Pure Plastic Art,* New York 1945; republished in Mondrian 1986, 324–30, here 326.
9 Piet Mondrian, "L'Expression plastique nouvelle dans la peinture" [The New Plastic Expression in Painting], in *Cahiers d'Art* 1 (1926), 181–83; English translation in Mondrian 1986, 202–04.
10 Ibid., 203.
11 Christina Lodder, "Transfiguring Reality: Suprematism and the Aerial View," in Dorrian/Pousin 2013, 95–117, here 101.
12 Fernand Léger, "Les Réalisations picturales actuelles" [Contemporary Achievements in Painting], in *Les Soirées de Paris* 25 (June 15, 1914), 349–56; English translation in Léger, *Functions of Painting,* ed. Edward F. Fry, New York 1973, 11–19.
13 Ibid., 12.
14 Ibid., 11.
15 See Mondrian 1918 (see note 3), English translation, 64.
16 Léger 1914 (see note 12), English translation, 12.
17 Michael White, "Advertising as Fine Art," in White 2003, 77–102.
18 Vilmos Huszár, "De reclame als beeldende kunst," in *De Reclame* 8,4 (1929), 167; English translation in White 2003, 96.
19 Letter from Theo van Doesburg to J. J. P. Oud (February 4, 1920), quoted in Mondrian 1986, 124: "[Mondrian] is deeply absorbed in his Boulevard chronicle. It took considerable persuasion on my part, for, while liking the idea, he had many reservations. This noon, happily, we were on the Boulevard des Capucines, where we observed the working of the incredible machine that is Paris."
20 Piet Mondrian, "De groote boulevards" [Les Grands Boulevards], in *De Nieuwe Amsterdammer* 273 (March 27 and April 3, 1920), 5; English translation in Mondrian 1986, 126–28.
21 Piet Mondrian, "Little Restaurant: Palm Sunday" (1920), in Mondrian 1986, 129–31.
22 Ibid., 129.
23 Benjamin H. D. Buchloh, "Social Silence," in *Artforum* 34,2 (October 1995), 124.
24 See Janssen 2022.
25 Mondrian 1926 (see note 9), English translation, 204.
26 Janssen 2022, 58.
27 See *Léger: Modern Art and the Metropolis,* exh. cat., Philadelphia Museum of Art, 2013.
28 Letter from Piet Mondrian to Theo van Doesburg (October 21, 1919), quoted in Janssen 2022, 79 (translation modified).
29 Letter from Piet Mondrian to Lodewijk van Deyssel (March 18, 1932), quoted in Mondrian 1986, 133.
30 Janssen 2022, 53–55.
31 Piet Mondrian, "De Jazz en de Neoplastiek" [Jazz and Neo-Plastic], in *Internationale revue i10* 1,12 (December 1927), 421–27; English translation in Mondrian 1986, 217–22, here 221.
32 Mondrian 1920 (see note 20), 128. Translation by Sterre Barentsen.
33 See Pyotr Demianovich Ouspensky, *Tertium Organum: The Third Canon of Thought; A Key to the Enigmas of the World* (1911), trans. Nicholas Bassaraboff and Claude Bragdon, London 1934, 48; see also Lodder 2013 (see note 11), 107–08.
34 "De architecten van den ‚Stijl' te Parijs," in *De Telegraaf* (October 23, 1923); English translation in Mondrian 1986, 206.
35 Linda Dalrymple Henderson, "Abstraktion, der Äther und die vierte Dimension: Kandinsky, Mondrian und Malewitsch im Kontext," in Düsseldorf 2014, 37–55, here 48.
36 Mondrian 1927 (see note 31).
37 Ibid., English translation, 222.
38 Piet Mondrian, "A Folder of Notes" (ca. 1941), in Mondrian 1986, 370.
39 See William A. Shack, "Le Jazz Cold: The Silent Forties," in *Harlem in Montmartre: A Paris Jazz Story between the Great Wars,* Berkeley 2001, 107–27.
40 See Hanna Diamond, *Fleeing Hitler: France 1940,* Oxford 2007, 2.
41 Letter from Piet Mondrian to Barbara Hepworth (July 4, 1940), quoted in Sophie Bowness, "Mondrian in London: Letters to Ben Nicholson and Barbara Hepworth," in *Burlington Magazine* 132,1052 (November 1990), 782–88, here 787.
42 "The Blitz," in *Encyclopaedia Britannica,* https://www.britannica.com/event/the-Blitz (accessed on November 7, 2024).
43 See Janssen 2022, 371–74.
44 Wiegand 1961, 65.
45 Sidney Janis, "The School of Paris Comes to the US," in *Decision* 2,5–6 (November/December 1944), 85–93.
46 Harry Cooper, "Looking into the Transatlantic Paintings," in Cambridge 2001, 24–66, here 32.
47 Wiegand 1961, 65.
48 See Dickerman 2023.

An Art Without Content? Hard Edge Painting, 1958–1968
Jeremy Lewison
pages 50–65

[1] For a discussion of the impact of American art on European painters and its political consequences in the postwar period, see Jeremy Lewison, "The Shape of Freedom? International Abstraction after 1945," in Potsdam 2022, 10–27.

[2] Darby Bannard, "Present-Day Art and Ready-Made Styles," in *Artforum* 5,4 (December 1966), 30–35, here 30.

[3] Lawrence Alloway, "Introduction," in *6 American Abstract Painters,* exh. cat., Arthur Tooth and Sons, London 1961, unpaginated.

[4] Jules Langsner, "Four Abstract Classicists," in *Four Abstract Classicists: West Coast Hard-Edge,* exh. cat., Institute of Contemporary Arts, London 1960, unpaginated. The same text was published the previous year in the San Francisco catalog.

[5] Lawrence Alloway, "London Letter," in *Art International* 4,2/3 (1960), 60–62, here 60.

[6] Ibid.

[7] See his description of that process in Langsner 1960 (see note 4).

[8] Barbara Rose, "ABC Art," in *Art in America* (October–November 1965), 57–69, https://www.artnews.com/art-in-america/features/abc-art-barbara-rose-1234580665/ (accessed on August 22, 2024).

[9] Ad Reinhardt, "Monologue," in *Art as Art: The Selected Writings of Ad Reinhardt,* ed. Barbara Rose, Berkeley 1991, 23–29, here 24. "Monologue" was excerpted from a 1966 interview with Mary Fuller and published in *Artforum* in October 1970.

[10] Ad Reinhardt, "25 Lines of Words on Art: Statement" (1958), in Reinhardt 1991 (see note 9), 51–52. The original text is written in all capital letters.

[11] Michael Fried, *Three American Painters,* exh. cat., Fogg Art Museum, Harvard Art Museums, Cambridge, MA, 1965, 5.

[12] Clement Greenberg, "Avant-Garde and Kitsch," in *Partisan Review* (1939), republished in *Horizon* (1940); quoted in Greenberg 1986, 5–22, here 18.

[13] Clement Greenberg, "The Case for Abstract Art," in *Saturday Evening Post* (August 1959), quoted from Greenberg 1993, 75–84, here 80.

[14] Kenneth Noland quoted from "Hitting the Bullseye," in *Newsweek* 59,16 (April 16, 1962), 108; quoted in Moffet 1977, 49.

[15] Mollie R. Berger, "Centres of Energy," in *Gift 1961–2 by Kenneth Noland,* Tate Research Publication, 2016, https://www.tate.org.uk/research/in-focus/gift-kenneth-noland/centres-of-energy (accessed on August 29, 2024).

[16] Fried 1965 (see note 11), 30–31.

[17] Lippard 1966, 149.

[18] See "Frank Stella (1984)," in David Sylvester, *Interviews with American Painters,* London 2001, 183–200, here 194.

[19] Lippard 1966, 158.

[20] He was perhaps mistaken in this aspect as many abstract paintings of this period relied heavily on symmetry.

[21] Leonard B. Meyer, "The End of the Renaissance: Notes on the Radical Empiricism of the Avant-Garde," in *Hudson Review* (Summer 1963), 169–86.

[22] Susan Sontag, "Against Interpretation," in *Evergreen Review* 8,34 (December 1964), 76–80.

[23] Robbe-Grillet's *Pour un nouveau roman,* a collection of previously published essays, was published in French in 1963. His novels *Le Voyeur* (1955) and *La Jalousie* (1957) were translated into English in 1958 and 1959 respectively. *Dans le labyrinth* appeared in 1959 and was translated in 1960.

[24] Lawrence Alloway, "On the Edge," in *Architectural Design* 30,4 (April 1960), 164–65, here 164–65.

[25] See David Mellor, *The Art of Robyn Denny,* London 2002, 75.

[26] Norbert Lynton, "London Letter," in *Art International* 7,5 (May 25, 1963), 59.

[27] For a discussion of Stella's references to the Holocaust in this and the *Polish Series* of the early 1970s, see Godfrey 2007, 79–111.

[28] Robert Rosenblum, "Frank Stella, 1958–1965," in Rubin 1986, 16–23; reprinted in Rosenblum, *On Modern American Art: Selected Essays by Robert Rosenblum,* New York 1999, 170–80, here 172. Rosenblum acknowledges that this idea was first aired by Brenda Richardson in her catalog introduction to Baltimore 1976.

[29] See Godfrey 2007, 23–49.

[30] Quoted in Al Filreis, *1960: When Art and Literature Confronted the Memory of World War II and Remade the Modern,* New York 2021, 5.

[31] Brian O'Doherty, "The New Nihilism: Art Versus Feeling," in *New York Times* (February 16, 1964), section 2, 15; quoted in Irving Sandler, *American Art of the 1960s,* New York 1988, 66.

[32] Irving Sandler, "The New Cool-Art," in *Art in America* (January 1965), https://www.artnews.com/art-in-america/features/archives-new-cool-art-63525/ (accessed 29 August 2024).

[33] Meyer Schapiro, "The Liberating Quality of the Avant-Garde," in *ARTnews* 56,4 (Summer 1957), 36–42, here 38.

[34] Ellsworth Kelly, from his application for a John Simon Guggenheim Memorial grant, November 1951; quoted in Clare Bell, "At Play with Vision: Ellsworth Kelly's 'Line, Form and Color,'" in New York 1996, 66–79, here 68.

[35] Alloway 1961 (see note 3).

[36] Alloway 1960 (see note 24), 164.

[37] Peter Brook, *The Empty Space,* London 1968, 9.

[38] Lawrence Alloway, "Introduction," in New York 1966b, 17–18.

[39] Andrew M. Goldstein, "Ellsworth Kelly on his His Singular Career, and the 'Great Joy' of His Art," in *Artspace* (December 29, 2015), https://www.artspace.com/magazine/interviews_features/qa/ellsworth-kelly-final-interview-53394 (accessed on August 29, 2024).

[40] Ibid.

[41] Al Held, quoted in a biographical summary at https://www.whitecube.com/artists/al-held (accessed on August 29, 2024).

CATALOG OF EXHIBITED WORKS

Spirit and Technology: Geometry in Abstract Art

Max Boersma
pages 68–73

1. Wassily Kandinsky, "Reminiscences" (1913), in Kandinsky 1994, 357–82, here 373.
2. Wassily Kandinsky, "Cologne Lecture" (1914), in Kandinsky 1994, 392–400, here 394.
3. T. J. Clark, *Farewell to an Idea: Episodes from a History of Modernism,* New Haven 1999, 285.
4. See Lodder 2004.
5. Aleksandr Rodchenko, "Notepad," in *Aleksandr Rodchenko: Experiments for the Future; Diaries, Essays, Letters, and Other Writings,* ed. Alexander Lavrentiev, New York 2005, 90.
6. Liubov Popova, "Statement from the Catalog for the 'Tenth State Exhibition: Nonobjective Art and Suprematism,'" in Dmitri V. Sarabianov and Natalia L. Adaskina, *Popova,* London 1990, 347.
7. Gough 2005, 21–59.

Universal Language of Abstraction: Bauhaus and Concrete Artists

Max Boersma
pages 98–103

1. Kandinsky 1947, 83.
2. See "The Language of Form and Colour," in Kandinsky 1977, 44–78, esp. 45–46; and John E. Bowlt and Nicoletta Misler's contribution to this catalog, 18–27.
3. Richard Paul Lohse, "Lines of Development 1943–84," in *Systems,* ed. Edward A. Shanken, London 2015, 153.
4. Quoted in Brigitte Ulmer, "A Leap Out of the Grid," in Haemmerli/Ulmer 2024, 136.
5. Max Bill, "Wassily Kandinsky," in *Werk: Die Schweizer Monatsschrift für Kunst, Architektur, Künstlerisches Gewerbe* 33,4 (April 1946), 128–32, here 130.
6. Max Bill, "Einführung," in Wassily Kandinsky, *Punkt und Linie zu Fläche: Beitrag zur Analyse der malerischen Elemente,* Bern 1986, 7–10, here 10.

Straight Lines, Flowing Forms: International Abstraction in Paris

Sterre Barentsen
pages 124–29

1. See Piet Mondrian, "De Jazz en de Neo-plastiek," in *Internationale revue i10* 1,12 (December 1927), 421–27, English translation in Mondrian 1986, 217–22; and Janssen 2022, 61–71, 139–40.
2. Stanley William Hayter, "The Language of Kandinsky," in *Magazine of Art* 38,5 (May 1945), 178–79.
3. Vivian Endicott Barnett, "Kandinsky and Science: The Introduction of Biological Images in the Paris Period," in New York 1985b, 61–88, here 77.
4. See Kandinsky 1947, 39.
5. See New York 2022.

Balanced Forces: Constructivist Utopias in British Art

Altair Brandon-Salmon
pages 154–59

1. Read 1934, 19.
2. Alloway 1954, 6.
3. See Spalding 2022, 290, 317, 349.
4. Sam Gathercole, "The Geometry of Syntactics, Semantics and Pragmatics: Anthony Hill's Concrete Paintings," in *Tate Papers* 31 (Spring 2019), https://www.tate.org.uk/research/tate-papers/31/anthony-hill-concrete-paintings (accessed on May 17, 2024).
5. Alloway 1954, 13, 32.
6. Ibid., 10.
7. See Alan Fowler, "Constructive and Systems Art in Britain after the Second World War," in Southampton 2005, 74–75; and Hilary Floe, "Concrete," in London 2022, 168–69.
8. Sam Gathercole, "The Lost Cause of British Constructionism: A Two-Act Tragedy," in *British Art Studies* 18 (2020), https://www.britishartstudies.ac.uk/issues/issue-index/issue-18/the-lost-cause-of-british-constructionism (accessed on May 15, 2024).

The Essence of Form: Hard Edge Painting and Minimalism

David Max Horowitz
pages 184–89

1. Clement Greenberg, "Modernist Painting" (1960), in Greenberg 1993, 85–93, here 85.
2. Clement Greenberg, "Introduction to an Exhibition of Morris Louis, Kenneth Noland, and Jules Olitski" (1963), in Greenberg 1993, 149–53, here 153.
3. Lippard 1966, 161.
4. Lucy Lippard, "Top to Bottom, Left to Right," in Philadelphia 1972, unpaginated.

Space Age: Op Art in the Sixties

Sterre Barentsen
pages 218–23

1. See New York 1965, 7–8.
2. Lucy R. Lippard, "New York Letter," in *Art International* 9,4 (March 1965), 52–59; Barbara Rose, "Beyond Vertigo: Optical Art at the Modern," in *Artforum* 3,7 (April 1965), 30–33, here 31; and Rosalind Krauss, "Afterthoughts on Op," in *Art International* 9,5 (June 1965), 75–76, here 75.
3. On the appeal of television, see, for example, Jacques Ellul, *The Technological Society* (1954), New York 1964; and Lee 2004, 183–92.
4. Thomas Hess, "You Can Hang It in the Hall," in *Art News* 64,2 (April 1965), 41–43, 49–50, here 43.
5. Quoted in Bridget Riley and E. H. Gombrich, "The Use of Colour and Its Effect: The How and the Why," in *Burlington Magazine* 136,1096 (July 1994), https://www.burlington.org.uk/archive/article/the-use-of-colour-and-its-effect-the-how-and-the-why (accessed on August 23, 2024).
6. Paul Klee, "Analysis of Movement in 1932/s2: City Castle of KR," in Klee 1961, 234.

List of Exhibited Works

JOSEF ALBERS
1888, Bottrop, Germany –
1976, New Haven, CT, USA
Mostly active in Weimar; Dessau; Black Mountain, NC; and New Haven

28
Homage to the Square: Mitered Square, 1967
Oil on Masonite, 122 × 122 cm
Inscribed on lower right: A67
Inv. 9/198
Josef Albers Museum Quadrat Bottrop

29
Homage to the Square, 1967
Oil on Masonite, 81 × 81 cm
Inscribed on lower right: A67
Inv. 9/215
Josef Albers Museum Quadrat Bottrop

30
Study for Homage to the Square: Reticence, 1965
Oil on Masonite, 81 × 81 cm
Inscribed on lower right: A65
Inv. 9/279
Josef Albers Museum Quadrat Bottrop

31
Study for Homage to the Square: Corona, 1968
Oil on Masonite, 81 × 81 cm
Inscribed on lower right: A68
Inv. 9/263
Josef Albers Museum Quadrat Bottrop

32
Study for Homage to the Square, 1965
Oil on Masonite, 81 × 81 cm
Inscribed on lower right: A65
Inv. 9/120
Josef Albers Museum Quadrat Bottrop

EDNA ANDRADE
1917, Portsmouth, VA, USA –
2008, Philadelphia, USA
Mostly active in Philadelphia

105
Color Motion 4-64, 1964
Oil on canvas, 121.9 × 121.9 cm
Inv. 2003-94-1
Philadelphia Museum of Art; Gift of Frederick R. McBrien III, 2003

RICHARD ANUSZKIEWICZ
1930, Erie, PA, USA –
2020, Englewood, NJ, USA
Mostly active in Cleveland, New Haven, New York, and Englewood

118
Orange Delight, 1969
Acrylic on canvas, five parts, overall: 306.1 × 306.5 cm
Inv. 69.176a-e
Whitney Museum of American Art, New York; Gift of the artist

119
Monument Valley, 1970
Acrylic on canvas, 121.9 × 121.9 cm
Estate of Richard Anuszkiewicz

120
Untitled, 1972
Acrylic on canvas, 153 × 153 cm
Inv. HH0399
ASOM Collection

121
Metamorphosis of Cadmium Red—Blue Line, 1979
Acrylic on canvas, 213.4 × 213.4 cm
Estate of Richard Anuszkiewicz

JO BAER
b. 1929, Seattle, WA, USA
Mostly active in New York, London, Ireland, and Amsterdam

100
White Side Bar (blue line), 1972–75
Oil on canvas, 183 × 183 cm
Inv. 916
Louisiana Museum of Modern Art, Humlebæk, Denmark; Gift from the Riklis Collection of McCrory Corporation

MAX BILL
1908, Winterthur, Switzerland –
1994, Berlin, Germany
Mostly active in Zurich, Ulm, Hamburg, and Berlin

33
reflections from dark and light, 1975
Oil on canvas, 120 × 120 cm
diagonal: 170 cm
Dr. Angela Thomas, Haus Bill, Zumikon, Switzerland, www.maxbill.ch

ALEXANDER CALDER
1898, Lawnton, PA, USA –
1976, New York, USA
Mostly active in Paris; Roxbury, CT; and Saché, France

54
Untitled, 1963
Iron wire and painted aluminum sheeting, 152.4 × 182.8 × 76.2 cm
Inv. FGA-BA-CALDE-0001
Fondation Gandur pour l'Art, Genève

ENRICO CASTELLANI
1930, Castelmassa, Italy –
2017, Celleno, Italy
Mostly active in Brussels and Milan

98
White Surface No. 18, 1964
Acrylic on canvas, nails, 180 × 180 cm
Mercedes-Benz Art Collection

ILYA CHASHNIK
1902, Lyutsin, Russian Empire (now Ludza, Latvia) – 1929, Leningrad, USSR (now St. Petersburg, Russia)
Mostly active in Vitebsk and Leningrad

2
Suprematist Cross, 1923
Oil on canvas, 133.2 × 133.4 cm
Inv. MMA.CC.157
MOMus—Museum of Modern Art—Costakis Collection, Thessaloniki

GENE DAVIS
1920, Washington, DC, USA – 1985, Washington, DC, USA
Mostly active in Washington, DC

86
Black Popcorn, 1965
Acrylic on canvas, 296.5 × 292.4 cm
Inv. 2014.136.102
National Gallery of Art, Washington; Corcoran Collection (museum purchase and exchange)

JO DELAHAUT
1911, Vottem, Belgium – 1992, Schaerbeek, Belgium
Mostly active in Liège and Brussels

52
Clostra, 1950
Oil on canvas, 100.5 × 80.7 cm
Inscribed on lower right: delahaut 50
Inv. FGA-BA-DELAH-0001
Fondation Gandur pour l'Art, Genève

SONIA DELAUNAY
1885, Gradizhsk, Russian Empire (now Ukraine) – 1979, Paris, France
Mostly active in Paris and Madrid

53
Bing, 1967
Wool, 203 × 165 cm
Inv. 31175
Sainsbury Centre, University of East Anglia

WALTER DEXEL
1890, Munich, Germany – 1973, Braunschweig, Germany
Mostly active in Munich, Jena, Magdeburg, Berlin, and Braunschweig

23
Composition 1924 VI, 1924
Oil on canvas, 92 × 64 cm
Galerie Berinson, Berlin

24
Composition 1924 II, 1924
Oil on canvas, 55.5 × 47.5 cm
Inscribed on lower right: W DEXEL 24
Inv. HK-5166
Hamburger Kunsthalle

BURGOYNE DILLER
1906, New York, USA – 1965, New York, USA
Mostly active in New York

46
Third Theme, 1946–48
Oil on linen, 106.7 × 106.7 cm
Inv. 58.58
Whitney Museum of American Art, New York; Gift of May Walter

THEO VAN DOESBURG
1883, Utrecht, the Netherlands – 1931, Davos, Switzerland
Mostly active in Leiden, Weimar, and Paris

39
Composition in Gray (Rag-time), 1919
Oil on canvas, 96.5 × 59.1 cm
Inv. 76.2553 PG 40
Peggy Guggenheim Collection, Venice (Solomon R. Guggenheim Foundation, New York)

CÉSAR DOMELA
1900, Amsterdam, the Netherlands – 1992, Paris, France
Mostly active in Ascona, Paris, and Berlin

43
Neoplastic Composition 5a, 1924
Oil on canvas, 58 × 58 cm
Inscribed lower left: NG; and verso: Domela 1924
Triton Collection Foundation

ALEKSANDRA EKSTER
1882, Białystok, Russian Empire (now Poland) – 1949, Fontenay-aux-Roses, France
Mostly active in Paris, Kyiv, Moscow, and Odesa

12
Construction of Colors, 1921
Oil on canvas, 88 × 72 cm
Inv. GE636DL
ALBERTINA, Vienna—Private collection

BORIS ENDER
1893, St. Petersburg, Russian Empire – 1960, Moscow, USSR
Mostly active in Leningrad (now St. Petersburg)

11
Abstract Composition, 1919–20
Oil on canvas, 104 × 100 cm
Inv. CC-0022/B.Ender-/13.78 verso-8
MOMus—Museum of Modern Art—Costakis Collection, Thessaloniki

JOHN ERNEST
1922, Philadelphia, USA – 1994, Exeter, UK
Mostly active in Sweden, Paris, and London

69
Relief: Triangular Motif II, 1959
Aluminum, Formica, hardboard, and wood, 42 × 45 × 7.5 cm
Inv. 31573
Sainsbury Centre, University of East Anglia; Bequeathed by Joyce and Michael Morris, 2014

76
Mosaic Relief III, 1964
Aluminum, Formica, plexiglass, and wood, 100.5 × 111 × 10 cm
Inv. 31547
Sainsbury Centre, University of East Anglia; Bequeathed by Joyce and Michael Morris, 2014

WOJCIECH FANGOR
1922, Warsaw, Poland – 2015, Warsaw, Poland
Mostly active in Warsaw; Washington, DC; Paris; and New Jersey

110
M37, 1967
Acrylic on canvas, 132.5 × 132.5 cm
Inv. J.175
ASOM Collection

111
M70, 1966
Acrylic on canvas, 132 × 132 cm
Inv. HH0496
ASOM Collection

112
B13, 1964
Oil on canvas, 131 × 131 cm
Inv. HH0389
ASOM Collection

113
B15, 1964
Oil on canvas, 131 × 131 cm
Inv. E.107
ASOM Collection

TERRY FROST
1915, Leamington Spa, UK – 2003, Newlyn, UK
Mostly active in London, St. Ives, Leeds, Banbury, and Reading

77
Red, Black and White, 1977
Acrylic and collage on canvas, 122 × 81.2 cm
Inv. 03/604
Royal Academy of Arts, London

NAUM GABO
1890, Bryansk, Russian Empire – 1977, Waterbury, CT, USA
Mostly active in Munich, Kristiania (now Oslo), Moscow, Berlin, Paris, London, and Connecticut

20
Linear Construction in Space no. 2, 1969
Plexiglass with nylon monofilament on a plexiglass base, 40.5 × 40.5 cm
Inscribed on top: Gabo
Triton Collection Foundation

FRITZ GLARNER
1899, Zurich, Switzerland –
1972, Locarno, Switzerland
Mostly active in Zurich, Paris, and New York

47
Relational Painting, 1949–51
Oil on linen, 165.1 × 132.1 cm
Inv. 52.3
Whitney Museum of American Art, New York

48
Painting (white), 1945
Oil on canvas, 74 × 71 cm
Inscribed on lower left: GLARNER-45
Inv. 1979/0072
Kunsthaus Zürich; Bequest Louise Glarner, 1979

JEAN GORIN
1899, Saint-Émilion, France –
1981, Niort, France
Mostly active in Paris and Nantes

45
Spatio-Temporal Plastic Composition, 1962
Wood and paint, 152.5 × 45.5 × 45 cm
Inv. KM 118.480
Kröller-Müller Museum, Otterlo, The Netherlands

CAMILLE GRAESER
1892, Carouge, Switzerland –
1980, Wald, Switzerland
Mostly active in Stuttgart and Zurich

35
1 : 2 : 3 : 4, 1969
Oil on canvas, 120 × 120 cm
Inv. B 1969.7
Courtesy Camille Graeser Stiftung, Zurich

AL HELD
1928, Brooklyn, NY, USA –
2005, Todi, Italy
Mostly active in New York and Paris

89
The Dowager Empress, 1965
Acrylic on canvas, 244.5 × 183.2 cm
Inv. 66.3
Whitney Museum of American Art, New York; Purchase, with funds from the Friends of the Whitney Museum of American Art

JEAN HÉLION
1904, Couterne, France –
1987, Paris, France
Mostly active in Paris, New York, and Virginia

50
Abstract Composition, 1932
Oil on canvas, 64.9 × 49.8 cm
Inv. FGA-BA-HELIO-0014
Fondation Gandur pour l'Art, Genève

51
Untitled, 1935
Oil on canvas, 116.7 × 81.7 cm
Inv. FGA-BA-HELIO-0013
Fondation Gandur pour l'Art, Genève

BARBARA HEPWORTH
1903, Wakefield, UK –
1975, St. Ives, UK
Mostly active in Leeds, London, Paris, and St. Ives

58
Conoid, Sphere and Hollow III, 1937
Marble, 32 × 35.5 × 30.5 cm
Inv. 7368
UK Government Art Collection

79
Orpheus (Maquette I), 1956
Brass with cotton strings, 52.2 × 22.5 × 18.9 cm
Inv. PAC 43
Pier Arts Centre, Stromness, Orkney

AUGUSTE HERBIN
1882, Quiévy, France –
1960, Paris, France
Mostly active in Lille and Paris

49
Good, 1952
Oil on canvas, 130 × 89 cm
Inscribed on lower right: herbin 1952
Inv. FGA-BA-HERBI-0003
Fondation Gandur pour l'Art, Genève

CARMEN HERRERA
1915, Havana, Cuba –
2022, New York, USA
Mostly active in Havana, Paris, and New York

91
Diptych (Green & Black), 1976
Acrylic on canvas, 114.9 × 210.8 cm, each panel 114.9 × 101.6 cm
Inv. HERR76002
Estate of Carmen Herrera; courtesy private collection and Lisson Gallery

ANTHONY HILL
1930, London, UK – 2020 England
Mostly active in London

65
Progression of Rectangles, Version II, 1954–59
Plexiglass and wood, 40.5 × 40.5 × 4.5 cm
Inv. 31539
Sainsbury Centre, University of East Anglia; Bequeathed by Joyce and Michael Morris, 2014

73
Five Regions Relief, 1960–62
Aluminum, hardboard, and plastic, 61 × 54.9 × 9 cm
Inv. 31193
Sainsbury Centre, University of East Anglia

PAUL HUXLEY
b. 1938, London, UK
Mostly active in London and New York

87
Untitled no. 51, 1966
Acrylic on canvas, 274 × 274 cm
Studio Paul Huxley

JOHANNES ITTEN
1888, Südern-Linden, Switzerland –
1967, Zurich, Switzerland
Mostly active in Vienna; Weimar; Herrliberg, Switzerland; Berlin; and Zurich

25
Sticks and Planes, 1955
Oil on hardboard, 100 × 72 cm
Mercedes-Benz Art Collection

DONALD JUDD
1928, Excelsior Springs, MO, USA –
1994, New York, USA
Mostly active in Marfa, TX; and New York

102
Untitled, 1969
Steel and plexiglass, 15 × 69 × 61.5 cm
Staatliche Museen zu Berlin, Nationalgalerie, Marzona Collection

WASSILY KANDINSKY
1866, Moscow, Russian Empire –
1944, Neuilly-sur-Seine, France
Mostly active in Munich, Moscow, Weimar, Dessau, and Paris

1 (p. 13)
White Sound, 1908
Oil on cardboard, mounted on panel, 70 × 70 cm
Inscribed on lower right: KANDINSKY
Private collection

3
White Cross, 1922
Oil on canvas, 100.5 × 110.6 cm
Inv. 76.2553 PG 34
Peggy Guggenheim Collection, Venice (Solomon R. Guggenheim Foundation, New York)

21
In the Black Square, 1923
Oil on canvas, 97.5 × 93.3 cm
Inv. 37.254
Inscribed on lower left: K 23; and verso: K/No 2591023
Solomon R. Guggenheim Museum, New York, Solomon R. Guggenheim Founding Collection, by gift

22
Emphasized Corners, 1923
Oil on canvas, 130 × 130 cm
Nahmad Collection

27
Light in Heavy, 1929
Oil on cardboard, 49.5 × 49.5 cm
Inscribed on lower left: VK 29
Inv. 2682 (MK)
Collection Museum Boijmans Van Beuningen, Rotterdam

38
Arrow Toward the Circle, 1930
Oil on canvas, 80 × 110 cm
Nahmad Collection

55
Red Knot, 1936
Oil on canvas, 89 × 116 cm
Inscribed on lower left: VK 36
Collection Fondation Marguerite et Aimé Maeght, Saint-Paul de Vence, France

57
Accompanied Center, 1937
Oil on canvas, 114 × 146 cm
Nahmad Collection

78
Above and Left, 1925
Oil on cardboard, 70 × 50 cm
Inscribed lower left: VK 25
Private collection

80
Silent, 1924
Oil and ink on canvas, 55.3 × 49.3 cm
Inscribed on lower left: VK 24
Inv. 2678 (MK)
Collection Museum Boijmans Van Beuningen, Rotterdam

103
Two Crosses, 1929
Oil on cardboard, 49 × 70 cm
Private collection

125
In the Black Circle, 1923
Oil on canvas, 130 × 130 cm
Private collection

ELLSWORTH KELLY
1923, Newburgh, NY, USA – 2015, Spencertown, NY, USA
Mostly active in New York, Paris, and Spencertown

88
Blue Yellow, 1968
Oil on linen, 171.8 × 217.8 cm
Private collection

IVAN KLIUN
1873, Bolshiye Gorki, Russian Empire – 1943, Moscow, USSR
Mostly active in Moscow

9
Red Light: Spherical Composition, 1923
Oil, sand, and concrete on wooden panel, 69.1 × 68.9 cm
Inscribed on top left: И Клюн
Inv. MMA.CC70
MOMus—Museum of Modern Art—Costakis Collection, Thessaloniki

10
Non-Objective Spherical Composition, 1920–25
Oil on canvas, 101.8 × 70.7 cm
Inscribed on lower left: Клюн
Inv. CC-0180/I.Kliun-/83.78-10
MOMus—Museum of Modern Art—Costakis Collection, Thessaloniki

KATARZYNA KOBRO
1898, Moscow, Russian Empire – 1951, Łódź, Poland
Mostly active in Moscow, Warsaw, and Łódź

17
Spatial Composition (6), 1931
Steel and oil paint, 64 × 25 × 15 cm
Inv. MS/SN/R/1
Muzeum Sztuki, Łódź

JEAN LEPPIEN
1910, Lüneburg, Germany – 1991, Courbevoie, France
Mostly active in Dessau and Paris

26
LXVIII, 1949
Oil on canvas, 99.6 × 72.3 cm
Inscribed on lower left: Jean Leppien 49
Inv. FGA-BA-LEPPI-0001
Fondation Gandur pour l'Art, Genève

ALEXANDER LIBERMAN
1912, Kyiv, Russian Empire (now Ukraine) – 1999, Miami, USA
Mostly active in New York and Paris

92
Blue Opposite Red, 1959
Oil on linen, 131.1 × 208.3 cm
Inv. 52.3
Whitney Museum of American Art, New York; Gift of the Trust of Alexander Liberman

EL LISSITZKY
1890, Pochinok, Russian Empire – 1941, Moscow, USSR
Mostly active in Vitebsk, Moscow, Berlin, Dresden, and Hanover

13
Proun 30, 1919–20
Mixed media on cardboard, 49.5 × 39.5 cm
Inv. MOI00320
Kulturstiftung Sachsen-Anhalt, Kunstmuseum Moritzburg Halle (Saale)

14
Proun 93 (Conic), ca. 1923
Pencil, black ink, pen, gouache, colored pencils, 49.9 × 49.7 cm
Inv. MOIIH00454
Kulturstiftung Sachsen-Anhalt, Kunstmuseum Moritzburg Halle (Saale)

18
Untitled, 1919–20
Oil on canvas, 79.6 × 49.6 cm
Inv. 76.2553 PG 43
Peggy Guggenheim Collection, Venice (Solomon R. Guggenheim Foundation, New York)

VERENA LOEWENSBERG
1912, Zurich, Switzerland – 1986, Zurich, Switzerland
Mostly active in Zurich

34
Untitled, 1965
Oil on canvas, 121 × 121 cm
Private collection, Switzerland; Courtesy Henriette Coray Loewensberg, Verena Loewensberg Stiftung, Zurich

RICHARD PAUL LOHSE
1902, Zurich, Switzerland – 1988, Zurich, Switzerland
Mostly active in Zurich

36
Thirty Vertical Systematic Color Series in a Yellow Rhombic Form, 1943/1970
Oil on canvas, 165 × 165 cm
Richard Paul Lohse-Stiftung

37
Center of Four Squares as a Result of the Four Cross Surfaces, 1952/1971
Oil on canvas, 120 × 120 cm
Richard Paul Lohse-Stiftung

KAZIMIR MALEVICH
1878, Kyiv, Russian Empire (now Ukraine) – 1935, Leningrad, USSR (now St. Petersburg, Russia)
Mostly active in Moscow, Kursk, St. Petersburg, and Vitebsk

4
Architectons and Figurines, late 1920s
Plaster, 90 × 70 × 23 cm
Inv. SK157DL
ALBERTINA, Vienna—Private collection

AGNES MARTIN
1912, Macklin, SK, Canada – 2004, Taos, NM, USA
Mostly active in New York and New Mexico

99
Summer Sky II, 1967
Acrylic and silver pencil on canvas, 183 × 183 cm
Private collection

KENNETH MARTIN
1905, Sheffield, UK – 1984, London, UK
Mostly active in London

67
Mobile Reflector, 1953
Aluminum and painted metal, 100 × 230 cm
Inv. 16934
UK Government Art Collection

68
Mobile Reflector: Elliptic Motif, 1955
Aluminum, steel, and duralumin, 70 × 96 × 75 cm
Inv. 31571
Sainsbury Centre, University of East Anglia; Bequeathed by Joyce and Michael Morris, 2014

MARY MARTIN
1907, Folkestone, UK – 1969, London, UK
Mostly active in London

63
White-Faced Relief, 1959
Paint, plywood, plexiglass, and wood,
64 × 94.5 × 11.5 cm
Inv. 31209
Sainsbury Centre, University of
East Anglia

64
Climbing Form, 1957
Plexiglass, steel, and wood,
35.5 × 7 × 7 cm
Inv. 31631
Sainsbury Centre, University of
East Anglia; Bequeathed by Joyce
and Michael Morris, 2014

70
Pierced Relief, 1959
Plexiglass and wood, 30 × 39.5 × 8 cm
Inv. 31562
Sainsbury Centre, University of
East Anglia; Bequeathed by Joyce
and Michael Morris, 2014

71
Rotation, 1968
Glass and polystyrene, 13 × 13 × 9 cm
Inv. 31589
Sainsbury Centre, University of
East Anglia; Bequeathed by Joyce
and Michael Morris, 2014

72
White Diagonal, 1963
Stainless steel, Formica, and wood
construction, 85 × 85 × 10.4 cm
Inv. 18270
UK Government Art Collection

74
Spiral Movement, ca. 1971
Fiberglass and plastic,
29 × 29.5 × 6 cm
Inv. 31588
Sainsbury Centre, University of
East Anglia

LÁSZLÓ MOHOLY-NAGY
1895, Bácsborsód, Hungary –
1946, Chicago, USA
Mostly active in Budapest, Berlin,
Dessau, Amsterdam, London,
and Chicago

19
Composition Z VIII, 1924
Distemper on canvas, 114 × 132 cm
Inv. NG 5/59
Staatliche Museen zu Berlin,
Neue Nationalgalerie

PIET MONDRIAN
1872, Amersfoort, the Netherlands –
1944, New York, USA
Mostly active in Amsterdam;
Domburg, the Netherlands; Paris;
Laren, the Netherlands; London;
and New York

40
Composition with Yellow and Blue,
1932
Oil on canvas, 55.5 × 55.5 cm
Inscribed on lower right: P M 32
Inv. 78.3
Fondation Beyeler, Riehen/Basel,
Beyeler Collection; Acquired with
the generous support of Hartmann P.
and Cécile Koechlin-Tanner, Riehen

41
Composition with Yellow, 1930
Oil on canvas, 46.5 × 46.5 cm
Inscribed bottom right: P M 30
Inv. 0164
Kunstsammlung Nordrhein-Westfalen,
Düsseldorf

FRANÇOIS MORELLET
1926, Cholet, France –
2016, Cholet, France
Mostly active in Cholet and Paris

93
3 Double Grids 0° 30° 60°, 1971
Oil on wood panel, 80 × 80 cm
Inv. FGA-BA-MOREL-0001
Fondation Gandur pour l'Art, Genève

94
2 Wire Grids −4° +4° (# 19 mm), 1972
Acrylic and mesh on plywood panel,
80.3 × 80.4 × 2.2 cm
Inv. FGA-BA-MOREL-0002
Fondation Gandur pour l'Art, Genève

95
The 1st Unique and Inexpensive Work,
1970
Screenprint on paper, 30 × 30 cm
Inscribed on lower middle: œuvre
unique et pas chère 1ter Morellet
Inv. FGA-BA-MOREL-0004
Fondation Gandur pour l'Art, Genève

96
Untitled, 1970
Screenprint on paper, 29.8 × 29.8 cm
Inscribed on lower right: A Morellet c A
Inv. FGA-BA-MOREL-0005
Fondation Gandur pour l'Art, Genève

97
Unique and Inexpensive Work 1 (6), 1970
Screenprint on paper,
30 × 30 cm
Inscribed on lower right: œuvre
unique et pas chère 1[(6)] Morellet
Inv. FGA-BA-MOREL-0003
Fondation Gandur pour l'Art, Genève

MARLOW MOSS
1889, London, UK – 1958, Penzance, UK
Mostly active in London, Paris, and
Cornwall

42
Composition in White, Red and Gray,
1935
Oil on canvas, 56 × 56 cm
Private collection, The Netherlands

44
Relief, 1957
Aluminum, wood, and paint,
51 × 108 × 12.5 cm
Inv. KM 112.222
Kröller-Müller Museum, Otterlo,
The Netherlands

AURÉLIE NEMOURS
1910, Paris, France –
2005, Paris, France
Mostly active in Paris

101
Composition (Divide), 1961
Oil on canvas, 116 × 81.1 cm
Inv. FGA-BA-NEMOU-0001
Fondation Gandur pour l'Art, Genève

BEN NICHOLSON
1894, Denham, UK – 1982, London, UK
Mostly active in London, Paris, and
St. Ives

59
1934 (painting), 1934
Oil on board, 37 × 45 cm
Inv. PAC 41
Pier Arts Centre, Stromness, Orkney

60
1934 (painted relief), 1934
Oil on composite board, 92.5 × 92.5 cm
Inv. HERUH375
University of Hertfordshire Art
Collection

61
1939 (painted relief), 1939
Oil on carved board, 91.4 × 82.6 cm
Inv. PAC 43
Pier Arts Centre, Stromness, Orkney

62
Painting 1937, 1937
Oil on canvas, 79.5 × 91.5 cm
Inv. P.1984.AH.286
Courtauld, London
(Samuel Courtauld Trust)

KENNETH NOLAND
1924, Asheville, NC, USA –
2010, Port Clyde, ME, USA
Mostly active in Black Mountain, NC;
Paris; Washington, DC; New York;
and Vermont

83
Half-Time, 1964
Acrylic on canvas, 177.8 × 177.8 cm
Inv. HH0541
ASOM Collection

VICTOR PASMORE
1908, Chelsham, UK –
1998, Gudja, Malta
Mostly active in London and Malta

66
Transparent Relief Construction
in Black, White & Ochre, 1956–57
Paint, plywood, plexiglass,
68.5 × 79 × 17.5 cm
Inv. 31296
Sainsbury Centre, University of East
Anglia; Purchased with support from
the V&A Purchase Grant Fund, 1988

ANTOINE PEVSNER
1886, Oryol, Russian Empire –
1962, Paris, France
Mostly active in Moscow, Kristiania
(now Oslo), Berlin, and Paris

15
Construction in the Third and Fourth
Dimension, 1961
Bronze, two parts, overall:
99.5 × 60 × 54 cm
Inv. 993/1963
Lehmbruck Museum, Duisburg

16
Column of Peace, 1954
Bronze, 130.5 × 80 × 45 cm
Inv. KM 114.109
Kröller-Müller Museum, Otterlo,
The Netherlands

LIUBOV POPOVA
1889, Ivanovskoye (now part of Moscow), Russian Empire – 1924, Moscow, USSR
Mostly active in Moscow

5
Spatial Force Construction, 1920–21
Oil with marble dust on wood, 112.6 × 112.3 cm
Inv. MMA.CC.79
MOMus—Museum of Modern Art—Costakis Collection, Thessaloniki

7
Painterly Architectonics, 1918–19
Oil on canvas, 73.1 × 48.1 cm
Inv. CC-0755/L.Popova-/180.78-76
MOMus—Museum of Modern Art—Costakis Collection, Thessaloniki

8
Spatial Force Construction, 1921
Oil with marble dust on plywood, 71 × 63.9 cm
Inv. MMA.CC64
MOMus—Museum of Modern Art—Costakis Collection, Thessaloniki

PAUL REED
1919, Washington, DC, USA – 2015, Phoenix, AZ, USA
Mostly active in Washington, DC; and Arlington, VA

82
Coherence, 1966
Acrylic on canvas, 264.2 × 114.3 cm
Inv. 2011.131.1
National Gallery of Art, Washington; Gift of Bill McGillicuddy in memory of Thomas W. Reed and Robert A. Reed

BRIDGET RILEY
b. 1931, London, UK
Mostly active in London

104
Tremor, 1962
Emulsion paint on wood, 122 × 122 cm
Inv. XII, 2
Lambrecht-Schadeberg Collection, Museum für Gegenwartskunst Siegen

123
Clepsydra 1, 1976
Acrylic on linen, 202 × 257 cm
Inv. XII, 19
Lambrecht-Schadeberg Collection, Museum für Gegenwartskunst Siegen

124
Shih-Li, 1975
Acrylic on linen, 160.7 × 355.6 cm
Inv. HH0547
ASOM Collection

ALEKSANDR RODCHENKO
1891, St. Petersburg, Russian Empire – 1956, Moscow, USSR
Mostly active in Moscow

6
Linearism, 1920
Oil on canvas, 110.5 × 78 cm
Inv. MMA.CC.77
MOMus—Museum of Modern Art—Costakis Collection, Thessaloniki

MIRIAM SCHAPIRO
1923, Toronto, Canada – 2015, Hampton Bays, NY, USA
Mostly active in Iowa; New York; and Santa Clarita, CA

90
Jigsaw, 1969
Acrylic on canvas, 203.2 × 183.2 cm
Inv. 69.46
Whitney Museum of American Art, New York; Purchase, with funds from Mr. and Mrs. Harry Kahn

JULIAN STANCZAK
1928, Borownica, Poland – 2017, Seven Hills, OH, USA
Mostly active in Cleveland and New Haven

114
Green Light, 1973
Acrylic on canvas, 152.4 × 152.4 cm
Collection of the Estate of Julian Stanczak; courtesy of The Mayor Gallery, London

115
Firefly, 1973
Acrylic on canvas, 152.4 × 152.4 cm
Collection of David and Kathryn Birnbaum

116
Repulsive Attraction, 1965–66
Acrylic on canvas, 134.6 × 167.6 cm
Courtesy of Neil K. Rector & the Rector Artwork Trust

117
Ephemeral Movement, 1965
Acrylic on canvas, 167.6 × 134.6 cm
Collection of the Estate of Julian Stanczak

122
Late Glow, 1977
Acrylic on canvas, 203.2 × 177.8 cm
Collection of the Estate of Julian Stanczak

FRANK STELLA
1936, Malden, MA, USA – 2024, New York, USA
Mostly active in New York

81
Slieve More, 1964
Metallic powder in polymer emulsion on canvas, 195.6 × 206.4 cm
Inscribed on verso: F. Stella 64
Private collection, Switzerland

84
Double Scramble, 1978
Acrylic on canvas, 180 × 350 cm
Private collection

85
Sacramento Mall Proposal #4, 1978
Acrylic on canvas, 262.5 × 262.1 cm
Inv. 1982.53.1
National Gallery of Art, Washington; Gift of the Collectors Committee

SOPHIE TAEUBER-ARP
1889, Davos, Switzerland – 1943, Zurich, Switzerland
Mostly active in Munich, Zurich, Strasbourg, and Paris

56
Twelve Spaces with Planes, Angular Bands, and Laid with Circles, 1939
Oil and pencil on canvas, 80.5 × 116 cm
Inv. 1958/0024
Kunsthaus Zürich; Gift from Jean Arp, 1958

VICTOR VASARELY
1906, Pécs, Hungary – 1997, Paris, France
Mostly active in Budapest and Paris

107
Yabla, 1961
Vinyl paint on wood panel, 159 × 90 cm
Inscribed on lower right: vasarely–
Inv. E.304
ASOM Collection

108
Vegaviv II, 1955
Vinyl paint on wood panel, 113.7 × 76.2 cm
Inscribed on lower middle: vasarely–
Inv. FGA-BA-VASAR-0004
Fondation Gandur pour l'Art, Genève

109
Boglar I, 1966
Vinyl paint on wood panel, 250 × 250 cm
Inscribed on lower middle: vasarely
Inv. HH0440
ASOM Collection

MARY WEBB
b. 1939, London, UK
Mostly active in Newcastle, London, Norwich, and Suffolk

75
Fritton, 1971
Oil on canvas, 152.5 × 152.5 cm
Inv. 31417
Sainsbury Centre, University of East Anglia; Donated by East England Arts

MARGARET WENSTRUP
1930, Stanford, KY, USA – 2008, Cincinnati, OH, USA
Mostly active in Indianapolis, Cincinnati, and New York

106
Whirligig, 1964
Oil on canvas, 96.5 × 96.5 cm
D. Wigmore Fine Art, Inc., New York

Compiled by Sterre Barentsen, Anna Heling, Chen Min Loh, and Céline Véronique Marten

Intersecting Realms

Geometric Abstraction Exhibitions and Scientific Breakthroughs

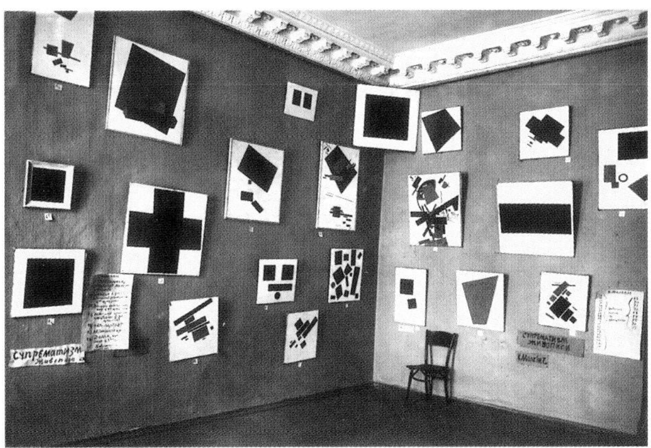

0.10: The Last Futurist Exhibition of Paintings

Dobychina Gallery, Petrograd
December 20, 1915 – January 19, 1916

Catalog: Petrograd 1915

The exhibition *0.10: The Last Futurist Exhibition of Paintings* took place at Dobychina Gallery in Petrograd from late 1915 to early 1916. This event marked the first public presentation of Suprematism. The movement, characterized by its concentration on fundamental geometric forms, was founded by Kazimir Malevich in 1913. In addition to paintings by Malevich, works by Vladimir Tatlin, Liubov Popova, Ivan Puni, and Olga Rozanova were also on view. Some of these artists had studied in Western Europe and now wanted to demonstrate that they had emancipated themselves from the influence of European centers of art, especially Paris. The exhibition title suggests a break with the past ("0") and the dawn of a new artistic era ("10"). The rivals Malevich and Tatlin exhibited in different rooms. Malevich showed thirty-nine non-objective paintings with geometric planes on a white ground. The works were hung close together on two adjacent walls. *Black Square* (1915, Tretyakov Gallery, Moscow) received special emphasis through its placement in the upper corner of the room, where an icon is traditionally located in Russian Orthodox households. This positioning provoked a scandal and was interpreted by the press and the public as a sign of nihilism. Tatlin, in contrast, presented three-dimensional *Counter-Reliefs.* These sculptures, assembled from a variety of everyday materials, were affixed to the wall, their forms projecting out into the room. Both Malevich and Tatlin experimented with the effect of geometric planes in three-dimensional space. Painting, which until now had always referred to objects in the external world, could now freely develop in form and color. CVM

Anonymous,
installation view of *0.10: The Last Futurist Exhibition of Paintings,* 1916.
Works shown: Kazimir Malevich

Skies Above, Shapes Below: The Birth of Aviation

On December 17, 1903, the Wright brothers completed the first sustained, powered flight at Kitty Hawk, North Carolina. Although it lasted only twelve seconds, it marked the beginning of a new era. The media reception was initially skeptical, and it was not until the brothers' public demonstrations in France in 1908 that aviation sparked worldwide interest. This enthusiasm soon reached Moscow and St. Petersburg, influencing avant-garde artists such as Kazimir Malevich. His 1927 Bauhaus publication, *Die gegenstandslose Welt* (The Nonobjective World), included aerial photographs of cities and images of airplanes in flight. He described this new perspective as the environment that inspired Suprematism. Malevich distinguished it from the urban environment that characterized the Futurists, which included locomotives and zeppelins. Through these aerial photographs, he explored how the high-altitude viewpoint flattened three-dimensional structures, reducing architecture to essential geometric forms. This new vision of the world aligned with Malevich's Suprematist aesthetics, which sought to distill forms to their pure essence. Vladimir Tatlin built his own flying machines in the 1920s. Drawing on studies of bird anatomy, he built three *Letatlin* prototypes and conducted several test flights. Tatlin's designs were inspired by organic shapes, as he believed that the world of technology should incorporate natural elements. Intended for mass production, *Letatlin* was envisioned as a means to revolutionize mobility in the Soviet Union. However, this vision of a flying proletariat was never implemented due to technical challenges. Through their work, these artists sought a visual language that transcended physical limitations, reimagining human movement, nature, and technology. SB

Further reading:
Lodder 2004, Metz 2013, and Vujošević 2017

Anonymous,
presentation of Vladimir Tatlin's *Letatlin*
at a glider show in Moscow, 1933

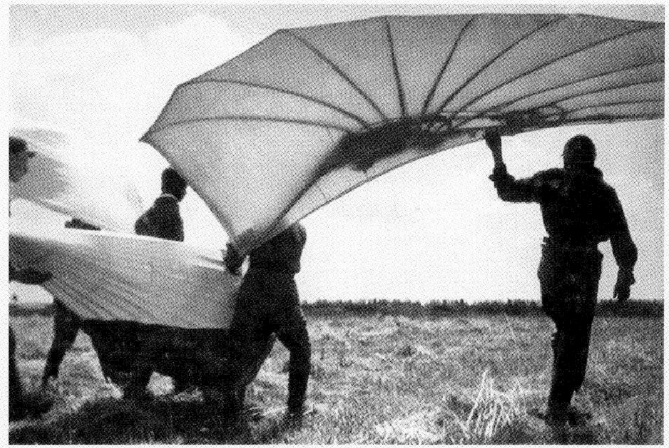

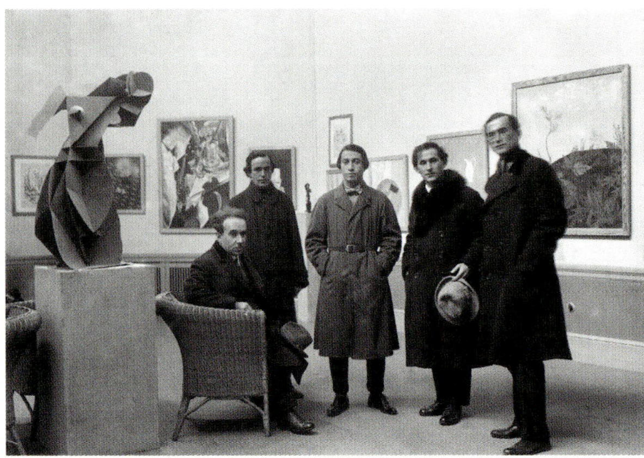

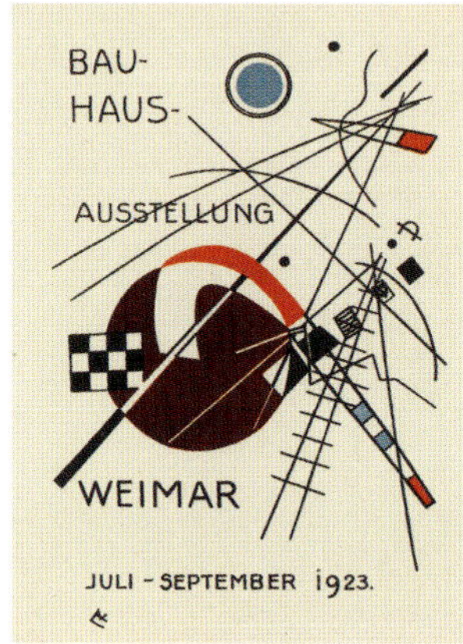

First Russian Art Exhibition

Galerie van Diemen, "Paintings by New Masters" branch, Unter den Linden 21, Berlin (October 15 – late December 1922); Stedelijk Museum Amsterdam (April 29 – May 28, 1923)

Catalog: Berlin 1922

The *First Russian Art Exhibition,* mounted at Galerie van Diemen in Berlin in 1922, presented art from Russia and the former czarist empire. Due to an international boycott of the Soviet state since 1917, recent artistic developments in Russia were little known in Germany. The preparations for the exhibition dated back to 1918, when the Art Collegium of Petrograd and Moscow sought exchange and collaboration with the artistic avant-garde in Germany. The initial contact was probably established by Wassily Kandinsky, who had close connections in Germany. However, it was not until 1922, when Germany finally recognized the Soviet government, that an exhibition could be arranged. For this purpose, Galerie van Diemen, which specialized in Old Masters, opened a branch for contemporary art in a city palace in Berlin. A range of artistic currents were represented in the exhibited works, which had been created since around 1905 and were intended to demonstrate the diversity of artistic approaches. Yet it was above all the Constructivist and Suprematist works—largely unknown in Germany up to then—that received special recognition and continue to be associated with the exhibition to this day. The work of progressive artists such as Aleksandra Ekster, Wassily Kandinsky, Kazimir Malevich, and Liubov Popova was shown, and Malevich's Suprematist paintings were exhibited outside of Russia for the first time. However, since most of the works on display still adhered to traditional styles and the exhibition thus reflected a more conservative approach, many visitors who had expected a stronger presence of revolutionary art expressed disappointment. Reviews of the exhibition were mixed: some critics emphasized the radicality and intellectual rigor of the avant-garde, while others criticized the lack of clarity and coherence in the presentation of the new art. Although it was originally planned that the exhibition would travel to other cities in Europe and North America, it was ultimately shown only at the Stedelijk Museum Amsterdam in the spring of 1923. Despite its more traditional artistic orientation, the *First Russian Art Exhibition* played a decisive role in achieving international recognition for the Russian and Eastern European avant-garde. CVM

Willy Römer,
installation view of the *First Russian Art Exhibition,* 1922.
Work shown: Naum Gabo

Bauhaus Exhibition 1923

Weimar
August 15 – September 30, 1923

The importance of exhibitions as a central activity of the Bauhaus had already been emphasized by architect and director Walter Gropius in his Bauhaus manifesto of 1919, in which he outlined the principles and pedagogical methods of his new art school. Yet it was also political pressure from conservative elements in the provincial city of Weimar, and later in Dessau, that caused him to present the products and educational results of his new approach to the public. From 1920 on, works by artists such as Theo van Doesburg, Lyonel Feininger, Wassily Kandinsky, and Oskar Schlemmer were shown in exhibitions at the Landesmuseum in Weimar and the Anhaltischer Kunstverein in Dessau in an effort to emphasize the school's artistic legitimacy. The first comprehensive exhibition organized by the Bauhaus, featuring works by students and teachers, took place in Weimar in the summer of 1923. Its purpose was to present a comprehensive view of the art school, with the exhibition serving as a survey of the developments and results of its first years. One of the posters was designed by Kandinsky and produced in the Bauhaus printing shop. Within the school building, workshop spaces for wall painting and stone sculpture were included in the exhibition, while paintings and three-dimensional works were shown at the Landesmuseum. The first architectural project of the Bauhaus in Weimar—the Haus am Horn—was also presented as part of the exhibition, demonstrating how the design and theoretical approaches of the school's various workshops could be translated into reality. The exhibition was preceded by "Bauhaus Week," a five-day cultural festival with theater performances, concerts, and lectures. Kandinsky gave a talk entitled "On Synthetic Art." The show provoked controversy in the press: while liberal and progressive voices expressed disappointment that the goals for the new art school formulated by Gropius in 1919 had not been fulfilled, conservative circles felt confirmed in their rejection of the Bauhaus. The transregional publicity, however, contributed to the fame of the Bauhaus and the dissemination of its aesthetic ideas. CVM

Wassily Kandinsky,
postcard for the *Bauhaus Exhibition,* 1923

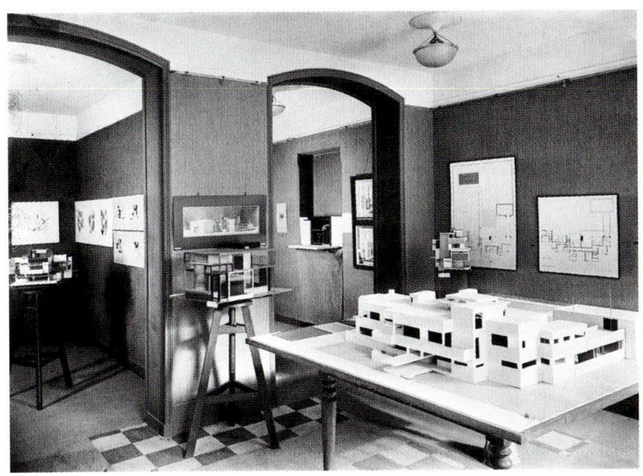

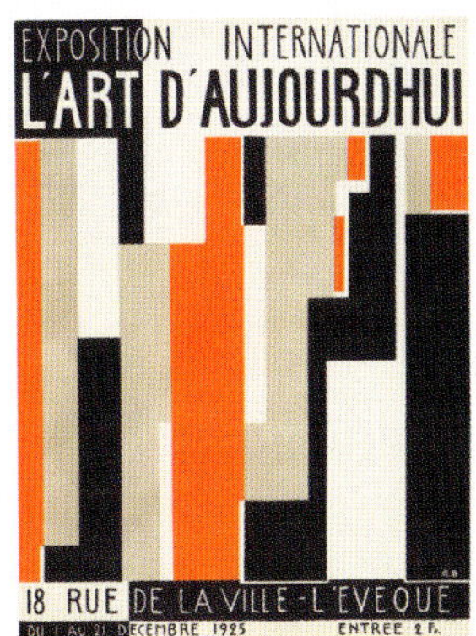

Les Architectes du groupe "De Styl"

Galerie L'Effort Moderne, Paris
October 15 – November 15, 1923

In 1923 influential art dealer Léonce Rosenberg invited artists of the De Stijl movement to present their newest architectural projects at his Galerie L'Effort Moderne in Paris. The show would be the first and only exhibition devoted explicitly to the work of the group during the years of its existence (1917–31). The artistic ideas and principles of De Stijl had been formulated since 1917 in the magazine of the same name as well as in other publications, manifestos, and essays by the group's members. Within only a few years, they succeeded in disseminating their notion of the cooperation of various artistic disciplines throughout Europe, beyond the borders of the Netherlands. Rosenberg, who promoted avant-garde movements and above all Cubism in his gallery, took an interest in the group's ideas and in 1923 commissioned the artists to create a building. Cornelis van Esteren was to design it, Piet Mondrian and Theo van Doesburg would develop the color concept, and Gerrit Rietveld would produce the interior furnishings. In the end, however, due to conflicts within the group, only Van Doesburg and Van Esteren participated in the project, and the building was never built. But its designs were presented in Rosenberg's gallery in the form of sketches, models, photographs, and drawings, along with those of other De Stijl projects. The designs for a private house (*hôtel particulier*) and an artist's house (*maison d'artiste*) by Van Doesburg and Van Esteren drew considerable attention from critics. Ludwig Mies van der Rohe was also represented with a photograph of a model for a glass skyscraper from 1922. Rietveld presented a design for a jeweler's shop, and J. J. P. Oud showed plans for two public housing projects in Rotterdam. Works by Vilmos Huszár, Jan Wils, and Willem van Leusden were also on view. The participation of Mies van der Rohe and Van Leusden, who are not usually associated with De Stijl, demonstrates that the group's membership was not fixed, but rather constituted a dynamic movement. CVM

Anonymous,
exhibition view of *Les Architectes du groupe "De Styl,"* 1923.
Works shown: Cornelis van Eesteren, Theo van Doesburg, and Gerrit Rietveld

L'Art d'aujourd'hui: Exposition internationale

Chambre Syndicale de la Curiosité et des Beaux-Arts, Paris
December 1 – 21, 1925

Catalog: Paris 1925

The *L'Art d'aujourd'hui: Exposition internationale,* organized by Polish artist Victor Poznański, presented the newest currents in contemporary art. With over sixty artists from a variety of countries, the exhibition was one of the most important avant-garde shows of the interwar years. In the catalog, Poznański emphasized the emergence of a new artistic movement that had developed out of Cubism. The works on display were nonobjective: Poznański asserted that they were intended not to serve as intermediaries between nature and the viewer but to move the soul through form and color. He compared the ideal experience of these works to that of music, requiring an attitude of openness and immersion. The first rooms of the exhibition featured the art of Pablo Picasso and the Cubists, followed by the turn toward abstraction in the works of Neoplasticism and Constructivism. Many of the international participants resided in Paris, including Russian exiles Aleksandra Ekster, Natalia Goncharova, and Mikhail Larionov. American artists who studied at the art academies in Paris, such as Patrick Henry Bruce and Florence Henri, took part in the exhibition. The De Stijl movement was prominently represented by Dutch painters Piet Mondrian and Theo van Doesburg, while England was represented by Winifred and Ben Nicholson. Also Surrealists such as Max Ernst and Joan Miró were also on view in the main hall as representatives of an emerging avant-garde in Paris. *L'Art d'aujourd'hui* not only marked a decisive moment in the development of nonobjective art; it also contributed to the commercial success of a number of its participants, with artists such as Constantin Brâncuși, Alexander Archipenko, Piet Mondrian, and Fernand Léger achieving greater recognition for the first time. Some critics, however, dismissed the artists as adherents of French Cubism or proponents of a new academicism. The opening of the exhibition provided the international artists with an important opportunity for mutual encounter and exchange. The glamorous reception, at which collectors from the United States were also present, attracted considerable attention. SB

Gustave Buchet,
poster for *L'Art d'aujourd'hui: Exposition internationale,* 1925,
Fondation Gustave Buchet, Lausanne

Group exhibitions of the artist associations Cercle et Carré and Abstraction-Création

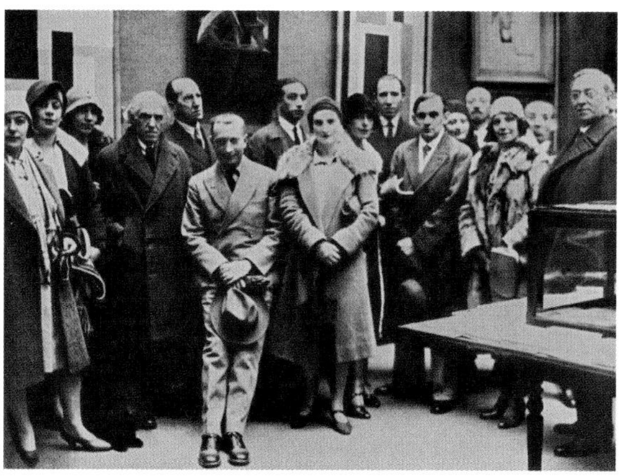

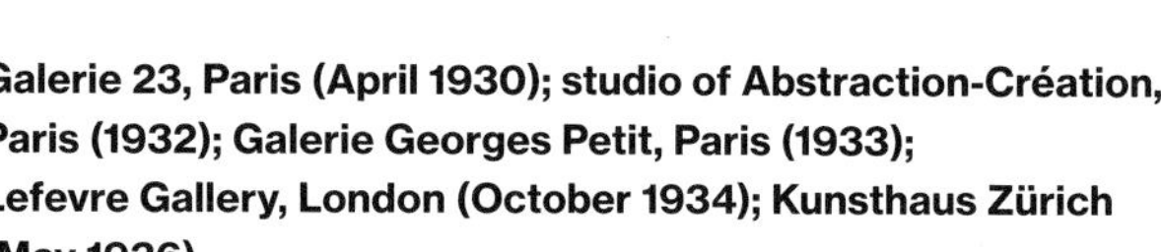

Galerie 23, Paris (April 1930); studio of Abstraction-Création, Paris (1932); Galerie Georges Petit, Paris (1933); Lefevre Gallery, London (October 1934); Kunsthaus Zürich (May 1936)

In 1929 a group of international abstract artists founded the association Cercle et Carré (Circle and Square). The initiators—draftsman, poet, and art critic Michel Seuphor and painter Joaquín Torres-García—sought to counter Surrealism, the dominant movement in Paris at that time. The name Cercle et Carré stood for the fundamental forms of the visual language of abstraction. The group organized only one exhibition, which took place at Galerie 23 in Paris in April 1930 and is considered the first international group exhibition of abstract art. Forty-six artists participated, including Wassily Kandinsky, Piet Mondrian, Antoine Pevsner, and Jean Arp. The 130 exhibited works exemplified both biomorphic and strictly geometric tendencies. Since neither the Cercle et Carré exhibition nor the magazine of the same name elicited any substantial response, the group disbanded after only a year. Shortly thereafter, on February 15, 1931, Theo van Doesburg, Arp, Albert Gleizes, Jean Hélion, Auguste Herbin, František Kupka, Léon Arthur Tutundjian, Georges Valmier, and Georges Vantongerloo founded the group Abstraction-Création with the intent of unifying all the variants of abstraction. Most of the former members of Cercle et Carré joined Abstraction-Création, as did those of the group Art Concret, which had been founded by Van Doesburg in 1929. The goal was to champion abstraction as the true expression of reality and spirituality, as opposed to the illusion of figurative art and above all to Surrealism with its focus on the unconscious. The group soon comprised around four hundred members from twenty different countries. The members of Abstraction-Création cultivated a lively exchange, and in addition to publishing an eponymous almanac organized exhibitions that contributed decisively to their public visibility. The first show took place in 1932, followed by an exhibition at the prestigious Galerie Georges Petit a year later. In 1934 the group opened its own gallery in Paris, while shows in London and Zurich strengthened its international network. The persecution of "degenerate" artists under the Nazi regime and differences of opinion regarding the future of abstraction brought an end to the activity of Abstraction-Création in 1937. AH

Anonymous,
exhibition view of *Cercle et Carré* with participating artists, 1930

Thesis, Antithesis, Synthesis

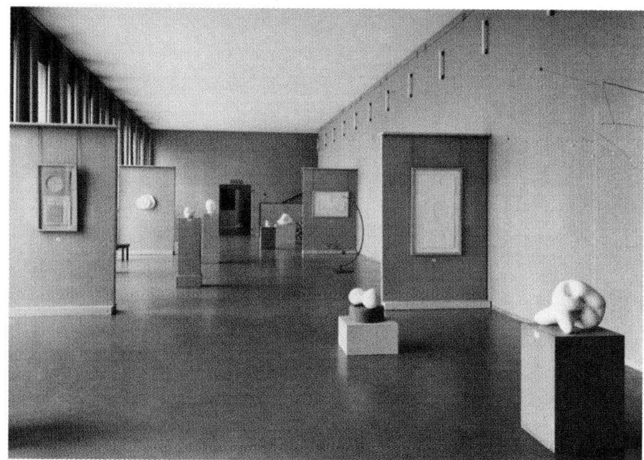

Kunstmuseum Luzern, Lucerne
February 24 – March 31, 1935

Catalog: Lucerne 1935

The Kunstmuseum Luzern was founded in 1932. Its first exhibition with international impact was presented in the spring of 1935 under the title *Thesis, Antithesis, Synthesis,* featuring ninety-five works of Dada, Surrealism, Cubism, Constructivism, and abstraction. The show was organized by Swiss painter Hans Erni, with the support of communist philosopher Konrad Farner. Erni was a member of the artist group Abstraction-Création in Paris and thus interacted with many of the international proponents of abstract art whose works he included in the exhibition: Jean Arp, Alexander Calder, Jean Hélion, Wassily Kandinsky, Paul Klee, Piet Mondrian, Ben Nicholson, and Sophie Taeuber-Arp. The presentation of *Thesis, Antithesis, Synthesis* in Lucerne, in politically neutral Switzerland, offered curatorial freedom to show art movements vilified by the Nazis as "degenerate." The exhibition was intended to introduce contemporary artistic developments to the public in a systematic form. Its title alludes to the dialectical method of philosopher Georg Wilhelm Friedrich Hegel, according to which an initial position (thesis) and the response to or negation of it (antithesis) interact to produce a new, more fully developed position (synthesis). As the exhibition catalog indicates, the concept of thesis and antithesis served as a simplifying model to help differentiate the "intellectual origin" of contemporary art movements. The "conscious" approach of abstraction was contrasted with Surrealism and its emphasis on the unconscious, while their synthesis was discovered in "elements of a new art." Against the backdrop of the increasing suppression of abstract art by the Nazi regime, the exhibition played a significant role in its furtherance on the eve of World War II. AH

Anonymous,
installation view of *Thesis, Antithesis, Synthesis,* 1935.
Works shown: Jean Arp, Alexander Calder,
Alberto Giacometti, and Ben Nicholson

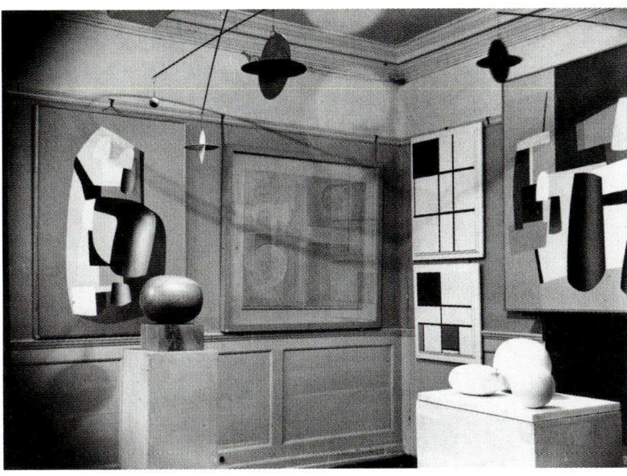

Abstract and Concrete: A Survey of Modern Art

41 St. Giles', Oxford; Liverpool School of Architecture; Lefevre Gallery, London; Gordon Fraser Gallery, Cambridge February 15 – June 13, 1936

Catalog: London 1936

The group exhibition *Abstract and Concrete: A Survey of Modern Art* was a turning point in the development of British abstraction. Art historian Nicolete Gray, only twenty-four years old at the time, made it her goal to curate the first exhibition of international abstraction in Great Britain. She established contact with artists in Paris such as Jean Arp, Jean Hélion, Wassily Kandinsky, and László Moholy-Nagy in an effort to include them in the project. Artists in London such as Ben Nicholson, Eileen Holding, Barbara Hepworth, and John Piper, as well as Piet Mondrian and Naum Gabo, were also presented. Gray received financial support from patron and collector Helen Sutherland, while Myfanwy Piper, editor of the art magazine *Axis,* likewise played an important role by facilitating contact with artists, finding additional supporters, helping with hanging, and devoting an issue of her publication to the exhibition. In this way, *Abstract and Concrete* was essentially the achievement of a group of women. Myfanwy Piper viewed the ordered stringency of geometric abstraction as the answer to the turmoil of the modern world, while for Nicolete Gray, abstraction signified the representation of spirituality and the creation of visual harmony. In their view, England was making an important contribution to international art for the first time since the eighteenth century. Their aim was to establish abstraction as a serious, trendsetting movement. Ultimately, forty-three works by sixteen artists were shown; yet they achieved little in the way of financial success. The auction house Christie's considered the works of practically no value. The show *Abstract and Concrete* was the first exhibition of Mondrian's work in Great Britain; of his three paintings offered for the price of fifty pounds, two were purchased by Nicolete Gray and Helen Sutherland themselves. Aside from that, two works by John Piper found buyers. AH

Arthur Jackson Hepworth,
installation view of *Abstract and Concrete: A Survey of Modern Art,* 1936.
Works shown: Alexander Calder, Jean Hélion, Barbara Hepworth, Piet Mondrian, and Ben Nicholson

Microcosms: Organic Forms in Abstract Art

The invention of the microscope in the seventeenth century made it possible to study life-forms invisible to the naked eye. By the early twentieth century, microscopic images gained popularity through magazines, inspiring many artists with the structures of cells and microorganisms. Fascinated by these minute life-forms, Wassily Kandinsky studied illustrations in books such as *Art Forms in Nature* (1904) by Ernst Haeckel and collected newspaper clippings of diagrams and microscopic photographs. His paintings from the Paris period (1934–44) feature shapes reminiscent of embryonic beings and cellular bodies, marking a shift from the geometric style he developed at the Bauhaus to a more "biomorphic" visual language. The term *biomorphic* was coined by critic Geoffrey Grigson in 1936 to describe a new phase of abstraction. It was soon adopted by curator Alfred H. Barr Jr. in the catalog for *Cubism and Abstract Art*. In 1930s and 1940s Paris, both abstract and Surrealist artists embraced biomorphism, as seen in the works of Jean Arp, whose forms—bridging both styles—recall the fluid outlines of amoebas. Cells, as fundamental units of life, came to symbolize transformation and new beginnings. British abstraction during this period also explored organic forms. Popular science publications featuring microphotographs and illustrations were widely circulated, aligning with the scientific reform initiative known as New Biology. This movement proposed that organisms are holistic systems governed by a "life force" beyond the scope of physics or chemistry. The gently curved sculptures of Barbara Hepworth and Henry Moore evoke cellular forms, embodying life in its state of emergence and transformation. Amid technological progress and wartime destruction, these organic forms served as poignant reminders of life's resilience and capacity for renewal. AH

Further Reading:
Botar/Wünsche 2011, Juler 2015, and Taylor 2020

Wassily Kandinsky,
Succession, 1935,
Phillips Collection, Washington, DC

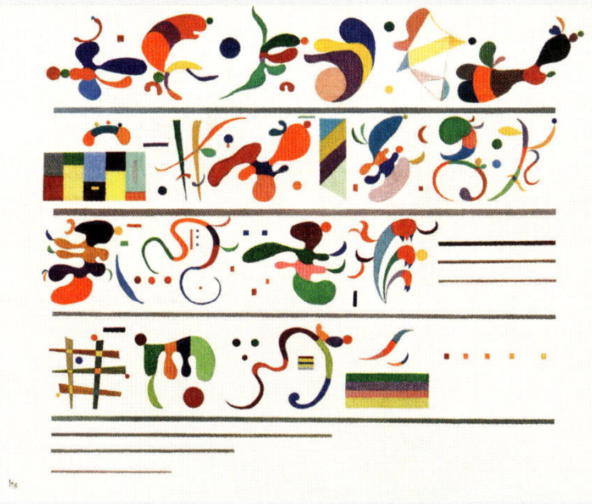

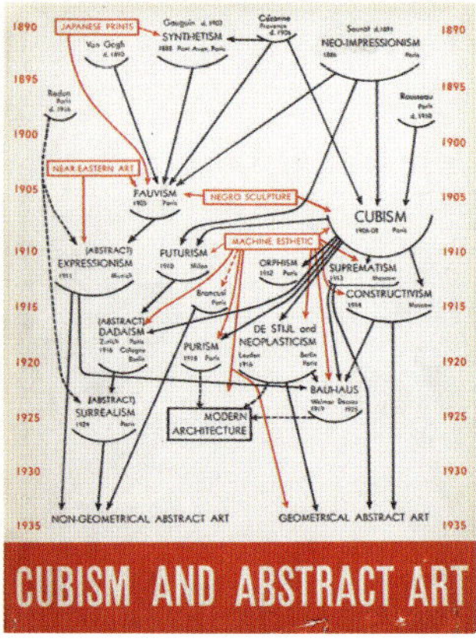

Museum of Modern Art, New York
March 2 – April 19, 1936

Catalog: New York 1936

With *Cubism and Abstract Art,* Alfred H. Barr Jr., founder and director of the Museum of Modern Art in New York, curated one of the most important exhibitions in the museum's history. His goal was to represent the chronological development of Cubism under the influence of other artistic currents and its evolution into geometric and nongeometric abstraction. In order to visualize the various artistic directions and their origins, Barr produced a flow chart of European art movements since the 1890s. He traced nongeometric abstraction back to Vincent van Gogh and Paul Gauguin; geometric abstraction, on the other hand, he derived from Paul Cézanne as well as from Georges Seurat, Cubism, Futurism, Constructivism, Orphism, Purism, and De Stijl. Barr also presented the "influence" of non-Western art on European "isms," though without reflecting on the issue of appropriation. In the exhibition itself, stylistic influence was visualized through the juxtaposition of different works. The multimedia approach was unusual: in addition to painting and sculpture, the show also integrated media including design, typography, photography, and film. The exhibition featured a total of four hundred works by a wide range of European artists. Barr had visited Germany in 1932–33 and had observed the incipient threat that Nazism posed to abstract art. With *Cubism and Abstract Art,* he took a decisive stand in its support. The systematic narrative of the show offered a didactic line of orientation through the diverse currents of art that had developed almost simultaneously in the first decades of the twentieth century. With its story of progress, in which the development of contemporary art was based on innovation, *Cubism and Abstract Art* shaped art historical writing and exhibition practice. It elevated abstraction to a place in the art historical canon, making a decisive contribution to its public recognition. AH

Alfred H. Barr Jr.,
cover of the exhibition catalog
Cubism and Abstract Art, 1936

From Atom to Antenna: The Revolution of Communication

Once considered the smallest indivisible unit of matter, the atom had symbolized stability and certainty. This view was upended in 1897, when physicist J. J. Thomson observed rays that deflected in electric and magnetic fields, leading him to conclude that atoms contain negatively charged particles, now known as electrons. This discovery profoundly disrupted a long-standing confidence in the physical foundations of reality and expanded the possibilities of remote communication. Wassily Kandinsky later reflected on how the electron's discovery transformed his perception of reality. Equally, the invention of telegraphy—an innovation that transmitted signals via electromagnetic waves rather than wires, eventually leading to radio—captivated his imagination. Kandinsky saw a parallel between the vibrations of these electromagnetic waves and his aspiration for art to "transmit" emotional vibrations directly to the viewer's soul. Hungarian artist László Moholy-Nagy extended this concept of art as a means of transmission even further. In 1923, shortly after joining the Bauhaus faculty, he envisioned a project of entirely mechanically produced art. Completed the following year, the project consisted of three enamel paintings he claimed to have commissioned over the phone, directing a local factory in composition and color remotely. The resulting minimalist compositions, featuring bold black bars intersected by smaller red, yellow, and black forms, stand as pioneering examples of art created through technological mediation. As television technology boomed in the 1960s, it further shaped the intersection of art and electronic media. While cathode ray tubes had been invented in the late nineteenth century, they became widely accessible in the 1950s and 1960s as a feature of televisions, where they directed electrons onto fluorescent screens to produce images. The flickering, pulsing energy of this new medium found a visual echo in Bridget Riley's Op Art paintings, which, not unlike Kandinsky's work, aimed to transmit a charged, immersive experience to the viewer. In this way, artists of the electronic age translated the dizzying effects of modern media into their work, capturing the dynamic energy of a rapidly changing world. SB

Further reading:
Henderson 1983, Gamwell 2002, and Lee 2004

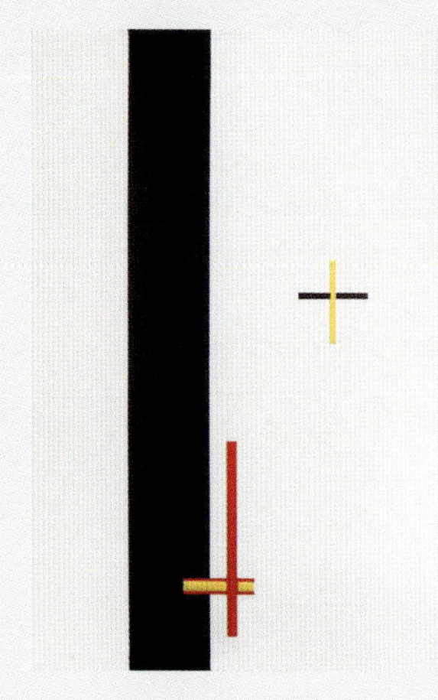

László Moholy-Nagy,
Telephone Picture EM 2,
1923, Museum of Modern
Art, New York

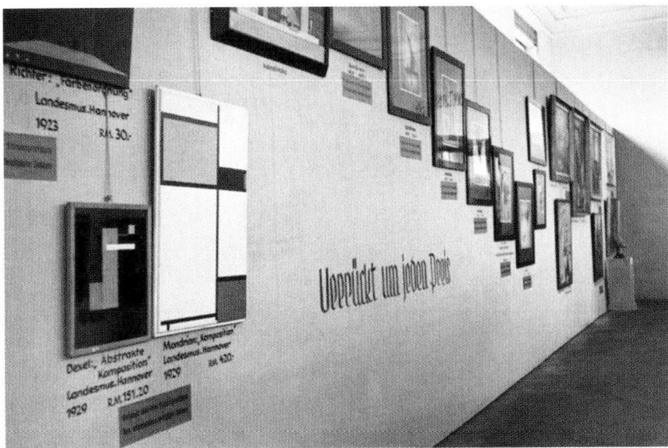

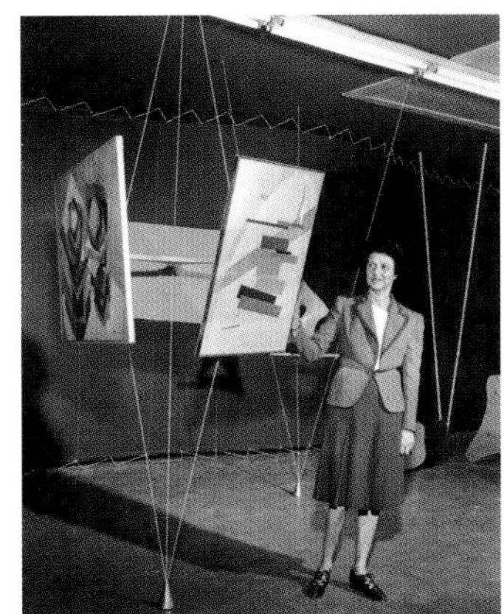

Entartete Kunst (Degenerate Art)

Hofgarten arcades of the Archäologisches Institut, Galeriestrasse 4, Munich
July 19 – November 30, 1937

Also shown in Berlin, Leipzig, Düsseldorf, Salzburg, Hamburg, Stettin (now Szczecin), Weimar, Vienna, Frankfurt am Main, Chemnitz, Waldenburg (now Wałbrzych), and Halle an der Saale

Catalog: Munich 1937

In Nazi Germany, avant-garde art movements were vilified as "un-German" and "degenerate" and their proponents forbidden to engage in professional activity or exhibit their work. The abstract art of Constructivism or the Bauhaus was considered an "expression of cultural decline." As early as 1933, German museums began showing exhibitions aimed at discrediting the works of the avant-garde. In 1937 the Nazi defamation campaign reached a climax when the Reich Ministry of Propaganda under Joseph Goebbels was commissioned to remove works of "decadent art" from museums all over Germany. From July 1937 on, the first confiscated works were shown in the exhibition *Entartete Kunst* (Degenerate Art) at the Hofgarten arcades in Munich. It attracted more visitors than any other art exhibition that had taken place in Europe up to that point. From then until 1941, the show was presented in twelve other cities including Berlin, Hamburg, Düsseldorf, Salzburg, and Vienna. The first version in Munich included more than seven hundred works by over 120 artists of Impressionism, Expressionism, Dadaism, and New Objectivity as well as Constructivism and the Bauhaus. The exhibited pieces were crowded together on the walls and were accompanied by vilifying inscriptions intended to stir up antisemitic, racist, and anticommunist prejudices in the public. The works were staged in such a way as to provoke indignation. The Nazis' contempt for abstract styles was reflected, for example, by hanging works by Wassily Kandinsky upside down or failing to include their titles. Abroad, however, the success of *Entartete Kunst* and the negative presentation of the exhibited works led to increased interest in the proscribed artistic movements, which could now be considered an expression of resistance against the Nazis. With the acquisition of abstract works, American museum directors such as Alfred H. Barr Jr. at the Museum of Modern Art and Hilla von Rebay at the Museum of Non-Objective Painting (now the Guggenheim Museum) were able to position themselves in opposition to Nazi Germany on a cultural-political level. CVM

Arthur Grimm,
installation view of *Entartete Kunst* (Degenerate Art), 1937.
Works shown: Walter Dexel and Piet Mondrian

Art of This Century

Art of This Century Gallery, New York
Opened October 20, 1942; gallery existed until May 1947

Catalog: New York 1942

American patroness Peggy Guggenheim actively supported and promoted modern art throughout her entire life. In Paris of the interwar years, she stood in close contact with Surrealist and abstract artists, whose works she collected and exhibited from 1938 on in her gallery Guggenheim Jeune in London. With the Nazi occupation of France in 1941, Guggenheim was forced to leave the country along with her art collection. She returned home to New York, where on October 20, 1942, she opened a gallery in Manhattan with the programmatic name "Art of This Century." Here she would exhibit what she considered the relevant contemporary artistic currents from Europe—Surrealism and abstraction—while also networking with emerging abstract artists from the New York scene. Three rooms—the Abstract Gallery, the Surrealist Gallery, and the Kinetic Gallery—presented Guggenheim's collection, while the Daylight Gallery was devoted to changing exhibitions. The spaces were designed by Austrian émigré architect Frederick Kiesler. He created individualized forms of presentation that were meant to translate the content of the art into the architectural space and evoke active participation from visitors. Some of the walls were curved or revolving; the paintings could be raised by turning a crank or could be viewed through peepholes. The Abstract Gallery, with walls consisting of undulating waves of blue fabric, featured works of Cubism and abstraction, while sculptures by Jean Arp or Antoine Pevsner were placed on organically shaped benches. Ropes spanning from floor to ceiling created geometric forms and supported paintings by El Lissitzky, Wassily Kandinsky, Jean Hélion, and others, liberating the canvases from the confines of the wall. Kiesler's goal was to abolish the hierarchy between architecture, sculpture, and painting and allow them to merge into a modern *Gesamtkunstwerk*. The opening exhibition of Art of This Century drew throngs of visitors, not least of all on account of its extraordinary mode of display, and received many positive reviews. The gallery, which existed until 1947, set new standards for the presentation of contemporary art and made an essential contribution to establishing New York as a new artistic hub, especially for Abstract Expressionism. AH

Tom Fitzsimmons,
installation view of the Abstract Gallery at Art of This Century, 1942. Works shown: El Lissitzky (cat. 18)

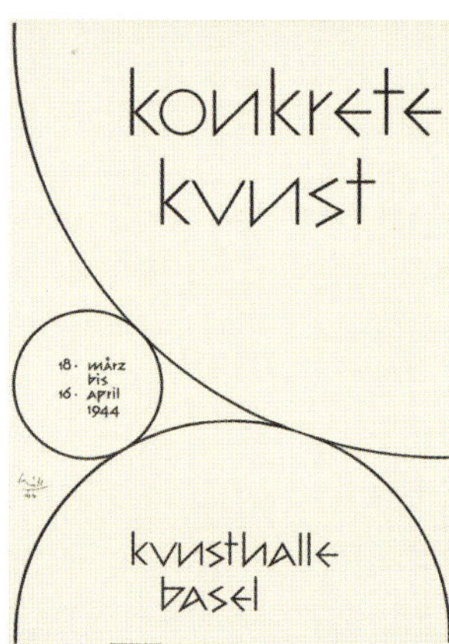

konkrete kunst (Concrete Art)

Kunsthalle Basel
March 18 – April 16, 1944

Catalog: Basel 1944

Curated by artist and designer Max Bill in 1944, *konkrete kunst* (Concrete Art) at the Kunsthalle Basel marked the first use of the term *concrete* in an exhibition title. Amid the devastation of war-torn Europe, Kunsthalle Basel remained a crucial venue for contemporary art and innovation, having previously shown geometric abstract works at the *Konstruktivisten* (Constructivist) exhibition in 1937. The term *concrete* was coined by De Stijl artist Theo van Doesburg in the 1930 manifesto "Art concret." Van Doesburg argued for *concrete* rather than *abstract* painting, asserting that art should be created from purely visual elements such as lines, colors, and forms, without imitating or abstracting from the natural world. The exhibition *konkrete kunst* featured fifty-one artists, including Bill's Swiss contemporaries Verena Loewensberg, Richard Paul Lohse, and Sophie Taeuber-Arp, while also paying tribute to predecessors such as Kazimir Malevich, Wassily Kandinsky, Paul Klee, and Piet Mondrian. Bill selected works characterized by precise composition, many of which were inspired by mathematical or scientific principles. With its historical references and international perspective, the exhibition was highly influential, particularly in a wartime context. It attracted large crowds and received support from collectors in Basel, Bern, and Zurich, who contributed works, along with pieces loaned directly by the artists. In the exhibition catalog, Jean Arp described the show as a call for a new art that does not imitate nature but is created by artists in a manner uninfluenced by sensuality or sentiment and as natural as plants bear fruit. CML

Max Bill,
poster for the exhibition *konkrete kunst* (concrete art), 1944,
Basel Poster Collection

The Art of Space-Time: Einstein's Fourth Dimension

In 1905 Albert Einstein revolutionized the understanding of space and time with his theory of relativity. He identified time as the fourth dimension, intertwined with the three spatial dimensions to form spacetime, which can bend and stretch under the influence of speed or massive objects. By the time *Relativity: The Special and the General Theory* was first published in 1916, Einstein had become a household name, inspiring artists to explore new approaches to make the temporal dimension perceptible. Kazimir Malevich and Wassily Kandinsky, who approached the fourth dimension from a spiritual rather than a mathematical, physical standpoint, drew inspiration from theosophical writings, including Helena Blavatsky's theories and P. D. Ouspensky's *Tertium Organum* (1912), which described the fourth dimension as a transcendent plane beyond the visible world. Both artists sought to convey an awareness of this transcendent reality through their abstract works. A completely different perspective on the fourth dimension was presented in the *Realistic Manifesto,* published in 1920 in Moscow by Naum Gabo and his brother, Antoine Pevsner. Influenced by Einstein's theory of relativity, their constructivist art aimed to incorporate the dynamics of time. That same year, Gabo created his first *Kinetic Construction,* a metal rod set in motion by a motor, creating the illusion of a three-dimensional shape. The sculpture went beyond depicting movement to becoming dynamic itself. In 1922 Hungarian artist László Moholy-Nagy created his *Light Prop for an Electric Stage,* later known as the *Light-Space Modulator,* while working at the Bauhaus. This motor-driven rotating sculpture, made of reflective metal, plastic, and glass, cast shifting patterns of light and shadow throughout the space, offering a striking expression of Einstein's spacetime concept. By the 1950s, kinetic sculpture—pioneered by artists such as Gabo and Moholy-Nagy—had become a favored medium for artistically engaging with Einstein's groundbreaking discovery of the space-time continuum. AH

Further reading:
Henderson 1983, Gamwell 2002, and Henderson 2007

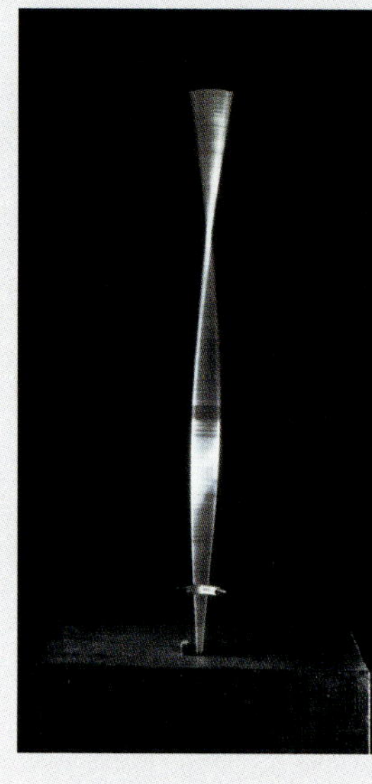

Naum Gabo,
Kinetic Construction (Standing Wave), 1919–20,
replica 1985, Tate

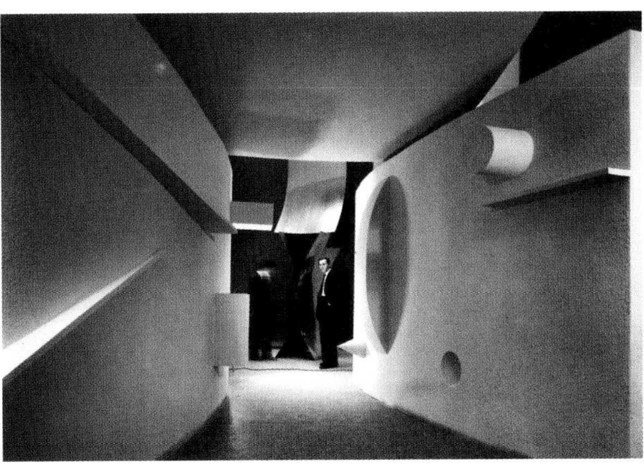

Whitechapel Art Gallery, London
August 9 – September 9, 1956

Catalog: London 1956

The exhibition on view at Whitechapel Art Gallery in London in the summer of 1956 was self-confidently entitled *This Is Tomorrow.* It represented the collaboration of thirty-eight artists seeking to bring together their various disciplines: painting, sculpture, art theory, architecture, and design. About half of them belonged to the Independent Group, founded in 1952, which focused on contemporary consumer and popular culture. The others worked primarily in an abstract-constructivist vein. The idea of the exhibition was a shared exploration of modern life in order to develop conceptions of the art of the future in relation to architecture. The participants were divided into twelve interdisciplinary groups, each of which designed a chapter of the exhibition. The projects involving abstract art concentrated first and foremost on the relationship between space, structure, and perception. With built-in partitions accentuated by narrow relief elements created by Mary Martin, the room of Group Nine resembled an abstracted gear wheel; in the center hung a kinetic mobile of wire rods by Kenneth Martin, which echoed the spiral design of the space. This fusion of architecture and sculpture also characterized the installation by sculptor Robert Adams, engineer Frank Newby, and architects Colin St. John Wilson and Peter Carter (Group Ten). They created a passageway with geometric, three-dimensional forms between inward-bending walls and a bowed ceiling, tapering toward an ensemble of curving aluminum planes. In their works and catalog texts, the abstract artists made reference to Russian Constructivism and the Dutch movement De Stijl, which was unusual in Great Britain at that time. The exhibition at the Whitechapel Art Gallery caused a sensation and was attended by thousands of visitors. It provoked discussion of the future role of art, asking how it should respond to an ever more rapidly changing society, and how it should contribute to new ways of thinking and seeing. AH

John Maltby,
installation view of *This Is Tomorrow, Group 10 exhibit,* 1956.
Works shown: Robert Adams, Peter Carter, Frank Newby, and Sir Colin St. John Wilson

Molded Modernity: The Rise of Plastics

The 1950s saw a boom in plastic production across Western Europe and the United States, leading to its widespread use in everyday objects. However, as early as the mid-nineteenth century, the chemical modification of natural substances had begun, resulting in the creation of semisynthetic materials such as celluloid. By the early twentieth century, fully synthetic plastics became feasible, revolutionizing both industrial and artistic production by making it possible to imitate and mass-produce costly materials including marble and ebony. In response to this new synthetic trend, reform movements such as the British Arts and Crafts movement and the German Werkbund promoted artisanal production with natural materials. In contrast, the Constructivists embraced plastics as symbols of technological progress. As early as 1917, Naum Gabo experimented with assembling celluloid sheets into sculptures, though these proved too fragile. Only the more stable acrylic glass developed in the 1920s by Otto Röhm and others, which became more widely available in the 1930s under brand names like Plexiglas or Perspex, was easier to work with and could be shaped through heat. Gabo used colorless, transparent plastics to impart a sense of dynamism and lightness to his sculptures, aiming to integrate the surrounding space. Across Europe, artists explored the potential of these new materials. For instance, members of the Dutch De Stijl movement adopted plastics in their work. César Domela incorporated acrylic sheets in his reliefs, while Georges Vantongerloo crafted mobiles and sculptures from plastic rods to express energy flows and force lines. By the 1960s, acrylic paint, initially developed for industrial applications, brought new color intensity and smooth surfaces to art, especially in the precise shapes and patterns characteristic of Minimalism, Hard Edge Painting, and Op Art. The development of plastics, from celluloid to acrylic, not only expanded material possibilities but also challenged traditional notions of the unique artwork. AH

Further reading:
Arghir 1988, El-Danasouri 1992, and Van Oosten 2002

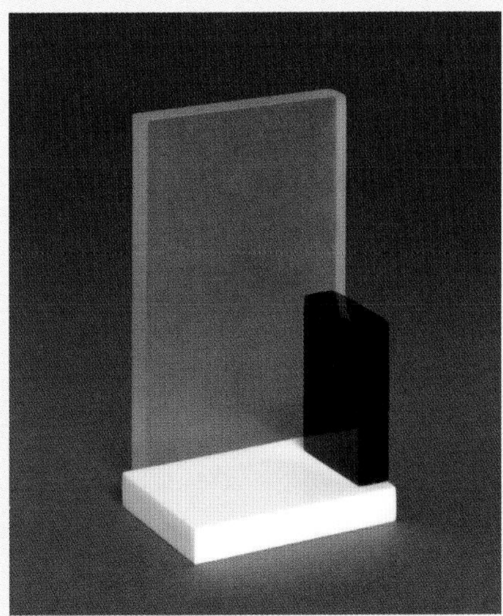

Mary Martin,
Perspex Group,
1963, Tate

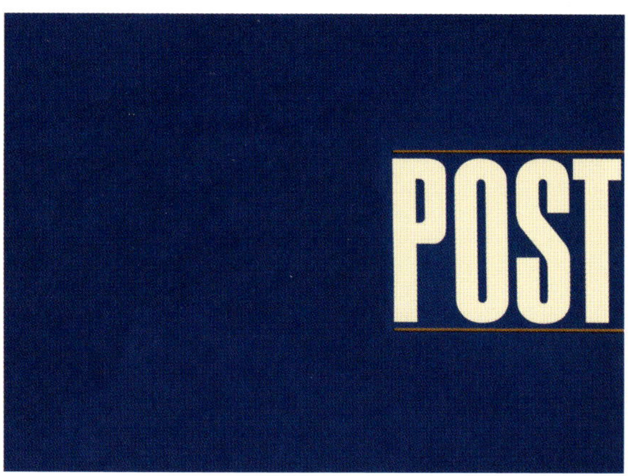

Post Painterly Abstraction

Los Angeles County Museum of Art
April 22 – June 7, 1964

Catalog: Los Angeles 1964

In 1964 the Los Angeles County Museum of Art (LACMA) mounted the exhibition *Post Painterly Abstraction.* It was curated by Clement Greenberg, one of the most influential American art critics of the postwar years, in collaboration with LACMA curator James Elliott. The exhibition featured thirty-one artists including Sam Francis, Helen Frankenthaler, Morris Louis, and Kenneth Noland. The title of the show was derived from Greenberg's essay "After Abstract Expressionism" from 1962. Greenberg saw the continuing development of modern painting as a turn away from the gestural techniques of Abstract Expressionism toward a more rigorous form of abstraction. Instead of applying the paint in an expressive manner, the artists shown in *Post Painterly Abstraction* concentrated on linearity and planes of pure color. Although the works were not strictly representative of the style known as Hard Edge Painting, they were distinguished by an emphasis on formal qualities such as color, shape, and surface. Greenberg's selection for the show was broad, yet he rejected movements such as Pop Art and Neo-Dada, finding them too strongly influenced by popular culture and irony. The exhibition also constituted a critique of the dominance of New York in the American art scene. Greenberg, who is often credited with having established New York as the center of the modernist movement, gave space to artists from other regions, including many from the West Coast and Canada. Although some critics felt that Greenberg had placed more emphasis on adherence to his stylistic criteria than on artistic quality, the exhibition enhanced the reputation of many of the participating artists. Furthermore, it also marked the turning point from Abstract Expressionism in the United States toward the geometric abstraction of the 1960s. SB

Cover of exhibition catalog
Post Painterly Abstraction, 1964

Beyond Earth: Art in the Age of Space Exploration

The Space Race reached its first peak in 1957 with the launch of the first satellite, Sputnik 1, by the Soviet Union. Over the following years, one milestone after another was achieved: in 1961 Yuri Gagarin was the first human in space, and by 1969 Neil Armstrong and Buzz Aldrin took the first steps on the Moon. The Space Age permeated popular culture and design around the globe. In the year of the Moon landing, pop star David Bowie released his album *Space Oddity,* featuring a painting by Victor Vasarely on the UK album cover. The Hungarian artist's paintings use geometric shapes resembling coded patterns and are often named after stars and constellations. In 1982 French cosmonaut Jean-Loup Chrétien took one hundred of Vasarely's numbered silkscreen prints on the Soyuz T-6 mission to the Salyut 7 space station, making Vasarely the first truly universal artist. Motifs of speed and industrial design from the Space Age also influenced the wedge-shaped canvases of Frank Stella. With their dynamic, converging stripes, these works evoked streamlined forms, suggestive of rockets and spacecraft. Stella used metallic industrial paints, transforming his canvases into gleaming surfaces that echoed the latest feats of engineering. During the 1960s the first color photographs of Earth were captured from space, Mars was photographed up close for the first time, and the Moon's surface was mapped and photographed in unprecedented detail. Inspired by this surge of imagery directly from outer space, Polish artist Wojciech Fangor created paintings evocative of celestial bodies. Together, these artists reflected the sense of wonder, technological progress, and limitless exploration that defined the Space Age. SB

Further Reading:
Kraków 2012 and Frankfurt am Main 2018

Victor Vasarely,
Vega 200, 1968,
Michèle Vasarely collection

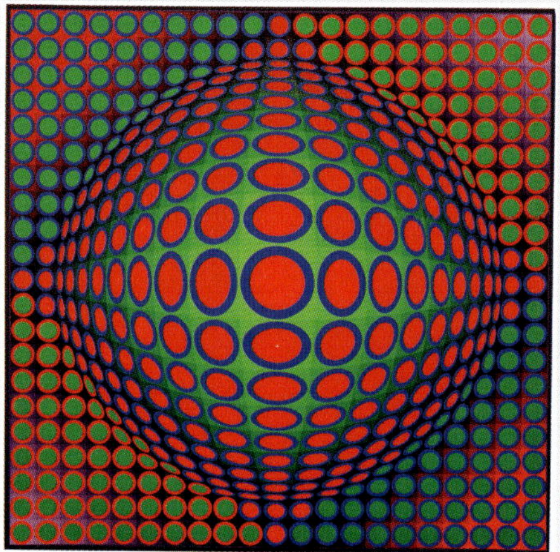

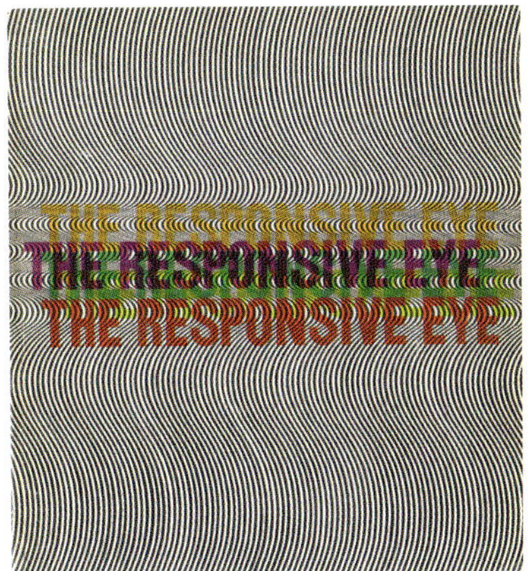

The Responsive Eye

Museum of Modern Art, New York
February 23 – April 25, 1965

Also shown in St. Louis, Minneapolis, Seattle, Pasadena

Catalog: New York 1965

From February 23 to April 25, 1965, the Museum of Modern Art in New York mounted the exhibition *The Responsive Eye,* curated by William C. Seitz. With 180,000 visitors, the show drew the largest crowds in the history of the museum. Although artists had experimented with optical effects before the 1960s, not until the 1965 exhibition did Op Art establish itself as an independent artistic movement. On view were 123 works by seventy-five artists including Richard Anuszkiewicz, Wojciech Fangor, François Morellet, Bridget Riley, and Victor Vasarely, all revolving around the theme of "perceptual abstraction." Their works tested the boundaries of visual perception, in many cases using patterns of repeating or superimposed geometric forms that seemed to flicker and pulsate in the eye. The exhibition also illuminated the art-historical interest in optics, especially in the Renaissance and Postimpressionism. Particular attention was devoted to Pointillist Georges Seurat, who had explored the division of color hues and their optical fusion when viewed at a distance in order to manipulate visual phenomena. His work inspired Op Art as well as the experiments with color contrasts in the work of former Bauhaus instructor Josef Albers, whose influential series *Homage to the Square* (cats. 28–32) received a space of its own in the exhibition. The shimmering, flickering effect of Op Art was perceived by many visitors as dizzying or even painful, while reviewers largely dismissed the works as empty showmanship. Still, *The Responsive Eye* attracted enormous attention—the visual effects of Op Art required no previous knowledge on the viewer's part and could be experienced by anyone. Their visual language was translated into every area of art and design and found entrance into pop culture and everyday life. AH

Bridget Riley,
Current, 1964,
illustration on the cover of
the exhibition catalog *The Responsive Eye,* 1965,
designed by Joseph Del Valle

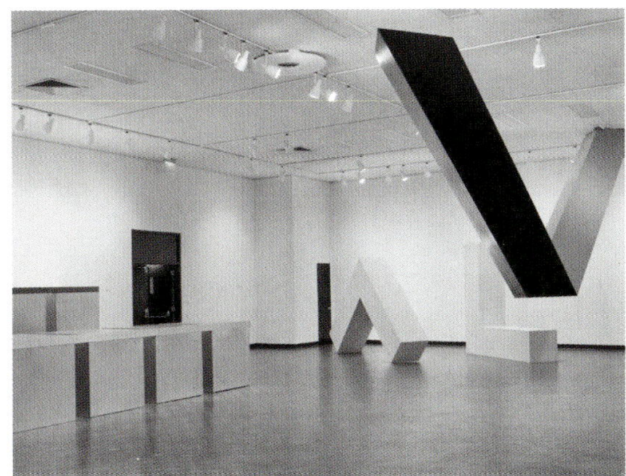

Primary Structures: Younger American and British Sculptors

Jewish Museum, New York
April 27 – June 12, 1966

Catalog: New York 1966a

Upon entering the exhibition *Primary Structures: Younger American and British Sculptors* at the Jewish Museum in New York, visitors must have initially felt a sense of astonishment. The works on view consisted of objects reduced to basic geometric forms reminiscent of everyday items—beams, boxes, struts, or panels—and arranged into sculptural forms. The show, curated by Kynaston McShine, was the second group exhibition of Minimalist art following the presentation of *Black, White and Grey* at the Wadsworth Atheneum in Hartford, Connecticut, in 1964. The show *Primary Structures* was originally conceived by McShine as a focused examination of the artists defined as Minimalists; ultimately, however, he expanded the exhibition to include a broader overview of contemporary geometric-abstract sculpture. McShine formulated a principle of organization in which Minimalist art was divided into two tendencies: on the one hand, the continuation of the modernist tradition as represented by the asymmetrical sculptures of Anthony Caro, and on the other the reduction to geometric forms exemplified in the sculptures of Tony Smith. The latter direction, to which artists such as Carl Andre, Dan Flavin, Judy Gerowitz (later known as Judy Chicago), Donald Judd, Sol LeWitt, and Anne Truitt also belonged, left the greatest impression on critics of the exhibition. The sculptures of these artists, radically reduced to geometric shapes, often consisted of industrial, seemingly unworked materials such as metal, aluminum, plastic, or glass. The Minimalists were interested in the essence of the form in its spatial relationship to the viewer: as one moved through the space, the sculptures could appear to change. *Primary Structures* was *the* New York exhibition event of 1966 and effected a breakthrough for Minimalism as a "museum-worthy" style. The title of the show came to serve as an umbrella term for the Minimalist sculpture of the 1960s. AH

Rudolph Burckhardt,
installation view of *Primary Structures:*
Younger American and British Sculptors, 1966.
Works shown: Robert Grosvenor, Donald Judd,
and Robert Morris

Translated from German by Melissa M. Thorson

Selected Bibliography

Aarau 2014
Sophie Taeuber-Arp: Today Is Tomorrow, exh. cat., Aargauer Kunsthaus, Aarau 2014.

Alloway 1954
Lawrence Alloway, *Nine Abstract Artists, Their Work and Theory: Robert Adams, Terry Frost, Adrian Heath, Anthony Hill, Roger Hilton, Kenneth Martin, Mary Martin, Victor Pasmore, William Scott,* London 1954.

Amsterdam 1999
Jo Baer: Paintings 1960–1998, exh. cat., Stedelijk Museum Amsterdam, 1999.

Amsterdam 2013
Kazimir Malevich and the Russian Avant-garde: Featuring Selections from the Khardzhiev and Costakis Collections, exh. cat., Stedelijk Museum Amsterdam, 2013.

Appleyard 1989
Bryan Appleyard, *The Pleasures of Peace: Art and Imagination in Post-War Britain,* London 1989.

Arghir 1988
Anca Arghir, *Transparency into Art: Acrylic Glass as a Medium,* Cologne 1988.

Baer 2010
Jo Baer, *Jo Baer: Broadsides & Belles Lettres: Selected Writings and Interviews 1965–2010,* ed. Roel Arkesteijn, Amsterdam 2010.

Baltimore 1976
Frank Stella: The Black Paintings, exh. cat., Baltimore Museum of Art 1976.

Bann 1974
Steven Bann, ed., *The Tradition of Constructivism,* New York 1974.

Basel 1944
konkrete kunst, exh. cat., Kunstmuseum Basel, 1944.

Basel 2013
Piet Mondrian—Barnett Newman—Dan Flavin, exh. cat., Kunstmuseum Basel, 2013.

Basel 2014
Kazimir Malevich: The World as Objectlessness, exh. cat., Kunstmuseum Basel, 2014.

Basel 2021
Sophie Taeuber-Arp: Living Abstraction, exh. cat., Kunstmuseum Basel, 2021.

Battcock 1968
Gregory Battcock, ed., *Minimal Art: A Critical Anthology,* New York 1968.

Becks-Malorny 1993
Ulrike Becks-Malorny, *Wassily Kandinsky 1866–1944: Aufbruch zur Abstraktion,* Cologne 1993.

Beijing 2012
Constructivism in Europe: From Malevich to Kandinsky, exh. cat., NAMOC—National Art Museum of China, Beijing 2012.

Benson/Forgács 2002
Timothy O. Benson and Éva Forgács, eds., *Between Worlds: A Sourcebook of Central European Avant-Gardes, 1910–1930,* Cambridge, MA, 2002.

Berlin 1922
Erste Russische Kunstausstellung, exh. cat., Galerie van Diemen & Co., Berlin 1922; reprint, ed. Eberhard Roters, Cologne 1988.

Berlin 2004
Light and Colour in the Russian Avant-Garde: The Costakis Collection, exh. cat., Martin-Gropius-Bau, Berlin 2004.

Berlin 2009
Bauhaus: A Conceptual Model, exh. cat., Martin-Gropius-Bau, Berlin 2009.

Berlin 2010
Color Fields, exh. cat., Deutsche Guggenheim, Berlin 2010.

Berlin 2014
Vassily Kandinsky: Teaching at the Bauhaus, exh. cat., Bauhaus-Archiv/Museum für Gestaltung, Berlin 2014.

Berlin 2019a
Original Bauhaus, exh. cat., Bauhaus-Archiv/Museum für Gestaltung, Berlin 2019.

Berlin 2019b
Bauhaus Imaginista: A School in the World, exh. cat., Haus der Kulturen der Welt, Berlin 2019.

Berlin 2021
Alexander Calder: Minimal/Maximal, exh. cat., Neue Nationalgalerie, Staatliche Museen zu Berlin, 2021.

Bern 1984
Die Sprache der Geometrie: Suprematismus, De Stijl und Umkreis—heute, exh. cat., Kunstmuseum Bern, 1984.

Bern 2021
Max Bill Global: An Artist Building Bridges, exh. cat., Zentrum Paul Klee, Bern 2021.

Besant/Leadbeater 1905
Annie Besant and Charles Leadbeater, *Thought-Forms: A Record of Clairvoyant Investigation,* London 1905.

Blotkamp 1986
Carel Blotkamp, *De Stijl: The Formative Years, 1917–1922,* Cambridge, MA, 1986.

Blotkamp 1994
Carel Blotkamp, *Mondrian: The Art of Destruction,* London 1994.

Bois 1990
Yve-Alain Bois, *Painting as Model,* Cambridge, MA, 1990.

Botar/Wünsche 2011
Oliver A. I. Botar and Isabel Wünsche, eds., *Biocentrism and Modernism,* Farnham, UK, 2011.

Bowlt 2017
John E. Bowlt, ed., *Russian Art of the Avant-Garde: Theory and Criticism, 1902–1934,* London 2017.

Bowlt/Washton Long 1980
John E. Bowlt and Rose-Carol Washton Long, eds., *The Life of Vasilii Kandinsky in Russian Art,* Newtonville, MA, 1980.

Bowness 2011
Sophie Bowness, *Barbara Hepworth, The Plasters: The Gift to Wakefield,* Farnham 2011.

Bowness 2017
Sophie Bowness, *Barbara Hepworth: The Sculptor in the Studio,* London 2017.

Bristow 2013
Roger Bristow, *Terry Frost: A Painter's Life,* Bristol 2013.

Brooker et al. 2013
Peter Brooker et al., eds., *The Oxford Critical and Cultural History of Modernist Magazines,* vol. 3: *Europe 1880–1940,* Oxford 2013.

Brucher 1999
Günter Brucher, *Kandinsky: Wege zur Abstraktion,* Munich 1999.

Brussels 2016
Theo van Doesburg: A New Expression of Life, Art, and Technology, exh. cat., BOZAR, Brussels 2016.

Buchloh 2003
Benjamin H. D. Buchloh, "Kelly's Matrix: Administering Abstraction, Industrializing Color," in *Ellsworth Kelly: Matrix,* exh. cat., Matthew Marks Gallery, New York 2003.

Buchloh 2013
Benjamin H. D. Buchloh, "Painting as Diagram: Five Notes on Frank Stella's Early Paintings, 1958–1959," in *October* 143 (2013), 126–44.

Buffalo 1989
Abstraction, Geometry, Painting: Selected Geometric Abstract Painting in America Since 1945, exh. cat., Albright-Knox Art Gallery, Buffalo 1989.

Button 2007
Virginia Button, *Ben Nicholson,* London 2007.

Cambridge 2001
Mondrian: The Transatlantic Paintings, exh. cat., Harvard University Art Museums, Cambridge, MA, 2001.

Cambridge 2002
Enrico Castellani, exh. cat., Kettle's Yard, Cambridge, UK, 2002.

Chemnitz 2016
Revolutionary: Russian Avant-Garde Art from the Vladimir Tsarenkov Collection, exh. cat., Kunstsammlungen Chemnitz, 2016.

Chemnitz 2023
"Das Kreative geht dem Unbekannten kühn entgegen": Willi Baumeister und sein Netzwerk, exh. cat., Museum Gunzenhauser, Kunstsammlungen Chemnitz, 2023.

Churchward 2013
Charles Churchward, *It's Modern: The Eye and Visual Influence of Alexander Liberman,* New York 2013.

Cincinnati 1974
Warren Hall, Coletta Martin, Robert Michener, Patricia Renick, Janet Rappoport, Margaret Wenstrup, exh. cat., Cincinnati Art Museum 1974.

Cologne 2010
Kasimir Malewitsch und der Suprematismus in der Sammlung Ludwig, exh. cat., Museum Ludwig, Cologne 2010.

Cologne 2020
Russische Avantgarde im Museum Ludwig: Original und Fälschung; Fragen, Untersuchungen, Erklärungen, exh. cat., Museum Ludwig, Cologne 2020.

Colpitt 1990
Frances Colpitt, *Minimal Art: The Critical Perspective,* Seattle 1990.

Columbus 2007
The Optic Nerve: Perceptual Art of the 1960s, exh. cat., Columbus Museum of Art, 2007.

Cooke/Kelly 2011
Lynne Cooke and Karen Kelly, eds., *Agnes Martin,* New Haven 2011.

Davos 2010
Sophie Taeuber-Arp: Movement and Balance, exh. cat., Kirchner Museum Davos, 2010.

Dickerman 2023
Leah Dickerman, "Mondrian's Boogie Woogie," in *October* 185 (2023), 118–38.

Van Doesburg 1930
Theo van Doesburg, "Art concret: Groupe et revue fondés en 1930 à Paris," in *Art Concret* (1930), 1–16.

Dorrian/Pousin 2013
Mark Dorrian and Frédéric Pousin, eds., *Seeing from Above: The Aerial View in Visual Culture,* London 2013.

Douglas 1994
Charlotte Douglas, *Kazimir Malevich,* New York 1994.

Douglas/Lodder 2006
Charlotte Douglas and Christine Lodder, eds., *Rethinking Malevich: Proceedings of a Conference in Celebration of the 125th Anniversary of Kazimir Malevich's Birth,* London 2006.

Dresden 2019
Visionary Spaces: Kandinsky, Mondrian, Lissitzky and the Abstract-Constructivist Avant-Garde in Dresden, 1919–1932, exh. cat., Albertinum, Dresden 2019.

Droste 1990
Magdalena Droste, *Bauhaus, 1919–1933,* Cologne 1990.

Duisburg 2009
Für eine neue Welt: Georges Vantongerloo und seine Kreise von Mondrian bis Bill, exh. cat., Wilhelm-Lehmbruck-Museum, Duisburg 2009.

Düsseldorf 1977
Werke aus der Sammlung Costakis: Russische Avantgarde 1910–1930, exh. cat., Kunstmuseum Düsseldorf, 1977.

Düsseldorf 1980
Wassily Kandinsky: Drei Hauptwerke aus drei Jahrzehnten: Eine didaktische Ausstellung; Bilder, Fotos, Texte, exh. cat., Kunstsammlung Nordrhein-Westfalen, Düsseldorf 1980.

Düsseldorf 1992
Konstruktivistische Internationale Schöpferische Arbeitsgemeinschaft, 1922–1927: Utopien für eine europäische Kultur, exh. cat., Kunstsammlung Nordrhein-Westfalen, Düsseldorf 1992.

Düsseldorf 2013
Alexander Calder: Avant-Garde in Motion, exh. cat., Kunstmuseum Nordrhein-Westfalen, Düsseldorf 2013.

Düsseldorf 2014
Kandinsky, Malevich, Mondrian: The Infinite White Abyss, exh. cat., Stiftung Kunstsammlung Nordrhein-Westfalen, Düsseldorf 2014.

Düsseldorf 2024
Hilma af Klint und Wassily Kandinsky träumen von der Zukunft, exh. cat., Stiftung Kunstsammlung Nordrhein-Westfalen, Düsseldorf 2024.

Edinburgh 2019
Bridget Riley, exh. cat., Scottish National Gallery, Edinburgh 2019.

El-Danasouri 1992
Andrea El-Danasouri, *Kunststoff und Müll: Das Material bei Naum Gabo und Kurt Schwitters,* Munich 1992.

Essen 2000
Bauhaus: Dessau—Chicago—New York, exh. cat., Museum Folkwang, Essen 2000.

Fer 1997
Briony Fer, *On Abstract Art,* New Haven 1997.

Follin 2004
Frances Follin, *Embodied Visions: Bridget Riley, Op Art and the Sixties,* London 2004.

Forgács 2020
Éva Forgács, "The New Aesthetic of the Late Nineteen Twenties: Reconsidering the Periodization of the Interwar Avant-Gardes," in *Tomus* 61 (2020), 201–16.

Forgács 2022
Éva Forgács, *Malevich and Interwar Modernism: Russian Art and the International of the Square,* London 2022.

Frankfurt am Main 1989
Wassily Kandinsky: Die erste sowjetische Retrospektive. Gemälde, Zeichnungen und Graphik aus sowjetischen und westlichen Museen, exh. cat., Schirn Kunsthalle, Frankfurt am Main 1989.

Frankfurt am Main 1995
Okkultismus und Avantgarde: Von Munch bis Mondrian, 1900–1915, exh. cat., Schirn Kunsthalle, Frankfurt am Main 1995.

Frankfurt am Main 2007
Op Art, exh. cat., Schirn Kunsthalle, Frankfurt am Main 2007.

Frankfurt am Main 2018
Vasarely: In the Labyrinth of Modernism, exh. cat., Städel Museum, Frankfurt am Main 2018.

Gamwell 2002
Lynn Gamwell, *Exploring the Invisible: Art, Science, and the Spiritual,* Princeton 2002.

Gassner/Kersten 1991
Hubertus Gassner and Wolfgang Kersten, "Physikalisches Weltbild und abstrakte Bildwelten bei Wassily Kandinsky," in *Moderne Kunst: Das Funkkolleg zum Verständnis der Gegenwartskunst,* ed. Monika Wagner, Hamburg 1991.

Geneva 2023
Verena Loewensberg, exh. cat., MAMCO, Geneva 2023.

Godfrey 2007
Mark Godfrey, *Abstraction and the Holocaust,* New York and London 2007

Gough 2005
Maria Gough, *The Artist as Producer: Russian Constructivism in Revolution,* Berkeley 2005.

Gouma-Peterson 1999
Thalia Gouma-Peterson, *Miriam Schapiro: Shaping the Fragments of Art and Life,* New York 1999.

Glimcher 2012
Arnold Glimcher, *Agnes Martin: Paintings, Writings, Remembrances,* London 2012.

Gray 1962
Camilla Gray, *The Great Experiment: Russian Art 1863–1922,* London 1962.

Greenberg 1986
Clement Greenberg, *Clement Greenberg: The Collected Essays and Criticism,* vol. 7: *Perceptions and Judgments: 1939–1944,* ed. John O'Brian, Chicago 1986.

Greenberg 1993
Clement Greenberg, *Clement Greenberg: The Collected Essays and Criticism,* vol. 4: *Modernism with a Vengeance, 1957–1969,* ed. John O'Brian, Chicago 1993.

Grieve 2005
Alastair Grieve, *Constructed Abstract Art in England after the Second World War: A Neglected Avant-Garde,* New Haven 2005.

Grieve 2009
Alastair Grieve, *Victor Pasmore,* London 2009.

Grohmann/Allen 1966
Will Grohmann and Robert Allen, *Willi Baumeister: Life and Work,* New York 1966.

Haemmerli/Ulmer 2024
Thomas Haemmerli and Brigitte Ulmer, eds., *Circle! Square! Progress!: Zurich's Concrete Avant-Garde; Max Bill, Camille Graeser, Verena Loewensberg, Richard Paul Lohse and Their Times,* Zurich 2024.

Hahl-Koch 1993
Jelena Hahl-Koch, *Kandinsky,* Stuttgart 1993.

Hamburg 2007
Das Schwarze Quadrat: Hommage an Malewitsch, exh. cat., Hamburger Kunsthalle, 2007.

Hamburg 2013a
Rodtschenko: Eine neue Zeit, exh. cat., Bucerius Kunst Forum, Hamburg 2013.

Hamburg 2013b
Jean Leppien: From the Bauhaus to the Mediterranean, exh. cat., Hamburger Kunsthalle, 2013.

Hamburg 2014
Mondrian: Farbe, exh. cat., Bucerius Kunst Forum, Hamburg 2014.

Hammer/Lodder 2000
Martin Hammer and Christina Lodder, *Constructing Modernity: The Art & Career of Naum Gabo,* New Haven 2000.

The Hague 1994
Piet Mondrian 1872–1944, exh. cat., Gemeentemuseum Den Haag, The Hague 1994.

Harrison/Wood 1993
Charles Harrison and Paul Wood, eds., *Art in Theory, 1900–1990: An Anthology of Changing Ideas*, Oxford, UK, and Cambridge, MA.

Hastings 2021
Victor Pasmore: Line & Space, exh. cat., Hastings Contemporary, 2021.

Henderson 1983
Linda Dalrymple Henderson, *The Fourth Dimension and Non-Euclidean Geometry in Modern Art,* Cambridge, MA, 1983.

Henderson 2007
Linda Dalrymple Henderson, "Einstein and 20th-Century Art: A Romance of Many Dimensions," in *Einstein for the 21st Century,* ed. Peter Galison et al., New Jersey 2007, 101–29.

Hoberg/Friedel 2008
Annegret Hoberg and Helmut Friedel, eds., *Wassily Kandinsky,* Munich 2008.

Hock et al. 2019
Beáta Hock et al., eds., *A Reader in East-Central-European Modernism 1918–1956,* London 2019.

Houston 2004
Kenneth Noland: The Nature of Color, exh. cat., Museum of Fine Arts, Houston 2004.

Howard 2006
Jeremy Howard, *East European Art, 1650–1950,* Oxford 2006.

Howarth 2019
Lucy Howarth, *Marlow Moss,* Bath 2019.

Humblet 2007
Claudine Humblet, *The New American Abstraction, 1950–1970,* Milan 2007.

Humlebæk 2016
Eye Attack: Op Art and Kinetic Art, 1950–1970, exh. cat., Louisiana Museum of Modern Art, Humlebæk 2016.

Ingolstadt 2018
Über das Geistige in der Kunst: 100 Jahre nach Kandinsky und Malewitsch, exh. cat., Museum für Konkrete Kunst, Ingolstadt 2018.

Janssen 2022
Hans Janssen, *Piet Mondrian: A Life,* London 2022.

Janssen/White 2011
Hans Janssen and Michael White, *The Story of De Stijl: Mondrian to Van Doesburg,* Brussels 2011.

Jena 2009
Punkt und Linie zu Fläche: Kandinsky am Bauhaus, exh. cat., Kunstsammlung Jena, 2009.

Judd/Murray 2019
Donald Judd Interviews, ed. Flavin Judd and Caitlin Murray, New York 2019.

Juler 2015
Edward Juler, *Grown but Not Made: British Modernist Sculpture and the New Biology,* Manchester 2015.

Kandinsky 1947
Wassily Kandinsky, *Point and Line to Plane: Contribution to the Analysis of the Pictorial Elements* (1926), trans. Howard Dearstyne and Hilla Rebay, New York 1947.

Kandinsky 1977
Wassily Kandinsky, *Concerning the Spiritual in Art* (1912), trans. Michael Thomas Harvey Sadler, New York 1977.

Kandinsky 1994
Wassily Kandinsky, *Kandinsky: Complete Writings on Art,* ed. Kenneth C. Lindsay and Peter Vergo, Boston 1994.

Kandinsky 2024
Wassily Kandinsky, *Concerning the Spiritual in Art* (1912), trans. Ruth Ahmedzai Kemp, London 2024

Karlsruhe 2019
The Whole World a Bauhaus, exh. cat., ZKM—Zentrum für Kunst und Medien, Karlsruhe 2019.

Kentgens-Craig 1999
Margaret Kentgens-Craig, *The Bauhaus and America: First Contacts, 1919–1936,* Cambridge, MA, 1999.

Kiaer 2008
Christina Kiaer, *Imagine No Possessions: The Socialist Objects of Russian Constructivism,* Cambridge, MA, 2008.

Klee 1961
Paul Klee, *The Thinking Eye: The Note-books of Paul Klee,* ed. Jürg Spiller, trans. Ralph Manheim, New York 1961.

Kraków 2012
Wojciech Fangor: Space as Play, exh. cat., Muzeum Narodowe w Krakowie, Kraków 2012.

Krauss 1986
Rosalind E. Krauss, "Grids," in Krauss, *The Originality of the Avant-Garde and Other Modernist Myths,* Cambridge, MA, 1986, 8–22.

Lee 2004
Pamela Lee, "Bridget Riley's Eye/Body Problem," in Lee, *Chronophobia: On Time in the Art of the 1960s,* Cambridge, MA, 2004, 154–214.

Leiden 2009
Van Doesburg and the International Avant-Garde: Constructing a New World, exh. cat., Stedelijk Museum De Lakenhal, Leiden 2009.

Leimer/Wünsche 2022
Miriam Leimer and Isabel Wünsche, eds., *100 Years On: Revisiting the First Russian Art Exhibition of 1922,* Vienna and Cologne 2022.

Levinger 2022
Esther Levinger, *Constructivism in Central Europe: Painting, Typography, Photomontage,* Leiden 2022.

Lewison 2025
Jeremy Lewison, *Paul Huxley,* London 2025.

Lippard 1966
"Questions to Stella and Judd: Interview by Bruce Glaser," ed. Lucy Lippard (1966), in Battcock 1968, 148–64.

Liverpool 2014
Mondrian and His Studios: Colour in Space, exh. cat., Tate Liverpool, 2014.

Lodder 1983
Christina Lodder, *Russian Constructivism,* New Haven and London 1983.

Lodder 2004
Christina Lodder, "Malevich, Suprematism and Aerial Photography," in *History of Photography* 28,1 (2004), 25–40.

Lodder 2005
Christina Lodder, *Constructive Strands in Russian Art, 1914–1937,* London 2005.

Lodder 2019
Christina Lodder, *Celebrating Suprematism: New Approaches to the Art of Kazimir Malevich,* Leiden and Boston 2022.

Łódź 2019
Composing the Space: Sculptures in the Avant-Garde, exh. cat., Muzeum Sztuki, Łódź 2019.

London 1936
International Exhibition of Abstract Painting, Sculpture and Construction, exh. cat., in *Axis: A Quarterly Review of Contemporary "Abstract" Painting & Sculpture* 5, London 1936.

London 1956
This Is Tomorrow, exh. cat., Whitechapel Art Gallery, London 1956; reprint, ed. Nayia Yiakoumaki, London 2010.

London 1968
Four Artists: Reliefs, Constructions and Drawings: John Ernest, Anthony Hill, Malcolm Hughes, Gillian Wise, exh. cat., Victoria and Albert Museum, London 1968.

London 1983
Anthony Hill: A Retrospective Exhibition, exh. cat., Hayward Gallery, London 1983.

London 1984
Mary Martin, exh. cat., Tate Gallery, London 1984.

London 2006
Kandinsky: The Path to Abstraction, exh. cat., Tate Modern, London 2006.

London 2008
Breaking the Rules: The Printed Face of the European Avant-Garde, 1900–1937, exh. cat., British Library, London 2008

London 2009
Rodchenko & Popova: Defining Construcivism, exh. cat., Tate Modern, London 2009.

London 2012
Mondrian/Nicholson: In Parallel, exh. cat., Courtauld Gallery, London 2012.

London 2015a
Sonia Delaunay, exh. cat., Tate Modern, London 2015.

London 2015b
Agnes Martin, exh. cat., Tate Modern, London 2015.

London 2015c
Barbara Hepworth: Sculpture for a Modern World, exh. cat., Tate Britain, London 2015.

London 2017
Revolution: Russian Art 1917–1932, exh. cat., Royal Academy of Arts, London 2017.

London 2022
Postwar Modern: New Art in Britain 1945–65, exh. cat., Barbican, London 2022.

London 2023
Hilma af Klint & Piet Mondrian: Forms of Life, exh. cat., Tate Modern, London 2023.

London 2024
Expressionists: Kandinsky, Münter and The Blue Rider, exh. cat., Tate Modern, London 2024.

Los Angeles 1964
Post Painterly Abstraction, exh. cat., Los Angeles County Museum of Art, 1964.

Los Angeles 1986
The Spiritual in Art: Abstract Painting, 1890–1985, exh. cat., Los Angeles County Museum of Art, 1986.

Los Angeles 2002
Central European Avant-Gardes: Exchange and Transformation, 1910–1930, exh. cat., Los Angeles County Museum of Art, 2002.

Lucerne 1935
These, Antithese, Synthese, exh. cat., Kunstmuseum Luzern, Lucerne 1935.

Madden/Spike 2010
David Madden and Nicholas Spike, *Anuszkiewicz: Paintings & Sculptures, 1945–2001: Catalogue Raisonné,* Florence 2010.

Madrid 2017
Kobro and Strzemiński: Avant-Garde Prototypes, exh. cat., Museo Nacional Centro de Arte Reina Sofía, Madrid 2017.

Madrid 2018
Victor Vasarely: The Birth of Op Art, exh. cat., Museo Nacional Thyssen-Bornemisza, Madrid 2018.

Madrid 2022
In the Eye of the Storm: Modernism in Ukraine, 1900–1930s, exh. cat., Museo Nacional Thyssen-Bornemisza, Madrid 2022.

Mansbach 1999
Stephen Mansbach, *Modern Art in Eastern Europe: From the Baltic to the Balkans, ca. 1890–1939,* Cambridge, UK, 1999.

Metz 2013
Vues d'en haut, exh. cat., Centre Pompidou-Metz, 2013.

Meyer 2001
James Meyer, *Minimalism: Art and Polemics in the Sixties,* New Haven 2001.

Milan 2001
Enrico Castellani, exh. cat., Fondazione Prada, Milan 2001.

Milwaukee 2014
Kandinsky: A Retrospective, exh. cat., Milwaukee Art Museum, 2014.

Misler 2002
Nicoletta Misler,"Vasilii Kandinsky and the Russian Academy of Artistic Sciences," in *Experiment* 8,1 (2002), 173–85.

Moffet 1977
Kenworth Moffet, *Kenneth Noland,* New York 1977.

Mondrian 1986
Piet Mondrian, *The New Art, the New Life: The Collected Writings of Piet Mondrian,* ed. Harry Holtzman and Martin S. James, Boston 1986.

Moscow 2018
Goncharova and Malevich: In Three Dimensions, exh. cat., State Tretyakov Gallery, Moscow 2018.

Munich 1937
Führer durch die Ausstellung Entartete Kunst, exh. cat., Haus der Deutschen Kunst, Munich 1937.

Munich 1976
Wassily Kandinsky, 1866–1944, exh. cat., Haus der Kunst, Munich 1976.

Munich 1984
Russische Avantgarde aus der Sammlung Costakis, exh. cat., Städtische Galerie im Lenbachhaus, Munich 1984.

Munich 1995
Vasily Kandinsky: A Colorful Life, exh. cat., Städtische Galerie im Lenbachhaus und Kunstbau, Munich 1995.

Munich 1996
Die russische Avantgarde: Sammlung Costakis, exh. cat., Haus der Kunst, Munich 1996.

Munich 2006
Against Kandinsky, exh. cat., Museum Villa Stuck, Munich 2006.

Munich 2008
Kandinsky: Absolute, Abstract, exh. cat., Städtische Galerie im Lenbachhaus und Kunstbau, Munich 2008.

Munich 2011
Mondrian, De Stijl, exh. cat., Städtische Galerie im Lenbachhaus und Kunstbau, Munich 2011.

Münster 1978
Abstraction—Création, 1931–1936, exh. cat., Westfälisches Landesmuseum für Kunst und Kulturgeschichte, Münster 1978.

Münster 2014
Die Revolution entlässt ihre Bilder: Von Malewitsch bis Kandinsky, exh. cat., Kunstmuseum Pablo Picasso Münster, 2014.

Murnau 2007
Bauhaus-Ideen um Itten, Feininger, Klee, Kandinsky: Vom Expressiven zum Konstruktiven, exh. cat., Schloßmuseum, Murnau 2007.

Nakov 1975
Andrej B. Nakov, *The Laboratory Period (1919–1921) of Russian Constructivism,* Paris 1975.

Nakov 2010
Andrej B. Nakov, *Malevich: Painting the Absolute,* Farnham 2010.

New Haven 1979
Mondrian and Neo-Plasticism in America, exh. cat., Yale University Art Gallery, New Haven 1979.

Neuy 1984
Heinrich Neuy, *Bauhaus: Der Weg zur abstrakten Malerei,* Cologne 1984.

New York 1936
Cubism and Abstract Art, exh. cat., Museum of Modern Art, New York 1936.

New York 1942
Art of This Century: Objects, Drawings, Photographs, Paintings, Sculpture, Collages, 1910 to 1942, exh. cat., Art of This Century, New York 1942.

New York 1945
In Memory of Wassily Kandinsky, exh. cat., Museum of Non-Objective Painting, New York 1945.

New York 1963
Vasily Kandinsky, 1866–1944: A Retrospective Exhibition, exh. cat., Solomon R. Guggenheim Foundation, New York 1963.

New York 1965
The Responsive Eye, exh. cat., Museum of Modern Art, New York 1965.

New York 1966a
Primary Structures: Younger American and British Sculptors, exh. cat., Jewish Museum, New York 1966.

New York 1966b
Systemic Painting, exh. cat., Solomon R. Guggenheim Museum, New York 1966.

New York 1983
Kandinsky: Russian and Bauhaus Years, 1915–1933, exh. cat., Solomon R. Guggenheim Museum, New York 1983.

New York 1985a
Contrasts of Form: Geometric Abstract Art 1910–1980: From the Collection of the Museum of Modern Art Including the Riklis Collection of McCrory Corporation, exh. cat., Museum of Modern Art, New York 1985.

New York 1985b
Kandinsky in Paris, 1934–1944, exh. cat., Solomon R. Guggenheim Museum, New York 1985.

New York 1985c
Liubov Popova: Spatial Force Constructions 1921–22, exh. cat., Rachel Adler Gallery, New York 1985.

New York 1990
Burgoyne Diller, exh. cat., Whitney Museum of American Art, New York 1990.

New York 1991
Liubov Popova, exh. cat., Museum of Modern Art, New York 1991.

New York 1992
The Great Utopia: The Russian and Soviet Avant-Garde, 1915–1932, exh. cat., Solomon R. Guggenheim Museum, New York 1992.

New York 1995
Kandinsky Compositions, exh. cat., Solomon R. Guggenheim Museum, New York 1995.

New York 1996
Ellsworth Kelly: A Retrospective, exh. cat., Solomon R. Guggenheim Museum, New York 1996.

New York 2002a
The Russian Avant-Garde Book: 1910–1934, exh. cat., Museum of Modern Art, New York 2002.

New York 2002b
The Minimalist Years, 1960–1975, exh. cat., Dia Center for the Arts, New York 2002.

New York 2009
Bauhaus 1909–1933: Workshops for Modernity, exh. cat., Museum of Modern Art, New York 2009.

New York 2011
Kandinsky and the Harmony of Silence: Painting with White Border, exh. cat., Solomon R. Guggenheim Museum, New York 2011.

New York 2012
Inventing Abstraction, 1910–1925: How a Radical Idea Changed Modern Art, exh. cat., Museum of Modern Art, New York 2012.

New York 2014
Vasily Kandinsky: From Blaue Reiter to the Bauhaus, 1910–1925, exh. cat., Neue Galerie, New York 2014.

New York 2016
Carmen Herrera: Lines of Sight, exh. cat., Whitney Museum of American Art, New York 2016.

New York 2021a
Alexander Calder: Modern from the Start, exh. cat., Museum of Modern Art, New York 2021.

New York 2021b
Vasily Kandinsky: Around the Circle, exh. cat., Solomon R. Guggenheim Museum, New York 2021.

New York 2022
Americans in Paris: Artists Working in Postwar France, 1946–1962, exh. cat., Grey Art Gallery, New York 2022.

Nicholson 2019
Ben Nicholson, *Ben Nicholson: Writings and Ideas,* ed. Lee Beard, London 2019.

Norwich 2011
Mary Webb: Journeys in Colour, exh. cat., Sainsburg Centre for Visual Arts, Norwich 2011.

Norwich 2021
Rhythm & Geometry: Constructivist Art in Britain Since 1951, exh. cat., Sainsbury Centre, Norwich 2021.

Ochmanek/Kitnick 2021
Donald Judd, ed. Annie Ochmanek and Alex Kitnick, Cambridge, MA, 2021.

Van Oosten 2002
Theo van Oosten, *Plastics in Art: History, Technology, Preservation,* Munich 2002.

Paris 1925
L'Art d'aujourd'hui: Exposition internationale, exh. cat., Chambre syndicale de la curiosité et des beaux-arts, Paris 1925.

Paris 1984
Vassily Kandinsky, exh. cat., Centre Pompidou, Paris 1984.

Paris 2004
Aurélie Nemours: Rythme, Nombre, Couleur, exh. cat., Centre Pompidou, Paris 2004.

Paris 2005
Jean Hélion, exh. cat., Centre Pompidou, Paris 2005.

Paris 2018
Chagall, Lissitzky, Malevich: The Russian Avant-Garde in Vitebsk, 1918–1922, exh. cat., Centre Pompidou, Paris 2018.

Paris 2021
Elles font l'abstraction, exh. cat., Centre Pompidou, Paris 2021.

Paris 2024a
Auguste Herbin: Le Maître révélé, 1882–1960, exh. cat., Musée de Montmartre, Jardins Renoir, Paris 2024.

Paris 2024b
Jean Hélion: La Prose du monde, exh. cat., Musée d'Art moderne de Paris, 2024.

Pedde 2014
Brigitte Pedde, *Willi Baumeister, 1889–1955: Creator from the Unknown,* Berlin 2014.

Petrograd 1915
Poslednyaya futuristicheskaya vystavka kartin 0,10 (Nol'-desyat') [0.10: The Last Futurist Exhibition of Paintings], exh. cat., Dobychina Art Bureau, Petrograd 1915.

Philadelphia 1972
Grids Grids Grids Grids Grids Grids Grids Grids, exh. cat., Institute of Contemporary Art, Philadelphia 1972.

Poling 1982
Clark V. Poling, *Kandinsky—Unterricht am Bauhaus: Farbenseminar und analytisches Zeichen,* Weingarten 1982.

Poppe 2016
Birgit Poppe, *Kandinsky und seine Zeit,* Leipzig 2016.

Potomac 2023
Ellsworth Kelly, exh. cat., Glenstone Museum, Potomac 2023.

Potsdam 2022
The Shape of Freedom: International Abstraction after 1945, exh. cat., Museum Barberini, Potsdam 2022.

Read 1934
Herbert Read, ed., *Unit 1: The Modern Movement in English Architecture, Painting and Sculpture,* London 1934.

Riehen/Basel 1998
Farben—Klänge: Wassily Kandinsky und Arnold Schönberg, exh. cat., Fondation Beyeler, Riehen/Basel 1998.

Riehen/Basel 2003
Mondrian+Malewitsch: In der Mitte der Sammlung, exh. cat., Fondation Beyeler, Riehen/Basel 2003.

Riehen/Basel 2015
In Search of 0,10: The Last Futurist Exhibition of Painting, exh. cat., Fondation Beyeler, Riehen/Basel 2015.

Riehen/Basel 2022
Mondrian Evolution, exh. cat., Fondation Beyeler, Riehen/Basel 2022.

Riley 1996
Bridget Riley, "Mondrian: The 'Universal' and the 'Particular,'" in *Burlington Magazine* 138,1124 (1996), 751–53.

Rome 2000
Wassily Kandinsky: Tra Monaco e Mosca, 1896–1921, exh. cat., Museo Centrale del Risorgimento, Rome 2000.

Roskill 1992
Mark Roskill, *Klee, Kandinsky, and the Thought of Their Time: A Critical Perspective,* Urbana and Chicago 1992.

Rotterdam 2019
Netherlands—Bauhaus: Pioneers of a New World, exh. cat., Museum Boijmans Van Beuningen, Rotterdam 2019.

Rubin 1986
Lawrence Rubin, *Frank Stella: Paintings, 1958–1965; A Catalogue Raisonné,* New York and London 1986.

Sandler 1970
Irving Sandler, *The Triumph of American Painting: A History of Abstract Expressionism,* New York 1970.

Sarab'ianov/Avtonomova 1994
Dimitrii Sarab'ianov and Natal'ia Avtonomova, *Wassily Kandinsky,* Moscow 1994.

Shatskikh 2012
Aleksandra Shatskikh, *Black Square: Malevich and the Origin of Suprematism,* New Haven 2012.

Schindler 2017
Viktoria Schindler, "Color Theories from Western Europe and the United States in the Writings of Ivan Kliun," in *Experiment* 23 (2017), 253–66.

Schmidt 2002
Christiane Schmidt, *Kandinskys physikalische Kreise: Kunst als Medium naturwissenschaftlicher Erkenntnis; Untersuchung der Schriften des Künstlers und seiner abstrakten Bildwelt der zwanziger Jahre unter Heranziehung von Gesichtspunkten moderner Physik,* Weimar 2002.

Schuldenfrei 2024
Robin Schuldenfrei, *Objects in Exile: Modern Art and Design across Borders, 1930–1960,* Princeton 2024.

Schwerin 2006
Von Kandinsky bis Tatlin: Konstruktivismus in Europa, exh. cat., Staatliches Museum Schwerin, 2006.

Seuphor 1962
Michel Seuphor, *Abstract Painting: Fifty Years of Accomplishment, from Kandinsky to the Present,* New York 1962.

Sidlina 2012
Natalia Sidlina, *Naum Gabo,* London 2012.

Southampton 2005
Elements of Abstraction: Space, Line and Interval in Modern British Art, exh. cat., Southampton City Art Gallery, 2005.

Spalding 2022
Frances Spalding, *The Real and the Romantic: English Art between Two World Wars,* London 2022.

Stephens 2015
Chris Stephens, *Terry Frost,* London 2015.

St. Ives 2020
Naum Gabo: Constructions for Real Life, exh. cat., Tate St. Ives, 2020.

St. Petersburg 2000
In Malevich's Circle: Confederates, Students, Followers in Russia, 1920s–1950s, exh. cat., State Russian Museum, St. Petersburg 2000.

St. Petersburg 2003
Russian Paris, 1910–1960, exh. cat., State Russian Museum, St. Petersburg 2003.

St. Petersburg 2022
Russian Avant-Garde: Revolution in the Arts, exh. cat., State Hermitage Museum, St. Petersburg 2022.

Stuttgart 1974
Der Konstruktivismus und seine Nachfolge, exh. cat., Staatsgalerie Stuttgart, 1974.

Stuttgart 2013
Op + Pop: Experimente amerikanischer Künstler ab 1960, exh. cat., Staatsgalerie Stuttgart, 2013.

Sweeney 1948
James Johnson Sweeney, "An Interview with Mondrian," in Sweeney, *Mondrian,* New York 1948, 15–16.

Taylor 2014
Brandon Taylor, *After Constructivism,* London and New Haven 2014.

Taylor 2020
Brandon Taylor, *The Life of Forms in Art: Modernism, Organism, Vitality,* London 2020.

Thomas 1993
Angela Thomas, "Max Bill: The Early Years, An Interview," trans. Susan Ernst-Peters, in *The Journal of Decorative and Propaganda Arts,* 19 (1993), 99–119.

Troy 1983
Nancy J. Troy, *The De Stijl Environment,* Cambridge, MA, 1983.

Troy 2013
Nancy J. Troy, *The Afterlife of Piet Mondrian,* Chicago 2013.

Tupitsyn 2009
Margarita Tupitsyn, *Rodchenko & Popova: Defining Constructivism,* London 2009.

Vaduz 2021
Russian Avant-Garde from the Tsarenkov Collection: The Permanent Loan at Kunstmuseum Liechtenstein, exh. cat., Kunstmuseum Liechtenstein, Vaduz 2021.

Vienna 2001
Kasimir Malewitsch, exh. cat., Kunstforum Wien, Vienna 2001.

Vienna 2004a
Wassily Kandinsky: Der Klang der Farbe, 1900–1921, exh. cat., Kunstforum Wien, Vienna 2004.

Vienna 2004b
Pop Art & Minimalismus, exh. cat., Albertina, Vienna 2004.

Vienna 2005
Piet Mondrian, exh. cat., Albertina, Vienna 2005.

Vienna 2016
Chagall to Malevich: The Russian Avant-Gardes, exh. cat., Albertina, Vienna 2016.

Vienna 2019
Vertigo: Op Art and a History of Deception 1520 to 1970, exh. cat., Museum moderner Kunst Stiftung Ludwig Wien, Vienna 2019.

Vujošević 2017
Tijana Vujošević, *Modernism and the Making of the Soviet New Man,* Manchester 2017.

Warsaw 2017
The Other Trans-Atlantic: Kinetic and Op Art in Eastern Europe and Latin America, exh. cat., Muzeum Sztuki Nowoczesnej, Warsaw 2017.

Washington 1992
Theme & Improvisation: Kandinsky & the American Avant-Garde (1912–1950), exh. cat., Phillips Collection, Washington, DC, 1992.

Washington 2008
Color as Field: American Painting, 1950–1975, exh. cat., Smithsonian American Art Museum, Washington, DC, 2008.

White 2003
Michael White, *De Stijl and Dutch Modernism,* Manchester 2003.

Wiegand 1961
Charmion von Wiegand, "Mondrian: A Memoir of His New York Period," in *Arts Yearbook* 4 (1961), 57–65.

Zurich 1984
Kandinsky in Russland und am Bauhaus. 1915–1933, exh. cat., Kunsthaus Zürich, 1984.

Zurich 2009
Verena Loewensberg: Druckgraphik, exh. cat., Graphische Sammlung der ETH Zürich, 2009.

Zurich 2011
Complete Concrete: Over 100 Years of Constructive, Concrete, and Conceptual Art, exh. cat., Museum Haus Konstruktiv, Zurich 2011.

Zurich 2017
Marlow Moss: A Forgotten Maverick, exh. cat., Museum Haus Konstruktiv, Zurich 2017.

Zurich 2020
Camille Graeser: The Making of a Concrete Artist, exh. cat., Museum Haus Konstruktiv, Zurich 2020.

Authors

Sterre Barentsen, assistant curator at the Museum Barberini in Potsdam since 2023–24, studied art history at the Courtauld Institute of Art in London and the University of Oxford. She received her PhD from the Humboldt-Universität zu Berlin for the dissertation *From Acid Lakes to Miningscapes: An Environmental Art History of the Late GDR* (2023). Barentsen cocurated the Moscow International Biennale for Young Art (2020) at the Moscow Museum of Modern Art and has contributed to the exhibition catalogs *Wolfgang Mattheuer / Stan Douglas* (2022), *Clouds and Light: Impressionism in Holland* (2023), and *Maurice de Vlaminck: Modern Art Rebel* (2024).

Max Boersma, postdoctoral fellow at the Kunsthistorisches Institut of the Freie Universität Berlin since 2023, has a doctorate in the history of art and architecture from Harvard University for the dissertation *Technical Difficulties: Abstraction's Entanglements in the World, 1918–1933* (2023). He has published articles in the journals *Grey Room, Les Cahiers du Musée national d'art moderne,* and *October.* His research focuses on interdisciplinary, transnational, and transcultural histories of abstract art and the intersections of art, craft, and design, particularly in Germany, Russia, and France.

John E. Bowlt is a professor in the Department of Slavic Languages at the University of Southern California, Los Angeles, where he also directs the Institute of Modern Russian Culture. He is a specialist in the history of modern Russian art, particularly Symbolism and the avant-garde, and curator or cocurator of exhibitions such as *L'avanguardia russa, la Siberia e l'Oriente* (2013), *A Game in Hell* (2014), and *Avant-Garde Theatre: War, Revolution and Design* (2014–15), as well as the retrospective *Léon Bakst* (2016). He was Slade Professor at Cambridge University in 2015 and is the author of *Begstvo form: Russkoe iskusstvo nachala XX veka* [Flight of Forms: Russian Art of the Early Twentieth Century] (2019) and editor of *Khudozhniki russkoi emigratsii v Amerike* [Russian Émigré Artists in the United States] (2023).

Altair Brandon-Salmon, lecturer in the Civic, Liberal, and Global Education program at Stanford University since 2024, has degrees in art history from Oxford University and a doctorate in art history from Stanford University for a dissertation on how bombsites in London shaped postwar British art and architecture. He has published articles in *Art History, Art Journal,* and the *Oxford Art Journal,* and was a guest lecture at the Courtauld Institute of Art, University of York, and Paul Mellon Centre for Studies in British Art in London. He is the curatorial assistant at the Sheldonian Theatre, University of Oxford, and a guest curator with Projects Twenty Two in Cornwall. He was previously assistant curator at Campion Hall, University of Oxford.

Anna Heling, student assistant at the Museum Barberini in Potsdam since 2023, studied art history, history, and theater studies at the University of Leipzig, where she also worked as a student research assistant. She previously completed an internship at the Kunsthalle Bremen. Her research focuses on the exhibition history of Surrealism. Since 2024 she has been pursuing a master's degree in art and visual history at the Humboldt-Universität zu Berlin.

David Max Horowitz has been assistant curator at the Solomon R. Guggenheim Museum in New York since 2015, where he curated *Marking Time: Process in Minimal Abstraction* (2019–20) and *Jean Dubuffet: Ardent Celebration* (2022), cocurated *R. H. Quaytman + ×, Chapter 34* (2018–19), and was part of the curatorial team for *Agnes Martin* (2016–17) and *Hilma af Klint: Paintings for the Future* (2018–19), for which he also contributed to the catalog. Other contributions to exhibition catalogs include *Joan Mitchell* (2021), *Alex Katz: Gathering* (2022), *Harmony and Dissonance: Orphism in Paris, 1910–1930* (2024), and *Hilma af Klint* (2024).

Jeremy Lewison has been a freelance art historian and curator in London since 2002, after serving as director of Kettle's Yard, Cambridge (1977–83) and holding various positions at the Tate Gallery, London (1983–2002), ranging from curator and deputy keeper of the modern collection to director of collections. He has curated numerous exhibitions, including *Circle: Constructive Art in Britain, 1934–1940* (1982), *Ben Nicholson: The Years of Experiment, 1919–1939* (1983), *Sol LeWitt: Prints, 1970–1986* (1986), *Anish Kapoor: Drawings* (1991), *Brice Marden: Prints, 1961–1991* (1992), *Ben Nicholson* (1993), *Jackson Pollock, 1912–1956* (1999, with Kirk Varnedoe and Pepe Karmel), *Barnett Newman* (2002, with Ann Temkin), *Turner, Monet, Twombly: Later Paintings* (2011), *Alice Neel: Painter of Modern Life* (2016), and *Helene Schjerfbeck* (2019), and is author of many publications in the area of modern and contemporary art, among them the monographs *Karl Weschke: Portrait of a Painter* (1998), *Interpreting Pollock* (1999), *Looking at Barnett Newman* (2002), and *Paul Huxley* (2024).

Chen Min Loh, intern at the Museum Barberini since 2024–25, studied arts and culture at Erasmus University Rotterdam. She is currently a research master's student in art history at Utrecht University, and she previously worked as a research intern at the Netherlands Institute for Art History (RKD) in The Hague. Her research focuses on early twentieth-century abstract painting, with her master's thesis examining Piet Mondrian and his exile in London.

Céline Véronique Marten, student assistant at the Museum Barberini in Potsdam since 2023, studied German studies, art history, musicology, and curatorial studies in Dresden, Paris, and Frankfurt am Main. She is a PhD candidate at the University of Bonn with the dissertation topic "Narratives of Modernism during the Cold War: The 'Brücke' Artist Group in Collection and Exhibition Policy in Germany, 1945–1989." She was exhibition assistant at the Brücke Museum, Berlin, for the presentation *Biographies of Modernism: Collectors and Their Works* (2024).

Maria Mileeva is a lecturer in modern and contemporary art at the Courtauld Institute of Art, London. Her research and teaching center around post-colonial and decolonial narratives of the Russo-Soviet imperial projects and Soviet multinationalism. Mileeva's current book project interrogates the linkages between the cultural policies of Socialist Realism and socialist internationalism in the postwar period. An aspect of this research was published as "Imagined Solidarities: Cairo-Moscow and the Struggle for Realist Art," in *Art History* (November 2022).

Nicoletta Misler, emeritus professor of Russian and Eastern European art at the Università di Napoli "L'Orientale," in Naples, is a specialist in the visual culture of Russian modernism. She has published monographs on Pavel Filonov, Francisco Infante, Solomon Nikritin, Alexander Ponomarev, and Wassily Kandinsky. She was curator or cocurator of numerous exhibitions, including *Kandinsky tra Oriente e Occidente* (1993), *Kazimir Malevič* (1993), and *Marc Chagall: Les Années russes, 1907–1922* (1995); and academic consultant for exhibitions such as *Filonov und seine Schule* (1990) and *Pavel Filonov: Seer of the Invisible* (2006). Misler's current research focuses on the evolution of free dance in early Soviet Russia. She organized *In principio era il corpo . . . L'Arte del movimento a Mosca negli anni '20* (1999–2000) and authored many publications including *Beyond Vision: Essays on the Perception of Art* (2002) and *The Art of Movement in Russia, 1920–1930* (2017).

Image Credits

Exhibited Works

Estate of Richard Anuszkiewicz: cat. 120 • photo: Fred Charles: cat. 119 • photo: Loretta Howard Gallery: cat. 121
ASOM Collection: cat. 83, 107, 109, 111, 124 • photo: Rafal Maslow: cat. 110, 113 • photo: VAN HAM Kunstauktionen/Saša Fuis Photographie: cat. 112
Galerie Berinson: cat. 23
akg-images, Berlin (photo: André Held): cat. 125
bpk, Berlin: Hamburger Kunsthalle/Elke Walford: cat. 24 • Kunstsammlung Nordrhein-Westfalen, Düsseldorf/Walter Klein: cat. 41 • Solomon R. Guggenheim Foundation | Art Resource, NY: cat. 21 • Nationalgalerie, SMB/Jens Ziehe: cat. 19
Staatliche Museen zu Berlin, Nationalgalerie, Marzona Collection (photo: Jens Ziehe): cat. 102
Josef Albers Museum Quadrat Bottrop: cats. 28–32
Lehmbruck Museum, Duisburg (photo: Bernd Kirtz): cat. 15
Scala, Florence: 2025 digital image, Whitney Museum of American Art/Scala, Florence: cats. 46, 47, 89, 90, 92, 118 • photo: Philadelphia Museum of Art/Art Resource/Scala, Florence: cat. 105
Fondation Gandur pour l'art, Genève: photo: Sandra Pointet: cats. 26, 49, 54, 108 • photo: André Morin: cats. 50–52, 93–97, 101
Kunstmuseum Moritzburg Halle (Saale): photo: Punctum/Bertram Kober: cat. 13 • photo: Kulturstiftung Sachsen-Anhalt: cat. 14
University of Hertfordshire Art Collection (photo: © Rob Harris): cat. 60
Louisiana Museum of Modern Art, Humlebæk: cat. 100
Studio Paul Huxley (photo: Anna Arca): cat. 87
Muzeum Sztuki, Łódź: cat. 17
Richard Paul Lohse-Stiftung: cats. 36, 37
Courtauld, London (photo: © Courtauld): cat. 62
Royal Academy of Arts, London (photo: Prudence Cuming): cat. 77
Mercedes-Benz Collection: photo: Andreas Freytag: cat. 25 • photo: Uwe Seyl: cat. 98
Nahmad Collection: cats. 22, 38, 57
Lisson Gallery, New York: cat. 91
D. Wigmore Fine Art, Inc., New York (© photo: Noel Allum): cat. 106
Sainsbury Centre, University of East Anglia, Norwich: cats. 53, 63–66, 68–71, 73–76
Kröller-Müller Museum, Otterlo: photo: Marjon Gemmeke: cats. 16, 44 • photo: Tom Haartsen: cat. 45
Private collections: cats. 1, 42, 78, 103 • photo: Courtesy of Lévy Gorvy Dayan: cat. 81 • © photo: Johannes Maria Haslinger: cats. 84, 99 • © photo: Wes Magyar: cat. 115
Fondation Beyeler, Riehen/Basel (photo: Robert Bayer): cat. 40
Museum Boijmans Van Beuningen, Rotterdam (photo: Studio Tromp): cats. 27, 80
Fondation Marguerite et Aimé Maeght, Saint-Paul de Vence (© photo: Claude Germain—Archives Fondation Maeght): cat. 55
Museum für Gegenwartskunst, Siegen (photo: Philipp Ottendörfer) cats. 104, 123
Ellsworth Kelly Foundation, Spencertown, NY: cat. 88
Estate of Julian Stanczak: photo: Christopher Burke: cat. 114 • photo: Julian Stanczak: cat. 116 • photo: Jacob Koester: cats. 117, 122
Pier Arts Centre, Stromness, Orkney: photo: Alistair Peebles: cats. 59, 61 • photo: Mike Davidson: cat. 79
MOMus—Museum of Modern Art—Costakis Collection, Thessaloniki: cats. 2, 5–11
Triton Collection Foundation: cats. 20, 43
UK Government Art Collection: cats. 58, 67, 72
Peggy Guggenheim Collection, Venice (photo: © 2024 Solomon R. Guggenheim Foundation, New York): cats. 3, 18, 39
ALBERTINA, Vienna: cats. 4, 12
National Gallery of Art, Washington: cats. 82, 85, 86
Haus Bill, Zumikon, digital image courtesy Hauser & Wirth: cat. 33
Camille Graeser Stiftung, Zurich: cat. 35
Kunsthaus Zürich: cats. 48, 56
Verena Loewensberg Stiftung, Zurich (photo: Philipp Hitz): cat. 34

Comparative Images

artvee.com: p. 222, fig. 3
© Succesió Miró S.L., Barcelona: p. 129, fig. 4
Basel Poster Collection: p. 274 left
akg-images, Berlin: p. 21, fig. 4; p. 25, fig. 8; p. 48, fig. 13; p. 73, fig. 4; p. 101, fig. 2 • De Agostini/V. Pirozzi: p. 26, fig. 12 • FAF Toscana—Fondazione Alinari per la Fotografia: p. 70, fig. 1 • fine-art-images: p. 267 left and right; p. 271 right; p. 272 right; p. 276 right • Heritage Images/Fine Art Images: p. 27, fig. 13; p. 32, fig. 6; p. 39, fig. 3
bpk, Berlin: p. 46, fig. 11; p. 273 left • CNAC-MNAM: p. 268 right • CNAC-MNAM/Georges Meguerditchian: p. 270 left • Kunstbibliothek, SMB, Photothek Willy Römer: p. 268 left • Kunsthalle Mannheim/Cem Yücetas: p. 159, fig. 4 • Nationalgalerie, SMB, Verein der Freunde der Nationalgalerie/Jörg P. Anders: p. 60, fig. 12 • Solomon R. Guggenheim Foundation | Art Resource, NY: p. 44, fig. 9 • Staatsbibliothek zu Berlin: p. 32, fig. 5 • Staatsgalerie Stuttgart: p. 127, fig. 2 • Städel Museum: p. 54, fig. 5 • Jewish Museum of NY/Art Resource, NY/Rudolph Burckhardt: p. 277 right
Staatsbibliothek zu Berlin—Preußischer Kulturbesitz: call no. Ny 7456/100-11: p. 20, fig. 2; p. 73, figs. 7 and 8 • call no. Nr 500/60-1927,1/3(N=2): p. 37, fig. 10 • call no. 2"@Nr 499/50: p. 37, fig. 9 • call no. Na 10944/90: p. 25, fig. 9 • call no. 4"@Lc 35473-1912: p. 27, fig. 14

© Gustave Buchet. Familles Bron Bersier Biber (photo: © Musée cantonal des Beaux-Arts de Lausanne/Étienne Malapert): p. 269 right
President and Fellows of Harvard College, Cambridge, MA: p. 220, fig. 1
DNP Art Communication: p. 40, fig. 4
Scala, Florence: Photo Fine Art Images/Heritage Images/Scala, Florence: p. 72, fig. 3 • 2025 Digital image, Museum of Modern Art, New York/Scala, Florence: p. 29, fig. 2; p. 48, fig. 14; p. 49, fig. 15; p. 51, fig. 1; p. 52, fig. 2; p. 53, fig. 4; p. 59, fig. 10; p. 187, fig. 2; p. 272 left; p. 277 left • 2025 digital image, Whitney Museum of American Art/Scala, Florence: p. 55, fig. 6; p. 58, fig. 9
Universitätsbibliothek Johann Christian Senckenberg, Frankfurt am Main (call no. Wq 389): p. 35, fig. 7
Studio Paul Huxley (photo: Anna Arca): p. 60, fig. 11
© Museum Associates/LACMA: p. 276 left
Arts Council Collection, Southbank Centre, London: p. 223, fig. 4
Mercedes-Benz Art Collection: p. 102, fig. 3
Bayerische Staatsbibliothek, Munich (call no. Res/Art. 434): p. 29, fig. 1; p. 31, fig. 3
Gabriele Münter- und Johannes Eichner-Stiftung, Munich: p. 21, fig. 3
© Eric Firestone Gallery, New York: p. 189, fig. 4
© New York Public Library for the Performing Arts (photo: Friedman-Abeles): p. 63, fig. 14
Kröller-Müller Museum, Otterlo (photo: Marjon Gemmeke): p. 186, fig. 1
Roger-Viollet, Paris (photo: Albert Harlingue): p. 42, fig. 6
picture alliance/ASSOCIATED PRESS (photo: Tom Fitzsimmons): p. 273 right
PWB Images/Alamy Stock Photo: p. 42, fig. 5
RIBA Collections (photo: John Maltby): p. 275 left
© Collection Nieuwe Instituut, Rotterdam: C. van Eesteren archive, EEST 3.360: p. 269 left
Ellsworth Kelly Foundation, Spencertown, NY (photo: Ron Amstutz): p. 188, fig. 3
Tate: p. 45, fig. 10; p. 52, fig. 3; p. 100, fig. 1; p. 126, fig. 1; p. 157, fig. 2; p. 221, fig. 2; p. 274, fig. 2; p. 275, fig. 2; p. 271 left
RKD—Netherlands Institute for Art History, The Hague: p. 37, fig. 8; p. 39, figs. 1 and 2; p. 47, fig. 12
Collection of the Library of the Faculty of Psychology, University of Warsaw: p. 22, fig. 5; p. 23, fig. 6; p. 24, fig. 7
Hirshhorn Museum and Sculpture Garden, Washington, DC (photo: Lee Stalsworth): p. 56, fig. 7
Wikimedia Commons (photo: Stephan Jockel): p. 31, fig. 4
Courtesy of New Art Centre, Wiltshire: p. 56, fig. 8
Zentralbibliothek Zürich, Manuscript Department, Estate of K. Farner, call no. 66.3: p. 270 right

Images were reproduced from the following publications:
Jelena Hahl-Fontaine and Kate C. Kangaslahti, eds., *Kandinsky: A Life in Letters, 1889–1944,* Munich 2023 (fig. 10): p. 19, fig. 1

© for all works by the following artists: Josef Albers, Richard Anuszkiewicz, Jean Arp, Max Bill, Peter Carter, Enrico Castellani, Gene Davis, Robyn Denny, Jo Delahaut, Burgoyne Diller, Walter Dexel, César Domela, Terry Frost, Camille Graeser, Al Held, Jean Hélion, Auguste Herbin, Anthony Hill, Johannes Itten, Fernand Léger, Jean Leppien, Richard Paul Lohse, François Morellet, Gabriele Münter, Aurelie Nemours, Kenneth Noland, Victor Pasmore, Antoine Pevsner, Ad Reinhardt, Alexander Rodtschenko, Frank Stella, Victor Vasarely, Mary Webb: VG Bild-Kunst, Bonn 2024; Edna Andrade: courtesy Locks Gallery; Gustave Buchet: Gustave Buchet. Familles Bron Bersier Biber; Alexander Calder: 2024 Calder Foundation, New York / Artists Rights Society (ARS), New York; Ilya Ehrenburg: Ilya Ehrenburg Estate; Wojciech Fangor: FANGOR Foundation; Konrad Farner: Sybille Farner; Naum Gabo: Nina & Graham Williams/Tate; Fritz Glarner: Estate of Fritz Glarner, Kunsthaus Zürich; Barbara Hepworth: Hepworth Estate, Bowness; Carmen Herrera: Lisson Gallery; Ludwig Hirschfeld-Mack: Kaj Delugan; Paul Huxley: Paul Huxley; Donald Judd: Judd Foundation/VG Bild-Kunst, Bonn 2024; Ellsworth Kelly: Ellsworth Kelly Foundation; Verena Loewensberg: Stiftung Verena Loewensberg, Zurich; Morris Louis: All Rights Reserved. Maryland College Institute of Art/VG Bild-Kunst, Bonn 2024; Agnes Martin: Agnes Martin Foundation, New York/VG Bild-Kunst, Bonn 2024; Kenneth Martin, Mary Martin: Paul Martin; Henri Matisse: Succession H. Matisse/VG Bild-Kunst, Bonn 2024; Joan Miró: Successió Miró/VG Bild-Kunst, Bonn 2024; Robert Morris: Estate of Robert Morris/VG Bild-Kunst, Bonn 2024; Barnett Newman: Barnett Newman Foundation/ VG Bild-Kunst, Bonn 2024; Ben Nicholson: Angela Verren Taunt. All rights reserved/ VG Bild-Kunst, Bonn 2024; Pablo Picasso: Succession Picasso/VG Bild-Kunst, Bonn 2024; Bridget Riley: 2024 Bridget Riley. All rights reserved. Courtesy the artist and David Zwirner; Miriam Schapiro: Estate of Miriam Schapiro/VG Bild-Kunst, Bonn 2024; Peter Sedgley: Peter Sedgley; Julian Stanczak: Estate of Julian Stanczak; Margaret Wenstrup: Estate of Margaret Wenstrup

Details of images were used on the following pages:

pp. 2–3
Frank Stella, *Double Scramble,* 1978, private collection (cat. 84)
pp. 4–5
László Moholy-Nagy, *Composition Z VIII,* 1924, Staatliche Museen zu Berlin, Neue Nationalgalerie (cat. 19)
pp. 16–17
Wassily Kandinsky, *In the Black Square,* 1923, Solomon R. Guggenheim Museum, New York (cat. 21)
pp. 66–67
Wassily Kandinsky, *White Cross,* 1922, Peggy Guggenheim Collection, Venice (Solomon R. Guggenheim Foundation, New York) (cat. 3)
pp. 96–97
Wassily Kandinsky, *Light in Heavy,* 1929, Collection Museum Boijmans Van Beuningen (cat. 27)
pp. 122–23
Wassily Kandinsky, *Accompanied Center,* 1937, Nahmad Collection (cat. 57)
pp. 152–53
Wassily Kandinsky, *Above and Left,* 1925, private collection (cat. 78)
pp. 182–83
Wassily Kandinsky, *Silent,* 1924, Collection Museum Boijmans Van Beuningen, Rotterdam (cat. 80)
pp. 216–17
Wassily Kandinsky, *In the Black Circle,* 1923, private collection (cat. 125)
pp. 252–53
Wassily Kandinsky, *Arrow Toward the Circle,* 1930, Nahmad Collection (cat. 38)

The assertion of claims according to section 60h UrhG for the reproduction of images of the exhibited works is carried out by VG Bild-Kunst.

It was not possible to locate or successfully contact copyright holders in all instances. Any legitimate claims will be resolved in the framework of the usual agreements.

Colophon

This catalog is published in conjunction with the exhibition

Kandinsky's Universe: Geometric Abstraction in the Twentieth Century
Museum Barberini, Potsdam
February 15, 2025–May 18, 2025

Editors:
Ortrud Westheider, Michael Philipp, Nerina Santorius

Exhibition and Catalog:
Sterre Barentsen

Assistant Curator:
Anna Heling

Catalog Editing:
Sterre Barentsen, Anna Heling, Annette Krüger, Chen Min Loh

Image Editing:
Anna Heling

Museum Barberini, Potsdam

Director: Ortrud Westheider
Assistant to the Director: Dorothee Entrup
Finance and Administration Director: Janine Meyer
Assistant to the Finance and Administration Director: Nadine Müller
Chief Curator: Michael Philipp
Curator and Head of the Impressionism Collection: Nerina Santorius
Research Associate Provenance: Linda Hacka
Assistant Curators: Sterre Barentsen, Valentina Plotnikova
Registrars: Annelies Legein, Anna Seidel
Intern: Chen Min Loh
Communications and Marketing: Achim Klapp, Marte Kräher, Valerie Maul, Carolin Stranz
Digitization and Information Security: Stefan Scholze
IT Administrator: Sebastian Semmler
Educational Service: Dorothee Entrup, Isabel Acosta, Andrea Schmidt
Events: Katharina Mench, Deniz Lusch, Kaspar Winkler
Ticketing: Yvonne Benesch, Daniela Schaube
Accounting: Heike Kraeft
HR Administration: Julia Pauline Nowak
Security Coordination and Guest Management: Nikolaos Dokalis, Verena Daub
Guest Management: Angela Winkler, Roswitha Waldheim, Catrin Berendsen
Building Services: Carsten Loeper, Frank Altmann, Dennis Kokert

In collaboration with:

Conservation: Felicitas Klein, Berlin Friederike Beseler, Berlin
Exhibition Design: Philipp Ricklefs, Berlin BrücknerAping, Büro für Gestaltung, Bremen
Museum Shop: Museum Barberini. Der Shop, Jörg Klambt
Transport: Hasenkamp, Berlin

Catalog

Munich · London · New York, a member of Penguin Random House Verlagsgruppe GmbH
Neumarkter Strasse 28
81673 Munich

produktsicherheit@penguinrandomhouse.de
(The above information is also mandatory information according to GPSR)

Editorial Direction, Prestel: Markus Eisen
Graphic Design and Typesetting: BrücknerAping, Büro für Gestaltung, Bremen
Copyediting: Tas Skorupa, New York
Project Management: Annette Krüger, Hamburg
English Translations: Melissa M. Thorson
Production Management, Prestel: Cilly Klotz
Color Separations: Reproline Genceller, Germering
Printing and Binding: Printer Trento, Trento
Typeface: Neue Haas Grotesk
Paper: Garda Matt Ultra, 150 g/m²

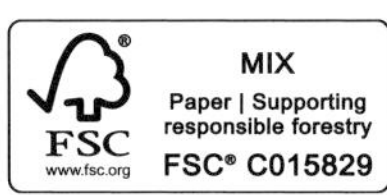

Penguin Random House Verlagsgruppe
FSC® N001967

Printed in Italy

A CIP catalog record for this book is available from the British Library.
Library of Congress Control Number: 2024952717

ISBN 978-3-7913-7790-2
(German trade edition)
ISBN 978-3-7913-7791-9
(English trade edition)
ISBN 978-3-7913-9146-5
(German museum edition, Museum Barberini, Potsdam)
ISBN 978-3-7913-9147-2
(English museum edition, Museum Barberini, Potsdam)

www.prestel.de
www.prestel.com

Russian and Ukrainian transliterations of names in this book follow the Library of Congress system. A more common spelling was used for first names with identical equivalents. Apart from a few exceptions, diacritical symbols were used in the bibliographic entries in the notes and bibliography. Dates with days and months are cited as listed in each individual source, following either the Julian or Gregorian calendar.